What ʿĪsā ibn Hishām Told Us

Letter from the General Editor

The Library of Arabic Literature series offers Arabic editions and English translations of significant works of Arabic literature, with an emphasis on the seventh to nineteenth centuries. The Library of Arabic Literature thus includes texts from the pre-Islamic era to the cusp of the modern period, and encompasses a wide range of genres, including poetry, poetics, fiction, religion, philosophy, law, science, history, and historiography.

Books in the series are edited and translated by internationally recognized scholars and are published in parallel-text format with Arabic and English on facing pages, and are also made available as English-only paperbacks.

The Library encourages scholars to produce authoritative, though not necessarily critical, Arabic editions, accompanied by modern, lucid English translations. Its ultimate goal is to introduce the rich, largely untapped Arabic literary heritage to both a general audience of readers as well as to scholars and students.

The Library of Arabic Literature is supported by a grant from the New York University Abu Dhabi Institute and is published by NYU Press.

Philip F. Kennedy
General Editor, Library of Arabic Literature

About this Paperback

This paperback edition differs in a few respects from its dual-language hardcover predecessor. Because of the compact trim size the pagination has changed, but paragraph numbering has been retained to facilitate cross-referencing with the hardcover. Material that referred to the Arabic edition has been updated to reflect the English-only format, and other material has been corrected and updated where appropriate. For information about the Arabic edition on which this English translation is based and about how the LAL Arabic text was established, readers are referred to the hardcover.

What ʿĪsā ibn Hishām Told Us

or

A Period of Time

by

Muḥammad al-Muwayliḥī

translated by

Roger Allen

foreword by

Maria Golia

volume editor

Philip F. Kennedy

NEW YORK UNIVERSITY PRESS

New York

NEW YORK UNIVERSITY PRESS
New York

Library of Congress Cataloging-in-Publication Data
Names: Muwayliḥī, Muḥammad author. | Allen, Roger, 1942– translator. | Kennedy, Philip F. editor. | Muwayliḥī, Muḥammad. Ḥadīth ʻIsā ibn Hishām. English. | Muwayliḥī, Muḥammad. Ḥadīth ʻIsā ibn Hishām.
Title: What 'Isa ibn Hisham told us or, A period of time / Muḥammad al- Muwayliḥī ; translated by Roger Allen ; foreword by Maria Golia ; volume editor, Philip F. Kennedy.
Other titles: Period of time
Description: New York : New York University, 2018. | Series: The library of Arabic literature | Includes bibliographical references and index.
Identifiers: LCCN 2017046583 (print) | LCCN 2017045494 (ebook) | ISBN 9781479840915 (paperback) | ISBN 9781479836710 (Ebook) | ISBN 9781479820993 (Ebook)
Classification: LCC PJ7850.U9 H313 2018 (ebook) | LCC PJ7850.U9 (print) | DDC 892.7/35—dc23
LC record available at https://lccn.loc.gov/2017046583

New York University Press books are printed on acid-free paper, and their binding materials are chosen for strength and durability.

Series design and composition by Nicole Hayward
Typeset in Adobe Text

Manufactured in the United States of America

10 9 8 7 6 5 4 3 2 1

MIX
Paper | Supporting responsible forestry
FSC® C013604

Contents

Foreword

MARIA GOLIA

In 1898, when Muḥammad al-Muwayliḥī and his father Ibrahim began publishing the weekly *Miṣbāḥ al-Sharq* ("Light of the East"), the Egyptian press was thriving. Seventy years had passed since the appearance of the Middle-East's first official gazette, *Al-Waqā'i' al-Miṣriyyah* (*Egyptian Events*, Bulaq Press) announcing affairs of state in Turkish and Arabic. Newspapers had proliferated following the 1882 bombardment of Alexandria and subsequent occupation by the British, many with the intent of fueling nationalist sentiment, others the natural outcome of several decades of break-neck development. The wealth Egypt accumulated by exporting cotton when America was mired in the Civil War, was wisely directed towards infrastructure improvements like railways, the telegraph, telephone, and entire new cities built around the country's first modern mega-project, the Suez Canal, all of which attracted immigrants from Europe and elsewhere. By the 1890s, newsstands in Cairo and Alexandria overflowed with dailies and periodicals, including cultural, scientific and religious journals in Arabic, Greek, French, Italian, and English, a number of them produced by and for women and circulated throughout the Arab world.

Despite its diversity, readership of the Egyptian press was small, elite and largely foreign; an 1897 census (when Egypt's population was about eight million) estimated male literacy at 20 percent in Cairo and Alexandria and in the countryside it was certainly far less. In those pre-radio days however, pubic readings in cafes and at other gatherings made the printed news available to the unlettered. One wonders if Muḥammad al-Muwayliḥī thought to reach this larger audience as he wrote the articles collected here. By loading traditional story-telling forms (descriptive dialogues, nested narratives and pithy poetic asides) with details of familiar places and personages, he delivered not only the news but a call for awareness of history and for the questioning of authority, ethics and self. However "classic" the presentation, al-Muwayliḥī's acerbic, insider observations rendered the writing fresh, entertaining and daring.

Shy and perceptive, Muḥammad al-Muwayliḥī was a natural-born scholar thrust into the world by family and politics. His people were wealthy, his education superb, his father a confidante to royalty, and just fifteen years old when Muḥammad was born. Ibrahim, who was deeply involved in anti-colonialist political and religious movements, treated his son as a trusted collaborator, at one point making him his emissary to the Ottoman Sultan in Istanbul. Beginning in his teens, Muḥammad partnered with his erudite and outspoken father in publishing endeavors that espoused nationalist agendas and consequently placed them in harm's way. At age 22, Muḥammad was arrested for distributing an anti-British pamphlet his father had authored, taken before a judge, tried and sentenced to death. Thanks to the intervention of a high-ranking family friend he was exiled (temporarily) instead. But being subjected to such harsh and expedient justice is an alarming experience for anyone, however well connected, and it surely colored the scathing accounts of the Egyptian judiciary he later wrote for the *Miṣbāḥ al-Sharq*.

Muḥammad was forty when he composed this series, a seasoned writer, editor and publisher who had travelled widely, met with heads of state, and was largely unimpressed. He generally preferred books to people, whose interactions he nonetheless found fascinating. As a member of the elite, Muḥammad enjoyed access to Cairo's worlds within worlds, from aristocratic salons to dicey downtown dance halls. In the series presented here which he called, "A Period of Time," he shares his observations and barbed social commentary via fictional conversations conducted by one ʿĪsā ibn Hishām. Named for a character lifted from the pages of classical Arabic literature, ʿĪsā is Muḥammad's alter ego. Well-mannered, multi-lingual and exceedingly well-read, ʿĪsā presents himself by stating that "my profession is the art of writing." The scholarly ʿĪsā meets his main interlocutor, the Pasha, in a cemetery where the elderly man was recently resurrected by some mysterious means, after having spent a half-century in the crypt.

A personification of the classist conservatism of his day, the Pasha, who lived and died in privileged proximity to the court of Muḥammad ʿAlī, barely recognizes the Cairo he finds on his unexpected return. Restyled as a "Paris on the Nile," the heart of the capital is literally foreign to him, as are the behaviors and perspectives of the people he meets. Seen through the eyes of the disoriented Pasha, Cairo's quotidian is rendered extraordinary. ʿĪsā is a patient and knowledgeable guide, offering explanations of things that however familiar to the readers of *Miṣbāḥ al-Sharq*, baffle the Pasha whose astonishment serves to pull a not-too-distant history into focus. ʿĪsā's elucidations, alongside discussions with characters from all walks of life, illumine the workings of contemporary society while obliging readers to step back, pause and recapitulate, to assess the pace—and price—of change.

In the course of their odyssey of rediscovery, ʿĪsā and the Pasha exchange roles as student and teacher while exploring intuitions, events and attitudes. We overhear self-serving ministers discussing the expansionist war in Sudan and hypocritical sheikhs bickering in the religious courts. We learn of a recent outbreak of plague, the perfidy of lawyers, bureaucratic opacity, the perils of stock market speculation, science versus superstition, east versus west, pyramid climbing, and the unseemly greed of guests at a sumptuous wedding party buffet. ʿĪsā and the Pasha are appalled by the stench and vulgarity of the taverns in Opera Square where "belly-dancing" is performed, a topic to which some twenty pages of quivering outrage are assigned. Women make tellingly rare and disparaging appearances in these wide-ranging articles. Only feminine beauty is acknowledged, albeit as embodied by a statue at the entrance of the Paris *Exposition Universelle* of 1900. ʿĪsā and the Pasha's exploration of the exposition (in the wake of Muḥammad al-Muwayliḥī's visit) with its modern inventions and treasures of ancient art, forms the substance of ten probing, piquant episodes that must have delighted the readers back home.

Presented here as they originally appeared in *Miṣbāḥ al-Sharq* (as opposed to an edited version issued in 1927 as a high-school textbook), these articles hold enduring appeal, not only for their insights into the "period of time" the author portrays but for how they reveal the author's character. Roger Allen has negotiated the translation of this unusual work—part chronicle, part literary compendium—with studied grace; even occasionally pedantic passages read effortlessly and the author's voice rings true throughout. Curmudgeonly and companionable, Muḥammad al-Muwayliḥī reserves his praise solely for greatness, which he finds in Nature and the splendor of Cairo's gardens, in the architecture of Paris, and in classical Arabic literature, excerpts from which are strategically dispersed throughout the text, as are priceless anecdotes and turns of speech.

Perhaps the most engaging aspect of this book is what ʿĪsā ibn Hishām didn't tell us but that readers now, as in the past, must ask themselves; notably, what is it exactly, aside from material accoutrements, that distinguishes us from our forebears? Much of Muḥammad al-Muwayliḥī's world, in terms of human behavior, is perfectly familiar, as is his tacit yet resounding admonishment that history, if left undigested and unresolved, will always return to haunt us.

Maria Golia
Downtown Cairo

Introduction

The Author: Muḥammad al-Muwayliḥī

Muḥammad al-Muwayliḥī was born on the 30th of March, 1858, into an illustrious family that traced its origins to the town of Muwayliḥ on the coast of the Ḥijāz in the Arabian Peninsula. His father, Ibrāhīm al-Muwayliḥī (1843–1906)—only fifteen years older than his son, had inherited the family silk business along with his brother ʿAbd al-Salām, and both brothers were closely involved in the political life of Egypt during the reign of the Khedive Ismāʿīl (r. 1863–79).

For a brief period at the age of ten, Muḥammad attended the famous school at Khurunfish in Cairo which was run by the Jesuit order and catered for the sons of the aristocracy, but from the time he was fifteen he was taught privately. As a young man he made the acquaintance of many of his father's friends, among whom Jamāl al-dīn al-Afghānī and Muḥammad ʿAbduh.[1] Muḥammad later attended ʿAbduh's lectures at al-Azhar, the same institution that he was to criticize with such vehemence in the newspaper articles that were later to be published in edited form as *Ḥadīth ʿĪsā ibn Hishām* (*What ʿĪsā ibn Hishām Told Us*). He also had occasion to meet other important figures in Egyptian cultural life of the times, including Shaykh Ḥusayn al-Marṣafī and Maḥmūd Pāshā Sāmī al-Bārūdī, the famous statesman and poet, both of whom took an interest in his education.[2]

In 1872, Ibrāhīm's fortunes suffered a severe setback. He had been attracted to the newly founded Stock Exchange, and in the course of speculation lost the 80,000 pounds which had been bequeathed to him by his father.[3] Leaving ʿAbd al-Salām to manage the business as best he could, Ibrāhīm retired to his house for three months. We learn from various sources that when the Khedive Ismāʿīl heard about this, he summoned both brothers to the palace, gave each the title of Bey and 3,000 pounds, and ordered his entourage and harem to dress themselves exclusively in al-Muwayliḥī silks.[4]

Following the financial crisis of 1879, the Khedive Ismāʿīl was forced to abdicate and went into exile in Naples. He invited Ibrāhīm al-Muwayliḥī to join him as his private secretary and tutor to Prince Aḥmad Fuʾād (later King Fuʾād the First).[5] Putting Muḥammad in the care of his uncle, ʿAbd al-Salām, Ibrāhīm left Egypt for Italy. Through his uncle, Muḥammad met Ibrāhīm al-Laqqānī, a barrister and writer who was also a friend of Ibrāhīm al-Muwayliḥī. Al-Laqqānī introduced Muḥammad to some of his own friends, amongst whom were ʿAbdallāh Nadīm and Ḥasan Mūsā al-ʿAqqād. These three men were the protagonists of the "Egypt for the Egyptians" movement, and Muḥammad wrote regularly to his father in Italy describing the discussions he heard and the general political situation in Egypt.[6] On April 5, 1882, Muḥammad became a clerk in the Ministry of Justice, but he did not remain in the post for long. In June, ʿAbd al-Salām al-Muwayliḥī left for Syria to convalesce from an illness, and Muḥammad was left on his own during the turmoil which led up to the revolt of Aḥmad ʿUrābī, the riots in Alexandria, and the subsequent British landing and occupation. Ibrāhīm had sent his son a leaflet he had written in support of the Nationalists, entitled *Al-Jannah taḥta ẓilāl al-suyūf* (*Paradise Under the Shadow of Swords*), and Muḥammad was arrested distributing copies of this document. Put on trial before a military court on the orders of ʿUthmān Pāshā, the Minister of the Interior, he was condemned to death. However, Buṭrus Ghālī Pāshā, a friend of the Muwayliḥīs who was Permanent Under-Secretary to the Minister of Justice (*Wakīl al-ḥaqqāniyyah*), interceded on Muḥammad's behalf with the Khedive Tawfīq, claiming that Muḥammad had been encouraged by his father, that his uncle—who was his official guardian—was convalescing in Syria, and that he was not old enough to be considered politically troublesome. The sentence was commuted to exile.

Muḥammad now joined his father in Italy, where he learned Italian and some Latin, and continued his studies of French with a lawyer friend of his father. He also helped his father to produce the newspaper *Al-Ittiḥād*. But the Ottoman Sultan wrote in 1880 expressing his displeasure at the views published by the newspaper, so the Khedive Ismāʿīl was compelled to order Ibrāhīm to stop printing. In 1884, Ismāʿīl sent Ibrāhīm to Paris from Italy, and Muḥammad accompanied his father. In the French capital both Ibrāhīm and Muḥammad al-Muwayliḥī helped Jamāl al-dīn al-Afghānī and Muḥammad ʿAbduh with the publication of *Al-ʿUrwah al-Wuthqā*. This newspaper was to have a tremendous influence in the Arab Middle East, not only because of its outspoken attacks on the British presence in Egypt and the evils of excessive Westernization, but also because of its advocacy of the idea of Pan-Islam based on the Ottoman Caliphate. The Muwayliḥīs were later to support all of these points of view with vigor in their own newspaper following their return to Egypt.

The fourth issue of *Al-Ittihād* was circulated in Europe, Turkey and Egypt, and its criticism of the Ottoman Sultan caused a considerable stir. The Ottoman court contacted its ambassador in Paris, and, despite protests in *Le Figaro*, Ibrāhīm was expelled from the country and traveled to Brussels.[7] Al-Afghānī wrote from London at that time, and suggested Ibrāhīm and Muḥammad come to England. Father and son accepted the invitation. Once there, they assisted al-Afghānī in the publication of further issues of *Al-ʿUrwah al-Wuthqā*. Ibrāhīm himself produced further issues of *Al-Ittiḥād* and *Al-Anbāʾ* as well as a new newspaper called *ʿAyn Zubaydah*. During their stay in London, the Muwayliḥīs were introduced to Lord Randolph Churchill and Lord Salisbury, but any further entrées into British political society were cut short by another turn of events.

Ibrāhīm had been changing his tack somewhat by supporting the Ottoman government in his newspapers through fierce attacks on the policies of Gladstone's government, and this seems to have pleased the Sultan. Hagopian Pāshā, the "Nāẓir al-Khaṣṣah al-Sulṭāniyyah" (Supervisor of the Sultan's Entourage) was sent to London in January 1885. We learn that he, together with Qastākī Pāshā, the Ottoman ambassador in London, tried to persuade Ibrāhīm to go to Istanbul where, they asserted, he would discover that the Sultan had forgiven him for the unfavorable comments he had made in his newspapers in the past. But, with the memory of his recent expulsion from France still fresh in his mind, Ibrāhīm was (not unnaturally) dubious about the Sultan's intentions, and sent Muḥammad to Istanbul to find out the real terms of the invitation. When Muḥammad confirmed that the Sultan's offer was sincere, Ibrāhīm came to Istanbul and was appointed a member of the Education Council. Ibrāhīm soon made the acquaintance of Munīf Pāshā, the Minister of Education, who allowed Muḥammad to use the Fātiḥ Library with its large collection of manuscripts. Among the works which Muḥammad al-Muwayliḥī transcribed were *Risālat al-ghufrān* (*The Epistle of Forgiveness*) by the famous poet, Abū l-ʿAlāʾ al-Maʿarrī, several treatises by al-Jāḥiẓ (including one on magnanimity, *al-Nubl*, and another on envy, *al-Ḥasad*), and the *Dīwān* of Ibn al-Rūmī. Another friend of Ibrāhīm whom Muḥammad met at this time was al-Shinqīṭī who is one of the dedicatees of *Ḥadīth ʿĪsā ibn Hishām*.[8] In addition to all this, Muḥammad found time to write some articles for the newspaper, *Al-Munabbih*, at the invitation of ʿAbdallāh al-Mughīrah.

In 1887, Muḥammad left his father in Istanbul and returned to Cairo where he helped ʿĀrif Bey al-Mardīnī (the private secretary of Mukhtār Pāshā, the Ottoman Commissioner in Cairo) to edit *Al-Qāhirah al-Jadīdah*, a daily newspaper which had first appeared in 1885 but ceased publication when al-Mardīnī was invited back to Istanbul by the Sultan a few months after Muḥammad's return to Egypt.[9] Muḥammad continued to write articles for other newspapers in Egypt; *Al-Muqaṭṭam*, for example, he wrote under a variety of pseudonyms such as "an Egyptian who knows his country" and "*al-Badī'*." At the head of these articles he was described as "a distinguished man of letters in Egypt whose eloquence will fascinate all those who are fond of literature." In them he broached a variety of topics including the Nationalist Party, slavery, and the Legislative Council and its schemes.[10] On his return from Istanbul, Muḥammad had renewed his acquaintance with Ibrāhīm al-Laqqānī and Buṭrus Ghālī. These two men were among the circle of friends who would meet regularly at the house of Princess Nāzlī Fāḍil, the niece of the ex-Khedive Ismā'īl and wife of Salīm Abū Ḥajib, the Mufti of Tunis. This circle served as the meeting place for a remarkable collection of figures from Egyptian political and intellectual life, and of some non-Egyptian ones as well; we are told that Lord Cromer attended occasionally.[11] In addition to those already mentioned, the members included Muḥammad 'Abduh, Sa'd and Aḥmad Fatḥī Zaghlūl, Qāsim Amīn, Muṣṭafā Fahmī, 'Alī Yūsuf, and Ḥāfiẓ Ibrāhīm, a list which includes some of the leading spirits in the movement to reform Egyptian society. There seems little room for doubt that much of the discussion which must have taken place at the meetings of this circle is directly reflected in the series of articles that al-Muwayliḥī was to publish under the title *Fatrah min al-Zaman*. Another interesting figure with whom Muḥammad al-Muwayliḥī was acquainted at this time was the Englishman, Wilfrid Scawen Blunt, who had been very closely involved in the defense of 'Urābī after the collapse of the 1882 revolt. Blunt mentions the "Moelhis" many times in his *Diaries*, and from this source we can obtain some interesting pieces of information about Muḥammad's activities during this period. Blunt tells us for instance that Muḥammad was a close friend of Mukhtār Pāshā: "To these Arabist visitors from Cairo were gradually added other sources of native information, the most important of whom were my old friends Aarif Bey and Mohammed el Moelhi, nephew [sic] of my old friend Ibrahim el Moelhi, both of whom were now much in the confidence of the Ottoman High Commissioner in Cairo, Mukhtar Pasha Ghazi."[12] Blunt also tells us that 'Abd al-Salām, Ibrāhīm, and Muḥammad al-Muwayliḥī were all involved in the intrigue of 1893, as a result of which Muṣṭafā Fahmī was dismissed as Prime Minister by the Khedive ʿAbbās the Second and replaced for a period of days by Fakhrī Pāshā.[13] Ibrāhīm may have been informed about these events through correspondence with his son, but in any case, Muḥammad was a frequent visitor to Istanbul during this period; in 1892, he was there to be decorated as a Bey (second class), and again in 1893 when Blunt went to Istanbul in an unsuccessful attempt to gain an interview with the Sultan. In this same year, Muḥammad delivered a lecture to the Language Academy (*al-Majmaʿ al-ʿIlmī*) on the acquisition of the talent for creative writing by learning poetry.[14]

In 1895 Ibrāhīm al-Muwayliḥī decided to leave Istanbul. He had made many friends in the Ottoman capital, including al-Shinqīṭī, Munīf Pāshā, and Ibrāhīm Bey Adham, for whose newspaper, *Al-Ḥaqāʾiq*, he had written several articles describing state occasions. He had, however, grown tired of the court intrigues and decided to return to Egypt. He was unable to keep this fact a secret from the Sultan's spies, and Sultan ʿAbd al-Ḥamīd sent someone to find out why he wished to leave. Ibrāhīm sent back the reply that he wished to return to his own country and see his son and friends again. The Sultan seems to have been satisfied and did not prevent him from leaving. In 1896, Ibrāhīm collected the articles which he had written about life in Istanbul and published them at the Egyptian *Al-Muqaṭṭam* press under the title *Mā Hunālik*. When copies of the book reached Istanbul and were brought to the Sultan's attention, however, he dispatched a letter to Egypt with the order that they should all be collected and sent to him in Istanbul. Ibrāhīm had no wish to incur the Sultan's hatred and set about collecting as many copies of the book as he could, which he duly sent to Istanbul.[15]

In December 1895 Muḥammad had been appointed Muʿāwin of the province of Qalyūbiyyah and later Maʾmūr of the district of Burullus, but he resigned the latter post after a short while and in 1898 joined his father in producing his new newspaper.[16] The first issue of *Miṣbāḥ al-sharq* appeared on April 14, 1898, and the paper soon established a high reputation for itself. This was due in no small part to the fact that the majority of the content was written by the Muwayliḥīs and indeed was frequently unsigned, a fact which was later to give some of Muḥammad's enemies the opportunity to dispute the authorship of the articles that eventually became the book *Ḥadīth ʿĪsā ibn Hishām*. The paper contained news from Istanbul and items of local interest as well as extracts from Arabic literature, including essays of al-Jāḥiẓ and poems from the *Dīwān* of Ibn al-Rūmī which Muḥammad had transcribed in Istanbul. The leading articles dealt with such topics as the Pan-Islamist movement, the British occupation of Egypt, the war in the Sudan, the religious reform movement, and the comparison of Oriental and Western customs. Muḥammad also caused a considerable furor in the literary world of Cairo by publishing a series of articles in which he subjected the *Dīwān* of the famous Egyptian poet, Aḥmad Shawqī (1868–1932), together with its introduction, to some exacting but constructive criticism.[17] Such material as this was rarely found in newspapers of the time, and many writers have acknowledged the effect which its contents and style had on them; Muḥammad Kurd ʿAlī says that "*Miṣbāḥ al-sharq* was the best weekly," while Salāmah Mūsā tells in his autobiography how he acquired "a taste for artistic beauty" by reading the articles it contained.[18]

In November 1898, Muḥammad began to publish under the title *Fatrah min al-Zaman* the lengthy series of articles that form the text of these volumes; later, after much editing, these articles became the book *Ḥadīth ʿĪsā ibn Hishām* (their precise history is discussed in the section "A History of the Text" below). They appeared each week on the front page of the newspaper. At first they were unsigned, but, when Ibrāhīm began to publish his own story in a series of articles entitled "Mirʾāt al-ʿĀlam," Muḥammad signed his name with the letter *mīm* and Ibrahim used an *alif*. Muḥammad continued to publish these articles until June 1900, when he went to London to cover the state visit of the Khedive to the homeland of Queen Victoria (in whose honor Ibrāhīm composed an ode which was printed in the newspaper). Muḥammad sent back an article describing this visit,[19] and then went to Paris to visit the Great Exhibition (*Exposition universelle*), which he described for the readers of *Miṣbāḥ al-sharq* in a series of episodes entitled "Paris."[20] In describing his visit to the French capital, al-Muwayliḥī was following the precedents set by such figures as al-Ṭahṭāwī, al-Shidyāq, and ʿAlī Mubārak. Unlike these writers, however, he confined most of his descriptions to the Paris Exhibition of 1900.

Although *Miṣbāh al-sharq* was officially owned and edited by Ibrāhīm al-Muwayliḥī, Muḥammad gradually took over the management of the newspaper, and Ibrāhīm became a political adviser of the Khedive. In 1902, Muḥammad found himself at the center of a social scandal. While sitting in a café, he appears to have insulted a young nobleman, Muḥammad Bey Nash'at (whom ʿAbd al-ʿAzīz al-Bishrī—a friend and young protegé of Muḥammad al-Muwayliḥī—describes as "a frivolous fool"). Apparently the whole thing was intended to be a joke, but it seems to have been misinterpreted because the irate young man slapped al-Muwayliḥī on the face.[21] ʿAlī Yūsuf, the editor of the newspaper *Al-Mu'ayyad*, then published a series of reports of the incident which considerably dramatized the whole affair and cast a slur on Muḥammad. Muḥammad wrote a rather stupid and vitriolic reply in *Miṣbāḥ al-sharq* called "Al-Jarīdah al-ʿĀmmiyyah" ("The Plebeian Newspaper") in which he declared that *Al-Mu'ayyad* represented the gutter press and was read only by the lower classes of society.[22] ʿAlī Yūsuf countered his attack with a regular column in his newspaper called "ʿĀm al-kaff" ("The Year of the Slap"). Al-Bishrī points out that many people in Cairo had suffered from the barbed pens of the Muwayliḥīs and thus there was no shortage of material with which ʿAlī Yūsuf could fill his column. Indeed, the poet Ismāʿīl Ṣabrī (1854–1923) was among those who composed poems for this purpose.[23] ʿAlī Yūsuf kept the column going for twelve consecutive daily issues of the newspaper and continued to taunt Muḥammad for not replying to his critics.[24] Eventually however, the common friends of both men including, no doubt, many members of the Nāzlī circle which both men attended, appear to have arranged a cease-fire, and no more was heard of the subject—for a while at least.

According to his closest friends, Muḥammad was deeply affected by this campaign against him; based on descriptions of his retiring nature and hatred of crowded places, this seems very likely. To some degree, his generally unsociable temperament can be attributed to the chronic stammer from which he suffered; apparently it was so bad that he would often be unable to finish a sentence at all and would have to resort to an embarassed silence. This fact may not only explain why he preferred to be educated at home as a boy, but also may provide a clue to the drastic effect which this incident in the café had on him. It is certainly true that the gradual decline of *Miṣbāḥ al-sharq* and *Abū Zayd* (a satirical magazine started by his father) can be traced to this period. The articles on topical subjects written by the editor, which had been a hallmark of the earlier issues and had accounted for much of the paper's popularity, became less frequent and were replaced by long extracts from French newspapers, some of which extended over several issues. Advertisements and announcements were allowed to take an ever-increasing amount of space in a paper which had only four pages to fill. It may have been at this time that Muḥammad decided (or perhaps it was suggested to him) to collect the episodes of *Fatrah min al-Zaman* into book form, so he closed down the newspapers to allow himself more time to concentrate on his revision of the text. Whatever the cause of closure may have been, *Miṣbāḥ al-sharq* ceased publication on August 15, 1903.[25]

The Muwayliḥīs continued to write for other newspapers. Ibrāhīm sent articles to *Al-Mu'ayyad* and *Al-Muqaṭṭam*, and in 1905 even founded a new newspaper called *Al-Mishkāt* in the name of his son Khalīl and Ḥamdī Bey Yakan.[26] Meanwhile, Muḥammad saw revenge taken on ʿAlī Yūsuf. In 1904 the latter was involved in a scandal when he proposed to Ṣafiyyah al-Sādāt, a woman of high birth, and was refused by her father, although the woman herself had consented to marry him and seemed to want to do so. The woman's father based his refusal on the fact that 'Alī Yūsuf was an Upper Egyptian (Ṣa'īdī) and was not worthy of his daughter because he was not a *sharīf*. The case was taken to court, and 'Alī Yūsuf lost both the initial case and the subsequent appeal.[27] During all this, the daily newspaper *Al-Ẓāhir* printed a column with the title "'Ām al-Kuf'" ("The Year of Equality")—an obvious echo of the series of articles against Muḥammad mentioned above, except that this series continued for thirty-four consecutive issues.[28] In poems that appeared in the column, 'Alī Yūsuf's suitability for such a marriage was questioned, his claims to be a *sharīf* were ridiculed, and he was made out to be a person totally unsuitable to take over the supervision of the Ṣūfī *waqf* properties, a post for which his name had been put forward.

Ibrāhīm al-Muwayliḥī fell ill in December 1905 and died on January 29, 1906. It was also in that year that 'Abbās the Second decorated Muḥammad with the order of Bey second class (Mutamayyiz), but Muḥammad now appears to have preferred to remain at home as he had done as a boy, reading and holding discussions with his friends. Among the people who used to frequent his house during this period were 'Abd al-'Azīz al-Bishrī and 'Abbās Maḥmūd al-'Aqqād, both of whom have left descriptions of the friends who used to come to these discussions—Ḥāfiẓ Ibrāhīm, 'Abd al-Salām al-Muwayliḥī, Muḥammad Tawfīq al-Bakrī, Muḥammad Bey Rashād, and 'Alī Yūsuf (with whom Muḥammad appears finally to have been reconciled).[29] Muḥammad left his house rarely and wrote very little. The series of articles *Fatrah min al-Zaman* appeared in book form as *Ḥadīth 'Īsā ibn Hishām* in 1907. On February 9, 1908, an article entitled "Kalimah Mafrūḍah" ("An Obligatory Word") appeared under his name in *Al-Mu'ayyad*. The occasion of this article's appearance is described by Sir Ronald Storrs:

> The Italians of Alexandria have chosen this juncture for proposing that the Municipality should erect a large statue

> to Dante, which plan, seeing that Dante placed Muhammad and *Ali* in hell with the other Schismatics, cleft from chin to tank with their insides hanging out, is meeting with frantic opposition from united Islam.[30]

Muḥammad's article was an important contribution to this united Islamic front. He began by quoting in Arabic for the readers of the newspaper exactly what Dante does say about Muḥammad in the *Divine Comedy*, and from there went on to demand that all Muslims should rally to the cause of their religion instead of sitting back lethargically and watching while it suffered such a gross insult. It is almost certainly significant that a few pages later Storrs records the disgust of Princess Nāzlī herself with what Dante had written. In the following year, Muḥammad allowed himself to be drawn even further out of his seclusion and retirement when he accepted an invitation to attend the opening of the Ḥijāz railway, traveled to Medina and is said to have been one of the anonymous contributors to the series of articles on the railway which appeared in *Al-Mu'ayyad* at the time.[31]

On May 15, 1910, he was appointed Director of the Waqf Administration. Al-ʿAqqād records that al-Muwayliḥī found the work very tedious, and so it is hardly surprising that he resigned from the position four years later, and retired to his home again. He apparently felt that his talents were being wasted and that a man of his standing should not have to work in such a fashion.[32]

From now on, he seems to have lived a modest life which at times descended to poverty, but the pride which had prompted him to leave his post in the Waqf Administration apparently helped him to live through such trials with dignity.[33] He ventured into print only once more before his death in 1930. On December 30, 1921, an article of his appeared in the newspaper *Al-Ahrām* under the title "Ṣawt min al-ʿUzlah" ("Voice from Retirement") in which he began by giving his reasons for retiring from a life of journalism and then proceeded to express his feelings about the second expulsion of Saʿd Zaghlūl from Egypt. He pointed out that the situation was one which could bring Egyptians together as one nation and that Jamāl al-dīn al-Afghānī would rejoice at the thought. Apart from this article, Muḥammad divided his time during the remaining years of his life between his home and Alexandria with occasional visits to sporting events such as horse racing. In 1925, "the owner of a well-known newspaper" (unfortunately anonymous) is said to have asked him to write two articles expressing a certain point of view on a subject for the sum of eighty pounds, but Muḥammad's alleged reply sounds typical enough: "Al-Muwayliḥī's pen is not for sale."[34]

In 1927, *Ḥadīth 'Īsā ibn Hishām* was published as a textbook by the Ministry of Education for use in secondary schools. Muḥammad undertook an extensive revision of the work before its publication (see more details in the following section). In this process, he excluded many of the book's most controversial pages and included the episodes from Paris mentioned above as "Al-Riḥlah al-thāniyah" ("The Second Journey"). He also began to work on the production in book form of a set of essays on various philosophical topics, most of which had also appeared on the pages of *Miṣbāḥ al-sharq*. A few weeks after finishing work on these essays, on February 28, 1930, he died in Ḥulwān, and it was left to his brother Khalīl and his friend Salīm Abū Ḥājib, Princess Nāzlī's husband, to prepare the book for publication. It appeared as *'Ilāj al-nafs* (*Cure for the Soul*)—also a school text—in 1932.[35]

A History of the Text

Ḥadīth 'Īsā ibn Hishām, Muḥammad al-Muwayliḥī's famous turn-of-the-century narrative, was an instant success when it appeared as a series of articles under the title *Fatrah min al-Zaman* between 1898 and 1902 in the family's Cairo newspaper, *Miṣbāḥ al-sharq*. It became even more successful when it appeared as a book in 1907, now under the title *Ḥadīth 'Īsā ibn Hishām*. Multiple editions of the work have been published in the century or so since that first edition—the most recent of which is edited by me—appeared as part of a collection of the author's complete works in 2002.[36] While all these editions of the work may be considered as versions of the text, they are by no means all the same. Behind that fact lies a tale that I would like to relate in this section of the Introduction.[37]

As noted in the previous section, the Muwayliḥīs—father Ibrāhīm and son Muḥammad—had been vigorous participants in Egyptian political and cultural life beginning in the reign of the Khedive Ismāʿīl (r. 1863–79). The father had held prominent positions, and his son often joined his father in such activities. Both men were acquainted, for example, with the renowned Islamic activist, Jamāl al-dīn al-Afghānī, and his colleague, Muḥammad ʿAbduh, who was to become a major figure in the Islamic reform movement in Egypt.[38] As a direct result of the Muwayliḥīs' involvement in such controversial debates, activities, and intrigues, Ibrāhīm al-Muwayliḥī clearly felt it wise to accept the Khedive Ismāʿīl's invitation to travel with him when he was exiled in 1879, and Muḥammad was also compelled to leave the country when he was arrested for distributing leaflets written by his father during the 1882 ʿUrābī Revolt, a direct consequence of which had been the British occupation of Egypt. Thereafter father and son traveled widely, to Italy, to Paris, to London, and finally to Istanbul when, as noted earlier, Ibrāhīm received an "invitation" from the Sultan ʿAbd al-Ḥamīd to come to the Ottoman capital—an invitation, one suspects, it would have been unwise to turn down. Both Egyptians spent a number of years in Istanbul, and Ibrāhīm wrote a famous account of his time there (*Mā Hunālik*) which was published in Cairo following his return in 1896 and immediately banned. Now that father and son had returned to their homeland, their broad acquaintance with the intricacies of Egyptian political and intellectual life, their wide experience of European culture, their exposure to life in the Ottoman capital, and, in the case of Muḥammad al-Muwayliḥī, long hours spent reading texts and manuscripts in Istanbul's Fātiḥ Library, were all qualities that made them ideal candidates for the foundation of a new weekly newspaper, one that would join an already crowded field that included, besides *Al-Muqaṭṭam*, the long-established *Al-Ahrām* (founded in Alexandria in 1875 by the Syrian Taqlā brothers) and the more populist *Al-Mu'ayyad* (founded in 1889 and edited by ʻAlī Yūsuf).

The al-Muwayliḥī newspaper, *Miṣbāḥ al-sharq*, soon established a wide reputation, not only for its trenchant commentary on current events and political developments, but also for its elevated style.[39] As if to emphasize the erudition of the composers of the articles (which were not initially signed), readers may have been somewhat surprised when issue number 21 of the 8th of September 1898 contained an article—published as section 0.1.1 in this edition—that begins with a line of poetry and then introduces the name of ʻĪsā ibn Hishām as the narrator of a sarcastic piece in the form of a fictional conversation between three well-known Egyptian political figures and holders of Egyptian ministerial office, Fakhrī Pāshā, Buṭrus Pāshā, and Maẓlūm Pāshā, about the latest developments in the Sudanese War. Quite apart from the obviously critical posture that the article adopts, of interest here is the process of fictionalizing the commentary and also the invocation of an illustrious name from the heritage of Arabic pre-modern narrative, ʻĪsā ibn Hishām, the narrator of and often participant in the famous collection of *maqāmāt* composed centuries earlier by Badīʻ al-Zamān al-Hamadhānī (358–98/969–1007). Given that the contents of newspapers usually brought (and indeed bring) almost instantaneous reactions from their readerships, we have to assume that the initial foray into this type of composition was well received, in that it was followed in quick succession by three others, all of them relating to the Sudanese War and the involvement (or rather non-involvement) of the Egyptian government and its ministers in what was projected as a joint enterprise (the so-called Anglo-Egyptian Sudan). The significance of these four initial articles introduced by ʻĪsā ibn Hishām is firstly that they are directly concerned with one particular aspect of Egyptian political life in the final years of the nineteenth century—the Sudanese war—which is completely missing from the published book text of *Ḥadīth ʻĪsā ibn Hishām* to appear later (1907). In addition, the final article of the four appears just one week before the first "episode" of *Fatrah min al-Zaman*, the series that, in heavily edited and rewritten form, was later to become the text of *Ḥadīth ʿĪsā ibn Hishām*. One is left to wonder whether this initial set of four articles (*Miṣbāḥ al-sharq* 21, 23, 24, and 30) was a kind of "dry run" for what was to become a much longer project—even though it is almost certain that, at this initial stage, Muḥammad al-Muwayliḥī himself could have had no idea of the runaway success that was to greet his work nor the length of time that weekly publication of episodes would involve.

The first episode of the series of articles entitled *Fatrah min al-Zaman* appeared in issue 31 of *Miṣbāḥ al-sharq* (November 17, 1898). The new title and the fact that ʿĪsā ibn Hishām, the narrator who is wandering in a graveyard, encounters a Pāshā from the era of Muḥammad ʿAlī, clearly implies that something new and different is intended, although the existence of the four previous articles also implies a clear and continuing linkage to current events. Another feature that marks this episode as being something different is the author's virtuoso use of the traditional style known as *sajʿ*, literally the cooing of a dove, but used to represent the ancient style of cadenced and rhyming prose that is first encountered in the pre-Islamic era in the utterances of preachers and soothsayers, then found as the primary stylistic feature of the Qur'anic revelations, and later adopted by Badīʿ al-Zamān al-Hamadhānī in his innovative narrative genre, the *maqāmah*. Over the course of the series—spread out over four years in total—almost every original episode begins with an extended passage of *sajʿ*, more often than not setting the scene and establishing the context.

The initial four episodes of *Fatrah min al-Zaman* were published in a flurry, one week after another, suggesting that their author had a basic "plot" in mind for at least the initial encounter of his Egyptian narrator and the resurrected Pāshā with the complexities of Egyptian law—a French-based system being applied to Egyptians during a British occupation. At the same time however, he clearly needed to assess the reaction of the continually growing readership of the newspaper to this new experiment, one that combined astute observation of late nineteenth-century occupied Cairo with a style redolent of the most famous of pre-modern Arabic narratives.[40] Bearing in mind the reaction to both the original episodes and the subsequent book, one has to assume that the response was extremely positive. The episodes therefore continued after a five-week gap. The trials and tribulations of the Pāshā following his arrest for assault—his court case and eventual acquittal, and his quest for the misappropriated endowment that he had bequeathed to future generations—were recounted in a series of articles that take us to March 1899. What is significant in view of our current concern with the textual history of the narrative is that the publication sequence is interrupted with an episode in *Miṣbāḥ al-sharq* 40 (January 19, 1899) which is entitled "The Sudanese Government Monopoly" and involves yet another conversation between a newspaper reporter and a minister in the Egyptian government about events in the Sudan; in other words, we see a return to the topic dealt with in the four episodes preceding the opening episode of *Fatrah min al-Zaman*. Here is how this intrusion is justified by the author:

> ʿĪsā ibn Hishām told us: I heard a story about a minister concerned with that topic which is on everyone's mind at the moment. This happened when a newspaper reporter came to see him to try to get the benefit of his enlightened views and learn some accurate information about the new government in the Sudan. Because it seems to me so remarkable, I have decided to relay it to our readers immediately before we go back to the story of the Pāshā and his trial.

The insertion of this article into the sequence of episodes involving ʿĪsā ibn Hishām's narration of the Pāshā's encounter with the Egyptian legal system is certainly a symptom of the vagaries of serialized publication—as the careers of earlier generations of novelists in Europe can readily illustrate. But the insertion also shows that the situation in the Sudan was a preoccupation of the Egyptian press at the time when Muḥammad al-Muwayliḥī began to publish his narrative, and that it is clearly reflected in the original sequence of articles.

This concern with the Sudan is also responsible for another break in the publication sequence, but this time for a different reason. In ʿĪsā ibn Hishām's *Fatrah min al-Zaman* narrative, the Pāshā is both emotionally and physically exhausted after his experiences with the law. A period of rest and contemplation is recommended, and it coincides with an actual occurrence of the plague in Egypt. Several episodes are thus concerned with medicine, the plague, and a resort to literature as a source of relaxation and contemplation. This brings the publication sequence of episodes to June 1899, at which point Muḥammad al-Muwayliḥī pauses. The gap is filled by his father, Ibrāhīm, who publishes three episodes of a narrative of his own, *Mirʾāt al-ʿĀlam* (*Mirror of the World*), where there is also an intense focus on the poor conditions under which the Egyptian army is laboring in the Sudan and, as experienced by Ibrāhīm directly, on the perils of speculation on the Stock Exchange.[41]

When Muḥammad al-Muwayliḥī resumes his narrative (*Miṣbāḥ al-sharq* 63, July 13, 1899), it is with a visit to a wedding hall, as part of which there is a section devoted to a lengthy history of singing. At the conclusion of an episode, the protagonists encounter a number of different social groups who have gathered at the wedding celebration—al-Azhar shaykhs, merchants, royal princes, and civil servants. Each of these categories subsequently becomes the topic of a later episode in *Fatrah min al-Zaman*. These shifts in narrative focus, each one involving a gap of varying duration in the publication of the articles, give us a hint as to how al-Muwayliḥī's responded to reader interest in the way he composed and sequenced episodes, again a replication of the circumstances under which novelists like Charles Dickens frequently functioned in composing and publishing novels. It is in the episodes that follow the description of these "meetings" (*majālis*) that al-Muwayliḥī comes up with his most inspired creation, the provincial *ʿumdah* (village headman) who comes to the rapidly Westernizing capital city from the countryside in search of fun and is mercilessly exploited by a duly Westernized fop (*Khalīʿ*, which I have translated as "Playboy") and his accomplice, a Merchant. The juxtaposition and confrontation of traditional mores and Western fashions is explored through a number of different venues and situations: restaurants and food, bars, tourism, money borrowing, and the theater. After a visit to the Pyramids, ʿĪsā ibn Hishām, the Pāshā, and their "Friend" (*ṣadīq*) leave the other group to their own devices and return home (*Miṣbāḥ al-sharq* 107, June 8, 1900). Given that Muḥammad al-Muwayliḥī was leaving almost immediately for Paris and the *Exposition universelle*, it is not surprising that, in what was at the time a final episode in the series, the Pāshā expresses to ʿĪsā his desire to see Western civilization firsthand. Plans are made to travel to France.

As already noted, Ibrāhīm al-Muwayliḥī made use of his son's journey to France to publish further episodes of his own narrative. Not only that, but *Miṣbāḥ al-sharq* 107 also contains the following announcement:

> ʿĪsā ibn Hishām: Muḥammad al-Muwayliḥī is traveling to the Paris Exposition this coming Sunday. Once he has gathered his impressions of the entire scenario and its details, *Miṣbāḥ al-sharq* will be publishing his description of its marvels and curiosities.

Muḥammad al-Muwayliḥī traveled first to London in order to write about the Khedive's visit to England,[42] but he then traveled to Paris. The first Parisian episode of *Fatrah min al-Zaman* was published in *Miṣbāḥ al-sharq* 116, August 17, 1900, with the following preface:

> This is the first episode of *Ḥadīth ʿĪsā ibn Hishām* concerning the visit to the Paris Exhibition. It has been sent to us by Muḥammad al-Muwayliḥī following his previous report on the visit of the Khedive of Egypt to Her Majesty the Queen of England.

Among the things to note from this introduction is that the series of episodes, originally (and still) called *Fatrah min al-Zaman*, has now acquired another title, *Ḥadīth ʿĪsā ibn Hishām*, which had been used on a few occasions in announcements before, but seems to have become the preferred title—indeed the one under which the eventual book was to be published in 1907. This trend is further emphasized by the fact that Ibrāhīm al-Muwayliḥī's narrative is assigned the subtitle *Ḥadīth Mūsā ibn ʿIṣām*, invoking the name of his own narrator and at the same time echoing in the clearest possible way the emerging title of his son's work.

Eight episodes describing (and, more often than not, harshly criticizing) the *Exposition universelle* in Paris were published between August and December 1900.[43] The last of them finishes with the usual statement, "To be continued," followed by the letter "M." Muḥammad al-Muwayliḥī had used this formula at the end of his articles ever since his father had begun publishing them. And yet the articles didn't continue. Or, at least, nothing followed until February 1902 (in other words, long after his return to Cairo) when, without any further explanation, three further episodes of *Fatrah min al-Zaman* were added. The first simply opens with the following statement:

> 'Isa ibn Hisham said: Our coverage of the visit we paid to the mother of all European capitals and our stay in the hub of civilization finished with a description of the Great Exhibition: the different people we met there, the strange happenings day and night, the variety of exotic items, the precious and creative objects of every conceivable kind of craft that were on display, the nightclubs and music halls scattered across the grounds, the splendid views it afforded visitors, and the undesirable subtext out of sight. The Pasha, our Friend, and I had emerged from it with a mixture of feelings: praise, criticism, and outright condemnation. We were still in the company of the sage Frenchman, his temples whitened by his willingness to share with us his culture and learning.[44]

These three articles, which form an uninterrupted continuum and only the first of which contains an example of their author's virtuoso use of *saj'*, offer a detailed description of the French system of government—its presidency, election processes, senate, and chamber of deputies. The third of these episodes ends again with the usual "To be continued," and yet nothing followed. And this time it was indeed the end of the *Fatrah min al-Zaman* series the author had initiated four years earlier.

For whatever combination of reasons, al-Muwayliḥī was to take his time in converting his series of newspaper articles into book form. It seems clear that he had already been receiving encouragement to do so from the enthusiastic response of readers of the newspaper, not to mention many of his literary colleagues, including the renowned nationalist poet, Ḥāfiẓ Ibrāhīm (1871–1932). Indeed the latter's own contribution to the neoclassical revival of the *maqāmah* narrative *Layālī Saṭīḥ*, first published in 1906, contains an extract from al-Muwayliḥī's as yet unpublished book (and incidentally concentrates heavily on the situation in the Sudan, not surprising in view of the fact that the poet served as an Egyptian army officer there).[45]

The first edition of *Ḥadīth 'Īsā ibn Hishām* was published in 1907, *Fatrah min al-Zaman* becoming its subtitle. In the introduction to this (and only this) edition, al-Muwayliḥī explains his method and rationale:

> After reviewing the articles carefully—a process that has demanded revisions and corrections, as well as alterations, substitutions, omissions and additions, I have now converted the story into book form. After all, the contents of newspapers are by definition ephemeral, mere thoughts of the day. They cannot claim a place in a book that will move with the times and be read over and over again.[46]

A comparison of the text of the 1907 edition of *Ḥadīth 'Īsā ibn Hishām* with articles in the series *Fatrah min al-Zaman* does indeed corroborate the author's description of the conversion process. The wording of individual phrases is changed, and clarifying detail is often added; the major emphasis is on expansion and clarification rather than contraction. For the second edition of 1912, the author adds a glossary at the end of the text. However, what is most striking about the first edition of the book is that it does not include any of the material in which the Sudan situation is the primary topic; secondly, the original sequence of episodes is altered, requiring a good deal of rewriting and reorganization. In the original articles the visit to the wedding hall comes much earlier in the sequence and is followed by visits to the series of assemblies (*majālis*), whereas in the book version the assemblies come first in the ordering of episodes. Furthermore, completely new material is included about the plague, derived from a factual article, "Al-Akhlāq fī l-Wabā'" ("Ethics During the Epidemic") that was published in *Miṣbāḥ al-sharq* 221, September 13, 1902. The first edition (and the two subsequent ones, 1912 and 1923) all finish with the expressed desire to add "the second journey" (*al-riḥlah al-thāniyah*)—the episodes describing the visit to Paris—to the first (*al-riḥlah al-ūlā*) at some point in the future. Meanwhile the first three editions of *Ḥadīth ʿĪsā ibn Hishām* were and are only concerned with the Egyptian context. A further addition to the third edition (1923) was that of titles to the newly established "chapters" created either from the contents of the original articles or, more often, by consolidation of articles into larger units.[47]

At some point in the 1920s, *Ḥadīth ʿĪsā ibn Hishām* was adopted as a text for secondary school, and al-Muwayliḥī was invited to prepare a new fourth edition, which was published in 1927. I have not thus far found any specific evidence as to instructions that the author may have received regarding expectations for such a school text, but it is clear that the revision process he undertook before publication of this fourth edition radically altered the critical tone of the work—one that had already been somewhat muted by the process of converting the newspaper articles into a book. His now twenty-year-old wish to include the Paris episodes (*al-riḥlah al-thāniyah*) to the book was also finally fulfilled. Thus the second part of post-4th edition versions of *Ḥadīth ʿĪsā ibn Hishām* was added to the list of several previously published contributions by Arab visitors to the analysis of European civilization—in the case of Egypt a trend initiated in the nineteenth century by Rifāʿah Rāfiʿ al-Ṭahṭāwī (1801–71) with his *Takhlīṣ al-Ibrīz fī Talkhīṣ Bārīz* (*The Purification of Gold Concerning the Summary of Paris*), originally published in 1834. However, along with this addition to the text, some extremely significant omissions were made. Two complete "assemblies," one devoted to the shaykhs of al-Azhar discussing the heretical sciences of philosophy and geography and the other to the princes of the royal family who were squabbling with each other over expensive racing stallions, were completely omitted, along with a number of uncomplimentary anecdotes about Muḥammad ʿAlī, founder of the dynasty to which the current Egyptian ruler—now called "king"—belonged. One can only surmise about the decision-making process involved in these omissions, and whether they were made on the author's own initiative or as the result of a "recommendation" from some official channel, possibly because it was now almost thirty years after the time when the original articles had been composed. Indeed the none too subtle criticism in these episodes may have been reckoned inappropriate for the Egyptian teenage minds who would be studying *Ḥadīth ʿĪsā ibn Hishām* for the secondary-school examinations known as the *thānawiyyah ʿāmmah*.[48]

Whatever the case may be, the book version of Muḥammad al-Muwayliḥī's narrative *Ḥadīth ʿĪsā ibn Hishām*, originally published in 1907 and the one that has become the best known through a number of subsequent editions and reprints, already differs considerably from the original newspaper articles, and its fourth edition of 1927 takes the process of change still further. When I was asked by Professors Gaber Asfour and Sabry Hafez in the 1990s to prepare a new edition of the author's complete works (and those of his father) for a new series, *Ruwwād al-Fann al-Qaṣaṣī* (*Pioneers of the Narrative Art*) to be published by al-Majlis al-Aʿlā li-l-Thaqāfah

(Supreme Council for Culture) in Cairo, I was already aware of the differences between the various editions of this work which had long since come to be regarded as a foundational contribution to the development of modern Arabic narrative—looking both forward and backward in time, a genuine "bridge-work." It was on that basis that I prepared the text for publication, using the resources that I had myself collected—in handwritten form—as part of my Oxford doctoral research in 1966. That work was published in two volumes in 2002. However, with advancements in computer technology and research methods, I have now been able to access the complete archive of the al-Muwayliḥī newspaper, *Miṣbāḥ al-sharq*, and have discovered that even what I thought was a "complete" edition of the text is in fact not entirely complete.

I am grateful to the Library of Arabic Literature (LAL) for giving me the opportunity to produce for the first time a version of the sequence of all the episodes of the original series of articles al-Muwayliḥī wrote and published that are introduced by a narrator named ʿĪsā ibn Hishām, whether or not they are part of the series called *Fatrah min al-Zaman*. That decision on my part, of course, raises some significant questions. Al-Muwayliḥī's description of his own revision process in converting the original articles into book form clearly indicates an aspiration on his part to turn something that was published in a context that he describes as "ephemeral" into a more permanent form. However the notion of ephemerality that he associates with newspaper publication and invokes to explain his rationale for revision is only part of the story. If we examine the sequence of the original articles closely and follow his lead in omitting entirely the "dry run" set of four articles devoted to the Sudan (and the somewhat curious return to the topic inserted in the initial sequence of *Fatrah min al-Zaman*), then the series seems to fall into four subseries: the Pāshā's initial encounter with the Egyptian legal system in which both he and ʿĪsā ibn Hishām are centrally involved in the action; the period spent away so as to avoid the plague and allow the Pāshā to recover, in which there is considerably less action; the series of "assemblies"; and finally the episodes involving the ʿUmdah and his two colleagues—in both these last two sequences ʿĪsā and the Pāshā fade almost completely into the background once the context has been established. Thus, if one is to apply some notions of Western narratological analysis to the resulting book text, one can say that al-Muwayliḥī's careful reworking of the newspaper articles does provide for a more convincing sequence of "events," but does little or nothing to affect the varying roles of two of the principal "characters."

Several Egyptian critics have tried to make of *Ḥadīth ʿĪsā ibn Hishām* an incipient novel, but I would suggest that an investigation of the work's origins ties it as closely, if not more so, to the more episodic model of the classical *maqāmah* genre that is deliberately being invoked by the use of ʿĪsā ibn Hishām as a participant narrator, duly derived from al-Hamadhānī's tenth-century model. To the episodic nature of the individual articles can be added yet another feature of al-Hamadhānī's creations, namely their resort to "prosimetrum," the regular inclusion of lines of poetry within a cursive prose narrative. One might even go on to suggest that, if al-Muwayliḥī's attempt at producing a more logically sequenced narrative out of the original article series *Fatrah min al-Zaman* was a reflection of his acquaintance with and understanding of fictional models of that era, then the episodic and even fragmented nature of the story in its article format is a much closer reflection of his "classical" model in al-Hamadhānī's *maqāmāt* and may indeed emerge therefrom as almost postmodern.

This translation, the first ever in book form to include all the original articles narrated by a nineteenth-century Egyptian called ʿĪsā ibn Hishām and published in *Miṣbāḥ al-sharq* at the turn of the nineteenth century, will thus re-establish their author's text firmly within the political and cultural context within which they were conceived and on which they regularly commented. The availability of different versions of this famous narrative—the original articles of *Fatrah min al-Zaman*, the collected works of Muḥammad al-Muwayliḥī, and the various editions of *Ḥadīth ʿĪsā ibn Hishām*—will make it possible to examine in detail the role that this "bridge-work" played in linking the pre-modern heritage of Arabic narrative to his lively portrait of a tumultuous and changing present in nineteenth-century Egypt and the ways in which the story has been transformed during a timeframe that now exceeds a century.

Note on the Translation

In view of the complex textual history, it should again be made clear that the translation presented here is *not* based on any published book version of Muḥammad al-Muwayliḥī's *Ḥadīth ʿĪsā ibn Hishām*. Rather it offers for the first time a translation of the series of articles, entitled *Fatrah min al-Zaman*, which were originally published over a four-year period (1898–1902) in the al-Muwayliḥī newspaper, *Miṣbāḥ al-sharq*, and later converted by the author—after significant editing, into the book, *Ḥadīth ʿĪsā ibn Hishām*, first published in 1907.

It might seem more appropriate to select *A Period of Time* as a title, that being a literal translation of the original Arabic title for the series of articles. However, since I had already used that title for my published study and translation of the third edition of *Ḥadīth ʿĪsā ibn Hishām* (1923—originally my doctoral thesis at Oxford submitted in 1968, published originally in microfiche form in 1974 and later in a second edition in 1992), I have decided to use another title, *What ʿĪsā ibn Hishām Told Us*, my aim being to reflect the fact that the contents of this version involve *all* the articles that he published in *Miṣbāḥ al-sharq* that are introduced by a narrator named ʿĪsā ibn Hishām, both those that made their way, albeit in altered form, into the book *Ḥadīth ʿĪsā ibn Hishām* and those that, for a variety of reasons, were not included.

Muḥammad al-Muwayliḥī, through his mostly private education, his travels, his interests, and his research in libraries, was extremely erudite, as indeed was his father, Ibrāhīm al-Muwayliḥī. That much is abundantly clear from the elevated style that characterizes the articles published in their newspaper *Miṣbāḥ al-sharq*, and thus in the works in which those articles were assembled in book form. Whereas some of their contemporaries—such as Jūrjī Zaydān (1861–1914) and Muṣṭafā Luṭfī al-Manfalūṭī (1876–1924)—may have striven to develop a less elaborate and more accessible style with which to attract a broader readership to their works and especially the newspaper and journals in which they published, such, it would appear, was not a goal of the Muwayliḥīs in their choice of style.

In the particular case of Muḥammad al-Muwayliḥī and the text that makes up this translation, we are dealing with a conscious revival of a pre-modern narrative genre (including its narrator by name) and its characteristic stylistic features. Like al-Hamadhānī many centuries earlier, al-Muwayliḥī has a narrator and a main character (the Pāshā) travel to various places where they react to and comment on what they encounter, in this case the Egyptian legal system, the onset of the plague, the wide variety of meeting venues in Cairo, the clash of indigenous and imported values exemplified by the tastes of the ʿUmdah and the "Playboy," and, at a later stage, the various pavilions of the Paris Exhibition of 1900. Also like his illustrious forebear, al-Muwayliḥī indulges in a variety of pastiches of other forms of discourse: among many possibilities, we might mention the overblown rhetoric of the groomsman's speech at the wedding (20.10), and the absurdly complex and obscure reasoning of the newspaper article allegedly written by the al-Azhar shaykh (22.14–22.18). But from the point of view of this text and its translation into English, the most prominent feature of the *maqāmah* genre was its revival of the ancient style known as *sajʿ* and the resort at the same time to the use of "prosimetrum," the inclusion of lines of poetry and sometimes complete poems in what is otherwise considered to be a work of "prose." A comprehensive history of the stylistic phenomenon of *sajʿ* within the literary heritage of the Arabs has yet to be written, but the style is certainly to be found during the pre-Islamic era and is the primary characteristic of the Qurʾanic text; indeed in his important study *Introduction to Arabic Poetics*, the Syro-Lebanese poet and critic Adūnīs (b. 1930) suggests that in the Arabic literary tradition, *saj'* may not be the first manifestation of poetry per se, but is certainly the first manifestation of the poetic. Here is not the place to explore these issues in detail, but merely to point out that the linkage of *saj'* and poetry in Arabic, and in the writings of al-Muwayliḥī with which we are concerned here, can be traced back to the very origins of its literary history.

The articles narrated by 'Īsā ibn Hishām which al-Muwayliḥī published in *Miṣbāḥ al-sharq* are characterized by a very elevated style of prose writing, and they also replicate the drama genre to a degree by including lengthy examples of dialogue, still composed of course, in the same elevated style. However, the initial paragraphs of each original article also involve the kind of virtuoso displays of style that are an intrinsic feature of *saj'*. As any learner of Arabic soon discovers, the language is one in which morphological patterns are not only widely prevalent but form the very basis of its lexicography (one might even suggest that the entire process is not a little "algebraic," algebra being itself a subdivision of mathematics and indeed the term itself being of Arabic origin, *al-jabr* [contraction]). The *saj'* style exploits this feature to the maximum: not only is there regularly a sequence of phrases with a rhyming syllable at the end (thus replicating the prosodic system of Arabic poetry), but it would also appear that the rhythmic cadence of each phrase also needs to parallel the others in each rhyming sequence (which, when done by a virtuoso composer of *maqāmāt* such as al-Ḥarīrī [1054–1122], might extend for eight consecutive phrases). An almost axiomatic consequence of these "expectations" of the *saj'* style (one that admittedly has been scantly analyzed by scholars, perhaps because of the presence of the phenomenon in the Qur'an and the notion of that text's "inimitability") is that the same incidents and images are depicted numerous times with different phraseology, allowing the composer not only to display his linguistic virtuosity but also to exploit Arabic's myriad possibilities in the realms of morphology and synonyms.[49] When we add to this al-Muwayliḥī's acknowledged erudition and wide exposure to both Arabic and European cultural and literary traditions, the challenges that confront the would-be translator of this text seem clear.

Turning now to the translation process itself, I have to acknowledge that, even when faced with the challenges a text such as that of al-Muwayliḥī presents to both the translator and the anticipated reader of the resulting translation, I still find myself resorting to the logic presented by the renowned German theologian, philosopher, and commentator on translation, Friedrich Scheiermacher (1768–1834) when he states:

> Either the translator leaves the author in peace as much as possible and moves the reader towards him, or he leaves the reader in peace and moves the author towards him.[50]

While there are, of course, a number of theoretical and practical issues that any translator has to resolve in the process of "transferring" a text from one culture and reading public to another, I have as a basic principle always much preferred the former of these two possibilities, that of "foreignizing the reader" rather than "domesticating the text." With that in mind, I should therefore state clearly that, when I have been confronted, for example, at the beginning of each article in this text with a series of phrases in Arabic *saj'* which portray with multiple variations the same image or create a scenario—that being the most usual function of the introductory paragraphs in each article, I have resorted to a process of repetition and a copious use of synonyms which is perhaps not characteristic of English-language discourse, but a clear replication (translation) of the original Arabic text. Meanwhile, the often lengthy passages of cursive Arabic prose have been rendered into what I hope will be regarded as an appropriate level of English discourse. It is only in the marginally more spontaneous sections of dialogue (especially those involving the 'Umdah and his two companions) that I have made any attempt at a more "conversational" style, but even there the constraints of al-Muwayliḥī's choice of Arabic language register do not encourage any efforts at producing a series of more spontaneous exchanges.

To conclude, al-Muwayliḥī's long-acknowledged masterpiece—whether in its original newspaper article form as in this edition or in one of the many and varied book editions of the work—is not only a wonderfully trenchant survey of turn-of-the-century Egypt under British occupation as it was involved in a complex process of cultural assimilation and transition, but also a conscious attempt to link developments in Arabic language and its literary forms during the nineteenth century (a movement generally known as the *nahḍah* [revival]) to the Arabic heritage of the pre-modern centuries. For that reason I have already characterized here it as being a genuine "bridge-work," one that adopts a kind of Janus-like posture, looking in two directions simultaneously. It can be argued, and indeed several Egyptian scholars have argued, that the editorial process al-Muwayliḥī undertook before the publication of *Ḥadīth ʿĪsā ibn Hishām* in 1907 may have been an attempt to turn the text into a kind of "proto-novel." However, as I have also endeavored to show previously (especially in *A Period of Time*, 1992, Section III), the revised text is less than successful in meeting even the minimal goals of such a designation. While one may be able to offer different views within that critical generic context, there can be little doubt that the original newspaper articles, published here for the first time in their original format and sequence, are the clearest possible reflection of the political, social, and cultural concerns that were the central focus of both al-Muwayliḥīs in their newspaper. That is, it seems to me, their enduring value, added to which is the fact that the vast majority of the text that was eventually to be published as *Ḥadīth ʿĪsā ibn Hishām*—with either its "first journey" only (1907, 1912, and 1923) or both journeys (1927 and thereafter)—is present in the current text, albeit in a different sequence.

Given the multiple cultural and cross-cultural references in the text, I have provided both a Glossary of Names and Places and a series of detailed endnotes. The latter includes references to the equivalent chapters of the book version of *Ḥadīth ʿĪsā ibn Hishām*, as well as citations of as many of the sources of the copious amount of poetry in the text as I have been able to find. In that context, I have to express particular gratitude to Professors Geert Jan van Gelder, James Montgomery, Maurice Pomerantz, Bilal Orfali, and Philip Kennedy, all of whom have allowed me to tap their knowledge of the Arabic poetic tradition in quest of the identities of the many unidentified poets whose lines are cited in this text. I would also like to thank my colleague, Professor Joseph E. Lowry, for his assistance with the identification of the legal sources that are cited in the text.

In conclusion, I would like to avail myself of this opportunity to express particular thanks to Professor Philip Kennedy, the General Editor of the Library of Arabic Literary series (and also editor of the project that consists of these two volumes) and the other members of the project's Editorial Board.

Roger Allen

Notes to the Introduction

1 Ibrāhīm's dealings with al-Afghānī are fully covered in Keddie, *Sayyid Jamāl ad-Dīn "al-Afghānī,"* 235ff. and 246ff.

2 Al-Bishrī, *Al-Mukhtār*, 1:246.

3 The al-Muwayliḥī newspaper *Miṣbāḥ al-sharq* is full of articles concerning the perils involved in speculation on the Stock Exchange and the wiles of brokers in tricking the unwary. The topic of speculation is also a major theme of Ibrāhīm al-Muwayliḥī's *Mir'āt al-ʿĀlam* discussed below.

4 It should be pointed out that the most detailed source of information on the lives of Ibrāhīm and Muḥammad al-Muwayliḥī is Ibrāhīm al-Muwayliḥī the younger, and that, although the family anecdotes do throw considerable light on various aspects of the lives of the two men—and particularly the atmosphere of political intrigue which is further illuminated by al-ʿAqqād in "Mā warā' al-tarājim"—many of these stories may have been embellished to some degree in order to amplify the influence which Ibrāhīm al-Muwayliḥī is alleged to have had.

5 Ibrāhīm al-Muwayliḥī the younger quotes a letter written by Ibrāhīm to Muḥammad on March 15, 1880 asking for junior grammar books to be sent to Italy. See *al-Risālah* 6 (1938): 617ff.

6 *Encyclopaedia of Islam*, 2nd ed., s.v. "Arabi Pasha"; Landau, *Parliaments and Parties in Egypt*, 94ff.

7 *Le Figaro* (Paris) 331, November 26, 1884.

8 "Ihdā' al-Kitāb," in all editions of *Ḥadīth ʿĪsā ibn Hishām*. Al-Shinqīṭī died in Cairo in 1904.

9 Tarrāzī, *Ta'rīkh al-ṣiḥāfah al-ʿarabiyyah*, 4:165. ʿĀrif Bey later rose in the Ottoman administration and became governor of Sūriyā (Damascus).

10 These articles appeared irregularly in *Al-Muqaṭṭam* between December 8, 1887 and November 19, 1894.

11 Muḥammad Farīd comments in his unpublished memoirs that the Princess had a penchant for British officers. The setting for these meetings is well described by Sir Ronald Storrs in his *Orientations*, 87ff. The circle is discussed in greater detail in my "Writings of Members of the Nazli Circle."

12 Blunt, *My Diaries*, 1:14.

13 Ibid., 1:106. See also Lord Cromer, *Abbas II*, 7ff.

14 Published in *al-Muqaṭṭam*, August 18, 1893.

15 The Arabic text of this work was (re-)published in Ibrāhīm al-Muwayliḥī, *Al-Mu'allafāt al-kāmilah* in 2007. My English translation of this work is published as *Spies, Scandals, and Sultans.*

16 The former of these two appointments was announced in *Le proche Egyptien*, December 3, 1895.

17 The articles are reprinted in al-Manfalūṭī, *Mukhtārāt al-Manfalūṭī*, 139ff. I discuss both the articles and the accompanying furor in "Poetry and Poetic Criticism at the Turn of the Century."

18 Kurd ʿAlī, *Memoirs*, 89; Mūsā, *The Education of Salāma Mūsā*, 38.

19 *Miṣbāḥ al-sharq* 112, July 12, 1900.

20 *Miṣbāḥ al-sharq* beginning August 17, 1900.

21 Al-Muwayliḥī's version of the incident is given in "Ḥādithat Darāktūs," *Miṣbāḥ al-sharq* 229, November 8, 1902.

22 *Miṣbāḥ al-sharq* 230, November 15, 1902.

23 Ismāʿīl Ṣabrī, *Dīwān*, 94ff.

24 *Al-Mu'ayyad*, November 9–30, 1902.

25 The last issue of the newspaper to appear (August 15, 1903) contains the following announcement: "Apology: the editor of this newspaper has fallen ill and must have a change of air and some relaxation for a while. He asks the esteemed readers of the newspaper to accept his apologies for being away from work for a period of thirty days so that

he may recover, God willing." No formal announcement of permanent closure was made, and there was no comment on the subject from the rest of the press.

26 Tarrāzī, *Ta'rīkh al-ṣiḥāfah*, 4:185.

27 For further details of the case, see *Al-Kātib* 28 (July 1963, 74). For one of the poems on this subject, see Ḥāfiẓ Ibrāhīm, *Dīwān*, 1:256.

28 *Al-Ẓāhir*, August 2–October 3, 1904.

29 Al-Bishrī, *Al-Mukhtār*, 1:244ff.; al-ʿAqqād, *Rijāl ʿaraftuhum*, 79ff.

30 Storrs, *Orientations*, 74.

31 Al-Bishrī, *Al-Mukhtār*, 1:249.

32 Al-ʿAqqād, *Rijāl ʿaraftuhum*, 82–4.

33 One of the articles by Zakī Mubārak published in *al-Risālah* (10:995ff.) contains a section called "The Captive of Poverty and Hardship."

34 Mubārak, *al-Risālah*, 10:1049.

35 Al-Muwayliḥī, *ʿIlāj al-nafs*.

36 Al-Muwayliḥī, *Al-Mu'allafāt al-kāmilah*.

37 This history of the text should be regarded as a much-updated version of the section in my earlier study and translation of the text: Allen, *A Period of Time*, 32–48.

38 For fuller details on the two men's involvement in Egyptian and Ottoman politics, see Allen, *A Period of Time*, 1–14.

39 I must take the opportunity here to express my gratitude to my colleague and friend, Professor Gaber Asfour. While he was serving as Secretary-General to the Supreme Council for Culture in Cairo, I arranged for him to meet (now Dr.) Marie-Claire Boulahbel, at the time a French doctoral student writing a dissertation under my supervision on the works of Ibrāhīm al-Muwayliḥī at INALCO in Paris. He provided her with a CD-ROM of the complete run of issues of *Miṣbāḥ al-sharq* in the Dār al-Kutub newspaper archive that she subsequently catalogued and of which I now possess a copy. I need to express my gratitude to her as well for making access to the materials that much easier. All my subsequent research on the works of the Muwayliḥīs has been based on the ability to consult the original articles in the newspaper.

40 While Aḥmad Fāris al-Shidyāq includes examples of the *maqāmah* genre in his famous work, *Al-Sāq ʿalā al-sāq fī-mā huwa al-Fāryāq*, al-Muwayliḥī uses the *sajʿ* style as an opening feature to all his articles. For a virtuoso translation of al-Shidyāq's work, see Humphrey Davies's recent translation of al-Shidyāq, *Leg Over Leg*.

41 The complete text has been published in Ibrāhīm al-Muwayliḥī, *Al-Muʾallafāt al-Kāmilah*, 161–202. My English translation of the text has appeared in the journal *Middle Eastern Literatures*, 15, no. 3 (December 2012): 318–36; 16, no. 3 (December 2013): 1–17. It would seem that the father was willing to subordinate the publication of his own story to that of his son, in that, after publishing an initial three episodes in June–July 1899, he was willing to wait an entire year before publishing the remainder (while his son was traveling to Paris to report on the *Exposition universelle*).

42 Al-Muwayliḥī was clearly not enamored of English weather: "To Almighty God is the complaint about London weather! The sun has vanished and the moon is nowhere to be seen. Do you have any information to share with me about the sun or news of the moon? It has been such a long time, and I can only hope that God will compensate me for London weather with better in Paris. Farewell." *Miṣbāḥ al-sharq* 112, July 13, 1900.

43 *Miṣbāḥ al-sharq* 116, 117, 118, 121, 123, 126, 130, and 133.

44 *Miṣbāḥ al-sharq* 192, February 14, 1902.

45 Ḥāfiẓ Ibrāhīm, *Layālī Saṭīḥ*, 29.

46 Cairo: Maṭbaʿat al-Maʿārif, 1907.

47 Where original articles are combined to make a single chapter in the book version, the beginning of the second original article can easily be identified by its opening with a characteristic passage of *sajʿ*.

48 While conducting research for my Oxford doctoral thesis in Cairo in 1966, I had occasion to ask many Egyptians for their opinions of *Ḥadīth ʿĪsā ibn Hishām*. Their reactions were very similar to my own regarding the work of Geoffrey Chaucer, namely that, while it was and is recognized to be a great work, the very fact that it had been a "set text" for important examinations (and thus involved dealing with

considerable linguistic complexities at a certain age), had radically affected their views of it.

49 An exception to this situation is Stewart, "Sajʿ in the Qur'an: Prosody and Structure."

50 Quoted in L. Venuti, *Translation Studies Reader*, 2004, 49.

What ʿĪsā ibn Hishām Told Us

Miṣbāḥ al-sharq 21, September 8, 1898[1]

Three things shine in glorious splendor on this earth: 0.1.1

The noonday sun, Abū Isḥāq, and the moon.[2]

ʿĪsā ibn Hishām told us that in his dreams he saw three rulers conversing over their meal. As you will see, this is what he dreamed:

Buṭrus (*making a show of his refinement, full of good cheer, and feigning elegance*) Where, O where, I ask, are those orators of olden times, men of eloquence, poets who could sing paeans of praise, littérateurs who would record people's names for all time? Where are Ibn al-Walīd and Abū Tammām, Firdawsī and al-Khayyām, Euripides and Homer, Horace and Virgil? Who will record the part we have played in this great victory and our share of the glory? Who will note down the marvelous record in the archives of time and make the white pages of our history glow with stories of the conquest of Sudan, the lands of the blacks? At this moment, the Sirdar[3] and we ministers resemble Julius Caesar himself when he sent back from Asia the news of his rapid victory to a Roman senate which must have been much like our own tripartite meeting here. Caesar used just three crisp words: "*Veni, vidi, vici.*"[4] 0.1.2

Maẓlūm (*astonished and baffled*) Tell me for heaven's sake, my friend, why on earth are you speaking in Latin? What does it mean?

Buṭrus It's not Latin! It's pure Arabic. Whenever victories, campaigns, and battles are to be recorded, such are the demands of description and panegyric. But I can describe it for you in another way which might be more appropriate:

> "To your Egypt has her Khartoum been returned."
> The year 1316.[5]

Our fortune has been fulfilled, and destiny has come to our aid. The conquest of the Sudan has occurred during our blessed and orderly period in office. Now the tyrant has gone, Maẓlūm. So all praise be to God who has reserved these gifts for us and afforded us such a wonderful conclusion to events!

0.1.3 MAẒLŪM (*who still seems baffled, like a miser who has just lost a ring on the ground*) I can understand that you're talking about the Sudan. But why this jubilant celebration that's making you rhapsodize like a soothsayer? What benefit will we Egyptian ministers get from this victorious conquest?

BUṬRUS (*arrogantly*) We've now become ministers who are in charge of twenty-four million people. That's the benefit we get from it all. Our names are to be proclaimed over huge areas, and we will have wide dominion in a place where the earth is virgin and the soil is pure gold.

MAẒLŪM (*disdainfully and in utter contempt*) The only advantage that I can see would involve us getting a salary raise equivalent to the territorial expansion.

BUṬRUS (*exasperated*) God forgive you! How can you talk about a salary increase when people are already criticizing and excoriating us for the little work we do and the piles of money we get for it? Even so, if there's to be substantial benefit gained from it all, then it will be in shares in English companies which are now at our disposal.

MAẒLŪM (*revealing a set of pearly white teeth*) Whom do we know who is *au fait* with companies and shares?

BUṬRUS Don't you realize that those companies will only be able to colonize the country if the Egyptian government gives them permission? As long as the Egyptian flag is flying over the Sudan, you can impose restrictions through the Finance Ministry.

Fakhrī (*distressed*) Please don't mention "flags" in my presence; the very word makes me shudder in horror. As it is, your hopes and expectations and my own anxieties are quite enough. God has willed that I should twice hold ministerial office: once as a real minister for a single day, and once as a deputy minister for several days. When I was a real minister, fate decreed that Egypt was not able to make a single move or change any ministry without consulting the occupying power, and this was recorded in the Blue Book.[6] When I was a deputy minister, the English flag was raised over the Sudan, as everyone knows full well. 0.1.4

Buṭrus (*trying to console him and make light of the situation*) Calm down, my friend! Some people who have no idea of the difficulties involved may look on your two ministries as you do, but those of us who know the real situation can acknowledge the great expertise that you possess. It's because of you that this ministry has carried on for so long without incident, that is as long as the occupying powers has been happy with it. But then, it's so easy for our ministers to keep the occupying forces happy; they'll stay on forever, as long as the occupation lasts. Actually the English flag was only raised during the memorial service for Gordon and not on the occasion of the annexation of the Sudan to England. There's nothing for you to be ashamed of on either count; your twin ministries did not cause us any grief.

Maẓlūm (*leaning forward attentively*) Where did you both get the news about the English flag being raised over Khartoum? We haven't received any official word.

Buṭrus From the telegram which the Sirdar sent to the General commanding the occupation army. Then the papers picked it up. As usual, they started denouncing it at length, and so we got to hear about it.

Fakhrī My dear Ministers, can't you both see how determined and prudent the English are? In everything they do, they abide by the dictum: "To get what you want, make full use of secrecy." Just like ants crawling noiselessly around, the English run the Egyptian government among themselves in such secrecy that the only way we get to hear about things is when newspapers get information and start croaking. Then people start maligning us by suggesting that we're involved in the secret sessions too.

MAẒLŪM Why do we need to know such things as long as the minister among us gets paid his salary?

FAKHRĪ (*with a sigh*) How can you possibly know as much about it as I do?! If you'd tasted, as I have, the sweet savor of absolute authority that we had in our ministries before the occupation, you'd realize that being starved of government news, when we are supposed to be in charge, detracts from the respect which simple ignorant people feel for us.

MAẒLŪM (*baffled*) What was that sweet savor you used to taste?

0.1.5 FAKHRĪ Delegations would crowd your door, and people with petitions would head for your ministry.

MAẒLŪM (*horrified*) Stop, stop! Spare me such sweet delights! In actual fact it's all bitterness and loss.

FAKHRĪ The horror that you envisage from all those delegations and people with petitions that seem to aggravate you so much are nothing when compared with the pleasure to be gleaned from the way people bow and throw themselves at your feet. They crane their necks to make their pleas and strain their ears to hear a single word from your mouth. I don't want either shares in companies or a salary raise. I'm quite content with my small house in al-ʿAbbāsiyyah which is like a primitive place in Omdurman when compared with the huge mansions all around it. I've no desire to have it lit by electricity, or to have asparagus and chicory on my table. My own worldly pleasures now reside in more spiritual realms.

MAẒLŪM Your withdrawal from worldly affairs like some ascetic and your obsession with spiritual pleasures gives me the impression that they surpass all other pleasures. So, tell me, how can we find it and make use of what they have to offer?

Fakhrī The days of absolute authority are over. All that remains is for us to hear about what is going on in the government before anyone else. All we can do is to ask God to inspire the occupying power to let us know about our government's affairs before the newspapers get hold of it.

Everyone Amen to that!

Buṭrus (*as he takes his leave, he is talking to himself and shrugging his shoulders*) This flag business is very serious. It's a difficult problem to shrug off. But then, we've heard and seen a good deal. How often have we managed to save ourselves and others?!

(Since Buṭrus Paulus was in charge of the Khartoum treasury when Gordon and his men were killed and was the only one to escape the Darwīsh slaughter, it should not be too difficult for Buṭrus Ghālī to rid himself of silly games like these which people in politics call "difficulties.")

Miṣbāḥ al-sharq 23, September 22, 1898

0.2.1 War engenders its own folk whom God leads astray;
When it summons them to its turmoil, they leap.
I am not of such people; I abhor what they wreak;
Neither conflict nor plunder give me pleasure.[7]

0.2.2 ʿĪsā ibn Hishām told us: I heard that a newspaper correspondent spotted one of our senior ministers walking around the courtyard in a spa abroad. From his prancing gait he gleaned that it was the Minister of War. As the common expression has it: such a gait is detested everywhere except in the sphere of conflict. So this reporter went up to beg him for something: not for money, but rather for information. He told himself that he would now be getting the news from the very source. At the same time he kept thinking about his fellow reporters who would be roaming around in the deserts of the Sudan, wandering in the steaming heat of the midday sun, far away from their families and relatives, as they sweated in seas of humid air—their only water a mirage; their only food bitter-tasting colocynth. They would be sleeping on prickly thorns, and their only shade would come from flags fluttering over the army. They would be doing the rounds of caves and forests, just like anemones in plant-life and chameleons among animals as they encountered the sun's disk hovering over the horizon until evening sunset. Then conflict would erupt, fighting would flare up, heroes would battle each other, and men would confront their foes. Fates would rush in to snatch away hopes and put an end to all activity. The reporters meanwhile would be eager for news, like insomniacs craving the light of day. The entire saga would then proceed to recount its tales of dead and wounded, those slain and maimed. But fate has indeed been kind to me, he told himself, and my lucky stars have come to my aid. I have achieved my goal and escaped the hardships and risks that my colleagues are facing; and all that in this luxurious European spa. But then, that's the way of the world: the layabout who stays home gets all the luck, while those who ride their mounts into danger have to suffer.

The reporter then went up to the Minister and said:

Reporter Your demeanor leads me to believe that you're an Egyptian and a war veteran. Will you allow me to interview you so that I can publish some news about events in the Sudan in the newspapers? That will bring your name to people's attention and enhance your prestige. 0.2.3

Minister of War (*arrogant and contemptuous*) I'm the Egyptian Minister of War.

Reporter (*encouraged*) I'm sure you've only recently left Egypt, Sir. You must only have come here for a rest after enduring severe hardships and difficulties during the Sudanese campaign.

Minister (*flustered*) Yes, I was there. But that was two months before the conquest.

Reporter (*astonished*) How can that be? Can the Minister of War simply stop supervising the campaign when it's at its height and slip away for a holiday abroad?

Minister There's nothing wrong with the Minister doing that. He can supervise everything from abroad. After all, an army general directs operations from the rear.

Reporter That's quite true, but it doesn't stop him from directing operations and knowing what's going on. Do you get news as quickly as he does then?

Minister (*boastfully*) You should realize that I have two deputies in the Ministry of War: the Minister of Finance and the

Permanent Undersecretary of War. They both make a point of keeping me informed from San Stefano as soon as anything happens.

Reporter (*seeking information*) San Stefano? Is there a place of that name in the Sudan?

Minister (*explaining*) It's not in the Sudan; it's a spa in Alexandria. You know full well that time and distance mean absolutely nothing now that telegrams are available. One chess player can play with another in a different country. In fact war is itself the very foundation on which that particular game is based, so how can you have any doubts that I can get the news in the same way?

Reporter So tell me then, what's today's news?

Minister The weather's fine; there's a cool breeze and clear sky, and the sun is shining brightly.

0.2.4 Reporter (*with a smile*) Easterners are certainly quick to imitate Westerners, aren't they? Talking about the weather! We used to think amirs and ministers were in a class of their own when it came to prevarication and ruses to get rid of newspaper reporters who were trying to get some information out of them. May I suggest, Minister, that I stop using tricks to get information from you and you in turn stop hedging; that way we won't waste any more time. If you're agreeable, would you mind telling me what you think about al-Taʿāyishī?

Minister (*offering a prediction*) If he goes to Kordofān, he's a dead man; if he escapes to Darfūr, he'll be obliterated for sure; if he comes back to Omdurman, he won't find for protection any remand; and, if he goes back to Khartoum, then for that city it's doom.[8]

Reporter So far you've not told me anything I didn't know already. But I'm not going to press you to reveal any secrets; you have a right to keep them to yourself. Disclosing such information might prevent his being captured. I'll leave that point and ask you about the most significant news of all; the fact that the Sirdar is heading for Fashōda.

Minister (*derisively*) The Sirdar's actions can be easily explained. He wants to get back to Egypt to enjoy his triumph and is just resting for a while.

Reporter (*sighing regretfully*) I see you're still dodging the question.

Minister (*making excuses*) I assure you, someone such as myself doesn't tell lies after agreeing to talk frankly.

Reporter (*exasperated*) Then how can you say that things are so simple? It's a matter of great importance, one that is preoccupying all the ministers of the European powers and especially those of Egypt! How can you say that the Sirdar is coming back to Egypt from Fashōda? He only went there after entering Omdurman in order to complete the conquest of the Sudan. It's quite near the source of the Nile.

Minister (*laughing scornfully*) You're obviously wrong. If Fashōda is really at the source of the Nile, then it must be at the cataract where the dam is being built.[9]

Reporter (*amazed and increasingly angry*) I'm not mistaken, 0.2.5
my dear Minister. I see you've changed your tactics now; instead of hedging, you're feigning ignorance. Fashōda is more than four hundred kilometers above Omdurman on the White Nile. Tell me, what do you know about it and Marchand?[10]

Minister (*relieved*) Now I see why the Sirdar is moving towards this Fashōda place—it's because of this *marchand d'esclaves*![11]

Reporter (*angrily*) My dear Minister, I'm fed up with talking to you. Marchand is a Frenchman who's come with a French force to take control of some areas close to the source of the Nile. The aim is to try to prevent England from controlling the whole of the Sudan.

Minister (*using his memory*) Yes, he failed. He was delayed in Ethiopia and gave up; he never occupied any part of the Sudan.

Reporter (*furious*) Good grief! Here I am talking about Marchand, and he's talking about Bonchamps!

Minister Don't lose your temper, my dear sir! I'll tell you the complete truth in a couple of words. If you were talking about Marchand, then the Sirdar is going there to put an end to slavery in the Sudan. If it's Bonchamps you were referring to, then he is heading for Fashōda to choose some lands which can be used for cultivation and settlement.[12]

0.2.6 Reporter (*tearing at his clothes and losing all patience*) My dear Minister, Marchand and Bonchamps are proper names belonging to famous people; they're not being used as nouns with semantic connotations. When people are called Mazlūm, Ghālī, and ʿAbbāʾī, it doesn't mean there's any reference to tyranny, overcharging, or heavy loads.[13]

Here we are with a Minister of War who knows nothing about fighting and is not even supervising the campaign. What bad luck! I'm wasting my time. I came to get information and I end up giving it instead! The nightmare of this confrontation makes me envy my colleagues who are facing death on the Sudan battlefront. At least they will have got what they want after some hardships, whereas all I've got are still more problems after thinking I had found what I was seeking! That's what happens when you stay aloof without getting involved in the task at hand.

Three in One and One in Three

Miṣbāḥ al-sharq 24, September 29, 1898

ʿIsā ibn Hishām told us: I heard that the deputy *qāʾim maqām* had a visit from one of his coterie. When the latter came in to ask for the latest news, he found his friend with his head lowered, deep in thought. He was frowning and scowling and looked disheartened. Sweat was glistening on his forehead, and he was wiping it off with his left and right hand in turn. He began to mutter and grumble to himself. His visitor asked him what was the matter: 0.3.1

Visitor How is it I see you looking so pensive and worried? Surely nothing's happened to make you so anxious? 0.3.2

(*The deputy pays no attention but remains deep in his own thoughts.*)

Visitor Maybe you're racking your brains to work out what will be the result of the negotiation between the two powers on the Fashōda question?

Deputy (*scornfully*) The papers are fussing about that.

Visitor Then perhaps you're thinking about what will happen over the question of the raising of the British flag?

Deputy That's for people in Istanbul and London.

Visitor Then you must be busy contacting the Khedive over the arrangements for the Emperor's arrival?

Deputy That's a job for one of his aides.

Visitor Could it be then that, along with the Minister of Works, you're involved in organizing the precautionary measures to be taken against the Nile flood this year?

Deputy That's for local authorities to worry about.

Visitor Then maybe you're trying to come up with an excuse for selling off the Sudanese Railway.

Deputy Suarez is working on that. I'm not concerned with any of those public interest items you've just mentioned. It's a purely private matter.

Visitor Could it be that Mr. Rollo has authorized the sale of his house in Bāb al-Lūq to you for the three thousand pounds that you've offered, when he'd been asking for twelve thousand?

Deputy It's not that either. Two things are bothering me: the term of tripartite rule has come to an end; and secondly my own term as deputy *qā'im maqām* is over. All I can do is to try to find some way of keeping alive the memory of my period in government, something that'll give me pleasure in retirement, something my children can wear as a badge of pride. Then after my death, my descendants can assume the Fakhrī mantle.[14]

Visitor What a marvelous idea.

0.3.3 (*The deputy continues to rack his brains. After a while, he leaps to his feet in joy. "I've found it," he yells, just like Archimedes before him.*)

Visitor What secret treasure have you uncovered? What cherished dream have you now realized? Why such a radiant smile on your face?!

Deputy Three in one and one in three.

Visitor Why didn't you tell me at the start that it was an engineering or algebra problem you were trying to solve?

Deputy That's it: three in one and one in three.

Visitor I understand. But tell me, what is this problem which has been bothering you—one that manages to combine arithmetic with keeping memories alive?

Deputy Now you'll understand the import of the decree that you see in front of me.

VISITOR You're just making me even more confused and baffled.

DEPUTY This will solve the riddle.

(*The deputy takes out a pen, writes something on a piece of paper, then hands it to his visitor. It concerns the important matter involving the appointment of the chairman of the Railways Commission. Here's how he has written it out:*)

By order of His Excellency the Khedive from the Prime Minister:

FAKHRĪ FAKHRĪ

Minister of Public Works

FAKHRĪ.[15]

VISITOR Hasn't it occurred to you that in future people may think there were three people with the same name in the Egyptian government at the same time? 0.3.4

DEPUTY Do you imagine that the fates would allow there to be three people like me at any one time? Haven't you heard the words of the poet:

Small chance that time will ever produce his peer;
with people of his ilk it is miserly indeed![16]

VISITOR Thank God you have been able to devise this plan. It's like a three-way mirror in which the Minister can see himself three times at once!

Ministers and Equality

Miṣbāḥ al-sharq 30, November 10, 1898

0.4.1 ʿĪsā ibn Hishām told us: I was keen to hear from people about various aspects of the current situation: the mixture of organization and chaos, of war and peace, and agreement and discord. So I made for a market. It was so crowded there that you could barely put your foot on the ground. What I found in fact was a showroom of oaths rather than of faith; everyone was breaking their word and infringing regulations so that they could get rid of their merchandise and sell their wares. When I failed to get what I wanted, I changed my plans and retraced my steps.

On the way I came across a tram moving along like fate itself descending from heaven. I got on and found myself among a whole variety of people. Some were standing, others sitting, and people kept getting on and off. There were women and babies, wives with their husbands, good-looking men and women and ugly ones too, and some drunken fools as well. They were all yelling and screaming, arguing, or whispering to each other, bickering with the conductor over the fare and then agreeing when the ticket was handed to them. Others were reading newspapers or else making eyes at pretty girls.

0.4.2 Next to me sat an imposing man who was so bulky that he filled up the entire space. He seemed to value the simple life and was keeping himself amused by listening to people talking about themselves and then covering his face with his handkerchief every time such talk made him laugh. He was particularly happy when two passengers who were squeezed together started arguing. Eventually one of them swore and cursed at the other and then proceeded to cuff him. The police would have been called then and there if the driver had not told the injured party that the person who had cursed and cuffed him had to be shown great respect since he was a minister's servant. The man at whom the curses had been aimed immediately apologized profusely and tried to make amends while the curser gave him an arrogant stare.

As we proceeded on our way, the tram ground to a halt with a whistle. There were two men alongside each other, one riding a bicycle and the other quite out of breath from keeping up with him. They had barely reached the tram before the man next to me stood up respectfully and accepted their greetings. The man who had been walking took a seat, looking as though he were mounting a splendid steed like some horseman on the battlefield. The man who was riding the bicycle stayed on his machine and pedaled alongside the tram. I was sitting between them. I had no idea who they might be until they greeted each other with an air of authority, from which I gathered that they were ministers. From their conversation, it emerged that the passenger sitting beside me was the Permanent Undersecretary of Justice, the person who had been walking was the Minister of War, and the man on the bicycle was the Minister of Finance. I will now give you a version of the conversation I heard; they were speaking sometimes in Arabic and at others in French: 0.4.3

PERMANENT UNDERSECRETARY (*to the Ministers of War and Finance*) Why are you both walking and riding like this? What's happened to your horses and carriages? 0.4.4

MINISTER OF WAR (*chuckling*) They've been sequestered by the Ministry of Finance!

UNDERSECRETARY (*almost skipping a heartbeat from shock*) How can they sequester the Minister of Finance's carriage? He's the guardian of the country's treasury after all. They can't do that to the Minister of War. After all it was his horse and foot which helped conquer the Sudan.

MINISTER OF WAR We've overlooked sharing the revenues accrued from both of them, so the occupying powers were eager to show how just they were by applying the principle of equality and by treating us in exactly the same way as they do ordinary people. They confiscated the carriages on the spot, and we've rushed to oblige them by walking in the streets and riding on trams. By so doing, we can show how compliant we are to their wishes and thus ingratiate ourselves to them.

UNDERSECRETARY We should be delighted by the present situation. The occupying powers have restored the principle of equality from the very first days of Islam that we've all been hearing about. In those days of old, amirs used to descend to the same level as the people. The way you're riding on a tram is no different from the way Marwān came into Damascus riding a donkey during the caliphate of Abū Sufyān ibn Hishām; he had objected to his procession and the way it contravened a sense of equality.[17]

MINISTER OF WAR In which book did you find that story?

UNDERSECRETARY I didn't get it from a book; I don't have any time to read such things. I heard it from the Minister, and he in turn heard it from his teacher, Shaykh Ḥaddād.

MINISTER OF FINANCE (*looking right and left over his bicycle*)

> "For all the things you've mentioned,
> there are several you've overlooked."[18]

There is something else which goes far beyond the benefits we get from merely complying with this idea of equality. If we ride on trams, the price of shares in the tramway company is bound to go up. People will start crowding each other out so that they can all ride on trams and have an opportunity to see us and copy everything we do. The price of shares will rise; people who are lucky enough to own shares in them will make a large profit.

MINISTER OF WAR If the tramway company did what it has promised to do and introduced first-class carriages, that would be fine. Then we wouldn't have to mix with common people and run the risk of their hearing our conversations about secret government matters while we're riding with them. 0.4.5

UNDERSECRETARY The first-class compartments would be bound to get overcrowded as well.

MINISTER OF WAR People who ride in first-class carriages are from the upper class. It doesn't matter if they hear some of the secret business we're discussing. The people to worry about are the common folk who don't read newspapers.

MINISTER OF FINANCE Every time you come up with a way of making a profit, you miss another one. Don't you realize that it costs more to ride in first class than it does in second? Sound economics won't allow such extravagance.

MINISTER OF WAR Don't you think we should forget this whole idea? After all, we already have an example of a way to remedy it. When His Excellency Fakhrī Pāshā, the Minister of Public Works and Public Education, used to travel by rail from Ramla to Alexandria, he would cut his ticket in half. If the inspector asked him, he completely nonplussed him by replying that he was a minister. As such, he was entitled to travel at half fare and to be exempted from the return half. I'm sure the tramway company here will be more amenable on this point than the Ramla Railway Company.

Our narrator told us: When the time came for us to part company, I got off and so did they. We all went our own ways. I left them to their dreams of profit, economy, and flattery. They meanwhile left me with their conversation, achieving thereby the cherished goal of distinction between the curser and the cursed and of equality between ruler and ruled. 0.4.6

Miṣbāḥ al-sharq 31, November 17, 1898

1.1 ʿĪsā ibn Hishām told us: In a dream, I saw myself walking among the tombs and gravestones in the Imam Shāfiʿī cemetery. It was a brilliant moonlit night, bright enough to blot out the stars in the sky; in fact, so gleaming was the light, one could have threaded a pearl and watched a speck of dust. As I stood there amid the graves atop the tombstones, I contemplated man's arrogance and conceit, his sense of his own glory, his pride, his total obsession with his own pretensions, his excessive desires, his sense of self-aggrandizement, and the way he chooses to forget about the grave. In his deluded arrogance he hoists his nose into the air and endeavors to pierce the very heavens with it. Then he can boast about the things he has collected and use what he owns to claim some kind of superiority. But then Death always coerces him. Once it has enshrouded his artificial splendor and glory beneath its slabs of stone, it uses that very same nose to block up a crack in his tomb.

1.2 Deep in thought I continued my walk. I recalled the words of the sage poet, Abū l-ʿAlāʾ al-Maʿarrī:

Tread lightly, for methinks the surface of the earth
is made only from these bodies.
It would be wrong of us to treat our forefathers
and ancestors lightly even if they lived long ago.
Walk slowly abroad, if you are able,
and do not strut over the remains of God's people.[19]

So I repented and trod lightly. Among these numerous corpses and remains of the dead there would be mouths. For a single kiss from them, lovers in the past would often have changed course and bartered the very sweetness of Kawthar for their sweet taste. But now they are blended with the dust of the earth, and their teeth mingle with pebbles and small stones. 1.3

I also remembered those cheeks the rose so envied that it wept dewy tears, which would arouse people's hearts to a fiery passion. The beauty spot on their surface looked exactly like the faithful companion Abraham in the fire, or the black-skinned Nuʿmān of al-Ḥīrah in the midst of red anemones. Through them flowed the glow of modesty and youth's gushing spring, but now fate has folded away their beauty just as one shuts a book; by destiny's decree they have become a mere layer on the earth's surface. The lashes of those eyes ensnared mighty kings, so that the rulers of people became the subjects of girls. They bewitched Hārūt and Mārūt in Babel and humiliated the majestic tyrant as he sought some glimmer of approval in their glances. There he stood, crown in hand. Beads of perspiration on his forehead were evidence of his shyness; he was like a beggar seeking alms. These same eyes have now become soil within the tombs; it is as though they had never infatuated anyone. That luxuriant black flourish of hair whose glitter dazzled both heart and eyes to the core has been plucked from its roots by Time's hand, and from it fate has woven a funeral shroud.

Those breasts, that once seemed like boxes of silver decorated with pearls or balls of snow with a pomegranate flower at center, now look like leather bags with food for worms in the grave. 1.4

> How many a maid who withheld her cheek from a kiss
> has had her cheek mastered by the earth!
> How many a girl whose neck now carries the weight of the earth
> used to complain of the unbearable weight of a necklace.[20]

Those decaying bones, remains of mighty kings who considered the earth too paltry a domain and tried to attain regions bordering the very stars; those chests which contained courageous and prudent hearts; those lips which often uttered orders of war and peace; those fingertips which used to sharpen quills for writing and trim necks with the sword; those faces and heads which enslaved bodies and souls and which were described as full moons at one moment and as suns at another; among the dead, such rulers are peers of the ruled, nor is there difference or distinction between the lowly and mighty.

He is Death for whom rich and poor are both the same;
a man who knows his way is like another who has gone astray.
In his judgment, the warrior's shield and maiden's shift are both alike;
an emperor's dwellings are mere spider's webs.
Such folk are trodden in the dust, while misfortune rides rampant;
among people fate is still the best rider.
The bier is like a ship casting its contents to drown in the sea of death,
piling up and up.[21]

1.5 As part of such sobering notions, I was considering the remarkable things that happen and marveling at the way in which times change. Deep in thought about the extraordinary things which fate brings about, I was trying to probe the secrets of the resurrection. Suddenly, there was a violent tremor behind me which almost brought my life to an end. In terror I looked behind me. I discovered that one of the graves had opened, and a man had appeared. He was tall and imposing, carried himself with dignity and a majestic aura, and displayed all the signs of nobility and high birth. I felt as stunned and terrified as Moses on the day when the mountain was destroyed.[22] Once I had recovered from the shock, I noticed that he was walking toward me. He shouted to me like an army commander issuing orders. The conversation went as follows:

GHOST Come closer. 1.6

ʿĪsā ibn Hishām said: My whole body shook, but I could see no way out, so I obeyed his instructions and moved closer.

GHOST What's your name and profession? What are you doing out here?

This man must have been interrogated recently by the two Questioning Angels, I told myself; that is why he is using their procedure. I asked God to rescue me from these dire straits and come to my aid so that I could escape the arguments of the Day of Reckoning and be protected from this terrible punishment. Then I turned in his direction and answered:

ʿĪSĀ IBN HISHĀM My name is ʿĪsā ibn Hishām, my profession is the art of writing, and I came here to find some inspiration by visiting the tombs. I find it more effective than listening to sermons from pulpits.

GHOST Well then, secretary ʿĪsā, where's your inkwell and notebook?

ʿĪSĀ IBN HISHĀM I'm not a secretary in the Treasury or Secretariat, I'm an author.

GHOST Never mind! Go then, my good author, and look for my clothes and bring me my horse, Daḥmān!

ʿĪSĀ IBN HISHĀM But where's your house, Sir? I don't know it.

GHOST (*in disgust*) Tell me, for heaven's sake, which country are you from? You can't be an Egyptian. There's no one in the whole country who doesn't know where my house is. I'm Aḥmad Pāshā al-Manīkalī, the Egyptian Minister of War!

ʿĪSĀ IBN HISHĀM Believe me, Pāshā, I'm from pure Egyptian stock. The only reason why I don't know where you live is that houses in Egypt are no longer known by the names of their owners, but by the names of their street, lane, and number. If you would be so kind as to tell me the street, lane, and number of your house, I'll go there and bring you the things you've requested.

AL-MANĪKALĪ (*annoyed*) It's clear to me, my good author, that you're out of your mind! Since when have houses had numbers to be known by? What are they? Some kind of government legislation or army regulations? Anyway give me your overcoat to wrap myself in and your tarboosh and sandals too. Then accompany me till I reach my house.

1.7 ʿĪsā ibn Hishām said: Since it was only my overcoat, tarboosh, and sandals that were involved, it was fairly easy. Usually it is highwaymen who rob passersby, but now here was this ghost, a grave-dweller at that, doing it to me as well.

Al-Manīkalī took the coat and put it on with a reluctant disdain:

Al-Manīkalī Well, "Necessity has its own Rules!"[23] But then, I have disguised myself in even shabbier clothes than this while accompanying our late revered master, Ibrāhīm Pāshā, on the nights he used to spend in the city so that he could see for himself how people were faring.

Īsā ibn Hishām said: We started walking, but then he stopped abruptly.

Al-Manīkalī But what's to be done?

ʿĪsā ibn Hishām What do you mean?

Al-Manīkalī I've forgotten that it's nighttime. There's no one on duty who'll be able to recognize me in this overcoat. How can we get the gates opened when we don't have the password?

ʿĪsā ibn Hishām You've just told me, Sir, that you don't know anything about houses having numbers. Well, I don't know anything about a "password." What is it?

Al-Manīkalī (*laughing contemptuously*) Didn't I say you had to be a foreigner? Don't you know that the "password" is a word issued each night from the Citadel to the officer of the watch and all the guardhouses and gates? No one is allowed to travel at night unless he has memorized this word and can repeat it to the gatekeeper, whereupon the gate is opened for him. It is given out in secret to the people who ask the government for it so that they can carry on their business at night. It's changed every night. So, one night, it will be "Lentils," the next night "Greens," the next night "Pigeons," the next night "Fowl," and so on.

ʿĪsā ibn Hishām It's clear to me that you're the one who's not Egyptian. The only use we have for such words is as food. We've never heard of their being used to convey permission to travel at night. In any case, it's almost dawn, so we'll have no further need of such words or any others.

ʿĪsā ibn Hishām said: So we went on our way. The Pāshā began to tell me more about himself. He told me tales of wars and battles which he had either witnessed himself or heard about and then went on to recall any number of exploits of Muḥammad ʿAlī and the great courage of Ibrāhīm. We continued in this fashion till we reached the Citadel Square, by which time it was daylight. The Pāshā halted in humble respect, recited the Fātiḥah to Muḥammad ʿAlī's tomb and then addressed the Citadel: 1.8

Hail to thee, source of bounties, treadmill of the violent Mamluk tyrants, haven of sovereignty, fortress of royal sway, source of might, birthplace of power, and height of glory. You are the refuge of the pleader for help, protection for him who seeks it, treasure-house of people's desires, goal of their aspirations.

O Cairo Citadel, how many people who came to you in search of kindness you have obligated with your charity! How many pompous men have you coerced, and how many swords have you drawn. You combined power and generosity, and could decide as alternatives between life and death.

ʿĪsā ibn Hishām said: Then the Pāshā turned towards me. "Hurry to my house with me," he said. "I can put on my proper clothes, buckle my sword, and mount my horse. Then I'll return to the Citadel and pay my respects to his exalted highness, the dispenser of bounty." 1.9

All this astonished me, and I decided to follow his story to its conclusion.

Miṣbāḥ al-sharq 32, November 24, 1898

2.1 Leaving the Citadel Square, we walked downhill. As we proceeded, we found our path blocked by a donkeyman pulling his donkey behind him. The rogue had the animal trained to stand in the way of passersby and block the road. So, every time we tried to move on, we found the donkey in front of us and the Donkeyman shouting at us in a hoarse voice. Eventually he grabbed the edge of my companion's coat:

2.2 DONKEYMAN Get on my donkey, Sir—you've kept me from my business. I've been walking behind you.

PĀSHĀ (*to the Donkeyman*) You miserable wretch, do you really expect me to ride your donkey? I've never had the slightest desire to ride it, nor have I hailed you at any time while I've been walking. How could someone such as myself possibly mount a braying donkey rather than a rearing thoroughbred?

DONKEYMAN How can you deny summoning me with the gesture you made with your hand while you were talking to your companion on the way from the cemetery? I've been hailed by travelers several times since then, but I didn't respond or pay any attention to their calls because I was obligated to you by that gesture of yours. Either get on my donkey or else pay me the charge for hiring me.

PĀSHĀ (*pushing the Donkeyman with his hand*) You insolent devil! Go away! If I had my weapon with me, I'd kill you.

Donkeyman (*defiantly*) How dare you talk to me like that! Either you give me my charge, or else come with me to the police station. You'll find out there how they'll deal with you for threatening to kill me!

Pāshā (*to 'Īsā*) I'm surprised you're being so patient with this bumptious yokel who is being so persistently rude and cheeky to me. Get on and kill him for me; that way we'll relieve him of his life and ourselves of him!

'Īsā How can I possibly do that? What about the law and the authorities?

Pāshā Heavens above, am I really to believe that fear has cleft your heart in two and cut short your breath? Are you really afraid in my company? That's incredible!

Donkeyman (*scoffing*) Oh, begging your pardon, Sir, begging your pardon! Who do you think you are, or who is anyone else for that matter? We're living in an age of freedom now when there is no difference between a donkeyman and a Pāshā.

'Īsā I'm not going to hit anyone, and, as long as you're with 2.3
me, you're not going to kill anyone either. You must realize that if we commit an infraction, misdemeanor, or felony, we will be punished for it. So don't be surprised that I am so patient and long-suffering. I will say to you exactly what al-Khiḍr told Moses (peace be upon him): «You will not be patient with me, so how can you endure things of which you have no experience?»[24] The way to get rid of this insolent fool is for me to give him some dirhams. Then he will bother someone else. I just pray that we reach home safely.

Pāshā You'll not give this barking cur a single dirham. Beat him! If you won't do it, then I'll have to stoop so low as to beat him myself and teach him a lesson. The only way to improve a peasant's skin is by flogging.

With that the Pāshā grabbed the Donkeyman by the neck and started hitting him.

Donkeyman (*yelling for help*) Police! Police!

ʿĪsā (*doing his best to rescue the Donkeyman from the Pāshā's clutches*) O God, save me from this ill-starred day full of disaster! I spoke to the Pāshā: Show the fear of God, Amir, in your treatment of His servants!

2.4 I had barely finished saying this to him when I saw his temper get the better of him. His whole expression changed, his eyes began to roll, his lips tightened, his nostrils expanded, and his forehead contracted into a frown. I was afraid that his crazy temper would lead him to do me an injury as well as the Donkeyman. I tried a more rational approach. I told him that a personage of his eminence should not demean himself by behaving in such a manner; he was far too exalted a figure to foul his noble hands by touching a corpse like this one. Using such a stratagem I managed to calm him down. I went over to the Donkeyman and put some dirhams into his palm without the Pāshā knowing. I asked him to go away and leave us alone, but that only made the wretch shout all the louder for the police to help him.

Pāshā (*to ʿĪsā*) Didn't I tell you that peasants can only be reformed by beating? Don't you realize that the only thing he can do to get rid of the pain he's going through is to yell for help to Shaykhs and Saints! But tell me, is this "Police" he keeps shouting for and asking to help him some new kind of saintly figure?

ʿĪsā Well, yes. The "police" is the agency responsible for public order and vested with the government's executive powers.

Pāshā I don't understand. Explain to me what this "police" you're talking about really is.

ʿĪsā It's what you used to call "Kavvas."[25]

Pāshā So where is this kavvas who cannot hear all this yelling and screaming?! I want him to appear so that he can receive my orders regarding this wretch.

Donkeyman Police! Police!

Pāshā (*to ʿĪsā ibn Hishām*) Come on, let's help him yell for the kavvas!

ʿĪsā ibn Hishām said: I asked myself how I could possibly yell for the police when I was really thanking God because I'd managed to quiet him down. All the while, the Policeman was standing close by, not paying the slightest attention to the shouts for help.

I turned to the Pāshā and told him that there was no point in yelling and screaming; as he could see, the Policeman was preoccupied with the fruit seller.

When the Donkeyman spotted the Policeman directly in front 2.5
of him, he dashed over to speak to him. All the spectators who had gathered round us followed. They found the Policeman standing there holding a red napkin full of various oddments which he had collected from the market traders during the course of his supervision of the "regulations." He was busy talking to the owner of the shop, instructing him to put inside the shop the stalks of sugarcane which he had on display outside. In one hand, he was holding a stalk of cane and threatening the owner with it, shaking it in his face like a spear. At the same time, he was looking in another direction, and giggling and babbling at a baby on a woman's shoulder.

He carried on like this till we all came towards him, then turned round with the napkin in one hand and the sugarcane in the other:

Policeman (*to everyone*) What's all this row about in the early morning? Why so much yelling and commotion? Anyone would think that every single person had to have his own private policeman at his service.

Donkeyman Please help me, Sergeant Sir. This man here assaulted me and has refused to give me my charge. You know me on this beat and realize that I'm not one to argue or pick a quarrel for nothing.

Pāshā Guard, take this insolent wretch and lock him up in prison till someone brings you my orders concerning him.

Policeman (*to the Donkeyman*) Tell me, Mursī, from where did this man ride with you?

Donkeyman From the Imam district.

Pāshā Why are you being so slow about carrying out my instructions? Take him to prison at once!

Policeman (*with a scoff*) My dear fellow, it seems to me you must be from the lunatic asylum in the Imām district. Come to the station with me. Your scruffy clothing makes it quite clear that you're penniless and cannot pay the charge.

2.6 'Īsā ibn Hishām said: The Policeman dragged my companion along by the arm. The Pāshā almost collapsed in astonishment; he had no clue about what he was doing. The Policeman handed the fruit and other things he was holding to the man whom the Donkeyman had asked to take care of his donkey. My companion was dragged along to the police station on the Policeman's arm. The Donkeyman followed behind them and the crowd came along at their heels.

They all reached the station and climbed the steps. At this point, the Donkeyman started yelling and screaming again. One of the policemen on duty came up and hit him; he had to quiet him down because the Precinct Adjutant was sound asleep. He went into the Sergeant-Major's room to enter the charge, but found him there with his pen in his ear, eating; he had taken off his tarboosh, removed his shoes, and undone the buttons on his uniform. At his side were two peasants whom I presumed to be relatives of his; they were seeing for themselves the enjoyable way he could exercise his influence in the country's capital city and seat of government, the extensive authority which he had over people whether important or of little significance, and the power he had to imprison anyone, whoever he might be, and to use whatever testimony took his fancy as evidence against accused people.

At this point we were all ejected from the room until he had finished eating, so we went outside in the hall to wait. The Pāshā was so distressed that he needed somewhere to lean against. He propped himself up against the wall, but unfortunately his hand gave way and he fell right on top of a policeman out of uniform who was sweeping the floor. This policeman started cursing and swearing, then rushed into the Sergeant-Major's office and told him that the accused person against whom the Donkeyman was bringing a charge had assaulted him "during the course of the execution of his duties" and had kicked him. The Sergeant-Major ordered the Pāshā to be brought in, called for his police clerk, and told him to take a statement for an infraction charge and another for a misdemeanor. He dictated some technical jargon to him, but I didn't understand a single word of it.

The Policeman whom we had accompanied to the station gave his evidence on the infraction which helped the Donkeyman substantiate his charge, and then the Sergeant-Major himself testified on the misdemeanor charge that he had seen the accused assault one of the station personnel during the course of his duties. The two charges were thus completed. The Sergeant-Major then gave orders for the accused to be taken to the measuring-beam and his identification dossier to be drawn up. The Policeman who had brought the charge against the Pāshā came up, took my companion by the right arm and carried out the order himself, subjecting the Pāshā to all manner of pain in the process of measuring him. While all this was going on, the Pāshā looked like someone who has just fainted from sheer bafflement and distress. But eventually, when he had roused himself a little from his stupefaction, he turned to me and said:

Pāshā I can only imagine from the situation I'm in that today 2.7
is Judgment Day itself, that I'm dreaming, or else that His Mighty Excellency is so furious with me that he has given orders that I be humiliated in this dire fashion.

ʿĪsā The only thing you can do is to resign yourself and be patient till we can escape safely from this misfortune.

Policeman (*to ʿĪsā ibn Hishām, after he has placed the measuring beam on the accused's head*) Look at the scale, Sir, and read off the number.

ʿĪsā ibn Hishām said: Once I had done that, he took my friend to the 2.8
office secretary to put together the Pāshā's identification dossier. The

secretary asked him whether he had anyone to stand bail for him. I put myself forward as surety for him, but they wouldn't accept my offer without verification from the Shaykh of the Quarter. I was at a loss as to what to do; where could I find the Shaykh of the Quarter at a moment's notice? One of the policemen whispered in my ear that I should go outside; I would find the Shaykh of the Quarter at the door. I should give him ten piasters, he said, for verifying the bail. The policeman caught up with me, pointed out the Shaykh of the Quarter, and even acted as go-between in handing over the fee for the verification. When I returned to the secretary's office with the Shaykh of the Quarter, it was to discover that the policeman, who had been inflicting the most pain on God's people and had seemed the most eager to ensure that the Adjutant was allowed to sleep in peace now, was rushing to the door of the Adjutant's room, shoving it with all his might, and going in. He shook the bed vigorously. The Adjutant woke up with a start to be informed that the Inspector had been seen entering the station gate. He rushed over to his uniform, put it on in a trice and rushed out to meet the Inspector. He stood there at attention, but unfortunately for him he had put his tarboosh on carelessly with the tassel over his forehead instead of putting it on the right side. In addition to that, there was a fresh growth of hair on his cheeks because he had not yet found time to shave. The Inspector glared at him, went into the room in a rage, and began to write out a report charging the Adjutant with contravening "standing regulations regarding dress and turnout."

2.9 When the Pāshā noticed that the beating and yelling had stopped all of a sudden and witnessed the alarm and confusion among the policemen, let alone the actions of the Adjutant, he asked me what was the significance of this man whose entry had caused such a flurry of activity. I told him that the Inspector came to the station to inspect and supervise "conditions," to look into people's complaints, and to make sure that the actions of officials conformed with the demands for law and order. The Pāshā then asked that we go inside and bring to his attention the insult we'd endured.

We went in and stood in front of him. We found him writing his report. He turned towards me and asked us our business. But no sooner had we begun to tell him our story than he ordered one of the policemen to remove us from his presence. When he had finished writing the report, we saw him put it into his pocket. With that, he rushed away without bothering to inspect or supervise anything, apart, that is, from the Adjutant's turnout.

When he had left, the beating, yelling, and general din resumed in every part of the station with an even greater intensity than before his arrival. One of the people who had been severely beaten and was in intense pain yelled out that he fully intended to make a complaint against the station officers at the Parquet Office. One of the policemen went in to tell the Adjutant what the man had said. Placing my ear to the door, I could hear the Adjutant talking to himself:

"What's the point of this job," he was saying, "and all the humiliation I have to suffer? God's curse on the need to earn a living! Even so, thank the Lord this Inspector is English and not a native Arab. He's much better than they would be. He doesn't understand Arabic and knows absolutely nothing about the job. All he's worried about is inspecting my tarboosh and beard. If he were an Arab, he'd have managed to find out what a chaotic state the court cases are in and the way the station officers break all the rules."

He then turned to the policeman and listened as he told him what 2.10
the man who was determined to complain to the Parquet Office had said. At this, he became even more worried and annoyed. He issued orders that all the suspects were to be imprisoned for twenty-four hours, including my friend, the Pāshā. I went to see the Adjutant and requested that he release the Pāshā after I had stood bail for him. He refused and told me with a frown that the best thing was for the Pāshā to remain at the station till the next day so that his previous convictions could be investigated. Then he would be sent over to the Parquet Office.

With that, the Pāshā went to prison.

Miṣbāḥ al-sharq 34, December 8, 1898

3.1 ʿĪsā ibn Hishām said: I left my companion in prison and went home. I lay awake all night, feeling restless and unable to sleep because I was so worried at the way fate had struck the Pāshā down with such a succession of blows. There he was, utterly baffled and bewildered, unaware that time had passed. He was completely unfamiliar with the present state of affairs, and had no idea that, with the passage of time since his own era and the decline of the dynasty of his time into the folds of decay, things had changed. I had intended to tell him about all this when I first met him by explaining the circumstances involved, but then fate had struck us a blow by landing us in the chain of events which had befallen us. Afterwards, I had thought for a while and decided that the best plan would be to let him remain ignorant about the way things were until his misfortunes were at an end. The fact that he had been unaware that conditions had changed would serve as a pretext in clearing him of the charge against him.

I decided not to leave his company until I had managed to show him the things he had not seen, tell him about the things he had not heard, and explain those aspects of modern history which he did not know or might find perplexing. In that way, I would discover what his opinion was of the present in comparison with the past, and learn which of the two was of greater worth and brought more benefits, and in what ways one was superior to the other.

Early the next day I went to the station, taking with me some suitable clothing for my companion to wear when he came out of prison. I found the policeman ready to take the Pāshā to the Register of Convictions in the Government Building. As soon as he spotted me, he started yelling at me:

PĀSHĀ What's the meaning of all these misfortunes and calamities? I imagined that the sufferings I endured yesterday were the result of His Mighty Excellency's anger at his obedient servant, that my enemies had managed to devise some kind of plot against me, or else that people who envy me had trumped up some false story. So I endured the things which necessity decreed I had to suffer and submitted myself to these indignities till such time as I would be able to present myself at the doorstep of the palace and appear before the master of all slaves. Then I would dispel all suspicions, banish any doubts, and show him that I was innocent of whatever charges slanderers and calumniators had trumped up against me. I would make clear to him how genuine was my devotion and loyalty to him. As a result he would be doubly pleased with me because of the dignified way in which I had submitted to this humiliation. 3.2

> Long was my endurance.
> I imagined I was grasping miseries hotter than coals.[26]

Thereafter I would make it my business to inform everyone of the penalty of death and crucifixion that I proposed to wreak on those insolent wretches and ignorant scoundrels in recompense for the way they treated me and ignored my status in society. But I heard in prison—what a dreadful thing to hear!—that dynasties have succeeded one another, conditions have changed, and that you really are living in a different time from the days of old, and in a state of anarchy in which the Donkeyman's assertion that both he and a Pāshā are of equal standing is true. This is something that:

> Deafens the hearer, blinds the person who sees;
> we ask deliverance from the like of it.[27]

Oh God, by Your pardon and forgiveness, has the last day come, is 3.3
this the Day of Gathering? Have classes disappeared and dynasties

disintegrated? Is the mighty man on a par with the lowly, the powerful dignitary the equal of the small, the great man the equal of the despised, the servant the equal of the master? Has the Qurayshī no longer any superiority over the Abyssinian,[28] and is a Turkish amir not of higher status than a mere Egyptian? This cannot be true! It is quite beyond the powers of comprehension.

And as for you, my good fellow, I want you to know that, compared with your outrageous conduct, I consider the crime those insolent wretches have committed against me to be nothing more than a grain of mustard seed as compared with a rock, a mere drop in the ocean. You have kept me in the dark and even introduced me to a country where this is the state of affairs. So God protect me from the likes of you and all the devil's demons.

ʿĪSĀ «Don't blame me for my forgetfulness, nor burden me with any difficulty in my affairs.»[29] When you emerged from the grave, I was so scared and bewildered that I behaved stupidly. I wasn't able to tell you about present conditions and the way in which things have changed since your own lifetime. I hardly had an opportunity to tell you about it before the Donkeyman started bothering us, and we were beset by these misfortunes. I've done nothing wrong, and you should accept my excuse. Endure whatever you may encounter and put up with the situation in which you find yourself. Accept fate with a good face and don't grieve over the past in order to atone for your present misdeeds.

POLICEMAN (*to the Pāshā*) Come on, we're going to the Register of Convictions.

PĀSHĀ The Lord be praised! I do believe my suffering is over and my misfortunes have been driven away. I have regained my former status, and they have brought me my retinue and horse![30]

ʿĪSĀ That word doesn't mean rearing steeds and neighing thoroughbreds. It's a department where they record the features and characteristics of the accused and find out if he has committed any previous offences.

Policeman (*to the Pāshā, as he drags him along*) Stop all this chatter. Come with me quietly and in an orderly fashion.

Pāshā (*holding back*) What can one do in the face of predestined fate? How can I escape? Who will dispatch me to death a second time and return me to my grave?

ʿĪsā (*pleading*) I beg you, in the name of the one who is buried in the Citadel and by the clash of your swords in battle, please take my advice and behave as I suggest. Don't resist or object. Reluctance will serve no purpose and only make our misfortunes worse. When we have no choice in the matter, the sensible thing to do is to resign ourselves to fate and to wear the appropriate garments for every situation, whether cheerful or miserable.

ʿĪsā ibn Hishām said: The Pāshā heard what I had to say and reluc- 3.4
tantly accepted the decree of fate. We duly accompanied the Policeman until we reached the Register of Convictions and Substantiation of Identity. There the Pāshā endured enough identity procedures to give anyone heart failure and turn his hair white. They stripped him of his clothes, examined him limb by limb, measured his face and body, stared into his eyes, and did all kinds of things to him. He just kept sighing deeply until they had finished with him. They asked about bail and discovered that he had none because the Adjutant—God curse him!—had refused to accept the verification of his bail which the Shaykh of the Quarter had provided, so that he could legally keep him in prison for the night.

With that, they sent us over to the Parquet with the Policeman. When we entered, we found the Parquet Attorney with a load of cases on his hands and hordes of litigants waiting their turn. So we went over to one side to wait our turn as well. My companion turned to me.

Pāshā Where are we now? Who's this young fellow? What's this mob of people?

ʿĪsā We're in the Parquet office. This man's a member of the Parquet, and all these people are litigants.

Pāshā What is this "Parquet?"

'Īsā In this new legal system, it's the judicial authority responsible for bringing criminal charges against offenders, acting on behalf of society. It was introduced so that no crime should go unpunished. Its duties are to uphold the truth and prove the guilt of the guilty and the innocence of the innocent.

Pāshā What is this "society" on whose behalf it acts as deputy?

'Īsā The people as a whole.

Pāshā Who is this mighty person whom the people agree to act as their deputy?

'Īsā The man you see in front of you is not a man of enormous importance. He's just a peasant's son whose father has sent him to schools where he's obtained the certificate. He's thus entitled to act as an attorney of the Parquet. His authority to deal with people covers matters of homicide, property, and finance.

Pāshā In God's eyes the martyr has an exalted status; in heaven, he occupies the very highest position.[31] But you seem to have lost your mind! How can you suppose that martyrdom in the way of God and life here on earth can both apply to one man at the same time? What is even stranger and more confusing is that a peasant can have authority over people, and a farmer is the community's deputy! I've gone from one misfortune to another but still remained calm and patient. But I can't do so any longer in the face of this incredible state of affairs. What an utter disaster! What a terrible catastrophe! I've no patience left. Will someone help me return to the oblivion of the grave?

3.5 'Īsā You must realize that this "certificate" does not mean the same thing as martyrdom in holy war. It's a piece of paper received by students at the end of their studies to confirm that they have studied and achieved excellence in the various branches of learning. Sometimes people who want to get one have to pay one thousand five hundred francs.

Pāshā Oh, I see! You mean the certificate awarded by scholars at al-Azhar to the students who have studied with them and achieved distinction. But I never heard of such expenses in my time, nor have I heard of the noble al-Azhar dealing in francs.

ʿĪsā The subjects they study are not the traditional al-Azhar ones, but Western ones which they learn in Europe. The franc is the French unit of currency, and they call that amount the fee for the certificate. It is a trifling sum when you bear in mind the many advantages it brings. In this system, the basic principle is that "a certificate without any learning is better than learning without any certificate." Anyone with a certificate can present it to the government department and have the right to receive a salary and continuing increments.

Pāshā I almost follow you now. I think this certificate corresponds to the tax-farm lists and ledgers of treasury officials in the time of our government.

ʿĪsā ibn Hishām said: While we were chatting, two young men sud- 3.6
denly appeared. They looked very suave and elegant as they strutted their way through the crowd. Their sleeves exuded perfume into the air. Conversing volubly with each other, they managed to ignore everyone around them. One of them kept cleaving the air with his cane, while the other fiddled with his spectacles. Everyone stared at them agog. The Policeman walked ahead of them, pushing people out of their way. Eventually they reached the door of the Attorney's office. He told the litigants in the various cases to leave, whereupon the usher proceeded to force them all out, cursing and swearing as he did so. Meanwhile the Attorney himself set about finishing up the minutes and removing the inkwells. Having cleared the entire place, he made ready to welcome the two young men. The Pāshā asked me:

Pāshā (*to ʿĪsā*) It looks to me as if these two young men must be the sons of very important princes, or else they are inspectors of the Parquet like the police station Inspector whom we saw earlier.

ʿĪsā No, I think they're just friends of the Attorney from his college days paying him a visit. That's clear enough from their general appearance.

I wanted to find out more about the two of them. So, while everyone else was milling around, I took the opportunity to sneak up close to the door behind the curtain from where I could both see and hear. This is the conversation I heard:

3.7 First Visitor (*after greeting the Attorney and sitting down*) Why did you leave us yesterday before the game was over?

Attorney It was long past midnight, and I had so many cases to deal with that I had to get up early.

Second Visitor Whoever heard of cases keeping anyone away from his friends' company? That excuse is only handy when you're talking to people who aren't familiar with the Parquet's business! I personally am acquainted with a colleague who only spends an hour a day on cases! He's satisfied just to look them over for a moment. He doesn't bother to peruse them, but relies instead on a combination of his sheer mental acumen, his alert intellect, and his wide experience in order to discover the relevant facts. Not only that, but now that there's no longer any disagreement or bad feeling between the Parquet and the police, the best idea is to make do with police evidence or else send it back it to them for completion. There's no point in reopening inquiries and wasting time on something which may lead to more bad feelings and arguments all over again.

Attorney That's exactly what I do, but one has to adhere to outward appearances as far as possible.

First Visitor Haven't you got a secretary who can take over and save you all the bother?

Attorney You're right. The secretary can do it perfectly well. The real reason why I stopped playing and left yesterday was that I'd already lost the month's salary I had with me, and it's still only the beginning of the month.

First Visitor You're always claiming to have lost, however much you've won. In my entire life the only thing I've ever heard you say is that you've lost. Didn't you win five pounds off me on the last hand we played?

Attorney I swear to you on my honor, conscience, and future career, that I'd lost money when I left yesterday.

Second Visitor Never mind! Tell me, are you still going to keep your appointment with us to go to our friend's house to see that famous belly dancer?

Attorney I can't make it. In the first place, I don't like that type of dancing. Only locals and peasants enjoy that sort of thing. Secondly, I've invited Mademoiselle X, the opera star, and two of her colleagues to dine with me at "Santé" in the Ezbekiyyah Quarter. Afterwards, we're going to have some fun and visit Khān al-Khalīlī, Qaṣbat Ruḍwān, the Tombs of the Caliphs, and other ancient sites in the city.

First Visitor You were just claiming you didn't have any of 3.8
your month's salary left. How are you going to afford such expenses?

Attorney I forgot to mention that a lawyer and his friend, the *'umdah*,[32] are coming with us.

Second Visitor How can two such people make any pretense of liking French soirées or getting the slightest enjoyment out of them? They don't know a word of the language or any European phrases.

Attorney My dear friend, don't you realize that lawyers want to keep the company of the judiciary, and peasants want to brush shoulders with us? But both alike dearly want to attend French soirées, even though the cost is so high and they get no benefit or enjoyment whatsoever.

Second Visitor (*tersely*) Where did you get that cravat?

Attorney I didn't buy it, *monsieur*. It came with my clothes from my tailor in Paris.

First Visitor Did you hear that X has resigned?

Second Visitor Have you seen those electric carriages?

Attorney I've found out for you why Suarez's son committed suicide.

First Visitor I know—love!

Attorney No.

VISITOR Money?

ATTORNEY No.

VISITOR Was he ill?

ATTORNEY No, the poor chap was copying the latest rage in Paris!

FIRST VISITOR And I've found out for you why 'Uthmān Bey Ghālib was fired from his post.

ATTORNEY Was it his conduct?

VISITOR No.

ATTORNEY His job?

VISITOR No.

ATTORNEY His French?

VISITOR No, his English!

3.9 'Īsā ibn Hishām said:[33] I found this terse and vacuous conversation boring, so I took advantage of the guard's entry to leave my hiding place and return to my companion, the Pāshā. I found a lawyer's agent beside him. He had come over and was talking to him. So I stood at a distance. Here is some of what I heard him say:

AGENT You should realize that the lawyer can direct the judiciary exactly as he wishes, punishing and acquitting anyone according to whim. The members of the Parquet, the courts, and judges merely follow his instructions. No decision can be made unless he says so and no verdict can be reached without his instructions. You're a stranger here, someone who deserves sympathy and forbearance. Mere human decency forbids me to let you fall into the clutches of some low-class lawyers who regularly use deceitful and crafty methods and make false promises that raise all kinds of hopes, and all that merely to rob people of their money. My colleague on the other hand is honest and reliable, a well-known man of principle who is highly regarded by princes and government officials alike. He's the inspector's friend, the counselor's companion, the judge's intimate companion, the attorney's confidant, and the prince's agent. If only you could see him just once, my dear Sir, when he meets them for a late-night chat. You would immediately notice the informal atmosphere they share as they enjoy themselves in each other's company and watch him as he eats and drinks with them, chats and jokes, debates and gambles. You would then be convinced that every request he makes is granted and no one would refuse to do what he orders. As a result, the guilty man can be innocent in accordance with his wishes, and the innocent man guilty. So tell me, how much can you afford to pay in advance?

Pāshā I know nothing about advance or arrears. My friend didn't mention this powerful arbiter you describe. So once I've asked him about it—

Agent (*interrupting*) There's no need to ask anyone! Here comes the lawyer now.

(*The Agent greets the Lawyer with the lavish respect due to a prince.* 3.10
As he clears a path toward the Pāshā, he is whispering in the Lawyer's ear.)

Lawyer (*raising his voice*) I cannot possibly take on anybody else's brief these days. I have piles of work and a colossal number of cases. There's no time left to eat and drink. (Maybe the truth of the matter was that he had nothing left at all, not just time.) How can you expect me to take on your friend's brief in such a trifling case, when I've already turned down five major cases this very morning?

Agent For humanitarian reasons and in the name of the sanctity of chivalry and your inborn sympathy and pity for the weak, I beg you to allow one of your office staff to handle this case. Even if you cannot demean yourself so far as to handle it yourself, all that's needed is the influence that your name brings to the court.

Lawyer Out of regard for you and sympathy for your friend, I can see no objection.

(*The Lawyer shakes hands with the Pāshā, then turns away and leaves.*)

Agent (*to the Pāshā*) Come on, that'll be twenty pounds.

Pāshā I haven't a single dirham on me.

Agent Then give me a check from a relative or acquaintance.

Pāshā I don't understand what you mean. Go away, I'm fed up with you!

Agent How can I leave when you have just reached an agreement with the Lawyer right in front of me?

Pāshā I made no agreement with anyone. Go away!

Agent How can you possibly deny shaking hands with the Lawyer and reaching an agreement with him?

Pāshā How can anyone tolerate this situation? I gestured while talking to my friend, and that resulted in the disaster with the Donkeyman. Now I shake the Lawyer's hand, and I'm twenty pounds in debt! What kind of world am I in?

3.11 ʿĪsā ibn Hishām said: I noticed signs of anger on the Pāshā's face and was afraid there would be another disaster, this time with the Agent. I rushed over. After reprimanding the Agent for his trickery, I proceeded to threaten him, saying that I would raise the matter with the Public Attorney. He went away and left us alone.

The usher who was supervising plaintiffs gave a shout. We went inside and found the Attorney still chatting merrily with his two visitors. They indicated that we should go to talk to his secretary, so I went along and began to explain the case on my companion's behalf. I told him about the bad treatment we had received from the police and the shocking way they had trumped up the charges. The Attorney turned to his secretary and told him not to allow any statement against the police; he should accept their statements and investigation. With that, he looked at his watch, found that it was the time for his appointment, grabbed his stick, put on his tarboosh, and left in a hurry with his two colleagues.

I must go now, I told my companion, and look for one of my friends who is an honest lawyer.

3.12 Pāshā Tell me, what's a lawyer in this system of yours?

ʿĪsā He's the one who speaks on your behalf on matters in which you have no competence. He will defend you in areas you know nothing about, and testify for you about things which normally would not occur to you. His is a noble profession practiced today by many excellent people. However, certain other people have entered the profession who aren't worthy of it and who use deceit and trickery as a means of making a profit, like this lawyer and his agent. It is people like them whom ʿAlāʾ al-dīn ʿAlī ibn Muẓaffar al-Kindī has in mind when he says:

Whenever they litigate, legal attorneys
    are simply all-powerful Satans.
They are a people who find they have evil to spare,
    so they sell it off to mankind.

Miṣbāḥ al-sharq 35, December 15, 1898

4.1 ʿĪsā ibn Hishām said: When the day of the court session arrived, I went to the court with my friend. In the courtyard outside I found people who looked pale; their expressions were grim. They breathed heavily and lifted their hands towards the heavens in despair. We watched in amazement as falsehood was passed off as truth and truths were denied. In all the commotion, we noticed some people complaining and making menacing remarks, a criminal currying favor, and a witness hesitating. A policeman kept uttering threats. Elsewhere, an orderly was taking matters into his own hands, and a lawyer was making his preparations. A mother was wailing, a baby crying, a girl fretting, and an old man grumbling. I heard people making incompatible and contradictory statements, and saw the lawyers who were about to defend the two parties sharpening their tongues and rousing their spirits, as they prepared to enter the arena of verbal combat and conduct the defense in cases of dispute, so that both of them could take away as their spoils from the legal battlefield an acquittal and the removal of suspicion and guilt.

With my friend I withdrew to a corner. At my side, the lawyer kept talking about the requisite principles, subsidiary issues, various other points and circumstances, and also mentioning the various phrases, articles, and sections dealing with misdemeanors and infractions. Then he thumbed through his notes, turned his files over, and gave us a solemn promise that the Pāshā need have no worries about being acquitted of the charge. Meanwhile, I was answering all my companion's questions as the situation demanded. When he asked me questions about this particular slaughterhouse, I informed him that it was actually the court itself.

Pāshā The memories I have of the Shariah Court and the judge's residence are certainly different from what I see now. Has Time included it among the things on which it has wrought such a major transformation and upheaval? 4.2

ʿĪsā This is the Native Court, not the Shariah Court.

Pāshā Is there some other form of jurisdiction besides the Shariah Court?

ʿĪsā In this country you can take your pick! The judiciary operates through numerous courts and a variety of committees. These include Shariah Courts, Native Courts, Mixed Courts, Disciplinary Tribunals, and Consular Courts, not to mention the Special Courts.

Pāshā What is this utter confusion? Have Egyptians divided into different sects and parties, tribes, and family groups? Have they turned into people of different species who live in discordant groups and divided classes, so that they've had to establish a special court for each one? This isn't how I remember them in days of old, even though dynasties may have changed. Is the noble Shariah extinct? Have the centers of judicial authority been eradicated? Oh God, forgive me and curse the devil!

ʿĪsā Things are not the way you think or surmise. Egyptians are not split into groups; they are a single people and a single government. It is the organization of things that demands this kind of arrangement. I'll explain it to you as I always do:

The role of the Shariah Court is now restricted to matters of personal status: marriage, divorce, and things like that. 4.3

Pāshā By God, things really have decayed; all semblance of organization has vanished! How can people live in stable surroundings without God's holy law? Are we really living in an age which the poet meant when he said:

In their time the holy law was abrogated.
 If only they had been abrogated like their holy law![34]

ʿĪsā The noble Shariah has not been abrogated; on the contrary, it lasts for ever, as long as there is any justice in the world and honesty exists among peoples. But it is a treasure ignored by its own folk, a jewel neglected by its own merchants,

> Or a precious pearl, no sooner did a diver see it
> than he rejoiced and sank in prayer.[35]

4.4 Nowadays people pay no attention to the various aspects of its structure and formulation. Instead they prefer to adhere to the branches at the expense of the roots and to dispense with the kernel for the husks. They argue about regulations, concentrate assiduously on insignificant matters, and devote themselves to paltry and worthless matters. Their greatest aspiration and goal is to obscure the clear truth and complicate our liberal faith. They've never grasped what the laws of time demand. Every era has an order of its own which requires that the provisions of the Shariah be adjusted. Instead they are preoccupied with insignificant issues, in the apparent belief that that's the way of the world; Destiny and Time follow their course for a while and then come to a stop. As a result, they're a primary reason for the charge that's leveled against the noble Shariah—may it be purified and sanctified!—namely that its legal authority is deficient, its obligations are weakened, and it lacks fairness. They are all entirely happy with this appalling situation. Instead of upholding the law, they fool around with it. The kind of thing that they bother about now is: "During the ritual ablutions, is it legitimate to wipe your shoes if they are made of glass"—weird things like that. Everything has ground to a halt, whence the need to create the Native Court alongside the Shariah Court.

4.5 Pāshā Shariah scholars must have an obvious excuse. They've been faced with either the objections and arguments of opponents or the oppressive tyranny of a powerful ruler. This has prevented them from following the right course and made them choose this pernicious path instead.

ʿĪsā It was nothing of the kind. People are free to choose and can form their own opinions independently. By so doing they may obtain peace of mind. The source of corruption is not the laws of time or unforeseen happenings. It's the consequence of faulty education and moral decline, something to which they're happily reconciled. It's reached such a stage now that any attempt to extricate themselves from this situation is regarded as a trial and any return to the genuine tenets of the religious law is seen as heresy. The diseases of mutual envy, hatred, discord, and rancor have spread among them; cowardice, lassitude, weakness, dissatisfaction, slackness, tedium, and laziness are now deeply ingrained inside them. As a result we've now reached the stage that you're witnessing. Since we've all done these things ourselves, the sin and responsibility is ours; we're the ones to blame.

Pāshā I realize that you're exaggerating. But, even if we're to suppose that the corruption that you describe is widespread, isn't there some rare individual to point out to you the need for the law to be upheld and to guide you toward the true bases of your faith? Is there no one to offer you such guidance?

ʿĪsā Oh yes, we have such judicious counselors. There are scholars, men of virtue, intellectuals, true believers, and pious folk. But, whenever any of them takes a stand, he's immediately accused of being a deviant heretic. They call him a recalcitrant apostate. Such are the moral postures so deeply ingrained in the souls of people in the grip of conservative tradition. So the forward-looking person thinks twice, and ambitious ideas falter. Virtue is so lacking among us that people's ideas are scoffed at and their statements are despised. Not only that, but it's always easier to do nothing rather than take action; a life of ease is more convenient than one of exhaustion. I've not been exaggerating in my description, as you're about to see for yourself.

ʿĪsā ibn Hishām said: While we were conversing like this, the whole place was reverberating with the noise of people surging around in 4.6

crowds. Then the Judge appeared. He was in the prime of his youth, still quite young, his face radiantly handsome. His stance made him look like a tree branch; with his light, energetic stride he seemed to be flying. When he entered the court, I went to ask when our case was coming up, then returned to my companion. He asked me to continue our conversation, and I duly responded to his request:

ʿĪSĀ The Native Court is the judicial authority that passes judgment on subjects today in all litigations in accordance with the stipulations of the law.

PĀSHĀ Do you mean the Humāyūnī law code?[36]

ʿĪSĀ The Imperial Code.

PĀSHĀ I don't remember you speaking in a foreign language or using obscure terms like that before!

ʿĪSĀ I'm doing neither. It's the Code of Napoleon who was Emperor of France.

PĀSHĀ Have the French returned to Egypt and subjected you to their regime again?

ʿĪSĀ No. We're the ones who subjected ourselves to their authority. We chose their legal code to replace the Shariah in our country.

PĀSHĀ Are this code's regulations consistent with those of the noble Shariah? If not, then you are being governed with something which was not sent down to earth by the Almighty.

4.7 ʿĪSĀ That's what Shariah scholars state in private confidential discussion. However, it seems that it is compatible with the holy law. As proof, one can cite the pronouncement made by a scholar of great eminence who swore a mighty oath on a legal decision which he'd given at the time of its promulgation to the effect that this French code was not at variance with the Islamic holy law, even though there's no punishment specified in the French code for adultery or homosexuality, provided that the object of affection agrees and is one day over twelve years of age; nor for anyone who commits incest with his mother, provided she assents and is unmarried. This is the legal code which considers a brother guilty of a criminal offense when he risks his life in the defense and protection of his sister's honor, and the same with the rest of her family beyond her husband; which decrees that debtors shall be compelled to pay interest to creditors; which is willing to accept the testimony of a single woman against a man; and which does not punish the husband who steals from his wife, nor the reverse, nor son from father, nor the reverse.

The Mixed Courts, which have foreign judges, specialize in investigating litigation between native people and foreigners, and amongst foreigners themselves on matters of civil rights, by which I mean cases involving money. Foreigners have a greater right to wealth because they are serious and work harder. Egyptians on the other hand deserve to be poor because they are negligent and leave everything to foreigners. As a result, the majority of cases in which these courts have competence to pass judgment inevitably result in Egyptians being deprived of their money and property. 4.8

Disciplinary Tribunals deal specifically with the punishment of officials who fail to carry out their job properly. They're usually made up of the same officials who charge the offenders. The severest sentences which they can impose are dismissal from office and loss of livelihood. The remaining degrees of sentence are referred back to be dealt with by the Native Courts.

Administrative Tribunals deal with the punishment of anyone who contravenes edicts, orders, and decrees. It would take ages to explain. 4.9

Military Courts are concerned with the punishment of officers and troops on a charge. They also have authority over people in questions of conscription and the like.

Consular Courts cover the supervision of misdemeanors committed by foreigners against Egyptians and by one foreigner against another of the same nationality. If a foreigner commits a felony against an Egyptian, the courts have no jurisdiction or power of punishment in Egypt; none of these courts which I have explained to you has any special authority in this matter. The offender is returned to his country of birth and homeland for trial. When judges there look into the case, they inevitably end up acquitting the criminal for "lack of confidence in the Egyptian police's investigation," "loss of data relevant to the case," and "lack of sufficient witnesses."

Special Courts handle punishment for people who assault foreign troops.

PĀSHĀ You keep on giving me curious bits of information and explaining things I don't understand. When did Egyptians ever assault troops?!

4.10 While we were talking, our case was called. The Pāshā was summoned and entered the court with the Lawyer. The Attorney of the Parquet stood up and asked for a conviction against the accused, in accordance with articles 124 and 126 of the Penal Code, for an assault on a member of the judicial police during the execution of his duty, and with article 346, dealing with misdemeanors, for a minor assault on the Donkeyman.

JUDGE (*to the accused*) Did you commit the offence with which you have been charged?

LAWYER He did not.

4.11 'Īsā ibn Hishām said: They then brought me forward as a witness. The Judge proceeded to question me about my knowledge of the whole affair. I responded to his questions.

'ĪSĀ The whole thing is a most peculiar tale. It started like this—

JUDGE (*interrupting*) There's no need to go into details. Just tell me what you know about it.

'ĪSĀ What I know is that one night at daybreak I was visiting the graveyard in search of spiritual counsel and reflection.

JUDGE (*getting irritated*) There's no need to speak at length, just answer the point I asked you.

'ĪSĀ That's what I was doing. I was telling you what happened. I saw a man coming out of—

Judge (*fidgeting*) I've just told you I won't accept any elaborate accounts of what happened. Did the accused strike the police officer and the Donkeyman?

'Īsā The accused did not strike the Donkeyman; he merely pushed him away because the Donkeyman was being so persistent. He didn't hit the policeman either. He was feeling faint and simply fell on him by accident. He's quite unaware—

Judge All right, that's enough! Call the Attorney.

Attorney This Pāshā stands accused of assaulting a member of the police during the course of his duties at the police station, and also of injuring Mursī the Donkeyman. The charge is substantiated by the witnesses' testimony in the dossier on the case. The court has enough information about all this. On that basis therefore, the Parquet demands that sentence be passed against the accused according to article 346 dealing with misdemeanors. It demands that the court must prove its integrity by showing no mercy in its sentence. The accused's attitude demands no less. He seems to be under the impression that his status exempts him from the authority of the law and gives him the right to regard the rest of the population as being less important than himself. So he disciplines them himself without regard to their rights and the sanctity of the law. He must undoubtedly be punished severely so as to provide an example and warning to people like him and to ensure that justice will be unbiased. I commit the case to the court. 4.12

Judge (*to the lawyer*) Now the defense, and make it brief. 4.13

Lawyer (*after clearing his throat and fumbling among his papers*) We are indeed amazed that the Attorney of the Parquet has summoned us here today describing us as the accused. What we say, your worship, is that, since desert civilization and the barbarian ages, the origin of the occurrence of crimes according to the law in this world was meant—

Judge (*in disgust*) Would my learned friend be brief and get to the point?

Lawyer It is well known, your worship, that the system of organization in the classes of human society demands—

Judge (*irritated*) My dear Sir, be brief.

Lawyer But the point at issue requires that—

Judge (*grumbling*) There is no need for all this.

Lawyer (*flustered*) The Attorney has said . . . (*here he quotes something from the Attorney's speech*), however, we claim that, were we to concede for argument's sake—

Judge (*annoyed*) That's enough, sir. Get to the point!

Lawyer (*stuttering and confused*) May it please the court, this accused man who now stands before the Judge is a man of importance and an amir of considerable standing in days of old. His story has been published in the papers; here are the numbers of *Miṣbāḥ al-sharq* for you to examine.[37] While he was walking, a donkeyman kept blocking his path, so he pushed him aside. Now we're all well aware of how persistent and uncouth donkeymen and uneducated people like them can be—

Judge (*losing all patience*) Listen, my good Sir, I've told you to be brief!

Lawyer (*sweat pouring off him*) When the accused reached the police station, he fainted and fell unintentionally on a policeman out of uniform who was sweeping the station floor. The integrity of the court therefore demands that no attention be paid to the police claims. There can be no charge against the accused whatsoever. He lived in an age different from our own; in his day the whole system was different. He has never heard of the demands of the law, so he is unaware of its regulations. Your worship knows the situation best of all, and if—

Judge (*pounding the desk with his hand in annoyance*) The court has been enlightened, so there's absolutely no need for all this talk. Get on with your demands.

Lawyer (*suppressing his own anger*) We have two demands. We ask that the accused be acquitted as a matter of principle. If the court decides otherwise, then we hope that, in accordance with article 352 of the Penal Code, it will show due clemency.

ʿĪsā ibn Hishām said: The Judge proceeded to deliver his verdict. In accordance with the two articles of the Penal Code as cited, he condemned the Pāshā to a year and a half's imprisonment and fined him five piasters with costs as stipulated by the article on misdemeanors also mentioned above. I found this too much to bear; the world darkened before my eyes. I would certainly have joined my companion in a swoon of astonishment, had not the Lawyer given us every possible assurance that the Pāshā was bound to be acquitted at the Court of Appeal because of the fairness of its members. However, he told us that, besides that, we would have to raise a grievance with the Committee of Surveillance so as to present the case in a favorable light when it was considered at the appeal. "I want you to realize," he told me, "that the Judge kept interrupting and hurrying me on because he's been invited to the banquet of a friend of his at 1 p.m. He's got thirty cases on his agenda, and intends to pass sentence in all of them before his appointment." 4.14

ʿĪsā ibn Hishām said: God Almighty alone is the possessor of power and might! What could I say other than quote the words of the wise poet, al-Maʿarrī: 4.15

> I forbid you to pursue controversy or to be seen
> as linked to preaching or mosque-imam.
> Abandon princedom and using a whip in the city,
> thinking it a champion's sword.
> These things have I despised in relatives
> and friends alike. It were better to stint your own self.

Miṣbāḥ al-sharq 39, January 12, 1899

5.1 Our Lawyer forwarded a petition to the Committee of Surveillance and suggested that we should go to inquire about it. He told us that he would like to deal with it himself, but he was prevented from so doing by the realization that the Judge who was the subject of the complaint because of his continuous interruptions during the evidence phase might well make a determined effort to do him some harm in the future. He would be aware that the Lawyer was the one who had lodged the complaint with the Committee or been its primary instigator. Lawyers, he told us, must always avoid annoying judges and foster their goodwill.

When I urged the Pāshā to follow the Lawyer's suggestion, he shied away, adamantly refusing to come and being persistently obstructive. This is what he kept saying:

PĀSHĀ I've had enough. The utter humiliation, injustice, damage, loss of honor, and lack of respect that I've endured as a result of the Creator's predestined decree are more than enough. I couldn't bear the thought of putting up with two humiliations at once: enduring oppression and submitting to injustice on the one hand, while making weak and humble complaints on the other. Just leave me alone! Don't give these misfortunes any more encouragement; don't serve as the key to open up any more troubles. One should complain to God alone, and through Him alone comes recompense. «Lord, I prefer prison to the thing to which they are summoning me.»[38] God knows, I would have sought release from my worries through suicide, were it not for the punishment of hell-fire. I only wish that the prison sentence could be changed to one of death, so that I could escape from these dreadful misfortunes. Throughout my life I never heard of a prison sentence being given to any amir. In our time, it was only applied as a punishment to the plebs and lowest classes. At least amirs had this special privilege: if the question of sentence ever arose, it was execution. It would be far easier to face death rather than gloomy prisons.

ʿĪsā I've never noticed such panic and fear in a person like you, nor do I expect to encounter such cowardly resignation from you, the dauntless, courageous hero. Courage consists merely of showing endurance in the face of adversity, and confronting the circumstances in which you find yourself with a cheerful and calm equanimity. 5.2

Hearts will often panic because of something
which can be resolved like the untying of a cord.[39]

In my opinion, you're a man of the very soundest resolve and steadiest intellect. Intelligence involves the effective use of thought to rid oneself of misfortunes and devising a scheme to put an end to anxieties. At our disposal today we have a variety of sanctioned and prescribed courses of action. We will suffer no disgrace or harm by making use of them. You must realize that changing times and the fickle vicissitudes of life alter the basis of things and bring about modifications in the way in which one looks at them. What was considered a virtue in the past is regarded as depravity on the morrow; behavior which was regarded as a failing in past ages is now considered a virtue. In the past, nobility may indeed have derived its splendor from forceful authority and used brute strength to support itself, but today nobility in every sense demands submission to the regulations of the law. Come on then, and let's follow this course of action! We may eventually be rid of these misfortunes and escape safe and sound from the troubles we are experiencing.

PĀSHĀ The taste of violent death would be easier for me than what you suggest. I would rather drink boiling water than suffer such humiliation.

5.3 ʿĪsā ibn Hishām said: We continued this discussion, but the various suggestions I made to change my companion's stubbornly defiant attitude failed to achieve anything. I was on the point of giving up my attempt to carry out my intention of advising and guiding him. Just then, we heard a newspaper vendor shouting in a voice so hideous that it was even worse than a donkey braying: "*Al-Muʾayyad* and *Al-Muqaṭṭam*, *Al-Ahrām* and *Miṣr*, all four for a piaster."

PĀSHĀ What incredible things I keep hearing! Have mosques, mountains, monuments, and countries become things one can purchase by auction in the market?

> Without a doubt mankind has been disturbed;
> so be serious about time, or else make sport with it.[40]

ʿĪSĀ Those names aren't monuments or countries! They're used as titles for daily newspapers.

PĀSHĀ By newspapers do you perhaps mean the lists and daily sheets used by money changers, or are they lists of tax farms? But what's the point of these obscure titles?

ʿĪSĀ Things are not as you think. Newspapers are sheets of paper printed daily, weekly, or monthly, in which news and stories of public interest are collected and reported, so that people can find out about public affairs. They are one of the aspects of Western civilization that we've imported into our own society. The purpose of issuing papers is to publish articles which give due credit for value and merit; and to rebuke depravity, to criticize bad actions and encourage good ones, to draw attention to points of imperfection, and to urge people to correct mistakes. They are meant to tell people what the government is doing on their behalf, so that it doesn't drag them into anything against their interest, and also to let the government know about the people's needs so that it can endeavor to satisfy them. To sum up, those who run the press occupy the position of "those who command good deeds and prohibit bad deeds" as referred to in the Islamic Shariah.

PĀSHĀ We used to hear about something of the kind in our time called "Gazette." One of them was published in Turkish called *The Daily Record of Events.* Eulogies and congratulations were recorded in them, and there were notes about movements of the Viceregal entourage. But, if the status of newspapers today has been raised to the level you claim, then the most eminent scholars and important shaykhs must be involved in their production. It is an excellent means of informing people about things which will benefit them in their present life and help them in the hereafter. So let me take a look at one of them. 5.4

'ĪSĀ Our scholars and shaykhs are of all people the least likely to follow this course and pursue the journalistic profession. They consider working in it to be heresy. They've dubbed it innovation (which the Shariah forbids) and interference in matters of no concern to anyone. So they ignore newspapers and often disagree as to whether or not it's even permissible to read them. But other people have chosen it as a profession, some of them worthy, others unworthy. Some have used it as a means of earning a living by all possible means. So you'll find them no different from tradesmen and market vendors. They are all as fraudulent, treacherous, lying, hypocritical, cunning, and crafty as one another when it comes to looting and murdering:

> They have peopled the site of hypocrisy among themselves,
> but the haven of loyalty lies in ruins.[41]

The original intentions of the press and the respect which it commanded have foundered ever since its standing fell among the élite and the benefits expected from it proved to be less than the damage it caused. Some sensible people still hope that one day the situation can be rectified and the profession elevated to the noble and worthy position it deserves. The whole question lies in the hands of readers.

They must focus on what is beneficial and reject what is harmful. «Dross metal disappears as rubbish; what benefits people remains on the earth.»[42]

5.5 I called out to the vendor and bought papers from him. I opened one of them to read some items of news to my friend. There was some news about the sentence passed on Aḥmad Sayf al-dīn, the sympathy people felt for him, and the attempts to obtain a pardon. It described the coarse clothing and poor food he was having to deal with in prison, enough to bring tears to the eyes when contemplating the fate of this young man, a scion of princes and rulers. Once I had finished reading, I turned to the Pāshā and said:

ʿĪsā Just observe how circumstances have made us equals. You've just heard about the sentence passed on Prince Aḥmad Sayf al-dīn by the court judge. Having heard that, how can you still refuse to submit to the law, conform with its regulations, and make use of its channels to get out of the situation in which you find yourself?

Pāshā What's this word "prince," and who's Aḥmad Sayf al-dīn?

5.6 ʿĪsā "Prince" is a foreign title given to heads of the Roman Empire before they had the audacity in the face of the populace to adopt the title of Emperor. Later on, it came to be used in Europe to apply to members of the royal family and to heads of petty governments. Today male and female members of the Khedive's family call themselves by it, even though it's not included in the list of official Ottoman titles. Aḥmad Sayf al-dīn is in fact Aḥmad ibn Ibrāhīm ibn Aḥmad ibn Ibrāhīm ibn Muḥammad ʿAlī, the latter the ancestor and founder of the present Khedive's family. He committed a felony, was dragged before the courts, and incurred the penalty laid down by the law. The Court of First Instance sentenced him to seven years' imprisonment. He appealed, asking the Court of Appeal judges for clemency. They reduced his sentence to five years. Then he asked the Court of Cassation for assistance, but obtained none. Efforts were made to arrange for members of the Khedive's family to request that he be pardoned. His mother went this way and that, trying every possible means of asking for clemency, but the law applies to everyone. So how can you deem it proper to hold yourself aloof by refusing to submit a grievance petition? Now that you have heard about the history of princes, are you still too proud to pursue your case with the Committee of Surveillance and the Court of Appeal?

PĀSHĀ Lofty mountains must inevitably crumble when the whitefooted mountain goats are brought down. Graves must be split asunder and the trumpet be blown when all ideas of dignity have vanished and all values have been debased. The words of the Almighty have come true with regard to Egypt: «And We have made its highest parts into its lowest parts.»[43] As long as you tell me that Muḥammad ʿAlī's descendant is in prison, is conforming with the law's regulations, and using these avenues for submitting a petition, while his mother tries to intercede on his behalf, then I can see no disgrace in what you're asking me to do. So take me wherever you wish. I only hope that they will accept my wish to act as ransom for the son of my masters and benefactors. Then his sentence can be added to mine.

ʿĪsā ibn Hishām said: The Pāshā accompanied me to the Ministry 5.7
of Justice. He kept dragging his feet and choking back his tears. We entered the place where the Committee of Surveillance sat. They directed us to the inspectors' room and we tried to enter, but an orderly stopped us and asked the Pāshā for his "carte."

PĀSHĀ What does that foreign word mean?

ʿĪSĀ The "carte" is a small piece of paper on which visitors write their name. They're supposed to show it before entering an office. The person being visited can then decide whether to receive the visitor or avoid seeing him.

PĀSHĀ In our day, channels for complaint were open to anyone who wished to use them. How can this restriction be in keeping with the equality of rights and justice in matters of law that you've been talking about?

ʿĪsā That system provides no safeguards against visits from idle callers or importunate petitioners. So this method has been evolved to give authorities enough time to perform their duties.

Pāshā But isn't the very prestige and kudos that people in authority have sufficient to prevent the kind of people you have mentioned from stopping in and bothering them?

5.8 ʿĪsā ibn Hishām said: I wrote a little slip with the Pāshā's name on it. The orderly came back to tell us we could go in. We entered and found in front of us a young man with a premature growth of beard; signs of his youth welled up like a spring beneath it just as light swells in the midst of the moon's halo. As we moved a little closer, I noticed that he had an account sheet in his hand which he turned over and other papers that he kept piling together and pounding. Then he put his hand to his forehead like someone trying to remember a figure which is missing from his calculations. On his right was a foreign book, on his left an Arabic book. I took a look at them: the former was by Voltaire, the French atheist philosopher; the latter by Muḥyī al-dīn Ibn ʿArabī, the monist Ṣūfī. When the Inspector asked us our business, I told him the whole story and mentioned the way the Judge had kept interrupting the testimony of the defense lawyer. I described for him the petition that we had presented. At this point the Pāshā interrupted me and spoke to the Inspector:

Pāshā The worst thing at the trial, the bitterest stroke of all in the entire matter, was that the man whom you call the Attorney of the Parquet considered my rank to be sufficient cause to insult me. Never in my dreams did I imagine that the rank that I obtained by rushing without regard into perilous missions and enduring great hardships would turn out to be an unpardonable crime, something that would in his view provide a conclusive proof to support his claims, something to be used as a pretext for demanding that the sentence be more severe. Tell me, by God, since when has this noble rank of mine deserved punishment and vengeance?

Furthermore, where do you belong within the various species of mankind?

ʿĪsā ibn Hishām said: At this point another visitor came in. I thanked God that his entrance had interrupted the Pāshā. But for that, he might well have said things that could not have been put right. Once the visitor had offered his greetings, he asked what news there was at the start of the day. The inspector expressed his great admiration for a speech he had been reading for amusement and handed it over to him. He had only just turned his attention to us again when a foreign inspector came to see him and showed him a drawing on a piece of paper which he claimed to have drawn during a legal discussion in which he had been involved in arguments and disputation. The young man looked at it and laughed, admiring the fine craftsmanship, then got rid of him so that he could attend to us. He addressed the Pāshā in a sympathetic tone that showed his noble background and good breeding. He finished by saying: 5.9

INSPECTOR (*to the Pāshā*) I've already studied the angles of the case in *Miṣbāḥ al-sharq*. The Judge may well have a good reason for interrupting the lawyer. Some of them make a habit of including the history of mankind's creation, the formation of human society, and other similar matters, into their defense speech. Such antics lead to lengthy expositions and have no relevance whatsoever to the point of the case. Such lawyers will often insist on using such devices in the simplest and most trifling cases in order to convince their client that no word has been left unsaid in his defense, regardless of whether the case is won or lost. Thus, one finds some clients who believe that the lawyer only earns his fee by the amount said, just like an article that is costed according to its weight. One of them once refused to pay his lawyer the fees in arrears even after winning his case, claiming that he had not heard him make a long enough defense speech to deserve the fee, regardless of whether it achieved good or bad results. The judge's time is both short and valuable, so the only thing he can do is to interrupt any lawyer who makes lengthy speeches. The judge will also interrupt the witness in order to direct his attention to the facts of the case so that he will not omit anything by getting off the point. In short, the judge in no way contravened the law in the way in which he treated you.

5.10 PĀSHĀ Now that you've explained away the Judge's interruptions, I wish I knew what excuse there can be for putting me in the prisoner's dock and making me stand for every question. I'm an old man who spent his life filling the highest positions in the Egyptian government and gave his blood freely in the service of the Khedive's family. Why did he show no consideration for my age and no respect for my position? What law is there in the world to prevent him from doing that? Reverence for age is something inborn; respect for people of high rank is something innate. God Almighty says in the Qur'an: «We have raised some of them above others in degrees.»[44]

INSPECTOR The law stipulates that as well. It's based on the concept of equality. In the eyes of the law, there's no difference in either age or status. This is exactly in accordance with the commands of the noble Shariah and applies in particular to members of the Khedive's family and people in authority when one of them commits a crime indictable under the law. So you have suffered neither ignominy nor disgrace in standing up before the Judge. You merely stood before the representative of His Excellency the Khedive who holds the highest rank of all.

PĀSHĀ If that constitutes your opinion about the Judge, then what about the member of the Parquet who saw fit to reproach me for my noble rank?

5.11 INSPECTOR I haven't studied the files on the case and the details of the defense yet. But the part of the Attorney's speech which has been published in *Miṣbāḥ al-sharq* is not intended to convey any idea of reproach because of your rank. On the contrary, its aim is to make it clear that it is not the right of people of high rank, however important they may be, to completely override the rights of the weak and use it to claim precedence over other people before the law. The scope of rank is limited purely to its possessor, without giving him any advantages over those who do not have it. Thus you have no reason to complain about the things which the Attorney said on this point. That's the way things normally happen in this age.

Pāshā Well then, if the Judge and Attorney can both be excused, what's the point of my coming to see you and submitting a petition of complaint? Wouldn't it be proper to summon the Judge and Attorney, reprimand them both, then examine the case, verify the falsity of the accusation, and on that basis quash the sentence in their presence?

Inspector That's not within our sphere of jurisdiction. If a court official acts contrary to the dictates of his office, the investigation of the case is in the hands of the Disciplinary Committee. A senior person has no recourse against a subordinate except through a court decision. Thus, I'm extremely sorry to say that we can't act in your case. The decision rests with the Court of Appeal alone since it is the entity charged with annulling verdicts.

ʿĪsā ibn Hishām said: As this conversation proceeded, I was watching another young inspector at our side. His bright red tarboosh was tilted to one side. His expression showed signs of authority, and he kept raising and lowering his hand to and from his glasses. His appearance confirmed the fact that he was well organized and astute. When our conversation reached a certain point, he hailed the orderly, signs of regret and sympathy imprinted on his expression: 5.12

Second Inspector Bring me Dalloz and Garraud.

The Pāshā turned to me and asked: Are those the names of the Judge and Attorney? Has the time come for me to get fair treatment from them both?

ʿĪsā They're the titles of two books on civil jurisprudence, instead of Ibn ʿĀbidīn and Al-Hidāyah on Shariah jurisprudence.

The librarian fetched the two books, but the Inspector gave one of them back to him. "Not Baudry," he said. "I asked for Garraud." When they brought him that book, he began to delve into the two works for a long time. He looked despairingly at the librarian. "Get me Faustin Hélie," he said, whereupon the librarian brought him another book. After studying this book for a while, he began to argue with his colleague in French. Eventually, when they finished, they spoke to the Pāshā:

5.13 Your only recourse in this case is the Court of Appeal. As far as the Judge and Attorney are concerned, we will make a note of it and refer it to the Board when it meets. If they find the slightest fault in their conduct, they will send out a circular to all courts ordering this practice to be discontinued in future.

With that, they both bade us farewell with reverence and respect. As we left, the Pāshā spoke to me:

PĀSHĀ Every time I've set foot in one of this government's departments, I've found myself faced with young people conducting its business. Have Egyptians been created afresh, or are they living in heaven where all ages are equal? My heart is almost completely exhausted from the way these worries and anxieties keep piling up against me.

> I have seen sorrows obscuring sorrows
> just as one line is written over another on paper.[45]

5.14 ʿĪSĀ Don't be surprised that young men are appointed to government positions; in this era the system requires it. They claim that men in middle and old age cannot bear the burdens of responsibility because they lack the necessary knowledge about modern sciences and the skills they demand.

> Were God to see any good in old age,
> The devout would abide near Him, old-aged for all eternity.[46]

PĀSHĀ How can they possibly claim that knowledge is the sole province of the young to the exclusion of older people? I've only encountered genuine learning in people whose backs have been bent by old age and whose hairline has been whitened by experience. It's only then that reason and culture shine forth in all their brilliance.

'Īsā Knowledge and learning are not the exclusive province of one age group or one period of life. Young men are often more effective in the scientific sphere and can gather more information on various subjects because of the sharp intellect and quick comprehension which is characteristic of people of their age. As a result, when they apply their energies to learning with determination, they can take in materials that are no less abundant than those possessed by men in middle and old age. Indeed their swift comprehension of things may enable them to achieve the same as older men have done after lengthier experience. You should not deny young people the knowledge they acquire nor challenge their right to assume high office.

> Youth is not something to prevent one from learning;
> learning may exist in both young and old.[47]

Pāshā So far I've followed your line of reasoning and taken your advice. We've presented our case to the Committee of Surveillance. But, as you can see, we've emerged without success. After going to all this trouble, we can only trust in despair. With today's events behind us, you have no plausible reason for dragging me into making any further efforts to lodge a complaint before the judges. 5.15

'Īsā Don't despair or lose heart. We still have the Court of Appeal before us. I've great faith in the fairness of its judgment. And, even supposing that our hopes were to be dashed there, the gate still remains open for us to try to obtain a pardon through the Minister of Justice.

Pāshā From now on, don't mention any ruler or minister. I've had enough of standing in front of these young men, however much you exaggerate and quote poetry to describe them.

'Īsā The Minister of Justice I'm describing is not at all like these young men. He prays devoutly, devotes all his attention to 5.16

extra recitations and remembrances of God, and spends the night standing in prayer and the day fasting. There's a pact of understanding between his fingers and the rosary, and a firm connection between his forehead and the prayer mat. All in all, in this modern age he reminds us more than anyone else of the old times you knew. His father was in fact one of the great men of your day, Ḥasan Pāshā al-Manāstirlī.

PĀSHĀ Al-Manāstirlī! He was my greatest friend and companion, my colleague in government service. Why didn't you tell me about the son of this companion of mine right from the very beginning? You'd have preserved the color in my cheeks and saved me this abuse and degradation.

'ĪSĀ I didn't forget. It's just that he wouldn't have been of any help in avoiding the misfortunes in which we've been involved. He'll only be useful in the final stages of the process. We can't expect any assistance from him until after the decision of the appeal regarding the request for a pardon is published.

Sudanese Government Monopoly

Miṣbāḥ al-sharq 40, January 19, 1899

ʿĪsā ibn Hishām told us: I heard a story about a minister concerned with the topic that is on everyone's mind at the moment. This happened when a newspaper reporter came to see him to try to get the benefit of his enlightened views and learn some accurate information about the new government in the Sudan. Because it seems to me so remarkable, I've decided to relay it to our readers immediately before we go back to the story of the Pāshā and his trial. 6.1

The Reporter said: I inquired when the Minister of War would have some free time from all his responsibilities. They told me that he was too busy carrying out his ministerial duties, but they also went to great lengths to explain how stubborn and secretive he was; he excelled at saying nothing. Many newspaper reporters like myself had tried in vain and had left frustrated and disappointed. However, I paid no attention to these statements and ignored their advice. I reminded myself that he might be reluctant to meet newspaper owners through fear of their criticisms; as a result he would regularly refuse to help them or give them information. On the other hand, any reporter who pretended to praise him to the very heavens as a way of offering him support against bitter critics, thus playing the role of a genuinely loyal helper in the face of slanderous falsehoods, would find that the minister had no cause to hide his innermost feelings and secret thoughts or offer the usual excuses. 6.2

After all, people love making excuses for themselves, whatever they happen to be doing.

6.3 So I headed for the Ministry and asked for an audience with the Minister. The curtains were pulled back for me, and I went in. He was standing towards the door in welcome, lighting the fire to keep warm in the winter cold:

> Approaching him, you glow in the warmth of his blazing fire;
> there you find the best of fires, and to tend it, the finest kindler.[48]

I stood where I was. He seemed completely distracted and did not even notice me. I watched as he gestured with his hands and stamped on the ground, then started banging his head and mumbling to himself about his sorry plight. In front of him was a long spear and gleaming sword while by his side was a coat and rosary. He spoke in a hoarse voice:

6.4 MINISTER (*talking to himself*) How futile are people's dreams, how erroneous their understanding! They keep watching me closely, hatching all kinds of plots, all in order to have me relieved of my post so they can step into it themselves. If only the silly fools knew the things I have to tolerate and suffer through! We spend the whole day being despised and looked down on, and then worry all through the night. They should feel pity and sympathy rather than envy and hatred!

> He who envies a poor wretch his livelihood is himself despicable;
> Death itself is less burdensome than many a life.[49]

The Sudan has been conquered in my name, subjugated by the Egyptian army under my authority. Now, everyone's earned their laurels and come home victorious. However, I'm out of luck. Everyone but me has their share of booty, a portion of the prizes and gifts:

> To East and West, a full moon has lit up the earth;
> but the place where my foot has stepped is as black as pitch.[50]

Kitchener has been given the title of Lord, and twenty-five thousand pounds to boot, not to mention an embossed sword. He's gained the kind of fame and prestige that he would never have dreamed of in his entire life. Lord Cromer has been made a Viscount, and Buṭrus Pāshā a Knight—and there's obviously a world of difference between the Foreign Ministry and the Ministry of War! Wingate has been promoted to Major-General after ten years of waiting, and Colonel Rhodes has been allowed the privilege of returning to the ranks of the British army after being cashiered for Wingate's campaign in the Transvaal. Zubayr has the reward of seeing his sons going back to the Sudan as amirs after being thwarted for so long. Hunter has got the Second Class 'Uthmānī decoration and Griffith the Third Majīdī. All their officer colleagues have been decorated, and Omdurman has been open to the Sudanese soldiery for three full days. Everyone who participated in the conquest has got two months' pay as a reward and those who didn't got one month's, right down to the military draft councils in the various provinces. But even though the Minister of War, the head of this splendid army, is in charge and signs the documents, he has no share in this bounty. All he can do is to repeat these lines of poetry: 6.5

> Is it not incredible that someone in my position
> watches as his inferiors stay aloof from him?
> In his name the whole world is being subdued,
> and yet none of it comes into his hands.[51]

I seek God's forgiveness! This weapon and these clothes they've given me as reward constitute my entire share in the spoils of victory, with all its glory and honor. They're the kind of thing that the Mahdī would previously give to those people whom he was encouraging to follow the path of true guidance and avoid temptation. This is all the reward I get for assuming so much responsibility and enduring so much blame and criticism. My foes have even accused me of neglecting my job, going against the canons of patriotism and disregarding the people's interests. 6.6

6.7 The Reporter went on to say: The Minister became quite upset and started sobbing. He quoted al-Mutanabbī's line to himself:

> What have I ever got from the world? Most incredible of all
> is that people envy me for something which makes me weep.[52]

I felt sorry for him so I coughed. The Minister turned towards the door with a jump. I went over to him and offered my greetings. He asked me how long I had been standing there; I hedged and gave an ambiguous answer so that he would think I had not been eavesdropping on him and not seen him sobbing. When he accepted that, he sat down in a chair which was an imitation of one in the English War Ministry and chewed a Havana cigar like the one the American general Miles had in his mouth when he entered that city. He put one foot on top of the other, brought the seal of office out of his pocket and started fiddling with it. He began counting his fingers and sifting papers on his desk in the pretence of being busy. All the while, he kept sneaking glances in my direction. After carrying on like this for some time, he asked me what I wanted. I responded as follows:

6.8 Reporter You are well aware, Sir, that the Sudanese problem is the primary event of the day and the focus of everyone's attention. I'm fed up, and so are our readers, with all the confusion and bungling, not to mention the slanderous criticisms being leveled at you. I've come to get some idea of the situation from you since you have a complete mastery of the whole picture. I can then pass it on to our readers and claim distinction from my colleagues by providing plausible statements and clear rationales. That will rid you of all the criticisms and abuse. As the saying has it, if you want information, ask someone who knows.

6.9 Minister The whole thing is quite straightforward; there's no cause for concern and nothing for people to be worried about. The Sudan is being governed jointly by the Egyptian government in which we are ministers and the British government represented by Lord Cromer. At the moment, we are considering together ways of organizing the government there and introducing Western culture and civilization instead of the primitive barbarianism which subsists there at the moment. We are entirely unconcerned about the stupid prattle of those ignorant meddling fools who are unable to grasp what lies in the inscrutable future. Sudan is going to be a veritable garden for Egypt; it will provide us with all our wants. It is the place where we find the source of Egypt's Nile and so it will also be the source of its welfare and mainstay of its power and pride. The Sudanese people are still primitive; they don't have ingrained in them the customs of Oriental civilization with all its futilities, delusions, opulence, and luxury. The corrupt character and nasty traits which are so common in Oriental countries have not become so deeply rooted in their nature; in fact, quite the opposite, their thoughts are like their own land, virgin. All this bride lacks is a dowry made up of the jewels of civilization. The country will then reveal its true beauty and shine radiantly over all other ideas. It's as if you are planting a seed in their soil; the fruit it produces will be better than any other fruit.

The Sudanese are not like the Egyptians. They're serious and energetic; they have a sense of purpose and élan, they persevere with whatever they're doing and have a strong willpower. It won't take them long to reach a quite sophisticated level of civilization. In Africa their position will become like that of the people in South America. In this era of ours what project is more worthy, glorious, memorable, and long-lasting than this one? Every time I think about the enormous pride and prestige it brings, I find it easy to ignore the idiotic things people say, the envy that people feel, and the criticisms of my detractors. All the yelling and screaming, fault finding, and prevarications are of no import. The whole of the Sudan is in Egyptian hands; the only trace of the occupation is two hundred English soldiers.

Reporter Since you seem to be so enthusiastic about the 6.10
future of the Sudan, Sir, and so concerned about its administration and coordination of government arrangements, how is it that

you haven't traveled to Khartoum along with the others to put your concern to work and confirm reports by seeing everything for yourself?

MINISTER I don't have to put up with the hard journey all the way up there. The late Sa'īd Pāshā only stayed there for half an hour even though it had taken him months to get there. Lord Cromer is representing the British government, the Financial Adviser is representing the Egyptian government, and the Sirdar is my personal representative.

REPORTER Were you happy about Lord Cromer's speech? Did it conform with your intentions?

MINISTER Certainly! The device Lord Cromer has come up with to put the Sudanese government under the control of the Sirdar instead of the British and Egyptian governments is a very subtle maneuver which shows considerable shrewdness. By so doing, his intention is that the Sudanese government will be rid of the fetters imposed by capitulations, treaties, and debts. He couldn't say it had been annexed by England because that would have involved the violation of company contracts, and he didn't want to have it declared as annexed to Egypt since that would put it under the same restrictions as our present government. So he put it under the Sirdar's control, or, in other words, under martial law. In that way, things can be organized without any opposition or objection—what a marvelous way of doing things!

6.11 You're aware of the story about the Greek general who was in charge of the Athenian government? One day, people met as was the custom in their republic. The general asked them if they knew who ruled the world. When they said they didn't, he told them that it was the little boy who was standing at his side, his son. He pointed out that the boy ruled his mother, his mother ruled him (the general), he ruled Athens, and Athens ruled the world. One day, I should ask the Egyptian people if they know who rules the world's great continent. When they say they don't, I'll reply that

I'm the Egyptian Minister of War, I have authority over the Sirdar, he rules the Sudan, and Sudan commands Africa.

Reporter If you realized, Sir, that I was standing by the door all the time you were talking to yourself, watching and listening to you, you wouldn't carry on pretending like this.

Minister All is lost! As if I didn't have enough to worry about! My chamberlain is so negligent and doesn't use his wits to keep people out of my office. In that case, I've no alternative but to ask you to keep everything you've heard a secret and not publish any part of it in the newspapers. I hope you'll be kind enough to turn a blind eye to my dissimulation. Such things are forced on me by the prestige of the office I hold. This is what happens when the occupying power does all the thinking and arranging. Their actions are all like cast iron whereas we keep weaving excuses for ourselves like a spider. Meanwhile, all the other people get the rewards and presents.

Reporter Don't be so sad and resentful that they're the ones getting rewards and not you. They can quote a number of reasons for their good fortune. The Sirdar has got his for putting up with so many troubles in the war, for the stratagems he's devised against the enemy, and for saving his country the need to gather a large force together for the battles in the Sudan. He's only been using a token number so as to give some semblance of their being there as part of a cooperative effort during the battle, whereas in fact it's Egyptian soldiers who do all the work. Lord Cromer has got his title for advising his government to lend the Egyptian government eight thousand pounds at a time of desperate need and then forgoing it at the right moment so that it could be used as capital for setting up the Anglo-Egyptian Company to control the Sudan. Buṭrus Pāshā got his title because he didn't object to receiving this gift from Cromer's government so that the latter could make full use of this opportunity. Zubair secured the return of his sons because he gave advice which proved useful in the conquest of the Sudan. Wingate 6.12

got his promotion for his efforts to keep track of enemy information. They've all been rewarded for good reasons, but they couldn't come up with anything you've done to help them in the Sudanese campaign.

6.13 MINISTER Let's leave aside the question of rewards. Why didn't they at least maintain some semblance of form in their dealings with me? It wouldn't do them any harm. They could have taken me with them to the Sudan and suggested on my recommendation that the Minister of Finance be appointed to the cabinet, instead of appointing him over all our heads direct from London. In everything Lord Cromer has done, said, and projected regarding the Sudan he seems to have wanted to bring the nineteenth century to a strange end; namely to get the Sudanese government to reintroduce the feudal system and tax farming just as it was during the Middle Ages. It's as if he's tired of organizing the Egyptian government along the lines of contemporary Western civilization and is eager to try something new by turning a loathsome and objectionable concept into something commendable. But I can't believe in the inversion of basic truths. Something that people unanimously condemn continues to be unacceptable. In any case, the upshot of it all is my chief concern and that comes within my responsibility. Talking of responsibility. . .

6.14 The Reporter said: The Minister pressed his bell button, and the chamberlain came in. The Minister instructed him to call the accounts secretary. The chamberlain came back after a while and told him that the secretary was busy with the Adjutant General and could not come. The Minister told him to go back and inform the secretary that he very much hoped he would be able to come; it was a private matter, not government business. As soon as the secretary had finished his business with the Adjutant, he came in. The Minister told him that he wanted him to forward his salary to the National Bank. The Minister turned to me and told me that this salary was all he got in return for his considerable responsibilities. He told me that he still cherished the hope and continued to dream that, if they came across al-Taʿāyishī's treasure, they would make him a gift of the Mahdī's fur or the lion skin which al-Taʿāyishī used to sit on while carrying out his functions as governor. He asked me, in view of what I'd learned, whether I could envisage anyone casting an envious eye on his situation or thinking that his office was worthy of aspiration.

The chamberlain came in to say that the council had left. So I said farewell and left too.

Miṣbāḥ al-sharq 41, January 26, 1899[53]

7.1 ʿĪsā ibn Hishām said: The time came for the appeal. We went to the court to seek a fair hearing. Each one of us was intent on his own business and occupied with his own aspect of the judicial contest. The Pāshā was considering the misfortunes he had suffered and complaining about his tribulations; the Lawyer was arranging his material and keeping a mental note of his fee; for my part, I was asking God to deliver us from life's intrigues. We reached the Ismāʿīliyyah quarter.[54] When the Pāshā saw the mansions, houses, palaces, and villas, he was entranced by the gardens and bowers which had grown around them and the neat layout of the streets with their trees. He stopped us and broke the silence by asking in astonishment what place this gleaming paradise occupied in the city of Cairo! Once we had given him a description of it, he said:

7.2 PĀSHĀ All praise be to Almighty God, Glorious and Powerful! This district used to be in ruins; there were no houses or mansions in it. The only plant life was the barren acacia tree; the only flowers the tragacanth and sayal thorn; the only birds owls, crows, falcons, and eagles. Of wild beasts there would have been foxes, wolves, hyenas, jackals, and lizards. The only humans would have been plundering brigands, murderers, or lurking cutthroats. What wonders the Egyptians have accomplished! Fate has clearly smiled favorably on them by giving them these flowers in exchange for thorns and housing them in these lofty mansions instead of those shattered ruins.

LAWYER My dear Amir, don't envy the Egyptians their good fortune. Rather join us in bewailing their misfortune. They don't own any of the houses in this paradise where they could settle down. Everything you see in this area belongs to foreigners.

PĀSHĀ Heavens above! How can foreigners claim this beautiful paradise, such a superb residential area, for themselves and keep native Egyptians out? Are you speaking in riddles? Are you perhaps being deliberately vague in your explanation?

LAWYER There's no riddle involved, nor is anything vague. 7.3
Egyptians have brought it on themselves by exchanging their happiness for misfortune. As their lot in life they're satisfied with whatever is paltry and inferior. Each one of them makes do with his meager, pathetic share. In the shadow of his own negligence, sloth and apathy, he remains deprived, leading a wretched life full of degradation and bewilderment. Meanwhile foreigners keep working hard; they take their job seriously. They acquire goods and want more; they store and collect things. Alongside them, Egyptians squander and waste everything. They get distressed, then fritter their time away; they become helpless, then grow conceited; they become poor, and start boasting. Our rulers and men of influence, our governors and amirs, all of them help foreigners rule and dominate us. They use their power and authority to assist foreigners and use them as allies and helpers against Egyptians. In that way they can make use of them to humiliate the Egyptians even more. Eventually however, they too have fallen into the clutches of foreigners; now they too have become their prisoners. Masters and servants are now on equal footing, envier and envied are alike, and exalted and unapproachable people are on a par with the despicable and lowly. We are all participants in the varying degrees of hardship and suffering; a distinguished and powerful man now suffers the same fate as a weak and lowly person. Such are the consequences for anyone who gives in to the avaricious. "He who assists a tyrant will find himself oppressed":

If a hunter uses a lion as a falcon,
the lion will surely count him amongst its prey.[55]

7.4 ʿĪsā ibn Hishām said: My two companions had only just finished their conversation, with its questions and answers, when a cyclist came speeding past us like a viper in the depths of the sand. He was swaying like a man intoxicated by wine and bending over like branches in the early morning breeze. The Pāshā was utterly flabbergasted and asked us about this acrobat. I informed him that it was a new bicycle, something that people chose to ride in preference to carriages and horses. What they liked about it was that it didn't eat or drink, nor did it become bored or tired. The intention of such riders was to exercise their limbs so that mind and body were in equilibrium. That particular rider, I surmised, was none other than one of the judges. We all stared after him, only to witness the rider fall off his bicycle. The ensemble had fractured into three separate entities which were lying on the ground; rider, bicycle, and tarboosh. He stood up again and brushed himself off. He tried to get back on the bicycle, but was unable to do so, so he started pushing it by hand and walking alongside it.

7.5 PĀSHĀ How I wish we could go back where we've come from, at liberty and with no encumbrances. How can judges or governors fare when this is the kind of image they project in full view of everyone? Were people ever judged in court without pomp, chamberlains, and impressive displays? In our day, no judge or governor would ride anywhere without an escort of soldiers and cavalry, preceded by servants, retinue, and aides. People's hearts would shudder in awe and respect. No one would dare commit a crime which involved appearing before such a judge.

ʿĪSĀ Yes indeed! Poets have gone to great lengths to depict such status, weaving it into their figurative creations. Here is what al-Mutanabbī has to say:

Time is defiant, there exists no pleasure
that is unsullied, no complete joy,
Not even Abū l-Faḍl ibn ʿAbdallāh. To see him may be one's
dearest wish,
and yet it is also an awesome experience.[56]

Lawyer It's time to stop this chatter, we've reached the court. 7.6

ʿĪsā Let's hope, God willing, that we find it in its proper place. I'm getting so used to going from one place to another that they will seem like Bedouin's tents:

One day in Huzwa, another in al-ʿAqīq, another
in al-ʿUthyab, and another in al-Khulayṣāʾ.[57]

We approached the place where the building was supposed to be and actually found it! There we stood for a while awaiting our turn. Eventually we were summoned. We stood before three judges. One of them was a shaykh who displayed the august demeanor of a judge and the law. The Pāshā admired his appearance and took comfort from his aspect. The judge who was a foreigner stood up and began reading the summary of the case in a foreign accent, without bothering to articulate the consonants fully.

Reader of the Summary This man stands accused of an assault on X, the policeman, during the course of his duty on such and such a day of such and such a month. The accused denies this. The plaintiff has testified in person, and medical evidence has shown the existence of marks on his person from the assault. The Court of First Instance sentenced him to a year and a half in prison according to articles 124 and 126 of the Penal Code. The convicted person has appealed.

ʿĪsā ibn Hishām said: I asked the Lawyer about this peculiar summary. "It's normal practice here," he replied. "Foreign judges like this one adopt the same style of preamble as was used in the initial trial, and turn it into a summary. They write it down in its Arabic 7.7

form but in foreign characters, so that they can read it before the court."

The chief judge of the court now turned to the Pāshā. He asked him, as was customary, his name, age, profession, and place of residence. He then invited the Parquet Attorney to address the court.

7.8 The Attorney began to explain the case as suited his fancy. This time, however, I heard no interruptions from the chief judge as had happened in the Court of First Instance, the reason being that some of the judges who had not read up the notes of the case in the appeal needed to hear about it from the Attorney's speech. So they allowed him to go on with his accusations at length. Once the Parquet Attorney had finished his expatiations, the chief judge allowed the Lawyer to speak briefly. The latter began to go into details about the aspects of the accused's defense. Every time he reached the crucial point, the chief judge told him to get to the point and make his demands. When this happened again, I saw one of the judges make a cryptic gesture in order to inform the chief judge that the Lawyer was actually talking about the point. (However, one had to excuse the chief judge because he did not know the details of the case.)

CHIEF JUDGE The case has now been heard. Sentence will be passed after deliberation.

7.9 ʿĪsā ibn Hishām said: We went outside to wait while the session moved to the deliberation chamber. I asked the Lawyer how long the deliberation usually took.

LAWYER Usually no more than an hour.

ʿĪSĀ What's the average number of cases per session?

LAWYER Ten on average.

ʿĪSĀ Is that enough time to study all the papers which go into criminal cases?

LAWYER Certainly, although when a criminal case involves the possibility of a death sentence or hard labor, it may take two or three hours. I've often perused case files which have been returned from the judge who sums up to the secretary's office for the lawyer's perusal. We found a mark on them with one of these letters A, C, and E. A stood for acquittal, C for conviction, and E for endorsement of the verdict of the first court. The judge writes these signs so that he won't forget his opinion on the case when he presents it to his colleagues during the deliberation process. In that way, when he gives them his opinion, he doesn't waste time on discussion and argument.

But, since the criminal judge has absolute discretionary inde- 7.10
pendence to decide on the verdict according to his own conscience, he has to check the proofs of confirmed guilt and innocence for himself. After that, he deliberates the entire matter for himself without any personal feeling about innocence or guilt. Once he's convinced of the proof, he passes sentence according to the weight of evidence. In so doing, he isn't giving way to someone else's opinion or making do with the verdict of another. However, the final verdict is settled based on one of those three letters which the summarizing judge skims over in the seclusion of his own home.

As we were talking, the court resumed its session. We went back 7.11
in to hear the verdict. The chief judge pronounced the Pāshā innocent because the case against him was not proven and there were cogent mitigating circumstances which kept him apart from the claims of the law. With that we left, feeling overjoyed at this piece of good fortune after so much bad luck.

Pāshā Today I cannot deny that justice still exists. But it's so slow. This slowness is an intolerable burden on the innocent. In these trials, with all their arguments and deliberations, it would be better for the conclusion of the case to be reached at the beginning. Then people like myself would not have to suffer the shame and degradation of imprisonment, comings and goings, permissions and chamberlains, all the while being labeled and treated like a criminal. If I'm happy to be found innocent, it's not because I feel any genuine pleasure, but rather that I feel relieved of real pain.

Lawyer I congratulate you on your acquittal. It is my hope that you may continue to be free from the trials of being under suspicion. May you emerge from every trial like an arrow from a bow and a sword from a scabbard! My defense of you is now complete, so it only remains for you to pay me.

Miṣbāḥ al-sharq 42, February 2, 1899[58]

'Īsā ibn Hishām said: The Lawyer kept on nagging us to give him his fee. The Pāshā promised it to him by the end of the month, by which time one of his servants and retainers would be able to bring him some money from his estates and property. But the Lawyer rejected the idea of deferred payment and demanded payment on the spot. 8.1

LAWYER (*to the Pāshā*) Do you imagine such promises can take the place of cash in a country where there are so many expenses and daily needs keep increasing, a place where profits are as scarce as common decency, and the dirham is more valuable to a father than his own son and vice versa? This case has exhausted me in two ways: fingers and heart. The only relief I can get from such exhaustion is for you to pay me with some of that ringing gold stuff. Don't dismiss me with promises, even though you are a man of integrity; but rather with cash—then I'll be grateful. I don't want to be in the position that the poet al-Mutanabbī describes in his line:

> I'm rich, but my wealth is all in promises.[59]

Don't get to the end of one case simply to start another and be rid of one misfortune only to fall into another. That's not the kind of thing for intelligent men to do; people of discretion should not embark upon such a course.

'Īsā ibn Hishām said: I noticed the Pāshā was rapidly losing his temper, so much so that he could hardly speak. At this point I 8.2

prudently intervened between the two of them. There was no form of humble petition that I did not try, no kind of polite request that I did not essay. Eventually my pleadings and fawnings persuaded the Lawyer to agree to a deferment of payment till the Pāshā's circumstances changed from difficulty to ease and from crippling poverty to wealth and affluence. I told him all the usual things about generosity and magnanimity: how one should show consideration to people in trouble; that, whenever anyone pauses to consider the role of fate and the lessons of time, his temper calms down and his obstinacy gives way. Between a man's ascent and descent, the rising and setting of his fortunes, his wealth and poverty, his happiness and grief, there lies only the distance of that fatal judgment from the heavens.

8.3 PĀSHĀ A fine friend and companion you've turned out to be! How dare you label me "poor" and try to win me the sympathy of weak people? I'm a high ranking amir, a man of great wealth. Where are the things I treasured and stored up in my lifetime, my money and real estate, the silver and gold, mansions and farms, ornaments and belongings that I owned? My wealth was proverbial. If you haven't got any information about me, then simply ask people. Go and bring me news of all the other things I collected and hoarded. How can it be that you and the Lawyer have no idea about the money and estates I possessed and about the time I spent collecting and treasuring objects? I left no ruse untried and no means neglected in order to gain wealth. Eventually I had amassed a huge store of the things which are divided up amongst mankind. I used it to support myself, a safeguard against the misfortunes that my destiny might bring down upon me, and as a treasure for my sons and grandsons, an inheritance for my descendants. Then, after my demise, they could be protected against the humiliation of need and could live comfortably in an earthly paradise, free of poverty and involvement in wrongdoing. When I left them, it was with a feeling of security and self-satisfaction, because in people's memories I would remain exalted and revered.

ʿĪsā ibn Hishām Oh yes, you amirs, members of the ruling class, we're all too well aware of how you spent your lives collecting ephemeral objects. You plied power and authority as your trade, using them to gain riches. The only point you could see in having authority was in order to amass money, to deprive people of their rights, and to snatch food out of the mouths of widows and orphans. It didn't matter whether you obtained the money by fair means or foul; it was all the same to you. You showed no concern for the wretched weakling and felt no pity for the humble disabled person. Instead you wronged the innocent and set guilty people free. As a result, you amassed for yourselves whatever bounty God had apportioned to His servants and whatever nourishment He had divided among them. You condoned all kinds of sin and took the burden of guilt on yourselves. Afterwards, you deprived yourselves of any enjoyment of what you had collected and acted like misers. You did not number among those people to whose wealth beggars and the needy have an acknowledged right. You failed to carry out the duties which God has enjoined regarding your wealth or to render it pure by giving alms and charity.[60] It was the ringing of dirham against dirham and the hushed sound of dinars clinking against each other that thrilled you. 8.4

In order to rob, despoil, and hoard as you did, you devised all sorts of ways abhorred by God and utterly condemned by mankind. In so doing, you acted in sin and willfully disobeyed the Prophet's injunctions. You dared to flout the commands and prohibitions of God Almighty and forced religious scholars to interpret His authority as you fancied. They fulfilled that role for you because you had exclusive control over their salaries; they needed the surplus from your way of life to provide food for themselves. So the burden of guilt is on you and on them, but it is greater and heavier on you. Eventually when your life came to an end when the moment of death arrived, you bequeathed what you had left behind to your young sons and daughters who had grown up in your midst in a state of deprivation. You didn't enlighten them with any kind of education, nor did you 8.5

allow them to be taught and instructed by the inexorable passing of days and nights. In their eyes, you were like a watchdog in front of the door of a treasure chamber, and they were forever making schemes to get rid of it by killing it—as the saying goes. When death or murder finally relieved them of your presence, they tore your wealth apart out of vengeance on it and you. So it happened that worms and inheritors had a race over your buried remains as well as over your hoarded ones, and the inheritors beat the worms coming and going. More and more money disappeared, estate after estate, mansion after mansion, till only the house in which they were living was left. Then they started selling off the furniture, and pawning the jewels and necklaces off the girls' very necks. They kept working on the house, room by room, and creditors entered step by step until all vestiges of it and every detail about it disappeared. The name of the original builder who had committed so many crimes in order to keep it standing was forever lost, and all that remained was a separate curse for each of two circumstances: the first for being rid of him by committing him to the grave; the second for their regret that he'd failed to teach them anything when they were still young that would help them live useful lives.

8.6 This then was the way, you amirs, that your money and property came to nought after your death. If only your children and grandchildren had mitigated the crime you had committed in amassing this wealth from the blood of Egyptians by spending and squandering it in their midst. That at least would have been akin to restoring some rights to the proper owner. But the worst misfortune of all is that all this wealth has fallen into the hands of foreigners and aliens. It seems as if fate put the Mamluks in authority over the Egyptians in order to rob them of their wealth and deprive them of their properties, then God put other people in command in order to rob the Mamluks of what they had collected. He then put their descendants in control, and they've proceeded to hand it all over to foreigners to enjoy in front of the very eyes of Egyptians who have more right to at least part of it. The only thing which has led your descendants to submit like this is their reverence for foreigners and the utter contempt for the Egyptian people which they've inherited from you. You weren't satisfied just to be masters of the Egyptians! You had to bring in foreigners as your partners in this domination. The result was that they beat you at your own game and forced you to join the Egyptians in their subjection.

You need to know, Amir, that the mansions of your wealthy friends and companions from your era whom you used to count in the thousands are all in ruins. Their descendants just stare at them. If you want to find out about your wealth and estates today, then inquire under the surface of that millstone. Oh the sheer futility of those who collect and hoard with such relish! You had no need to indulge in such avarice, depriving yourselves in this world and earning hellfire in the next. 8.7

Man says: "I have invested my wealth," and to the heir alone
belongs the money which the earner has invested.
He holds himself to account for it in his lifetime, then bequeaths it
as booty for those whom he cannot hold to account.[61]

Pāshā In my opinion you've exceeded all reasonable bounds in your opprobrium and hypercritical comments. I have thought of you as a friend; ever since we have been together, I have never made such a series of rash and deceitful statements. How am I supposed to earn a living now that all the money has disappeared and, as you point out, we no longer have any authority? The only way out of my difficulties which I can see is to allow my soul to return to the grave and rest in deathly peace again. How serene everything felt just yesterday, how soothing to the soul! How fair is the shadow of the tomb, and how foul the light of this sun!

'Īsā Someone in your circumstances can only expect sorrow and pity from us. You members of the ruling class have come to believe that the power to exert authority which you happened to have at one time is a general phenomenon on which to base existence, in that it provides an instrument for earning a living wage, 8.8

just like any other craft or job. But, once authority falls from your grasp, you lose the means of earning a living, just as a craftsman becomes unemployed when his hand is paralyzed. He can no longer function and becomes a weight on everyone's shoulders. Like you, his only wish is to die. It's as though you members of the ruling class are a group apart, with a guaranteed share of some form of livelihood to the exclusion of everyone else. You have to be on top, either of a golden throne or a bier. A poor chap who was one of the leaders in your profession wrote the following line while he was in low spirits in prison:

> We are a people for whom there's no middle course:
> For us it is either the forefront over others or the grave.[62]

In the profession of authority and order, you know full well how little is raised to prominence and how much is left to be contained in the grave. It would be more appropriate if you were to behave like other people by earning a living. Everyone has a particular method, trade, profession, and machine which enables him to earn a decent living wage. If you step down from your thrones, you can join the other members of our society doing something useful and also gaining some rewards.

PĀSHĀ By God, all the harm I have suffered at the hands of the police, Parquet, the two courts, and the Committee is far less worrying and distressing than this bitter advice of yours. What's to be done? My life has long since passed, save for a very little. I've no time left for crafts and hard work. The moral you draw may be sound enough, but it's meant for somebody who's on the way up rather than passing on.

8.9 ʿĪsā ibn Hishām said: The Pāshā's mood saddened me, and I started feeling sorry for him. I tried to think of ways he could earn a living. Every time an idea occurred to me that might work, my hopes were dashed when I thought about it more carefully. Sometimes the Pāshā stared at me as I was thinking, at others he thought for himself. We stayed like that, but then he suddenly leapt to his feet and grabbed my coat.

PĀSHĀ I've come up with a way to ward off poverty and suffice for my old age.

'ĪSĀ What have you thought of?

PĀSHĀ In former times rulers used to save their necks from hellfire and purchase a place in heaven by building a public fountain, mosque, and Qur'an school. To cover the costs they would use a building or lands to provide an endowment. I followed the same plan and copied their precedent; like them I erected a "forgiveness factor." Come with me, and let's find out what I built and endowed.

Miṣbāḥ al-sharq 43, February 9, 1899[63]

9.1 ʿĪsā ibn Hishām said: The Pāshā and I kept on going round in circles, trying one course after another in an attempt to find these endowments. We questioned passersby and travelers about mosques and fountains; it was like seeking verdant meadows in an arid desert or a thirsty man in quest of a pool of water. We could not find anyone to guide us to the object of our search. At this point the Pāshā began to remember the location of streets, alleyways, and houses; he would say that the endowment was here and then there, and that what the Almighty brings about is glorious. He kept shortening his pace and prolonging his sighs as he wept at the sight of the ruins and old houses, like the lovers of ʿAzza or Nawār:

> Question these ruins and make your weeping an answer;
> in tears you find both question and answer.[64]

9.2 After spending ages wandering around and walking hither and yon, we eventually reached a narrow lane at the end of the road. The Pāshā came to a halt in front of some ruined dwellings, derelict walls, and a small mosque. The front part consisted of a wine shop, and there was a perfumer's shop in one corner. Alongside these two were some other shops of various shapes and sizes. The Pāshā looked up and stared at them intently, but was not sure whether he was right or wrong. A long close scrutiny led him to see an old man sitting cross-legged by himself on a bench. He looked weak and timeworn, and seemed very despondent, as though he had resigned himself to his lot. His forehead looked like an old papyrus sheet, showing signs of dreadful hardship that time had inscribed on it. The Pāshā's uncertainty now changed to conviction. From a distance he yelled over to the man as a master would to his slave. The man leapt to his feet remarkably quickly and ran towards him in answer to his summons. From the fearsome yell and the manner of response I assumed a prince seated on his throne was summoning one of his courtiers. When the Shop Owner reached us, he stood humbly in front of the Pāshā. After collecting his thoughts and staring intently at the man, the Pāshā spoke to him:

PĀSHĀ Aren't you Aḥmad Aghā, the groom? Weren't you a 9.3
member of my entourage? Don't you know who I am?

SHOP OWNER If it weren't for the fact that death is a thick and impenetrable screen separating the surface from interior of the earth, I would have said that you were my master and amir. God is my witness that, every time I look at your face and hear your voice, my mind almost takes flight. I am utterly bewildered, so closely do you resemble my late master.

PĀSHĀ I am indeed your master. Here's the mark on my body that you'll recognize. I got it as a result of a javelin contest you saw on that notable games day.

The Pāshā uncovered his leg and showed him the mark. The man was so amazed that he fell to the ground. He started kissing the Pāshā's foot, tears cascading from his eyes.

SHOP OWNER How can there be life after death? You're a miracle indeed! Even so, I'm not surprised by what I see. In my lifespan I've witnessed remarkable transformations and alterations which pens cannot describe nor notebooks contain within their covers. From now onward the sun may well start rising in the West and the earth release the dead from its graves!

ʿĪsā ibn Hishām said: 9.4

> Every day is an object of wonder
> so that nothing it brings forth can amaze.[65]

"You must realize," I said, "that all things are possible." I then told him the Pāshā's story from the very beginning. With that he uttered a cry and started weeping and moaning:

Shop Owner If only my mother had never borne me! Would that I knew whether the force that resurrected the Pāshā after his death would also bring back the era in which he lived as well. Failing that, how can he possibly make a living in this age? It would be far better for him to retrace his steps to the shrouds of the grave.

9.5 ʿĪsā ibn Hishām said: He started telling us his own story, what had happened to him after the Pāshā's death and what had befallen the Pāshā's house and his peers who were both colleagues and friends. Turning to face the Pāshā he went on:

Shop Owner Master, not a single trace of your wealth remains. Lands, money, wealth, and possessions—they're all gone. For a long time I was able to live on the profits of the endowment that you bequeathed to your household and retinue, along with this mosque and fountain, both of which you established to perpetuate your memory. But before too long, the endowment collapsed through prolonged neglect. We were all left in dire need. As you can see for yourself, the fountain has turned into a wine shop, its water into wine, the mosque is now a dye works, and the Qur'an school is a storehouse. I became a farrier after being a groom, and took over this shop from the endowment's property as a way of earning a living.

Pāshā But aren't there any of my descendants left to supervise the endowment?

Groom The last I heard of them was when I went to see one of them about this shop. I mentioned to him the position I'd held in your entourage, but he paid me no attention, upbraided me, proceeded to throw me out, and sent me away with a rebuke. However, my desperate needs forced me to persist, so I went to see him several times. He rid himself of my tiresome and persistent pleas by sending me to a European he had with him who had taken control of what was left of his wealth after the cash had dwindled and the well had run dry. The European sent me to the wine-shop owner. He had purloined the endowed property and taken it over. No one dared to do anything about it without his sanction for fear of litigation at court. So I went to the owner of the wine shop and agreed on a fixed rent with him. I've stayed in this shop struggling against a fate which in turn struggles with me, as I search for food that I can't find and crave the hour of my death which keeps delaying me. God is almighty, alone in His might and outstanding in His wisdom.

PĀSHĀ Where's this disobedient child who's acting contrary to my wishes? The stipulations of the endower are as fixed as the text of the giver of the Shariah itself. 9.6

GROOM At present, he's staying at the "Hotel."

PĀSHĀ What's a "hotel?"

GROOM The locanda.

PĀSHĀ And what's the "locanda?"

'ĪSĀ IBN HISHĀM The hotel is a residence available to strangers, foreigners, and travelers with no home of their own to stay in for a fixed price. It's like the hostel that you'd recognize from your times.

PĀSHĀ Has this reprobate now stooped so low as to stay in a hostel? Praise be to the One whose deeds human minds cannot comprehend! How can the poor man lead an agreeable life under such conditions after living a life of great luxury and prosperity? Was this resurrection of mine, something decreed upon me by fate, meant to serve as a form of torture for the excessive offences I committed against God? May He be praised! Isn't there something in the punishment of hellfire in the world to come? To me that's preferable to shame in this world! O Lord, Hell is an easier punishment to endure than what I'm hearing about loss of both money and family.

If only a child died at the hour of its birth
and never suckled from its mother in childbed.[66]

'ĪSĀ IBN HISHĀM Today it's not a sign of poverty and humiliation to live in a hotel. Quite the contrary, it's an indication of 9.7

considerable importance and wealth. The expenses for a few days spent there would be enough for a month's stay in the very largest mansions, complete with maids, servants, courtiers, and retinue. Your children were attracted to this trend by their crazy desire to copy foreigners exactly and imitate everything they do as precisely as possible. Today fortunate and wealthy children of amirs sell their property and pawn their estates in order to afford a stay in this hostel. Some of them stay at home because they are scared that foreigners will raise cases against them, so they have food brought to their house from the hotel even though they have cooks downstairs and cooking maids upstairs.

Pāshā (*to the Groom*) I hope you'll give my friend directions to this hotel so we can go there and meet this fellow. I must meet him.

Groom God forbid, my dear Amir! How can you talk to me about giving directions? Do you imagine that I'd leave your retinue or desert your company whatever changes may have been brought about by the vicissitudes of time? So come! It's your prerogative to give instructions.

9.8 ʿĪsā ibn Hishām said:[67] The Pāshā asked me to go with him, and we set off with the Groom plodding along behind us. He had a smooth walking stick that he had used so much that it looked quite polished. Eventually we stopped by the lofty structure of one of the best-known hotels. As the Pāshā went in, he was amazed by the beautiful building itself, the lovely furniture, the splendid decorations, and the politeness of the waiters. He imagined we had made a mistake and entered a consular residence from his own era. I gave him details about the hotel and, after leaving the Groom outside, we inquired about his long-lost descendant. One of the waiters gave us the number of the suite. The Pāshā did not bother to ask for permission to enter or even wait for a response. He simply pushed the door open, and we entered. In front of us we discovered a group of amirs' sons, divided up into different groups. Some were playing dice while others were looking at pictures of racing horses. A group of them were clustered round a middle-aged woman neither old and ugly nor young and beautiful; she made full use of what little beauty she possessed by embellishing herself to the maximum extent possible with all kinds of makeup and finery. Her face was almost aglow with the glint of necklaces and ornaments, while her forehead sparkled with the pearly glimmer of jewels and gems. The middle of the room was occupied by a table with different types of wine in flagons and glasses, along with various expensive vessels. Laid out on top were an inkwell and paper, a pen inlaid with diamonds, and foreign books adorned with gold—all prepared for display, not for learning or culture. Sheets of regulations were scattered all over the floor, and newspapers were strewn about under people's feet still intact and unread save for the title or racing news. They all had their heads uncovered, and their hands were gloved. They were all jabbering away in foreign languages, making sure not to speak Arabic unless it involved the names of Arab horses, in which case the *kāf* sound was used instead of *qāf* and *hā'* instead of *ḥā'*.[68]

When they noticed us, they started frowning and scowling and looked put out. A young boy left the woman's side, hurried over to the door, and addressed us in French: 9.9

Young boy How dare you enter without permission!

'Īsā ibn Hishām We were prompted by a father's desire to see his offspring.

The youth asked me to explain.

'Īsā ibn Hishām A is enquiring after B.

Young boy The latter is my name, but who is this other person who is enquiring after me?

I started telling him the entire story and the issues it raised, but he interrupted me with a scoff.

Young boy Get out of here! I don't have to listen to such childish lies. I have no father or mother, and no relatives close or otherwise. I am certainly not one of those people who's going to believe such fairy stories or give credence to made-up tales. I'm someone who's learned to deny the possibility of resurrection after death, so how am I supposed to believe in it when I'm still alive?

With that he turned and addressed his brothers, interrupting his words with frequent guffaws:

Come on, brothers, just listen to this weird tale! Just take a look at this scruffy bashibozuk beside him.[69] (*He points at the Pāshā.*) He's claiming to be one of my ancestors and relatives; he's demanding that I give him part of his bequeathed wealth and payment for his endowment. Have you ever heard anything more peculiar than the events of this morning? Fate isn't satisfied any more merely to disturb our lives with creditors' claims. Now it's started raising the dead from their graves to demand back their wealth, inheritance, and endowments. My friends, isn't that the best joke of all at the end of this century!

And with that, the entire assembly burst out laughing.

9.10 When the Pāshā kept questioning me about his grandchild, I asked him to wait till the talking stopped. He had no idea of what was being said and could not feel the impact of the sarcastic barbs. Once the laughter came to an end, they yelled to the servant to eject us. At this point the Pāshā's descendant turned round to discover that one of his closest friends and brothers had slunk off with the girl whom they were treating as though she was their wife. The two of them kept flirting, the brother making advances while she toyed with him. He swooped down on the two of them like a hawk, and a fierce quarrel broke out that turned more and more bitter. Everyone gathered round. I listened as the Pāshā's descendant scolded the woman while the woman's friend kept offering excuses. But the woman herself would have none of it:

"How dare you scold anyone like that?" she yelled in rebuke. "Only men who take care of me and respond to my wishes and needs are permitted such rash displays of temper. Only yesterday, I asked you to buy me that necklace that the jewelers received from Paris in the last post. At first you promised to buy it, but then you refused claiming you were hard up. Then today I find out you've bought a stallion for a huge sum of money. How can you expect me to keep myself only for you, when other men who are infatuated by me are eager to respond to my demands?"

I listened now as the Pāshā's descendant replied, with sweat pouring off his brow and panic cutting short his breaths: 9.11

"I swear by God," he said, "I haven't bought anything. In fact, I've had to sell some things to get enough cash to buy you the necklace. Don't be deceived by the things they're saying about how wealthy this vile and treacherous friend is or by rumors about my poverty and my lands being in pawn. You know very well how much money is coming to me from the profits of the court cases I have pending. The lawyer keeps telling you all about it."

No sooner had his colleague heard him call him by those two epithets than he flew into a terrible rage and gave him a resounding slap. The target of his curses promised in his turn to appoint seconds. Now a further commotion arose at the gaming table between two friends, one of whom had won and the other lost. Elsewhere one of them was asking his brother for a loan, and another who was bankrupt was asking a wealthy man for a loan that he would not be repaying. The quarrel eventually resorted to fisticuffs and yet again ended up with the appointment of witnesses. Still another dispute occurred in the corner of the room where people were looking at pictures of racing horses. One of them kept saying his horse had won and the other man's came next; his groom was intelligent and was the son of an intelligent father; the other man's stallion was short whereas his was tall; you have to admit, one of them claimed, that there's a clear difference in their weights. The quarrels and insults kept getting worse, and the conversation degenerated into a fight. All the while the woman was flitting from one circle to another like a slinky viper. At her whim, the fire of discord was put out, but then she would rekindle it again for her own vicious intentions.

I dragged the Pāshā out by the arm and left the room. As we hurried toward the street, I felt sad to see the degree of sheer ignorance mankind had reached. I gave him a version of what had transpired, 9.12

and that made him even more annoyed. The only thing that managed to calm him down was to hear that they had decided in the end to resolve their differences by fighting each other.

"Maybe fate can remove this misfortune from me," he said with a sigh. "The duels may at least relieve me of sons and descendants."

"Unfortunately," I told myself, "your sons inherited neither your money nor your ethics. They don't possess enough courage to embrace danger so as to expose what's wrong. For them, dueling's a word spoken at night and forgotten about the next day."

The Pāshā now remembered that he needed to pay the Lawyer's fees. Turning to the Groom, he asked:

Pāshā What about my close friends? Are any of them still alive?

Groom Only X, Y, and Z are left.

Pāshā Well, take us to X's house first!

9.13 ʿĪsā ibn Hishām said: So we went where he indicated. We were beset by anxieties, and constant worry reduced us all to silence. The Fates were not working in our favor, and problems would not let us be.

Miṣbāḥ al-sharq 44, February 16, 1899[70]

ʿĪsā ibn Hishām said: So we set out to look for one of the Pāshā's three friends and companions who were still alive. After a long walk, we reached the amir's house. Its grounds were so extensive that it looked like a square in its own right; looking at its height you would have said it was a fortress. The Groom stopped us at the door, greeted the servants and asked them about their master. With a frown they replied in a surly fashion that he could be found in the reception hall. We proceeded across the central courtyard. In the middle we noticed a tree with thick branches. Time's relentless progress had bent it over, and it now looked like a bereaved woman who in sheer grief lets down her hair at a funeral. In its shade a horse was tethered but clearly full of energy; beside it was a ram with thrusting horns. Strutting around them was a fighting cock with talons as sharp as spears: 10.1

Red and pitch black; nimble as the legs
of the herd of the Banū al-Sayyid.
In the heat of the battle, attack is glorious in their eyes,
where the weak would find flight more attractive.
And when the weak would be useless, defiance is there,
keeping honorable women protected.[71]

We reached a lofty hall with spacious alcoves. On one side was a spring with water flowing from the mouths of statues. The ground was covered with Persian carpets and the skins of wild animals, 10.2

while the walls were hung with arms of various sorts: daggers, swords, and spears. Above these were a number of rows of shelves supporting precious objets d'art and ancient Chinese vessels along with pipes made of jasmine branches. We removed our shoes and moved forward. We found the amir with a group of people sitting cross-legged around him listening. Their faces gleamed with the light of age and dignity, and a splendid and proud bearing irradiated from them. When we entered, the conversation stopped while they greeted us. Once greetings had been exchanged, the conversation picked up from where they had left off.

10.3 When we were settled in our places, I whispered in the Groom's ear and asked him to tell me the names of the people I was looking at.

GROOM The person presiding is X, the owner of this mansion. He was a great friend of my master, the Pāshā, in the Khedive's esteemed household. As you can see, in his later years he has devoted himself entirely to the pious observance of prayer to God and a life of abstinence and asceticism. He seeks favor with God through continual rituals of prayer and renunciation of the world through prolonged periods of piety and prostration. He has vast resources at his disposal which he spends on shaykhs, Ṣūfīs, and dwellers in holy places who tour around various parts of the country. By so doing, he hopes that God will forgive him the sins he has committed and will add his name to the company of His blessed saints. To his right is C who used to be a distinguished member of the Judicial Committee in Muḥammad ʿAlī's time. Next to him is one of the most eminent religious scholars and shaykhs. The person on his left is General Y, famous for his battles and victories, and next to him is Z, the retired governor. At the back of the gathering, the person you can see is A, a merchant in Khān al-Khalīlī.

10.4 ʿĪsā ibn Hishām said: Once I had taken in what the Groom told me, I looked at the Pāshā and realized that he was in no hurry to reveal his business until the people present had finished their conversation. So I sat there listening along with the other people present. Here is part of what the General had to say:

General Muḥammad ʿAlī Pāshā the great (whose place is in heaven) was the marvel of his age. He was a shrewd man possessed of a lofty ambition, farsightedness and firm grasp of management, added to which was a unique ability to win over people's hearts and train their minds to serve him faithfully. He had at his disposal capable men who served him loyally and were prepared to risk their lives for him. From among their number I would single out Muḥammad Bey Lāẓoghly who masterminded the annihilation of the Mamluks in the space of a single hour. My late brother who witnessed this dire event told me that the Mamluks realized that there was a plot to wipe them out, that everything had been fixed, and that they were surrounded on all sides. So they set about looking for Muḥammad ʿAlī in every nook and cranny of the palace, but they could find no trace of him because Lāẓoghly had taken enormous precautions to keep him hidden. At the time in fact he occupied the same position—if this comparison is permissible—as ʿAlī ibn Abī Ṭalib did for the Prophet of God (peace be upon him) on the night of the hijra.[72] It was from that same period that Muḥammad ʿAlī inherited the unnerving shout which never deserted him thereafter. In his council chamber he used to roar like a lion; the effect was enough to stop your heart beating. It caused the death of a European painter for whom the late master was sitting for a portrait. They had warned him in advance, but it was so loud that the poor man could not stand it and died on the spot. Where are there governors like Lāẓoghly today, and where will you encounter shouts of such a kind in other men like him?

Member of the Judicial Committee Yes indeed! The procedures used by the late Muḥammad ʿAlī to train men to serve him were too subtle for mere words and concepts. Some of them were even won over by him with a single word which impressed them so much that they served him faithfully for the rest of their 10.5

lives. Such was the case in the story which our late friend Rāghib Pāshā told me:

"When I was one of the secretaries in the late Pāshā's entourage, I was reading over some pages with him. While I was reading, Sāmī Pāshā came in and stood beside us. Muḥammad ʿAlī asked him what he wanted, but he hesitated, as though he wanted me to leave so that he could be alone with the Pāshā and then tell him his news. 'Tell me your news immediately,' the Pāshā ordered him. 'I keep nothing from Rāghib. The secretaries in my entourage are like my own children.'"

Now tell me, gentlemen, in your experience can gifts of estates, distributing money as bounty, or the award of titles and decorations serve as an appropriate substitute for words such as those when it comes to persuading people to serve you faithfully and reliably?

The late Rāghib Pāshā often used to compare these words with the kind of thing he witnessed when he was serving Muḥammad ʿAlī's successors, Ismāʿīl Pāshā for example. When Rāghib was Egyptian Minister of Finance, Ismāʿīl would leave him with papers in front of him and go into another room for a private conversation with some grocer or moneylender. Rāghib would be left there waiting hour after hour with pressing government business in his hands until the private conversation came to an end. Naturally enough, when it came to comparing the two experiences, one brought him a beneficial reward while the other merely exasperated him.[73]

10.6 Just consider how Muḥammad ʿAlī perfected the art of geniality. Kings need not possess any other skill. If they can perfect just this one, then their subjects' goodwill and affections will be under their exclusive control. I heard of another instance from history involving the Abbasid Caliph, al-Manṣūr, which shows how skilful and adroit he was in the art of monarchy. One day he was eating with a shaykh who was one of his generals. His two sons were at his side. Being an old man, the shaykh had lost all his teeth. While he was eating, bits of food kept falling out of the side of his mouth. The two young princes kept winking at each other at his expense. When the Caliph looked in their direction and saw what was causing their amusement, he stretched out his hand, gathered up the bits that had dropped to the floor and ate them. The general stood up. "My fealty is all I have to offer you, Commander of the Faithful," he said, "so command me to do as you wish."

Retired Governor Let me tell you another story about the 10.7 late Muḥammad ʿAlī. This one will show you how gentle his policies were and how sympathetic he was towards the common people. One particular governor wanted to outdo his colleagues in a display of dutiful service in order to gain his amir's esteem. He proceeded to collect money from his province with great zeal and exceeded all normal bounds in the methods he used. By such means he managed to collect in one fell swoop everything people owned. The hue and cry grew ever louder, and the people's complaints became increasingly vociferous. Eventually there came the day when they reached the ears of Muḥammad ʿAlī, the dispenser of bounty. He ordered the governor to appear before him. When the governor came into his presence, Muḥammad ʿAlī told him to come closer. When the governor came up to him, Muḥammad ʿAlī grabbed him by the neck and started pulling out one hair at a time from his head, neck, cheek, and eyebrow until he had collected a little tuft; all of which caused the governor little pain—he hardly felt it. Then the amir turned to his beard and from one side pulled out all at once a tuft as large as the other tuft of separate hairs, which caused blood to well up beneath it. The governor let out a yell of pain. "Let that serve as a demonstration," Muḥammad ʿAlī told him, "of the different ways of dealing with people when you're taxing them. When you take a dirham at one moment and then another dirham at a later date, people can tolerate it and don't notice any hardship. But when you demand this large amount all at once in one lump sum, it causes them a lot of suffering. In the same way, you can see the difference between pulling hairs out individually and pulling them out in a clump. In both cases the amount is the same, but the suffering involved is completely different. From now on, make sure you don't treat people in such a way that they resort to complaints and begin sending pleas for help."

10.8 I can cite you yet another example of his talent for succinctness. He gave orders that Ḥasan Pāshā al-Injirköylü was to be appointed governor of the Sudan. The latter declined the post, pointing out that he couldn't speak Arabic. "How can I govern and regulate the affairs of a people," he asked, "when I don't know a single letter of their language?" "You don't need to know the language in order to supervise the laws," Muḥammad ʿAlī retorted. "It's not a requirement for sound government; the regime can be quite effective without it. For your job, you only need to know two Arabic words to keep on the tip of your tongue, *fulūs* and *kurbāj*."[74] Had Ḥasan Pāshā bothered to recollect that Muḥammad ʿAlī himself managed to rule the Egyptian people for a long time and to conquer Arab lands without ever speaking Arabic or being prevented thereby from running government affairs efficiently and maintaining his authority, he would never have invoked such an excuse.

10.9 On this particular topic, one of the most incredible stories tells how Muḥammad ʿAlī ordered the citizens of the capital to form a military reserve, and appointed officers of military rank to command them. One day, some officers from Būlāq came in; at the time, Ṣubḥī Pāshā was acting as interpreter. Muḥammad ʿAlī addressed some words to them in a manner which demanded some expression of appreciation. One of them said: "Thanking you kindly, Sire," an expression which was commonly used by the populace at that time to express pleasure and approval. Muḥammad ʿAlī looked very angry; he'd taken it in its Turkish sense, "What an ass!" Ṣubḥī Pāshā hastened to interpret, then Muḥammad ʿAlī fell flat on his back laughing.

So tell me, what's the point of knowing Arabic when Arabs use these low and uncouth phrases when addressing their amir? Actually, quite a few people have governed the Egyptian people without knowing their language, Nūbār Pāshā and others among them.[75]

SHAYKH (*quoting*) 10.10

Spend not too long recalling times long past.
That is an age gone by; this is another.[76]

May God have mercy on what is past, may He protect us from the present, and give us a safe refuge against the future! Amirs, however far you've gone in describing his virtues and enumerating his good qualities to fulfill all the obligations of dutiful remembrance, I still feel that you've failed to do full justice to our late master. Of all his good works, which need neither summary nor explanation, showing both his expertise and sense of priorities, it's enough to remember that he always fostered and revered the religious scholars, kept them close to him, and showed them great respect. He answered their needs and asked for the blessing of their prayers. I myself had a genuine vision about him which gave him the promise of a place with God in the next world and a residence in paradise as a reward for his good deeds.

ʿĪsā ibn Hishām said: During this conversation one of the people from Mecca (known as the Circumambulators or Guides) came up to the owner of the house.[77] After kissing his hands, he handed over a purse of green silk, along with some dates, a comb, a jar of kohl, a rosary, and some henna. He recited the Fātiḥah and then spoke to the Amir: 10.11

MECCAN Amir, I've brought the piece of the holy *kiswah* as you requested, and also some dates from the blessed palm tree that Fāṭima planted with her noble hand.

AMIR (*to the attendants*) Fetch the chief clerk, Master Masīḥih, for me and get him to bring the purse so that we can give this traveler his reward.

ʿĪsā ibn Hishām said: Master Masīḥih came in and approached the amir. When he set eyes on the blessed gift in front of the Amir, he prostrated himself face to the ground, kissed the gifts one after the other, and then spoke to the Amir:

Master Masīḥih By God, it was this blessed kohl which saved my son from going blind. Only this pure henna managed to cure his mother of malaria.

Shaykh (*after testing the dates and registering approval*) Yes indeed, my dear man, you are right. Heaven is assured to anyone who fasts and then breaks the fast with dates from Medina.

10.12 ʿĪsā ibn Hishām said: The Pāshā was seated at my side muttering and fuming, and I could tell that he was getting furious. He was about to speak, but just then the owner of the house turned to the Groom to ask what was causing all the angry muttering. I stepped forward to tell them the story. I explained how the Pāshā had emerged from the grave. Some of them believed me, others did not. With that, the Shaykh cleared his throat and spoke to them:

Shaykh Indeed, there are no limits to miracles and supernatural phenomena, nor should you entertain any doubts about man's return to life after death; to do so is to display a lack of conviction concerning the resurrection of buried men. It's an incontrovertible fact that one returns to life after disappearing into oblivion; that is something which God in His omnipotence accords to those people whom He wishes with the blessing of holy men and saints. The closest thing I can quote to you on this subject comes from the books of *Glorious Deeds of the Crown of Saints and Proof of Holy Men* by the divine leader and everlasting refuge al-Sayyid ʿAbd al-Qādir al-Jīlānī. Let me quote you his text word for word:

10.13 In the *Treatise on the True Nature of Realities*, he tells the story of how a woman's son was drowned in the sea. She came to the Mightiest Refuge[78] and said to him: "My son has drowned in the sea, and I'm utterly convinced that you can bring my son back to life." "Return to your house," he replied (God be pleased with him), "and you'll find your son there." So she went home but didn't find him there. She came back again and begged him. "Return to your house," he told her again, "and you'll find your son there." She went home again but failed to find her son. Yet again she came back and entreated him in tears to bring her son back to her. This time he watched closely and bowed his head. Then he raised it again. "Go to your house," he said, "and you'll find your son there." She went home again and found her son. The Mightiest Refuge addressed God in the manner of those who are beloved to Him: "Lord, why did You embarrass me twice in dealing with that woman?" Back came the word from the Almighty Provider: "When you spoke to her, it was the truth. On the first occasion, the angels collected his different parts; on the second, I brought him back to life; and on the third, I extracted him from the sea and brought him to her house." To this the Refuge replied: "But Lord, with the command 'Be!' You created worlds before which there was neither time nor epoch. At the moment of resurrection You gather and muster the infinite different parts of these beings in the flash of an eye. It's a trivial matter for You to collect the parts of a single body, revive them, and then send them to this woman's house. So what was the point of this delay?" From God Almighty came the reply: "Ask anything you wish. We bestow it on you as a recompense for breaking your heart." At that, the Mightiest Refuge placed his face to the ground and replied in supplication: "Lord, I am created, and so it is fitting for me to make requests by virtue of my createdness. You are a Creator, and so it is right that You should give in proportion to Your might and being Creator." "Everyone who sees you on the day of communal prayer will be a close friend," God replied. "Whenever you look at the ground, it will turn into gold." "But these things are of no use to me," the Refuge replied. "Give me something of greater worth to leave behind, something which can serve in both worlds." "I have made your names as meritorious and influential as My own," God replied. "Anyone who recites one of your names is doing exactly the same thing as someone who recites one of Mine."

There is another story in this book from al-Sayyid the great 10.14
Shaykh Abū l-ʿAbbās Aḥmad al-Rifāʿī (may God be pleased with him). One of the servants of the Mightiest Refuge died. His wife came to the Refuge and begged him to help get her husband's life

back. The Refuge turned to observe and consulted the world of the unseen. He saw the Angel of Death (blessings upon him) going up to heaven with the souls which he had snatched away that day. The Refuge said: "Angel of Death, stop and give me the spirit of my servant." (He gave his name.) "I take away spirits by divine decree," replied the Angel of Death, "and conduct them to the gate of His glory. How can I give you back a soul which I've snatched away at my Lord's command?" The Refuge repeated his request to be given back the spirit of his servant and was again refused. The Angel of Death had a spiritual container in his hands which looked like a palm-leaf basket. In it were the souls he had snatched that day. By the power invested in him as a beloved of God, the Refuge tugged the basket and snatched it from the Angel's hand. All the souls were scattered and returned to their bodies. The Angel of Death (blessings upon him) confided in his Lord: "Lord," he said, "you know best of all what has occurred between myself and your beloved associate, ʿAbd al-Qādir. He forcibly removed the souls that I snatched today." "Angel of Death," God (may His splendor be exalted) replied, "the Mightiest Refuge is My beloved and My desire. Why didn't you give him his servant's soul? Because of your actions many souls have escaped your grasp for the sake of just one. On this occasion, you are the loser."

(Here ends the quotation from *Manāqib tāj al-awliyāʾ wa-burhān al-aṣfiyāʾ al-quṭb al-rabbānī wa-al-ghawth al-ṣamdānī al-Sayyid ʿAbd al-Qādir al-Jīlānī*, printed at the expense of Shaykh ʿAbd al-Raḥmān al-Niyāzi, Shaykh of the Qādiriyya House in Alexandria, pp. 20–22.)

10.15 ʿĪsa ibn Hishām said: Barely had the Shaykh finished talking before the Pāshā leapt up before my very eyes, anger, sorrow, and regret written all over his face. This is what he had to say:

PĀSHĀ My brothers, pardon from God the merciful and a place in heaven, you should realize, are not to be gained by prolonged fasting, eating dates, seeking blessings from relics, or by protecting oneself with pious recitations. The only way to win an exalted position in God's eyes is to be just and charitable, to practice good and avoid evil, and to show mercy towards those of God's creatures who are weak and poor. During my own life here on earth, I too was deceived by the very same things which are now deceiving you. Before I died, I too used to listen to the kind of things this Shaykh has been saying; all of which made me think nothing of committing the most outrageous acts and condoning terrible wrongs in the way I treated people. I felt I could rely on a day of fasting and a night spent performing prayers, or on an amulet I would carry around with me and some relic or other which I would kiss, as a way of atoning for all these wrongs. As a result, I put my trust in such beliefs and slept with a clear conscience. However, when the mighty omniscient God sent me to my death and I became an inhabitant of the grave, I learned things which I didn't know before. All my prayers, fasts, and supplications did not spare me from God's judgment at all. The only thing which alleviated the terrors of the grave and made the angels' interrogation easier to bear was a single act of charity which I'd performed when someone who had been wronged asked for my protection when he was almost under the executioner's sword, and I'd given it to him. My advice to you then is to make sure that you all behave in a just and charitable manner. Show fear of God in the way you treat mankind and spread kindness and goodwill among His creatures. Don't follow that side of your nature which suggests an evil course of action; in that case, you'll rely on being deluded by vain hopes and will have to ask for forgiveness without having done anything worthwhile. God Almighty has said in the Qur'an: «Whoever does one atom's weight of good, God sees it.»[79] Also bear in mind 'Alī's words (may God be pleased with him): "Many people who fast only get hunger and thirst from their fasting; many a man who performs prayers at night merely loses sleep and wears himself out." Here is what the wise poet has to say:

> Doing good is not just a fast that makes fasters waste away,
> nor prayer, nor wearing wool on the body.

It involves utterly rejecting all evil
and ridding your heart of malice and envy.[80]

10.16 SHAYKH I think you must be Satan in human form, or else a heretic masquerading as someone who has risen from the dead. A curse on this age with its enormous follies, a plague on its utter trivialities! There's only one other miracle still in store for us: for a dead person to come out of his grave and tell us the things he's seen and heard!

OWNER OF THE HOUSE (*to the Pāshā*) I beg you to tell us, by God, in which language did the two angels interrogate you? Was it Arabic, Turkish, or Syriac?

SHAYKH I implore you in God's name not to talk to this man alone! He's one of the accursed Devil's temptations.

10.17 ʿĪsā ibn Hishām said: The Pāshā was in a seething temper. He turned his back on them and rushed out in a fury, asking God for help and protection. As I departed the assembly and rushed out after him, I left behind the fat Shaykh about whose type the Caliph ʿUmar ibn al-Khaṭṭāb once said: "God hates fat men of religion." I repeated to myself Abū Turāb's words (may God honor his aspect): "I complain to God about a community living in ignorance and dying in error. In this community nothing is as hard to sell as the Book of God when it is recited properly, and no article is a more saleable commodity than God's book once its meaning has been distorted. Nothing is less well-known than what is approved, nothing more well-known than what is abhorred."[81]

As we left, the Groom and Merchant who had been with us in the assembly called out to us and so we waited for them. The Merchant came up to the Pāshā and leaned over to kiss his hand.

MERCHANT Master, I call God to witness that I believe your story. Aḥmad here has told me about your situation and the needs that brought you to this assembly. You refused to draw attention to it while you were standing up for God. I'm a wealthy man, and I owe it to God and yourself for a favor that I'll never forget. The prosperity that I now enjoy comes from your generosity, kindness, and blessed fortune. I can never forget that the fame that has brought me this wealth came as a consequence of your spending a short while sitting in my shop one day after you had tripped during a visit to the al-Husayn mosque. As a result, my own fortune and reputation both grew, and people flocked to my place because you had deigned to sit there for a while. They assumed that I'd some personal connection with you and your vast influence. So, in the name of God, I beg you to accept enough money from me to satisfy your needs and rid yourself of the claims of this Lawyer.

'Īsā ibn Hishām said: The Merchant now produced a full purse and offered it to the Pāshā, shaking all the while in case he refused his offer. The Pāshā took it and said: 10.18

Pāshā I'm deeply grateful to you for your kindness, and I ask God to give you a worthy reward. Come now, write yourself a check for the amount. I'll repay you when I get my endowments back.

Merchant God forbid that I should be one of those people these days who don't trust anyone. Brothers no longer trust each other, a father will distrust his own son, and relatives and friends will not rely on one another. People will squabble over a mere dirham, and everyone insists on legal transactions, witnesses, and checks. I'm still one of those people from that age when no merchant would do business without trust and confidence, and there was no need to write notes or demand guarantees. Everyone trusted everyone else, and there was no deceit or trickery. Checking is only necessary when one suspects dishonesty. We all seek refuge in God from such circumstances!

'Īsā ibn Hishām said: So the Pāshā repeated his thanks to the Merchant. "Come on," he said to me, "let's go to the Lawyer and get him off our backs after so much trouble." 10.19

As we left the Lawyer's office, the Pāshā told me that now the time had come to bring a case in the Shariah Court to recover his endowments.

"What we need first," I replied, "is to find a Shariah Court lawyer."

He then asked me to take him to consult a competent lawyer. So we were now out the clutches of one lawyer, only to fall into another's. We ask God to deliver us in the end.

Miṣbāḥ al-sharq 48, March 23, 1899[82]

ʿĪsā ibn Hishām said: I went with my friend to look for an acquaintance whom I could ask for advice in our search for a Shariah Court lawyer. While we were proceeding on this difficult quest, I spotted a friend of mine and asked for a minute of his time. 11.1

"What's the problem?" he asked.

"A court case," I replied, "in the Shariah Court."

Barely had he heard the words before he started weeping. We both bewailed the situation and realized how hopeless it was. "I've already suffered such a misfortune," he said, "and I've yet to recover. If you're the litigant, my advice to you is to drop your summons and accept your sufferings with patience. If you're the defendant, then you've no choice since prescient planning is of no avail against the course of fate."

"Even necessity has its own rules," I replied. "I'm asking you for guidance in choosing a lawyer who is highly regarded for his impartiality and famous for his honesty. We need someone who will not break promises, a person who has not the slightest trace of a crooked character in him and who will not make agreements with the opposition or ask for extortionate fees."

"Of all kinds of impossibility," he replied, "ask rather that ants carry mountains, but don't look for such a collection of qualities in a lawyer! You'll only finish up in despair and despondency. Try climbing on the back of the Phoenix instead; that's a much easier task, one that allows you more scope than what you're asking! When it comes to choosing Shariah Court lawyers—God protect you! They're like the teeth in a comb or a donkey's molars. In fact, they're just like al-ʿIbādī's two donkeys: to the question as to which one was worse, he responded: 'This one, then that one.' On the basis of sincerest affection I can swear to you that I don't trust any one of them. How can you ask me to choose one wolf from among a whole pack? Were I to do so, I would have to shoulder the burden of blame. Please absolve me from making such a choice, and may God protect you from all misfortunes!"

11.2 Soon after he said farewell and went on his way, leaving me on tenterhooks. I moved on too, feeling sad and discouraged. I continued to look for someone else to advise and help us. When I discovered that none of my friends was prepared to select a lawyer whom we could trust, I went to see someone who was known to me because of the many litigations he had undertaken. I told him of our search for a lawyer who could get us out of our unfortunate situation. "You should realize," he told us, "that there are various types of Shariah Court lawyer. Some can see, others are blind. In their ranks one finds wearers of the tarboosh and wearers of the turban—may God give you protection![83] I'll direct you to one whose evil ways are the easiest to contend with and who will cause you the least harm. He knows more than anyone else about the ruses of the Shariah. Go and see X." With that he gave me directions to the lawyer's house and went on his way.

We made our way along twisting roads and winding alleyways crowded with people. Eventually we came to the door of a house which looked as though it was tarred with pitch. It was blocked up with mounds of filth and surrounded by piles of rubbish. At the entrance we noticed some children playing with the earth. Among them was a little girl whose face was covered with so many flies that it looked as though she had donned the veil before her time. As we walked past them, we were hit by the stench of the lavatory, and rested for a moment on a pile of debris. Alongside it there was a mule's feeding trough with ducks and geese crowding round it. We found our way to a room to the right, and saw a baker in front of us shouting out his wares.

We asked for the owner of the house, and he pointed to the room. We went inside and found a carpet covered with dust and small stones, a couch without any padding or covering left. In one of the corners was a lamp which was too weak to pierce through the thick smoke. On the topmost shelves were piles of books and scrolls; a spider's web acted as their protective covering and binding, and the mildew which clung to them stopped them from splitting and falling apart. On the floor were discarded bottles of ink, while the white walls had been covered by the black scribblings of children at play. There we saw a man: 11.3

> Henna had altered his grey locks;
> but can it change his back once bent?[84]

The Lawyer was still sitting on his prayer mat; at times he was praying, while at others he would keep talking to a woman. He was speaking to her as follows: "May God shower His blessings on you and find you another husband! How can you claim that I've overcharged you for the divorce and for devising a strategy for getting you a legal separation? Haven't I rid you of a husband you loathed, so that you could marry a man you love instead?"Just then he noticed that we had entered behind his back and started reciting his prayers all over again. The woman jumped up, put up her veil, wrapped her shawl round herself and departed. We were left with a man who was deceiving people with his long prayers, and reciting the Surahs of the Cow and the Sheep during his prostrations.

> Should he who prays wish to deceive,
> the one who intentionally stops praying is closer to God.[85]

For a while we just sat there; we were waiting for ourselves to be rid of this trouble, for him to stop this hypocrisy, and for the two questioning angels to finish with his black list. All the while he was fussing about and hurrying to perform the evening prayer. 11.4

Meanwhile, we noticed that he kept glancing furtively towards the door as though he too were waiting for someone. Eventually an Assistant came in. "How long are these devotions going to take?" he shouted. "You've already worn out the prayer mat. People have put their cases in your hands, leaving it to you to carry out what is in their best interests. His Highness the Prince has been waiting for you since the afternoon prayer, not to mention the Director of Religious Endowments who is asking you to rescue him from his plight." The praying Lawyer paid no attention to all this. Instead he recited the verse from the Surah of the Sheep: «And thus have we tested some of them with others so that they may say: Are these the ones among us to whom God has been gracious? Is not God most knowledgeable about the thankful?»[86]

His Assistant sat down, wiping the sweat from his brow. Who, we asked ourselves, could guarantee that this praying and glorification would ever come to an end? We were so upset that we were on the point of getting up and leaving. Just then the Lawyer Shaykh completed his prayers with the necessary concluding phrases. He then turned toward us. "Greetings to you," he said. "What is the cause of your litigation?"

"It concerns a religious endowment," we replied.

"Are you seeking the income from it," the Assistant asked, "or do you wish to sell it?"

"Can religious endowments be sold?" we asked.

"Certainly," he replied, "Mount Jabal Qāf itself is on the market!"

11.5 The Shaykh cleared his throat, coughed, spat, took some snuff, and blew his nose.

Lawyer Don't take any notice of my Assistant. Tell me what right you have to the endowment. What's the circumstance of the endowment's donor? What's its current cash value so that the fees can be calculated accordingly?

ʿĪsā The endowment belongs to my friend here, but certain factors are preventing him from obtaining it. Other people have laid their hands on it. We want to initiate a suit to reclaim it from them.

Lawyer I asked you what its cash value was.

ʿĪsā I don't know exactly; certainly in thousands.

Lawyer Then the advanced charges will certainly be X pounds. You need to pay half in advance.

ʿĪsā My dear Shaykh, isn't that too much. We can't possibly pay it.

Assistant How can you say such a thing and refuse to pay? Don't you realize that this business involves subscriptions, and that secretaries and clerks all charge search fees? Apart from my master, the Shaykh, how do you expect to find anyone else who can guarantee you success in the case and profit from the suit? That should make it easy to pay all the fees he asks for? Is there anyone else so knowledgeable about the ruses of the Shariah? He stands head and shoulders above everyone who's written on the subject. Other than he who else can win over the opposition lawyer?

ʿĪsā This is all the money we have with us now. We'll write you a check when the case is won. The delay won't be a problem as long as you're prepared to guarantee the success of the trial at all events.

The Lawyer now took the purse and counted the money.

Lawyer (*after counting the money*) I accept this paltry sum 11.6
from you now, desiring that great reward which God reserves for His servants who act in the service of Muslims. But you're responsible for providing two witnesses for the warrant of attorney.

ʿĪsā And how, pray, do we obtain a warrant of attorney?

Lawyer You need to produce two witnesses to testify before the court that "A, son of B, son of C, appoints D as attorney for the purposes of proceeding at law, making defense speeches, conducting cross examinations, settlements, payments, receipts and consignments; for appeals, expenditures, undertakings, in fact anything in which the warrant of attorney is permissible according to the Shariah law; and to subcontract the suit to someone else and dismiss him, to do this repeatedly whenever he deems it fit, time after time." So tomorrow, God willing, you'll appear with the two witnesses and the record of the endowment.

ʿĪsā At this point, we've only one witness who knows about the Pāshā's origins and lineage.

Lawyer's Assistant This is stage one in the expenses of the case and its various difficulties. You'll probably realize the cost involved. We'll find someone for you who knows your friend and his origins and can witness to that effect before God.

ʿĪsā We don't possess the record of the endowment either.

Lawyer In that regard one has to produce a copy of the "official" record (said in a particular tone of voice). This is stage two in the expenses of the case.

11.7 ʿĪsā ibn Hishām said: At this point, the Lawyer brought his conversation with us to a close. Facing the qiblah, he placed his right hand on his brow and started praying the evening prayer. My companion and I got up to leave and walked out. I was amazed at the subdued calmness and patient resignation I had noticed in the Pāshā. I told myself that nothing educates and trains the soul in the paths of virtue so quickly as the experience of misfortune and a struggle with disaster. It was only a short time ago that he had been cantankerous and quick-tempered, finding it necessary to kill someone for the most trifling lapse and the least pretext. After succumbing to this series of calamities, he had become meek-tempered, magnanimous, approachable, and patient; so much so that he no longer scorned and grumbled about everything we saw that day. He had nothing to say, but had instead turned into a wise philosopher who habitually observes people's manners and customs in the course of his dealings with them. I became further convinced that the people with the worst natures who lead the most miserable lives are those gullible fools who are pampered and spoilt by their luxurious existence and who have never been taught how to live by the bitter experience of adversity nor learned any lessons from the misfortunes of time.

11.8 As we walked, the Pāshā merely said the following to me:

Pāshā I want you to know, my dear friend, that, were it not for the great respect and veneration which I have for shaykhs and wearers of the turban who are the bearers of God's holy book, I would have asked you to take me to a Shariah Court lawyer who wears a tarboosh.

'Īsā One must take things as they come, you should realize, and in any case it's all God's will! Beneath the tarboosh you'll often find some people more ferociously destructive than wild beasts. I myself know a tarboosh wearer who swore in my presence that he would pronounce the threefold divorce on his current wife and every wife he would marry in the future, all that in order to deny something which he had in fact said in a company at which I was myself present. By so doing, he was mocking the lawgiver's authority, relying instead on the words of the poet who said:

> If they make me swear to divorce my wife,
> I will return to her, our relationship better than before we separated.
> Should they make me swear to free a slave,
> my slave 'Ubayd knows he will not be freed.[87]

'Īsā ibn Hishām said: The days went by. Every day we went to see the Lawyer Shaykh, but never found him. If we went to his house, we were told he was in court; and if we went to court, we learned that he was at the royal palace or a mansion owned by some important personage. Eventually our feet were sore, and we grew tired of waiting. We decided to lie in wait for him in front of his house during the last hours of darkness, so that we could catch him before he left. We sat at a distance from the door. Eventually he emerged riding a donkey. "Please forgive this delay," he said. "The real fault lies with the numerous problems and lawsuits involving princes with which I'm dealing." We accepted his excuse and accompanied him to the court. He went with us to the testification clerk—and may God preserve you from such circumstances! We found him sitting there in resplendent attire: red shoes on his feet, blue coat on his shoulders, yellow belt around his waist, and a white turban around his head: 11.9

His colors were so numerous, he looked like a rainbow.[88]

11.10 The Lawyer Shaykh had left us with his Assistant. The clerk gave one of the witnesses a doubtful look. "He's young and under age," he told us. "He's this and that." The Lawyer's Assistant leaned over and whispered something in his ear, whereupon he immediately accompanied us to the assize judge to hear the testification. The Assistant meanwhile let us know that this was stage three in the expenses of the case. Through God's grace and concern for us, the testification was completed in a single day. As we were leaving, we were told that we would have to submit a petition to his honor the judge requesting permission to investigate the original charter of the endowment in the archives of the Public Records Office. That would show the number and date of the original charter, and from whose agency it came (implying the name of the scribe who had originally drawn it up). So we went looking for the groom, who might conceivably know a way of getting hold of what we needed. Once we found him and told him what we needed, he told us that he had a scroll with the number of the original charter on it. He had obtained it by various means after a good deal of time and effort in order to confirm his rights to the endowment's proceeds. He went to his house and came back with the scroll, but we discovered that it only mentioned the number and date; the name of the scribe who executed the document was not recorded on it.

11.11 We accompanied the Lawyer's Assistant to the court once again. We wrote the petition and presented it to his honor the judge. On the page he wrote instructions to the chief clerk to investigate the problem of the case. They asked for witnesses, stipulating that they had to be from the Pāshā's generation in order to confirm his personal identity, to testify that he was the possessor of the endowment, and that other people had laid their hands on it. The entire process left us completely baffled, but the Assistant undertook to produce such witnesses as well, not before he had informed us that this was stage four in the expenses of the case. They looked at the petition and noticed that we had not given the name of the clerk of the agency in it. We were informed that, without that information, it would be impossible to look into the records at the Registry Office. With only the number and date, we'd have to wait for years and years till we came across a copy of the original endowment. This information distressed us greatly, but the Assistant told to us not to give up hope. "I'll help you to complete the business quickly," he told us, "and God willing, I'll come to the Registry Office with you, that being, of course, stage five in the expenses of the case." The wretch continued to count out the stages for our benefit. At each stage, we counted out some dirhams for him, asking God, as we did so, to rescue us from fate's decree which had struck us so hard and to bring the case to a speedy conclusion before our very lives came to an end.

Miṣbāḥ al-sharq 49, March 30, 1899[89]

12.1 ʿĪsā ibn Hishām said: We applied ourselves eagerly to the search, and the Lawyer was just as assiduous in keeping out of our way. We spent ages trying to visit him, but eventually we gave up and tried instead to look for his Assistant. After a good deal of searching we eventually got hold of him and used both incitements and threats to keep him with us. "I'll tell you the truth," he said, "and nothing but the truth. Knowing only the date and name of its owner, it's absolutely out of the question to find the text of the endowment in this case. We also need to know the name of the scribe who wrote it out. One just cannot envisage the Records Clerk coming across it amongst all these piles of papers. He would need to be inspired, and days and years would have to pass. If you don't believe me and still doubt my word, come with me. I'll show you things which will dispel any uncertainty you may have and convince you of what I'm saying." And with that, he set off, jumping and skipping his way to the Records Office.

12.2 Once we had passed through the doorway where all the clerks were sitting, we found piles of timber propped up against other blocks of strong wood, and trestles with goatskin rugs spread out over the filth and dust. It was so dark in this gloomy place that you could not distinguish one man from another. The darkness was so intense that it reminded the Pāshā of the grave which he had only just left, and so he turned back and decided to wait for us in the daylight outside. The Assistant leaned over and whispered something in the ear of one of them. I could not make out what it was he said, but in any case the man got up hurriedly and went away with the Assistant. I tagged along behind them. After just a few steps, a veil of darkness descended and daylight vanished. I could not see where I was going and stopped where I was. The Assistant grabbed me by the hand; I had no idea where I was going in this terrifying and dangerous place. I kept feeling something under my feet that crunched and sagged like chaff trodden into the soil. We made our way through this cellar until I imagined that I was either in the midst of the graves of ancient Egyptians, involved in the sacred mysteries in Roman temples, or else in the course of examination by Freemasons.[90]

My heart leapt. I was panic-stricken and scared in case a trap had been set or some sort of trick arranged. I was so frightened at first that I could not say a word, but then I plucked up my courage and spoke to the Assistant: "What do you want by bringing me into this gloom? I don't have any silver or gold. There's no reason why you should be planning to commit murder." 12.3

The blackguard guffawed and then swore to divorce his wife, all in order to assure me that we were simply walking between the sacks of ledgers and bundles of scrolls. "Just remain calm," he told me. "You'll see the truth with your own eyes." The wretch had barely finished explaining things to me when I tripped over a package and fell over on to a pile of scrolls. All of a sudden, someone started shouting from underneath them.

"What's the matter with you, you blind idiot?" this personage yelled at me in haughty disdain. "Can't you see straight? After all, we're still in broad daylight."

I pulled myself up again and recited to myself the following line of poetry:

> A gloom in which everything is alike
> and people's sex is unknown until they shout.[91]

As I looked again, a specter suddenly appeared, wiping the dust off his head and beard with the edge of his cloak or gown. I was seized with panic. "Who's this man?" I asked. "Just one of the records clerks," the Assistant replied, "unearthing a scroll in the records of title deeds."

"But how can he find such things in this pitch darkness?" I asked."These are people," he replied, "who are used to working without any light; they can see in complete darkness. With habit comes guidance; every mortal gets his accustomed due from fate.

If all mankind walked like this,
then the blind would not envy those who can see."[92]

12.4 Turning to our right we noticed the outline of a hall. Patches of light gleamed in it like fireflies' wings, the rays of the sun as they poured in through a hole in the roof of this pit. Various types of microbe kept making ripples, like straw on water or as if the sun were trying to penetrate and traverse this space but was scared of the dark, so it was leaning on a cane. I rubbed my eyes and looked carefully. What did I see, you ask?

I have never heard, and I cannot see myself ever hearing
of a desert with a gate.

In front of me I saw an area piled high with old scrolls and frayed ledgers, looking for all the world like towering hills and lofty mounds. The difference was that, whereas the latter bear fruit and are productive, these were moth-eaten and threadbare; while the latter are verdant and fertile, and, if watered by plenty of rain, will produce lush plants, these were black and arid; dampened by moisture they would produce insects:

The earth spreads leaves on the earth's cheek
as carpets are spread on the edge of the soil.
The wind emits perfumed breaths
like scent mixed with rose water.
But these scatter paper over the earth,
but only for moths and decay to consume.

Whoever inhales their scent is only left with disease,
as though he were inhaling the grave's own soil.[93]

After a while I managed to make out the face of the clerk who was accompanying us. He was short and wore a large turban. His face was masked by a pale coloring, and his eyes were bloodshot. He had wrapped up his coat behind him and pulled it up on his back like a quiver. In his belt he was carrying a brass inkwell, while between the folds of his turban were scrolls with dates and numbers on them. I turned and spoke to the Assistant: 12.5

ʿĪsā Come on! Take us back to the door so that we can return to the light of day. I've given up. Now I believe what you've been telling me. Even supposing we had a thousand dates and numbers for the original scribe, how on earth would this clerk be able to make out all these crumbling manuscripts in such pitch darkness?

Lawyer's Assistant Don't assume that people like him cannot find things in total darkness! Don't be put off by the scattered ledgers and piles of scrolls. They're all arranged and codified in his memory. Thanks to his father and grandfather he knows the whereabouts of every one of them. It is just like pilots in Alexandria who inherit the ability to guide ships at the entrance to the harbor on the basis of information about the shape of the sea bed that they've learned from their fathers. If only we knew the name of the scribe, the search would be easy, and we'd get what we wanted.

Clerk Yes indeed! God bless you—please don't assume that I can't find things in my search through the scrolls. God knows that this Records Office has been imprinted on my mind from earliest childhood according to the very best methods of arrangement and description. They are subdivided into a number of records. There is firstly the record of the Sublime Porte in which saleable objects which have not been inherited are written down; the record of the military division in which saleable inherited chattels are recorded; the record of title deeds in which defined properties are recorded (such as a bequest which is specially allotted or sold by auction); 12.6

the record of notifications detailing those articles in which all kinds of regulations of the Shariah Courts are published; the record of accounts, in which the accounts of trustees in matters of endowment and other things are put down; the record of the endowment system, where the original endowment charters are recorded, and the warrants of attorney, wills, and authentification are entered.

'Īsā All glory be to the Opener and Provider! Let's go back to the door!

Clerk Then there's the record of the High Committee, recording the decrees dealing with the appointment and dismissal of consuls, and the proclamations published by the Egyptian Appeals Committee in the form in which it is presented by the Shariah Court judge or his deputy together with all the great religious scholars from all sects; the record of the Arab division, where the inherited chattels particular to *dhimmīs* are noted down.[94]

'Īsā I believe you! But that's enough. We're short of time...

12.7 Clerk (*enlarging on the subject*) Then there's the record of confiscation of villages, in which lands and villages seized by amirs are registered. In the city of Cairo, there were District Courts in which the ruling authority was the judge appointed by the Sultān. Each court kept a record (and they've all been kept in this Records Office) in which all kinds of things were written down. They had offices in various areas: Bāb al-Sha'riyyah, Qanāṭir al-Sibā', Ibn Ṭulūn's mosque, and Qayṣūn's mosque.[95]

'Īsā Enough Sir! There's no need to go to such lengths in your explanation. We have to leave.

Clerk (*continuing with his list*) In Darb Sa'ādah, Bāb al-Khalq, Ṣaliḥiyyah, Najmiyyah, Aḥmad al-Zāhid, al-Barshamiyyah, old Cairo, and Būlāq.

'Īsā I've told you that we don't need all this detail!

Clerk The Mosque of Al-Ṣaliḥ, the Mosque of Al-Ḥākim, and the Court of the Sublime Porte. That is the most important court of all, and the judge has authority over every one and is appointed from Constantinople. The court of the army division, the judge of which is appointed every year from Dār al-Saʿādah, as is the judge of the Supreme Court—he is known as "The Ordainer," and his function is restricted to various kinds of legacies, and—

ʿĪsā ibn Hishām said: I grabbed the Assistant by the arm so we could escape from this predicament. I had totally lost patience with this place and this prattling clerk. We had no hope of getting what we needed, so there was no point in hanging around. 12.8

ASSISTANT Don't give up or lose your temper! Wait a bit till I've consulted the Shaykh. He may be able to help us solve our problem and help us escape from our misfortunes.

With that, he leaned over and had a word with the Shaykh. I heard him say:

ASSISTANT Surely you wouldn't turn down a chance for all of us to make a profit. After all, the influential people involved in this case are full of kindness and generosity.

CLERK Just a minute! The mention of that word "generosity" almost permits me to recall the name of the scribe of the endowment. The drafting process provided a story which is still famous because of the munificence of the gifts involved. Even today, the family and descendants of the clerk who wrote it still own some remnants of the robes of honor which were presented to them. His name was the late Shaykh X. It's up to you to deal with the people involved in the case. Come to an agreement with them to write the scribe's name on the document with the date and number as though it came from you. By helping Muslims we all gain benefit from God.

The Assistant came over to me and said:

ASSISTANT (*to ʿĪsā*) Things are now becoming easier through God's sanction. We've found the way to get the name of the scribe who produced the copy. All we have to do is to act on it as the sixth phase in the case.

ʿĪsā ibn Hishām said: The Assistant went on in front and pulled me along behind him till we emerged from darkness into the light 12.9

of day—through God's bounty. I was blinded by the sunlight and couldn't see anything till I had gone backwards and forwards between the light and darkness several times. When I met my friend the Pāshā, he asked why I had been away for so long. I did not want to add any more misfortunes to his troubles by recounting the terrors I had faced, so I told him how the situation had improved. We reached an agreement with the Assistant that he would deal with the recording of the scribe's name on the document and then return next day to the clerk in the Records Office to bring us the copy of the endowment document. We then paid him some more money.

Now, days and months went by. We kept going back to the Records Office, sometimes with the Assistant, other times without him. At last one day the Assistant brought us the news that the text of the endowment had been found. We were overjoyed; our feelings were the same as those of a diver who beneath the buffeting waves finds a pearl fit to be used in a royal diadem. We accompanied him to the Records Office and found the clerk congratulating himself on his skill at finding the document in such a short time. We offered praise to God for our good fortune and happy outcome, and then congratulated him for his outstanding zeal and splendid work. From underneath his armpit he produced some ragged, tattered, and torn documents; no one sheet was level with the one next to it. The writings on them were disjointed and could only be deciphered by someone with a profound knowledge of the techniques for solving riddles. Not only that, but we discovered that the ends of lines were cut off.

12.10 I told the clerk that it would be even trickier and more complicated to translate the documents than it had been to unearth them in this murky desert. To which he responded that such problems were solvable through constant practice. He went on to tell me that he had also inherited from his late father the ability to read these scripts and to supply endings for lines which had been erased. Only one form of expression is used almost without variation in every type of record.

We said farewell and went on our way. After several weeks the Lawyer's Assistant came back and told us that the copy of the endowment had been completed. He asked us to pay the fee and to bring two witnesses to testify to its receipt. He promised to bring two of them after notifying us that this was the seventh phase in the trial's expenses. We duly conformed with his wishes.

Miṣbāḥ al-sharq 50, April 6, 1899[96]

13.1 ʿĪsā ibn Hisham said: As a result of the events described in the previous chapter, we now had a copy of the endowment in our hands. After a good deal of argument and opposition, the Assistant proceeded with the eighth phase. He went to the Petitions Clerk to make an appointment for one of the sessions and to draw up a subpoena calling for the presence of the opposing parties on a particular day. He returned with the good news that the clerk had agreed with the session Judge; our session would take place on Sunday. With that we kept nursing our hopes, until the appointed day dawned. Good fortune willed that the Lawyer Shaykh should be close by; he had been staying out of our way for some time as he went to and fro:

> Perhaps God had brought the two pieces together
> after they had become convinced that they would never meet again.[97]

13.2 He accompanied us to the court where he could use his expertise to rid us of the wrongs we had suffered. We all made our way to the Shariah Court, haven of law and fair judgment, where justice would be dispensed in accordance with divine inspiration and the Prophet's own practice. This was the place where the pulpits of divine guidance are located; there the minarets of piety are established, and the light of truth and justice shines forth. In it, the murky paths of heresy and error are exposed, the oppressed person gets back the things which are taken away from the oppressor, and the ruled receive justice from their ruler. Yes indeed, this is the place where all are equal and frivolity and fancy vanish into thin air; the poor widow with her orphaned children is considered more important than the knight with his spear and sword, and the defenseless plaintiff has more power than someone bristling with arms. In the court's eyes, the indigent weakling has more power than any monarch seated in a throne; the owner of a tiny sheep and a camel stands above the lord of Al-Khwarnaq and Al-Sadīr.[98] Yes indeed, this is the seat inherited from the Prophet who was sent to us, and where matters are conducted according to the Sunna and verses of the Qur'an. It always aids the lowly against the powerful, sometimes following the practice of ʿUmar ibn al-Khaṭṭāb, and at other times the practice of ʿUmar ibn ʿAbd al-ʿAzīz.[99] It is also regarded as the residence of all awe and majesty, the font of piety and perfection, the seat of purity and fidelity, the source of decency and respectability, the focal point of all devoutness and humility, and the place where obedience and submission are to be found.

When we reached the court, we found the courtyard crowded 13.3
with carriages pulled by rearing steeds. At their sides stood prancing mules and asses with silver and silk trappings on them. We thought these must be the mounts of important men and amirs in splendidly decorated retinues. But, when we inquired to whom these carriages belonged, we were told that they belonged to the group of secretaries, to which our only reaction was: Praise to the Lord, the Almighty provider, who gives unlimited benefits. We went up to the door; alongside it we found a Shaykh bowed down by age; the hand of fate seemed to have passed him by. He was both deaf and nearsighted, and plagued by senility and disease. We were told that his job was to guard the court against the adversities of Fate. After climbing the stairs, we found the whole place teeming with people of various shapes and sizes. They kept exchanging insults and abuse, punching and walloping one another, flashing and fulminating, and cursing and swearing at each other. The majority of them were grabbing

other people by the collar, pounding them against the walls and falling over each other on the floor.

13.4 With turbans tumbling and rolling around us, we kept pushing our way up the stairs until God graciously released us and enabled us to escape from this mass of people crammed together in such a crushing bottleneck. Once we had reached the lower hall, we found a pregnant woman by the door writhing around on the floor like a snake. She kept asking the people around her to witness to the fact that her husband refused to acknowledge her pregnancy. We endeavored to move forward a step, but were unable to do so, faced with a torrent of clashing waves. A headlong flood of women kept shouting and screaming, howling and wailing laments; with all their screeching and complaining it was as though they were performing the last rites for the dead, an occasion when their eyes would normally become sore and their voices hoarse. Among them was a woman with her face partly uncovered and arms and head exposed, sitting cross-legged in the heat of the sun, while her sister deloused her. She had bared her breasts and was suckling an infant in her arms. Another woman was preceded by her divorced husband and followed by her lover; she was wishing the former good riddance with curses and abuse, and beckoning the latter with her hand which was decorated with dye. Yet another was suckling two children facing each other while her husband kept hitting her on the head with his shoe. Still another kept clutching the hair of her husband's second wife while her child was yearning for her milk. We noticed a cloistered wife walking with her eunuch, but he could hardly keep her protected in the thick of such a fray. Among the mob we spotted a whole crowd of wanton lechers and girl-chasers, flirting with every lithe maiden and hassling every pretty girl who passed by. They tried to settle the arguments and disagreements between the women and girls whose glances had bowled them over. Thus it happened that winks became intermingled with urging hands, all argument and controversy ceased, and everyone began talking amicably.

One of the most incredibly awful things we saw was a man and woman challenging each other to produce more obscene language and going to utter extremes in vulgarity. They were dragging a boy along by the hand, almost as though they both wanted to divide him up and keep part of his limbs for themselves. The boy was in severe pain and kept crying. For our part, we asked God who hears and knows everything to rescue us from this Hellish torture. Among the utterly dreadful things we heard was something spoken by a weeping woman with tears sprinkling her veil. "If we women had female judges," she said, "we would never have reached this miserable state. Men always favor the members of their own sex and help each other against women." With that, we asked the Lord of the Holy Book to help us. We climbed the next flight of stairs, but found that it was just like the first floor, seething with people going up and down like an ant's nest or bee hive. Eventually we finished up in a hall filled with various types of salesmen. One was shouting "bread and cheese," another "tobacco and coffee," another "butter and honey," and another "beans and onions." An ice vendor was clanging liquorice juice cups together while a sheep seller was cutting open the animals' skulls. There was a café where people with cases could relax, each one of them surrounded by witnesses in scores like insects. The crowds here were even bigger and the arguments were that much fiercer than before. Lawyers' assistants ran to and fro between the litigants, using every trick they knew to dupe people and play false with them. They were living with the wolves and crying with the shepherds. 13.5

We went into a small secretarial room, but were driven out by the army of flies on the vendors' trays. The Lawyer's Assistant now took us to another large room. He told us to sit down and have a rest, and found us some seats between two clerks and assistants; every clerk here had an assistant who deputized for him in implementing lawsuits and recording sentences. I heard the clerk to my right swear a solemn oath that his donkey would never have lagged behind A's donkey during the race if he had not been hampered by 13.6

the tramcars and the narrowness of the square, while his companion at his side swore by his grandfather and most revered relatives that, if he had not tightened the reins, he would have beaten every other donkey and won the bet. "You should know, dear sir," the companion said, "that we have it from our ancestors that, when the grey hair is in good trim, even air cannot grasp the donkey's tail. It will fly its owner to the highest heavens." Turning now to my left, I spotted another posh gentleman in the prime of his youth whose clothes exhibited the most exquisite taste. He positively glistened in silk brocade; such was their profusion of shapes and sizes, he looked as though his clothes had been assembled from a montage of all the flowers in the garden. The scent he was wearing inundated everyone's noses and permeated the air all around. In front of him, a man was spreading out and folding a pile of clothes which he had in his hand, while the gentleman was taking them from him, then discarding them. He was speaking to him:

13.7 GENTLEMAN I don't like these clothes at all I won't accept any of them. Whoever cut them is no good.

TAILOR My dear Sir, how can you possibly say such a thing? I swear to you on the noble Qur'an that they are larger than the suits being worn by those two gentlemen, 'Abd al-'Azīz and 'Abd al-Ḥamīd.

GENTLEMAN By the Lord of the Kaaba, you're lying. The curve of the sleeve is too narrow, and the neck is completely out of fashion.

TAILOR What am I supposed to do? That's the width of the fabric. If we were dealing with the old style, my dear Sir, you could have put two or three of your friends into the folds of your present clothes.

LITIGANT May God bless the gentleman with kindness and generosity.

WITTY CLERK (*making a pun*) No, but rather with horses and livestock.[100]

Litigant May I ask you, Sir, to give me the notification of the judge's verdict.

Gentleman Go away till the assistant comes.

Witty Clerk (*punning yet again*) Go and look him out in Umm al-Ghulām street; you'll find him sitting there, literally under the signposts.

ʿĪsā ibn Hishām said: These stupid jokes and vulgarities set me all aquiver, so I stopped listening and looked round in other directions. I saw all the clerks talking and joking with one another. One was crushing opium in his hand, another rolling his majoon between his fingers. Sometimes the assistants busied themselves with their papers, at others they shared jokes. Meanwhile the poor people who had entrusted their affairs to them were being upbraided and pushed aside with promises and delays. I overheard one clerk arguing with a litigant about terms: "How can you give the assistant such a paltry sum?" he asked. "Do you think he's your slave? Do you expect him to record and work for you when he has no wage or salary from the court and gets no profit from it? How utterly incredible!" When the judge's messenger came in searching for one of the head clerks, he found him sound asleep. Some of them suggested waking him up, but others advocated letting him be, pointing out that for a long time the clerk in question had made a habit of staying asleep till the opium was circulating in his veins alongside the blood. They all agreed that the messenger should go back and say he hadn't been able to find the Shaykh where he was supposed to be, but then he had heard that he'd gone down to the Records Office. A while later, the sleeping clerk woke up, yawned, and stretched himself. He then resumed his slumber, reciting the lines of al-Maʿarrī as he did so: 13.8

> The primary virtue of sleep is that it takes the sleeper
> out of this world, one molded in suffering.[101]

13.9 When he finally woke up, it was to find a bookseller waiting for him.

CLERK Have you brought the books I requested?

VENDOR Yes. I've managed to get you some priceless old volumes, including *The Solution of Riddles for Opening Treasure Chests, The Principles of Ritual in Unraveling Mysteries, The Perfect Guide for People to Extract Gold from Copper, The Proverbial Truth about the Effects of Incense,* and...

CLERK Didn't you find any books on the invocation of spirits?

VENDOR Yes, I've brought you two: *Jewels of Pearl and Coral Concerning the Invocation of Demons,* and *The Best Times for Seeing Devils.*[102]

CLERK May God bless you and reward you well! I've got a defective copy of the latter work. Come home with me and we'll compare them and make corrections.

13.10 ʿĪsā ibn Hishām said: With that, the clerk got up and went off with the vendor. I got up too, feeling utterly disgusted at such rampant ignorance. Meanwhile, the Lawyer's Assistant beckoned us to get up as our case was about to be heard. We went out and stood by the door of the room where the session was being conducted. Both inside and out we saw the most appalling crowds of people, and heard the orderly shouting loudly sometimes and softly at others. I asked the Assistant about this. He replied that the orderly lowered his voice so that the litigant would not hear all the shouting; if that happened, the entire case would have to be annulled out of sympathy and consideration for the defendant. In addition to this, the orderlies could bring in and keep out people as they saw fit. Our turn was called. We went inside, accompanied by the witnesses to our acquaintance whom the Assistant had brought for us as one of the stages he kept counting out for us. The session, we discovered, consisted of three members along with the chairman, each one of whom sat apart from the others. There was so much noise from people shouting and raising their voices that you could barely hear what someone next to you was saying. The clerk of the session who was dressed up like a peacock now pranced his way in and sat down. I stood in a position where I could see what he was writing. He took the pen in his fingertips, put it in the inkwell at one moment and then put it down. He kept on fussing with his clothes.

The Pāshā now moved forward with the lawyer and witnesses. 13.11
I could not hear anything being said to them because there was so much noise and shouting. I could only see the clerk writing in the minutes book. I quote it word for word:

The plaintiff, lawyer, and witnesses appeared before the session. The plaintiff stepped forward and introduced himself as A, son of B son of C. He then identified two witnesses to tesify to knowing him, they being P son of Q son of R son of S resident in such and such an area and ward. Each one of them testified separately to the effect that he knew the aforementioned plaintiff and pointed him out, as being the aforementioned A. Then the plaintiff said: "I have a claim to make against B son of C son of D son of E concerning the administration of an endowment. I have the documents concerning my claim with me." The defendant did not appear even though he had received notification of the application which clearly laid down that he should appear before this session.

The court then ordered us to leave so that they could discuss the 13.12
case and inspect the documents. We stood in a corner of the room waiting along with the other people. After a while we were summoned. They told us that the court wished to acquaint us with the contents of article 72 of the code which stipulates (so the Lawyer informed us) that the defendant shall be granted a statutory deferment of the hearing. The Lawyer informed us that we were obliged to submit such a request to the court, since it could only authorize such a deferral if the Lawyer made such a request. Once we had such a request and the court had granted it, there would follow one deferral after another. And may God suffice you against the misfortunes of fate, protect you from the evils of this building, and rid you of every trial and tribulation that it involves!

Miṣbāḥ al-sharq 54, May 11, 1899

14.1 ʿĪsā ibn Hishām said: May God never afflict you with disaster or lead you away from the road to abundance! We now started on a round of warnings and deferments one after another. On each occasion, the court representative kept returning with the same news of failure. He informed us that the servants of our opponent in this case had only received him with contempt as did other servants of amirs' children. Eventually the time limit of the last deferment was reached. We assumed that it was merely a case of the representative's negligence and inefficiency, and decided to check his story by going with him to find out for ourselves how it was possible to treat the messenger of Muslim Holy Law with such contempt. We followed the representative, along with two witnesses to testify that he had issued a deferment to A son of B son of C. One of them had clasped the other by the shoulder in a manner enough to incite the wit of any sarcastic mocker; they were scuffing the ground with their shoes and then rubbing out the marks with their cloaks. They kept loitering and then speeding up, as if they were hurrying to get a bowl of meat broth. We sauntered along behind them at a reasonable pace, but then hurried along, with prayers to the all-powerful God, in quiet resignation until they were almost out of sight.

14.2 We might well have lost track of them altogether, if one of them had not tripped over the tram lines and lost his turban and shoes. He turned around to look for them, but before he knew it, along came a tram with the driver ringing the bell for all he was worth.

The man was not even aware of it till the tram had almost reached him. It would almost certainly have killed him if his companion had not dragged him back. His turban and shoes were lost, and he was left standing there with nothing to cover his head or feet. He asked someone to help him save them, but without any success; and so the three carriages passed over them. Meanwhile we had caught up with them. The poor man looked pale with fright and was in despair, but we were able to give him the good news that his clothes had in fact been saved. He put his turban and shoes on again, praising God for this happy outcome. We in turn offered our own praises since this delay had slowed them down, and we had been able to catch up and could now carry on walking behind them.

This brought us to a mansion in the centre of a garden, the beauty 14.3
of which belittled the very mansions of Baghdad and Ghumdān. It was bedecked with different kinds of flowers which looked like sapphires and other jewels. In the center was the mansion itself which looked like a white pearl or the full moon among the stars in the sky:

> As though it were a neck, and its garden around it
> a beautifully arranged necklace.[103]

What can we say about a garden so decorously woven by the earth's hand for the day of its festive decoration: a place garlanded in a cloak through which to relish its own radiant beauty?

> It is clothed in a garment made by downpour and dew;
> needlework, though not real, and striped cloth, though
> not such.[104]

In its wafting breezes, girls could dispense with the scent of musk, while the cool winds could save them the bother of perfuming themselves with ambergris:

> With plants like young virgins, and soil
> whose surface seemed rose water on musk.[105]

14.4 Their dearest wish would be to make ring-stones from the flower blossoms and amulet chains from the tree buds; they would long to be clothed in a glittering gown made from the silken brocade of its earth, and to be adorned with brilliant earrings from the jewels of its plants:

Whenever morning rain falls, its top parts
sway with scattered pearls and jewels of dew.
When greeted by the sun, the shining surface
of a gleaming marguerite reflects its light.[106]

In this garden fruit-laden branches took the place of buxom companions; flowers like serving maids with pitchers and cups who were pouring the remains of the dew from those cups and carrying the moisture's nectar as they swayed from side to side in the winds' flirtatious breezes:

Anemones carrying dew, as though they were
childhood tears on young girls' cheeks.[107]

14.5 Seeing this garden, we could only imagine that we were at some wedding feast where all means of arousing pleasurable and delightful sensations were gathered. Here the clouds had erected their pavilion and the intertwined plants had laid out their cushion. Flowers bloomed in the branches gleaming like lights, and birds perched on the trees vied with each other in their songs and chants, warbling melodies enough to sever the listener's heartstrings and attract even the wary beast of prey to hear them:

They saw the blooming flowers, and were roused by a lute,
the strings of which were delicate sinews and limbs.[108]

As the breeze rustled and blew, it played its own tunes in beats both light and heavy. The leaves clapped their hands, and the branches stood up to dance, swaying to the moisture's intoxicating effect and showing a smile that revealed a well-ordered daisy to put to shame the teeth of young girls. Swaying on their slim figures, they collected drops of rain. Beneath their garments, the brook trickled and flowed falteringly. Water coursed along in their shade and was channeled in different directions; it was as though its pebbles were pearl and coral on beauties' necks or golden necklaces on the finest singing girls:

> Its stones so amaze bejeweled virgins,
> they touch the edge of the well-strung necklace.[109]

Once we felt completely sated and overwhelmed by this earthly paradise, we intoned our praises to the only all powerful God, realizing as we did so how incapable mankind is of expressing its gratitude for His bounty. Just then, we noticed some people at the door of the mansion. They seemed both desperate and despondent, their expressions were gloomy, and their faces were covered in dust. All of them were either weeping, sobbing, or shouting angrily. As each one announced his purpose, I took a closer look: they all seemed utterly frustrated, thwarted, and discouraged. A Jew was talking with a sense of total failure: 14.6

JEW Woe is me! My money is all gone, and I've lost all hope. 14.7

MERCHANT What misery! If I'd known this was going to happen, I would never have fallen into such a trap.

VENDOR Too bad for me! I've been duped by high rank, and now I've lost the means of supporting my family.

JEWELER Woe to anyone who lets himself be deceived by superficialities and loses his jewels as a result!

PHARMACIST I'm prepared to swear that I'm not going to lose the costs of his medicine, even though he be suspended from the outermost limits of the heavens.

WINE SELLER A plague on this swindler who takes a fancy to my wine bottle and then disappears.

BUTCHER I'm not giving up my rights even if they put a knife to my throat.

TAILOR I won't quit this door till I've torn the clothes off him.

SHOEMAKER By the head of his father and grandfather, I'm going to get the cost of his shoes from his own skin.

BARBER "I'm someone well known and ambitious."[110] My trade brings with it many privileges and benefits. If only I could have marred his face and spoiled his features, I would have torn his moustache off and shaved his eyebrows. By God, I'm going to tackle this unpleasant dunderhead, block all the entrances and exits, and stick to him morning and evening even if he takes off into the sky.

14.8 While all this was going on, the servants were refusing to acknowledge that the owner was at home. They kept swearing he did not have a dirham or dinar left. If a creditor tried to enter, the servants stopped him; if someone simply ignored them, they pushed him away. We observed the scene in amazement. Contrasting the beauty of the place with the misfortunes of its inhabitants, we felt we were being roasted and turned on the embers of our own worries. Just then a European man emerged from the inner sanctum; he was seething with anger. He addressed the Doorkeeper: "I have made my demands, but he has explained that he is bankrupt and unable to pay. There is no alternative but to impose distraint on the property. Here is a detailed list. Make sure nothing is lost or damaged." Barely had this usher of the Mixed Courts finished and left before the usher from the Native Courts arrived, panting with fatigue. He handed a warning notice to the Doorkeeper who took it from him while repeating the same story about bankruptcy and inability to pay. That usher departed too. By now the midday heat was intense and the sun's rays were scorching their faces, so everyone present followed him. We seized this opportunity. Our court official moved forward, informed the Doorkeeper of his status at the Shariah Court, and handed him the warning notice. The Doorkeeper pushed him in the chest and refused to take the notice. "This is the only court we haven't heard from!" So saying, he turned his back on us and closed the gate. The court official now took the two witnesses by the hand and stood between them as he shouted the following statement in an official tone:

"The Qadi of Egypt orders you, A son of B son of C, to present 14.9
yourself at the court on Sunday next, the purpose being to investigate a claim of unlawful seizure of the endowment now filed against you by X son of Y son of Z. Should you not be present on the specified day, then a deputy will be appointed on your behalf to hear the claim in his presence and judgment will be passed upon you *in absentia*."

With that, we bade the official and the two witnesses farewell, and they went on their way. The Pāshā and I were still utterly staggered by the things we had seen and heard. We both felt very despondent. The Pāshā leaned on the garden wall and spoke to me:

PĀSHĀ Ever since Fate has placed me in such difficulties and misfortunes, I've begun to see more clearly the inner significance of things as they really are. So much so that I've become convinced today that worldly matters work on the basis of deception and untruth; they all involve the use of falsehood, fabrication, fraud, and swindling. Try to find anyone, for Heaven's sake, who can look at this mansion—with its glittering decorations and its retinue of servants—without being overwhelmed by a feeling of jealousy toward the people who live there and by a desire to enjoy the same good fortune and happy life as they do. As a result, such a person will resent the lot he has in life and his particular fate in this world!

ʿĪSĀ Yes indeed, you're still pursuing the path of prudence and 14.10
good judgment; you speak the truth as you see it. If you discovered what the situation is really like for the majority of wealthy people you're seeing and the kind of life they lead, you'd discover something that demands compassion and sympathy rather than envy and jealousy. You'd realize that any employee who earns his daily livelihood through the sweat of his brow is happier and more comfortable than these people are. The more flashy and splendid the exterior, the gloomier and darker the interior. I know one of them personally who may actually be extremely worried and anxious.

And yet, the more that's the case, the more you'll see him pretending to be happy and faking laughter. The poorer and more bankrupt he is, the more he risks lavish expenditure.

PĀSHĀ In my day, it was exactly the opposite. The richer someone was, the more needy he appeared; he was never as happy as when he made a display of his grief and misfortune.

14.11 ʿĪsā ibn Hishām said: We went on talking like this for quite a while. I was delighted to notice that the Pāshā was now regularly applying rational investigation and logical principles to obtain insight into the inner aspects of character. I became more than ever convinced that men in important positions remain totally inexperienced and ignorant; it is only when they happen one day to fall into the snares of misfortune that from the realities of their current situation they come to realize how futile their past way of life has been.

At this point we happened to glimpse over the wall and noticed the retinue of servants gathered round in a circle, chattering and arguing with each other. We heard the Doorkeeper start by saying:

DOORKEEPER How I wish my mother had never given birth to me and my father had never taught me how to write! My hand's sore from signing all these warning notices and statements. Hardly a day passes without my signing signatures and receiving papers. I've despaired of this life and the sorry state in which I find myself. How I wish I could be included in these clusters of creditors! Then at least I'd be able to escape with part of my salary which has been piling up for months. Who can help me get away from this house where distraint spreads like a plague of locusts? The people who live here are being constantly harassed by the voices of creditors. I myself am scared of court ushers who keep perching themselves on my clothes trunk.

14.12 CLERK I've no idea what the young man is going to do. How can we earn a living with him when he has absolutely nothing left? If I'm right, then the outcome will be the worst imaginable. He's been very restless of late, and I've the impression that he's devising some escape from this situation, but it'll be a poor way out and a vile end. God knows that, if it weren't for the things I pick up here and there while doing jobs for him, I couldn't afford to provide food for my family now that I've had difficulty getting my monthly salary. Yesterday he sent me off to sell a sapphire ring. It was valued at a hundred pounds, but the jeweler would only give me twenty-five for it.

SERVANT Now I can see things clearly. Yesterday I noticed 14.13
that he had some gold with him, but I'd no idea of where he'd got it from. He gave me ten pounds. I used it to purchase from his brother the dog which you've seen him playing with since this morning.

SECOND SERVANT And he gave me eight pounds that I used to buy him the parrot from his son-in-law. I also bought him a ticket for a box at the Opera.

THIRD SERVANT And I spent one and a half pounds on perfumes from Jacquin.

CLERK If that's the case, then he has only a pound and a half left. Only this morning I took four pounds to pay the owner of a well-known newspaper to keep quiet. He's been threatening every day to expose the young man's true situation and blacken his name.

DRIVER While he still has some cash left, I'll go to see him as well to collect the cost of the bristles and sponge he promised me.

FOURTH SERVANT You're well off now thanks to the profit you've made from these purchases and sales. But we other servants have to make do with food and drink as our only salary. We've put up with this situation out of a sense of loyalty to this illustrious house. If only this prosperity would last! You've heard the butcher's threats today, and only yesterday you heard the baker's messenger issue a warning too.

FIFTH SERVANT I think our only course of action is to ask him to transfer our wages to the profits of the endowment, which is the only thing which has escaped confiscation and court notices so far!

DOORKEEPER Your thoughts and hopes are all in vain. The endowment on which you were all relying has now been taken to court as part of legal proceedings. The representative of the Shariah

Court came today with the third notice of deferment. All that remains is for a verdict to be reached removing the endowment from your master's possession.

Everyone What a calamity!

A shout came from inside the house, to the effect that the master had woken up and wanted to take a ride.

14.14 ʿĪsā ibn Hishām said: They all leapt to their feet. For our part, we left feeling deeply unsettled by what we had heard, inasmuch as we were going to court on Sunday.

The day appointed for our session in the Shariah Court arrived, so we went there once again. When the session opened, the contestants were summoned as usual. We duly responded with our agent, but the defendant was not present. Once everyone was seated, the session asked for the witnesses of cognizance. The Lawyer's Assistant produced two witnesses who gave their testimony regarding the defendant's particulars. The session then asked about the three deferments, and they were found to conform with all the established requirements. A deputy was now chosen for the defendant, someone reliable and well-known for protecting the rights of those not present. They asked him to explain the defendant's claims in his place. Our Lawyer began to check the text of the endowment which we had obtained from the Records Office concerning the endowment's assets. However, he could only identify a small fraction of the many assets we had enumerated for him. He was afraid that the court would only adjudicate the assets detailed in this copy of the document which was not worth all the trouble. With that in mind, he asked the court to postpone the hearing for a significant amount of time, so that in the intervening period it would be possible to investigate the rest of the endowed property. The deputy acting on behalf of the absent defendant agreed to this, and so the case was adjourned until after the year's judicial vacation.

14.15 We now left the session with the Lawyer. Both he and his Assistant now saw further scope for trickery opening up before them.

When we asked him where we might find out about the rest of the endowment property, he cleared his throat and said nothing. As we walked a short distance with his Assistant, he told us that the only likely place was the Department of Endowments since it had records in which such properties are registered. That would be particularly true if the defendant in this case had lost some of the endowed property and the Department of Endowments had taken it over. Almost certainly it would have recorded this endowment in its records.

He now asked us to come to a new agreement with the Lawyer, while he committed himself to carrying out this new plan. We agreed to this latest request. God deals with us on matters of endowment as He wishes.

Miṣbāḥ al-sharq 55, May 18, 1899[111]

15.1 ʿĪsā ibn Hishām said: At this point we were hoping for some help and good news as we hovered between the court and the Department of Endowments. It was our fervent prayer that God would suffice us as we confronted the dire situation with this particular department and that He would preserve us from the vicissitudes of fate. Our ears had been filled with grim reports about this particular administration; there seemed to be a consensus on its incompetence and dysfunction.[112] No one could agree on the diagnosis of its ills, and people had run out of ideas as to how to cure them. Everyone agreed on the need for reform; the faults had to be acknowledged and addressed before things got worse, the entire situation deteriorated, and a prolonged period of neglect and indifference led to the direst consequences. It was at this point that my friend the Pāshā suffered the fate of people who go through a prolonged period of tension and worry; he fell ill and kept on losing weight and energy.

Anxieties can render even the portly man thin,
and turn the youngster into a grey-haired old man.[113]

15.2 But every time I suggested seeing a doctor, he kept balking and refusing. What is the point of doctors, he would say, when the fates have their schedule and appointed time. I managed to convince him that a belief in the inevitability of fate need not stand in the way of a cure to illness. How many sick people have waited for ages, but the illness has lingered on; on the other hand, how many healthy folk have died young without ever being sick? To that the Pāshā replied that, if indeed there was a need to undergo treatment, then let it be a doctor who relied for his treatment on incense and amulets, writing charms and talismans, but not those types who rely on medicaments and plants and keep talking about herbs and compounds. In olden times, he told me, I used to know a lot of people from the Maghrib, fortune tellers and diviners. If you could find me one of them, I would entrust my treatment to them and trust them to cure me.

So I set about responding to his request and did my utmost to meet his wishes. After a prolonged search I came across someone from Morocco. After I had told him the Pāshā's story, the first thing he asked was to "measure a sample": in their practice that meant a piece of the invalid's clothing—something white or yellow which, they claim, can point to the origins of the patient's illness. Once he had acquired what he was looking for, he told me to come back in three days.

15.3 So I kept the assigned appointment. He asked me to pay for the necessary fumigants: musk and ambergris, to which was added the cost of saffron and sandalwood, so as to afford a gaze into the unseen. He told me that my companion had been "touched" and was afflicted by a madness induced by the daughter of the Salamander King. In order to invoke her, all seven kings had to be gathered together in the same place. Not only that, but there also had to be present Maymūnah and ʿĀqiṣah, Dahnish and Wāqiṣah, Rattler son of Shaker, Quaker son of Shocker, Storm and Flasher, along with other rowdies and assistants. They would also need every diver and flying beast from the boundless climes and the denizens of desert wastes. Each one of these would need to have their particular vapors, each with its acknowledged cost. I can point you, he told me, to the vendor who knows the potion and can reproduce it exactly; either that or else you can give me the full amount, and I'll take care of the whole thing for you. I now realized that what was being demanded was beyond my ability to pay, so I immediately gave him an agreed-upon amount, and he in turn asked me to delay for a few days until he could visit the invalid at a specified time of day.

15.4 He did indeed come at the appointed time and invoked the spirits. He now proceeded to count and record, to resolve and cense, to mutter and growl, to rant and babble. With praises and prayers to God he pulled out one of the sick man's hairs and moaned and groaned without saying a word. He then started turning the patient over to left and right till his joints and nerves almost fell apart. The poor sick Pāshā was on the point of drowning in a sea of sweat. Using water he wiped off the design he had made in the basin, then handed it to the invalid to quaff some of its contents. He started to swallow, but could hardly manage it. This "doctor" then demanded some water from a well untouched by sunlight and started chanting over it, sometimes loud, sometimes in a whisper. He kept turning it in his hands and then spitting a whole mouthful of saliva into it. Eventually he finished reciting this mumbo jumbo, while I was getting more and more aggravated and impatient. He now started spraying the invalid's face with this cold water, all the while chanting that in the name of God he was protecting him from all fiendish devils. The Pāshā stood up, then sat down, shivering and shaking; he then fainted clear away, whimpering as he did so. The Maghribi doctor now proclaimed: "God is Almighty! Success! We are now rid of the red king's daughter."

I too was close to fainting out of sheer panic and fright. "What have you done?" I shouted at him.

"Don't be afraid!" he replied. "Don't panic! It only remains for your sick friend to come round from his fainting spell. Now that the devils have left his body, he's feeling feeble and weak. Once the space is completely clear again, he'll be just as healthy as he was. Once he is in the hands of the righteous and devout helpers, they'll soon wake him up and restore him to consciousness. But they never perform this cryptic cure if there are human beings in the room. So we need to leave the house. Make sure you don't go back inside till day's end."

So I obeyed his instructions and followed him out of the house. This total phony now left me and went on his way, leaving me prey to sorrow and regret. I waited on tenterhooks till nightfall. God is my witness that the only reason I put up with this trickster's routine was out of respect for the Pāshā's naïveté when it came to traditional beliefs. Rushing headlong back to the house, I found my friend lying there between life and death and still unconscious as he ranted and raved. I immediately realized that the situation was very grave, and we needed to find a doctor. I was now certain that this Maghribi so-called doctor had tricked us simply in order to extort money from us and had left the Pāshā in this serious condition with its uncertain consequences. In a total panic I rushed over to a nearby pharmacy and asked for a doctor who could take on a severely sick patient and alleviate the symptoms of his illness. The pharmacist pointed to a man sitting beside him playing backgammon. "There you are!" he said. "What a lucky chance; the fates have smiled on you!" But the doctor kept making excuses and coyly refusing to cooperate. He stretched and yawned and then spoke to me: 15.5

DOCTOR Leave me alone! I'm far too busy to answer your request. 15.6

PHARMACIST But, my dear Doctor, the likes of you will surely not dash the hopes of one who asks for help. The traditional bond between God and mankind still exists.

DOCTOR Tell me, who's been treating him up till now.

'ĪSĀ IBN HISHĀM No one. I didn't realize he was sick till today.

DOCTOR Assuming I agree to go with you, where's the carriage?

'ĪSĀ IBN HISHĀM The house is close by.

PHARMACIST (*to his assistant*) Go and get a carriage. We need it at once.

BACKGAMMON PLAYER (*to the Doctor*) You realize that, if you leave before the game's over, the bet will be forfeited.

DOCTOR How can you say that when I had to wait three long hours yesterday with everything set up in front of me before you came back and finished?

BACKGAMMON PLAYER That was because you were bound to win that particular game.

PHARMACIST My dear Doctor, get in the carriage and go. I'll take your place in this game and guarantee to pay the bet myself if you happen to lose.

15.7 'Īsā ibn Hishām said: And with that we reached an agreement; there was no further cause for argument. The doctor and I got into the carriage. In my misery I was barely conscious and aware of my surroundings. Once we reached the sick Pāshā, we found that he had come round from his fainting spell and had no more spasms. The doctor went over, felt his pulse, tapped his chest, then put his hand on his forehead like someone deep in thought. The doctor frowned and shook his head, but did not utter a single syllable. Putting his hand in his pocket, he brought out a ragged folded piece of paper and opened it up. On it were some phrases in French. Taking a pen, he copied them exactly on to another sheet of paper, added his own signature at the bottom, and told me that this was the prescription. The Pāshā was to take one spoonful in the morning and another in the evening. Great care needed to be taken to make sure that there were no lapses and the medicine was taken on time. It was also essential that the medicine be bought from the very same pharmacy; the pharmacist was an honest, devout man, who would not adulterate the medicine or charge an exorbitant amount. Just as he was leaving, I spoke to him in French instead of Arabic in order to find out what exactly the sickness was without the Pāshā understanding how serious his condition was. The doctor did not respond, which made it clear to me that the only French he knew were the precise words needed for the prescription. Once I had handed over the agreed amount for the visit, he promised to come back every day until the danger was past. The doctor did continue to come and go, and the same prescription kept being renewed and repeated, but the patient was still suffering and groaning; and the disease stayed the same. Every time we asked the doctor why the disease and pain seemed to be getting worse, he replied that we must not have been following his instructions about food and drink.

I now complained to a friend of mine about this terrible situation. He told me that I needed to look for another doctor, someone who had been trained in Europe, who knew about both modern and ancient medicine, and treatments that were good or bad. I followed his advice and sought out such a doctor at his consulting office. I found one of his servants upbraiding visitors for coming so early. He told them that they were supposed to know that the doctor was always asleep in the morning. It made no difference whether death's arrows were carrying away the sick and people were suffering in patience, apologizing and waiting, till the time came when the sun emerged from behind the veil and showed itself in its finest garb. With that in mind, I waited till this mob had been dealt with, and then approached the doctor. I acted as a humble postulant and made use of the politest possible language to ask him to choose his own time for a visit. 15.8

Doctor Why are there these mobs of people? Why is everyone so insistent? What's the value of this kind of life when I've no time to eat and drink, let alone to relax and get some sleep? Are there no other doctors in this country, such that I'm the only one left? Or is it that everyone is sick now, and all the doctors are busy caring for them and sharing the burden. My dear Sir, please realize that my schedule only permits me to pay you a call in two days' time. 15.9

ʿĪsā ibn Hishām I beseech you by in the name of humanity not to reject my request. It is your repute that has led me to you, and I'm sure that at your hands the invalid can be cured.

Doctor You need to know that I won't take on a patient who has been sullied by the hands of other doctors. Provided that your sick friend is in the initial stages of his illness and hasn't been treated by them, then I can respond to your request. I'll come to see him tonight.

'Īsā ibn Hishām He's only been seen by one other doctor, but he's failed to treat him properly or cure him.

Doctor Then you should go back to him and leave me alone. I'm not one of those doctors who wait till other doctors have failed the sick, only to rush over and correct the mistakes they've made. I assume that this doctor was someone who has never left Egypt; he has only studied locally, has no idea about modern developments, and accepts a paltry wage.

'Īsā ibn Hishām I think that's right. But I've only come to see you because I've heard that you're the exact opposite of that. Things always become clear through their opposites.

Doctor And I suppose you've also heard about the different prices charged by them and us.

'Īsā ibn Hishām Yes. You'll get whatever you wish to charge.

Doctor In that case I see no reason why I shouldn't pay you a visit.

15.10 After fixing the appointment, I left him and returned to the Pāshā. When the doctor arrived in the evening, he went in to see the patient with his head uncovered and holding his nose. As he approached the bed, he was adjusting his hair-parting with his right hand and holding the patient's hand with his left as he felt his pulse. He kept looking distractedly toward the door as though he were trying to see what might be in the private quarters. It was not long before he wrote out a prescription and hurried away as quickly as he had come. Two days later another person arrived to ask how the patient was doing, saying that he was the doctor's assistant. This poor treatment and general lack of concern was enough to make me lose my temper. I slammed the door in his face, but not before telling him to go away: we have no need of you, I told him, or of the person who sent you. That done, I went out again, the signs of my state of mind clearly visible on my face. One of my neighbors spotted my angry mood and asked me what the problem was. I told him the whole story. This neighbor had recently been abroad. He told me that what had happened was no surprise. You have been relying, he told me, on local doctors; whoever suggested using them was giving you bad advice. I happen to know a Parisian doctor, he said, who came here on the same boat as myself. I'm sure he can cure your sick friend. He lives in such-and-such a place, and I can show you where it is.

Once we reached this doctor's residence, he gave us a friendly welcome and started using a variety of verbiage that had nothing to do with what we needed. He came to the house with us. Approaching the invalid, he proceeded to turn him over, examine him, take his temperature, and count his pulse beats with the second hand on his watch. After a lengthy examination, he wrote out a prescription and left, saying that he would come back in the evening. That is the way things stayed for several days, and the illness only got worse, sending us into a further panic. All I could do was to blame the person who had sent me to this particular doctor. When I met my neighbor, he had one of his friends with him. 15.11

ʿĪsā ibn Hishām Come with me and see what your foreign doctor has managed to do.

Neighbor What's he done? Hasn't he cured your friend's illness?

ʿĪsā ibn Hishām Just the opposite! The condition is even worse than it was, something that we never expected.

Neighbor How can that be? That doctor is one of the most famous doctors in Paris. Everyone trusts him and people regard him as being honest and reliable.

Neighbor's Friend (*talking to him*) Are you still so infatuated with everything Western and foreign. Do you still prefer such people to your own folk, your fellow countrymen? We have doctors in Egypt who are far superior to any foreigner in the breadth of their expertise and their long experience.

Neighbor I only recommended the foreigner to him after he had complained about the experiences he had had with local doctors.

Friend Such as who?

Neighbor Doctors X and Y.

Friend How can you possibly consider X and Y proper doctors? All your friend needs to do is to choose a truly competent local doctor, and I'll guarantee you that the patient will be cured in short order.

15.12 'Īsā ibn Hishām said: So I chose one of them, went to his house, and brought him back. Once he had completed his physical examination, he asked me about his cultural background, both present and past and his intellectual concerns. I told him the Pāshā's entire history. He then spoke to me as follows:

Doctor You should know that your companion doesn't have some hidden disease or chronic illness. It is the events that have happened to him that have had a negative psychological effect on him. The reason why he's grown so thin and lost his energy is that his mind has been suffering. In order to recover what he needs is a complete change of air and a release from his troubles, along with some healthy food and refreshing drink.

'Īsā ibn Hishām But what about all the doctors who have filled the house with bottles and drugs?

15.13 Doctor (*once he has been told about the various doctors and their medicines*) Every profession has its practitioners, both useful and useless; there are those who know and those who don't, people who are honest and others who are crooked. It is clear to me that the first doctor could not care less about the medical profession. He failed to diagnose the illness and decided that he could justify his fee by prescribing a medicine that was neither harmful nor beneficial and then leaving the entire illness to nature to cure. As long as the illness persisted, he would benefit from it. The second doctor found the symptoms of the illness too complicated, so he misdiagnosed it and chose a medicine in line with his own misdiagnosis. He didn't even realize the mistake he'd made. The third doctor realized what the problem was, but he chose to write out a prescription as he would do for someone from his own country without taking into account the difference in climate and the variations in physical constitution. So he too was wrong.

You should realize that there is no profession in the world that can rival that of medicine when it comes to honor, respect, esteem, pride, beauty, and significance. Medical practitioners who contemplate the nature of their profession and are guided by God to an awareness of its scope will feel their souls ennobled and their worth enhanced. As a result they'll eschew the trivialities of cupidity and abstain from all thought of wealth gained by exploiting this noble profession and making use of it to acquire money and hoard gold. It will be clear to them that the pleasure of it all lies in the profession itself. No other pleasures in the world, be they money, children, or whatever of life's delights and fripperies you wish to mention, can rival it. What status can possibly compare with that of a doctor who is responsible for people's bodily health and the guardian of well-balanced constitutions? Which other profession is preferable to the one that is closely modeled on the very creation of God, the Maker and Originator? There is the story of that famous Greek sculptor whose craft led him to boast about the image of man that he had created in marble. When he stood there contemplating the marvel that he had made, its very beauty made him fall in love with it, to such an extent that he lost his mind and started smashing it with his chisel till it fell in pieces. His wonderful creation ceased to exist because he was so upset that his perfect creation was unable to speak. 15.14

What must have been the level of pleasure that led this man to lose his mind and destroy his common sense? Compare that with the feelings a doctor will have as he watches human bodies being cured of diseases and purged of all kinds of malady; things will have been returned to their normal condition and the person's constitution restored to balance. However those doctors who ignore the 15.15

nobility of their profession and reduce it to the level of mere vendors and tricksters simply regard it as a means to make money with no consideration of the obligation to fulfill its mission and to perform its tasks as well as possible. I can see no essential difference between the doctor who examines a patient and decides to prolong the treatment as a means of making more money, and gravediggers who hope for as many dead people as possible in order to increase their revenue. One of the things that illustrates the behavior of such doctors and their exclusive concern with their own interests is that they spend a lot of time on worldly matters to the exclusion of the practice of their own specialized field in medicine. The only reason is that they want to broaden their revenue sources and earn more money. As a result they ignore their own profession and fail to trace a path toward its loftier compensations. They are wrong, and all they manage to do is to turn medicine and doctors into something to chew on. By God, there is nothing in this world that saddens me as much as what is both utterly true and at the same time painful, namely when people say that "when a patient's ill, it's often the doctor's treatment that's at fault."

15.16 ʿĪsā ibn Hishām said: I was completely convinced by what this doctor had to say and was optimistic about his treatment of my friend. I only wished that all doctors could be like him. He had advised me about the best place for the invalid to go to get a change of air and had designated the most appropriate food and drink and the best times to consume them. He then departed, but not before asking to stay in touch with the Pāshā until he was completely cured.

Miṣbāḥ al-sharq 57, June 1, 1899[114]

ʿĪsā ibn Hishām said: So in compliance with the decree of Fate, we decided to take a trip. The idea was to give the Pāshā a chance to recover from his illness by having a change of air. We stayed in a mansion in the suburbs of Alexandria with lush gardens. It was set in a sweet-smelling district. The only sound to be heard was the cooing of wood pigeons; when they sang, their song was in harmony with the rippling water. When the billows moistened the edge of the breeze and hovered over that smiling meadow, they scattered drops of water like pearls on the flowery diadems and bathed the eyes of the narcissus in tears. Lovers would have craved to borrow those tears and put them on their own eyelids so that they could soften the heart of their coy and distant beloved. Young girls would love to use pearls to make a necklace for their neckline or a belt for their waists. 16.1

> This place is an object of wonder;
>   the earth laughs at heaven's tears.
> Gold wherever we go, pearls
>   wherever we turn, and silver in the sky.[115]

Rather liken it to the Milky Way, where bright flowers have taken the place of glittering stars, clusters of vines the place of the Pleiades, and gleaming fruits the place of suns and moons. 16.2

So we stayed in this place, secluded from the world of people; for in this world there can be no peace save in the ascetic life, no escape from mankind except through seclusion and privacy. The most noble of people are those furthest from contact with mankind.

> My very separation from people saves me contamination
> whereas their proximity infects both mind and faith.
> Just as a line of poetry, if left on its own,
> cannot be affected by common faults.[116]

16.3 This pleasant sojourn would have led to my friend's complete recovery if the very devil in human form had not terrified us with the news of a plague. We reflected that all God's creatures are in His hands (glory and praise to Him). We kept nursing our soul's ills through an avoidance of disaster and misfortune, and yet calamities and griefs seemed to beset us wherever we went. We told ourselves that we had to flee from one of God's decrees to another, He being the One who tests His servants when He wishes for them a good outcome.

So we set out to return to Cairo after saying farewell to this beautiful spot. We knew that we could trust our friends and relatives who lived in the capital and that no jealous snoopers would be able to spread any false rumors there. We sat down in the train compartment next to some ministers, but, as it was nighttime, it was very dark and so we were able to hear their innermost secrets. As the train took us back to Cairo, we listened to their conversation. One of them was saying things neither contentious nor polished.

16.4 Minister of War By God, in the face of these worries and dangers all precautions are useless! I've been living on my nerves throughout the Sudanese campaign till it came to an end. Thank God I'm still safe and sound. I've spent the entire time in Europe, taking exercise and having a wonderfully relaxing time in Karlsbad. That aggravating newspaper reporter who kept asking me questions about things I knew nothing about was the only thing that bothered me while I was there.[117] But now, just when I've recovered from such dreadful perils, the plague has struck at a time when we can't leave the country or even get out of Alexandria where it's struck. If it weren't for this terrible judicial situation, we wouldn't find ourselves being shunted backwards and forwards between two towns like some weaver's shuttle. God is my witness that at this point I'd rather be in command of the army in the Sudan, riding to and fro along the ranks in the heat of battle, than be subjected to death by the plague in peacetime. At least in war, there is pride and glory to be won, not to mention decorations and booty, all of which lessens the impact of the dangerous situation. But what is there to make our situation with regard to this Shariah Court project easier to swallow? How can the risk of catching the plague be made even bearable? If there's any prestige to be gained, then it's the Foreign Minister who has got it all for himself while leaving us all empty-handed.

FOREIGN MINISTER By God Almighty, tell me, what's this 16.5
prestige I'm supposed to have acquired? All I know is that I've lost everything I've spent my entire life cultivating, namely the trust and affections of Muslims and their continuing favor towards me. Now they've started accusing me of interfering in their judicial affairs, something I was careful to avoid from the moment I took office. I could have avoided the entire situation if the Minister of Justice had treated me fairly. He could have taken the entire burden on his shoulders. Such is his piety, devoutness, probity, and asceticism that no Muslim would ever think of criticizing him.

MINISTER OF WAR If all you did was to stand up at the conclusion of your period in office and speak eloquently in the Egyptian parliament without being at a loss for something to say or faltering, then that alone would be enough to satisfy your quest for prestige during your earthly life.

FOREIGN MINISTER What kudos can you see in getting up to speak in front of the members of the Legislative Council?

MINISTER OF WAR I regard the art of oration as being a very 16.6
glorious and praiseworthy profession. People often associate it with war because of the perilous situations both involve. Even though

I've never had any experience of war myself, I've still gone through things which would turn your hair grey. When I was saying a few words in the general assembly about taxes, I got so completely distracted that, to this day, I don't know whether I kept to the point or not. As I left the building, I would have been thoroughly annoyed with myself if someone who specializes in the study of anecdotes from past eras had not provided some consolation by telling me a number of amusing tales about great orators. I'll tell you some of them now, and then you'll realize God's kindness to you in saving you from similar situations when you got up to make a speech and I felt so sorry for you.

16.7 When ʿAbdallāh ibn ʿĀmir ibn Karīz, a renowned homilist, faltered while standing in the minbar in Basra, he was upset. Ziyād ibn Abīhi who was standing behind him told him, "Do not worry, amir. If I put some of the ordinary folk up there first, they would be even worse off than you." When Friday came, ʿAbdallāh was late, and so Ziyād told the people that he was indisposed. One of the prominent tribal amirs was told to go up; when he reached the top, he was lost for words and said, "Praise be to God who feeds these folk," and then stood there in silence. They brought him down and sent up another prominent person. Once he was finally in place, he turned towards the people and spotted a bald head. "People," he said, "this bald-headed man has prevented me from speaking, so God curse his bald pate!" So they brought him down too and told Wāziʿ al-Yashkurī to go up and address the assembly. When he got up there and saw all the people, he said, "People, I was reluctant to come to the Friday prayer today, but my wife forced me to do so; I call you to witness that she is divorced three times." At that, Ziyād turned to ʿAbdallāh ibn ʿĀmir. "Do you see what I mean?" he said. "Now go up there and address the people."

16.8 Muṣʿab ibn Ḥayyān was giving a wedding sermon when he faltered. "Remember your dead; there is no God but He," he said on the spur of the moment. "May God hasten your death too," the bride's mother retorted. Similarly, when Marwān ibn al-Ḥakam faltered while delivering a sermon, he said: "O God, we praise You, seek refuge with You, and we offer You thanks."

And so, Minister, since you haven't encountered the same kind of problems as these prominent figures from Arab history who were masters of rhetoric and the spoken word, how can you deny that you've achieved a good deal of prestige and distinction. On the day you adopted your position on this matter, I can only imagine that the mummies of the Pharaohs, your ancestors, were quivering with delight. And even though their fame may have rested on getting people to drag huge stones around and erect artificial mountains, I'm sure they never imagined that, with someone like your eminent self in mind, they could surpass the Arabs in the rhetorical art delivered from the wooden portals of the minbar.

Foreign Minister Stop this sarcasm and let's be serious. What about what the Minister of Justice was saying?

Minister of Justice I'm amazed that the Shaykh Profes- 16.9
sor of al-Azhar has rejected the ideas I've put forward for this project and accused me of acting contrary to the Shariah. Everything I know about the subject I've learned from him; I studied with him and bear him no grudge. After all, the way he's behaving now is just like the way he behaved when we were students as a way of reprimanding us. It wasn't long before his anger and disapproval disappeared, and he was kind and sympathetic to us again. Every time I recall those days of my youth and the lessons I took with him, I long to be back there; and that takes my mind off his feelings towards me at the moment. Even so, I've done nothing unprecedented. I'll read out to you now the stipulations for the office of judge just as I've copied them directly from their books. Then you can decide whether or not I've contravened the Shariah as they claim I have:

"People eligible for the position of judge are those who are enti- 16.10
tled to testify as witnesses as it says in *al-Ḥawāshī al-Saʿdiyyah*; other qualifications for such people are adherence to Islam, intelligence, eloquence, freedom, non-blindness, and avoidance of slander.[118]

These are all conditions for the acceptability of his appointment and also of his jurisdiction thereafter."

No one denies that Court of Appeal judges fulfill these stipulations regarding the qualifications for judge. Who can claim that either of the two representative judges from that court is either a polytheist, insane, a slave, or blind, or anything else which would disqualify him from holding the office of judge? While they have insisted on accusing the two judges of immorality, our retort has come from the very same law books, namely that "the immoral person is still qualified to testify, so he is also qualified to be a judge. However, it should not be compulsory, and anyone who installs a judge in that way commits a sin. The *al-Qāʿidiyyah* chooses to restrict this point to a situation in which the appointer deems him to be truthful. So let this be memorized. [*Al-Durr*]."[119]

I am personally quite happy to accept this notion of sin, but why are they so opposed to the general idea? Why do they keep fussing when, if they turn the page in the very same volume, they'll find the following passage: "The second authority makes an exception for the immoral person who has both status and virtue. His testimony must be accepted." From the *Bazzāziyyah*, while in the *Nahr* we find "accordingly, he is not considered to be committing a crime if he appoints a person judge in such a condition."[120]

16.11 The people who keep arguing that the judges of the Court of Appeal are neither prestigious nor courteous object that the highest court in the land does not just pass judgments but also issues fatwas. They note that the mufti must be well versed in both the preferable and the acceptable, the weak and the strong, principles well known in the Ḥanafī school of law. These stipulations, they say, are not satisfied by the Court of Appeal judges, particularly since they're accusing them of depravity and backing up their statements with the following text: "The sinner will not be a good mufti because fatwas are religious matters and the sinner's word cannot be accepted on such matters," as Ibn Malak duly noted, amplified by

Al-ʿAynī, followed by a number of recent scholars, and specifically stipulated by the author of *Al-Majmaʿ*.

However, these people fail to recall that the author of *Al-Durr al-mukhtār* cites this phrase and then goes on to say: "Yes indeed, it is valid. In the *Kanz* there is an authoritative statement that offers an individual judgment on the relative nature of the fault involved.[121] There can be no disagreement about such a person's Islamic faith nor his intellect. Some scholars make alertness a criterion, but not freedom, being male, or ability to speak. Thus a speech-impaired person may issue a fatwa."

Now, thanks be to God, you are all aware that the judges of the Court of Appeal all prefer to be dumb. So how can their fatwas have no validity if such people are allowed to pronounce them?

The author of *Al-Durr* goes on to say: "The judge can issue a fatwa 16.12
even in a court of law, and it is still valid. In so doing, the judge in his role as mufti is exactly following the dictum of Abū Ḥanīfah, then Abū Yūsuf, then Muḥammad al-Shaybānī, then Zufar and al-Ḥasan ibn Ziyād who is the most authoritative and enlightened." Here ends the extract from *Al-Durr*.

It seems abundantly clear from what I've just read to you that, if these people are using such passages as those I have just read to you as criteria, then the Court of Appeal judges are fully qualified and no one can object. If they have authorized the judge to issue fatwas as a mufti, following the dictum of Abū Ḥanīfah without exception, then the criteria of "preferable and acceptable, weak and strong" have to be subsumed as well. Of all judges, I am inclined to believe that those of the Court of Appeal are the most cautious about committing errors. In avoiding mistakes, the most plausible method is to consult books on law. The Court of Appeal judges are so completely accustomed to basing their judgments on positive law that they go beyond the Ḥanafī school by itself and also consult works of the Malakī, Shāfiʿī, and Ḥanbalī schools too. And so, if they find themselves restricted to the Ḥanafī code in the Shariah Court, they'll be able to make use of their knowledge of the other schools and devote their attentions to mastering the Ḥanafī code.

16.13 But even apart from such considerations as these, what is the point of all this fuss? Not long ago, when they were training people who had no familiarity with the Shariah yet were to be appointed judge, they were quite happy to make use of the following phrase: "Evidence is required of a claimant; oaths are needed in a case of denial." They would regard that phrase as an all-encompassing rubric to justify the appointment and then excuse his ignorance of the Shariah by saying that the onus was on the mufti. If the mufti was learned, they said, one could overlook the fact that the judge was ignorant and didn't meet the criteria needed for his judicial position. In saying this, they apparently forgot that the late Ibrāhīm Pāshā appointed Shaykh al-ʿAbbāsī as mufti when that latter was still a student and was only seventeen. On that occasion, the excuse they gave was that the mufti's secretary was a scholar who was completely familiar with Ḥanafī legal practice and could draw up the fatwas; all the mufti himself had to do was put his seal on it. They can't deny that the two judges from the Court of Appeal—may God watch over them!—who have been delegated are certainly over seventeen years old and aren't the only ones who will be giving fatwas; indeed they will have with them three paragons of Shariah scholarship whose presence embellishes the bench of the Shariah Court. These luminaries can fulfill the same function with their Court of Appeal colleagues as the secretary did with Shaykh al-ʿAbbāsī. Then the two judges will be able to show their prowess in legal matters just as this great sage did in earlier times, becoming one of the most illustrious religious scholars, someone to be respected in his religion and celebrated by his countrymen.

16.14 Minister of War Blessed be the name of God the Opener, the Provider! Where have you acquired such learning and such an impressive array of arguments? By God, you've put me to shame. But where were these trenchant arguments on the day when we were arguing before the Legislative Council about this project?

Minister of Justice There's nothing particularly extraordinary about it. I simply went back to my studies with the Shaykh of al-Azhar. I conveyed it to you just as he did.

Minister of Finance God is my witness that it might just as well have been in Hebrew or Latin for all I understood of it. Here's the gist of what I know about this project: judges have a revered position, so much so that I looked on them as the world's greatest ascetics for the way in which they belittled money and were prepared to take a loss when they retired. I'm sure you'll be as amazed as I was when I tell you what it is that they lose. The judge's salary is 1,800 pounds a year; with nine years' service, he can make 16,200 pounds. Supposing that he stays in the service for six years more, he can save 27,000 pounds. Add to that a quarter of his salary to which he's entitled after this length of service (450 pounds a year) and assume that he'll convert it at the age of seventy-five, his share will be 6,750 pounds. Thus, in those six years, he'll collect a total of 33,750 pounds. If he uses that to buy land and invests it for ten years, he should get a similar amount in return. If he sells the land, he has almost one hundred thousand pounds which he can use to buy shares. You all know what profits can be made there; within a few years, he can have a million pounds. Tell me, by God, how can anyone who owns a million be so stingy when it comes to saying one simple word to the two nominated judges: "Admitted"?

ʿĪsā ibn Hishām said: At this point, the train reached Cairo Station. 16.15
I went home with the Pāshā and left him there. I went to see one of my friends on some business, but found him just on the point of going out. When I began to explain to him my reasons for coming to see him, he told me brusquely to go with him first to a Masonic meeting to attend a party there. I was forced to do as he asked. Eventually we reached the place and found a lot of people there. In the middle of the group was a circle of Court of Appeal judges who were discussing the project and their proposed secondment to the

Shariah Court. I listened to what they were talking about and heard one of them say:

First Judge How long are we going to put up with these Shariah Court people? Here they are slandering us and accusing us of apostasy at one moment and immorality at another; it's as if they've got some kind of monopoly on religion and can insert and extract whatever aspects of the law they feel like. As far as I know, Islam is unlike other religions, in that no one's allowed to proscribe other people or to withhold forgiveness from others. God's mercy is wide enough to encompass everything. Today they require those whom they are willing to accept to repent in a hurry, renew their adherence to Islam, put on a turban, grow a beard and not wear a gold watch or drink from a silver vessel. People like them are described in this verse:

> He forbids people to drink water from a silver container;
> but, if he acquires any silver, he consumes it.[122]

The knowledge which we have allows us to stand apart from their group, thank God. The blinkers have been removed from our eyes and so we can see things in sharper focus.

16.16 Second Judge What amazes me is that the people who keep calling us infidels and sinners, who refuse to accept our testimony and are claiming that, in making judgments, we are not using God's transmitted message, are the very same people who keep bothering us all the time with requests to make categorical decisions on judgments which they and their colleagues have already made, decisions based on the very same law that they're now using to call us infidels. In those cases they're very willing and grateful to accept our judgments!

Third Judge Don't forget too that talking about rights is one thing, but judicial authority is something else. They have introduced a number of new concepts into Islamic law where the concept of rights is not quantified. They have started making judgments on the basis of new criteria—probable and preferable, weak and strong, famous and obscure, statements based on a fatwa and others without such a basis, a disagreement between the Imam and the two people bringing the case, or even an inconsistency between the commentators and writers of the marginal notes. Heaven forbid that the Shariah should have to function amid such judicial chaos!

FOURTH JUDGE I hereby vouch to you, my revered colleagues, that I won't accept the nomination to the Shariah Court which the government has offered me. People are spreading all kinds of rumors about me and the other nominees to the position—that we never pray, that we go to nightclubs and sit around in cafés, and indulge in other kinds of debauchery, all of which suggest immoral conduct and ruin our reputation.

FIFTH JUDGE If I'm offered the job, I will certainly stipulate that no such rumors are to be circulated about me.

SIXTH JUDGE My friends, I'm going to tell you the truth: two judges from our court won't be able to do anything about reforming the Shariah Court. What are we supposed to do by way of reform when we already know that everything about it is in a hopeless mess and its administration is rampant with corruption. In my opinion the easiest way to reform the Shariah Court is not for us to move over but rather for the whole court to be incorporated into ours.

'Īsā ibn Hishām told us: It was so hot and crowded in the room that 16.17
I found it difficult to breathe. When they all left to go into this shrine for socializing, I took the opportunity to leave with one of my turbaned friends.[123] As we were walking along the road, he asked me whether I would like to spend some time that night at a shaykh's house. He reminded me that it was a long time since I had last seen him and that, in any case, he would have a group of shaykhs with him who would be sitting out in the open air in the courtyard of his home. I decided to accept his invitation in case I might hear what the group had to say to ease my anxieties about this project. Wherever I went, people seemed to have different ideas and viewpoints about it. When we reached the house, we found that it was

overflowing with shaykhs and religious scholars who were discussing the project at great length. I took my place with all the deference which the company demanded. One of the more prominent scholars was talking:

16.18 First Scholar God bless the Shaykh of al-Azhar! He's revived the practice of the Prophet and put an end to heresy! He has dispensed with all worldly considerations for the sake of his religion, and by so doing he's not sacrificed the life to come! No one can possibly censure his conduct. Any attempt to prod or intimidate him only reinforces his stance in defense of the Shariah. How wonderful that he's managed to shake off the dust of illusion. He's never flinched, even with the memory in mind of that infamous day when a hail of bullets fell on al-Azhar students with their notebooks and inkwells. Thank God, we're all united and rallying for his success. All of us support him, and God will support his servants as long as they in turn support their brothers. We're all a single hand, and the hand of God is with the community. Believers are like a buttressed building where one part strengthens another. As God Almighty says in the Qur'an: «If you help God, He will help you and plant your feet firmly.»[124] May God give the Shaykh a good reward on behalf of Islam. He's reinvigorated the practices of our pious ancestors that had become defunct. In his stance toward the Minister of Justice al-Manāstirlī he is behaving like Abū Ḥanīfah confronting the Abbasid Caliph, like al-ʿIzz ibn ʿAbd al-Salām with the Ayyūbid Sultan, and like Shaykh al-Mahdī al-ʿAbbāsī with ʿAbbās the First. Undoubtedly, the government won't be able to implement this project because they won't find any among us who's so attracted by the superficialities of this life that he's prepared to sell his life in the hereafter and accept the position of judge in this new court.

Second Scholar Well said, Sir! We are all with you! We'll stick together and help each other against the government, and then they'll be unable to carry on with their plan to fight the Shariah.

ʿĪsā ibn Hishām told us: At this point, a visitor came in; I think he was an important lawyer. He started looking around the company as though searching for something he had lost. When one of the scholars spotted him, he craned his neck and beckoned him over. The lawyer sat down beside him and whispered in his ear, but I could make it out: 16.19

Visitor I've brought the news you've been waiting for. I've confirmed that your name has been forwarded to the cabinet. You're being mentioned as one of the candidates for the post of judge, if you're not actually the first name on the list. Our friend is doing all he can to convince his colleagues to give you preference over the others.

Nominee Shaykh Do they still intend to nominate X and Y?

Visitor Yes, but there are a number of factors which will prevent them, God willing, from getting in our way. We hope you'll be the lucky one.

Nominee Shaykh (*now raising his voice, addressing the scholar who has been talking, and joining in the conversation*) God alone has the power and judgment! They say that one of the signs of the Day of Judgment is that the sun will rise in the West. To that I would add that another sign would be that, according to information which my friend has brought me, a Muslim judge has been nominated today to the cabinet to fill the post. The whole project is disgusting and will have a terrible effect on the Shariah. How it must soothe the devil's heart! 16.20

Shāfiʿī Scholar Yes indeed! They say that Jesus (peace be upon him) will only appear when all traces of the Shariah on earth have disappeared. Today this project is undoubtedly a sign of the appearance of the Anti-Christ before Jesus himself appears. Thank God nevertheless that they've got to appoint a judge from Egypt. Wouldn't it be possible for the government to find some way of seeing that all the major positions don't keep going just to Ḥanafīs? Isn't it enough that the salaries Ḥanafīs get are much higher than anyone else's, quite apart from the stipends they get from the endowments of Lady Zaynab and Rātib Pāshā.

Malakī Scholar I know of a venerable Shaykh who has spent nine years teaching Al-Bannānī's *Abridgment* of al-Saʿd's *Commentary* together with the *Account* of Al-Anbābī.[125] So far, he has been on half salary and, like so many of his colleagues, is still waiting for salaries to be raised so he'll receive the full amount. If the poor man were a Ḥanafī, his home would be full of bread to eat and he'd be able to sell the left-overs and keep the cash.

First Scholar All this world is just a game; the next world with God is better and more lasting. I make you all witnesses to the fact that I won't accept the nomination for the post of judge even if they offer it to me. I'm not comfortable with the ministers' assertion that "judicial supervision is over Egypt."

Nominee Shaykh How was it possible, Sir, for you to appoint the late Shaykh ʿAbd al-Raḥmān, and then let the late Ismāʿīl Pāshā state in the decree, which publicized his appointment on the basis of your nomination, that it was made "through the general authority invested in me"?

16.21 First Scholar I was actually ill that day and didn't attend the meeting. Furthermore, who would dare go against anything which Khedive Ismāʿīl wanted or even show any misgivings or signs of doubt about the things he did? He told us to select someone, and we did so for fear that something terrible might happen. We were acting in accordance with the Qur'anic text: «Do not give yourselves up to destruction.»[126] These days we don't get any instructions at all from the Khedive, so it's entirely up to us to uphold the Shariah; God forbid that we should ever willingly go against its tenets. After all, this world is just a vanishing shadow. How will we be able to look God in the face if we keep the things which our shaykhs have taught hidden inside us when there is nothing to stop us proclaiming them?

Nominee Shaykh They say the judge's salary will not be reduced; it'll stay at one hundred and fifty pounds. Fortunately, I don't need the salary they're offering for a post which disparages the very name of our religion, and I wouldn't accept it even if they tried to tempt me with mountains of gold. They say too in their analysis of the project that the decree authorizing the appointment of these judges will contain mention of this same phrase that Ismāʿīl Pāshā used, "through the general authority vested in me," and they may also add to that "Shariah authority as well." From the terminology of these two expressions, it's quite obvious that the Khedive has the right to make these appointments. However, the government is well aware that none of us will accept it. We've heard that the two judges to be appointed from the Court of Appeal are not content simply to leave their court and its positive law approach; they are offering their total repentance to God for their shortcomings. In that way the Shariah Court judge will be able to allow them to pass judgments.

First Scholar There must be at least a six-month period after their repentance before it's permissible for them to exercise canonical judgment. Surely you can appreciate that a drunkard can repent and God will forgive him. But when a judge repents, some time must go by so that his repentance can be shown to be genuine.

Nominee Shaykh In spite of all that, compliance remains 16.22
the major factor. God Almighty has said: «You who believe, obey God, the prophets, and those among you who are in command.»[127] All we can do is to guide people and proclaim the truth. «Let whosoever wishes be a believer, and whosoever does not, be an unbeliever»; «there is no compulsion in religion; the difference between sin and rectitude has been made clear»; «you do not guide those whom you love»; «whoever follows the right path, it is to his own benefit—whoever goes astray, it is to his own disadvantage»; «say, everyone acts in their own way.»[128] The analogy of adopting the lesser of two evils is well known; they're allowing one third to be destroyed in order to preserve the other two thirds. If we ignore them and have nothing to do with their project, how can we stop them bringing in an Indian judge?—perish the thought! After all,

the name Samīʿ Allāh Khān is still mentioned in our midst right up to today.

First Scholar My dear Sir, I can see that you're going in one door and out of another. Your statements are contradicting each other like "a need in Jacob's soul."[129]

Nominee Shaykh God forbid that my thoughts should seem to contradict what I've been saying; hypocrites cannot gain God's respect. I still stick to my original opinion in which I advised that the project be rejected and objections be raised to the imposition of any unqualified person in the domain of the Shariah. Every morning and evening, I repeat these verses to myself:

> Those who pass judgment without the Shariah are in error;
> their judgment is like that of Thamūd.
> They have thrust God's book behind their backs
> and publish judgments based on the Talmud.

16.23 ʿĪsā ibn Hishām told us: At this point the company broke up and left. The Nominee Shaykh got up and took the lawyer along with him. I heard the Shaykh talking as they were leaving: "Let's go and see our friend again. We'll ask him to help us again, and then I may be lucky enough to mount the hump of this judicial post. 'God gives to whoever he wishes without reckoning.'"[130]

Miṣbāḥ al-sharq 58, June 8, 1899

'Īsā ibn Hishām said: Once the Pāshā had recuperated his bodily strength and been cured of his illness, I congratulated him on his recovery. Reminding him that bodily health is the basis of man's happiness, I observed that, even if you offered a sick man all the riches in the world, money in plenty, and a lofty status, he would recoil like a lizard from water, like a man with an eye condition from bright sunlight, and like someone with stomach conditions from rich food. Someone who has a sore on their finger does not value the emerald ring as much as a grain of mustard seed. You may gather together all the might, power, and authority of a royal throne, but it will be of little value to someone with a crooked back or fractured skull. 17.1

> One who has a bitter taste in his mouth
> will still find fresh water bitter.[131]

Whenever I offered him more of this sensible advice, his reluctance to show any gratitude for the boon of good health only increased. I came to realize then that humans only recall periods of happiness when they are in trouble. When a human being is content, he forgets his worries; when he is healthy, he forgets about ill health, but he never forgets about good health when he's sick. He only realizes that his hand functions so well when it is struck by paralysis. Few indeed are the people who acknowledge their good fortune at the time or appreciate life's happiness until misfortune strikes. «When 17.2

some injury befalls man, he summons us to his side sitting or standing. When we have removed his injury, he passes on as though he had never summoned us to an injury that afflicted him.»[132]

As I was thus engaged, the Pāshā asked me why I was congratulating him on his recovery when he kept shifting from one problem to another:

> If I escape safely, I will not abide;
> but I have avoided one fate only to fall into another.[133]

The Pāshā now started asking me about the plague and its effects. I could tell that he was still behaving like everyone else, influenced by rumor and illusion; and that was in spite of the fact that he had experienced real pain during his life and savored the serenity of oblivion in the grave. That would explain his reasons for wanting to return to the grave when the onset of disasters increased the level of anxiety. Residing in the grave was not easier for him because of any courage he might possess; rather the cause was a weakness and inability to endure the agonies brought about by the vicissitudes of fate. People waste so much time in life worrying themselves about death:

> Fear of death led the People of the Cave to shelter there
> and taught Noah and his son how to construct boats.
> The spirits of Moses and Adam did not relish the experience,
> and both had been promised the Garden of Eden thereafter.[134]

17.3 I went on to tell him that these days the plague was a shadow of its former self, affecting only a handful of people. The dogged enemy has now disappeared. And I quoted for him the line of *rajaz* poetry:

> God has taken away the spear of the jinn
> and forever banished torture and criminality.[135]

17.4 Pāshā I've not found you to be someone who conceals the truth or falsifies things, so how on earth can you make such a claim?

The plague wreaks tremendous havoc in Egypt; it's enough to melt your very eyelids and split your heart in two. It's one of Egypt's endemic diseases, one that occurs each year with the changing seasons. Egyptians expect it every spring, so much so that they've given it the nickname "Season"; they say, for example, the "Season" has come when the plague appears. People become alarmed and start panicking. Their faculties dwindle, and they become utterly confused. It attacks and destroys, its course unhampered and unimpeded by any obstacle. It only abates when palaces are in ruins and graves have been filled. It turns children into orphans and women into widows; people are either mourning or being mourned, carrying someone to the grave or being carried themselves. One person will weep for his father, another will mourn his brother; one woman laments for her family, another for her husband. In my own time I heard about it from an old man who gave me the following account of the epidemic in the year 1205 [1791]:[136]

"The plague began in Rajab 1205, causing a huge panic among the 17.5
populace. It increased in intensity during the months of Rajab and Shaʿban. Countless people died—babies, young men, girls, slaves, Mamluks, soldiers, scouts, and amirs. The governors of twelve provinces died, among them Ismāʿīl Bey the Elder. It wiped out the marine contingent and Albanians living in Old Cairo, Būlāq, and Giza. So many people died that they used to dig pits in Giza near Abū Hurayrah's mosque and throw all the bodies into them; out of the amir's house would come five, six, and ten in a single funeral procession.

"People crowded into shops looking for things with which to prepare the dead for burial, and asking people to carry their coffins; but without success. So they fell to quarrelling and fighting each other about it. Death and everything connected with it were the only thing on people's minds. Everyone you met was either sick, dead, visiting or consoling someone, attending funerals, returning from a funeral service or a burial, busy with the preparation of a dead person or else weeping apprehensively for himself. In mosques and places of prayer, funeral services never ceased, and on each occasion the prayers were pronounced over four or five people at once. Only in rare cases did anyone who contracted the disease not die. The attack would appear quite insignificantly on the body. A man might be sitting somewhere, then he would suddenly shiver with cold and wrap himself up. If he ever came round, he would be delirious; otherwise he died the next day, if not that actual day itself.

"The plague continued to strike people down until the beginning of Ramadan, when the Āghā and Governor both died. Their two successors were appointed, and both died within three days, so others were appointed to succeed them as well. The legacy was passed on three times in seven days. An amir's house was locked up with a hundred and twenty people inside, and they all perished."

17.6 ʿĪSĀ The scene you've been describing sounds to me like one of the halting spots on the Day of Judgment, or one of the horrors of the Day of Resurrection which you yourself have witnessed.[137]

PĀSHĀ During the course of the plague, people's miseries were not confined to the epidemic itself. The schemes which the Europeans imposed on the rulers were even worse. They forced them to harass people with distressing regulations which, they claimed, would prevent the spread of the plague. So they separated people from one another, splitting up father and son, brother and brother, husband and wife. They tore down houses, burned clothes, and scattered incense, as though, in their ignorance, they imagined that these measures which only hurt people's feelings and thwarted their best interests would scatter the assembled jinn and break the tips of their spears. People went from one misery and grief to another, from one kind of destruction to another. In 1260 [1844], I saw with my own eyes things which would turn your hair grey. My brother recounted to me what he saw in 1228 [1813] while he was in the service of the late Muḥammad ʿAlī the Great, in which he said:

17.7 "On the tenth day of Rabiʿ al-Thani, Muḥammad ʿAlī, whose place is in heaven, ordered a quarantine to be put into effect in Giza, and decided to stay there himself. He had severe misgivings about the plague because a few cases had already occurred in Egypt. A French doctor and some Greek Christians had died of it, convinced that the quarantine was effective and would stop the plague. The Shariah judge who served as judge for the military ratified their statement and went along with their plan. It happened that one of the judge's followers in the court died, so he ordered his clothes to be burned and the place he lived in to be scrubbed and fumigated with various disinfectant vapors. The same thing was done to the vessels he had been using. They gave orders to the police to tell the public and stall owners to sweep, spray, and clean on every possible occasion and also to spread out their clothing. When they received written a message, they pierced the paper with knives and fumigated it before handing it over.

"On the day the Pāshā decided to impose quarantine on Giza, 17.8
he issued instructions that the people who lived there were to be told that anyone who had enough food for himself and his family for sixty days and who chose to stay could remain in the district. Otherwise he would have to leave and go to live where he wished. They were granted four hours' grace. The inhabitants of Giza were very alarmed; some left and others stayed. This was at harvest time, and the folk there owned pastures and had various forms of traffic with their neighbors in the village. Man's need of his home, family, dependents, and means of sustenance is well known. But, in spite of all that, they deprived these people of all these things, and even went so far as to block up cracks in walls and doors and stop the ferry boats running. The Pāshā meanwhile stayed in the Ezbekiyyah Palace and only met people in public on Fridays. On that day he went to Giza at dawn and entered the palace there. Two boats were posted, one on the Giza bank, and the other opposite it on the Old Cairo bank. When the town clerk or Muʿallim Ghālī sent a dispatch, the sender handed it to the designated receiver on the end of a javelin after fumigating the paper with wormwood, incense, and sulphur.[138] The other person received it from him on another javelin standing at a distance from them both, and then recrossed

the river. When he approached the other bank, the person waiting for him also took it from him on yet another javelin and immersed it in vinegar and fumigated it with the above-mentioned vapours. He then gave it to his Eminence the Pāshā by some other method. The Pāshā continued this practice for some days, and then travelled to al-Fayyūm. Later he came back and sent his Mamluks and those who he feared might die to Asyūt."[139]

17.9 ʿĪsā You need to know that in days gone by people didn't understand the true facts about the plague and the reasons why it spreads (in fact there are still people like them around today). Those very same precautions to which people were exposed with the goal of preventing its lethal infection are today the very things which protect us from violent epidemics, some of which you've just been describing for me. In your time people refused to acknowledge this type of protection and even ridiculed it.

Pāshā Tell me, by God, what's the connection between burning clothes and those stings which carry death; or between these vapors and plague fever? For the life of me I cannot understand, unless the aim is to placate the jinn's foul moods.

ʿĪsā You shouldn't forget that the common people's ignorance has meant that they were unaware of many facts. Very few people have specialized in science, and it has remained beyond the reach of other classes of society. However, when science began to spread and the facts which it could prove became evident, it began to show people things which they hadn't comprehended before and factors which had previously baffled them. In your time, people may well have believed that plague was the jinn pricking them with their spears and that there was nothing capable of staving off these invisible spears. But today, research has convinced them that the plague does indeed have armies which are invisible to the naked eye and a prick far worse than the kind caused by the tip of any sword or spear. However, with the aid of science, they have produced an instrument which magnifies minute objects and shows them up clearly. By using this instrument, they have discovered the facts about these armies, devised ways of guarding against them, and equipped themselves to rid people of the pain they cause.

PĀSHĀ How can careful precautions be of any use against predestined fate? 17.10

ʿĪSĀ "Some things you have remembered, but there are others that have escaped your notice."[140] Precaution is enjoined by the tenets of our revealed faith. The Prophet of God (peace and blessings be upon him) always fought between two pieces of chain mail in wartime. In the Qur'an, God Almighty says: «Prepare as much power for them as you are able.»[141] Today there's a whole variety of precautions one can take to ward off this unseen enemy. They call it the microbe, a tiny creature from the world of the atom. One can apply at least one of the jinn's attributes to it, namely the speed of its procreation and the broad scale of its onslaught in a very short space of time. There are two ways of protecting against it: using fumigants that dissolve its structure; and burning clothes and anything it has come into contact with as a means of stopping the spread of the infection.

PĀSHĀ You've provided me with a precise definition of the jinn's poisoned spears, one which I don't think anyone could have comprehended in the age in which I lived. Can we take a look at this remarkable instrument which can magnify tiny objects? Then I can increase my conviction by looking at the marvels of God's creatures.

ʿĪsā ibn Hishām said: So I took him to a chemical laboratory where I showed him a speck of water under a microscope. When he saw that it looked like a huge pool and noticed the thousands of thousands of creatures swimming around in it, he prostrated himself in reverence to the power of the Creator and in praise to the greatness of the Maker. For my part I praised God because the Pāshā was convinced by this clear proof and did not behave as a Hindu once did with a German scholar. When the latter showed the former a speck similar to this one and the creatures which it contained so as to convince him that drinking water is full of creatures which Hindus are 17.11

forbidden to kill and eat, the Hindu smashed his instrument because he sullenly persisted in his beliefs and refused to accept the truth.

The Pāshā was now convinced of what I had told him: science had defeated the plague's cohorts and destroyed its spears. But for that, people would be dying today in hundreds of thousands instead of in tens. Turning to me he asked:

17.12 PĀSHĀ No doubt the person who invented this instrument that can demonstrate so effectively the might and power of the Creator without recourse to an intermediary was a devout shaykh and learned doctor of the faith. We owe him our praise and gratitude for all time.

ʿĪSĀ IBN HISHĀM By God, His angels, and His books, I swear to you that, as was the case in your own time, our shaykhs know absolutely nothing about this instrument. As is their wont, they remain isolated from all these useful sciences and helpful inventions. None of them have seen this instrument, and most of them have never even heard of it. They would rather face bullet fire than submit to the necessity of taking precautions against these tiny microbes.[142] Their knowledge comes entirely from their termite-ridden books and their study groups where bugs, ants, lice, and fleas float around, and their grammatical examples in which the phrase "the fleas have eaten me" does the rounds.[143]

Miṣbāḥ al-sharq 59, June 15, 1899[144]

ʿĪsā ibn Hishām said: I was afraid that, if I left the Pāshā deep in reflection and a prisoner of his own anxieties, he might have a relapse and become ill again. A relapse after convalescence is the very worst thing that can happen with an illness. So I set about moving from one place to another, from garden to garden, as a way of putting a distance between him and his worries. Eventually we reached the Giza Palace and antiquities museum where tourists from all countries in the world can be seen. We saw a park with streams flowing through it as though it were heaven itself, and took in the sheer beauty of the palace itself, a building so staggeringly beautiful that it beggared description. We proceeded to explore it, seeking shade beneath its eaves. We found lions kept in private compartments and snakes locked up in bottles; tigers in separate quarters, baby ostriches in alcoves, jackals kept in domed buildings, and gazelles in tents. 18.1

When the Pāshā looked at the ground, neatly laid out and paved, he assumed that whole area was carpeted. He did not know what to do and was on the point of removing his shoes. I told him that it was just an ordinary path, not an upholstered carpet; mere stones and pebbles, not rugs and skins. He asked me who these gardens belong to, and how was it possible for animals to live there? He told me that he had never heard of wild lions being kept in girls' quarters before, nor of desert animals playing in secluded apartments. In reply I told him that the house belonged to Khedive Ismāʿīl. In 18.2

former times its chambers would often serve as the starting point on the path to the very moons in the sky; its stairs were stages on the way to lofty status. When the owner yelled "Servant," some people would be miserable, others happy. In fact, misery and generosity were both at his beck and call and responded quicker than the echo's rebound. Here decisions were made, rules were formulated, and orders cancelled and confirmed. The person who sought shelter in the shade of this wall was shunned by adverse fate. Necklaces of previous stones would mingle with scattered flowers and decorate silver streams. Here trinkets dropped from the bodies of beautiful girls were likened to fruit on tree branches. To the sound of lute and mandolin songstresses used to sing, and their songs would be answered by the cooing of turtle doves on the tree branches. But now it's been turned into a public garden, ground to be trodden by upper- and lower-class feet alike. The grounds are hired out, and the produce of the trees is bought and sold. The place resounds with the cries of vultures, the roars of lions, the howls of wolves, and the snarls of lynxes. All glory and esteem, all splendor, might, power, and authority have vanished. It has been truly spoken:

> In this house, in this place,
> on this throne, I saw that the king had fallen.[145]

18.3 I told the Pāshā about the former owner of the palace, the monarch of that age, also about the good fortune that he had initially enjoyed, the bad luck that beset him thereafter, and the great suffering he had endured in exile until his death:

> They enjoyed a small amount of pleasure and went away
> against their will; days of grace became that much worse.[146]

The Pāshā said to me, "I have recovered my endurance and now regard my own affairs as somewhat trivial. But allow me to weep over these ruins and contemplate the vicissitudes of time. Let me learn from one lesson after another and consider both beginning and end. At all events I thank God."

And with that he leaned his head against a rock in the shade of a tree and seemed to start talking to his ancient ancestor, invoking his tears at the doings of unjust fate. After a while, he became drowsy and fell asleep.

I left him asleep, trying to relieve his anxieties and hardships. 18.4
Moving to one side, I spotted two elegant and suave young men who both seemed quite amiable. In fact I already knew both of them; they were both Egyptians and adhered to the principles of the same school of law, but their political views and tastes differed. One of them had been educated in England, the other in France. As I approached them and offered my greetings, the conversation involved discussion of horse racing and pawning old clothing. One of them was saying, "That friend of yours has pawned all his lands and estates so that he can spend the money on horses and carriages. Someone else has sold all his wife's jewellery to buy himself saddles and bridles. They both keep boasting about their horses and carriages; it's as though the only sign of prestige left is to hear people saying what a wonderful horse someone had at the Gezīra race track."

"Forget about that," his colleague replied. "Let's hear what 18.5
everyone's talking about these days." He pointed to two turbaned men, both of whom I knew. I informed them that one of them was a merchant and the other a religious scholar. The two of them had removed their turbans and were sitting on the lush grass with a knife and melon in their hands. There were some chairs beside them, so we greeted them and sat down beside them. They were discussing current affairs:

MERCHANT What's today's news about the plague?

FRENCH-EDUCATED NATIONALIST Just look at this utter stupidity! See how the English are working their trickery and believing the futile lies and falsehoods of politicians. The plague is simply a trap which they're using to contain people's desires and aspirations. Surely you all realize that every time they want to trick and belittle Muslims, they simply bring in some germs from India with which to pester them and make them agitated. They then use it as an excuse for the way they insult us just to gratify their own feelings. They wanted to insult the al-Azhar mosque, so they used the epidemic as an excuse for firing bullets at it.[147] They've wanted to cancel the pilgrimage, so they've used the epidemic as an excuse for stopping it year after year. They wanted to mix canon law with positive law, but there they didn't succeed. Because of that, they were out for vengeance, so they've used this plague as a device to help them.

18.6 MERCHANT By God, what you're saying is quite right; it makes good sense. If that were not so, how come it keeps reappearing in Egypt time after time under British Occupation when for years we've never heard it mentioned except for some stories passed on from one generation to the next. You're well aware, of course, of the negative effect it has on trade with the outside world and commercial prosperity.

RELIGIOUS SCHOLAR «God has made an example of a town which was safe and peaceful. Its provisions came in abundance from every place; but its people denied the favours of God, and so he made them taste famine and fear for what they had done.»[148] You should realise that these troubles all stem from the way you have shown your contempt for religious scholars and their teachings. You show contempt for their status and keep ignoring the useful sciences concerning all things, preferring to rely instead on modern sciences which are harmful to both worldly life and religion and contrary to the basic principles of belief. Not only that, but now you've turned away and no longer ask us for our guidance in times of trouble. In so doing, you've gone against the words of God Himself: «Ask the people of the remembrance if you do not know.»[149] Can anyone other than religious scholars ward off such perils, remove all disasters, and confront calamities? If it weren't for our great Shaykh, the Shariah would have been abolished. Had he not mounted a steadfast defense on behalf of the faith and its law, they would have vanished without trace.

Merchant Yes indeed, what lofty ambition, what superb determination, what wonderful persistence, and what a splendid stand he took! Our religion's underpinnings have been restored and the Shariah law has retained its status. God is my witness that I spent many sleepless nights weeping and disconcerted. I was unable to enjoy the company of my family and dependents. Eventually I decided to take a risk and, with no desire for fanfare, signed my name to the telegram in which we complained about this dreadful calamity. Now I thank God that things have worked out well, and I've acquired some prestige. May He reward the Shaykh in every way possible on Islam's behalf! 18.7

Religious Scholar May God bless you and everyone who did the same. If only everyone respected the Shaykh as you do and recognised the qualities he has, especially the religious scholars themselves. The only time they say anything is when he does something they approve of, but then they start accusing him about his past conduct in office. They've started claiming that he's reckless and feels in no way bound by the rules of order in anything he does. He's supposed to have abandoned the principles of eligibility and merit, and brought forward many people who did not deserve such advancement. According to them, his methods involve favoritism, compliance, and graft. 18.8

French-Educated Nationalist God fight the English! Have you ever heard of anything like this happening in Tunis or Algeria? Do the French ever use the kind of ruses and deceits which the English employ here to get their own way? If only the Egyptians would appreciate these machinations and kept a closer eye on these ruses, they would not have been so adversely affected by English cunning, and the occupation forces would not be so firmly implanted in our country.

English-Educated Nationalist Heaven protect us against such sickly motives and caprices! Why is it that, every time some occurrence comes down from on high, there is an emergency of some kind, a weather event happens, or some other unforeseen 18.9

event takes place, you always talk in terms of British tricks and cunning? You have made the fates themselves subservient to British commands; as a result they can achieve their goals, big or small. If they did in fact possess the amazing power you attribute to them, they'd certainly not need to use any tricks or cunning. The fact is that the English are an uncomplicated and amazingly peaceful people; like everyone else, they need guidance in order to deal with things about which they know nothing. Things would go much better for you if you complied with their peaceful intentions and accepted them for the simple people they really are. Then you would be able to move forward and provide them with leadership as they aspire to initiate reforms, something from which we could all benefit. Far better that way than to call them arrogant forces of occupation and cunning tricksters every time they try to improve something that is wrong or put something faulty to rights. That only makes them think badly of you, and then any trust and cooperation between both sides is lost. They then have to devise projects which they have to think up for themselves as being in your best interests and force you to adopt and implement them. What they really need are some intelligent people from among you who realize their good intentions and can convince them that they are sincere in both word and deed. The English will then come to realise that there are no ulterior motives or influences to divert them from the truth and they'll come to trust each other. Then the English will begin to listen to their advice and act on their opinions. But now, whatever they do, all they see from your side is the very opposite.

18.10 The Shaykh of al-Azhar has held his post for some time and all he has done in that time is to comply and show leniency whether in his personal life or as part of his religious function. Now soldiers have attacked the noble al-Azhar with rifles and swords, the very Kaaba of Islamic learning. Rifles were aimed at men whose heads were filled with scholarship and whose very marrow was the book of God. Ink was mixed with blood. Then, lo and behold, the Shaykh's report exonerates the killer and the victim's blood is shed in vain;

and all to appease the people in power instead of venting his wrath on behalf of the weak:

> I am content and my killer is angry, so be amazed;
> the victim is happy but the killer is not.[150]

The Shaykh himself was at the meeting at which the Minister of Justice (a pupil of his) was talking about unifying the accounts of the endowments. He said that, if the Shariah was really as he had described it, then he would not act by it. The Shaykh simply swallowed the pill and said nothing; he said nothing to defend the religion as he was bound to do. He has been much too indulgent in the way he has handled the duties of his position, not bothering about the continuous incidents of fraud connected with the Department of Endowments and actually placating those committing these swindles in matters concerning both parties and his obligations to handle the monies properly. He has also been far too negligent about preserving the dignity of his office, to such an extent that he was prepared to overlook the way a lawyer wrote to him in an insulting and denigrating fashion, whereas a single word spoken to the Minister of Justice would be quite sufficient when it came to punishing anyone who shows the Shaykh such contempt. In summary he has been negligent in these and other similar matters. 18.11

The occupying power has been calling for a reform of the Shariah Court for ages and asking experts about ways of implementing such a proposal. They have been urging these experts to open the court's doors and let progress in. But, even though those experts were convinced of the need for reform, all the English have encountered has been obstruction and rejection. When they got tired of talking about it, they started opening the doors of reform with their own hands, relying entirely on their own knowledge and good intentions. But, before they could turn round, there was the Shaykh of al-Azhar standing up to defend Islam in complete contrast with his normal behavior. He started arguing, protesting, and expressing his opposition with a rashness that he's never shown before in any 18.12

number of other situations which were far more relevant to Islam than this court-reform project. He made his point at the Legislative Council and rejected the project in the name of Islam. However, the government is convinced that there's more in it than meets the eye; the Shaykh is governed by factors beyond the project per se or whether or not he agrees with it. So they've lost all confidence in his opinions and assumed that his aim is simply to frustrate the government and give people some gratification.

18.13 After all, if, before the project was presented to the Council, he'd said that he was looking into it and that he had certain things to point out which ran contrary to the Shariah, the government would have accepted his suggestion with alacrity and would have taken his advice and counsel. They would then have benefitted from his learning in the process of improving the project or might even have asked him to advise them in drawing up another project to incorporate the desired reforms. Let no one claim that the Shaykh didn't have an early opportunity to state his opinion on the subject. He's the Mufti of Egypt and, according to the requirements of his office, it's his duty to give the government guidance in any matter which has any relevance to the Shariah. If only he'd taken some of the time he spent composing his memorandum in going to see some members of the government and discussing it with them, they would have accepted his advice and none of this confusion and complication would have arisen.

18.14 No one should claim either that the Shaykh is slow when it comes to going to see members of the government. He often goes to visit them on trivial matters like the distribution of salaries and loaves of bread. He has even debased his position to the extent of going to see certain cabinet staff members and asking them to expedite documents concerning the raising of his own salary by ten pounds. The Shaykh is not offering the government advice in the way that he should. He's preferred for the project to linger in the Legislative Council, like some dogged adversary whose aim is to frustrate the government so he can then claim that it's deviating from the Shariah and turning from the true path of Islam.

As you're well aware, the ministers are all Muslims. The English are renowned for their respect for religions and their unwillingness to violate other people's beliefs in any way. It's quite inconceivable that they would insist on implementing the project if the Shaykh had given them some guiding counsel. Furthermore, anyone who claims that the occupying power has an ulterior motive in introducing this project—namely of reducing the Shariah's authority by joining its court to the secular courts—is talking rubbish. Their only motivation for saying so is their poor opinion of the British and an assumption of evil intent. To say that they exploit plague epidemics and use such disasters to serve their own purposes falls into the same category. This government is more prepared than anyone else to act in accordance with the dicta of Islam to show that it's adhering to the tenets of the Sharīʿa and not succumbing to the interests of foreigners. The English are most cooperative when it comes to listening to religious authorities; they implement their advice immediately so as to give people as much proof as possible of the fact that they're not trying to damage the religion of every country they occupy, because at this moment in time their own civilization has plucked from their hearts the spirit which their forebears had in the middle ages. There can be nothing more virtuous for a pious scholar than to give guidance to a people whose nature it is to respect religions. When they're sure that he has no ulterior motives, he can speak and they will act. He can prove his sincerity by serving the truth and providing reliable counsel. 18.15

Religious Scholar (*to the Merchant*) They have both made their point, haven't they? Young people today read so widely and can serve their country well by giving us such powerful arguments. 18.16

Merchant Leave mankind to its Creator. We ask God to preserve us all in safety and to grant us a happy outcome! Certainties are the worst possible intrusion into something which has no meaning.

French-Educated Nationalist How disappointing! How frustrating! What is this that I hear you saying? You two represent some of the most important segments of our population. Patriotism is a matter of faith. You and your peers should be complaining about the same things as we are. You need to make one principle the focus of your attentions and the fulcrum of your ideas and actions. Then you can join us in supporting that sublime word "homeland," something that no amount of prattling and eloquence can resist. Everything else is simply empty words. People have been tortured for love of their homeland as a matter of pride. Some of their stories are famous. Take for example the Roman who was taken prisoner by the Carthaginians. They sent him to Rome to arrange an exchange of prisoners, relying on his word of honor that he would return. When he arrived in Rome, he advised the Senate that it wasn't in their best interest to exchange prisoners, he being one of them. He then returned to Carthage, knowing full well the punishment which awaited him because of the sound advice he'd given his own governing body. Bodily torture was compensated by a spirit's delight.

18.17 Esteemed Shaykh, how about the Arab hero whose city in Azerbaijan was besieged by the Tartars; they had weakened it considerably and almost captured it. The Caliph Hishām ibn ʿAbd al-Malik sent Saʿīd al-Ḥarashī with a large troop of soldiers to relieve the beseiged city. The commander sent one of his companions ahead in secret to inform the people in the city that he was on his way and they were to wait patiently; he was afraid that he might not reach the city in time. The man left, but was captured by a group of Tartars. They interrogated him, but he told them nothing. They then tortured him, so he told them and made them believe him. The Tartars told him: "If you do as we ask, we'll release you." "What do you want me to do?" he asked. "You know your friends in the city," they said, "and they know you. When you arrive at the city walls, shout out that there is no help on the way and no one can save you. I've been sent as a spy." He told the Tatars that he'd do as they asked. Once he arrived at the walls, he stood where the people inside could hear him. "Do you know me?" he asked. They replied that they did. "Sa'īd al-Ḥarashī has reached such-and-such a place," he told them, "He has a thousand men with him. He orders you to stay steadfast and hold the city; he'll be with you either in the morning or evening." With that the people inside the city raised paeans of praise to Almighty God. The Tartars killed the man and abandoned their siege. When Sa'īd arrived, he found the city gates open and the people inside safe and sound. «May people learn to do likewise.»[151]

'Īsā ibn Hishām told us: The Pāshā had woken up by now and was shouting for me. So I hurried over to him in response to his call. 18.18

Miṣbāḥ al-sharq 63, July 13, 1899[152]

19.1 ʿĪsā ibn Hishām said: When the human eye becomes acquainted with a scenario that is manifestly shameful, the disturbance to that person's vision will lessen his evil intent. Both thought and vision will play a preventitive role. His soul will grow like a tree that bends. Habit will replace what is loathsome with what is kindly. Malicious heresy will now be seen as something permissible and good, approved by those familiar with it and rejected by those who are unaware.

> When man is familiar with something, he despises it,
> seeing in it neither bad nor good.
> He can find nothing to savor in a reconciled life
> nor in the taste of his own saliva.[153]

19.2 In such a context let me use the simile of a wretched woman dealing in sheep and camels in the dunes and depressions of the desert. All around her are raids and revenge missions, men seeking prisoners and spoils, fearsome warriors armed to the teeth—the grey of their swords stained with the red blood of victims. She meanwhile continues to cower on the hillside grazing her flocks. People then transport her from this fearful desert environment to the gleaming city. There they show her a Western dance party. She can see electric lights emitting brilliant beams on beautiful people, their faces gleaming like the sun on the moon's surface; lovely figures before which all others bow; cheeks whose very blush puts the rose to shame; bosoms revealing buxom breasts on which float pearl necklets; shoulders and necks exposed, as smooth as brows and peerless as crystal; lustrous wrists like date-clusters made of silver; hair like golden threads with jewels that glow like flame—as though the golden hair spread across the silvered brow were the very rays of the sun branching out across the vista of dawn.

Then she spots men of all ages—old, middle-aged, young, and 19.3
boys—strutting their way amid these beauties, bedecked in all their personal finery and relishing their fancy clothes. A young man acts like an aspiring student as he goes wherever beauty leads him. Standing in front of a beautiful woman, he bows like a tree branch, as though he were freeing a lovely cow from the protection of her father or a gazelle from beside her brother—plucking the girl from her lord and snatching the virgin maid from her family. As the melodies swell, the branches begin to sway; figures draw closer together and cheek touches cheek. Now hands are clasping waists and supporting backs. Feet are constrained as though in chains, and bodies are in turmoil like sandgrouse caught in a trap:

> He leans over her like a welt, pressing
> on her breast that appears in all its smoothness.[154]

Once the music comes to an end, they rush over to get a drink of 19.4
wine; the glasses toy with people's heads, and the entire blend plays with their minds. In a joust of hearts and glances passions now come together. The dancing recommences, people pirouetting to the scents of fragrant perfume, the sweet smell of flowers in a verdant meadow. Sweat now drops from the necks of beauties like rows of pearls scattered among them from rare and costly necklaces. Seeing all this, the Bedouin woman covers her face with her shawl, her nerves in a tangle in sheer embarassment at what she has witnesed. She runs away as fast as she can, needing to go back to her home in the depths of the valley at the desert crossroads. Bearing in mind what she has now seen, she sees her home as a safe haven, offering more seclusion and protection, more modesty and less shame.

19.5 On the other hand, if one of these Western lovelies was transported to an Egyptian women's gathering in a household where guards and chamberlains did the rounds, passageways were blocked, and doors were kept locked—the kind of place where a eunuch held sway with all the force of a soldier and gruffness of a policeman—she might hear the kind of chatter the women indulged in, usually restricted to talk about men. With their young daughters sitting in their laps and their sons in front of them, they would resort to the lewdest and foulest of verbiage. And, if a male relative should happen to be brought in by the eunuch, this Western women would watch as he yelled at them all to cover themselves up; and they would all duly wrap their faces in the hems of their garments and leave just a slit so they could see. Confronted with such behavior, the Western woman would be just as alarmed as the Arab woman was. In this dance hall she would consider herself to be behaving immaculately and showing the best of manners and the most seemly modesty.

19.6 This is the way things were between the Pāshā and me. Every time I showed him something with which he had not been familiar in his own lifetime and had never encountered before, he would object and turn away, showing me as he did so things that I had not previously noticed and making me aware of the evil underpinnings that lurk beneath the surface cover of habit and are shrouded by the veil of familiarity and acceptance. Once he had recovered from his period of illness, I would take him to a number of places that would delight the heart and to assemblies that would distract his attention from the succession of troubles and anxieties that had beset him, not to mention the good times in the past and the miseries of the present. I found that he would talk to me about everything; for each idea that I thought of to provide a serene setting he would produce some issue or concern. Eventually our routine involved an invitation to a wedding. Accepting the offer we hastened to the location after sunset and discovered two policemen guarding the door. They kept shouting and shoving people away to stop them getting inside. The Pāshā pulled me aside.

PĀSHĀ Wait a minute, my friend! Are you sure you haven't gone the wrong way and mistaken the intention here? Unless, that is, you plan to go to the police station with me again and through the entire court system. 19.7

'ĪSĀ IBN HISHĀM No, there'll be no police and no courts! This is the door of the house where the wedding is being held. The two policemen have been hired to keep out people who haven't been invited. They don't want crowds of noisy people. These days important people have adopted this practice.

PĀSHĀ It's a very bad one! In our day wedding celebrations were specifically intended for everyone to attend who wished to do so. Poor and indigent people were never excluded. People would spread out tablecloths for them; they would eat and drink and then watch the amazing games that were put on for the occasion: horse races, displays of horsemanship, wrestling, and sword drills. They would listen to people chanting the Qur'an and singing lovely Sufi liturgies. The respect that everyone felt for important people, their lofty status, and their august demeanor were all sufficient to prevent any likelihood of rowdiness and noise. Every person had their own internal monitor. Has high rank and status now sunk that low with you? Does the man of influence no longer appreciate his own status, so he is neither capable of maintaining his prestige nor of behaving in a way that will earn him respect? It seems that now the common people have lost their sense of reverence and no longer behave with any kind of modesty. As a result they despise the status of influential people, and that requires them to have policemen when they organize weddings just as they need soldiers and chamberlains in government departments.

'Īsā ibn Hishām said: Good heavens, I told myself, now we're finding things to grumble about even at weddings. Once we passed 19.8

through the front door, we noticed four young flashily dressed men. The Pāshā stopped me and asked:

Pāshā Incredible! Is it a custom among you now for four men to be married at one ceremony? Do they all have a single father, or is it that they're foreigners? How have they managed to earn those medals on their chests when they're so young?

'Īsā ibn Hishām Those four men are not the bridegrooms, nor are the things on their chests medals. They're simply friends of the groom who are helping welcome the guests and seating them in their places. They're wearing those pendants on their chests to let people know what their function is.

Pāshā Then how come they didn't bother to welcome us and take us to our seats?

'Īsā ibn Hishām They don't know us, and our clothes didn't impress them enough.

Pāshā That's a bad custom too. In my day the head of the household and his relatives stood by the door to welcome visitors. That way no one was ignored and left to his own devices as we have been here.

19.9 'Īsā ibn Hishām The person putting on this wedding ceremony has an excuse. The majority of such people want to put on stupid displays and demonstrate how famous they really are. So they send invitations to government ministers, important social figures, and religious scholars—people they don't know and have never even met. As a result they have to get people like these complete strangers to welcome guests. I know a merchant who spent half of his entire fortune on a wedding so he could invite senior ministers to attend. Afterwards his own ledgers were divided into two parts: one contained the various types of merchandise that he had; the other was a list of ministers who'd attended the wedding.

19.10 'Īsā ibn Hishām said: The Pāshā stared at the ground shaking his head in regret. We made our way into the courtyard. It was brightly illuminated and decked with floral arrangements; there were flags, woven carpets, and colorful drapes. We took a seat where we found an empty space; it was right alongside one of my more fashionable friends. The Pāshā started looking around him.

Pāshā Tell me, who are those people lounging on couches in the center? They're behaving like Persian monarchs in some royal enclave. How come they're doing nothing, neither talking nor moving? Are they too some kind of new-fangled embellishment to weddings, or are they instead a final touch to the decoration in these social soirées?

Suave Friend (*entering the conversation*) «Question them if they are able to speak.»[155]

'Īsā ibn Hishām They're provincial governors and local authority figures.

Pāshā So do these governors of yours now exert their authority at soirées and wedding celebrations and use them as a means of showing how important and powerful they are? Do they don the same garments of arrogance and pride as they do in government chambers as a necessary way to inspire people's awe and respect? I can clearly recall the effort I used to put into such things when I was part of the government. How I used to hate it! I cannot imagine a life more wretched than one in which you're constantly having to put on airs and act a part. In our times when a government official finished his period in office and returned to the evening gatherings in his own home, he greeted everyone with a smile, unknitted his frowning brow, and showed a joyful countenance. People are the foes of government and its governors. When the grind of government, the arrogance of power, and the adoption of phony airs are all combined into one, it makes no sense to greet everyone with the same gloomy visage, no matter what the occasion or the venue. That's why in the past you would notice people going to see government officials in their own homes, for the simple reason that people were afraid of dealing with the officials' august demeanor when they were in their seat of authority. Once the official was far removed 19.11

from his government offices, they could place more faith in his indulgent side and calm their fears by observing his more relaxed and open expression.

19.12 SUAVE FRIEND Yes indeed, these days things are the exact opposite of what you've been describing. Now government officials are in their homes, princes are at other people's houses, and the populace is in their offices. You can see any one of them in his government office where he is supposed to hold sway, but he's a picture of apprehension, caution, and diminished authority, all because he's afraid he's being watched and spied on even if it's by someone who's his junior in rank. He's just like a student in the classroom or taking an exam. If you were to visit such an official—and few people do so—you'd discover that he'd welcome you with open arms, respond nicely to your requests, apologize profusely, and send you away content, just the way you have been describing the rulers in your day inside their own homes and those of others. Once he casts off the chains of office and is free to return to people's normal assemblies and clubs, his open smile becomes a frown and his welcome turns into avoidance; what was easy is now difficult, and what was pliable now becomes defiant. May God bolster you! Today our government officials have such a low opinion of themselves and are so scared to reveal their sentiments in public that they make every effort to cover it all up with boasts and displays of pride. They fabricate phony illusions of conceit and arrogance and go to enormous lengths to enhance their dignity in the way they walk and make their image that much more daunting in the way they sit. Some of them even take lessons in front of a mirror on bodily movements that they like and spend some time perfecting them. They can all be compared with the illustrious Egyptian who was renowned for his stupidity. He was in love with a girl in a wine seller's shop. He went in and tried to hide from the other people sitting there so that his status and honor would not be affected. As he sat down, he leaned his back against a pillar in the middle of the store, assuming that he was out of sight, or like the proverbial ostrich: when it hears a lion roar or is startled by the hunter's voice, it puts its head under its wing and assumes that its entire body is now hidden.

In actual fact, however, they've sunk low instead of aspiring to be seen on high; what they hoped to keep concealed is now revealed. The absurd lengths to which they've gone in their pride and arrogance has now led people to investigate quite how much power they really have and what are the precise limits of their authority. That's allowing people to make comparisons between these realities and the efforts they make to claim an illusory greatness and to use their positions to frighten people. Now everything that was concealed is out in the open, and their decline is in direct proportion to the exaggerated assertion of prestige that they claimed for themselves. But, seeking God's forgiveness, I wonder what's the matter with these people alongside us; they keep fidgeting as though they're sitting on a bed of thorns. 19.13

PĀSHĀ You're right. They're acting just as you describe. Who are they and what's their problem?

FRIEND They're a group of Egyptian notables and merchants. They still base their behavior on vestiges left from the previous regime, namely of ingratiating themselves with members of the government and boasting about the very least connection they may have with such people. You can watch as they leap up with every new arrival. If they realize that the person is a senior official or a member of the government, they make a big display of awe and respect, all with the goal of boasting to their colleagues whenever they happen to receive a greeting of some kind from such people. On the other hand, if they discover that the person is not important, they sit down again. Just look at the way they're straining their necks and staring at the group of government officials in case someone who didn't greet them when they entered happens to look in their direction.

ʿĪsā ibn Hishām said: This subtle criticism made us look in their direction and pick up bits of their conversation. Our Friend was 19.14

truly amazing in the way he was helping us relieve our problems and calm our worries. Every time someone came in, and some of the company stood up to greet them, we dissolved in laughter. The Pāshā himself could not avoid smiling and hid his face in a handkerchief. The owner of the residence swept past us, and we heard someone ask:

An Attendee How much do you think the sponsor of the wedding has spent on this celebration?

Another Attendee He's spent all the money he has. When it's over, he'll be completely penniless.

Still Another Attendee God alone possesses the power and strength! Whatever made him go to such absurd lengths. When this is all over, how's he going to earn enough to support his household?

Yet Another Attendee May God protect you from the veils of hypocrisy and ill repute! We've heard that a truly lavish amount is being spent on this wedding. The only reason is so that he can boast to his colleagues.

19.15 ʿĪsā ibn Hishām said: No sooner had the host of the wedding celebration looked in their direction than the conversations ceased. They all stood up ready to greet him and pay him some attention. However he ignored them, preferring to pay attention to a group of young men who were cackling and joking as they conversed about women and other young men. "We're totally ignoring X's daughter and Y's son," they were saying, "and we don't even want to hear about them."

We looked round just in time to hear voices raised in yet another group; they were yelling and screaming about court cases, laws, and decrees. We discovered that they were a group of judges and lawyers. While we were listening to them, a cluster of religious scholars came rushing out of the inner parts of the house, ignoring everything going on around them and leaving the meal service behind. They were carrying some empty plates and leftovers with them.

Pāshā Who are these people rushing away? 19.16

ʿĪsā ibn Hishām They're a group of religious scholars.

Pāshā Has some disaster befallen our faith which requires them to leave in such a hurry?

Friend It's not that. What usually happens is that when they've eaten as much food as they want, they leave, reciting the Qur'anic injunction «Once you have eaten, then scatter» as they do so.[156] They justify their hasty departure after they've eaten by saying that it's inappropriate for them to sit in a company where there's to be entertainment and singing, which is considered loathsome.

Pāshā That's an admirable thing that they are doing! After all, they are the preservers of our faith and the living example for all Muslims.

Friend No, it's not like that. It's simply that they're worried about indigestion because of the wide variety of food with which they've stuffed their stomachs. It has nothing to do with a disapproval of singing or steering clear of gatherings like this. A few nights ago I saw with my own eyes a religious scholar in a Coptic house where a wedding was being celebrated. He stayed there till well past midnight, going in and out of the dining rooms behind a minister, eating, drinking, and listening to the singing. Scholars like him cling to the fringes of their faith in accordance with their personal likes and dislikes. They'll make a personal judgment as to what they consider forbidden, what one is allowed to hear in one place, and what's to be declared abhorrent in another. 19.17

Pāshā What's the truth about this issue. Is it permissible for us to stay here and listen to the singing?

ʿĪsā ibn Hishām said: No sooner had I started to explain the doctrine on this topic than the evening prayer was called. We all stood up to fulfil the obligation before returning to the topic. 19.18

Miṣbāḥ al-sharq 64, July 20, 1899[157]

20.1 ʿĪsā ibn Hishām said: Once we had come back to the wedding, regathering after performing the evening prayer, we returned to the topic of singing and whether it is permitted in Islam or not:

ʿĪsā ibn Hishām You should realize that the enjoyment of singing is something innate, deeply rooted in the makeup of all animals. They will become fond of it, relax to it, and be invigorated by it. When untamed wild animals hear music, they calm down, get used to it, and lose their more violent traits. Their natures are softened, their movements become less frenzied, their voices soften, and they can often be tethered. Take the elephant for instance, the biggest of all animals. When it hears a voice singing or melodious speech, its huge body starts shaking with pleasure even in the face of fire—just like a ringdove on a branch. When a camel, the animal with the hardiest disposition, is exhausted by a long journey and is expiring from thirst, the camel driver will sing to it. That makes it forget all its afflictions and takes its mind off the thought of water wells, even though it may be the animal's fifth or even tenth day without water. It'll then resume the journey with renewed energy.

20.2 People have often observed how the earth's reptiles leave valley depths and mountain passes and congregate in great hordes to follow armies on the march. A naturalist scholar who was investigating the reasons why these creatures behaved this way determined that they were attracted by the sound of music at the head of the column and felt compelled to leave their habitats and follow the army. There's also a well-known tale about a philosopher musician who was standing on a promontory by the seashore. He wanted to get to the far shore, but couldn't find anything to take him there. It occurred to him to start singing. All of a sudden a dolphin came ploughing through the sea towards him. As he sang, it kept coming closer until it was alongside the shore and stopped to listen. The philosopher realized that he had charmed it with his singing. Once he was certain of that, he had no qualms about climbing on its back and through the magic of singing using it as a willing vessel to take him wherever he wished. Another story tells how Ibrāhīm ibn al-Mahdī was able to control wild beasts through his singing for which he was renowned. This then is the situation regarding the effect that songs have on animals, and all that in spite of their weak powers of comprehension and their crude sensitivities. How much greater then will be the effect on mankind, which represents the highest level of animal life, possessing the most perfect disposition and distingushed by the greatest powers of comprehension, the power of speech, the purest essences, and the gentlest spirit of all?

Singing has always been something completely natural and most closely associated with the emotions. A group of philosophers has defined singing as the process of affecting the heart by subtle control of the voice and by use of the vocal chords in a manner that is soothing to the ear. Others have defined it as the stimulation of the souls of people who are endowed with higher faculties and serene temperaments. It's a force which can buttress the powerful effect of speech in influencing the listener. The ancients regarded it as a general language medium for all people to understand in spite of their linguistic differences. In their opinion, the student of philosophy needed a thorough grasp of the art of music in addition to mathematics. The two great philosophers, Pythagoras and Hermes, declared that the science of musical arrangement is universally applicable, and so they gave it the name *harmonia* which means "order," "arrangement," and from which was derived "singing." They all agree that, when it comes to instilling in man various 20.3

qualities and virtues and aspiring to the acme of perfection, nothing in the world can rival the effect of music. Anyone who isn't affected by it must, in their view, have some defect in his nature. Singing was implanted in man from the moment of his creation within nature's confines and his first bawling moments on earth. Nothing else can afford him rest.

20.4 In fact, the way in which singing moves people more than the spoken word is analogous to the superiority of eloquent poetry in its original language to unrhyming translation into another language. There are many events in history that demonstrate the powerful effect of singing. One story tells how the people of Switzerland used to condemn to death anyone who sang a particular tune when soldiers used to come down from the mountain peaks to enroll in the army. This song was one that shepherds used to sing in the mountains, and it would always provoke feelings of intense nostalgia for home in the soldiers' minds. They would lay down their arms and make their way back to their home pastures. A similar story tells about a revolt in Sparta which flared up and could not be quelled until singing had its usual effect on the instigators. When they heard the singing, all they could do was to shout for joy instead of in rancor. Yet another story tells of Abū Naṣr al-Fārābī and Sayf al-Dawlah ibn Ḥamdān. The philosopher began by making the ruler's council laugh, and then he made them cry. Afterwards he put them all to sleep and departed. He made use of the effects of singing for a number of useful purposes.

20.5 It is rare to find any belief system in any part of the world that doesn't use recitation, chanting, and singing in its liturgies. That is because of the way music invigorates man's soul and nourishes the spirit. A Sufi shaykh recalls from one of his forebears—God be pleased with them!—that, when they went into seclusion, if one of them was unable to complete the entire period, he would go outside, listen to some singing, and then return invigorated. You'll not be able to locate a single people, whether in the desert or urban society, primitive or civilized, and possessing armed forces, that doesn't make use of music as a weapon in wartime. It is used to confront danger, handle what fate decrees, and deal with the perilous situations that ensue. Roman orators used to compete with each other to make their voices sound more melodious when they were making speeches and to maintain a tuneful pitch so that the words would have a greater effect on people. One of the more famous orators used to make use of a musician while he was speaking. If he happened to go off pitch, the musician could notify him by using one of his instruments and bring him back to the original pitch. And in our own era the latest concern people have shown with the art of singing is that the government of Germany has decided that singing will be one of the basic subjects in schools beginning at the earliest stages when pupils are learning the alphabet and continuing until they finish studying philosophy.

This then is what research can tell us about singing. If we look 20.6
at it from a legal perspective, we discover that there is nothing reprehensible or hateful about it. Just take for example what is reported concerning the Prophet (peace and blessings be upon him). He heard women singing at a wedding feast and didn't stop them. Once, when he arrived back from a raid, some women of the Anṣār[158] came up to him with lutes and tambourines, singing in rhythm to the words:

> The full moon has risen over us,
> from the folds of departure.
> We should show our thanks
> as long as one still prays to God.[159]

He didn't stop them singing. Our pious forebears and Caliphs regularly listened to singing and attended musical sessions, and neither category denied themselves the pleasure nor proscribed it for other people. Consider the case of ʿUmar ibn al-Khaṭṭāb, who was well known for his rigid conformity in religious matters. When he heard singing, he did not disapprove. The following story is told on the authority of his most devoted follower, Aslam, who recounts how ʿUmar walked by as ʿĀṣim and he were singing. "ʿUmar stopped and asked us to sing it again," Aslam says, "so we repeated it. 'Tell us, Commander of the Faithful,' we asked him when we'd finished, 'which one of us is the better singer?' 'You're like al-ʿIbādī's two asses,' he replied. 'When he was asked which of his two asses was worse, he replied: "This one, then that one!"' 'Am I the first of the two?' I asked. 'No,' the Commander of the Faithful replied, 'you're the second.'" And in spite of ʿAbdallāh ibn Jaʿfar's close association and friendship with the Prophet of God, he's famous for frequently sitting down to listen to singing and enjoying it.

20.7 FRIEND That's a wonderful explanation and description, although you have gone into more detail than seems necessary; we could have made do with noting that God—may His greatness be exalted—out of His great virtue and beneficence assigned to every sense of mankind its own pleasure. For the eye, the pleasure of observing comes from the symmetry of visible objects and the arrangement of their components, namely beauty; for the tongue, the pleasure of tasting in the blending of food, which is sweetness; for the nose, the pleasure of sniffing a pleasant odor, which is perfume; for the hand, the pleasure of touch in the proportions of the parts of what is touched, which is smoothness; and for the ear, the pleasure of hearing in the harmony of the voice and the pulses of its rhythm, which is singing. It's almost as though those who would either forbid singing or declare it objectionable have it in mind to place a barrier between people and the enjoyment of a blessing that God himself has ordained.

PĀSHĀ Yes indeed, my friend has certainly expatiated at some length. However he's also engaged his noble soul so as to provide me with the lucid understanding, clear expression, and cogent evidence that I've needed. The issues are now firmly implanted in my mind, and there's no room for doubt or fanciful notions. Now that I'm old, for me he's been serving the same kind of role as a teacher who would draw on a slate when I was very young.

ʿĪsā ibn Hishām said: No sooner had we finished our discussion than the singers mounted their dais and took their seats. The Pāshā noticed something about them which he drew to my attention: 20.8

Pāshā How is it that these singers aren't behaving in the serious and dignified way that they're supposed to, at least if we bear in mind the nobility and status of the art as you've just been describing it? One of them is spitting and blowing his nose left and right, while another is guffawing and making jokes to the people sitting to listen to him. A third is yelling for coffee at the top of his voice, and still another is standing on the dais in sandals right in front of everybody. They're all of an age when they seem to have little energy or get minimal pleasure out of their art. It's as though they've been dragged into forced labor against their will, so they approach the task with gloomy expressions and sagging spirits.

ʿĪsā ibn Hishām People now look down on singing and regard its practice as something reprehensible and blameworthy. Singers themselves despise it too and disparage their noble art. They've become disheartened and don't bother about adopting the lofty standards and exalted learning that are associated with it.

ʿĪsā ibn Hishām said: While we were talking, four people made their way back and forth through the rows of listeners looking for the wedding host. Once they found him, they pulled him away. He rushed out after them, wiping the sweat from his brow as he did so and adjusting his clothing. When we looked in the direction where he had gone, we saw that he was coming back, his face beaming with pleasure and pride. He started pushing people in the chest to make way for the people entering behind him. They turned out to be a group of foreigners, men and women. Once they had all come inside, they made their way to the harem. The Pāshā turned to me in utter amazement: 20.9

Pāshā Who are these foreigners? Do you suppose the wedding host plans to put on some European entertainments for the attendees?

Friend No. This is a group of European tourists who attend Eastern celebrations to see what goes on. What usually happens now is that some dragomen obtain letters of invitation to a wedding, and they sell them for a very high price to tourists, who get the impression that this is an oriental custom. When they arrive at the wedding celebration, the owner gives them a lavish welcome, assigns them places of honor, and neglects everyone else of any repute who's at the reception. Once he's esorted the women into the harem, he makes sure to give the foreigners the best seats and devotes all his attention to them until it's time for them to leave. He then escorts them back to the door and bids them a fond farewell. All this happens even though he neither knows them nor they him. The foreign women often bring a camera with them and take a picture behind the harem screen showing what the women are doing during a wedding celebration. The wedding host happily accepts whatever the foreigners choose to do because he's convinced that their visit will enhance his status and increase people's respect for him.

Pāshā If this is now a custom at weddings, then it's a very bad one!

20.10 ʿĪsā ibn Hishām said: We now heard the sound of music outside, and the groom's procession came in. The singers fell silent, and noise filled the entire place. People who had been seated stood up, and others stood on chairs. The groom entered with a group of his friends, and they stood in the center. One of them now mounted the singers' dais and started his speech:

"Tonight is a time when paeans of joy rise over pulpits of delight, and kinsfolk of happiness and new moons rise upward from these heavens that are hearts and the earth that is the soul; a time when stars of good luck rise from the horizon of the eyes, and clouds of grief and downpouring rains of anxiety are swept out of our sight.

"I may be no gallant cavalier in this arena, riding to win the stakes of the wager; nor am I one to unsheathe swords of lectures and speeches with the edges of spears and the javelins of letters; not for me either the backs of the lean to ride in expounding eloquence, nor to swim in the seas of poetry and prose with every *kāmil* and *wāfir*, to withdraw anything in the garments of Saḥbān,[160] or to arm myself with the twin fortresses of concepts and eloquence when both entrenchment and advance are impossible. And yet I know that the groom is a man of learning and initiative; he possesses a firm foothold in the field of education, a love for his homeland, and a devotion towards his brothers. I am also aware of what is known about this gleaming sun who tonight is marrying the full moon in all its glory, the lovely gazelle well protected in the women's quarters, mistress in a house of prestige and learning, one honored then and now. I can also see all the kind, friendly expressions and the delighted looks on the faces of the people present. It is all this that has encouraged me to stand up in this cramped space amidst the surging sea of this wedding feast. I now beg you all to turn a blind eye to my shortcomings and excuse my gaffes. I ask you all to join me in raising your glasses to the groom's health: may he live in health and happiness, prosperity, and joy; may he enjoy marital bliss and produce many sons, so long as wood pigeons coo in garden meadows. Amen, Amen!"[161]

'Īsā ibn Hishām said: As we listened to this speech, we could barely suppress our laughter as one phrase followed another. I listened to two people standing beside me: 20.11

FIRST How eloquent he is! What a wonderful speech. Every Egyptian should be proud of him.

SECOND Do you really imagine that this young man produced such eloquence?

FIRST Then where did he get it from?

SECOND He obviously got it from some composition books.

FIRST We don't get such eloquent discourse from reading books like that.

SECOND You're right! We've never read anything like that in books from the past. But I've often observed this particular orator reading from more recent tomes. Maybe he prepared this speech based on the section "examples of eloquence" by an author named al-Mawrī in a book entitled *Keys as Openings to Thought, Selected from Prose Extracts Wrought.*

FIRST That must be it. It has to be from there.

20.12 ʿĪsā ibn Hishām said: Once they had taken the groom to the bride's harem, the host came back and invited everyone to get up and accompany him. We followed his lead. After he had asked the senior person present to open the ceremonies and he had done so, we entered a room where food and drink was served. This was no conquest such as al-Muʿtaṣim at the Battle of Amorium, or Muḥammad the Conqueror at Constantinople. People crowded around like the chaste receiving gifts and devout going to prayer; they were standing close to the tables like sufferers from drought who have just found lush pasture. The Pāshā was on the point of going back.

PĀSHĀ Good grief, what an insult! Have things with the wedding host now reached the point that he makes people go into the scullery to eat, and on the run at that?

FRIEND It's not the scullery. This is a place designated for eating and drinking. People can choose the things that suit their fancy and satisfy their tastes. They call it a "buffet."

20.13 ʿĪsā ibn Hishām said: The Pāshā watched as the crowding got worse. Feet were cramped, shoulders clashed, heads collided, hands competed, and voices were raised and got louder. One person was grabbing a bite to eat from every plate and a glass of wine from every bottle, while someone else was holding a glass in one hand and a piece of turkey in the other while at the same time chewing on a piece of lamb and asking the waiter to bring him some fish and other things as well. The waiter did not offer to fill the glasses, so the man simply put a whole bottle under his armpit and grabbed a glass. Still another person was sweeping things up and cracking jokes, while his companion stood there stuttering and cackling. Some people were trading compliments while others were complaining and grousing.

Pāshā I've now learned things about people that I didn't know before and seen things I've never seen in my life. I can only vouch for the fact that in my opinion this place is more horrifying to me than anything I've ever witnessed in war or on the battlefield.

ʿĪsā ibn Hishām said: The crowd and crush kept getting worse. No one could turn either to left or right without finding a glass of wine or a slice of meat either beside him or on his clothing. Eventually stomachs were filled, eyes turned red, necks began to droop, and people began to stare. Passions were roused, hearts abandoned all inner secrets, and the covers came off every kind of vice. While one person vomited words, another did the same with food. There was no food or drink left on the tables, so people began shouting to the wedding host to bring more drink. When he asked the servants, they told him that all they had left was a single case of wine which had just been requested in the harem. Even when the eunuch had cursed and sworn at them, they could not stop it going there. Hearing that, the wedding host apologized to everyone and clapped his hands to show that the dining room was now closed. People now went back to their seats. As they left the room, everyone was swaying and leaning on their neighbors. I spotted two friends who were so completely drunk that they started arguing by the door. One of them slapped the other, which made him trip and fall to the ground, reciting these lines as he did so: 20.14

I have drunk wine till my friends ask: 20.15
"Won't you come round after your foolish behavior?"
Till the only place to lay my head
is the dusty earth.
And till the buffet is shut in my face,
and I encounter contempt from my friends.[162]

I watched as the other one, puffed up with pride and strutting his way out, turned his head and stumbled his way through this line:

> I have drunk wine till I imagined
> I was Abū Qābūs or ʿAbd al-Madān.[163]

20.16 Once everyone had sat down to listen to the music, the Friend spoke to the Pāshā:

FRIEND Just look at the group of government officials and princes now. Before they were sitting motionless like idols, but now everything's changed and they're moving from one spot to another.

PĀSHĀ You're right. I can see them looking up into the sky and making a lot of gestures. It looks as though they're praying for some disaster to be averted or some wish to be granted.

FRIEND The men are all drunk, and so are the women. Windows have been opened and gleaming suns are now shining bright. Flirtatious threads have been dispatched to ensnare heartstrings below. You can see the oldest man looking up at the windows, raising his eyebrows, waving his hand, toying with his mustache, unwrapping and folding his handkerchief, then putting it to his eyelids so as to use his fake tears to entice the woman above. Down below everyone is utterly convinced that he's managed to win over the hearts of the beauties above with his handsome mien; he's plucked at their heartstrings with his suave appearance, and attracted their attention with his magical glances and subtle gestures. And just look up at the women above us, showing their faces and flashing their jewelry. One of them is waving with her fan, while another is flirting with her rosette; still another is toying with her cigarette while her sister is brandishing her glass like a bow. Then take a look at the way the singer is looking up at the windows as he sings about passion's complaints and the fiery heat of love. Notice the way eunuchs are going up and down with requests from the women for particular songs that fit the mood of love and serve their purpose. Having now witnessed all this, Pāshā, pray tell me if there can any longer exist any virtue on the earth's surface?

'Īsā ibn Hishām said: The Pāshā blushed scarlet in sheer embarrassment. Signs of fury began to show on his face, especially when the singer finished and a comedian of some kind started telling dirty stories and using the foulest possible language. The women kept laughing and asking for more, while the men below them were shouting and guffawing. The Pāshā made to leave, saying: 20.17

PĀSHĀ I've had more than enough grief here. It's high time we left. I can never find any pleasure in such a disgusting place.

'Īsā ibn Hishām said: We left behind him. Once outside we found people cursing and punching each other. The wedding host was asking for police assistance. All joy now turned to sorrow, and songs of celebration were replaced by lamentations. The police arrived to put an end to the fights, and people found themselves on the way to the courts. Thus end all joyous occasions. 20.18

Miṣbāḥ al-sharq 68, August 17, 1899

21.1 ʿĪsā ibn Hishām said: So the Pāshā and I spent some time in seclusion. We both relished the privacy it provided and were quite content to persevere with it. Like philosophers we lived in complete contentment and satisfaction, and enjoyed the feeling of release which came with being apart from the world and all its wrongs, avoiding all the tribulations that it forces us to endure. Now that we had seen some of the things people did, had heard and remembered some of the words they used, and had suffered discomfort from keeping company with them, it became second nature for us to live apart from them. Whether the matter was serious or in jest, it was rare for there to be no implications and no reproof involved. If you make a request, they attack you; if you come to terms with them, they oppose you; if you cooperate with them, they are hostile; if you make an agreement with them, they trick you; if you associate with them, you are not safe from attack; if you mix with them, you will find no lack of falsehood; and, if you demand your rights, how can your requests be heard by the deaf?

21.2 Then too bad for you if you go to the venues where judges are to be found! If you go to their gaming and sporting clubs, your harvest from this effort will be everything that is repulsive, loathsome, and annoying. When you go in, you will be happy and at ease; when you leave, you will be disgusted and appalled. In both situations, their way of life represents the very depth of sin and combines all conceivable faults and defects. It is the origin of all trickery and the source of all harm.

Had the Gemini experienced what I have,
they would not rise at all for fear of being tricked.[164]

So the Pāshā and I continued to live in seclusion. We broached all kinds of topics and moved from one subject to another. Sometimes in our readings I waded through the waves of the sea with him; at other times we traversed desert mirages together. We would see someone burning his boats so that he could induce his squadrons to hurtle headlong into the very face of death. We heard the cameleteer-poet in the desert wastes spurring on his camel and rhapsodizing about his beloved. His humble infatuation could not prevent him from boasting about the might of his noble colleagues or lead him to forget the mention of his passion when slaughter and death were in the air. And so he would mix boasting with love poetry and address his lady from the depths of the desert:

Hail to thee, Salmā! Respond to our greetings! 21.3
If you give water to noble people, then do so for us!
If you call the leader of noble men
to great and noble deeds one day, then call upon us!
If one day some objective spurs us to a noble deed,
then in our number it will meet both leaders and runners-up.
No chieftain of ours ever perishes
without our producing a young chieftain from among us.
On the day of battle, we place little value on our lives;
should we bargain for safety, then we raise the price.
With our white hair and our pots simmering,
we use our wealth to remedy the deeds done by our hands.
I am from a tribe whose chieftains were killed
by the cries of heroes asking: "Where are the defenders?"
When warriors in armour swerve to avoid being hit
by sword-tips, we grasp them with our hands.[165]

21.4 Beneath him you would see the camel relishing its own domain and yearning for a resting place. How it yearns, how it groans! He would hear its complaint as it pricked up its ears to listen to his conversation, responded to the echo of his voice with its bellowing, and delighted him in his passion with its replies. With a moan and sigh he would recite:

A phantom vision has visited and spurred me on.
Has a similar spectre visited this camel?
Perhaps sleep showed it the way in which it tugs
at the top of the acacia and lotus trees in al-ʿAqīq
and its grazing ground in dark green shade, as though
it were to reveal canopied ladies.
In longing they have recited psalmody sent down to them
in which patience is never permitted,
and sung an ode of animal poetry; in their passion
they have imbued it with every kind of speech.[166]

21.5 Then we would turn our attention to descriptions of famous battles and conflicts. Blood would be cascading in the valleys and lives ebbed away as the blood flowed from dying bodies. Death would stand there gathering up heads and collecting precious souls. Cavaliers would walk haughtily among the ranks piercing every gaping wound with their spear. Then they would recite the following verses to describe its effects and depth:

I stabbed Ibn ʿAbd al-Qays with a vengeful, penetrating thrust;
but for the spattered blood, the very wound would illumine it.
I have given my hand free rein, opening its gash still further;
whoever stands on this side of it can glimpse what lies
beyond.
It matters not to me that the wounds may repulse
nursing women's eyes, for I have lauded its dreadful effect.[167]

21.6 Up would flare the flames of war. The fiery heat would not abate till women were widowed and children orphaned. Money was plundered; booty and precious trinkets became stolen loot. Cities were rendered desolate, castles derelict and in ruins. Within them war remained dominant for the feeblest of pretexts. The weak were triumphant for reasons they did not even consider. War has caused dynasties to change and authority patterns to be altered. Thrones have been toppled and kingdoms have fallen even when their regime was well founded and their prestige extended far and wide. Their power may well have reached the heights and lasted for a long time. But, just when no one could conceive of the possibility of its collapse and decline, Fate descended and executed its decree. With that, the whole episode happened in the twinkling of an eye, when a commander committed an error and led an army one step forward or backward. However far its shadow stretches, every dominion is ephemeral and its reach is eventually limited.

Later I took him to visit the circle of a learned preacher whose forceful explanations attracted our attention. He managed to coax our minds with his clear proofs and captivate our hearts with his unrestrained tongue. His topic was the baseness and ignominy of wealth: "O you people, I esteem this world of yours less than that of a dog's bone in a leper's hand." He would also say: "The ability to choose between eschewing the world altogether and using it to enrich oneself is like having the choice between being ruler or ruled: 21.7

> Whoever is happy never to see things that distress him
> should not acquire anything he is afraid to lose."[168]

He would also say: "A pleasant life is one full of riches. Rich people are content because their wealth means that they don't have to rely on other people. Thus the richest people are the least in need of other people. That is why Almighty God is the richest of all!

> Wealth of spirit does not spare you the need to stave off want;
> should it increase, that same wealth turns into poverty."[169]

He also talked about character traits: "Generosity is honor's sentinel, reason is the filter of the foolish, and forgiveness is the best 21.8

justification for victory. To seek advice is the source of guidance, and to abandon one's desires is the finest wealth of all. Many a mind has been the prisoner of an amir's whim. Part of the road to success involves remembering one's experiences. Anyone with pliant wood has thick branches; anyone who uses gentle words must earn affection. Discord is the destroyer of reason." He then stated: "In this world mankind is a target for a struggle between fates, a helpless prey with misfortune hurtling headlong in its direction. In every gulp of liquid and mouthful of food there is something to choke him. No man receives a single act of kindness without losing another; no one is afforded a day in his life without losing another from his appointed time of death. We are all the fates' helpers; our lives are merely a signpost for death. How can we expect to be immortal? Day and night have never elevated anything without immediately rushing to destroy what they have built and to break up what they have gathered together."

21.9 He goes on: "The liar is as far removed from virtue as one can be and the hypocrite is even worse. The latter lies in his actions whereas the former merely lies in what he says—and actions are more definite than words. The self-satisfied person is worse than both of them. For, while the first two can see their own shortcomings and are prepared to conceal them, the self-satisfied person is blind to his faults and will even regard them as virtues and flaunt them." He continues: "I am always amazed at the way misers accelerate the very poverty they are trying to avoid. By so doing, they lose the things they want and live like poor men in this world while still being called to account like the rich in the next. I am equally surprised by the arrogant man who yesterday was just a sperm and tomorrow will be a corpse; by the person who forgets about death when he can see people dying all around him." He notes: "Never complain to anyone; if they are your enemies, they will gloat, and if they are your friends, they will feel sad. It is not a good idea either to delight one's enemies or sadden one's friends:

Do not complain to people, you will make them gloat, 21.10
like a wounded man complaining to eagles and vultures."[170]

He says: "The weakness is, in fact, twofold: firstly that of inadequacy when the thing was attainable, and the second is an eager, yet futile search for it once it has disappeared. The best kind of scholar is one who regards the ignorant person as a baby deserving sympathy rather than anger. As a result, he will excuse him when he makes an error but will never forgive himself for hesitating to give him guidance." He goes on to recite:

Religion involves being just to all peoples.
And what religion exists for the denier of truth when compelled?
Man cannot control his heart when it imparts good,
even though he be in command of a huge army.[171]

He finished his homily with the following prayer: "O God, protect me from the outrages of trustworthy people and the tricks that friends play."

At this point I turned away with the Pāshā in order to exam- 21.11
ine the traces of people obliterated by time and toyed with by the vicious hands of history. They had assumed that no one else could ever match their achievements, but destiny brought others to overrun them and left them as an object lesson for those who came after. However, these younger people had learned no lessons from their forebears; they were behaving in exactly the same way and were similarly deluded. «There came to them news as a warning, sound advice, yet it was of no avail.»[172]

Later I accompanied the Pāshā as we went to listen to talks given in literary circles and to joke with some close friends. We read enough of their pleasant inclinations and subtle anecdotes to brighten the gloom and clear anxiety's rust from our minds:

Words seemingly vested with the ability to make you drunk; 21.12
anyone memorizing a verse never regains consciousness.

They are eloquent and hearten whoever lends an ear;
a cure for the disease of cowardice and anxiety.
When a singer chants them to a coward,
he will face the fates without fear or terror.
If a thirsty man quotes them to rocks,
they will gush with sweet, clear water.[173]

21.13 In this way, I led the Pāshā from one book to another, and from one chapter to the next. With him I would pluck the most priceless gems from the bowers of pages, pick the choicest buds from fragrant texts, and choose pearls of literature from volumes. Then one day he told me:

Pāshā My greatest regret today is that I wasted so much of my life on totally useless and unprofitable diversions and amusements. If only I had had the foresight from my younger days to limit my aspirations to leading a life like this, and had concentrated on getting some benefit from learning, happy and content rather than jealous and envied. I could have read books, then moved on to confer with scholars, hold discussions with men of letters, and consort with men of virtue. Only God knows, every time I remember the things they used to tell me about learned societies and literary circles in the days of my period in office, how much I regret what I missed. I took no notice of such people and thought that the members of those circles were people of leisure, mere lazy idlers who sat down to study their books and journals, just as women do to their spinning and crochet. Now at the end of my days I can thank God who has revealed the truth to me. I can appreciate the extent of this blessing which has revived my love of life and made its difficulties easier to bear. Now that you know the help that this is to me, I don't imagine you will refuse to pursue this commendable course in my company. You can take me to literary circles, erudite communities, and scholars' clubs. I'll be that much more grateful for this favor than wasting time going to parks and wedding receptions. Such things have only increased my anxieties and left my nerves shattered.

ʿĪsā ibn Hishām My dear Amir (may God keep all misfortunes away from you), you shouldn't place any confidence in circles like these. Time has enveloped and buried them. No one alive today has any experience of them or displays the slightest interest. 21.14

Pāshā How can that be? I keep on hearing you talk about the large number of schools, the progress of sciences, the number of students, the ease of access to books, the abundance of printing presses, and the freedom to publish. If we compare all that to previous times, books were difficult to get hold of; not only that, but it was impossible to copy them because their owners were so miserly. It was as though they were the secret contents of treasure chests; an owner could be just as proud of having such-and-such a tome in his library as a victorious general would at having his enemy's weapons in his armory. In fact, even ignorant people, the kind who wouldn't get any benefit from books or understand their significance, would regard their acquisition as the ultimate form of luxury item and decoration they could boast about—as if they were sapphires and gems. Anyone who wanted to benefit from reading them couldn't do so unless he had enough wealth to either copy or purchase them. So it shouldn't come as a surprise that every Egyptian today should have a book to read; each one of them should be quite used to listening to talks and discussing things with other people. Learned circles and literary clubs would be proud to have such people as members. How can this happen, when the benefits of reading that you have let me savor during this short period have made me forget all other pleasures that the world has to offer?

ʿĪsā ibn Hishām It's perfectly true that in recent years sciences have indeed spread, the number of students has increased, printing presses have increased in number, and people can easily get hold of books. But in fact, few of us show any interest in buying and reading them. As a result, there's no market, and business is bad. The people who could benefit the most by reading books ignore them. Those who used to buy them as decoration now detest them because they are in such wide circulation and have become quite 21.15

common. Today everyone is caught up in a movement which is neither Eastern nor Western; they are all involved in each other's business. By way of destiny they are content with everyday occurrences, and so their learned circles and gatherings have become defunct, sources of knowledge have diminished, and literary springs have run dry. Instead they devote all their attention in their gatherings to reading newspapers and their ephemeral daily reports. How can they establish for themselves a place in a learned circle when they never stay in one place and are always moving around. You see them coming and going, traveling here, there, and everywhere. The one place where they spend the most time sitting down is in vehicles: steamboats, tramcars, horse carriages, and bicycles. Affluent people spend months of the year traveling abroad and wandering through Western lands and distant locations.

21.16 For them learning consists solely in the student's studying various types of science in school at an age when he's not yet reached maturity in either intelligence or comprehension, then memorizing it all like a gramophone recording and repeating it like a parrot. If the student puts all this scattered information that he has memorized together when he takes an exam and is lucky to leave with a degree under his arm, he'll then proceed to wash his hands of all that information and the burdens and problems it brings, and discard it all like so much tattered clothing. He'll abandon it like someone who offers his family brackish water and dry food. After finding a job and taking a post, he becomes yet another working man rather than a scholar who appreciates learning and its practitioners and loves literature and its works. If one of them has a God-given capacity for reading, it only goes as far as books that cover the principles relevant to their position. Scholarly and literary works are now considered something out of the ordinary and tedious. You'll find that, if any of these people can read a single page of a book, he finishes up with sweat pouring from his brow and feeling utterly exhausted, angry, and bored. He tosses the book aside like someone gratefully shedding a heavy load he has been carrying.

This inability to put ideas together in their comprehension of books and their sense of boredom has now infected their ability to converse. The only things that they're prepared to listen to are disconnected and fragmentary, or else brief and in extracts. For them the most bothersome things about gatherings are lengthy research essays, complex conversations, or elaborate stories. 21.17

Pāshā My friend, you're clearly exaggerating. I cannot conceive that this era can be devoid of the kind of literary circles that existed in our times. Whether we are talking about a desert or civilized culture, they constitute one of the requirements of society. For us they were a necessity, something without which life was lacking something; so much so that we noticed that amirs and important people who may have had no knowledge of sciences and literature would always include an illustrious religious scholar, an eloquent poet, a well-read sage, an amusing storyteller, a witty raconteur, or an experienced bard in their circle, people whose task it would be to entertain people and refresh their spirits after a hard day's work. And all this was in spite of the fact that books were scarce and scholarship was not easy to come by. So what's the matter with you people today?

ʿĪsā ibn Hishām I would include our important men and amirs in everything that I've already said. Foreigners have provided them with all kinds of ornamental devices, fancy goods, and other forms of entertainment. For example, you can find an important person carrying a stick that emits an electric beam. He will reckon that much more useful than all the people who offer enlightening ideas to people who need to be informed. 21.18

You have just reminded me of something I'd forgotten: I need to show you some of today's gatherings so that you can get an idea about the difference between the ones in existence today and the ones in your own time. Then you'll be able to judge for yourself quite how much my account has been exaggerated.

Miṣbāḥ al-sharq 69, August 24, 1899[174]

22.1 ʿĪsā ibn Hishām said: I now chose some contemporary clubs and public meeting places of various sorts to fulfil my pledge and let the Pāshā find out for himself what went on there, whether obvious to the eye or beneath the surface. I decided to take him to four separate meeting places where we would encounter people with different ideas and inclinations.[175] We would start by visiting those distinguished gentlemen, the Islamic religious scholars, those lights of our religion, luminaries of our faith, stars of spiritual guidance, and scourgers of apostasy. As upholders of truth and sincerity, they guide all those who wander from the path and renounce the faith. They call mankind to the knowledge of their Creator. That way the Pāshā would learn about the contents of their lectures and the goals of their conversations. Next we would pay a visit to a meeting of notables and merchants, glorious ornaments of cities, supporters of civilized society, upholders of industry and commerce, seats of truth and reliability, havens of resolve and poise, conveyors of wealth to states and kingdoms, modes of success in the preparation of ways and means. By listening to their talk the Pāshā could assess the true extent of their circumstances.

22.2 Then we would attend a session involving civil servants and government employees, people involved in the passage of laws and celebrated by pens and dossiers. Through them affairs are put on a straight path; on them depends the right functioning of the people's welfare. From them emanates the gleam of justice, and with their literary erudition cultural clubs find themselves adorned. They are indeed veritable mines of decency and integrity, sources of probity and honor. The Pāshā could thus learn about them and probe their depths. Finally we would attend a meeting of royal princes and other members of the ruling class, lords of territories, leaders of thought, controllers of peoples, masters of both sword and pen, dispensers of beneficence and gifts, possessors of prestige and honor, people associated with command and leadership, glorious and proud. By visiting their palaces the Pāshā could assess their state of affairs.

We began by heading for a meeting where all the most unique 22.3
and highly respected scholars used to gather with their students, a group of virtuous people with whom I had an acquaintance and remained in touch. We asked permission to join them, and they welcomed us. After greeting them we sat down. We found them involved in a conversation which was far removed from what we were seeking and bragging about things that neither quenched our thirst nor made for profitable listening. Having abandoned their chairs, they were all reclining on cushions; in front of them were snuffboxes and braziers instead of penholders and inkwells. They now went back to the conversation they were engaged in before we came in. Here is a summary:

First Shaykh My dear Sir, you are quite wrong to claim 22.4
that these days, ownership of land and dykes is better than that of buildings and houses. I've tried both as sources of income and have found that the returns from buildings are more profitable, especially if they are in a pleasant district, the site is good, and the householders are Europeans who have smaller families than Muslims and thus exert less pressure and weight on the building's structure. They don't bang, grind, pound, bake, wash, or take a lot of baths; nor do they welcome strangers and guests in their homes or fill the house with butlers and servants. All this refutes your previous assertion that buildings disintegrate quickly.

Second Shaykh My good Sir, as the saying goes, "For everything you know, there are several things you don't know."[176]

You're making a hasty judgment on this matter. What about fires, earthquakes, storms, and other disasters?

First Skaykh But when it comes to land, what about worms, damp, flooding, and inundation?

Second Skaykh I'll grant you that land can be affected by some of the things you've mentioned and identified. However, its value is permanent, and one can expect a loss one year to be compensated for by the following year. A building on the other hand can be destroyed by any natural calamity, something that can happen suddenly and catch you unawares. You suffer huge loss, and the only benefit you can get thereafter is by rebuilding it. That's why I've decided to sell my house here and buy the acreage next to the lands I already own. Then all the land'll be mine.

First Skaykh «You've your beliefs, and I've mine.»[177] My view remains unaltered, and I'm not going to change my mind.

22.5 Third Skaykh Commercial profits are better than either of these other two. They can be kept out of sight and free of unwanted interference. They're veritably encircled by prosperity and growth all the time. Which of you has ever made as much from lands and buildings as the late Shaykh X (may God have mercy on all people)?

Second Skaykh You're right. Commerce is just the way you describe it. If only there weren't so much effort and trouble involved. It takes up time which should really be devoted to study and involvement in scholarship.

Third Skaykh The late Shaykh—God have mercy on him!—was a merchant of great importance. That didn't stop him from achieving high office and ascending the ladder of scholarship. He helped students with his classes, his confirmations, his explanations, and commentaries. Pupils of his now adorn study circles and are an object of pride in learned gatherings.

Fourth Skaykh (*sighing regretfully*)

When the eyes of happiness look at you,
go to sleep; for all anxieties offer protection.[178]

Fifth Skaykh In situations like this, I think it's safer and more reliable to deposit cash and paper with a really good, trustworthy merchant one can rely on. He'll act on one's behalf in commerce, invest it, and double the profits. In that way one gets the whole thing without using brain power or tiring oneself out. 22.6

Sixth Skaykh I've heard Y Pāshā say that these days the best profits come from buying company shares. That's why he's restricting his involvement to that sector and is hardly bothering with anything else. What's your view on these shares? Are people allowed to deal in them or is it forbidden?

Seventh Shaykh The issue is controversial, and there's a lot of discussion on the subject. For my part, I know of no safer place to store my gold than the chest which I keep in my own possession; then it's under my own eyes and control. Speaking of Y Pāshā, do any of you have news about his daughter's marriage to Z's son?

Sixth Skaykh Yes, I've heard that their engagement has been arranged.

Seventh Shaykh When's the marriage ceremony?

Sixth Skaykh My dear fellow, don't expect to get presents from wedding ceremonies any longer. I've heard that a group of important and influential men have given two of our number who hold high offices exclusive rights to perform marriage ceremonies because they want to show off and enhance their reputation. Nobody else will gain anything even though they need such largesse much more than those two do. The only weddings left will be those whose gifts aren't worth anything.

Fifth Skaykh Duly noted. Have you all received invitations to A's wedding? 22.7

Everyone We all acknowledge receipt of the invitation.

Seventh Shaykh Yes, I must postpone my trip to the country till after the wedding banquet.

Fifth Skaykh That's a good idea. Courtesy demands that.

Third Skaykh If B Pāshā hadn't invited me to dinner that same night, I'd be there with you. I've heard from the Pāshā's carriage driver that he has an old stallion which he doesn't need. My own carriage driver's told me that it's of similar stature and coloring to my own stallion. Maybe I can buy it from the Pāshā—God bless him!—for a reasonable sum. But let's hope that this time he doesn't have anyone at his meeting like that fool who spoiled our gathering with his contentiousness. God thwart him, he was arguing with us about whether people were allowed to wear gold jewellery as ornaments. As his basis was citing the fact that one of our fellow religious scholars was wearing a gold watch without taking into consideration the fact that schools of law differ on this point. If the scholar he was citing were someone guided by the light of genuine scholarship, then fools like this man would have no way of arguing with us.

22.8 First Skaykh You can say whatever you like about these times when tarboosh wearers have the absolute effrontery to discuss, argue, disagree, and compete with turbaned shaykhs about their area of scholarship. Long gone are the good old days when scholarship and exalted religious scholars held a position of power and esteem. People used to follow their injunctions and keep quiet during their meetings. They would seek our favor—only to be expected in view of the reverence, respect, and honor that were our due. It was as if each one of them had the text of the following two noble hadith inscribed on his chest: "Religious scholars are heirs of the prophets," and "Religious scholars live long like the prophets of the Children of Israel." How can it be anything but a disaster of major proportions, how can eyes avoid shedding blood with no tears, when these braggarts are not content just to argue with religious scholars, but even go so far as to try to prove such scholars ignorant in their own field of learning? These days they introduce modern scientific ideas into scholarly circles so as to make religious scholars look like some of their students. Just see how far their sheer impertinence has led them, even though these sciences of theirs are utterly useless. God protect us! Such subjects are merely one stage on the road to error, a slippery slope that veers away from the straight path. It is Satan who entices them down it without their even being aware. For example a knowledge of the four principles of calculation dispenses with the need for thorough and detailed investigation. And yet, that is precisely what they do in arithmetic, the purpose being to gradually introduce the student to the hated science of philosophy and incite him to commit heresy and disbelief. May God protect us from such evil!

THIRD SKAYKH You can add history to the list of such subjects. Quite apart from the fact that it's based on tales and myths, it requires its practitioners to delve into hadith accounts of the Prophet's companions (God be pleased with them!) and the wars which broke out among them. That is something specifically forbidden by the Shariah in the text of the hadith: "When you come to mention my companions, then stop." For the purposes of this subject, it is enough just to understand the contents of *Al-Sīrah al-Ḥalabiyyah*. 22.9

SECOND SKAYKH What's the subject they call "geography"?

THIRD SKAYKH It's what we call country mapping. If that's all that was involved, it would be neither harmful nor useful. However, as it is, it does great harm and brings about disastrous consequences. It combines such things as the degrees of the earth's rotation and the sun's static position. Weather events are explained through contrived reasoning, something easily disproved by what the eye can clearly see is completely unfounded. They claim, for example, that rain from the skies comes from the depths of the sea and clouds are simply dense vapor. Such ideas can be easily dismissed by reference to the statement of Kaʿb al-Aḥbār, namely that clouds are the leaves of paradise. They also claim that thunder and lightning are caused by the clashing of clouds due to atmospheric pressure, something that can also be refuted by reference to the fact that thunder is the sound made by an angel pushing clouds while lightning is a spear flashing in his hand.

SECOND SKAYKH And what do you say about their claim that the earth is suspended in space? 22.10

FOURTH SKAYKH They're totally wrong—may God suffice them in their egregious error! How can they argue with the fact that the earth is supported on a bull's horn, and the bull in turn is supported on a rock which is supported on the back of a fish. The fish is swimming in water, and the very first thing that people in paradise eat is from that fish's liver. Were we to peruse their books, which they claim to be superior to anything else before or since and to have achieved an unprecedented level of knowledge of country mapping, we would discover that they lack the comprehensive and useful information to be found in *The Pearl of Wonders* by the Imām Ibn al-Wardī. We never hear any mention of the remarkable things to be found in *The Pearl*—the land of Wāq al-Wāq, for example, where the trees grow buxom beauties and lovely maids who hang down by their tresses from the branches. When the sun shines on them, they cry "Wāq Wāq, all praise to the Creator!"[179]

22.11 The same sort of thing is mentioned in the work, *Remarkable Blooms and Occurrences of Dooms*,[180] which tells how Shaykh Ḥāmid crossed the Black Sea on the back of a donkey that worshipped the sun and reached the source of the River Nile. When the sun shone on one of the riverbanks, the donkey headed for that bank and kept revolving with the sun until it reached the other bank. Shaykh Ḥāmid noticed that the river's flow in the sea was just like a white thread in a black gown. He discovered that it emerged from a red ruby dome beyond the mountain of Qāf and the water was whiter than snow and sweeter than honey. From this same dome emerged three rivers, the Sayḥūn, the Jayḥūn, and the Euphrates. Have they collected such information in any of their books?

FOURTH SKAYKH By God, we live in an age when adhering to one's faith in the face of these modern heretical sciences is like clasping red-hot coals. «He whom God leads astray will have no guide.»[181]

22.12 FIRST SKAYKH Tell me, by God, have the students of these new sciences learned anything or gained any benefit from them? Have you ever heard of one of them composing a commentary on a text, a marginal note on a commentary, or a report on a marginal note, let alone providing a lengthy precis or expatiating in brief?

SECOND SKAYKH They are quite incapable of such things. That is why you'll see them accusing us of wasting our time on such useful activities and striving to invalidate our studies. By your life, has any religion existed, has any faith become established, has any legal system been effective without the availability of commentaries and marginalia such as these? They are incapable of understanding them and are not gifted enough to comprehend and acquire them, and that's why they envy us so much and are determined to rob us of this greatest of all qualities and virtues:

> They envied the man when they could not match his efforts
> All were his enemies and foes.[182]

THIRD SKAYKH How right you are!

> Many a true word comes from a critic,
> His ruin is faulty understanding.[183]

SIXTH SKAYKH Let's not waste our time, by God, talking about these babbling would-be chatterboxes. They have their books and academies, and we have our sciences and schools too. On Judgment Day, God will decide between us. 22.13

FIFTH SKAYKH We could overlook their reprehensible conduct if they did not object to our views and publish them in the things they call newspapers. As it is, they fill them with critical attacks on us and gatecrash on matters of language and proper composition. Then they brag about how wonderful their writings are and how easily they've bested us. In fact, newspapers are themselves a grievous source of temptation. We could be writing such things if we so wished.

FOURTH SKAYKH Even so, some of our own students who have been tempted to write in newspapers have actually beaten them at their own game. Yesterday Shaykh X, the illustrious scholar, showed me an article. He's since published it in the newspapers.

It's an eloquent piece of writing, and I still have it in my pocket. If you like, I'll read it for you. Then you'll realize that those conceited idiots are in no way superior to us, nor do they have any distinctive qualities.

EVERYONE Let us hear it! By all means, let us hear it!

22.14 FOURTH SKAYKH (*reading*)[184] "The factors of divine inspiration take immediate effect by virtue of the moderation of a ruler toward his people and a people toward its ruler. Since natural laws lead to the protection of society's constitution from inroads of fate that respond to the call made to them by disunity and disruption (resulting from the premises of deviation, itself the very cradle of dissension and the breeding ground for disharmony), and since human beings incline by virtue of their upbringing to that factor which has the more immediate effect, every nation must have two things. The nation is the haven of perfection, the origin of beauty, and the meadow of authority. It constitutes the very source of sustenance, the basis of discourse, the point of debate, the perfection of the faulty, and the object of the gazer's eyes. It is the firmest bond and the most organized defense, possessing every good quality; every good is its gain, every wrong its loss. It stands for what is right and is a confederate of truth.

22.15 "I am struck by a universal principle and useful statement from the past, one uttered by thoughtful men of intellect and acumen in olden times, to the effect that the decline of nations originates in the enfeeblement of its intellectuals. How true, how very true! This demands that we take a look at certain intellectual principles that have outlasted their rivals so that the way to eliminate the damage caused by decline can be clearly delineated. That enfeeblement of intellectuals leads to a disruption of objectives, and that leads in turn to fragmentation among ordinary people. Bitterness prevails, the centers of civilization are enveloped in danger, and consumptive calamities breathe in them with sighs which are the beginning of all destruction and the origin of hatred between lover and beloved and steward and master. Furthermore, if the condition of moderation does not prevail, then dire consequences ensue.

22.16 "In every nation it is the intelligentsia who are the pillars of its glory, the supports of its structure, the gleams of its jet, the key of its locks, the measure of its status, the purge of its dross, and the lamp of its joys. Unity among such luminaries can provide a closer insight than it does among other people into the way that slackness proceeds to the limit of decline, which is the origin of futile principles, of sickly emotions, of damaged elements, and of dire plight. Simple folk merely follow the example that they provide. If they are in decline, then it involves flattery, humiliation, and feeblemindedness; whereas, if they are united and in agreement, prudence and civilization are invoked.

"People make use of their hearts and minds to produce flashes of thought in praise of God's name, through unorthodox ideas and in attainment of their desires. They make use of their ears to listen to the herald of truth in the realm of mankind through the publication of newspapers. They represent the tablet of admonition, the views of the observer, the cream of information, and the finishing line in the race. They are expected with patient longing, they are the program of events and mirror an age for the benefits of later generations, and they preserve what is past for what is to come.

22.17 "My fellow countrymen, it seems both regrettable and peculiar that foreigners are continually claiming that they are following the practice of the previous generation by respecting the tenets of the Shariah in all circumstances, whereas in fact a huge gap separates us from an adherence to it ourselves. What a fine claim that is! Unfortunately it is one that cannot be substantiated. Nevertheless it has brought forth fruit and produced a state of affairs that we must abandon, even though foreigners have never countenanced such a thing. Yet they actually have the right to make such a claim. For if this were not the way we have been characterized, our influence would not have been so diffused, nor would our authority have been weakened and our status worsened, such that we have now reached a lamentable state of affairs. But then it is God alone who wields power and influence! So where are we to find people who are devoted to the Shariah law? Where are those zealots, patriots devoted to their country, raised on the good things that she provided for them, people who have converted her into a rich pasture for foreigners? In such circumstances if we are not moved to action by these exigencies which confront us all the time, are we any different from dumb animals? What factors will allow us to criticize foreigners over the courses of action that they keep taking to suit their own political purposes?

22.18 "No, and again no! Ever since we ceased adhering to the example of the Shariah code, we have been beset from every quarter by deficiencies, until we have now reached the stage when we see a man stretching his hand out to water so he can transfer it to his mouth but without it ever actually getting there; or even like a blind man abandoned in the desert where lions come and attack him. This is our traditional posture, one that has now led to our own backwardness and the foreigners' advancement.

"In such a context I would suggest that unity implies the protection of the nation from the clutches of other people when they aspire to encroach upon its interests and interfere in its particular situation, something that is of no concern to them under any circumstances. I refer you all, for example, to two recent issues as a result of which our revered professor has been dismissed. As a genuine service to his country he stood up in support of the Khedive, and as a result they took concerted action against him. But for that, the same thing would have happened as occurred to the people of Muslim Spain, and matters would have gone from bad to worse. So all praise be to God, the arranger of circumstances, and He knows best!"

22.19 First Skaykh How amazing! God alone has the power and might! Superb! He has made the eyes of the envious bleed!

Second Skaykh The Prophet of God—God's prayers and blessings be upon him!—was right when he said "There is magic in eloquence."

Third Skaykh Yes indeed, this really is legitimate sorcery and the sweetest running water!

Seventh Shaykh God be blessed! What eloquence, what clarity, what pellucid discourse!

Fifth Skaykh God bless him! His mouth has produced a precious pearl!

Seventh Shaykh Didn't I tell you that we could write such things if we really wanted to do so? If we were to start revealing the glimpses of learning concealed within us, we'd strike any other speaker dumb and belittle every writer. But there's no point in wasting such jewels on people who don't realize their value or appreciate their true worth.

ʿĪsā ibn Hishām said: Throughout this session the Pāshā had kept on muttering and grumbling beside me. But at this point he leapt to his feet and dragged me out in fury. As we left, he was sighing and groaning. He joined me in reciting this comment on the people at this, our first gathering: 22.20

There is among them no one either pious or ascetic,
who does not entice to his own advantage;
A rock is worthier than the worthiest among them,
it neither deceives nor lies.[185]

Miṣbāḥ al-sharq 71, September 7, 1899

23.1 ʿĪsā ibn Hishām said: I tried coaxing the Pāshā into visiting one of the numerous clubs and associations where notables and merchants would gather, following our visit to the religious scholars. However, all I encountered was avoidance and dislike; he kept on resisting the idea and preferring to procrastinate. What he wanted instead was for us to stay by ourselves and avoid company. "Ever since I've joined up with you," he said, "I've always found you to have the best intentions. Any harm, you have uncovered and eradicated; any benefit, you have initiated and continued; any evil, you have removed and fended off. I remain grateful to you for your kindness during our seclusion and the way you rescued us from the situations that Fate brought about, all so as to fend off the terrible consequences you were anxious to avoid, not to mention the illness caused by such an accumulation of worries and the inevitable relapse that would have followed. With all that in mind, why are you even bothering to coax me into visiting clubs and meetings like these? They are all completely useless and lacking in benefit, far removed from any exalted purpose. They're enough to make the heart shrink, exhaust one's patience, and depress one—quite apart from the anxieties they cause."

23.2 "God grant you long life!" I replied, "My intentions were good; I only wished you well. I've watched the way these experiences have enhanced your generosity and discernment. Real exposure to things has given you an understanding and knowledge that replaces the gruffness, arrogance, narrow-mindedness, and pomposity you used to display. You would approach things in a brash and boorish fashion, with little expertise whether listening or speaking. My aim is for you to be able to look at those aspects of people's lives which would take your mind off your misfortunes and at scenes which would let you relax. The way you're studying people's actions, their comings and goings, their joys and griefs, their comforts and sufferings, their hopes and despairs, is not like that of the philosopher Heraclitus, but rather Democritus. The former saw the way people behaved and wept in grief. The latter looked at them and then scoffed with laughter. To back up his views, the former wrote:

> Funerals distract people from their world;
> clouds weep and thunder laments.

"While to support his point of view, the latter said:

> This life is a drama for the actor;
> night is a curtain and day is the stage.

"So don't allow yourself to feel sorry for them or shed any tears on their behalf. Come with me, and I'll make sure you enjoy your visit to a meeting that'll relieve your solitude and calm your fears."

With that he agreed that this was clearly the most satisfactory 23.3
plan and he followed my lead obediently. We made our way to an imposing, highly decorated building with high walls and wide pillars. At the door, a groom pushed past us carrying a baby on his shoulders and leading an obedient horse behind him. The anger on his face showed clearly what he was really thinking. "My God," he said, "I don't know, am I a groom or a wet nurse?" Behind him came another person carrying a tray piled high with pickled vegetables, the juice of which had soiled his clothing. "Why on earth should I have to slave and suffer in this house?" he was saying. "How long will this hardship continue? I don't know, am I a driver or mere excrement?" Once we got past the door, there was the doorkeeper with a bundle of clothes in his hand. "There's no way of stopping

Fate's decrees," he said, "and no hope for a comfortable life. I don't know, am I a doorkeeper or eunuch?"

23.4 Passing through the vestibule, we entered the alcove where we encountered a young servant sighing and moaning, tobacco and paper in front of him and an embossed book by his side. "By God, it's incredible," he was saying. "My father makes his son work at filling cigarettes and keeps him away from the lessons he's supposed to be studying. No wonder people's eyes overflow with floods of tears and their hearts are charred by agonizing flames. I don't know, by God, am I the house's valet or the owner's son?"

No sooner had he noticed our arrival than he sprang to his feet and came over to greet us. He went on in front to announce that we had arrived. The father asked who had come. No sooner had the boy explained things, than the father came over to us, swaying as he walked and stumbling over his coat. He bade us welcome, greeted us elaborately, and sat us down so we could listen to the conversation and hear what was being discussed. There we found a variety of people: they all looked different and were wearing a varied assortment of clothing. A turban wearer for instance was making sure his turban was tight, while another was refolding his and fastening the edge of it with a pin; he would then take hold of it and swivel it on his head. Elsewhere a tarboosh wearer had tilted his tarboosh over his forehead. Whenever he was afraid it might slip, he would raise his right hand to adjust it. As a result his hand never stopped moving, and he looked as though he were continually greeting people. We noticed that they were all deeply involved in conversation. Here is what they were talking about:

23.5 One of Them Yes, God has facilitated things and agreement has been reached with Mr. Suarez. Putting up another building alongside the current one will bring you the kind of profit you couldn't possibly make in commercial dealings. I advise you to give up being a merchant; nowadays there's no hope of gain from it. Trust in God, and work with us on buildings; they're much more profitable.

ANOTHER May God increase my good fortune and blessing! Where can I find the wherewithal to back such an enlargement? You know full well how weak my position is. Thank God for the boon of concealment; that's the most complete wealth of all!

FIRST My dear Sir, don't say such a thing! Instead you should say: «And as for your Lord's blessing, talk about it.»[186] You're just being modest when you claim you're in a weak position. God lavishes favors on you one after another.

SECOND My dear fellow, I beg God's forgiveness, but that's mere flattery on your part. The truth is that my affairs are not as prosperous as you imagine. I've told you that concealment is the most perfect kind of wealth. In any case, there's good fortune in commerce. My forefathers and ancestors earned their living that way, and concealed profits bring more luck than those which are public knowledge.

THIRD You're still sticking to your old erroneous ways! How 23.6
can you get any revenue or profit from commerce when you're competing with foreigners? Abandon such apathy and start operating with cotton in the Stock Exchange; your profits will be doubled, and you'll always have a livelihood at your disposal, one that'll provide you with a carefree life without trouble or hardship. How many poor people we've seen enter the Stock Exchange only to emerge rich and influential as a result of speculation! Take our friend, Mr. X the Jew, for example; some of you will remember his mother selling bread in the street and beans in the Jewish quarter. He went in for transactions like these and as a result he's become a really wealthy and important person. Meanwhile we keep on relying on what our fathers and uncles left us (God's mercy be upon them).

FOURTH You've forgotten, Sir, that this friend of ours whom you mention only attained such heights by working as a broker. You know full well the indignity that involves. Are you suggesting that one of us should stoop so low as to take that type of work after living our kind of life?

THIRD God forbid, Sir! That isn't what I meant. But you've noticed that this Jew entered the Stock Exchange as a broker without any money to his name, and has now become a very rich man. How much more do you imagine someone will earn when he's already wealthy at the start? After only a short while he's bound to emerge as the Croesus of his era.

FIFTH The only thing that can follow huge profits is huge loss. I've seen the results of working in the Stock Exchange with my own eyes: destruction of homes people live in, squandering of vast wealth and the collapse of ancient properties and lofty pillars. I think it's sheer idiocy to venture into such perilous undertakings. «God is the best guardian».[187]

23.7 SIXTH I'm following the Prophet's own statement: "No believer is ever stung twice from the same hole."[188] The lessons I've learned from the losses I suffered speculating on cotton are quite enough for me. All praise to God for saving me from ruin.

THIRD To God alone belongs the power and might! «You will not guide those you love.»[189] How can you worry about suffering a loss or have any qualms about dealings in cotton on the Stock Exchange? I'll do a little calculation for you which should satisfy your concerns about profitability just as surely as one is half of two. Suppose for example that the cotton yield is so many qanṭars a year, and you want to invest it at so many qanṭars. The return you'll get won't even cover your expenses; and then shares go up in price. In any case, as long as this ministry remains in power, the government is still in the hands of people who are in complete control of things; the road to reform is firmly established in our midst. So there's absolutely no need to be afraid of a collapse in share prices.

23.8 FOURTH How can you possibly claim any such thing? May God preserve you! We have before us the example of A who made such a calculation and concentrated on such things. He was tempted by greed, and now you can see him continuing to fall into the Stock Exchange abyss until his losses have plunged to the very depths.

And all that although, as far as you're concerned, he's still regarded as being immensely rich.

EIGHTH God be praised! Don't you all share my amazement at the false renown some people have for being wealthy, whereas that same wealth turns out to be poverty? How often have we heard that X the man of means is worth many thousands! Soon afterward the secret's revealed and hidden facts come to light; his actual wealth doesn't equal even a tenth of that false renown.

FIFTH You're absolutely right! Just consider the late Y. He was so envious when I attained my post that at every meeting where I had any standing he used to brag that he was wealthier than I and thus had a loftier status. However when he died, he didn't bequeathe enough to his children to keep his house open and for his name to be remembered. But that didn't stop him doing it. Praise be to God, the Everlasting!

FOURTH I beg you, for God's sake, stop talking about sons and inheritances. Every time I think about our children's morality in the current age and see what's happened to Y's wealth, how his sons have ended up in desperate poverty after squandering riches galore, in the process forgetting their own father's name in death after their anger at him while he was still alive—never visiting his grave or asking God to have mercy on him—I think nothing of spending all the money I have and enjoying myself while I'm still alive.

FIFTH Don't even say such a thing! What use are we in this 23.9
world if we don't leave our children an inheritance that will spare them the need to beg once we're dead? Don't put all the blame for squandering inheritances on the sons. In fact, the biggest fault of all lies with fathers who leave their wealth untended when they die. As a result the children can then spend the money as they see fit, totally ignorant of the realities of ownership which would enable them to benefit from the proceeds, keep the capital secure, and prevent the house's name from being obliterated. In that way none of the sons or the sons' sons would have any need to—

Sixth My dear Sir, forgive me for interrupting you. Didn't you hear what happened to the endowment of A, B, and others? The supervisors grabbed the rights of the claimants, and the endowment fell into ruin during the course of all the court cases and claims. Debts kept piling up until eventually the supervision and claim to it were given to Jews. The houses involved fell into ruins, all trace of it disappeared, and the owners' names vanished just as yesterday precedes today.

Seventh Yes, endowments have their uses. Inheritances can be preserved from loss and destruction provided they contain stipulations like those under which the late D made an endowment. He detailed part of the revenues for his children and stipulated that the remainder should be saved and deposited. Each time a large sum accrued from it, an estate was to be bought. This was then to be endowed and added to the original endowment. In that way the profits were always disposable since the endowment itself was continually growing as time and fate's misfortunes passed. That explains how the family possessed considerable wealth after its owner's death, far more in fact than it ever did in his own lifetime. This is clearly an excellent way of doing such things.

23.10 Third That doesn't make sense at all! Rather it shows extreme niggardliness, a mere delight in storing things away after one's death. The late gentleman didn't permit himself the enjoyment of his own money during his lifetime and then deprived his children of it after his death.

First I beg your pardon, Sir, and I trust I give no offence. Who says that the late gentleman was stingy and niggardly? By God, I was a close friend of his for a long time, and never saw him deprive himself of anything or be tightfisted throughout his lifetime. His table always had mutton, pigeon, or chicken on it—by your grandfather's right! He was merely a prudent man who only spent money on useful ventures.

Second Don't keep talking about endowments or possessions. The best thing which a father can reserve for sons is a good school education. In his own lifetime, he shouldn't let them get into the habit of spending money extravagantly, but instead should train them to economize and teach them the value of money and coin.

First But, my dear Sir, aren't these schools and the education they offer primarily responsible for all the troubles we're having with our sons? All it does is to make them boorish, discourteous, arrogant, and supercilious? Someone made me laugh yesterday when he complained bitterly about his son. Here's what he had to say: 23.11

"Ever since this boy finished school, he's been torturing me every day. He doesn't approve of anything in the house and talks gibberish to his family. When they bring him some water, he says it contains microbes; when they bring him bread and cheese, he tells them to bring the microscope. Then you'll see the wretch cutting up food into sections. Then he'll start giving you a lecture. He'll tell you that eggs and yogurt are excellent food, but vegetables are rotten and unbeneficial. The only useful purpose that rice and other grown commodities serve in the stomach is to burn like fuel. Any foods which exceed one's needs constitute fat, and that does more harm than good. Once watermelons are cut, they have to be eaten immediately because they produce poisonous bacteria so quickly. The wretch goes on like this till he has the whole house in a dither over his tastes in food and drink; to say nothing of the way he bewilders me with his various styles of dress and adornment. Every time his father disagrees with him, he gives a haughty look, pokes fun at him, and accuses him of being ignorant and brags about his own learning. So this is the kind of behavior that he has gained through this system of education. Children now look down on their fathers; and all this after times of old when the sons of the family were like young virgin girls who would never even look up at their father's face or speak to him except to respond to a question, and that from early childhood into their adult lives."

Second But you're forgetting that by educating our sons in schools we get one material benefit, one that compensates for every wrong, namely that they can enter government service and thus 23.12

rise in rank and prestige. If only our fathers had bothered to have us educated in schools, we could have avoided the drudgery of commerce and the demands of hard work—the humiliation involved in buying and selling, being nice to customers, unsettled markets, and the need to market things in instalments and on trust. Being a civil servant is the only decent way to earn a living. They get their salary in cash and pure gold coin at the end of each month; it comes as a lump sum safe in their hands with no delay, postponement, or partial payment. All this is as compensation for spending three hours a day sitting in various government departments; and part of that time is spent talking, joking, disputing, and carping. And that's to say nothing of the respect and veneration they command and the power they have to help their friends and to hold up anything they wish for years and ages upon ages. The only capital involved in all this is reading a few books in school. So tell me, by God, what commerce and what profit can possibly rival government service? Praise be to Him who divides the lots, may there be no blame or reproach!

23.13 FOURTH All this we know full well and acknowledge. But how do you foresee your son getting his certificate? You know the situation regarding the people in charge of schools. Most of our sons leave school without a certificate. Those who take the trouble to get a degree still don't get employed because of the people who, as you well know, control the government.

SIXTH Perhaps God will bring about a change. Then this government administration will fall and be replaced by a nationalist one. Then you'll see how our sons whose circumstances you're bemoaning move up in rank.

FIFTH (*to the Sixth*) How true! If there's a change of government and your friend returns to the administration, we'll be in luck. The skies of the future will gleam bright, and carefree times will be with us again. Should such times ensue, don't forget my son along with your own children. He was at the same school with them. He's always reading the papers and watching for the events which will bring about the downfall of this ministry.

Eighth I think you're misguided regarding your children in this life and after your death. Your ideas are wrong. For me the best course involves teaching them various subjects and sending them to schools, but not in order to wait for appointments to government service but rather to be models of knowledge and learning for their contemporaries. As regards keeping inheritances in their possession once we are gone, the best plan is not to restrict their spending when we are alive or to distance them from our own business; but rather to set aside a sum of money for them to invest by themselves under our supervision. They can then learn how to give and take and come to appreciate the pleasure of earning for themselves. They'll thus have instilled in them the desire for profit and will benefit from their learning in expanding their commercial reach. I've implemented this plan with my sons and hope, God willing, that they'll prove to be worthy descendants.

Sixth Has today's newspaper arrived? 23.14

Owner of the House (*shouting to his son*) Get us the newspaper and read it to us.

(*The boy opens the newspaper.*)

First Read the front page.

Boy The war between England and the Transvaal.

Sixth Is there a war?

Boy It's not clear from the beginning of the article.

Sixth Then read from the end.

Fifth What's the point of reading that, or whether there's a war or not?

Sixth God pardon us both! Don't you realize that we get 23.15 an enormous benefit? I've heard a great deal about it in the High Council. They concluded that this war will preoccupy the foreigners and reduce the pressures they're putting on our government. As a result, we'll have a free hand. Everything will be changed, and we'll get a Nationalist Ministry.

Fourth If that's the case, then I hope you'll not forget about the idea we've discussed, the project to establish a national company to purchase recognized plots of land and get monopoly control with this new government's help.

Fifth God willing, I might have a part share in this company.

Third Who's on the board, and who's the chairman?

Sixth The board members are A, B, and C and the chairman is D.

Third God forbid I should ever join a company with B! Have we all forgotten the mess he made of things?

Fifth And I won't accept D being my chairman in a company.

Second I'll never consent to participate unless my share in the foundation is larger than A's.

Seventh After what happened with that other notorious company, I won't agree to participate in any company unless I'm the one to mediate and come to agreements with government authorities.

23.16 ʿĪsā ibn Hishām said: They started a furious argument. Eyes bulged, and they all kept glowering at each other. They seemed to be nursing a whole store of grudges and hatred against one another. Every one of them seemed to be longing for the heavens to fall on his colleague or the earth to swallow him up. Leaving them raging at one another, we took our leave.

Miṣbāḥ al-sharq 72, September 14, 1899

ʿĪsā ibn Hishām said: Next we decided to visit the third meeting, this one involving major figures and exemplars of government and wisdom, people of both sword and pen, possessed of absolute power, and capable of making people either miserable or content. Being brought up in the cradle of learning and possessing extraordinary talents in all categories of expression and concept, they are characterized by their authentic ideas and fine organizational skills, the power of their perspicacity and the quality of their intellect. 24.1

We headed for a house of gleaming whiteness that dazzled us with its brilliance. Its very grounds exuded prestige and its gardens fostered felicity. Sheer loveliness had taken root there, and its garments had been decorated by finery's hand. As a result it showed itself in the most beautiful of guises, the most perfect of forms, like a lovely girl displaying all her charms on the day where she is bedecked in jewels. At the gate we were met by servants wearing eye-catching clothes. They welcomed us warmly and showed us great respect, then took us to a room on one side of the courtyard where people could wait at their leisure. Inside was a man who was only half awake; his head was a ball, one might say, and slumber was the polo mallet. No sooner had we approached him than he roused himself and started using his fingertips to rub sleep from his eyes. We gave him our greetings which he reciprocated, yawning and stammering as he did so. From his general appearance and dirty clothes, we gathered that he was a workman or servant of some kind. However, before long, it became clear to us from his remarks to the servant that he was a relative of some importance in this household. When the servant went away to ask permission for us to go in, he turned in our direction:

24.2 "May God wreak havoc on all servants!" he said. "They are a kind of affliction. The damage they inflict is ever present, whereas the benefits they bring are often lacking; and one has to tolerate them ad nauseam. They've aggravated many a patient man and irritated generous people. Many times they've destroyed something genuine and muddled up something which is quite clear! Many are the crimes and sins they've committed, and many the lies and wrongs they've perpetrated. How many locks have they opened, how many jewels have they pilfered, how often have they caused discord between people and thwarted an agreement, separating people from their families in the process, and stepping in between the branch and its root! They're parasites of corruption and sparks of hatred. May God's curse be on them in both worlds! The terrible misfortunes I've suffered because of them and the dastardly actions they've perpetrated against me have almost made me succumb to a most undignified aversion. My brother sees all this happening and yet is prepared to overlook it. He tolerates the most unsavoury behaviour from them, while they in turn blame him and come out on top. When he tells them to do something out of respect for me, they refuse. God is my witness, every time I see my brother's money being frittered away in their hands and notice the ever-increasing confidence he has in them, my heart melts away and flows out through my eyes mixed with tear drops. Where the house steward is concerned—and 'Who's that?' you may ask. Well, «We count on God, and good is the trustee.»[190] He's a young man whose hypocrisy never errs; he never misses a trick inside the house. Cunning and treachery, stirring up resentments and disputes, these are all among his favourite pastimes. He will please an infant to enrage a grown man, and tempt girls with trifles, all so as to maintain his own luxurious lifestyle."

He kept up this diatribe for some time, muttering and grumbling. The only thing that rescued us from this deafening cacophony was the servant's return with permission for us to enter. Praising God for His generosity and kindness in ridding us of his babbling row, we now followed the servant to a pleasant room lit by electric lights and laid out with costly cushions and superb furniture of various shapes and sizes. Eastern ornaments were positioned opposite Western objets d'art and gold vessels were paralleled by others made of wood. The house's owner greeted us with a cordial smile, sat us in a place reserved for his close associates, and welcomed us as though we were genuine friends. This meeting, we discovered, was made up of high-ranking members of the government, people of prestige and illustrious ancestry, along with others who had entered government service as a means of earning a living and were now indebted to it. The discussion was focussed on politics. One of them was swaying from side to side as he spoke: 24.3

One of Them Yes, the right thing to do is to support the French army against the other parties in France. Did you but know it, therein lies our own liberation and the end of our sufferings. 24.4

Another I'm most impressed by your far-reaching aspirations and incisive judgment. Why don't you tell us—may your father belong to God!—how your research has led you to this conclusion? How can thwarting French parties and supporting the army against them affect us?

First I can see that, when it comes to analyzing events, you don't appreciate the intricacies of politics and fail to show the necessary insight. May God give you correct guidance! Don't you realize that, if the army party wins, the Republican system will be overthrown? Then the monarchy and empire will be restored. They'll bring us back kings and generals like the ones who conquered East and West, overwhelmed the Mamluks, and subdued entire empires. They had supremacy over all the peoples of the world. No obstacle could keep them from their goals, and nothing stood in the way of their aspirations. From my association with French officials, some of whom I've actually befriended, what I know for sure is that, were it not for this Republic, we wouldn't have reached the state we're in, nor would we be suffering the degradation involved in having to deal with the absolute monopoly possessed by the people who've grabbed hold of the reins of our government. They're occupying all the major positions and earning huge salaries. All gates to promotion are shut in our faces; the wherewithal of progress is cut off. If only France could regain her former power and prestige, she could remove these people with a mere gesture and drive them away from us with a word. Then we could begin to run our government with our own hands.[191]

24.5 THIRD For God's sake, put such fancies aside and stop talking nonsense! You've nothing to complain about in the present circumstances. You're on close terms with the Counselor[192] and have a direct link to the Minister himself. You're on the verge of getting the position which you've set your heart on. Not only that, but you're wealthy; you've enough funds, whether inherited or current, so that you don't need to be a government employee. But what about those of us who are still forced by need to be chained to the government and to be constantly humiliated—the boss gets annoyed, the Counselor is displeased, the Minister is furious, and it's the subordinates who feel it. There's no sense of respect or esteem, no manners or modesty. God knows that if I didn't have to earn a salary and get a living somehow, I'd resign immediately and wouldn't stay in government service for a single day.[193]

FOURTH By God, I anticipate spending only half my life as a civil servant. Then I'll quit and save myself from this bondage, with all its humiliating hypocrisy, arrant deceit, and frenzied cover-ups. After that I intend to rely on commerce. It's a more pleasant way of earning a living, brings greater profit, and keeps one removed from degrading situations.

24.6 FIFTH What stupid, useless ideas! You can't deny that, whatever the case, government service is more prestigious and affords a higher status. No means of earning a living in this world is entirely devoid of aggravations, but government service provides the easiest conditions and causes the least hardship. For example, you can employ a merchant and laugh in his face so long as you have money at hand. But merchants always need the services of the most junior government employee, even if they're incredibly rich and well-off. If you only could see them boasting to each other about visiting the clerk, conversing with the adjutant, greeting the judge and addressing the governor, then you'd admit that government service holds a very prestigious place in the estimation of such people and of other classes as well. In much the same way, if you gave one of them the choice of either abandoning his wealth, property, trade, and lands, or joining the ranks of government employees, he would abandon everything like an arrow from a bow or a snake from its skin. What's abundantly clear is that the very pinnacle of happiness lies in what you regard as a terrible hardship and utter humiliation.

Sixth Take it easy! Don't turn the issue upside down and alter the truth. Don't assume that the ethics you observe among practitioners of industry, commerce, and agriculture stem from the essence of those professions. To the contrary, it results from ignorance, illusion, and feeble thinking. If one of them were to abandon his profession, he'd appreciate his own worth; with an understanding of his own status in life, he'd acknowledge the boon of independent action and freedom of thought. He's undoubtedly happier than someone who has to suffer the trammels of government service, selling his very soul in return for a few paltry dinars, in returns for which he has to spend hours each day and days each month working. Anybody working in those other professions makes more profit in a single day than we do in our position; and they're their own masters and in control of their own environment. If only our fathers had given some thought to teaching us trades and giving us some experience in commerce! Instead, what they did do and what they did leave to us is completely useless. If only they'd realized the status of government service today, and had not been misled by the extensive authority and jurisdiction which people in authority had 24.7

in days gone by, along with the power to acquire money by virtue of their high rank! If they'd realized that a time would come when high-ranking people in this government (in whose hands they were like orphans in the care of their guardian) would be like babies in the nursery or invalids in nursing homes—leave them and they'd die of hunger—then they'd have bitten their nails in anguish and shed blood instead of tears for the way they'd failed us.

24.8 FIFTH You are talking like a lot of old women, satisfied with a life that only provides threadbare clothes and poor food. What about our quest for the loftier ideals, bolstering our sense of pride and glory, rising to a high position and serving our country so we can do both good and harm? What of the poet's words:

> Were I striving for a lowly livelihood,
> a little money would suffice; I would not ask for more.
> But yet I strive for a noble glory
> and my peers achieve such a goal.[194]

We should complain to God about an age in which people's aspirations have dwindled, their resolves are dead, and all thought lies quiescent. People have lost all ambition; they are content to sit back in apathetic indifference and live a meagre life.

24.9 SIXTH Eminent Sir, I'm surprised that you can be so completely and utterly wrong. You seem to imagine it's a sign of authority and high rank, of honor and glory, to be a civil servant, whereas in fact it's simply humiliation and suffering, one trial after another. I'll explain things to you in detail. Then you'll realize that the reason why people like yourself remain in government service when you can in fact leave it, is that you're weak and incapable, totally unaware of the comforts of life.

I maintain that the desire to enter government service can be subdivided into four categories. The first is a need for money, by which I mean staving off poverty and earning enough to stay alive. Anyone into this category is in a state of compulsion whereby Fate has decreed that he should endure humiliation because of the need to earn a living as a matter of bondage and the contemptible status of hireling. All he can do is to swallow the bitter pill and endure such misery till he can find some way out. Like me, he envies the way of life of every craftsman, merchant, and farmer, and is forever longing to join their number, relishing their independence and freedom.

The second category involves a quest for prestige, by which I 24.10
imply high status, important rank, wide authority, and executive power. As you can tell, this is a far-reaching and expansive field without any limits to its goals. Within it the rearing charger will inevitably stumble and the sword will miss its target. Lofty position and high class have often been the cause of great calamities and disasters and the instigator of miseries and sorrows:

> High rank brings evil; how often did ʿAlī complain
>   of news while Qanbar made no such complaint.[195]

Even if we concede that the person who holds an important position is free from harm and danger, he still spends the rest of his life continually straining and worrying. Every time he rises a rank in status, he discovers another one above it and envies the person who has been promoted to the post. He continually admires what is above him and strives to achieve it while belittling what he has. He lives his life, distracted from the enjoyment of the pleasures to be gained from the status that he spent his entire life attaining. He's satisfied neither with himself nor with other people, and they in turn are dissatisfied with him. This is the ultimate in suffering, and the very crossroads where distress and sorrow meet.

> That man is frustrated and distressed even though
>   he may be reckoned among the fortunate.
> He considers all good fortune to be in his hands,
>   whereas it is as distant as the Gemini.[196]

How appropriate it is that someone who continually aspires to 24.11
gain something he doesn't have should be the most miserable person alive! That's why philosophers and wise men have always refused to

accept important positions and disliked getting involved in them. Intelligent people have made sure they didn't chase after such posts and tie themselves down. All this was in the time when public office was still a great honor and commanded extensive authority. One could only achieve such distinction by proving one's excellence and nobility; the path to such positions involved honor, prestige, courage, fortitude, moral virtue, and merit. However, as we see it today, the road to high office consists solely in currying favor, acting as intermediary, and pouring one's lifeblood away. The only people rising to such levels are those who display the very highest level of hypocrisy and graft; they've mastered the crafts of sycophancy and concealment, both of which demand their share of humiliation, subjection, and passivity and a willingness to endure such injustice. As you know, public office now involves a loss of authority, a lack of status, an inability to express any opinion, a loss of freedom, and an atrocious level of responsibility. Any one person of moral integrity should turn the other way and avoid it; that would undoubtedly be better for them. People of steadfast courage and honor are achieving the highest possible status by renouncing it.

24.12 The third group involves government service as a means of wasting time and spending hours of one's life doing something or other. In that way, one can fend off boredom and waste hours fussing over other people's needs. The only people in that category are vacuous individuals who are totally lacking in any kind of virtue; their minds are only preoccupied by trifling concerns and futile fancies. Such people have no depth to them; the worst thing for them is to have no serious problems to solve that can distract them from the self-isolation they feel. If they're left to their own devices, it's like being in a hornet's nest or a viper's lair. The poor fools can never achieve their goals. Anyone who cannot tolerate himself will find the world yet more intolerable.

24.13 The fourth category joins the ranks of the civil service out of a desire to serve the country and help its people. This is also a futile objective because the attitude needed to remain in office and the independence of thought required to be of service to the country are mutually incompatible. Anyone desiring to serve his country should not tie himself down with government chains. In fact, he'll be serving it better by working elsewhere, a situation in which he will have a free hand. To all that you should add the bitter feeling of being sacked in a country where people attribute every kind of virtue to officeholders, only to strip them of such attributes when they fall from office. As far as they're concerned, people are known by their positions, not the opposite. That's the reverse of the old adage:

> The amir is one who becomes
>   an amir on the day of his deposition.
> Even if his authority ceases to exist,
>   his control of his own virtue continues.[197]

That's why we have seen many people, whose reputations while they were in office were such as to lead you to believe that they were scholars and men of merit, but who turn out to be the people least endowed with such traits once they were dismissed from their jobs.

With all this in mind, why would any sensible person want to go into the civil service if he can find an alternative, unless, that is, God has led him astray? That is why I've vowed to choose another profession for my sons to practice, something they can use to earn a living as free men and that will be at their disposal wherever they decide to go and settle down. It will not be wrenched away by changed circumstances or political upheaval. They will be unaffected by either Zayd's anger or 'Amr's pleasure.[198] 24.14

Seventh By God, that was a splendid and clear explanation! I thoroughly agree with your verdict.

Second By God, stop voicing such distressing ideas. Let's change the topic and talk instead about something that'll take our minds off our situation. Don't use daytime's humiliations and nighttime's anxieties for a combined attack on us. My dear A, can you join me in some exercise and bicycle racing?

FIRST A better idea would be to bring the phonograph for us to listen to.

EIGHTH Or else come to X's wedding with us. I've heard there's going to be a spectacular "buffet."

FIRST I'm with you.

EIGHTH But only if you'll stay with me and listen to the singing.

FIRST No, I'm not up for that. Let's go to the buffet, then move on to the Ezbekiyyah to listen to some English music or Italian opera.

FOURTH I'm not going to join you. I'm going to the "Club."

SEVENTH Wait a minute while we look at the evening papers.

FIFTH If there are any French ones, let me have them. Their news is always more reliable, and they have more in them.

THIRD Read the Arabic ones first, one after the other, or else a bit at a time from each.

24.15 SECOND (*reading*) "Russia in China and America in the Philippines."

FOURTH My dear fellow, what's gone wrong with your mind? Turn the page. What possible interest can we have in those editorials? Our ideas are just as good as theirs.

READER (*turning the page and reading*) "Cables. Alexandria to our offices. Anyone who has read the news from Johannesburg will have concluded that war has started. The outcome will undoubtedly favor the wronged party, namely Transvaal, against England, the wrongdoer. Should the latter be victorious, then truth will win with the passage of time in any case. There are examples from past history"—

FOURTH Enough! Didn't we tell you not to read those editorials?

READER Fine, I'll stop reading them, and turn to the cables.

SEVENTH Forget about Alexandria!

READER "Zaqāzīq to our offices. The public are unanimous in their praise of the Municipal Superintendent for his attention to street cleaning."

Eighth May God bless him and provide us with more people like him to serve the country! Now, my friend, give us the local news.

Reader "X traveled by express train to Alexandria this evening, and Y arrived in the capital on the morning express."

Eighth Stop reading this manifesto as well!

Reader "We have mentioned previously that the Cabinet of Ministers has been looking into the question of cemeteries. We will now quote the full text of the report"—

Eighth May God afford it a resting place in Paradise! Now read us something else.

Reader "The Commander-in-Chief has arrived at Omdurman. We learn from a reliable source that he is mainly concerned at this time with the question of conditions in the Sudan."

Eighth Good heavens! I thought he'd be concerned with the Dreyfus case or the Siberian railway!

Reader "The police are poisoning dangerous dogs."

Eighth We ask God for guidance and safety for them all.

Reader "Someone has discovered a cure for death. He writes 24.16
to us to say that he is so fond of the genuine tone of our newspaper that he can't put it down, even in bed."

Eighth Praise to the Granter of success!

Reader "We have received a telegram to the effect that Islam has been struck, the pillar of the religion has collapsed, and the world has been wronged. The fates have plucked away Shaykh B after a life of ninety-six years spent on pious and charitable deeds. At the announcement of his death, sorrow and sadness fill the hearts of the people of his town in particular and of the whole region of Egypt in general."

Eighth Take a quick look at stock prices. With this news, shares prices will inevitably go into a steep decline!

Reader "We would like to notify our esteemed readers that investigations are still proceeding in the such of such-and-such, but nothing has been concluded so far. As soon as it is concluded, we will publish it immediately in accordance with our practice of publishing news as it happens."

Eighth May God benefit you!

Reader "We have omitted to mention that C was at the head of the mourners at the funeral last week of the late lamented D. We also omitted to congratulate our esteemed correspondent in Dayr al-Ṭawīl whom God blessed with the birth of a child. May God continue to give him happiness from children!"

Eighth Excellent indeed is he who neither overlooks nor forgets.

Reader "A scorpion stung a girl in the al-Wāylī district."

Eighth God forbid! This all stems from the government's neglect of hygiene precautions and police negligence in stopping this kind of incident!

24.17 Reader (*to the Eighth speaker*) My dear judge, that's enough of your sarcasm and mockery! Listen now to this important announcement.

Eighth Hearing is obeying!

Reader "We have learned today that the government is at this moment considering a project to open traffic streets. In expressing the views of the people and deputizing for the people of Egypt who are distressed by the idea, we would warn the government of the consequences of this dangerous project which would lead to the penetration of foreigners into the country. We will be explaining to our esteemed readers the harm which such a plan would cause. As the saying puts it, the future is never far away. . . ."

First I'm the only one who knows about this project. I've shared it with you, but how did it get into the newspapers?

Eighth Give us some news from other cables.

Fifth I'm warning you that, if secret information keeps being leaked like this, it's not out of the question that this government will start using guards instead of us; that would be a reversion to times past.

Fourth (*to Second*) Read the rest of the local news.

Second All that's left in the three newspapers is cables and announcements.

First Read the political cables. They have the most important news.

'Īsā ibn Hishām said: No sooner had the reader finished reading the political cables than everyone started arguing; opinions varied widely as they tried to interpret them. The argument became more and more heated; it was if they were all taking part in an exam where everyone had to prove the extent of his knowledge and virtue. No one agreed with anyone else, and there was a complete lack of unified opinion. As things heated up, we crept out, leaving them to meander through their politics and wander aimlessly in their delusion. 24.18

Miṣbāḥ al-sharq 74, September 28, 1899[199]

25.1 ʿĪsā ibn Hishām said: The time came for our fourth visit to these meetings, this one made up of amirs and important figures. Possessors of glory, prestige, honor, and majesty, they are people of purity and influence, of luxury and refinement, of ease and opulence, of power and felicity. We went to all their palaces one after another, till we had visited almost all of them. However, the only people we found living there were their eunuchs and servants. Every time we inquired as to their location, we were informed that the owners no longer lived in their own abodes; they did not shelter there at night. If you're trying to visit and see them by day, we were told, you need to go to the Gezira Palace or the Nile banks at sunset. In the evening, you need to go to their regular meeting place, the location they frequent in search of relaxation, namely the "Club." They treat it as birds do their nests, gazelles do thickets, and buxom maids do pavilions. However I now recalled that, if we were planning to go there, the only means of entry for someone who was not known to them was in the company of a member of their group.

25.2 So we decided to wait till the following afternoon before following our plan, in the hope of coming across a friend with the necessary status and prestige to take us. At the appointed time we took a walk in its illustrious location. We headed for the renowned Gezira Palace. It proved to be the very revelation of everything glorious and superb, the gathering point for contest and rivalry, the course for comparison and resemblance, the show ground for all kind of flirtation and dalliance, a haven fit for relaxation and enjoyment, a house for drinking wines and spirits. The Pāshā was duly amazed by the sheer beauty of the place and the decorations on the building. He asked me which wealthy profligate was the owner, and I replied that this was yet another splendid palace about which the earth used to boast to the stars in the sky. People both poor and prosperous emerged from it alike, and, at a mere gesture or signal, regional grandees would be subdued. Its firmament could hurl vengeful darts, while its rivulets could course with blessings. Its counterpane of refinement and luxury was covered in the acme of majesty and honor:

> Times there were when it was bedecked in royal pomp;
> In its gardens strutted would-be clowns.
> Days when its twin rivers bestowed both water and generosity:
> Ismāʿīl and the Nile.
> But now it is open for the world's masses,
> As you see, it is populated by tourists.

The Pāshā groaned in despair, made his complaint to God, then gave a deep sigh. "Whoever reckons himself happy," he declared, "is mistaken." "Don't gnash your teeth in regret," I replied. "This is one of destiny's laws in its inexorable forward path. Mankind may well experience good fortune on occasion, but thereafter misery will be waiting: 25.3

> How often has a prince descended from a rostrum
> and once again become part of the earth.
> Removed naked from his throne,
> he has left behind a kingdom laid bare.[200]

"So calm down! Dynasties fade away, and all human happiness is mere futile fancy!"

While we were talking, a marked carriage passed by, pulled by a set of beautiful steeds. The owner waved at us and told his coachman to come over to us. It was someone whom I knew well, a good friend for whom I had great affection. I was aware that he was 25.4

highly regarded and was a member of several clubs and gatherings. He greeted me and shook my hand. "What has brought you here?" he asked. "Are you looking for dubious haunts and dives?" "No," I replied, "not at all! You're actually the very person we need and the conveyance that I've come here to look for." I then told him about our quest for someone to accompany us on a visit to this "club" so we could fulfill our secret plan. "I understand your wishes," he replied, "and I'll be glad to do it. I'll serve as both helper and guide for this visit to the club. Come on up and sit with me; we'll go for a ride till the sun goes down." With that we hurried to respond to his invitation.

25.5 As the sun went down and the horizon darkened, our carriage careened on its way, racing others in the process. In an instant we had arrived and were stepping down. My friend went on ahead of us, and we entered behind him. The stairway led to a spacious hall decorated with a constellation of lights. From there one entered a number of rooms adorned with the most magnificent furnishings and objets d'art. They were crowded with all sorts of people, unsmiling and unfriendly, all of them dressed in dazzlingly beautiful clothes with ruby and diamond ornaments. They kept shouting and yelling as though they were at a bring-and-buy sale. Our friend began to show us round the various parts of the place and telling us the names of people there. After introducing us to X and Y, he proceeded to inform us that the first room was intended for conversation and drinking, the second for betting and gambling, and the third for discussion and conversation. So we started by going into the last of these and noticed a large table in the middle upon which books were spread out. A group of amirs was thumbing through them, their eyes mostly focused on the mirror so that they could enjoy the reflected view. They were talking in a foreign language, not Arabic, all as a way of showing off and looking superior. We took our seats to one side of them and listened attentively. One of them was speaking to a senior member of his family; from the frown on his face, it was clear that he was furious:

FIRST There's no point in blaming and reprimanding me. I refuse to accept your ideas or advice. God alone is aware of what secret schemes people harbor inside them. If you mean the best for me, then leave me alone! I know how to put things right for myself. That debt you're blaming me for is none of your business. I've enough possessions and property to honor it and pay it back. I don't interfere in your affairs, so why should you meddle in mine and spoil my life? The best thing you can do is to devote your entire attention to organizing your own wealth. Your need is greater than mine; you have to watch carefully in case your trustees and agents start pilfering it without you having the slightest idea. I much prefer to spend my money on things which give me pleasure and delight my eye rather than live in a state of deprivation while others filch and hoard it for their children to use later. 25.6

SECOND I shall ignore all this inane talk. However, as from today I warn you that, if you don't mend your ways and hand over to me the responsibility for managing your wealth so that your debts can be settled and your affairs put in order, then I shall demand immediately that your legal competence be withdrawn.

FIRST People like myself aren't going to be influenced by such threats. There's nothing about my affairs to justify withdrawal of legal competence. Debt is a widespread phenomenon; hardly any wealthy person is free of it. The government itself is in more debt than most people. I swear to you by everything I love and value that if you don't stop your attempts to prohibit my legal competence I'm going to hand over all my money immediately to some foreigner to invest for me. Then you won't get any of it.

SECOND You'll soon see which of us is going to win.

THIRD By God, my brothers, the way relatives keep meddling has made me detest my wealth. I've promised myself to leave not a solitary dirham to anyone when I die. 25.7

FOURTH Thank God, my wealth's all gone. I don't have to deal with it any more. I'm selling the rest of my lands so that I can enjoy the proceeds at the Paris Exhibition.

Fifth And I ask God to expedite a profitable verdict in the case I've brought against my mother before the exhibition finishes. Then I'll be able to come with you.

Fourth Don't you realize that the case will be pending in the courts for ages?

Fifth I'm going to visit the exhibition at any rate, even though the case may not be over. I have in my possession some letters and papers written by my sister. I've just stumbled across them. I've calculated that they're worth enough money to cover the cost of my journey. I've told her that, if she doesn't pay me that amount at once, I'm going to have these letters printed and published. Her devotion to her husband will undoubtedly force her to deal with the matter and buy them from me.

Sixth I envy you such a precious opportunity and ask God to give me similar good fortune with my aunt.

25.8 Seventh Forget about such feeble expedients. Come on now! Let's try to get a raise in salaries.

Sixth What's the point of that? The biggest salary raise would only be five hundred or a thousand pounds a year. A mere tailor or carriage merchant makes that much profit. However, we have to do all we possibly can to grab enough wealth so that each of us can maintain himself in a style appropriate to his exalted status and his prestige among his peers.

Second Don't waste mental energy on such fanciful dreams. The wells have all seeped away and the udders are dry. Gone are the days when wealth would flow in without any effort or difficulty. Our ancestors and forefathers got hold of it for us.

First I beg you, for mercy's sake, don't bring up our forefathers' conduct or claim that they managed to amass money and riches. They were content with trifling, paltry sums. They thought they had collected a huge amount of money. But just consider how small their ambition was and how enormous their folly! God knows, if we'd been in their shoes in those days, we'd have shown them how money should be collected and treasures stored away. What can you say about the dreams of people who had the Egyptians and their money at their command, complying with any order or gesture they made, but then left millions of acres for the Egyptians to enjoy today to our detriment? Would any of our ancestors have imagined that peasant *'umdas*, people who in their days had no idea of what life in this world was about and what money was useful for, would now be even richer than their own children? That was gross negligence on our ancestors' part, condemning their descendants to a miserable existence. Their fault, our loss.

Eighth (*looking at us*) You should avoid malicious talk when talking about Egyptians. Don't make a habit of it. These days it isn't an appropriate thing for us to do.

First May God protect you, why should that be so? What 25.9
good have Egyptians ever done for us that we need to mention them charitably? But then, maybe you too want an Egyptian peasant to marry your sister so that you can have the honor of being related to him.

Eighth No. But I've heard the eldest of our group say more than once that shrewd politics and our own interests dictate that we need to make a show of affection and sympathy toward Egyptians. They'll cling to our coattails and shower us with praise and gratitude. Then, if the foreigners get to hear about it, they'll be forced to respect our status. And you all know what such respect implies for us when it comes to finding ways to benefit from their lofty status, especially in these times when government revenues only come from their hands.

Fourth My mind cannot cope with such subtle politics. I don't relish the thought of showing love and affection to these Egyptians, even for fraudulent purposes. In that regard I'm not going to go against my natural instincts. I'm more inclined toward the foreigners. They're much more deserving of our affection, loyalty, and friendship, and indeed of our praise and commendation as well. All Egyptians put together are not worth the nail-clippings of a single foreigner. If it weren't for your father and his, we wouldn't be in this state in the first place and wouldn't need to lower ourselves like this. They're the ones who stole our money and wasted our inheritance.

25.10 Fifth I'd rather not start a quarrel by discussing our parents. I'm afraid it might arouse deep-seated resentments or malice. We can all barely control ourselves, and you know full well the harm which will be done if the conversation on this topic goes any further.

Foreigner (*entering and speaking to the first Amir*) I've brought your Highness the most precious invention of the end of this century. Take a good look at this picture and examine its different parts. For originality and sheer perfection it amazes the human eye. This is just a drawing; imagine how fantastic it looks going along the streets. Everyone who has looked at it agrees that to date they've never seen an electric carriage like it. Suffice it to say that the factory only produced two of this type; the German Prince of Hohelohenstein, a major prince in Germany, has taken one, and this second one is for you, Your Highness. His Highness your brother has been trying for ages behind my back to get a glimpse of this picture, but I've kept it from him as I know he wants to pre-empt you by buying it, and brag about it at your expense. I haven't granted him his wish, because I much prefer your Highness to him.

25.11 First I'm well aware of the attention you've been paying to my affairs, and I thank you for it. My only request is that you hurry up and bring this carriage. I like the picture very much. Tell me, how soon can you get it?

Foreigner Only the time it takes to cover the street.

First The best plan is for you to send a telegram rather than a letter.

Foreigner Hearing is obeying. Here's the bill. Would you be so good as to bother yourself by signing it?

First There's my signature.

(*The Foreigner thanks him and bows low. He then exits with the bill in his pocket. "That's it with this one," he tells himself, "now let's go and sell it to his brother."*)

First (*yelling to the Foreigner*) I'm sorry, my dear Sir! Would you tell me the exact cost. I've forgotten.

Foreigner Excuse me, Your Highness! The cost is a mere six thousand five hundred and thirty-six francs.

First I'd ask you to do me a service. Go to see my brother and tell him that I've bought it for fourteen thousand francs. Tell him too that there are no other models from this company.

Foreigner As you say, Sir! I'm always at your service, Your Highness. In fact I was already thinking along those lines before you informed me of your own intentions. I'll tell him that you've purchased it for thirteen thousand seven hundred and forty-two francs—to be precise.

First What a clever idea! How subtle you are!

(*With that, the Foreigner says his farewells and leaves.*)

First (*to his brothers*) I'm sure my brother will throw a fit 25.12
when he hears this news. He'll try to borrow yet more money to buy a carriage like this one. As you all know of old, he usually copies me in every way he can. Things are now so bad that he has to sell all his possessions.

Third What'll the poor chap do then?

Fourth He'll have to survive on his salary alone.

Third Didn't I just tell you that, when things get really bad, that salary is all we have left? It's all we have to live on. I can think of no better idea than trying to get it increased. Come on, let's agree on that amongst ourselves.

Fifth Haven't you heard that relying on one's salary suggests feeble intellect and little ingenuity?

Third Well then, God give you guidance, pray suggest some other way of acquiring wealth.

First I see it in speculation.

Fourth I see it in hiring out our names to companies.

Fifth I see it in serving embassies.

Seventh My idea is marrying Jewesses.

Eighth I think our best plan at this point is to go to the gaming room.

Everyone What a great idea! Let's go!

25.13 ʿĪsā ibn Hishām said: They all got up, and we followed them to watch what they did next. They went into the wine room and had as many glasses of wine as they wanted. One of them started betting his friend that he could drink more than his colleague. A group of foreigners was standing next to them, encouraging them to take the bet and laughing at them behind their backs. We watched as two of them boasted about who was stronger: one claimed he could lift the table with one hand, while the other bragged that he could bend a riyal piece double between his fingers. They spent quite a while in this fashion, boasting and showing off. Whatever the case, things always finished up with bets being made; we imagined that none of them ever ate unless it was for a bet. Conversation now took a number of turns. One of them stated that he had leapt from the back of a camel and landed on one foot. Another insisted that he spoke to his stallion, and it understood him. Still another maintained that his girlfriend had sworn that she'd not seen anyone in Paris who danced as well as he did. Leaning heavily on each other, they now went into the gambling room. It was not long before pockets were emptied and money was borrowed. If the successful player refused to grant a loan, the bankrupt player would turn to the waiters and ask them for help. Soon afterwards they started arguing and quarreling among themselves in a way which we feared could only bring dire consequences.

25.14 We hurried out in order to make a safe exit. The Pāshā followed me guffawing with laughter. "Where are your floods of tears and heavy sighs?" I asked him. "Fate has overruled grief or tears," he replied. "Have you forgotten the line of the wise poet that you've recited for me:

> This life is an actor's drama;
> night is a curtain, and day is a stage."

Miṣbāḥ al-sharq 80, November 9, 1899[201]

'Īsā ibn Hishām said: The Pāshā had been amazed by what he had seen in these gatherings and meeting places and what he had learned in the sessions involved. They had offered object lessons and counsel that could dispense with the need for lengthy experience. They had offered him some relief and relaxation, and as a result his sufferings at the cruel hand of fate and destiny had dissipated. Frowns had turned into smiles, and difficulties had now become that much easier. So it happens that those people who have experienced hardships find adversity that much less of a burden. Ever since we had moved from the gathering of religious scholars to that of princes, he had kept asking for more of the same and insisting that he gain more knowledge. I told him that the only meeting places and clubs left for us to try were the scandalous clubs in the Ezbekiyyah, with all their varieties of filth, corruption, lechery, and drunkenness. "I've too high a regard for you," I said, "to bring into contact with such things; I should keep you far away. I have too much respect for you to lead you down paths that would see accusations leveled against you and raise doubts about your probity. I value your status too much to drag you down to such dubious haunts; my concern for your age and status will not permit me to let you mix with such people and dive into such a fetid pond. You will of necessity follow their lead and copy their ways. Your noble self will have to endure the kind of things they do, things the like of which you've never experienced. And they are evil indeed!" 26.1

26.2 "How can you say such things?" he replied, "when you've provided me with a whole variety of scholarship and philosophy that has enabled me to scorn the reproaches and criticisms of ignorant fools? A pure and noble soul will never suffer harm from being close to an evil and corrupt one. One patient rarely infects another; a foul stench can rarely dispel the odor of perfume. A close look at sin and vice only serves to strengthen the virtuous soul's adherence to virtue. The genuine is defined by what is corrupt, and the value of what is good is only enhanced through contact with what is evil.

Things are defined by their opposites.[202]

"Anyone who decides to study ethics without conducting research for himself or probing their depths can only indulge in conjectures, like someone trying to foretell what will happen, an artist using the imagination, or a painter without a model. The appreciation of all this I owe to the good advice you've been giving me. In the time of our regime, it was considered appropriate for governors and senior officials to change their appearance, disguise themselves, and substitute unfamiliar attire for their usual uniform. They could then mix with people during their leisure time and hours of relaxation and chat with them. That way, officials could find out for themselves what social conditions were really like, rather than having to rely purely on reports and word of mouth. Such contact with the common people did nothing to affect their prestige or detract from their authority. In my own case, following my resurrection from the dead I've donned a garment which has placed a veil between me and the common people. So come on, take me to these places. I find that I'm eager to continue my research on the secret aspects of people's morality."

26.3 ʿĪsā ibn Hishām said: So I went along with his decision and complied with his request. I took him to the luxuriant and fragrant park in the Ezbekiyyah. When we reached the gate, we stopped at the turnstile where I put in the admission fee; it was just like putting votive offerings into a donation box. I took my turn in it and so did the Pāshā. Suppressing his anger he asked me why people entering these gardens were expected to go round in circles like an ox at a waterwheel. I replied that these days people distrusted each other and were excessively concerned about safety, so they had invented inanimate machines like this; it counted what the entrants paid at every turn, and so not a grain of dust was lost. We started strolling along the paths and then sat down on a bench. The Pāshā was overwhelmed by the sheer beauty of the place and expressed his delight. "God alone possesses power and might!" he exclaimed. "Which grandee owns this place?" "It belongs to everyone," I replied, "no one person owns it. The government has turned it into a public facility, so all kinds of people can take a stroll. Everyone can enjoy this park by paying a very small fee."

'Īsā ibn Hishām said: We started walking around the various parts of the garden, looking at the leafy trees, luxuriant branches, and pretty flowers. The Pāshā kept looking at everything in amazement, utterly thrilled by what he was seeing: 26.4

A spot that reveals the Creator to you
when you disclose your thoughts on its beauty.[203]

The Pāshā looked left and right and then asked me:

Pāshā Why isn't this place thronged with people? Why aren't they taking advantage of the shade and looking at the beautiful views and marvelous design? As long as the government has opened it up to everyone, as you've just told me, why does it look exactly the opposite? The only people I can see are those foreigners over there wearing their distinctive clothes with their wives and children by their side? Has the government reserved this place for Westerners to the exclusion of other people? Since we entered and started walking around, we're the only Egyptians I've seen.

'Īsā It's not the government's fault. It's just that Egyptians have grown accustomed to paying minimal attention to cultural 26.5

pleasures, to seeking solace by looking at lovely views and spectacular sights, and to gaining insight and mental stimulation from reading books about nature and the beauties of creation. You find that Egyptians have put themselves into some kind of prison and confined their thoughts about the universe entirely to material things. An entire lifetime may pass by without them looking up at the stars in the sky or observing the variety of trees and flowers that the earth produces before their very eyes, so beautiful and eloquent that:

> You shout at passersby: "Do you not see me?
> For then you will understand the logic of amazing creation."[204]

PĀSHĀ Excellent! But tell me, how is it that Egyptians don't appreciate such a blessing, the sheer delight of such contemplation? Why have foreigners achieved that, and not Egyptians?

26.6 ʿĪSĀ Foreigners are now accustomed to appreciating such things, so much so that it's part of their nature. They have come to regard such practice as one of the arts and sciences necessary for civilized society and culture. It flows in their bloodstream, and sons inherit it from their fathers. For example, a young child of theirs will pick flowers and gather scented plants from the house garden into a posy in his hand; for his family that will be the best possible present he could bring them. These noble feelings and lovely sentiments are now deep-seated in Western society; from natural truths they've moved on to drawings and man-made pictures. You'll see someone busy painting a picture of a flower, a twilight scene, a shepherd, or an animal. The value of those images is thousands of thousand times more than their original in nature.

26.7 You'll rarely enter a wealthy person's home without finding the walls decorated with paintings and designs on panels portraying nature scenes. In that way the house owner is never deprived inside his house of the beautiful vistas outside. This in turn has led them to develop a great passion for looking at ancient relics and a fierce competition to acquire them. They go to excessive lengths to keep them exclusively for themselves. How often have we seen pieces of dagger or other objects that we despise? Egyptians in general ignore them; they even put them out along with their domestic rubbish. That's the way it continues until foreigners start collecting them; at which point they become worth as much as a precious jewel in a crown or a solitary pearl in a necklace. How often have we noticed tourists putting up with all the hardships of travel, the terrors of the sea and dangers of the desert, spending thousands of dirhams and dinars in the process, and all that so that they can look at some ruins and remains in this part of the world. Meanwhile, Egyptians living in Cairo, where they grow up, pass through middle and old age, and finally become old and senile, never even set eyes on the Pyramids which are right next to them. If they do, it's only because of the picture on postage stamps! Often they'll not even see that.

PĀSHĀ Goodness me, how amazing! If things worked in pro- 26.8
portion, Egyptians would be in the very forefront of nations when it comes to enjoying the feeling of pleasure through contemplation of the wonders of creation and the beauties of mankind. They've an amiable disposition and a gentle character, and their hearts are rapidly touched and affected by emotion. God has favored them with a pleasant climate, temperate weather, clear skies, an abundance of water, and fertile soil. Their means of earning a living wage are limited to farming—ploughing, planting, and harvesting. Anyone who regards the area of Egypt as a green chrysolite amid the Sahara sands has to envy its people the fact that it's decorated with such a jewel from nature's necklace, and that the people can enjoy the contemplation of this wondrous spectacle that can clear the vision, gladden the heart, and nourish the spirit. In so doing, it can soothe their worries and anxieties and calm their souls. Then the soul can flit from the trammels of the lower world to a link with the rope to the upper world. There for a while they can find some respite from life's relentless struggle and varieties of sickness and disease, escaping for a short while from sorrows and miseries in order to come "face to face with your Lord, the possessor of honor and veneration."[205]

26.9 You should realize—and I've often benefited myself from an expression that you've used, so please allow me to use it this once, as what I'm saying to you now is based purely on good will and experience—that the difference between humans and animals is not limited just to their nature, for some things in their nature are similar; nor to the ability to speak, as some animals can speak; nor to cleverness, since some of the earth's vermin and birds can surpass mankind's prudence and organizational ability in that too. No! The quality which distinguishes humanity from all other animals is its awareness of the true nature of existence through close study and its prolonged contemplation of God's creatures so that it can be guided to a knowledge of their Creator. This is the spiritual happiness and pleasure which distinguishes mankind from other creatures. It's the noblest, purest, the most excellent, and most lasting of all pleasures. The closest a worshiper can come to God in terms of flattery, the most sublime mode of devotion that he can show to the Creator—may His visage be exalted!—is through contemplation of the sheer beauty and wonders of His creation. Only those who one day find themselves, like me, removed from the corporeal, ephemeral world to the spiritual, eternal one can fully grasp the true value of these spiritual pleasures. Only someone who has experienced it can tell you.

Furthermore, if things worked in proportion, Egyptians would be involved with these cultural scenarios, if not for the pleasant sensations involved, then at least as a consequence of the way they imitate Western people and copy their habits in different situations—posture, clothes, way of life, gestures, and repose. But then, perhaps there's some underlying reason that prevents them from extending their imitation into this sphere as well.

26.10 ʿĪsā There's nothing to stop them. It's just that Egyptians are too introverted, not only in material concerns but cultural ones as well. As you can tell, they imitate foreigners, but only in trivial and undesirable ways that incite lusts, false ostentation, and phony tinsel—the kinds of thing that only result in bodily disease and wasted money. But, when it comes to beneficial aspects of civilization, they're not merely ignorant of them, but they even disparage them. In summary one may say that the way Egyptians have adopted the habits of Western civilization is analogous to a sieve that retains all the worthless waste and lets through the useful things with any value.

ʿĪsā ibn Hishām said: As our conversation proceeded in this fashion, I found myself delighted on two accounts; I wasn't sure which of the two was the more powerful emotion: my delight in listening to my colleague and realizing with joy how far he'd progressed in his thinking, appreciation, and psychological state; or my own delight as I looked at the gardens bathed in the late afternoon sunlight. I recalled the lines written by a colleague to describe this lovely park and its gorgeous vistas: 26.11

> The Ezbekiyyah Gardens possess a beauty
> that delights the hearts of observers.
> Should you come there before sunset,
> you see a green emerald in a golden ring.[206]

We continued walking till we reached the artificial grotto in a section of the garden. We observed its beautiful shape and exquisite craftsmanship. As water gushed from clefts, the Pāshā was overjoyed, and we decided to sit down on some chairs placed there for visitors. No sooner had he looked round than he turned back to me quickly and asked: "Aren't those three people sitting over there Egyptians?" I turned round and looked. He was right. They were busy talking to each other, so we listened from our seats to what they were saying. From their conversation, we gathered that one of them was a country *ʿumdah,*[207] the second was a port merchant, and the third a dissolute playboy. We picked up the conversation the ʿUmdah was having with the Playboy: 26.12

ʿUmdah So where's the thing we came to these gardens for? Did you really mean for us to sit here under these trees, with all this humidity and polluted water? I can't see any difference between the view here and the swamp I left behind in my village. By my life, the ducks swimming in the swamp there are far more numerous than the ones swimming around in front of us here. What's the point of these useless trees that don't bear any fruit or help relieve your hunger! Come on, feed us some of that luscious fruit and fresh game you promised us!

26.13 PLAYBOY Steady on! You won't miss a thing. I didn't realize that these gardens would have been reduced to such a state of desolation. But then I've just asked a servant who happened to be passing by. I've learned that the government apparently has nothing else to do; the only way it can find to serve the people is by restricting access to these gardens as reformers demand. Such reforms involve preventing girls with veils and shawls from entering the gardens. With that in mind, I can only quote the newspapers' phrase when grumbling about government action: «We count on God, and good is the trustee!»[208]

MERCHANT In that case, gone are the days when this garden used to be a delight for the observer, a promenade for beauties, a playground for gorgeous maidens, and a sweet resort for those in quest of wine and beauty. I've often come in here by myself and have never left without ensnaring two, three or four hundred lovely little antelopes.

'UMDAH God knows, nowadays Cairo's turned into a place where you should only stay long enough to complete your business and then head back immediately to your hometown. If only things were restricted to these gardens; on this visit I'm feeling totally deprived. I spent last night in the company of X the government employee in such-and-such office. My plan was to take him around and give him a good time as usual so that I could achieve my purpose. But—curse him!—he dragged me to any number of places in the Ezbekiyyah that he likes to frequent, but, as you know, I didn't find anything I liked in a single one of them. I came out with an aching head from the wine and empty pockets from the gambling.

This wretch wasn't content to involve himself alone, but dragged his friends in as well, all of whom clustered around me. I had to pay for everything. Every time he noticed me turning away from one of them, he told me that the person was Y, someone who was able to deal with my needs.

MERCHANT But why did you spend so much and go along with his scheme, when you only needed one person? 26.14

'UMDAH You've every right to object. God has relieved you from the irksome problems we face. Your commercial business in the cities doesn't require the kind of fawning, dissimulation, compliance, and cautious strategizing that agriculture does in the provinces. A single word from a junior official can often bring about the failure of a big transaction. How are you to know that the person you disregard and ignore in the Ezbekiyyah one night will not turn out the very next morning to be a judge in court or provincial offices?

PLAYBOY If things last night weren't to your liking, then we'll make amends tonight.

'UMDAH Are we supposed to believe your story about amends when you weren't telling us the truth in inviting us to these gardens!

PLAYBOY Believe me! I'd no idea of the effect government regulations have had on these gardens. I've been spending a lot of time in Ḥulwān and came here assuming it was the way it used to be. But—God be thanked!—I've arranged a little soirée that will surpass all previous occasions. When it comes to frequenting night clubs, don't assume I'm like your friend of yesterday. I've come across someone who has shown me how to get to a cloistered maiden in B Pāshā's house. Come on, let's leave now! I'm going to have to make an effort to persuade her to receive me tonight. I'll keep you two a secret from her. Once she's arrived at the rendezvous of my choice, I'll send someone to bring the two of you. You can enter when she's not paying attention, so she won't be able to hide. Then we'll be able to sit and chat with her to our hearts' content. But I can't conceal from you both that the dirhams I have on me are not enough to make all the necessary preparations for this tête-à-tête. If I went home to get enough money, I'm afraid that my family would stop me from coming back.

'Umdah Don't worry! I've got enough dirhams and more.

26.15 'Īsā ibn Hishām said: With that they grabbed each other by the hand and went off in search of debauchery and immoral pleasure. The Pāshā was sitting beside me, listening and thinking to himself; at times he was laughing, at others invoking God. We too stood up and followed them.

Miṣbāḥ al-sharq 87, January 4, 1900[209]

ʿĪsā ibn Hishām said: Our description of the perfumed gardens had reached the point of the discussion between the Playboy, ʿUmdah, and Merchant. They had left it to indulge in some debauchery and lewd diversions. For my part I was still exercising caution in selecting crowded venues and places to visit, all in response to the Pāshā's request for object lessons from which to learn—even if that required us to descend into low haunts and mingle with the lowest levels of society. In order to achieve this goal and satisfy our question I could not imagine any more effective way than following this trio to notorious haunts. "This is a good opportunity," I told myself, "and a lucky chance that we should not miss." I had noticed that the crafty Playboy was a devotee of such nefarious places where entertainments and entertainers stoke the flames of passion. This particular con man was completely au fait with such venues; he knew where the best ones were and better than the sandgrouse how to get there.[210] I explained my plan to the Pāshā and told him what my intentions were. He agreed to go along with it. 27.1

We kept up with them so we could both see and hear them. We heard the ʿUmdah say, "I really need to exercise my body and while away some time playing a round of billiards in the Opera Bar or New Bar." No one could have been quicker than the Playboy to satisfy his demand and fulfil his request. "What a splendid choice!" he said. "Come on and wait for me at the Opera Bar while I go and carry out the promise I've made; it'll be an occasion combining all pleasures 27.2

into one and giving us total satisfaction. Once I've managed all that in accordance with my solemn pledge, I'll come back." With that they agreed to his plan and separated in the square with Ibrāhīm's statue.

"Now we know their plan," I told the Pāshā, "and where they're going. But stop for a moment and let me point out something to you that will be the greatest possible gift." "And what might that be?" he asked. I pointed at the statue of Ibrāhīm and said "That!" He stared at it for a moment and then stood to attention out of respect. "Hail to Ibrāhīm!" he said, quivering and shaking all over. He gave a bitter, sorrowful sigh and almost burst into tears. "Why so sad?" I asked him. "Are you nostalgic for times past with all their happy and bitter moments and the good and bad things that are long since past? Haven't you now pursued different paths—those of maturity and common sense—and started to display symptoms of prudence and sound judgment?"

27.3 "How can I not shed tears of sorrow?" the Pāshā responded, "and express my profound grief when I see before me this hero of Egypt, someone who raised triumphal banners, kindled and burned fires of battle, and waded through the floods of tumultuous war and swept them clean:

> In every pore of his body where a hair grew,
> there was a lion extending its claws towards the prey.[211]

"My lord and master, source of my honor and prestige, kindling of my fire! I cannot dissemble. How can they have erected his statue in this place infamous for its dreadful reputation? Woe to a people whose indifference has brought them so low that frivolity and scrapping are now regarded as manly and serious."

"Calm down!" I told him, "Enough with your sorrows and censure. You're a creature of your own times. Just take a look at this columned building."

"It is indeed splendid," he said. "To which grandee does it belong?"

"It's a playhouse built by Ismā'īl," I replied. "He was responsible for building its foundations and providing its seats. It was beautifully designed and constructed:[212] 27.4

> No one can know: was it humans that built it for the jinn
> to live in, or did the jinn construct it for humans?[213]

so much so that it has now become the cynosure of all eyes, the haven of delights, where all kinds of entertainment and wonders are assembled, plots taken from sagas of the ancients and tales of yore. Scenes are acted out before the audience and offer lessons for those who would learn. They offer gorgeous girls with all the allure of song and dance. All this imitates the way Western people do things in their countries and copies their traditions. The government has decided to spend people's money in this way in order to provide amusement for foreigners and tourists. The only logic involved in the building's construction seems to have been that its harm should be greater than its benefits."

When we reached the place where we were heading, our rendez- 27.5
vous point, the Pāshā looked at the crowds of people going in and out. "What's this colossal din about?" he asked. "Is this a funeral or a wedding?" "Neither," I replied. "It's the place we've been heading for, where we've agreed to meet our friends. It's a public meeting place where people crowd in order to spend the evening out and drink wine." With that we made our way inside and chose some seats so we could listen to the conversation. The 'Umdah was playing billiards with someone else, while the Merchant and others were playing cards. Alongside us four people had a row and started arguing and protesting. From their conversation it became clear that the group consisted of a stockbroker and a wealthy man, along with a plaintiff in a court case and a foreign lawyer's assistant. Here's part of the conversation that we heard as their arguments came to a close:

Broker (*to the Rich Man*) There's no denying the fact that 27.6
former patterns of wealth have vanished. The days of old are long

gone when a man could become rich with a word or gesture and find himself thereby the richest of the rich after being considered the poorest of the poor. Egyptians now live in an era when everything is poverty and need; no one is handing out estates, granting feudal rights, and dispensing largesse. Wealthy people remain indifferent, only investing through notes on which foreigners with their companies have a monopoly. You're all too aware that such sources of revenue are not sufficient to meet needs that keep increasing day by day. As a result people have to spend part of their inherited property. The losses to a person's wealth never stop. If he continues this way and then tries to divide his property among his children, they each land up with just enough to live on and that's all. You can be sure that, before a single generation has passed, the wealthy's family homes that are left will vanish. But you should know that there is one place now that gushes with money and guarantees wealth. It can unlock treasure chests and take the place of those palaces where a person could enter in poverty, then emerge that very day, or rather that very hour, as a rich man. I'm referring to the Stock Market.[214]

27.7 Rich Man Don't even mention the words "Stock Market." In just the last few days, I've heard what it did to X, Y, and Z. That's enough to give pause to any sensible person.

Broker Please, Sir, don't use the cases of X, Y, and Z as examples. The reason why they lost is obvious enough; it's not the Stock Exchange's fault, but rather what they did for themselves. The first resorted to speculation in his buying and selling, relying on advice from one of two fortune-tellers: one a Sudanese woman using seashells, the other a European with bits of paper. The second one heard a lunatic whom he trusted yelling in the street "Go away, Zayd!" At that particular moment, he was wavering between buying and selling. Taking those words as an omen, he rushed in his carriage to the broker and told him to buy twenty thousand qanṭars. The broker tried to counsel against it, but he refused to accept the advice; all the broker's attempts to prevent a loss were rebuffed. Prices fell, and the idiot had to swallow his curses as he lost all his money. The third relied entirely on what the newspapers had to say. None of the three treated things seriously or took their brokers' advice. Those brokers are the people with the best information on speculation; they're the best informed about its ups and downs.

Rich Man You may have just given me an expert argument and skillful proof, but you should know that I can't regard speculation on the Stock Exchange as anything but a very risky venture.

Broker But man takes risks in everything he does. Anyone 27.8
who tries to protect himself from danger will never leave his house, even though it too can be exposed to risks. But let me try to convince you on the basis of your own situation. You've just told me that your yield this year is three thousand qanṭars from six hundred feddans of land. This year you've planted cotton, and the qanṭars are being stored in your house in anticipation of a rise in prices. You haven't taken into account the fact that cotton loses weight, nor the threat of other hazards such as theft or fire. If you were waiting with your three thousand qanṭars till prices rise, wouldn't it be better to wait for the profits from thirty thousand "contracts"? You wouldn't have to buy land, spend money on ploughing, or worry about crop damage and all the bother about irrigation. You'd never need to get embroiled in legal actions and disputes or problems with neighbors and government officials. You'd have no fears of disaster, whether earthly or heavenly. Instead it's all clear profit. The only capital involved is the four letters which you write as your signature.

Rich Man No matter how many arguments you advance, I'm still wary of getting involved in the matter.

Broker I'm not going to involve you in anything major; I'm 27.9
only suggesting something to your advantage. All you have to do is to experiment by purchasing two thousand contracts. You can add them to your own three thousand, and then wait for the rise in prices for all of it. As long as you accept my advice, I can guarantee you a profit. To sum it all up, the difference in speedy profits between people who work on the one hand in commerce, agriculture, and industry, and on the other in the Stock Market is like the

difference between traveling by camel and flying on the wings of steam, between climbing stairs to an upper story and taking the elevator, or between two copies of the same book, one handwritten, the other printed. This being so, it's up to you to choose as you please.

Rich Man How are prices faring today?

Broker Exactly as they were yesterday, a golden opportunity to buy.

Rich Man Then take a thousand qanṭars.

27.10 ʿĪsā ibn Hishām said: With that, we left this sparrow who had just fallen into the snare, and listened to the continuing conversation between the plaintiff and foreign lawyer's assistant:

Assistant If you take my advice and agree with me, then don't bring your case before the Native Courts. Quite apart from the slow pace at which they function in situations like this, they rarely rule against the government; and even if they do, it's difficult to have the judgment imposed. The Mixed Courts, on the other hand, have no qualms about ruling against the government, using all their facilities in the process. Sentences are carried out quicker than a shot from a bow. In much the same way, the Native Court doesn't appreciate the importance of this case and its place in history, nor will it take into consideration the interest accrued from the time of seizure till now. I can assure you that you won't win this important case unless you take it to the Mixed Courts. But before anything else, tell me about the tree that's mentioned in the deed with its recognized historical name? Is your own descent traceable back to the endower?

Plaintiff It's mentioned in the endowment document as being on arable land and recorded as being "the Tree of the Virgin." My own descent can be traced back to a freedman of the endower, Sulṭān al-Ẓāhir Baybars, who had rights to it. But how can I bring the case before the Mixed Courts? How can I possibly afford a foreign lawyer when I'm well aware of the huge sums you have to pay them in advance fees?

ASSISTANT Don't worry about that! Bringing the case before the Mixed Courts is easy: it's simply assigned to a foreigner. With regard to the foreign lawyer, I'll guarantee I can persuade the lawyer with whom I work to accept the case without bothering about advance charges. All he'll request is half the amount of profit you get from the case. The foreigner to whom you'll submit the case is in our office ready and waiting to be made use of in cases like this. All you need do now is pay the costs and judicial fees. 27.11

PLAINTIFF That's all very well, but the problem is that I haven't any spare cash on hand to pay for such expenses. God knows, if I was confident of winning the case, I'd sell the portion of the property that I own. But I'm afraid I'll lose the case, in which case I and my children will lose our livelihood.

ASSISTANT If you knew how skilled my master was and realized what high standing he had in the Mixed Courts and how close were his contacts with the consuls of various countries, you'd be asking God for proper guidance in selling your part of the estate and making every effort to bring the case.

PLAINTIFF In which case I will indeed ask God for guidance. I like your plan.

ASSISTANT So then, you'll permit me to speak to my master. All you have to do is come tomorrow to settle the terms.

PLAINTIFF Give me some time to find someone to buy part of the estate for the appropriate price.

ASSISTANT You've plenty of time to do that. All we need for the moment is for you to bring the deeds and documents so that they can be perused.

PLAINTIFF We'll meet here at the same time.

ʿĪsā ibn Hishām said: At that, we left this fish as well to thrash around in the net. We were surprised to watch as the ʿUmdah played 27.12

a billiards shot that hit a hatted foreigner who was playing with the Merchant right in the face. The man was absolutely furious and got out of his seat, hell-bent on doing the ʿUmdah an injury. The Merchant intervened between the two of them, with the hatted gentleman muttering and snarling, while the ʿUmdah kept stammering and mumbling. This was a genuine case of hat versus turban, or raven against dove. The Merchant's mediation ended up with two bottles of champagne being opened at the ʿUmdah's expense as a way of resolving the issue. Now the ʿUmdah's billiard partner insisted that he finish the game. The ʿUmdah asked to be excused, but that was refused. He returned reluctantly to the table, his hand shaking as he did so. It was only two shots later that he hit the table cover with his cue and ripped it apart. The waiter yelled for the owner of the bar, and the other waiters hurried along behind him. The owner turned to them and scolded them for giving a billiard cue to such a clumsy idiot. "Now he's split the table and ruined it!" he told them. He then went over to the ʿUmdah and demanded compensation for the damage he'd caused. He estimated the cost at fifteen pounds. The ʿUmdah took out his purse and counted the contents; he only had thirteen pounds. The owner would only accept the full amount. The Merchant and several other people now interceded and asked him to accept the amount he had, and the owner finally agreed. The ʿUmdah meanwhile vowed that he would never play that game again; playing with adders, he said, was safer than using a billiard cue.

27.13 ʿĪsā ibn Hishām said: The ʿUmdah sat down, his only concern being to rid himself of his anxieties with drink. He kept asking, and the bar owner kept responding generously to his requests until he was drunk as a lord. Meanwhile the Merchant had finished his card game. He got up, claiming that he had lost three pounds, and made it clear to the ʿUmdah how much he regretted what had happened. "For heaven's sake, stop feeling so sorry for yourself!" the ʿUmdah told him. "At least the loser loses. Your misfortunes are not as bad as mine." He handed the Merchant a glass. While they were drinking, the Playboy came hurrying back all excited. He told them:

PLAYBOY It's time for our intimate little gathering. The night is blessed, the timing is right. Now I ask God to prolong this night for us and keep daylight far away. Our plans are complete. Let's go!

'UMDAH For our part, we ask God to shorten the night and bring daylight as soon as possible! Sit down, and we'll tell you what has happened to us while you were away.

As they both told him what had happened, he stared at them—right arm outstretched, lips drooping, and nostrils flared.

PLAYBOY Woe is me! I'm to blame for leaving you to get into this trouble in my absence. However, God has made provision and shown you His kindness. My problems on the other hand are much worse. What can I say or do? How can I pay? What excuse am I supposed to offer? I've arranged everything and managed to bring the object of our desire. The intimate soirée is waiting for us!

MERCHANT Things are much easier than you fear. What we miss tonight we can get tomorrow!

PLAYBOY Such things aren't always available. This particular occasion is totally unique for a secluded girl. How can I postpone our little gathering when it's well past midnight?

> How can I return her, when around her domed mansions
> there are brown spears poised attentively?[215]

I beg you both, please save me from the tricky situation I'm in.

MERCHANT You know the situation. What's the best solution? 27.14

'UMDAH By God, it would be terrible to be deprived of the intimate occasion that you've described, far worse in fact than any other misfortune we've suffered. If it were daytime, I'd hurry to the bank and get the cash we need.

MERCHANT Since you seem to be that keen, things are simple. I've got enough money on me now. I'll assume the bank's role for you. How much do you want, and what deadline can you set for repayment?

PLAYBOY Now that is true friendship indeed when circumstances are difficult! May God grant you a long life!

'UMDAH Just to be on the safe side, loan me twenty pounds.

MERCHANT Here's the balance, seventeen pounds. That's the twenty you're asking minus the three I lost here in front of you.

27.15 'Īsā ibn Hishām said: No one could have moved quicker than the Playboy in bringing inkwell and paper. He put it gleefully in front of the 'Umdah and asked him to fill out the check. Once he had signed it, the three of them left. The 'Umdah kept dragging the edge of his coat behind him and scratching his head. Meanwhile the Pāshā kept looking on in amazement and pondering. We followed them out to see how things would work out.

Miṣbāḥ al-sharq 88, January 11, 1900[216]

ʿĪsā ibn Hishām said: As we left, the Pāshā was saying: "What is going on with the things we see people doing? It's almost as though someone has soaked everyone in a jar containing a mixture of all the worst faults to be found in man or else dipped them in a pool full of the various categories of crime. With each step we take we seem to be encountering every conceivable type of fraud and deceit. Whenever we investigate something, we read whole chapters involving swindling and hypocrisy. Pity the poor devils who have to deal with them and live among them! How miserable their neighbours must be, and how delighted those who can elude them—so God help me against mankind in this era!" "Enough of such talk!" I replied, and quoted these lines to him: 28.1

In no age will people's affairs be in sound order,
nor have they ever been; here security, there alarm.
In no age do people uphold any right;
from Adam's time they were divided by caprice.[217]

Whether the era was backward or advanced, mankind was always this way; people now are exactly as they've always been, yesterday, today, and tomorrow. What can you possibly say about the descendants of Shaykh Adam and his wife Eve, when the angels have already had the following to say about them: «Do you put in it someone who will do mischief amongst them and will spill blood?»[218] How can you describe a society when, as you can see, 28.2

utterly despicable and insignificant people aspire to be ransomed for the very zodiacal sphere and galaxy of stars? What despicable behaviour, what lewd desires! How can you characterize a created species when its most outstanding members are the chief cause of mankind's and their own distress?

The best things in the heart destroy it,
so we seek refuge in God from its army.[219]

"The morsel inside the man's mouth is the best thing in it," as the saying goes. If another identical morsel could be made with a scorpion sting as its meat—may God protect you!—and viper spittle as its pigment—may God shield you!—it would still be less harmful and pernicious when juxtaposed with this type of language. How can you describe a species, one of whom God Himself has described in a verse of the Qur'an with nine epithets:

«An oath taker, despicable, a slanderer proceeding in his libel, a preventer of good, a transgressor and criminal, harsh as well and impure by birth»[220]?

So to blazes with their periods of day and night
and their two sexes, men and women!
Would that a child died at the moment it was born
and did not suckle from its mother in childbed!
It says to her before ever speech is granted:
All you will get from me is sorrow and complaint![221]

28.3 As you contemplate different aspects of morality, don't despair or lose your temper. And as you experience people's various traits, don't act so amazed! Don't you realize that the moral integrity of the people you have been watching is by far preferable to that of their social superiors? Perhaps the things you've noticed—rich men's greed, brokers at their tricks, lawyers' assistants using all their wiles, the Merchant's treachery, the 'Umdah's ignorance, and the Playboy's crooked schemes—all of which clearly reveal their secret intentions and convictions—are actually significantly less pernicious than the things influential men and amirs keep under a veil of phony affectation, hidden from their colleagues' eyes behind walls of dissimulation? Every time someone is promoted a rank and takes a step forward, he enshrouds the process in a veil of secrecy. You'll find the truth about humanity recorded under pages of artful dissimulation and buried beneath cascades of hypocrisy. Indeed, people completely devoid of moral virtues and laudable qualities will be the ones who go to the greatest lengths of pretence in order to be known and recognized for them. I once had a friend who, on the basis of his talk, you would have assumed to be a raging lion guarding his lair and protecting his cubs, feared and respected by Caesars and Chosroes'. However, when you probed a little and penetrated his mind, you discovered that he was a complete coward, like a sheep leaning over its lambs or a wet nurse bending over her infant. I know another man who's made the letters of the word "virtue" shout, so often does he use his pen to prick with it and his mouth to spit it out. And yet, should he hear that someone has swindled a mere penny out of him, he scratches his face in anguish and gets sore eyelids from weeping. He's adept at using such fakery in his facial expressions to adopt a variety of different moods and symptoms; he can produce tears at will, and smiles when needed.

One person once said to another: "How often the chessboard changes in appearance, then comes together!" to which the other replied: "The changing aspects of people are even more remarkable." The sordid and depraved side of their moral character remains hidden from view until something happens to bring it to light. Then the seal is broken and the veil ripped away, revealing a foul and ugly disposition. In dealing with people's character the clarifying factors are fear, sorrow, anger, and drunkenness. The last of those, drunkenness, is right in front of us now, so let's catch up with our three companions. 28.4

28.5 ʿĪsā ibn Hishām said: We caught up with them. They were engaged in conversation, and so we eavesdropped on them:

ʿUmdah I've had enough of this! The sparrows in my stomach are screaming! Apart for a morning snack, I haven't eaten a thing all day; and I ate that in a hurry. Let's go to the New Road.[222] We can go to al-ʿAṭfi's—there's plenty of good food to be had there, real butter and good fat meat.

Merchant What's this al-ʿAṭfī you're talking about? What about al-ʿAjamī's rice and kebab at al-Fār next door?

Playboy Look, what's the point of all those places when we're in the Ezbekiyyah, with the New Bar, St. James Bar, American Bar, and Splendid Bar close by. They've everything to please the heart and delight the eye, not to mention cleanliness, good service, and the prestige of their customers.

ʿUmdah No, forget about those places! Their food isn't rich enough. It won't be enough to assuage my hunger, especially when my stomach is so empty.

Playboy Well, whatever the case may be, I can't possibly leave this area and accompany you to the places you've mentioned. I'm afraid people I know might see me there, and then I'd go right down in their estimation.

Merchant If that's the case, then I'm with you.

Playboy (*to the ʿUmdah*) Well then, there's no question. Two weaks overrule a strong. Come on, let's go to the New Bar.

28.6 ʿĪsā ibn Hishām said: They went inside, and we followed behind. They sat down, and we took seats nearby. The Playboy took off his tarboosh, and immediately the ʿUmdah removed his turban and cloak. When the former beat on the table with his hands to call the waiter, the ʿUmdah clapped with his. The waiter came up with the menu. The ʿUmdah grabbed it, took a look, and then handed it to the Playboy. "Translate for me!" the ʿUmdah asked. The Playboy took it and perused the contents. "Where's the item I had yesterday?" he asked the waiter. "It was delicious." The Playboy now proceeded to list the various choices until he reached the end. The ʿUmdah was paying no attention, but the Merchant listened carefully.

PLAYBOY (*to the ʿUmdah*) What would you like to order?

ʿUMDAH Broth, and, to follow, grilled meat.

MERCHANT I'll have kebab, rice, and pumpkin.

PLAYBOY (*to the waiter*) First I'll take the hors d'oeuvres, then a meat omelette, rice with seafood, chicken with mushrooms, truffles, and asparagus with butter.

ʿUMDAH What are all those strange words?

PLAYBOY They're light foods. My stomach can't digest any other kind.

MERCHANT As the saying goes, eat whatever you like, but wear clothes that please other people!

ʿĪsā ibn Hishām said: The waiter came back with the hors d'oeuvre for the Playboy: olives, radish, salted fish, and butter. The ʿUmdah took a look at them, leaned over towards the slice of butter and gulped it down. "What's this weird mixure?" he asked. "Butter with fish?" The Playboy asked for some more. But no sooner had the waiter reappeared with the bowl of broth than he discovered that the ʿUmdah had already eaten all the bread that had been put there for him. He leaned across to grab the Playboy's share and gobbled it down. 28.7

ʿUMDAH (*to the Waiter*) Where's the bread?

The waiter duly brought him another piece. The ʿUmdah dunked it in the bowl of broth until it spilled on to the table. He gobbled that down too and asked for another bowl and some more bread, both of which he downed quickly. He asked the waiter to bring something else. All the while, he kept leaning over the Playboy's plate. He took a piece of chicken, put it down in front of him and tried to cut it with his knife. It fell on the floor. He got up from the table, picked it up in his hands, and ate it. He then took a piece of mushroom, nibbled at it, then put it back on the Playboy's plate. "What's this stuff?" he asked. "They may cook it here, but where I come from you can find it on dikes; children play with it."

28.8 The waiter came back with another bowl of broth. The ʿUmdah asked for more bread. With that the waiter lost his temper. "My dear Sir," he said, "this isn't the Ramali bakery, you know!"

PLAYBOY (*to the Waiter*) What's that stupid talk for, George? Everything's got its price here, hasn't it? With our money we can ask for whatever we want.

WAITER (*to the Playboy*) Excuse me, Sir! My remarks weren't directed at you.

PLAYBOY If they weren't directed at me, they were at my friend here. He's worth more to me than my own self.

ʿUMDAH Let him go and get the bread. Don't bother yourself with what he's saying.

MERCHANT (*to the Waiter*) Get on with your job and bring me some vegetables as well.

ʿUMDAH (*to the Playboy*) And bring an onion along with the bread. I fancy one—

PLAYBOY You can do anything you like tonight except eat onions. Don't forget that from here we're going somewhere where the smell of onions won't fit!

Once the Merchant had mixed the various things he had asked for and eaten them all, he yelled out and asked for some dessert and fruit.

ʿUMDAH If you've any dates, bring me some.

PLAYBOY I'll have some bananas and pineapple.

ʿUMDAH (*guffawing*) Who ever said you weren't a man of the people!

PLAYBOY (*to the Waiter*) Bring a bottle of white wine too.

28.9 ʿĪsā ibn Hishām said: While the Waiter was away, we watched as the ʿUmdah reached for the fruit bowl, grabbed a cluster of five bananas and put them in his pocket. Once they had all finished with the fruit and drink, the Waiter brought colored glass finger bowls to wash their hands. The ʿUmdah was about to drink from his, but the Playboy managed to stop him.

‘Umdah Why are you stopping me drinking that water? It smells like rose water.

Playboy My dear fellow, it’s for rinsing your fingertips.

Merchant Seeing is believing!

‘Umdah (*to the Waiter*) The check!

Merchant Coffee!

Playboy And a toothpick!

The Waiter brought all this. The ‘Umdah used a toothpick on his teeth, then took another and used it to clean out his ear. He wiped it off on the tablecloth and turned to the Playboy.

‘Umdah How much do we owe?

Playboy Thirty francs.

‘Umdah What’s this? That’s daylight robbery! If we’d gone to 28.10
one of the places I suggested before we came here, our stomachs would be full by now and we’d have had plenty of food for a moderate price. If I’d remembered that I’ve a pot of rice and pigeon that I brought up with me from my home town, we could have gone to the hotel. That would have been more than enough for all of us. This Waiter’s obviously trying to make fools of us, so he’s decided to overcharge us and keep the rest for himself. But I’m not the kind of person who’ll tolerate such negligence. I’m not going to pay this bill. I’ve eaten in lots of places like this, and it’s always obvious when the waiters are cheating. I’ll show you both how we’re being tricked. I don’t mind wasting ten pounds on nothing at all, but I won’t pay a single piastre for deceit of any kind.

With that, he clinked two glasses together to call the Waiter, and wine spilled all over the table. When the Waiter arrived, he was not at all happy at what he saw.

Playboy (*to the Waiter*) Is there some mistake on the check?

Waiter How can there possibly be a mistake? Everything you ordered is clearly listed.

‘Umdah What an explanation! But you’re the one who wrote the check.

Waiter I wrote it, and you ate it!

ʿUMDAH Did we eat thirty dishes to be charged thirty francs?

WAITER (*to the Playboy*) Please convince him, Sir!

ʿUMDAH Am I such a fool that he can convince me?

(*The Playboy now gets up to leave.*)

MERCHANT Where are we going now?

PLAYBOY I see they've put a new cable in the political cable sheet. I need to read it.

28.11 WAITER (*to the ʿUmdah*) Pay me the full amount and stop keeping me from my work.

(*The ʿUmdah puts twenty francs on the plate.*)

ʿUMDAH There's your check. I'm not going to pay any more.

WAITER This isn't a place where you haggle over the cost of food after you've eaten it.

MERCHANT Give him a couple more francs.

WAITER As long as this is the way you behave, you'd do better eating somewhere else.

MERCHANT Don't lose your temper, my good sir. This gentleman here eats in places like this and places even more important. But he likes people to be honest.

WAITER So I'm dishonest, am I?

(*He is so angry that he starts yelling in Greek, then goes away.*)

MERCHANT Modesty's obviously not his strong point!

ʿUMDAH By your life, I'm not afraid of him. What I've already paid is all he's going to get out of me.

The Waiter had now come back with the owner of the restaurant. The Playboy had also come back to his seat.

RESTAURANT OWNER What's going on here?

ʿUMDAH Your waiter here is overcharging us and being abusive.

RESTAURANT OWNER No one may say such things about our restaurant!

28.12 WAITER (*to the Playboy*) Up till now, I've only known you to keep company with charming, civilized people. What on earth are you doing bringing this shaykh to our restaurant tonight? His behavior's been criticized by everyone in the restaurant. He's swallowed butter, wrapped up bread, reached over other people's plates and put the remains of what he has eaten back on them; he's stained the table with gravy and wine, wiped his hands on the tablecloth, broken his glass, pilfered bananas and put them in his pocket, almost drunk water from the finger bowl, cleaned his ear with a toothpick and then wiped it off on the tablecloth. Many of our regular customers sitting nearby have walked out in disgust at the mere sight of such appalling manners. And not content with all that, he has even been flirting with some of the women and making lewd gestures at them. They've all got up and left in disgust.

RESTAURANT OWNER Indeed, if a shaykh like this one comes here again, people will stay away and our restaurant will be put out of business.

PLAYBOY (*giving the Owner a wink*) Don't address this gentleman as "Shaykh"! He's attained the second grade of honor and is entitled to be addressed as "Bey."

RESTAURANT OWNER My dear Sir, please excuse the Waiter. He's always at your service, and the place is entirely at your disposal.

'UMDAH Thank you!

(*He then addresses the Waiter.*)

'UMDAH You need to find out about people and learn from the Owner how to treat them properly.

(*He then turns to the Restaurant Owner.*) 28.13

'UMDAH By God, but for your kindness, I would only have paid twenty francs. But now I'll pay the amount you ask.

RESTAURANT OWNER (*to the Waiter*) Find out what they are drinking and bring us a round.

The Playboy now leaned over to the 'Umdah and suggested that he ask for two rounds of drinks to honor the Owner. The 'Umdah asked for wine, then for more. Then he paid the restaurant Owner the original amount, to which was added the cost of the things he had just been asking for. The 'Umdah stood up to leave, swaying, stretching, and yawning; he kept wiping his eyes and complaining to the Playboy about feeling very tired. The latter replied that this was all quite normal when one was full; the only way to relieve the feeling was to have a couple of glasses of cognac. "Come with us," the Playboy said. "Let's go to the bodega." With that they left. We followed to find out what would happen to them next.

Miṣbāḥ al-sharq 89, January 18, 1900[223]

'Īsā ibn Hishām said: They went on their way to the place which they had selected. As we followed behind them, we were lost in thought and assessing the situation. The Pāshā turned towards that great hotel, a veritable al-Khawarnak and al-Sadīr, and noticed the electric lights gleaming brightly like rising suns, so much so that darkest night shone in white raiment and its surface seemed like ebony embossed with silver. The street lamps resembled tree branches glowing with light rather than mere lamps. Each pillar seemed like a ray of dawn piercing the cavity of darkness—and what a piercing it was! In the pitch darkness the lights were like stars scattered throughout the dome of the firmament. Beneath these lights the Pāshā could see rows of men mingling freely with women. Favored by continuing good fortune and enveloped in a becoming opulence, they were sitting opposite each other and lounging on sofas, looking like an exquisite posy on a flowering branch caught by the rustle of the breeze. The sound of musical instruments could be heard. "Is this a reception for some sociable occasion?" the Pāshā asked me in amazement, "or a bridal procession? Has some house opened its rooms so that anyone can see what's inside? Or is it perhaps a festival night for a group of demons who are socializing with human beings like tame animals? They've forsaken the earth's interior for its surface, its belly for its lap." 29.1

29.2 "Yes," I replied, "these people are devils in human form. They traverse land and sea, cut through hard and rugged earth, and fly in the heavens. They can walk on water, penetrate through mountains, and pulverize mountain peaks, turning hills into lowlands, levelling mounds, making deserts into seas, and changing seas into steam. They make people in the East listen to sounds made by people in the West, and vice versa. They can bring down the remotest stars for you to see, magnify the tiniest spider into a mountain, freeze the air, melt stones, start gales, cure secret intestinal ailments, and discover unknown facts about the limbs."

29.3 My companion told me, "You're describing Solomon's jinn living in this era!"[224] "They're European officials," I replied, "steeped in civilized society. From their lofty perch they look down on us with utter contempt. From the perspective of power and prosperity, they regard us like an eagle perched on the peaks of Raḍwā and Thabīr staring down at desert grasshoppers and pool frogs. With regard to learning, it's like the great sage and teacher Alexander having to watch a boy spelling out his alphabet. In the sphere of arts and crafts, it's as though Pheidias the sculptor were placed alongside Euclas.[225] Concerning wealth, it would be like a man with a bunch of keys weighing down his waistband looking at a laborer wiping the sweat from his brow beneath a waterskin. Finally, if we investigate the finer qualities of mind, it would be like Riḍwān looking at the very Devil." "But wait a minute!" the Pāshā said. "Are they really the way they claim to be?" "Certainly not!" I replied. "They posture and show off, and keep bringing in innovations. Their activities are evil and their knowledge is pernicious. They're the people who rob others of their wages. They plunder territories, cross deserts and destroy common folk. They're the pirates of the high seas who make other people's blood flow. They're the ones who keep duping us with their finery and swamping us with their cheap trash. «They have bewitched people's eyes and terrified them; they have brought a mighty enchantment.»[226]

29.4 "When they travel abroad, they can be divided into two categories. The first consists of wealthy leisure classes with time to spare, people afflicted with the disease of boredom. They're so incredibly wealthy and so susceptible to the novelties of civilization that they're eager to separate themselves from their peers. As a result they're beset by the twin diseases of listlessness and boredom. The only way they can be cured is by staring at rocks and coming into contact with people in countries less civilized than their own, visiting their hovels and indeed rubbing shoulders with panthers and monkeys in their lairs. The second group consists of scholars who have used their knowledge to despoil countries and grab control of them. They can put up with hardships and be exposed to all kinds of danger in the earth's remotest corners and most distant lands, and all because people in their own homelands are so crowded and their salaries are so limited; everyone feels indentured and enslaved." The Pāshā told me that this was important information and a clear danger. The entire matter belonged to God alone.

ʿĪsā ibn Hishām said: By now we had reached the tavern. The three of them were lined up by the kegs. We sat down near them to record their conversation: 29.5

PLAYBOY Is the Prince here?

ʿUMDAH (*astounded*) Do princes come here? Is it right for us to sit drinking somewhere in the same company as them? Why did we come here? Let's go!

PLAYBOY Don't worry! Just wait and see what I'm going to do. You won't be leaving here without the Prince shaking your hand and sitting with you.

ʿUMDAH Don't crack jokes at my expense. What business do we have with princes?

MERCHANT (*to the ʿUmdah*) You should believe him. Some princes are quite decent and down-to-earth people. They like to deal with people on equal terms in their various meeting places and transactions.

ʿUMDAH (*to the Playboy*) What do you plan to do? Do you know him already?

PLAYBOY Of course! Otherwise how could I get to sit with him every night? I often accompany him to his palace.

ʿUMDAH You're exaggerating!

PLAYBOY No, I'm not. And here's the proof for you!

29.6 ʿĪsā ibn Hishām said: The Playboy stood up and went over to a table piled high with various sorts of wine and dessert. He leaned over to one of the people seated there who was busying himself with the offerings; one hand was holding his plate, the other his glass, and his mouth was full.

PLAYBOY May God grant His Highness the Prince all felicity!

PRINCE (*laughing merrily*) Hello to you, my friend! Where have you been? We've missed you.

PLAYBOY Please forgive me, Your Highness. I've been performing a service and under obligation. What's kept me away is these two companions of mine: one's a provincial ʿumdah and the other's a port merchant. I've known them before in their own towns, but they're both unfamiliar with Cairo. I promised them both that, when they came to Cairo, I would accompany them.

ONE OF THE COMPANY (*cracking a joke*) Don't you mean "drag them"![227]

(*The Prince laughs, then says:*)

PRINCE Oh, is there a cattle pen around here?

(*Everybody laughs.*)

EVERYONE What a terrific joke the Prince has just made!

PRINCE I've never learned how to crack jokes, but once in a while something will strike me.

ONE OF THE COMPANY (*to another*) Do you see, my friend, how subtle and refined the Prince's wit is, and what lofty phrases he uses!

ANOTHER MEMBER (*to his colleague*) By God, you're also being very eloquent tonight! Did you get those phrases from the papers?

29.7 PRINCE (*to the Playboy*) Come and sit down.

Playboy What about my two companions?

One of the Company They're relaxing.

Prince Are they known to be rich?

Playboy The 'Umdah owns a thousand feddans of land. The Merchant owns the biggest tavern in his town. The 'Umdah owns ten irrigation pumps and holds the second grade. The merchant owns a cotton mill, and is in line for the third grade.

Prince If that's the case, why not invite them to join us?

One of the Company (*to another*) That's all the aggravation we need. I can't stand staying here any longer. Let's go!

The Other Member Wait a bit until they bring the round of drinks we've ordered and the bowl of mussels the Prince asked for earlier.

The Playboy went back to his companions to bring them over to 29.8
the Prince's table. The 'Umdah got up to pay his respects, but, as he did so, dropped his cigarette holder on the marble floor. He bent down sadly to pick up the fragments, but the Playboy dragged him by the hand.

Playboy Don't bother about such trifles now! Can't you control yourself when the Prince is inviting you over?

'Umdah I'm only sorry because it was a memento I received as a present from the district's Municipal Superintendent when I presented him with a horse. That's why I valued it so highly. But let's leave that now. Tell me, has the Prince really invited me over? How did he even know me? What have you told him about me?

Merchant Yes, do tell us how it happened!

Playboy I said what I said. As the proverb puts it, "Send a wise man, but don't advise him."

'Umdah What was said about me during the conversation? I saw him laughing a lot.

Playboy I told him about the clever way you dealt with the cotton broker. Now he'd like to hear it from you in person.

Merchant Talking of brokers, has His Highness the Prince sold his cotton or is he one of the people holding back?

PLAYBOY (*to the 'Umdah*) Let's go!

When they reached the Prince's table, the 'Umdah extended his hand with a bow, then raised it to his head. The Prince smiled at him, gave him a greeting, and gestured to him to sit down. The 'Umdah declined and remained standing until the Playboy sat him down. With that everyone sat.

PRINCE (*to one of the company*) Remind me tomorrow about the picture of that horse. The Duke of Brook has written to me by way of his friend the Counselor asking me for a picture.

ONE OF THE COMPANY It would be better to have the picture taken in his presence the day after tomorrow when the Counselor comes with the Irrigation Inspector to the lunch to which you've invited them both.

The 'Umdah moved back a bit, and his chair leg hit the Merchant's toe. He leapt up angrily, but then sat down again, muttering to himself.

PRINCE (*to the 'Umdah*) What will you have to drink, my dear Shaykh, my dear Bey?

'UMDAH (*standing up*) If you'll excuse me, Your Highness, I won't have anything.

PLAYBOY In this case conformity takes precedence over good manners.

The Prince ordered a round of drinks, then at the Playboy's suggestion the 'Umdah did the same.

29.9 The Playboy reached for the cigarette box in front of the Prince and gave one to the 'Umdah and Merchant. The 'Umdah avoided lighting it in the Prince's presence, so he held it in his hand. Then a salesman came over and whispered something in the Prince's ear which made him guffaw. He told the Waiter to bring a glass for the salesman who drank it and left. The 'Umdah then clinked two glasses together to bring the waiter over to light his cigarette and ordered another round of drinks.

PRINCE (*to the 'Umdah*) What's the crop like in your area? How much cotton have you got per feddan?[228]

ʿUMDAH By your Highness's breath, I've been getting eight per feddan.

MERCHANT That's an excellent yield, but prices are falling. Has His Highness sold his cotton yet, or is he holding it back?

PRINCE (*to one of the company*) I'm not going to pay more than twenty pounds for that dagger I saw today.

MEMBER OF THE COMPANY What if the owner insists on thirty?

PRINCE (*to another member*) I'm still sorry about the dog that died and the parrot that flew away. Waiter, another round!

When the new round arrived and everyone had grabbed their 29.10
glass, the ʿUmdah brought out the bananas from his pocket. He wiped one of them with his handkerchief and offered it to the Prince, then distributed the rest among the people present. One of them found some wool sticking to his banana, so he discarded it and left it on the table.

ONE OF THE COMPANY (*to the ʿUmdah*) Are these bananas from your farm land? Do you ripen them in wool where you come from?

ʿUMDAH No, my dear Sir, they're from the New Bar. They've only been in my pocket for long enough for us to walk here.

(*The Playboy is disgusted. He collects all the bananas and hands them to the waiter. The ʿUmdah asks whether they should order champagne. His offer is accepted.*)

ʿUMDAH (*to the waiter*) Bring us some English champagne!

ONE OF THE COMPANY (*to his companion*) It looks as though the ʿUmdah's crop has actually produced ten per feddan!

COMPANION Yes, in the real-estate bank!

ONE OF THE COMPANY What does "English" mean?

COMPANION From the same nation as the pound.

Meanwhile the salesman came back. The Prince got up at once 29.11
and left. One by one the members of the company slinked out after him. The ʿUmdah leaned over the leftovers from the dessert trays and helped himself.

ʿUmdah (*to the Merchant*) Try some of this before the Prince comes back. It's delicious. But we don't have any bread.

Playboy The Prince got into his carriage and left.

Merchant I didn't see him pay any of the check.

ʿUmdah Maybe he has a standing account here.

Playboy Let's ask the waiter.

Waiter The Prince didn't pay anything.

Playboy How much is the check?

Waiter Including the food, seventy francs.

ʿUmdah I can't believe that His Highness would leave without paying his share of the bill. In that case, he must be coming back. Get the amount he owes from him when he comes back.

Waiter Whenever the Prince gets up and leaves like that, he usually won't be back that night. Even so, I'll add just the cost of what you've had to his account. That's normal as well.

ʿUmdah If I were going to pay for anything at all, it would only be for what his Highness the Prince had to drink.

29.12 While they were arguing in this fashion, a deputy governor entered. The ʿUmdah got up to welcome him and offered him his hand. He then turned to the waiter:

ʿUmdah Bring me a detailed bill listing exactly what his Highness the Prince had to drink and eat, how much the drinks cost for the Prince's companions, how much we drank with the Prince, and how much the Prince drank before we arrived. Bring me the check so that I can pay you the entire amount.

Waiter I've told you, Sir. It's seventy francs.

(*The ʿUmdah pays the waiter, and then asks the deputy Governor:*)

ʿUmdah (*to Deputy Governor*) What would you like to drink, Sir?

Deputy Governor A glass of cognac.

ʿUmdah Good heavens, no! You should only drink champagne just as his Highness the Prince did.

Playboy (*to the ʿUmdah*) Why haven't you introduced us to His Excellency in the proper way?

ʿUmdah Deputy Governor of our province, this gentleman (*pointing to the Playboy*) is one of Egypt's refined wits, and that gentleman (*pointing to the Merchant*) is an important merchant.

Playboy (*to the Deputy Governor*) How is the governor? He's 29.13
one of my friends, and I've often spent many enjoyable hours socializing with him.

ʿUmdah (*to the Deputy Governor*) I believe you've been working today on the Elections Committee.

Deputy Governor That's right. God willing, everything will turn out the way we want.

ʿUmdah (*to the Waiter*) Champagne!

Deputy Governor That's enough! I want to go inside to join my colleagues, judges and public attorneys, who are sitting over there. (*pointing*)

Playboy Don't move, Your Excellency. I'll invite them to join us. A and B are both good friends of mine.

Deputy Governor Don't bother yourselves. It would be more proper for me to go and join them.

ʿUmdah That being so, we'll all come with you, and the waiter can bring us a bottle of champagne.

Deputy Governor I've no objection to that, if you wish.

They all stood up and joined the other company. The waiter brought a bottle of champagne, and the ʿUmdah asked them to drink some. They declined and he insisted, but they still declined. Then he started swearing he would divorce his wife if they did not drink with him. He fell on his neighbor's hand and started kissing it. With that they all complied with his wishes. The ʿUmdah now grabbed a glass and stood up unsteadily alongside the Playboy in order to have a drink with them. But hardly had he put the glass in his mouth than he began to choke and could not stop himself. The

Playboy, assisted by the waiter, hurriedly pulled him inside to put his sorry state to rights.

29.14 ʿĪsā ibn Hishām said: Once our friends had gone inside, the Pāshā spoke to me:

PĀSHĀ At this point, if there's nothing left for us to see, then tell me about something that's been on my mind all this time. What is this "prince"?

ʿĪSĀ IBN HISHĀM "Prince" is a title conferred on royal children. We've talked about it before. The person you've seen here is one of them.

PĀSHĀ How can such a royal person enter a tavern? We've never heard before of such personages lowering themselves to mingle with common people in places like this. Has fate dealt badly with them? Are they so few that they can't hold soirées and parties in their own residences? God in heaven, the only thing more remarkable would be for the sun to rise in the West!

29.15 ʿĪSĀ IBN HISHĀM It's not a matter of either numbers or indigence. They're bored with being imprisoned inside their own palaces. Not only that, but they no longer have the necessary prestige to bring people flocking to their doors in order to attend their councils. They lead lives that keep them apart from ordinary people; apart, that is, from Western travelers in quest of financial gain and generosity. As a result princes consort with foreigners who play a whole variety of tricks on them—falsehoods, cunning, deceit, and hypocrisy—until all the princes' wealth is exhausted and their funds have dried up. You can find some of them who have become aware of this situation and learned from others' mistakes. Not content to leave things as they are, such people are keen to mingle with ordinary people; they adopt the behavior common to such assemblies and enjoy the conversation in gatherings of this kind. Since the majority of meetings in Egypt are like that, princes have also descended to that level and adapted themselves to their moral standards. The prince whom you've seen here may actually be more ethical, cultured, amiable, and pleasant than other princes who only consort with the European riffraff and recoil from any contact with their own countrymen.

'Īsā ibn Hishām said: At this point in our conversation we saw that 29.16
the 'Umdah had recovered from his drunken stupor. He staggered out between the Playboy and Merchant. We followed them to see what would happen next.

Miṣbāḥ al-sharq 90, January 25, 1900[229]

30.1 ʿĪsā ibn Hishām said: When they left the tavern, we followed behind, sticking closer to them than their own shadows. We heard the ʿUmdah tell the Playboy that he had worn them out. "Let's go to the place you promised us," he said. "That way we can make use of comely faces to clear the dirt from our eyes before morning changes everything." The Playboy looked concerned and distressed. He interrupted the ʿUmdah and palmed off his reproach by pointing out that, if someone has to wait too long, even the height of patience dissipates. Pampered maidens rapidly grow impatient if they have to wait for men and put up with aggravataion and sheer boredom. "We gave in to a whim," he told them, "and so we've lost an opportunity. Our hopes have been dashed and our goal has eluded us. While you were dozing, the girl sent me a message, complaining that she'd become utterly bored. She regretted ever coming and went on her way." "So then," the Merchant asked, "what can we get to compensate for what we've lost? Where can we sit together now and while away the night?" "At this time of night," the Playboy replied, "the only thing we can still do is head for one of those raunchy dance-halls. Perhaps we'll find some substitute there for what we've missed."

The ʿUmdah now took out his cash, jingled the coins, then put them back in his pocket. "Don't worry," the Merchant told him. "Friendly company is readily available!" He turned to the Playboy. "Lead the way!" he said. "For you, nothing's a problem!"

So, without further delay, the Playboy took them to a place close by. We followed them inside and sat opposite them. We soon realized that the place was a veritable battlefield, its fiery furnace all aglow; in fact, a theater of war involving opposing armies. On this battlefield smoke was the dust cloud; wine casks served as ramparts, pitchers and glasses as armaments. Here flutes and oboes were substitutes for drums, and the clink of jewelry far surpassed the clang of Mashrafi swords.[230] Glasses and bottles gleamed as bright as lance-tips and spears. Here the generals and commanders were managers and waiters; headcloths replaced helmets, shawls replaced battle standards, mantillas replaced armor, and handkerchiefs replaced carrier pigeons. The dancing platform resembled an inaccessible fortress, and the hall's owner played the role of guard on watch. Swaying buttocks and waists were like attack and retreat. The people seated were beseiged, a vanquished army, while singers were its warriors and foes, and women its defenders and cavaliers: 30.2

Agents of sweet oppression have wrought an evil tyranny,
turning to us in complaint.
Cavaliers of temptation, beacons of seduction,
they have met you bedecked in bangles.[231]

You observe every bare-breasted girl as she shouts, "Who's going to join us and compete?" Then she makes the rounds, prancing and strutting. Every man who desires to be in her company throws darting glances at her. She steers them all toward the wine casks, which proceed to gush forth with blood-red wine; she then splits open people's pockets which pour forth the blood of golden coins! 30.3

They have been sheathed in wrapping cloths,
but their sword-like glances are exposed.
They have used the flint of passion to kindle the flame,
gleaming with the fire of their jewelry.[232]

In the midst of this battlefield you could see a lewd tart in her dancing finery slithering around like a snake in its skin. She would toss her victims into an abyss, and you could watch people flattened like the stumps of desolate palm trees.

30.4 ʿĪsā ibn Hishām said: As we sat there for a while, we were aware that we could hardly breathe. Our lives seemed shortened because of the disgusting stench that wafted from all corners—the smell of wine dregs, body sweat, lamp oil, tobacco and hashish, coupled with drunken breath and lavatories unflushed by water. An equally foul stench rose from the floor which was littered with filth and dirt. When all these smells intermingled and clustered together like a black cloud from the ceiling, all kinds of pestilence rained down. People inhaled it and sucked it into their lungs; as a result their bodies became emaciated. It was enough to make light wicks go dim just as they do inside pits and caves. We almost choked and felt sick. The Pāshā got up to leave, but I grabbed him and said:

ʿĪsā Huh! If someone like me, a person who's never seen a battle in his life or witnessed the turmoils of war, can tolerate staying in a place like this, how is it that someone like you cannot stand it? You've been involved in wars, seen battles fought, and inhaled clouds of dust!

Pāshā True enough. I've inhaled clouds of dust, but that was in open and unconfined spaces. I've never had to inhale smells like the ones bottled up in this place. Even so, I'll grin and bear it like you. Then I won't miss anything and can carry through our intentions from beginning to end.

30.5 Hardly had the Pāshā finished talking before I noticed a friend of mine standing right beside me. He greeted me with a smile and expressed his surprise at finding me in such a place. I in turn expressed my surprise at finding him here as well. I immediately asked him:

ʿĪsā ibn Hishām What's brought you here?

Friend I'm looking for someone who's swindled me on a business matter. I'm well aware that places like this one are regular haunts for tricksters like him. So, even though I've been staying well clear of this place for some time, I've reluctantly come here again. When necessity calls, one must obey. Tell me, though, what's brought you to this den of Satan and nest of vipers?

ʿĪsā ibn Hishām We've come here to study and observe people's customs and morals. But, as you're aware, I'm a complete stranger here. Can you sit with us for a while and tell us about some of the covert and invisible things going on in this place?

ʿĪsā ibn Hishām said: My friend sat down with us both. After settling in his seat, he started telling us stories from the time when he used to frequent such haunts and giving us details about how they got started, how they were run, and how the government sanctioned their expansion. However, it was only a moment before a drunkard came in, staggering his way through the rows of seated customers. He stopped at a place between them and another group that was sitting there quietly, listening to a famous singer. They were all craning their necks and staring at her; it was as though they were sitting silently beneath a pulpit during a preacher's sermon listening to the most flawless of discourse. The drunkard kept making a fuss till he reached the stage set up for singing and dancing. He banged on it with a cane he was carrying. 30.6

"That's enough singing," he yelled. "Let's have some dancing instead." Some of the crowd agreed with him and yelled for dancing. The person who had originally asked for singing and those with him were furious. Along with everyone else, they kept yelling for more singing. The drunkard turned round and started cursing and mocking them, ridiculing their poor taste and stupid choice. Some fool answered back, whereupon the drunkard set about him with his stick. The proprietor got up from his seat, pounced on the drunkard, grabbed him by the collar, and dragged him toward the exit. The man who had wanted the song to continue swore at the drunkard and laid into him. The latter clung to his assailant's coattails, yelling "Police, police!" The waiters assisted the proprietor and dragged the drunkard towards the exit, but he kept clinging to his assailant's 30.7

coat until they reached the exit. A policeman had responded to his cries and was waiting there. He was intending to arrest both men, but the proprietor stopped him taking in the drunkard's assailant. "Just take this man away," he told the policeman. "He got utterly drunk somewhere else first, then came to my place and started picking fights." But the policeman would only arrest both men. The proprietor made a gesture to the policeman as if to give way to him. Just then one of the waiters came rushing over. "You needn't do anything," he said. "The Police Adjutant's here; he's sitting at the bar with his girlfriend X."

PROPRIETOR (*to the Policeman*) Now you've no reason to take them both to the police station. Come along, we'll all go in and see the Adjutant at the bar.

POLICEMAN This is obviously a trick. I realize you're trying to rescue your friend. How can the Adjutant be in the bar? Tonight's his shift at the station.

PROPRIETOR Just bring these two men you've arrested inside and see for yourself.

30.8 The Policeman agreed, so they all went inside, only to find the Adjutant sitting beside his girlfriend with his coat over her shoulders and his tarboosh on her head. He was giving her a drink from his glass while she did the same from hers.

PROPRIETOR (*to the Adjutant*) My dear Sir, business in my premises has been completely disrupted, and I'm sure that's not to your pleasing. This man arrived already drunk from somewhere else and didn't order anything in my place. He picked a quarrel, disturbed the atmosphere, and then proceeded to assault this gentleman who's one of my most regular customers. What's odd is that this Policeman has insisted on taking them both to the police station. This gentleman's someone of noble birth. It isn't appropriate for someone of his stature to be dragged off to court with this drunkard. The policeman refused to listen to me when I explained the story to him.

The Adjutant now put his tarboosh back on and called over the Policeman. The Policeman came over and gave a salute.

ADJUTANT (*to the Policeman*) Since this man's so obviously drunk, you need only take him to the station. As long as this gentleman did not instigate an assault, as the Proprietor tells us, there's no need to take him now and further disrupt things here. It'll be sufficient for the gentleman to promise us to come to the station tomorrow so we can take his deposition against the drunkard.

With that, the Proprietor pushed the drunkard towards the exit, accompanied by the Policeman.

POLICEMAN (*to the Proprietor*) It's all very clever for you to follow your waiter's cues. But then, the Adjutant isn't here every night; and there are always the days in between!

PROPRIETOR Never mind! Just put him in prison and don't think any more about it!

ʿĪsā ibn Hishām said: We went back inside and discovered the Pro- 30.9
prietor and the gentleman who had been in the fight with the drunkard sitting with the Adjutant. The glasses were being passed to and fro. We listened as the gentleman was ordering glasses and bottles:

PROPRIETOR (*to the Adjutant*) Why did you tell your girlfriend to leave when we joined you?

ADJUTANT I didn't tell her to do anything. She went off in a rage.

PROPRIETOR Why was she in a rage?

ADJUTANT It wasn't my fault. She found a way to annoy me and herself as well.

PROPRIETOR I'll call her back at once so I can help settle your disagreement.

ADJUTANT No, let her be! She won't come back willingly at this point. She's angry because the Policeman didn't take this gentleman to the police station along with that drunkard. The gentleman here is a friend of the singer while she's one of her enemies.

Proprietor I've given up on this girl; there's no limit to her stupidity. Every night she causes me some new headache, and I suffer losses that I can't make good. If it weren't for you, Sir, I wouldn't keep her here and put up with paying her the monthly salary of a deputy governor first-grade. If you could just see her, she's always arguing with people and squabbling with her female colleagues. In all that, she's relying on you and boasting about her acquaintance with you. Then you'd realize how stupid she is!

Adjutant What can I do about her stupidity? Even so, she's good-hearted and lively. I've often warned her to stop getting into arguments and quarrels because of me.

Proprietor You're right. And beyond that she really loves you.

30.10 At this point, the singing came to an end. The singer came down to the bar and found the gentleman sitting with the Adjutant and Proprietor. She sat down with them and asked what had happened to him because of her. He told her the entire story.

Gentleman I'm extremely grateful to the Adjutant for treating me justly, but I'm asking him to allow me to bring about a reconciliation between him and the other lady. Then her anger will disappear, and we can enjoy a pleasant evening again.

Proprietor I don't think the Adjutant will object to that idea.

While they were talking, the Adjutant's girlfriend came back in. No sooner did she spot the singer sitting with them than she flew into a fiery rage and started behaving like a lioness that has gone berserk because she has lost her cubs. She ranted, cursed, and swore, uttering obscenities and oaths, and then hissed and spat. She pounced on the singing girl, grabbed her veil and threw her to the floor where she punched and beat her. She threatened to file a complaint against the Adjutant and then vowed not to dance that night. She would make sure they all had to go to the police station.

30.11 The only thing the Proprietor could do was to deal with the situation. He dragged her forcibly to one side, while the Adjutant slunk out as quickly as possible. The Proprietor then spoke to her in no uncertain terms, making it clear that the Adjutant had gone back to the station. If she didn't start dancing again, he intended to send her with the singer to the station. Everyone in the place could testify that she had assaulted the singer for no reason at all. She would not find anyone to testify that the Adjutant himself had been there. He would be the one conducting the inquiry, and he'd have his revenge on her on his own behalf and that of the Proprietor. In reply she told him that this time she'd do it, but in the future . . .

ʿĪsā ibn Hishām said: With that she went back to the stage, and we returned to our seats so we could watch what other amazing things would happen next. 30.12

Miṣbāḥ al-sharq 91, February 8, 1900

31.1 'Īsā ibn Hishām said: Once the row was over, we had hardly taken our seats again and our Friend had only just started telling us things before the dancing started. People were yelling and screaming; there was both applause and whistling. When a brazen tart took to the stage, a wholesale hubbub ensued. She was emaciated and ugly, flat-nosed and big-mouthed, bleary-eyed and nearsighted. With penciled eyebrows, she presented a riot of color—red cheeks, white forehead, and dyed fingers. Using greasepaint she had decorated her face with a veil of makeup and plastered on it a false, multicolored covering in a variety of hues—from gleaming white to pitch black and deep red. In fact she displayed as many different colors as the chameleon in the midday heat of the desert. The exposed parts of her body and naked flesh were covered with necklaces, bangles, bracelets, supports, armlets, bells, belts, and anklets. She started skipping and dancing to the beat of the music, twisting and turning like a snake.

31.2 Alongside her stood an assistant so repulsive that we had no doubt that he was the accursed Devil himself. He had an ugly head placed on top of a disgusting frame. His features seemed carved out of rock, with eyes like a hawk, a nose like a vulture's beak, drooping lips, and a tightly twisted turban. In his hand he held a pitcher from which he kept pouring glasses of sheer fire, not wine. He gave her pitch and tar, and made her swallow boiling hot water. Every time he filled a glass for her, she whispered in his ear and then pointed her finger at someone sitting in the front row. He would then roar like a lion once it has spied its prey. Bottles in multiple pairs and rounds one after another would appear, and he would uncork them and arrange them in rows at her feet. Her assistant kept pouring glasses for her, and she would quaff them and ask for more. She seemed never to be satisfied; her thirst was unquenchable. It was as if he were drawing water from a well and pouring it into an arid valley, or filling a cracked jug with water from a gushing stream. Once the wine had seeped like an insect through her veins and lit a red hot fire inside her, she started her twists and gyrations again. Her leaps and pirouettes became more violent and her jumps and turns intensified. She kept toying with her neck like a tortoise and twisting like a snake.

Her assistant stood beside her, closer than her own shadow, 31.3
pliant as her own shoes. He kept making passes at her, flirting and dancing with her and exchanging suggestive pinches. Between her to-ings and fro-ings, she kept making lewd and disgusting comments to the audience, treating them to all manner of filth and lechery, and mouthing taunts and nonsense. Their mouths simply gaped, and their hearts were enthralled. Everyone was stunned and full of admiration; as they followed her every movement, they were all expressing their utmost pleasure. They kept asking for more and demanding an encore. Eventually her energy gave out; her eyes began to droop, her lips contracted, and her jawbone tensed. Sweat poured off her shoulders and sides, and foam thickened on her neck and mouth. Sweat blinded her and covered her chest, so she had to wipe it completely off. She took a handkerchief and used it to wipe her face and arms. It was stained with various types of makeup, as though all the sweat that came off her skin were a kind of rain that the handkerchief turned into a rainbow. As a result, the falseness of her appearance was exposed and the deception became clear; things that had been hidden were brought out into the open. She was transformed into the guise of a harpy appearing in a desert mirage, a ghoul grimacing and leaping around, or a bear quivering

and crawling. We turned away in utter horror and disgust, so powerful was our sense of revulsion.

31.4 The Pāshā asked: "Do people's minds really focus on vipers like this and stare longingly at them?"

FRIEND Yes, indeed they do! Hearts and souls have been riven and pockets shredded for her. This woman you're watching is so hideous that wild beasts would run away and Satan himself would take refuge from her. And yet the dupes in this audience regard her as a palace statue, a pearl of the era, the wonder of the age. She's taken piles of money from men and ruined their lives; for her sake honor and prestige have been lost. She's humiliated people and corrupted many governors. Many times she's broken up a man and his wife, and provoked disagreement between father and son and enmity between one brother and another. As she's worked her evil ways, she's managed to bring ruin to flourishing houses, to sully pure lineages, and to open the gates to litigation. Many's the distinguished and honorable man she's ruined; many's the noble and exalted person she's consumed in her flames. The people you see sitting in this plague-infested marsh spend night after night here every month, and month after month throughout the year. And please don't imagine that, because this place is so awful, they're from the lowest class of people. Quite the contrary, just look to your right. The man sitting there arrogantly among his comrades is an amir's son whose father died and bequeathed him piles of money. His evil companions, all of them idle loafers, have swarmed round him. Now he's started squandering the money by buying pedigree horses and sumptuous carriages. He spent an obscene amount on his wedding reception, and now he's ended up handing over what's left to whores and to this stinking tart in particular. But, when he comes here every night, the only thing he gets is to look at her while she neither looks at him nor even asks after him.

31.5 Now look to your left. Do you see that fellow over there twisting his moustache as he leers and makes lewd gestures with his eyebrows. He's the son of an important man too. When his mother died, she left him a substantial legacy. It was only a few weeks after her death that misfortune allowed him to fall into the clutches of this deceptive trickstress. He cannot stand not being with her; he comes here every night to see her while she proceeds to rob him of every single thing he's inherited from his mother—jewelery and costly furnishings, not to mention the gold that gets scattered on the floor of this place. Then look in front of you. The man who's being shown such deference and respect by his companions is an important provincial official; he's still totally besotted with this woman. The way she's treated him has been disgusting; she's robbed him of his honor and toppled him from his lofty position. And yet, in spite of all that, he still can't forget her or take his mind off her. Whenever he comes to Cairo, her house is the one place he heads for, and he always comes to the hall where she dances. When he goes back to his provincial seat, he's utterly distracted. The only way he can recover his senses is to devise ways of cajoling local ʿumdahs and notables into holding banquets, the sole purpose being to hire this dancer. Then look at that shaykh sitting by himself over there, with his hand wedged between his temple and turban. He's one of the leading men of the city, and yet, in spite of the sobriety and dignity of old age, things have redounded against him and the role of time has been reversed. Even in old age he's behaving like a youngster; he's crazy about this lewd temptress and is wasting everything that he'd kept for his latter years.

Pāshā God knows, I can't see any obvious female qualities in this woman that would justify the way people seem so infatuated with her. As far as I can tell, it should be exactly the opposite: people should be running away from her rather than looking at her. Can you give me some other explanation which is better not mentioned? 31.6

Friend The only reason is that people love to boast, compete, show off, and monopolize. This tart is famous for her perfect and matchless dancing. Ignorant people are passionately fond of phony prestige; they cling to it blindly and helplessly. In spite of this woman's obvious ugliness, people believe there's something distinctive about such a woman and regard it all as an object of pride, a primary virtue, and a stake worth pursuing. People tend naturally to imitate and copy each other. That explains why her arrows are so effective and her poison flows through their veins.

PĀSHĀ If things are as you say and people are that corrupt and their dreams so inane, is there no preacher to offer them guidance, no counselor to advise them, no restraint to stop them, or no government authority to impede them and keep them out of harm's way?

31.7 FRIEND There's neither preacher nor adviser, no authority or restrainer. People are too busy with their own affairs; very few of them bother to help other people. If anyone does offer advice, all he gets by way of response is laughter and mockery from lechers and debauchees. For example, consider the government's attitude and listen to what it has to say! All these things take place with its full cognizance and before its very eyes. It regards them with approval and accepts them. It's the government that's supposed to lay down the laws and administer them. It formulates bills and publishes decrees that keep governors busy and wear out judges, even though people's lives are much worse and they are faced with a dire plight. What can you say about a government which realizes that its wealth comes from the people and that its life depends on theirs, and yet approves of the spread of these vile practices that result in the squandering of wealth and the destruction of body and soul; a government which has fashioned for its capital city's centerpiece, a necklace of taverns, gaming rooms, and brothels. It's incredible that in the provinces the most junior government official has the authority to rid his region of these evil practices, but here—where the center of authority actually subsists, people in government look at the way evil and misery are on the increase, and yet have no opportunity at the very least to soften the violence of its impact. What's even more incredible and peculiar is that this government does not follow the example of either Islamic or foreign governments. It's well aware that all Islamic capital cities are completely devoid of brothels where Muslim women prostitute themselves; any such thing is strictly forbidden, and no one dares to contravene it. It also knows that, in countries like England, no brothels exist with the cognizance of the government; furthermore, that governments which are an exception to this rule and turn a blind eye to brothels put them in special places on the outskirts of towns far away from people's houses and well out of the way of clubs and meeting places. But this government (which is a Muslim government) has gone against all this and given Muslim prostitutes permission to open their houses in an area surrounded by quarters where respectable people live.

PĀSHĀ For some time now I've been seeing remarkable things and hearing strange information. My peregrinations have produced a series of contradictions while increasing my awareness of people's shortcomings. My perception and amazement has now reached a stage of resignation, or, perhaps even more, of apathy.

ʿĪsā ibn Hishām said: Once the dancer had finished her routine, 31.8
she went to change her clothes and put herself in order. After putting on fresh makeup, she came out and started walking falteringly among the crowd. Necks and eyes strained in her direction, hearts and minds yearned for her, tables were adjusted to accommodate her, and gifts were readied. Each group put out a chair, but she paid no attention to any of this and kept walking till she reached the place where the Proprietor was standing. She stood beside him for a while, joking and laughing playfully. We then noticed her assistant sitting with the coterie of the infatuated provincial official; he was joking, jesting, and making merry with him. When the dancer walked right past him and didn't sit down, the official whispered something in the assistant's ear and slipped him some coins. With that, the assistant leapt up and went over to the dancer standing beside the Proprietor. He whispered something in her ear, and we watched as she rejected the idea. He persisted and kept on at her till she softened her stance. He rushed back to give the official the good news, and she reluctantly followed him over. She sat next to

the official on a chair he had put out for her, and the waiter was soon back with four bottles of champagne. He opened all of them at once, and the bubbling liquid gushed all over the floor. The waiter bided his time and waited till the fizzing had stopped and there was barely anything left, barely a thimbleful to fill the glasses. The tart quickly touched all of them with her lips, and the waiter came back to collect the empty glasses. She told him to bring some more, and the waiter did the same thing with them too. This continued for four or five more rounds. All conversation had ceased, and all they could do was stare at the way she moved and sat and the kind of mayhem and obscenity she was causing; it was as though they were looking at a star or waiting for a new moon.

31.9 When the requests came to an end, the assistant was standing at a distance where she could see him. He kept gesturing at her, sometimes with his eyebrows, at others with the tip of his tongue. She was about to get up, and that flummoxed the provincial official. She gave him a playful slap on the neck and jokingly cursed his father to compensate for her departure. Everyone smiled at her as she slunk her way over to the place where her assistant had pointed. She joined a group to our right and spoke to the young man who had lost his money and forfeited his honor because of his passion for her. "What do you want with me?" she asked. "Why have you called me over and made me give up my seat?" The poor man had no idea what to say in reply. Feeling crushed, he tried to make amends by saying, "I just wanted to let you know how things stand between me and the lawyer regarding your case. We've reached a favorable conclusion to the matter. Won't you sit down for a moment and let me explain things to you and give you some peace of mind?" "Forget about money and peace of mind!" she told him. "Let me take care of my own interests and do what I have to do. The Proprietor's looking at me from over there, and you know what that means. I know how poor you are now; you don't have enough to satisfy him." He now began to remind her of their long acquaintance and their former love affair, the serene nights and earnest days they had spent together, and the beautiful memories and happy times they had shared. At that, she slapped his face like a school teacher. "Those days and nights of old are long past," she told him. "All that remains are the tales they tell. Instead let me tell you a cautionary tale with a message. It's the Tale of the Teeth, one that provides the basic framework in which women such as myself operate and the foundation of our craft:

"They tell the tale of a boy who loved a girl as much as she loved 31.10
him. Under love's wing they spent a happy time together. Then the boy had to leave on an unexpected journey that carried him far away from her in quest of money. On the farewell day the boy arrived with tears and sobs. When she had stopped sharing his tears and it was time for him to depart, she asked him to leave her a memento to remind her of him during his absence and give her a hint of his scent. 'I have nothing that is part of my very body and more precious to me than my own tooth.' With that, he extracted one of his teeth without flinching at the intense pain and handed it to her. Taking his final leave of her, he departed. Days and nights went by, and then the absentee returned from his journey. The girl had heard that he was emaciated and had no money left. Thus, when he knocked on her door, she would not let him in and claimed not to know him. 'But I'm A!' he told her. 'And who is that?' she replied. 'I'm your old beloved,' he told her, to which she responded that everyone is a friend for a while, then leaves. 'Which one are you?' she asked. 'I'm the one with the tooth!' he told her. 'Do I have a tooth of yours?' she asked him. 'Yes, you do,' he replied. 'Then come in,' she said. He went in, and she produced a small case from her box and opened it. It was full of teeth. 'If you can recognize your tooth among that lot,' she told him, 'then I'll know who you are.' So that's the way we are. Learn the lesson, and may God bring you happiness morning and evening!"

With that, she left him and went over to the Shaykh. He stood up 31.11
to greet her with a gleaming smile. As she sat down beside him, the hall waiter was standing right behind her. "Forget that for now," she

told him. "This gentleman's no stranger." Once the waiter had left, the Shaykh told her he was bringing the buttons she had asked for. There were six of them; and fortunately they were of better weight than monetary pounds because the latter was less valuable than the former. She laughed at him and stretched out her hand to take them out of his pocket. She got up with a smile, and the Shaykh seemed serenely happy as though there was to be a rendezvous. She went away to work her wiles and cast her net over someone else.

Miṣbāḥ al-sharq 92, February 15, 1900

ʿĪsā ibn Hishām said: We stayed where we were, observing the antics of this lecherous tart and the way she was tricking people. We were amazed that a woman like her could deceive men and hurl them into the abyss of sin and error. She had none of the trappings of beauty nor any redeeming features or qualities, but instead had been molded in a brazen form and kneaded from the sludge of all that was ugly and repulsive. She continued her rounds among the seated customers, meandering her way through the rows and going back and forth to the Proprietor; sometimes she would be lost to view, but then she would reappear. She kept freely mouthing obscenities and slander and reaching out to grab and steal. She often slapped and punched people with her outstretched hand, enflaming people's minds with her deceitful wiles and using her hand to grab and swallow glassfuls. Her every move was aimed at profit and gain. As she made her way amid her devotees, she would sometimes scowl and frown, and at others break into a smile. One moment she would turn aside, at another she would come back yelling and then sag. One minute she would look happy, then frown; be content, then aggravated. Each man received the treatment that suited him best, and she dealt with them all in the appropriate fashion. She had managed to attract their attention and excelled at keeping them in her clutches; she could play with their minds and had them all enslaved. For them, the clearest sign of her affection and inclinations came when she would use her shoes to give someone who 32.1

pleased her a cuff; with that he would assume that he had struck lucky and his dearest hopes would be granted.

32.2 Once she had achieved her objective by cuffing and slapping him—along with insults to his father and mother, she would then go beyond mere slaps with shoes and tear his shirt and pluck his beard as well. He would now be sure that his hopes were achieved and the hour of union had finally arrived. He would give all his assembled friends and colleagues a boastful look, one filled with arrogant pride and scornful disdain—in fact, like a champion during the cut and thrust of conflict or a victor with the spoils of battle, escaping the jaws of death with prisoners and captives. Showing the utmost pleasure and sociability he would now extend his hand to his purse while she would stretch hers to the wineglass. The waiter would still be poised behind her, pitcher in hand, pouring her one glass after another, as though her throat were some kind of canal and he were a scoop or waterwheel.

32.3 All this time her friend, the young inheritor, had been gazing at her and following her every move with his own gestures. But she completely ignored him and never looked in his direction or moved toward him. This made him angry, and he started muttering his complaints, asking people to intercede, and making a fool of himself. He gave her assistant something and caught the waiter's eye. He then called over the Proprietor and invited him to share some wine. He also showed all due modesty to the female steward and her assistant, invited them both to sit closer to him than all his friends and colleagues, and showered them with his generosity. He kept on cajoling and begging them, accompanied by abject sighs and pleas, until the assistant's heart softened. She stood up and went over to her mistress as though to acquiesce in what would please her. The dancer stayed where she was, undecided as to whether to accept or not, to be sympathetic or cruel. Eventually her assistant's mission was successful, but, using all her wiles after so much relentless pleading, the assistant insisted that twelve bottles of the very best vintage—the most expensive available—should be opened for her mistress. The man accepted her terms; she may have been annoyed with him, but now she seemed content. She sat down beside him on the edge of a seat, eyes closed and not saying a single word. He kept spluttering and fawning, twitching and swaying in an effeminate manner, all with the goal of gaining her affection and winning over her heart. Just then she told him bluntly exactly why she was so annoyed with him and kept avoiding him. "I've had that jewel assessed," she told him, "the one you said was so unique. It's much less valuable than the other one. I've come to realize that you're mocking and despising me, toying with my mind and doing your best to beguile me. I've asked you to let me use your carriage before, but your only response was procrastination and delay. I want you to know that, if you continue behaving like this and don't treat me properly, I'm going to throw you off and take another lover." The man now swore on his honor and dignity, on the revered head of his own father, on the grave of both his mother and grandmother—or else let this night see the end of it all—that if she accorded with his wishes this very night he would not refuse her anything, neither withholding his riches nor keeping his property, whether current or inherited, away from her. And so, now that the reasons for her refusal had been removed, everything ended on a serene note.

We happened to look round and saw the Playboy and his two 32.4
companions. The 'Umdah was leering and signaling with both eyebrows and hands. As he spoke to the Playboy, he seemed completely on fire with love and totally distracted:

'UMDAH We're in luck, and our patience has brought a happy conclusion! We may have missed out on the previous occasion, but now the present offers us a golden opportunity. But how can we get to this lovely woman whom everyone adores, their hearts and eyes unanimous in acknowledgment of her beauty and fascinated by her charms?

PLAYBOY

If you should happen to dispatch your gaze
as emissary for your heart, the sights would exhaust you.

You would espy that over all of which you had no control
nor indeed could you abide even a part.[233]

This woman is renowned for her numerous lovers and devotees. The only problem with her is the sheer number of people crowding around her and going to extravagant lengths to get to her.

MERCHANT She's certainly expensive goods! Whoever gets her is the winner! If it were still a time when commerce was good and there was plenty of trade, then people could fall for her and get infatuated, but, as it is these days, people have other things to think about.

'UMDAH Whatever the case, we shouldn't miss the chance to spend some enjoyable time sitting and flirting with her tonight. We can relax and have an intimate gathering, quenching our thirst with her words and soothing our eyes with her beauty.

PLAYBOY If only it were that easy to achieve what you're asking and get her to sit with us for a while tonight! But you can see for yourself how crowded the field is and how much competition there is in longing for her attention and paying the price. All that makes it difficult, if not impossible, to meet your request.

'UMDAH As far as the competition to pay her is concerned, everything's to hand. And, as long as we have your skill and renown at our disposal, the crowds all around her should not prevent us enjoying her company for a while.

MERCHANT In that case, there can be no doubt about it. Our friend here is the proverbial master of intimate gatherings, discretion, and good taste. Maybe our night will come to a pleasant conclusion.

PLAYBOY I'll have to try my very best. I've known her for a while, and that may give me an edge when it comes to enticing her. I'll begin by talking to the waiter.

32.5 'Īsā ibn Hishām said: The Playboy now called the woman's assistant over. He was about to give him some dirhams, but the Merchant got there first. The 'Umdah stopped them both and took their place.

The Playboy had a word in the assistant's ear, and they spent a long time whispering. The assistant went away and came back almost immediately with his mistress; there was no resistance and no hesitation involved. She greeted them all:

> She greets the drinkers with conciliatory banter,
> yet the guile is that of a warrior.[234]

She greeted the Playboy with a smile and asked him what had happened after she had left the party so suddenly; she wondered how things had worked out between them all. He interrupted the banter with a hearty laugh and started introducing her to the ʿUmdah and Merchant, describing their influential position in exaggerated terms. She welcomed them both, and the ʿUmdah responded by raising his hand to his head several times in gratitude. She spotted the ring on his finger with its gleaming stone, playfully leaned over his neck, and bent down to his hand, a move that made him think she was going to kiss it whereas all she actually kissed was the stone itself. The only thing that made him pull his hand away was the sound of corks popping from bottles. The waiter now kept going to and fro, his hands full of yet more bottles. Whenever the Merchant felt worried about this continual process and leaned over to whisper to the Playboy, the latter calmed his fears and stroked his shoulder as a way of reassuring him. With that the Merchant turned to his glass, drank it down and refilled it, then turned to the woman and started handing her things and joking and flirting with her.

The ʿUmdah was in a complete daze, utterly infatuated, while the 32.6
Playboy was preening himself and relaxed; one glass hardly left his mouth before another took its place. He looked to right and left as though to boast to his colleagues how he had managed to secure the woman exclusively for his gathering. The ʿUmdah took his pocket-watch out; he held it in his hand and was staring at it for a while. The woman saw it, took it from him, and looked at the time. "It's time to go," she said, "it's closing time." She got up to leave, but the ʿUmdah begged her to crown her kind gesture by extending their soirée

somewhere else till morning. She accepted the offer with a laugh, then slapped the Playboy across the mouth with her fan, then went back to the Proprietor and sat by his side. People now started to leave; the waiters piled up the chairs and closed some of the doors. The only people left were the infatuated men who thought they had assignations: the Provincial Official, the enamored Shaykh, the Young Man with the inheritance, and the totally deluded ʿUmdah along with the Merchant and Playboy. As time went on and everyone started to despair after inviting her again and sending her messages, they too started to leave, dogged by their anxieties and misery. The ʿUmdah was twice besotted:

> Two kinds of drunkenness: love and wine;
> drunk with both, when will anyone recover?[235]

32.7 The ʿUmdah stumbled to his feet, dragging his cloak behind him, and staggered over to the place where the woman was sitting. Standing right in front of her, he demanded that she keep her promise. She paid him no attention and scoffed at him, preferring someone else. He took nine pounds out of his pocket and thrust them at her. That only made her reject him even more strongly. Passion got the better of him, and he hurled himself at her, but she pushed him away with her foot. He fell to the floor, and all the gold he was holding scattered. The Playboy got up to collect it all, but the Proprietor stopped him. It was the woman's servant who picked it up. Once the ʿUmdah had struggled to his feet, he stretched out his hand and grabbed hold of the woman's plaits. Cursing and swearing she held on to the Proprietor. The ʿUmdah kept pulling on her hair till he fell flat on his face with the plaits in his hand. Meanwhile the woman kept shrieking from her seat. From a distant corner of the place a gruff-looking thug of a man sprang to his feet and came rushing over; he was brandishing a club in his right hand and bundle of clothes in his left. He set about the ʿUmdah and started pounding him, while the ʿUmdah used the plaits to ward off the blows. The Merchant now intervened between the two of them and stopped the man's assault. The Merchant asked the man what business it was of his. The man swore at him and said that he was the woman's husband; he was only defending his wife and was not to be turned away from his rival. With that the Playboy advised the Merchant not to object any further. This man, he told him, was a protected person; it was best not to antagonize anyone who was above the law. He could commit any crime he liked without incurring a penalty. As soon as the 'Umdah heard that, he asked the Playboy to rescue him from his plight. With that the wretch now stepped forward and spoke in turn to the husband, the wife and the Proprietor. The disagreement was settled on the understanding that the 'Umdah would relinquish the dirhams that the servant had picked up from the floor so as to mollify the woman after he had degraded her in such a fashion and to recompense her for the loss of her plaits.

The Proprietor now got up and called over the waiter who was busy putting out the lights. He asked him for the 'Umdah's check, and the waiter duly made it out for him.

PROPRIETOR (*to the 'Umdah*) Before anything else pay us 32.8
thirteen pounds for the drinks. Please make sure to add something extra to the total amount you're going to give us by way of compensation for all the business the establishment has lost tonight because of your childish behavior.

'UMDAH What's this check? What are you saying?

PROPRIETOR Yes indeed, your behavior tonight has certainly not been fitting for a person of your standing! Wine is the source of all evil. You had no business monopolizing this woman who's famous for her petulance, when there were plenty of other women in the place besides her. I only hope you won't hesitate to pay this paltry sum. I know that you're someone of fine morals and good reputation. I've no desire to insult you, and you certainly don't want to be involved in a scandal. Forgive this woman for rejecting you; her life and profession require her to do that. If you can't help falling for her, I'll try to make peace between the two of you, then she can be reconciled to you when you pay us the honor of another visit tomorrow night.

ʿUMDAH (*to the Merchant*) Do you still have enough money on you to settle this amount?

MERCHANT No, I don't. By your life and the sanctity of friendship, I've nothing left at all.

ʿUMDAH (*to the Playboy*) My friend, please settle this problem and find me a way out.

PLAYBOY I'm sorry we're in such a fix, but I can't think of a way out. If the Proprietor would accept this watch of mine as surety for the amount of the bill, I'd gladly leave it with him. But he may well say it's not worth the required amount. If only we had time to go and get the ready cash some way or other.

ʿUMDAH If things can be settled by leaving something as surety, this watch of mine is more valuable than yours; it's worth more to me than my own soul. I got it as a gift from the Princess's office on the day I sold her her property. It has the letters of her name engraved on it. A jeweler valued it at fifty pounds for me. He wanted to buy it, but I refused. Then Mr. X valued it at eighty pounds.

PLAYBOY In that case, you shouldn't leave it as surety. You've a ring that you can leave as surety instead.

ʿUMDAH That's a better idea. The ring's worth more than the watch.

(*The ʿUmdah hands the ring to the Proprietor. He takes it and turns it over.*)

PROPRIETOR That's not enough. I've no confidence in gleaming stones like these. I've been taken in several times by perfect copies. There's nobody in the business here at the moment whom I can trust to assess the stone's real value.

MERCHANT (*after coming over and scrutinizing the stone*) How can you say such a thing? It's made from antique diamond; it's worth a hundred pounds. I'm prepared to provide surety for it with fifty pounds. Wait here. I'll go to the hotel and bring back the amount you want.

Proprietor (*scowling*) I've no time to wait. It's time to lock up. The policeman standing here keeps telling me to hurry up and close so as to conform with government regulations.

Policeman That's correct. It's time for the place to be locked up at once. Look for something else to leave as surety so that you can solve this problem quickly.

Playboy (*to the 'Umdah*) Give him the watch and heaven help ... There's absolutely nothing to be worried about! We can redeem it tomorrow morning when you meet me in the *Mūskī* Café.

Proprietor (*after appraising the watch*) The watch just by itself isn't equivalent to the required sum. Leave the ring as well.

'Umdah That won't do at all! Assuming the check's correct, you're only asking for thirteen pounds.

Playboy Look, as long as we've made up our minds to redeem the surety tomorrow, it doesn't matter whether it's in one part or two. I hope, Sir, you'll excuse us the sum you asked for to make up for loss of trade in the place tonight.

Proprietor For your sake, Sir, I'll excuse you.

'Īsā ibn Hishām said: Now the policeman became even more emphatic, insisting that the place close immediately. The 'Umdah was forced to hand over his watch and ring. The woman was standing there watching and listening; she kept scoffing and jeering. Just then, as everyone was getting ready to leave, an ugly, ill-tempered man came scowling his way in. With a thick neck, bulging eyes, flared nostrils and flabby lips, he was certainly not a pretty sight. Looking to right and left and scanning everyone present, he went over to the woman, started cursing and swearing at her, then gave her a slap. "The hours have gone slipping by," he yelled. "The time for our rendezvous has passed. Now all the taverns are closed. I've been sitting in the house waiting, and here I find you not finished yet. So, you tart, where's this great man who's kept you here and made you forget about me?" "You can curse me all you like," she replied meekly, "but don't call me that! By your love, I've 32.9

not been distracted nor have I forgotten you. Instead I've had an unfortunate incident with an 'Umdah which has kept me here till now. He's insulted and beaten me, and pulled off my hair." Her husband and the waiter both corroborated the details of her story. "So where's this man?" he asked. "If you're not lying, show me where he is." Hardly had she pointed at the 'Umdah before he was hurrying toward the door with his two companions. The man was going to chase after them, but she begged him not to spoil their lives and to come home with her.

32.10 Once we had left that foul place, the Pāshā started talking to our Friend as we were walking. He was asking him about the things we had seen and heard:

PĀSHĀ Thanks be to God for taking us out of darkness into light! By God, tonight I've almost expired from the sheer horror of what I've been through. The foul atmosphere inside that place has made me feel short of breath; it's almost been the end of me. When it comes to filth, a hyena's den or a polecat's lair cannot be worse. What's amazing is how people can tolerate staying in that awful place night after night without being aware of the ruinous consequences. God knows, the stench of the grave itself is like a waft of perfume compared with the smells in that place.

FRIEND People can survive there because they frequent the place, make it a habit, and inure themselves to it. It's as if their bodies are being gradually poisoned, so they can tolerate its effects and ignore the harm and damage it causes. They resemble a sick person who can ignore pain by drinking an anaesthetic during a surgical operation on one of his limbs, or, according to stories told about Indians, resemble one who gradually increases his opium dose until his body eventually reaches the stage that, even if a scorpion stings him or a snake bites him, the poison has no effect on his body which has already been poisoned.

PĀSHĀ I'd like you to explain to me, my august informant, about the woman's husband and his protection and also about the other man who came in later. What's the story with them both? I find it all amazing.

FRIEND With pleasure! The husband is one of the Maghribī riffraff attached to a foreign government, a status that makes him immune to the authority of Egyptian laws. Prostitutes like this woman have habitually chosen to rely on men like him; they marry such a man and pay him a fixed amount on which to live. So while he's her husband in name, in fact she can be everyone's girlfriend. In return he serves and protects her. The woman sticks with her so-to-say husband so as to get foreign protection. Thus, whenever she happens to get into a situation in which Egyptian law will seek to punish her, the fact that she's married to this man will serve to protect her from the law. Whenever, in the name of modesty and decency, the government attempts to stop her dancing, behaving in a lewd fashion, and blatently promoting sex, she can't be stopped. If the government forces her, the crafty woman can go to the Mixed Courts because of her relationship with her husband and claim damages for being forced out of work. This manipulation of the system is not confined to prostitutes alone. By now people are quite used to seeing it used in other contexts as well. Certain newspapers adopt the same procedure as prostitutes—God have mercy on us all! As you know, newspapers are available to educate the public and to inculcate morality. Even so, you'll find the owner of a newspaper and its editor adopting the name of some Maghribi sandal-seller. They put his name on a sidebar and make him the owner. They'll then put in the newspaper whatever takes their fancy by way of abuse directed at the government, ruling authorities, government ministers, and important people. If any one of these people should think of taking the newspaper to court, the actual owner gets away with it because he claims that the person who cursed the government and abused upright people was none other than the person with his name on the sidebar. And, if you should try to find that person, you'd find him peddling sandals on the street. There's no 32.11

hope of bringing him to the kind of court with which princes have to conform just as readily as the lowly. To the contrary, the case is to be heard before the Maghribi's consul. Yet the consulate's doorman won't even give the sandal-seller the time of day, let alone the consul himself.

The man who came in later is the woman's actual beloved and soulmate, to the exclusion of all those other men who expire for love of her, beg for her affection, suffer agonies because of her anger, and sacrifice money and soul simply to please her. She is never satisfied; they long for her, and she turns them all down. The depraved soul will only feel comfortable with someone who treats it with equal depravity and cruelty; it will only respect a person whose evil morals are totally dominant. As you can see, this woman prefers this raging beast over all those other domestic animals. He hurts her, beats her, makes good use of all the money that she collects by various means. He retains his fixed place in her heart and waits patiently till she's finished her job each night. Then at night's end he comes here and beats her right in front of all these worshippers who have been falling over each other to please her. She then submits to him and is led away.

Perdition despises the one infatuated in his love for her,
and discards men whose glory has made them detested![236]

Pāshā May God be exalted! This is undoubtedly fate's verdict in punishing this type of prostitute who robs people of their money and destroys their spirits. Rarely in such cases is such a penalty brought forward into this lower world.

32.12 Friend Noble amir, don't imagine that this is the only punishment for their crimes. She and others like her are all constantly prey to anxieties, suffering, and pain. Anyone observing their real situation will mitigate the bitter feelings he has toward them. The spoils that they plunder and the money they pilfer enable them to spend it just as easily as it is to get it in the first place. You'll notice that each one of them has never-ending needs when it comes to makeup, jewelry, and clothes, not to mention expenditures on their companions and male protectors. She is continually up to her neck in a sea of debt. The necklaces and bracelets you see her wearing are all chains and fetters whereby goldsmiths and jewelers manage to keep her in a kind of imprisonment. Her entire life involves spending the night till early morning, as you've seen, drinking foul wine and contorting her limbs and muscles in a series of exhausting routines. She has to devote her attentions to being friendly with groups of people and finding ways of tricking them. That will often lead to nasty quarrels and arguments. Once she reaches home, she's utterly exhausted; her nerves are shattered and her body aches. She has no desire to eat and doesn't even look at food. Instead she throws herself on her bed, totally drunk, and in a place which may be even filthier than the hall itself and has a worse atmosphere. Next day she gets up at noon or later, with a terrible hangover. Once she's pulled herself together, she works on improving her appearance. Then she receives her daytime visitors. When evening comes, she starts the round all over again, and so on . . . The wretched woman thus goes round and round in a vortex of endless corruption. If she should happen to come to her senses and realize how bad her situation is, the whole world blackens in her eyes and she longs to be rid of all her tricks. She envies other women their lot in life; the thing she devoutly wishes for, the words most frequently on her lips are that she should repent of her disobedience, patiently endure the lowliest of social levels among honorable women, and live among such people in the worst possible conditions. This is the way she stays until old age catches up with her, still far removed from her family and relatives who have discarded her throughout her nefarious career. This is the worst agony of all and the harshest punishment. If only these prostitutes realized the wretched end to which they come, they would never leave their families, whatever the cause that pushes them into prostitution: poverty, seduction, poor upbringing, or lack of any moral restraining factor. It all boils down to a lack of initiative in Islamic religious education. If that worked effectively among men and women, if they encountered some moral force that would prevent them from following this evil course, if they were educated according to the precepts of the Islamic religion, then we would not see any of this corruption showing its face so blatantly.

32.13 ʿĪsā ibn Hishām said: At this point, the cock started to crow to announce the morning. We went on our way, begging the Lord of heaven and earth to forgive the sins of Muslims, men and women.

Miṣbāḥ al-sharq 103, May 11, 1900[237]

ʿĪsā ibn Hishām said: The last episode finished with the ʿUmdah, Playboy, and Merchant managing to escape from the dance hall, that den of lechery and debauched behavior, but only after the ʿUmdah had been utterly humiliated and had lost both his honor and money at the feet of a female dancer. He had been forced to pawn his valuables and possessions without getting the least enjoyment in return. However, they had decided to meet in a specific café so that the Playboy could use his talents to make some amends and put things to right. That would involve redeeming the ʿUmdah's pawned possessions. The Playboy would then be able to proceed with the rest of his plans that had yet to be implemented in full. 33.1

When it was daylight, we continued our quest for information and morally useful lessons. We found our Friend sitting in the café waiting for us, so we went over and sat down with him. As we looked round at the people sitting and standing there, we spotted the ʿUmdah and his two companions to our right, so we turned in their direction in order to see and hear what had transpired and to catch up with their news. We could tell that the ʿUmdah was in terrible shape after the dreadful night he had just spent; he had, as they say, "a wilting side and pallid color, yet flowing saliva." His frowning features seemed layered in dust, and his fingertips had a yellowish hue; his eyelids looked red, but his pupils were dry. His limbs hung lifeless and his breaths were short. At one moment he was opening his mouth, at another rubbing his neck. Anyone setting eyes on 33.2

him would have imagined he was a worn-out camel exhausted by night travel in the desert, or else a shift worker whose flesh had been beaten bloody with a cane or provoked with a whip. At his side, the Merchant kept rolling his eyes and licking his lips, finding it hard to swallow. His sighs sounded like fire, like a wolf about to strike and afraid of being attacked by shepherds, or a failed hunter whose traps have let him down so that his prey has got away.

33.3 Meanwhile the Playboy was keeping his thoughts to himself, head down. He kept scratching the ground as he tried to come up with a plan that would bring his wiles to a successful conclusion. He was faking a display of distress and disappointment while hiding his grins behind his hand. He was showing two separate faces and appearing in two different hues, like a chameleon flicking its tongue or a fox near a chicken coop trying to sneak in unnoticed. He kept on cooking up bits of trickery and preparing to inflict them on the Merchant and ʿUmdah. Next to them we noticed another group of people who kept their gaze riveted on our friends. When we asked my friend who they were, he replied that they were that cunning and ruthless mob of profiteers and scoundrels, middlemen and brokers. The Playboy kept giving them sneaking looks and then smiling to let them know that he had succeeded. He leaned over to the ʿUmdah, making light of the latter's plight and offering to help him solve his problem. Here's what he said as he continued his cheating ways:

33.4 PLAYBOY Don't worry, my dear fellow! Things aren't as bad as you think.

MERCHANT I don't think they'll make you a loan unless you pawn something else. These days people no longer trust each other in this age of speculation. If you have to pawn something, I think I'm the best person to offer you such a service, since I'll have your best interests at heart and can offer you a loan with less interest than what's generally on offer at the moment.

ʿUMDAH That would be satisfactory, provided there was enough time. I need money and cannot afford any wait or delay.

Such procedures now involve supervision, definition of time limit, valuation, assessment, recording, registration, documentation, and so on.

PLAYBOY And don't forget the terrible opprobrium, disgrace, and loss of reputation you'll face with people. Whoever said "selling something is better than pawning it; pawning is selling and swindling at the same time" was certainly speaking the truth. Praise be to God, you're famous and respected for your considerable wealth. Your signature alone will be enough for more than what you need and will avoid the bother of pawning anything.

MERCHANT If that could be done, it would be fine. But at the same time don't forget another adage: "Someone who makes you a loan on the basis of reputation is bound to take a month's interest in a week." Nobody with money to lend is prepared to risk it without security unless he's guaranteed huge interest and considerable profit. Even so, I don't think anyone's willing to lend money these days without some kind of pawn.

PLAYBOY I can personally guarantee that we'll get the loan at this very moment, in this café. There's no need to worry about huge interest rates when harvest time is close at hand.

'UMDAH This is the kind of facilitation that one expects from real friends like you! That's true friendship, thou master of good intentions!

MERCHANT I was just expressing my opinion, but then a counselor may have no other resort. We are all free to use our money as we like.

PLAYBOY (*to the 'Umdah*) Tell me then, how much do you want to borrow?

'UMDAH As I see it, a hundred pounds should be enough.

PLAYBOY How can that small sum be enough? Before anything else, you have to settle up with your friend here for standing security for your debt. Then you need money to redeem the watch and ring from the dance hall. To which I would add the money you'll need to rent the house where you'll want to stay in Ḥulwān and to purchase furniture and decorations. Then there are expenses for your leisure time. After all this worry and exhaustion you'll certainly need some relaxation and fun, particularly because you'll have to stay here for some time while you wait for the successful conclusion of your court case which, as you know, has been postponed from its anticipated date. With all that in mind, I can't see you needing less than five hundred pounds at the very least in the short term. In any case, the moneylenders I know won't lend a smaller sum.

33.5 With that, the Playboy gestured to the group of brokers. They came rushing over in a group, and he had a word in the ear of one of them. Then he spoke openly: "This Bey is 'Umdah X, an influential landlord, renowned for the lands and estates he owns. He's never borrowed before, has absolutely no debts, and is exclusive owner of his lands and possessions, with no rival claims or partnerships. Circumstances in Cairo have so turned out that he's used up all the money he's brought to spend. He needs to borrow five hundred pounds which he'll repay at harvest time. I don't want him to borrow a paltry sum like this from one of the big banks; they have to make lengthy inquiries and waste time. Their owners have no knowledge of key figures in the country."

33.6 One of the Brokers Yes indeed, we're all well acquainted with the Bey. We're well aware of the high repute and great wealth with which God has endowed him. In fact, my late father had dealings with his father in the past; when I was a small boy, I often heard my father say that, among the notables of the region, he knew of nobody who was so truthful and reliable, so noble-minded and generous as your late father. However you must realize that cash is hard to come by these days. Few people are willing to risk loaning such a sum without security equivalent to several times as much. If the decision were mine alone, I wouldn't hesitate for a moment. I would respond to your request without demanding any pledge of security or interest, all as a token of recognition of the former friendship between our two fathers and as a way of consolidating the friendship between us. But I have a European business partner who's a child of this age. He'll only agree to loan money when all the legal stipulations are properly met. Even so, I can satisfy him, firstly with my personal guarantee and secondly by letting him have the interest amount. So if you'll agree to the five hundred being valued at seven hundred till harvest time, I'll attend to the matter with him and serve the Bey here as I must.

MERCHANT Good grief! Seven hundred for five hundred! By the lives of our forefathers, I've never heard of anything like it! 33.7

BROKER (*to the Merchant*) My dear Sir, I think you must be a student at the noble al-Azhar. Only someone who believes that interest is forbidden would consider it too much, using as his basis the fact that usury is forbidden to us just as much as it is to you. But then, as the proverb has it, "Life's circumstances legitimize what is otherwise forbidden."

'UMDAH The gentleman isn't a student at al-Azhar. He's a famous merchant.

BROKER If that's the case, then he's surely as aware as anybody of how tight the situation is and how short the supply of money actually is. He must realize what the interest rate is for loans with no collateral. Then he's surely not unaware of the meaning of partnerships and bargains.

(*With that he gives the Merchant a wink.*)

MERCHANT Even so, two hundred pounds interest on seven hundred is a lot. In my opinion, it needs to be one hundred and fifty.

BROKER Dealing with merchants is always tricky! But, as long as that's your view, we'll have to go along with it. Out of respect for the 'Umdah I'm prepared to accept what you say. So be so good as to accompany me to the bank with God's blessing so we can conclude matters with my partner.

PLAYBOY We needn't all go. The 'Umdah can go with you, and we'll wait for you here.

'Īsā ibn Hishām said: The Broker got up and went off with the 'Umdah. We spent an hour in conversation with my friend, during 33.8

the course of which we learned a variety of things from his wide knowledge. Suddenly we spotted the ʿUmdah coming back alone, hand in pocket. Once in a while he smiled, but then he was scowling. The Playboy and Merchant welcomed him back and asked him how things had gone. The ʿUmdah told them:

ʿUMDAH God curse necessity! We could well have done without this ruin and desolation.

PLAYBOY Was the money stolen?

ʿUMDAH No, not all of it, but half of it was.

MERCHANT (*with a groan*) and PLAYBOY (*mouth agape*) How on earth did that happen?

ʿUMDAH I rode away with the Broker, and we went to the bank. He sat me down in a corner, wrote out the check, and I signed it. Then he went away arguing with his partner. After a while he came back and told me that matters were complicated and difficult. He'd done his utmost to convince his partner, begging and pleading, but he'd been unable to convince him to permit the offer. The Broker told me how much he regretted that his endeavors had failed. He suggested that I wait a few days till the crisis was over. I told him how desperately I needed dirhams at this moment and that I couldn't wait. I was about to come back so you could devise some other way of getting the money. At that point the owner of the place came up to me and said, "By God, I'm reluctant to reject your request, but you must be aware of the tight situation that is dogging the country's finances this year: the shortage of ready cash, the inflation caused by the war in the Transvaal, the low level of the Nile, the plague epidemic, the amount of speculation, and the spread of companies. So please forgive me and do not take my refusal as a sign of weakness. I swear to you, on my word of honor, on my own children and on the long-standing friendship that binds me to your honorable self through your father—God have mercy on him!—that at this moment the only cash I have in our place is four hundred pounds which represents a trust fund for an orphaned child related to us. We are investing it and letting it grow. I'm even more sparing and stingy about it than I am with my own money. Even so, I'm going to give it to you if you wish, so you can know the extent of my affection for you and the excellent opinion we have of you. Let this be the beginning of the service that I'm offering you."

I could see no way of refusing the money. The foreigner brought a purse full of cash and weighed it. He put it in front of me, and I counted out four hundred pounds exactly. Once I'd put it in my pocket, I asked him to alter my check because the amount on it was five hundred, not four hundred. He refused, using as his excuse that he intended to hold on to the difference, some of it for the orphan's profit and some of it for court expenses and lawyers' fees in case, God forbid, I failed to pay the sum by the time stipulated, as was usually the case these days. At that I became alarmed. I gave him back the purse and asked him to give me back my check. He ignored me and turned to talk to some other people who had come to see him. Meanwhile he left me on tenterhooks. Every time I beckoned him from a distance, he turned away in disgust. I had completely lost track of my companion, the Broker; he was nowhere to be found. I became even more worried, and my anger got the better of me. I grabbed the owner of the place and demanded that he give me back my check. He told me that he could not return it unless his partner, who had brought me there, was present. He asked me to wait a while till his partner returned. 33.9

While we were thus involved, Y Bey, our governor's brother-in-law, came in and stood right beside us. As soon as I set eyes on him, my knees gave way in sheer embarrassment. He greeted me with sympathy and respect and asked me what the situation was. I told him what had been happening to me ever since I'd come to this place with the Broker. "There's no need for disagreement or argument," he told me. "I know that you're someone of high standing in the province where you live, renowned for your generosity and kindness. This foreign gentleman is completely reliable and trustworthy; he's renowned for his fair dealings with people, as anyone will readily admit. If he has retained a hundred pounds in case of 33.10

court expenses, he'll certainly return them to you when the amount on the check is repaid at the stipulated time. With all the wealth that you have through God's grace, you won't need to postpone repayment. If you haven't done enough business with the esteemed foreign gentleman before to be able to confirm his reliability and trustworthiness, then I can vouch for his honesty and integrity."

At that point I had no alternative but to accept the cash. I bowed to the Bey. "By God, my dear Sir," I told the governor's brother-in-law, "if it weren't for your own initiative here and a pressing need that I have for this sum of money, something that I require as a down payment on lands that I've managed to purchase from some rich children whose property has been sequestered, then I wouldn't have been prepared to accept this swindle." "May God bless you in your commerce, both buying and selling," he replied and gave me a message of greetings to convey to the governor. I counted the amount again, then said my farewells to the Bey and the foreign gentleman. So, after I'd written a check for six hundred and fifty pounds, all I've got in my pocket is four hundred. That's what I meant when I said that half of it had been stolen.

33.11 ʿĪsā ibn Hishām said: While the ʿUmdah was talking, we had our eye on a man who was standing right in front of him waiting for him to finish. He kept stretching out his hand toward him. From his general appearance we gathered that he was the carriage driver. We heard him say:

Carriage Driver We've finished, my dear sir. While I've been waiting here, you've kept me from my work.

ʿUmdah I'm not going to use you any more. I've given you quite enough already.

Carriage Driver My dear Shaykh, whoever said that three piastres is payment for hiring a carriage for such a trip? I've taken you from one place to another, then brought you back to this café. But then, it's all my fault. I'd promised God that I'd never pick up these rustic shaykhs and ʿUmdahs any more.

Playboy Stop this stupid talk! Here's a fourth piastre.

Carriage Driver That's not enough. Either give me my fare according to the tariff, or else I'm calling the police!

'Umdah Here's another half-piastre. Now go away and leave us.

Carriage Driver How can I leave with just four and a half piastres for such a long ride? Have you included in the fare the ride from here to the bank, then the long wait, then another ride from the bank to the sheep trotters' shop where I waited while you ate, and finally the ride back here?

Merchant (*to the 'Umdah*) Sheep trotters' shop? Is that your idea of friendship, thinking only of yourself and forgetting your friends? So you leave us here starving ever since yesterday and go off to eat without us!

'Umdah By God, it was only my incredible hunger that led me to do such a thing. I was so hungry that I thought light was darkness.

Playboy (*to the Merchant*) Don't think badly of him! Forgive him! That's just the prelude; we'll get something else to eat with him later on.

Driver Please show me some mercy! This policeman's taking down the carriage number so he can write up a misdemeanor charge because I've left it unattended in the street while I was busy asking you for the fare.

Playboy Take another piastre and leave us. I'll get rid of the policeman for you. I know him and can get you off the charge.

The Playboy goes over and has a word with the policeman, but 33.12
he refuses to agree. The Driver now insists on rejecting the payment and asks for more money. Otherwise the 'Umdah will have to go to the police station with him. The Playboy makes do by handing him a card with the 'Umdah's name, title, and place of residence on it. The Driver takes it and leaves, saying that he intends to take his complaint to the police. The Playboy returns to the café and talks to the 'Umdah:

Playboy Praise God, all our problems are at an end. First of all, pay our friend here the amount you owe him on the check, then you can go back to the dance hall Proprietor to get back your pawned goods.

The ʿUmdah counts out the amount owed to the Merchant three times and puts it in front of him. The Merchant picks it up and puts it in his pocket. He then addresses the ʿUmdah:

Merchant I've just remembered that I don't have your check with me now. It would be better for you to keep the money till I can bring it back for you.

Playboy What's all this commercial talk between trusted friends? Heaven forbid that there should be talk of checks and contracts! As long as the money's in your pocket, it's all the same whether you bring the check or not. Come on, let's go to see the dance-hall Proprietor.

Playboy (*to the Merchant*) Do you see the way his mind's working? His passion's still dragging him toward the denizens of those haunts!

ʿUmdah To tell you the truth, I'm still very angry with that nasty female. I haven't forgotten the flirtatious way she rejected my advances, nor the kind of looks she directed at me when I pulled her by her plaits. I'd like to see her again and give her a thorough scolding.

Playboy I fully appreciate your intentions! What you're planning is for your scolding to be followed by a reconciliation; happiness after anger. But as a sympathetic counselor my advice to you is that, while that woman's at work at night, she's too difficult to get at and have to yourself. I've a plan to match your desires. After lunch we'll look for her assistant, give him some money, and come to an agreement whereby she'll eat lunch with us at the Pyramids. Then we'll have her all to ourselves.

(*The ʿUmdah agrees to the plan, and they all get up to leave.*)

33.13 ʿĪsā ibn Hishām said: They left us to marvel at mankind's treachery towards his fellow human beings, treachery such as no wild beast inflicts on other creatures. We too got up to leave, after agreeing to go to the Pyramids on the following day.

Miṣbāḥ al-sharq 104, May 18, 1900[238]

ʿĪsā ibn Hishām said: When we reached the Pyramids, we stood in awe and reverence before that landmark, one that bests all others, the mountain that overtops mountains and hills, that structure that in its pride rivals Raḍwā and Shamām. Their structure erodes the ongoing freshness of days, and their very permanence obliterates eras of time. They entomb people after people beneath their shadow, and centuries turn grey without affecting them in the slightest. Time's own clothing has become threadbare, and yet there they stand in fresh attire. Ages have been recycled and eras have passed, but they still remain, bumping stars and mocking meteors. As long as day and night follow each other in turn, they still provide an eyewitness account of man's talent for creating miracles of potential, of the ability of this weak and feeble creature to do amazing things, and to show how such a transitory and ephemeral creature can produce such an abiding and eternal structure. It is the index marker of the unity of the one and only God, the greatness of the glorious existent, in the construction of mankind who is both knower and denier, honest and corrupt, submissive and capable, scornful and powerful. He is great and small, mighty and lowly, glorious and contemptible, many and few, climbing and falling, high and low, ephemeral and permanent, happy and miserable—a veritable aggregation of opposites and types, of differing actions and deeds. You may see him ascending to the very heavens using the stairs of his own knowledge, getting his scale to weigh every single 34.1

body and applying his learning to the stars and their byways. But then you can watch as he may be struck by the slightest movement, scratch a minor itch, swallow his own spittle, trip over a stone in his path. You can watch him aspire to the tree of eternity, yet tumble instead into a mole hole.

34.2 For a time we each spent a while using our imaginations, deep in thought and contemplation. We then progressed from private thoughts to conversation, from silence to discussion:

PĀSHĀ In olden times when I used to treat things as givens, I regarded this structure as the crown of Egypt, something with which to boast over other territories, a marvel to be proud of, and as evidence of advancement in industry, culture, and civilization. However, now that I've been enlightened by knowledge and have used reason to contemplate the inner nature of things, I've come to realize that it's not the way I thought; they're just a collection of paved stones and neatly arranged rocks with no benefit that I can see and no return except that they're trying to emulate a mountain or hill. Do you two know of any hidden significance they have, something I haven't discovered?

34.3 FRIEND There's really no great secret behind them, nor have they any evident use. It's just that in olden times some ignorant and tyrannical rulers with their backward ideas believed that, after they died, they would return to this world; after spending some time in other bodies, their spirits would reenter their bodies. So their major concern in life was to preserve their bodies after death. They used to build their houses out of clay bricks, walk around naked and shoeless, and eat the coarsest of foods, and yet they enslaved the entire people in order to transport these rocks and erect them into this structure to serve as their grave after death, a place where their bodies would be preserved until they returned (whereas in fact they are kept in the Egyptian Museum in Giza). As a result, the entire population of Egypt was enslaved, all other work stopped, limbs were torn apart, blood was shed, and people's spirits were shattered beneath the weight of these rocks; all that because of the idiotic and fatuous beliefs of a single person, a ruler who imagined that he would get some benefit from it. No one can boast about it, and no mighty person can claim any kudos. It's just oppression, tyranny, enslavement, ignorance, delusion, falsehood, and futility. These two large Pyramids are simply a reliable witness to the injustice and ignorance we've been talking about. Were there to be the slightest evidence of the civilization of those monarchs in their own times, then these same rocks and stones would have been used to build viaducts, bridges, and storehouses for the benfit of the people. By God, to anyone who thinks about it, the builder of the Qanāṭir Khayriyya dam is far more worthy of praise, honor, and prestige than these ancient kings who were themselves both enslaved by delusion and enslavers of people.

The only other use for this first pyramid I know about is that it 34.4
was once used as a platform by another tyrant who climbed up it, then duped his armies with ringing words so they would be prepared to kill at his whim.[239] Today it's become a source of income for a group of Bedouin who work here rather than robbing people on highways. Something else recorded by historians is that, once it was completed, the king inscribed this challenge on it: "I built this structure in thirty years. If anyone after me claims power and might, let him destroy it in three hundred years." If the poor fool had only realized that the age would come when anyone could blast this building to pieces in a trice and use chemical components to turn it into powder like carded wool and scattered dust[240], he would not have used as a challenge a structure that he then committed to the hand of fate—and fate never offers any assurances. God knows, it's a wretched achievement, one that is based on prevalent ignorance. Egyptians should only look at it with flowing tears and broken hearts since it provides proof through the ages of the humiliation of their forefathers and the arrogance of their rulers.

ʿĪsā ibn Hishām said: While we were talking, we spotted the Play- 34.5
boy, Merchant, and ʿUmdah, and they had the woman with them.

They had set up a place to sit by the Pyramid. They were laughing and having fun drinking and eating sweetmeats. We were afraid of missing the conversation between them that we had come to hear, so moved closer and listened to what they had to say. The ʿUmdah was saying to the Merchant:

ʿUMDAH Do you know anything about the origin of these Pyramids?

MERCHANT How could I not, when I've learned their entire history in *The Stories of the Prophets,* where they talk about our Lord Noah (prayers and blessings on him and our Prophet), as follows[241]:

"Sodon was king of Egypt before the flood. One night he had an alarming dream and summoned the magicians, soothsayers, and astrologers. He re-counted to them how he had seen the stars scattered and the moon falling to earth. They responded that this dream foretold a great flood which would shortly cover the earth and leave nothing on it. In great alarm the king asked them what he should do to protect against this great disaster. They told him to build these pyramids so that, when disaster struck, he could transfer his treasures there and take refuge himself along with his family and retinue. So the king gathered thousands and thousands of people and set them to work on the task. They completed the structure for him in two hundred and fifty years. When it was finished, he covered it in brocade, carpeted it with silk, and transferred to it so many precious jewels and priceless treasures that for many months he wore people out carrying them all. Then he gathered all the magicians together, and they fortified it with charms and magic chants. When the time for the flood's advent approached, the king took refuge in the Pyramid with his entire family and retinue. The flood inundated everything. The only people to survive were those in the ark, ʿŪj ibn ʿUnuq, and these Pyramids.

34.6 "ʿŪj ibn ʿUnuq was Adam's grandson (blessings be upon him), who was born in his grandfather's lifetime and lived up to the time of Moses (God's prayers be upon him). It has been related that the flood (which overtopped mountains and the Pyramids) did not reach as far as his knee. He used to wade through the flood accompanying the ark. When he felt hungry, he would grab a fish from the sea bottom, roast it in the sun's eye, and eat it. Once the flood was over and civilization returned to the world, he wreaked havoc for a long time until God sent Moses. People complained to him about what 'Ūj ibn 'Unuq was doing to them. Moses asked God to deal with 'Ūj ibn 'Unuq's evil deeds. 'Ūj ibn 'Unuq had been carrying a stone on his head to hurl at the folk of any town with whom he was annoyed. So God Almighty sent a bird with a steel beak which kept on pecking at the center of the stone until it pierced it. The stone dropped down on 'Ūj ibn 'Unuq's neck like an iron collar that prevented him from moving around. Then Moses came up to him with his staff. He was forty cubits high—God's peace be upon him!—and so was his staff. He leapt forty cubits into the air, and struck 'Ūj ibn 'Unuq a blow that did not even get beyond his ankles. However, such was the strength of the blow that our Lord Moses dealt him that it threw him to the ground; for Moses was a man of great determination. 'Ūj ibn 'Unuq fell headlong into the Nile and removed it from Egyptian soil for a whole year. Wild beasts began to tear at his legs. Whenever someone passed by his head, he would say: 'When you get to my feet in God's safe keeping, please wave away those flies; they're bothering me.' When he died, they used his ribs as bridges for the Nile, and the beasts used his eyes, ears, and nostrils as caves and lairs to live in. Thus did God compensate the people for his evil deeds and corruption."

'UMDAH Praise be to God, the mighty Creator! Please get me a copy of this book that I can take back to my home town. Then the mosque imām can read it to us.

'Īsā ibn Hishām said: All this time, the Playboy had been busy chatting to the woman, drinking and laughing with her. When the Merchant had finished his story, the Playboy began an amiable banter with the 'Umdah, saying among other things: 34.7

PLAYBOY Have you ever witnessed a more pleasant and enjoyable day, one that offered more causes for happiness and laughter than this one?

'UMDAH Yes indeed, it's a delightfully happy day. But I'd have preferred our gathering to be indoors rather than out in the open; beneath a roof rather than the sky. You can see the hordes of tourists and Bedouin all around us. I'm sure you realize how it cramps our freedom for fear of being criticized.

PLAYBOY Don't worry about other people's criticisms and objections! Grab your pleasure with daring and resolution and don't bother yourself with other people. But if you'd like us to imitate the tourists for a while, there's no harm in climbing the Pyramids.

MERCHANT Forget that idea! What pleasure can you get from climbing mountains and putting up with the strain and exertion it involves, not to mention the risks you run?

PLAYBOY Everyone who visits the Pyramids does it; there's no danger or tiredness involved. Just look at those women on the way up, falling right into the Bedouins' clutches. Do you see them worrying about risks or bothering about the effort involved? Are we men less daring and audacious than them? At all events, we must go up at least a little way so that people around us will come to realize that, like them, we've come to visit the monuments and not just to enjoy ourselves.

'UMDAH I agree too. We can climb up a bit. Maybe on the way up we'll come across an ancient scarab like the ones I've often stumbled on at the Kufrī hill near my town. But how can we leave the lady by herself?

MERCHANT I'll stay with her and wait for you.

PLAYBOY No, no! She's coming up with us just like those other women!

34.8 'Īsā ibn Hishām said: They got up to start the climb. The Merchant kept dawdling and tried to lag behind, but the 'Umdah kept pushing him as hard as he could; he was jeering and poking fun at him for being scared. The Playboy and woman were urging him on too and laughing scornfully. However, they had only gone up a little way when the ʿUmdah turned and looked downwards. When he saw the distance between himself and the ground, he panicked. Turning pale and trembling to his very veins, he leaned on the Bedouin guide and asked for help getting down. Claiming that his gall bladder gave him problems, he apologized to his companions that he could not climb any further. The Playboy came over and helped the Bedouin support him so that he could continue the climb, but the ʿUmdah's strength gave out and he collapsed between the two of them. The Playboy put him on the Bedouin's back and he was carried back down. He had barely reached ground level again when we heard the woman higher up the Pyramid let out a shriek. From higher up she yelled to them all to come up and help her look for the precious stone that had just fallen out of the ring on her finger. The Playboy dashed up to her, and he and the Bedouin started looking around, but they didn't find anything. The Playboy brought her down, almost fainting from exhaustion and sorrow, and the ʿUmdah did his best to make light of the whole thing. It occurred to the Merchant that the stone may not have fallen out while they were climbing, but might be somewhere in the sand where they had been sitting. He asked the Bedouin to bring a sieve in case they might find the stone. Meanwhile the woman made no attempt to dry her tears, lower her voice, or stop crying and complaining. At times the Playboy was trying to calm her down, at others he was leaning over to the ʿUmdah, regretting that this mishap had occurred to ruin their fun; now their gaiety had turned into sadness. This, he said, was the way of the world; it was rare for any pleasure to conclude without sorrow of some kind. However, he suggested, as long as money could provide compensation for the feelings of the heart, this particular disaster could be easily remedied. After all, who is to know what lies hidden in the world of the unknown?

The Playboy kept pestering the ʿUmdah till the latter went over 34.9
to the woman and swore that, before the night was over, she would

have another stone even better than the one she had lost. She was still unhappy and inconsolable. "How can I get another one like it?" she asked. "It was a rare sapphire." But the 'Umdah repeated that the next day she would have on her finger a stone of equal value that he would be bringing her. He shook her hand to confirm his promise. He was so distressed to see a ring on her finger with no stone in it that he removed her own ring and replaced it with his own, the one he had just redeemed from the pawnbroker. With that, they returned happily to the spot where they had been sitting and resumed their amiable banter.

'Umdah What a delightful gathering this is! If only we could link our daytime with the night!

Merchant Could it be that you want us all to spend tonight in that awful tavern as we did last night!

Playboy Do you imagine we'd be able to enjoy such a good time as this and have our lady companion to ourselves without other people?

Merchant So what's to be done then?

Playboy If that's the way it has to be, then I'll tell her to say she's sick. I'll send someone to tell the Proprietor that she can't come tonight.

34.10 The Playboy now started cajoling the woman into agreeing to his plan. At first she declined on the grounds that, under her conditions of employment with the Proprietor, she had to pay him ten pounds compensation for every night she stayed away. The Playboy turned to the 'Umdah and waited for his opinion on that subject. The 'Umdah let him know that he was agreeable and undertook to pay such compensation. They now started discussing how to spend the night. The Playboy said that he could think of nothing better than watching the splendid new play being presented at the Arab Theatre. After that they could go and spend the rest of the time at the café on the Gezira island. The Merchant welcomed the suggestion, and they all agreed. The 'Umdah put his hand in his pocket to look at his watch and check on the time. He could not find it and let out a yell. They all made a big fuss searching for it, but without success. "That's the way it is with those Bedouin," the Playboy said, "They're all thieves. One of them stole the stone when she was leaning against him, and another stole the watch when the Bey was doing the same. We need to raise a complaint to the shaykh in charge of those Bedouin and compel him to recover the stolen goods. Let's go and see him now." They all stood up and went to see that shaykh.

ʿĪsā ibn Hishām said: So their cosy gathering came to an end. 34.11
Meanwhile our Friend was insisting that we should visit the Giza Palace before the day was over. We accepted his idea, at the same time deciding that we would go to the theater in the evening to see what had happened about their complaint and what would happen thereafter.

Miṣbāḥ al-sharq 105, May 25, 1900[242]

35.1 ʿĪsā ibn Hishām said: We left the Pyramids behind, duly lamenting and reproaching the people who had built them, and made our way to the museum building, the repository of antiquities. There we would be able to look at the preserved artefacts and documents and view the things that time had brought out of darkness into light after being hidden for ages. These were objects that had been saved from oblivion and extinction by being enclosed in graves, protected from destruction and ruin by the interiors of tombs; relics of ancient peoples and secrets of our ancestors that had remained hidden inside temples and places of worship. The veils of centuries had been removed, to reveal them as deposits made by our forefathers for their successors—hidden troves and buried treasures renounced by the earth, miracles of delicate art, marvels of exquisite workmanship, and curios of ancient craft. Nights and days had been exhausted keeping company with them; past ages had bent their backs to embrace them. Seas had become lowlands and lowlands mountains; depressions were now plateaus, buildings ruins, and ruins buildings. Floods were mirages, and mirages floods; deserts citified, cities desertified. Countries had vanished, others had appeared. Dynasty after dynasty had vanished one after another. Things happened, then passed on; actions became evident, then fell into obscurity. Yet all these things were preserved in the form and shape in which people had left them. A sincere person speaking from experience once wisely declared about times past that:

> Gone are life's traces, olden times that have vanished,
> records inscribed on them, eternal for all time.[243]

We started wandering about among the figurines and statues and looking at the pictures, jewelry, and decoration. We examined the precious stones, viewing the bodies on display, contemplating the fact that these scattered bones and skeletons were once kings who ruled over peoples, but then came to exist in a state of nothingness. We continued to look at things and follow the sequence of histories and biographies about rulers and accounts of their reigns. The Pāshā kept observing these valuable treasures and priceless relics from the vestiges of the ages, witnesses to their glory and prestige, without showing any particular amazement or surprise. I was somewhat nonplussed and wanted to find out what he was thinking. I spoke to him harshly because he seemed so reluctant to appreciate what he was looking at. He turned toward our Friend to ask him for an explanation. The Friend looked at me and scoffed: 35.2

FRIEND It's all very well for people like you to admire and boast, praise and exalt, express amazement and emotion when your imagination recreates these decayed artefacts as emblems without price, and those would-be afficionados have characterized them as key evidence and proof of the high levels that the earliest stages of civilization achieved in sciences, learning, arts, and crafts. But you shouldn't blame other people who look at the realities of the situation and evaluate them according to their real worth. They're unimpressed by illusions and refuse to be misled by their imaginings. Their vision is not clouded by tradition. God knows, anyone who is unpolluted by fancy and free of tradition can only regard them as children's toys with reference to the present era.

PĀSHĀ You're absolutely right. Bravo! In my view the situation is exactly as you've described it. What I've seen here is no more 35.3

significant than the goods on display in various market stalls. For me at least, these faded relics and decaying bodies are no more than overturned tombs, upended graves, and exhumed corpses. If the purpose in putting them on display is to offer a warning for people to consider, then people surely have a very present illustration every day when they witness kings descending from golden thrones into wooden biers, from silken cushions to stone pillows, from the backs of neighing thoroughbreds to the stomachs of lice and worms in the grave. All that has a much swifter effect on the senses and is more fruitful for the soul.

FRIEND That's the truth. The only reason why they reckon things like this to be priceless is that they're profoundly interested in antiquity and things that decay, and also because of the place these antiquities have in history and the ancient writings inscribed on them.

'ĪSĀ IBN HISHĀM Why shouldn't these objects be admired and highly appreciated when they're so incredibly precious and valuable; they're worth more than countless ingots of gold and silver? Were that not so, then these Westeners would not be so keen to acquire them, spending large amounts of money to buy a tiny stone, coming here from far-off lands to enjoy looking at these things and confirming the information they've heard. No one should assume that people of such learning and intelligence are spending their money and putting up with the hardships of travel just to look at things. There have to be other advantages and benefits that accrue in value in recompense for the amounts of money they spend and the risks that they're prepared to take.

35.4 FRIEND If these relics and corpses do indeed possess any value for Westerners, as you say, then, as I've just explained to you, it's all linked to their research in archaeology and their interest in the philosophy of history; to which should be added their love of acquiring things and their specialized interest in rarities. So for them antiquities have risen in value, and their price has increased. However, Egyptians get no benefit at all, except that they have a museum whose contents surpass anything to be found in Europe. If I paraded Egyptians in their thousands of thousands through this museum, they wouldn't get anything out of it. Only a small group would be useful to you: the small percentage of Egyptians who've studied with Europeans and have learned from them. For Egyptians it would be much better if God used the price that these antiquities bring to lessen the heavy burden of debt on their government and the weight of taxation and levies which contribute to their difficulties and restrictions. If they had to be kept here for purposes of ostentation and pride and that was the only benefit, then how I wish they did no harm even if they do no good, and how I wish that Egyptians could have them with neither positives nor negatives. But, as things are, their benefits are nowhere close to the material damage they cause. Every year Egyptians are forced to pay fixed amounts of money in order to look after them, preserve them, and conduct archeological digs underground. And that's not even to mention what's spent on transferring them from the places where they're found and on their storage firstly in the museum in Bulaq, then their transfer again to this museum, and finally to the brand new museum that's been built to house them in Qaṣr al-Nīl[244], costing thousands in pure gold.

ʿĪsā ibn Hishām Dear Friend, I realize that your verdicts are 35.5
profound and your investigations on this topic have been thorough. But you don't seem to be taking into account the way in which people's minds attach great importance to the unusual, even though it be harmful, and relish the prospect of abandoning their slavish reliance on illusions. You'll see museums in every single country, institutions that they cherish and protect. Even if the highest prices were offered, they would not be willing to sell or disperse them. So how is it that you see Egypt as being an exception to this principle when its relics are so incredibly valuable and significant?

Friend Yes, people in other countries cherish antiquities in their museums because they are symbols of victory and conquest, and because they don't need the money they could get from selling them. Also some of them are gifts which should not be sold. But with Egypt it's exactly the opposite. These relics didn't come to us by way of conquests and victories; to the contrary, they came from excavations and digging. We're the people most in need of their value. Not only that, but there are more of them as day follows day. Rarely does a year go by without archaeologists discovering enough materials for ostentation and display. So why not sell some of them, particularly when Egyptian rulers have been allowed to give them away as presents and turn a blind eye to their plunder. You can see them in European and American countries, not to mention their museums where a sizeable portion of them has been taken either by plunder or fraud, or else by way of requests or sheer favoritism. This then is our share in the process of preserving these monuments, spending money on them, and jealously protecting them.

35.6 We've seen countries sold, so why not relics? At the moment they're not being sold, as you can see, but rather divided up. The benefits all redound to foreigners, either by coming here to look at them or else by taking them back to their own countries. If God were to give the Egyptian government a modicum of inspiration, it would be marketing some of these relics which our digs and caves produce on a daily basis. They could then be a source of income, some of which could be spent on things that would benefit the Egyptian people: the spread of education, stimulating culture by printing books archived in the Egyptian National Library at the Amīriyyah Press (which has often helped people by printing useful books in the time of the previous government which was both ignorant and tyrannical).[245] Tell me, by God, what benefit can there be for an Islamic Egyptian people to put ancient Pharaohs on display in the Antiquities Museum and at the same time to keep the spirits of scholars, philosophers, jurists, literature scholars, and poets locked up in the National Library? If we're spending such huge sums of money, which of the two is more profitable and beneficial: putting on display a picture of Osiris or Isis, a statue of Ibis, the arm of Ramses and leg of Amenophis, or rather having at hand a work by al-Rāzī, a treatise by al-Fārābī, a chapter by al-Asfarayīnī, an essay by al-Jāḥiẓ, or poems by Ibn al-Rūmī? By God, in our country things only work in contradictions; they always operate contrary to what's in the public interest.

ʿĪsā ibn Hishām said: When our Friend reached this point, it was time for us to leave the museum, and we did so with the other visitors. While we were on our way out along with the crowd of tourists, we spotted a turbaned gentleman accompanied by a younger man in modern dress. From their conversation we gathered that the man was an important person in the city while the young fellow was his son who had studied Western subjects. The son was saying to his father: 35.7

SON Have you noticed how our glory is mirrored in these shrines to our prestige? Do you appreciate the level of civilization that our ancestors achieved? Are you aware of the lofty ideas and artistic perfection that our earliest forebears developed? God is our witness that, if ancestors from different nations were gathered for a day of debate and argument, the Egyptian would emerge as clear winner; he would win the seventh arrow in the betting.[246] In so doing, he would be holding these relics in his hand as he competed, argued, and adjured:

> These are our remains which point us out.[247]

FATHER I can see nothing in these pictures, statues, and stones to glorify. In my opinion they're just palace ruins, remains that have long since been effaced, traces that have vanished. If what people say about these statues—that they represent ancient persons on whom wrath and transformation descended, then any glorification of their memory is something that will annoy the Creator and displease human beings. To claim that these monuments were made by our ancestors and that these Pharaonic corpses are our own ancestors is a foul sin. «A dreadful word comes out of their mouths. They speak nothing but lies.»[248] Our forebears and ancestors are those noble

Arabs; it's through them that we have our pride and to their prestige and honor that we're connected. Talking about perfection of craft, there are many peasant children who labor making stones and relics like these. They may live in abject squalor, and yet their hands can craft objects far superior to the crystal objects stored in palaces.

35.8 SON (*silently*) «Forgive my father! For he is one of those who have gone astray.»[249] (*raising his voice*) If we had books written in our Arabic language like the many tomes in foreign languages, then you'd be aware of their many qualities and the public benefits that accrue because they're visible to the eye of the perceptive beholder. Just look at that statue of the village leader. Can't you tell how subtle, perfect, and accurate a portrait it is in sycamore wood?

FATHER I can see hundreds of shaykhs like him every day in flesh and blood. I don't need wood and stone.

35.9 'Īsā ibn Hishām said: We reached the exit. As we got into our carriage, the Friend said, "Did you hear that conversation about cultural superiority? It confirms for you everything that I've been saying and the correctness of my views on the topic." In reply the Pāshā said, "What you told us is obviously correct." With that we set off for the theater—the playhouse where lives and stories are presented on stage.

Miṣbāḥ al-sharq 106, June 1, 1900[250]

ʿĪsā ibn Hishām said: When sunset extended its snare to snatch away the sun from late afternoon, the orb was forced to flee to its hide. Dusk then arose from its terminal breaths as sunbeams slowly vanished along with the disk.[251] Twilight's sisters disappeared beneath the horizon's sleeves, and night's darkness sprouted its mustache and its edges turned grey. Now evening lamps were lit in the domes of darkness. We had arrived at the theater where plays are performed and portraits and imaginings invoked. We joined other people at the entrance, women and men of all shapes and sizes. Choosing seats underneath the boxes so that we could look easily in all directions, we decided to sit down so that we could observe the people in the audience. We found ourselves in the middle of groups of people who were wearing a variety of fashions and raising a hue and cry. Their idea of fun seemed to consist of cursing and swearing, punching and kicking each other. They kept banging on the floor with their feet and canes, while some of them were leaning over each other—men and boys, young men and parents—all of them making it clear that they were tired of waiting; they wanted the curtain to be raised. Looking up at the boxes, we noticed that the same kind of vulgar and loose behavior prevailed. We could see curtained boxes that revealed pearls and gems on the necks of cloistered beauties, queens of the women's quarters in palatial mansions, looking like brilliant stars glimpsed through gaps in the clouds. Wisps of hair were now 36.1

revealed on faces that glistened with highlights like the night beneath the moon:

> She was veiled in a light white cloud,
>   twixt concealment and display.
> Like a maid's breath on her mirror
>   her beauty was perfect, and she was not married.[252]

36.2 From below men looked up and stared on fire with passion. Their eyes never wavered, and they never turned away but continued their worship, gazing up at them with fixed attention. The girls kept laughing incessantly, gesturing and exchanging winks, while the men below kept making signs. Everyone was waving their handkerchief in ways that made words superfluous. Fans were employed to arouse passions and provoke longing. Fingers pulled back curtains so that messengers with flowers could pass through. Opera glasses turned towards other opera glasses, bringing distant things close and magnifying small objects. Every young man assumed that he was the focus of these glances and gestures; he would put on dashing airs and pretend to be modest and suave. At the very top there were other people, and what a mob they were! They were boxed in, horde upon horde, like people at a sheep market or wild animals on hillocks, pestering and making a fuss. We looked around the theater for our companions and located them in one room and the tart and her assistant by her side in another. She was making eyes at the 'Umdah and pinching him. Then they both stretched their hands and grabbed some glasses of wine; the 'Umdah was getting his from a bottle that the Playboy was serving, while hers came from the hand of her assistant. All the while the Playboy kept coming and going, disappearing from the 'Umdah's box and then reappearing; sometimes he would be in a box with her and then in another one.

36.3 While all this was going on, the bell was rung and the curtain went up. A group of actresses and actors appeared, chanting and singing in an unbearable fashion, a spectacle against which human nature revolted. They were using obscure and unintelligible language and sounded like camel drivers in the waterless desert or people attending a funeral. They were wearing contrasting costumes: their shapes matched, but there were too many colors. Their bodies clearly hailed from different countries.

The curtain came down, and then rose again on a middle-aged woman and an adolescent boy. They were embracing each other and sharing their tears. As he spoke to her, he was detailing his passionate love. "What lovely words!" he was saying. "Come now, let's unite in love." "My handsome boy," she replied, "that might come to pass if my mother, Nasīm, would help us. Think of something because I'm going to send her to see you." As they left, a man and woman came on stage talking to each other like a married couple. She had been working on a strategy to deal with the boy. "That boy is more persistent than a fly," he was telling her. "As far as I'm concerned, he's more pernicious than a swarm of demons and more repulsive than a pack of old nags. He won't leave lowly women alone, even if they're old and ugly." "My dear good husband," his wife replied, "don't get alarmed. Not all little birds get eaten! Our daughter is intelligent and pretty. She has nothing to fear from him, either in company or in private."

They both left the stage, and the lover and his girlfriend reappeared.

"Praise be to God, my dear," she told him. "Things have been resolved, and my mother's worked things out. Now all we have to do is to keep the housekeeper happy. Then she'll keep our secrets to herself. If not, she's going to regret it."

"You're right, you lovely daughter of noble-minded parents!" the boy replied. "If she won't agree, I'll make her savor the cup of death at the point of this sword. This purse of gold should satisfy every wish."

"Come with me, my fine fellow!" she told him. "I hear footsteps. Let's go where we can be alone and bathe in passion's waters after waking!"

"May you be preserved, sweet lady!" he went on, "source of my life and death! Now the sun of my good fortunes has risen, and the aroma of musk has perfumed my existence! In a while we'll take a stroll."

36.4 Their dialogue now completed, other actors came on stage. They discussed theft, fraud, betrayal, treachery, and murder at one moment, and then talked about committing various other crimes, such as embezzlement and kidnapping. They started making a colossal din and bellowing something that resembled a song. The audience greeted them with whistles and threw flowers at them. With that the curtain came down on the first act. The audience now resumed its pushing and shoving. I was about to get up in the middle of the crowd, but the Pāshā grabbed my coattails and started questioning me:

PĀSHĀ Haven't you had enough yet of these dance halls and nightclubs? Aren't we sufficiently bored with all these sights and scenarios. Surely by now we've seen enough to provide us with the experience and instruction we need.

36.5 'ĪSĀ IBN HISHĀM This place isn't a dance hall or a nightclub. This is a theater, something that Western peoples acknowledge as having educational and corrective qualities. It encourages virtues, exposes evil traits, and portrays the deeds of former generations so that people can be educated and learn lessons from them. In Europe theater is regarded as an excellent moral guide writ large so that it can achieve the same effects as narratives and stories. It portrays evil deeds for you and demonstrates the dire consequences of such actions however much help the person may get from fate and however hard he tries to reach his goals and achieve his wishes. By watching such things, the spectator is provided with a negative impression and a restraining force. Theater can also show you laudable deeds, which can encourage you to emulate them and lead you to do likewise. It can show you the happy outcomes that will ensue whatever troubles and difficulties are encountered on the way, whatever misfortunes you may suffer as a result, and whatever hardship, distress, and anxiety life may bring down on you. By watching such actions on stage you'll be encouraged to pursue what is good and behave in a proper and reasonable manner. Theater can also provide you with the best possible models culled from historical accounts which are brought out of obscurity for all to see. It thus endows you with examples of virtue such as generosity, courage, reliability, loyalty, gallantry, pride, resolution, audacity, prudence, and perseverance, along with a disregard for wealth and a tolerance of misfortune and sorrow. At the same time it separates you from the equivalent degree of evil deeds and qualities.

Pāshā That's amazing! How can you be making such claims 36.6
when what I've been watching here doesn't resemble in any way what you've just been describing? In fact, it's just the opposite. What I've seen here is just a repeat of what I've observed in the dance hall—drinking wine, flirting with women, portraying amorous situations in a highly suggestive manner, one that's designed solely to arouse people's passions, make such things more accessible and easy, and stir up lustful emotions. If these presentations are considered to be displays of virtuous and appropriate conduct, then it would be better for people to enter this theater with the firm conviction that they're coming to see something undesirable, something that pleases neither God nor people. Based on what I've just seen, there's absolutely no way that anyone can excuse himself for coming into this place on the pretext that it's a haven of virtue as you've just depicted it, a display of perfections, or a source of noble and refined qualities. Any such person is committing an error in coming here, and he will leave in the same state, even though he may try both to excuse himself and offer excuses to others by stating that he only came here in order to absorb virtuous deeds and avoid vice. His only reason for coming, he will claim, is to purge himself of faults and the pollution of evil.

ʿĪsā ibn Hishām Don't take the shortcomings you see here as 36.7
evidence that this art has no value for people. I've already explained that it's a Western art form, and it's Westerners who have perfected

it. I've described to you the degree of perfection it's achieved among Western people. Here it's still in its initial stages, the beginning of its emergence. For that reason we need to excuse the shortcomings that we can see here. People are unaware of its true essence and effects. Many of them regard it as some sort of farce, an excuse for frivolity and obscenity. Anyone who's acquainted with the plots translated from the most illustrious Western writers and intellectuals and who realizes the education and refinement that is offered will come to appreciate its benefits. Such people will find themselves affected and will strive to learn from it. Along the same lines, it can be said that these shortcomings are entirely due to the government. In Europe useful arts such as this are an aspect of knowledge that can only spread and develop with government support and the involvement of associations. If the same amount of money was being spent here as is the case with theater in Europe, then the government would be providing the location, costumes, and funding so that it could achieve the highest possible level of progress and success. However, our government has completely ignored it, and you can see the result for yourself. It's still not out of the question that one day the government will give it some attention, in which case people in the East will be able to gain some benefit from it as those in the West already do.

36.8 FRIEND My dear friend, I think you're simply repeating what people are saying rather than reflecting the true situation. How can you imagine that in the current circumstances this art is going to improve with government support—which implies government funding—so that, according to European claims, people can be educated by it? Even if we were to admit that it was indeed beneficial for Eastern peoples and there was no worry about the corruption that it might cause, how are we to plot its forward progress when everything in Egypt—from its earliest days to the present—has made progress except for this particular art? Ever since some Syrians introduced it here some twenty years ago, there has been no sign of improvement. No one has stepped forward to give it approval. As time passes, it seems bound to remain just as it is now, namely translations of weird Western stories like the dreadful translated text and clashing rhymes that we have just witnessed. The only people who tolerate it are the kind of regular customers here who regard it as a place for amusement and socializing, a special kind of soirée. The impact that this art form has on them is no greater than that of all the other types of entertainment presented by phony imitators and magicians. If we take an honest look at this art form as it exists in the West, we discover that it does not suit Eastern people and does not accord with their customs—most especially Muslims.

You're aware, of course, that when prudent researchers investigate matters connected with upbringing and moral education, they need to take into account local terrain and the construction of people's natural instincts and temperaments. They can tell, for example, that what works in Paris won't do in Beijing; what's approved in London won't be in Khartoum. Indeed it may be even worse than that. Something that's beneficial in one place may actually be harmful in another; what Westerners treat seriously may be regarded as a joke in the East, and what's true in one country may be false in another. The point that you're missing is that theater and acting involve plots that revolve around the topic of love. It's extremely rare for one of their narratives not to have two lovers as its beginning and end; and that's the way things are. It causes no great harm in Western societies because expressions of love are permitted by their customs, something that can be projected in public by their young men and women who see neither fault nor sin in it. Indeed it's one of the major bases for marriage. The basis for that custom lies in the judgment of that particular region that sentiments can remain fairly calm and that presentations such as these will not arouse and enflame the imagination to strong reactions. In Eastern countries by contrast the damage can be considerable. For that very reason love is kept secret, something to put under wraps. In certain quarters the mere notion of sin and disgrace has such a hold that, if a young man even proclaims his love for a girl, they will refuse to marry her to 36.9

him. They may even raise the matter with the ruler who will order that he be put to death with no possibility of retaliation or blood payment. Among Westerners, if a girl does not love her boyfriend, then she doesn't marry him. That provides a clear example of the difference in customs and the contrast in traits between one region and another. Love of this kind is the primary focus of this particular art, and so it must inevitably be rejected in the East. Otherwise corruption and disorder will spread, all of which may lead to all sorts of evils being committed and a nasty intercultural mix in which crude emotions will be rapidly stirred and lewd sensations will be kindled.

36.10 The supposed purpose of this art is for education and moral purification. The only way of achieving that is by making use of what is familiar and in accord with people's habits. The translation of stories that have been composed with specific moral standards in mind cannot have the same effect on another people as they do on the one for which it was originally intended. The promoters of this art must inevitably be drawn from the same people so that their presentations will serve to elucidate their own conditions and customs. The morality of the peoples of the East does not include this kind of exposure and representation, especially in matters relating to family and children. The codes of the Islamic faith do not permit women to involve themselves in this art because it forbids them to display themselves in public, quite apart from mingling with others. Indeed it commands them to turn their gaze away rather than the opposite. Nor is it any part of Islamic practice that we should be portraying its history and that of its caliphs and holy men, devising various plots, making up stories, and placing them in amorous situations. By so doing, we make them say things they never uttered and put them in unreal situations. Even so, that is what many non-Muslims are daring to do these days in our country. What can you possibly say about the Caliph Hārūn al-Rashīd singing, his vizier Jaʿfar al-Barmakī playing the flute, and al-Faḍl ibn al-Rabīʿ dancing? Without the slightest doubt it's an insult to our ancestors and a distortion of history.

All this presupposes that the origin of the theatrical art is in education, proper training, and a quest for perfection. However, if we take a closer look at it from the perspective of its benefits within the Western context, both intellect and observation make it clear that, even in their own cultural environment, the harm it does is clear enough while the benefits are nonexistent. The evidence of this lies in the fact that the art aims to reveal virtuous conduct by portraying evil and to illustrate chaste behavior through portraits of sheer lust. In order to achieve those aims, it has to exaggerate in its portrayal of illicit behavior and lewd desires and to portray them by using the tricks, falsehoods, and deceits that can be devised as a result of the plots and formats that the poetic imgination can devise. Not only does it not encourage the evil person to refrain from committing such acts, but it also leads him to get even further involved in such activities and to expand and enhance his expertise in its various aspects. Thus the thief learns further arts of theft, the villain learns how to commit crimes, the swindler learns how to trick and deceive, and the lecher learns all kinds of debauchery and fornication. While these are the effects on wicked people, the virtuous gain no benefits. The wicked person becomes yet more evil, and the spectacle may even cause harm to the virtuous person. 36.11

It only requires a little thought to discover that the process of providing detailed illustrations of the hidden aspects of evil and latent desire is actually harmful and unbeneficial. It turns what is not supposed to happen into something that actually might happen. That's why people say that the act of detailing particular crimes in law codes draws attention to them. A sage Greek lawgiver was once asked why he'd overlooked the provision of a punishment for parricide in his legal code. His reply was that he'd never imagined any Greek would ever dare to kill his father. That statement of his did more to prevent the occurrence of that crime than describing the various penalties for committing it. That lawgiver refused to mention parricide in his law code, so what can you say when the very same thing is acted before your very eyes. These theatrical plots 36.12

are loaded down with depictions of father-killers and men marrying their mothers or sisters, decrees requiring that a father drink his son's blood, and other similar criminal acts that we would never believe actually occurred were it not for these Western plays.

36.13 It's true enough that human beings may be affected when someone suffers a mishap if that mishap is occasioned by someone else. However, that affect is not enough to prevent him from committing a reprehensible act because man will act justly as long as the wrong comes from somebody else. If, for example, he witnesses a disagreement in which he's in no way involved, he will adopt a posture of justice and fairness and will steer clear of any personally harmful evil action as long as he has no personal interest in it. That's why a man with an ugly face will loathe ugliness on someone else's face even though he doesn't do so with regard to his own face. But if he has some benefit to gain and is somehow connected with it, then he'll be unable to resist. At that point he will tend to commit the evil act that is to his advantage and will deviate from the right course that his mind has been dictating to him. All of which makes it clear that the notion of theater as being effective in the acquisition of laudable qualities is by definition false. Passions cannot be cooled by enflaming them in the first place; moderation does not emerge from recklessness. We have a minor illustration right in front of us. If the woman who draws back the curtains in her box to flirt with men actually learned about chaste behavior from the play, she would be using her hand to pull the curtains closed again. But how can we claim she has learned something when the gaps in the curtains grow ever wider?

36.14 ʿĪsā ibn Hishām said: At this point people returned to their seats, and the din resumed at its former level. The curtain now rose on a desolate woodland scene. A voice was raised imitating that of a muezzin. The Pāshā was perplexed and asked me if the call to prayer was performed in the theater as well. Hardly had he finished asking the question before the young man from the previous act appeared carrying something and singing. Behind him was the middle-aged woman who kept looking behind her and stumbling as though she were running away and was afraid of being followed or chased by the police. Both of them were chanting, singing, and calling for help. It was only a moment or so before the man whom we'd seen in the previous act with his wife came rushing in, followed by the troupe who had closed the last act. They all surrounded the young man and his beloved. First there was an exchange of words, then argument, abuse, and fisticuffs. The young man now took out a revolver and fired it at the man who fell dead. He then fired it at another man, and he fell dead too. The rest of the men turned on their heels, while the woman fainted. With that the act came to an end.

We followed people out and headed for the theater bar. It was 36.15
very crowded, but we spotted the 'Umdah with his two companions and the tart sitting at a table with wine and full glasses in front of them. They had obviously drunk a lot. We moved to one side and had only been there for a few moments before we saw a man going up to them. He spoke to the woman: "Do you think that, by missing our appointment, you can put off paying the amount you owe me on the check? I'm exhausted having to search for you day and night in every possible spot. So now I've finally stumbled on you here! I'm not going to move till you give me what I'm owed; either that, or else you can give me back that necklace you're using to decorate your bosom in front of all your paramours and lovers!" With that he stretched out his hand to snatch the necklace from her bosom, but the Playboy stopped him by stepping between them. "This is not the right time," he said. "If she owes you something, then seek redress through the courts." But the man refused. "I'll not seek redress through the courts when my money's right there in front of me on her bosom." He stretched his hand out again, but the tart clutched her necklace. She leaned over in the 'Umdah's direction and begged him to come to her aid. Anger and self-respect got the better of him, and he pushed the jeweler away from her. "If you don't like the way I'm demanding my due," the jeweler said, "don't push me away. Pay

me yourself!" The 'Umdah inquired how much was owed, to which the woman replied that it was a mere forty pounds. He paid the jeweler the amount and grabbed the check in one hand and a glass of wine in the other. He offered them both to the woman, and she kissed the rim to show her gratitude. The jeweler meanwhile left with a smile.

36.16 They started drinking and chatting again. The 'Umdah suggested to his companions that they leave the playhouse which only youngsters found enjoyable and go to the cafés on the Gezira. They could sit in the moonlight in the gardens alongside the River Nile. They all approved of the idea and were about to leave when the Proprietor of the dance hall where the woman regularly performed was standing right in front of them, hands on hips and shaking his head in annoyance. "So this is the illness that's kept you from coming to work tonight, is it? Is this the hospital where you're being treated? I assume that the 'Umdah is one of the era's most accomplished physicians!" With that he grabbed her hand to take her back to the dance hall with him. The 'Umdah grabbed hold of her other hand. "What do you mean by this impertinence?" he asked. "Why are you treating her so roughly? You've already taken ten pounds as compensation for her not coming to work in the tavern tonight. Now you want her to go with you. That's arrant deceit and fraud!" "You're the ones indulging in deceit and fraud," the Proprietor replied, "you and she both. If you paid her that amount, then she's tricked you and kept the money for herself. I'm surprised at your own impudence, bringing business in my place to a halt and tempting her into staying away from her job so you could bring her to a place like this."

The row got worse, and things became so heated that one of the actresses who had no role to play that night started yelling for the police to eject them all for fear the evening would be ruined. The police duly arrived and decided to take them all to the station. We were intending to follow them, but the Pāshā absolutely refused to go. "I'm not going to any police station," he said firmly, "whether it's to lodge a complaint or merely to observe. I've already had some experience of both the visible and hidden aspects of it all. I'm well aware of what goes on there."

'Īsā ibn Hishām said: Since the Pāshā was feeling both tired and bored, we headed for the house as quickly as possible. 36.17

Miṣbāḥ al-sharq 107, June 8, 1900[253]

37.1 ʿĪsā ibn Hishām said: When we reached the house, the Pāshā made for his bedroom to rest after the tiring day. However he could not fall asleep and was restless. He called out to me, wanting to while away the remainder of the night talking. We had a conversation about times old and new. Night was in the final stages of its youth and was about to dispense with both shawl and veil; old age crept into its temples, and traces of daylight appeared on its skin. Disdaining necklets and jewelry and stinting on pearls and precious gems, it took off the rings of the Pleiades from its hand and removed the twin stars of Ursa Minor—its earrings. From its neck it cast away clusters of lustrous pearly stars and emerged as a grey-haired old woman tottering along on the stick formed by the Gemini. A former veiled, coquettish posture was now turned into one of vulgar insignificance. Night was now stripped of her veil and revealed in her common gown. Dawn took pity on her as sons do their mothers and covered her with its blue sheet. Ere long the laws of closure imposed their inevitable decree. Morning wrapped her in its white sheet, then shrouded her in the belly of space.

37.2 As soon as sunrise opened the gates to daytime and radiant light shone forth over the world's regions, our Friend arrived along with the sun according to the plan we had arranged the day before. He began by asking how we were after the way we had spent the night. We told him that we had continued talking, to which he responded by asking what we had been discussing and what topics we had broached. I replied by telling him that, every time the Pāshā recalled the amazing modernities he had seen, the strange statements and discussions he had heard, and the things he had witnessed during his travels that were unfamiliar to him in the era of his own dynasty, he would complain about the corruption and imperfection that he kept seeing. He was keen to find out what the underlying causes for the situation were. The Friend replied that the root cause lay in the way Easterners were imitating Western civilization. When compared with what could be seen and heard, he found it amazing that Westerners' minds could be so preoccupied and their lives could be so squandered on the creation of things that did only harm, and no good, on the devising of new phenomena that only serve to corrupt rather than provide benefit. I showed him that, whereas Westerners only see advantages and gains in their civilization, the peoples of the East have chosen to imitate them without any firm basis for doing so. They have only picked the thorns off the fruit tree and tasted the bitter fruit.

Friend You're absolutely right! This Western civilization 37.3
has reached the peoples of Eastern lands without any firm basis or acknowledgment of different regions, variant temperaments, and incompatible moral systems. People have failed to distinguish what suits them from what does not, and have not discriminated between the authentic from the phony. Quite the opposite, they have accepted it all willingly and have contented themselves with useless superficialities and utter trivialities. In so doing, they have abandoned all national norms and firmly rooted principles. As a result, structures and pillars have been weakened and links have been cut. You can see for yourself how severe is the resulting damage and how widespread the dire consequences. This patina of Western civilization has turned into a trap that Westerners can use to catch us unawares, a pickaxe to destroy our very foundations and undermine our walls. We're destroying our house with our own hands.

Pāshā I can't understand why peoples of the East have chosen to adopt the useless aspects of civilization rather than its true essence, the surface rather than the core. They seem to confine their attention to the shell rather than the pith, whereas in earlier times they were of all peoples the most steeped in civilization and culture.

37.4 FRIEND The only reason is that the natural consequence of periods of glory is recklessness and hubris, and they in turn engender weakness, indifference, slackness, and neglect. They are only willing to bear light loads and minimal responsibilities, things that don't require any hardship to achieve or exhaustion in their execution. While Eastern peoples paid no attention, Westerners were willing to undertake difficult assignments and to persevere doggedly in burdensome activities. As a result they've developed industries, made inventions, and scattered across countries far and wide. That has bequeathed them wealth and military power. The riches of the East have attracted them and its resources have flowed for them in abundance. They've sold the peoples of the East utter trash for gold. Meanwhile Westerners have benefited from their own civilization and have continued ever upwards while the peoples of the East have gained nothing from imitating them, but have rather continued their downward trajectory.

PĀSHĀ How I wish I could see this Western civilization in its homelands! I'd be able to examine both its external and internal aspects and investigate what parts of it are useful and harmful. Then one could make judgments based on eyewitness experience. But that's a big challenge and would involve a lot of trouble.

'ĪSĀ IBN HISHĀM The idea's not that remote; don't think it's so impossible! I'm still thinking of accompanying you one day on a trip to Europe so we can learn about the essence of this Western civilization and the benefits that progress has brought to its people. Then its effects will be as obvious to the eye as what you've been hearing with your ears.

37.5 FRIEND If that's your goal and intention, then no better occasion and opportunity exists for me to show you things than a trip at the present time to visit the *Exposition universelle* in Paris, mother of all Western capitals. You would be seeing civilization on display in its clearest form, culture shining forth in its brightest and most glorious guise.

PĀSHĀ What is this "*Exposition universelle*"?

FRIEND It's a huge market that has been built by Western governments to last for a few years. They invite the governments of the world to send people with their crafts and products, things that demonstrate the perfection of man's work. The world's products and crafts are on display for experts to examine, and the best examples are awarded prizes for their perfect craftsmanship. In that way people are stimulated and encouraged to perform well in their own work, to aspire to higher goals in learning and arts on the one hand, while on the other the government that created the exhibition earns a large profit along with its own people because hordes of people who can be counted in millions enter the grounds for a fixed fee. And you can add to that the commercial transactions and the large amount of buying and selling that occurs between the native population and visitors who come from the remotest parts of the planet.

The first people to create an exhibition like this were the English 37.6
in 1851; they were followed by the French in 1855. The French have followed the same pattern several times according to the circumstances of the period. Recently it's been decided to hold such an exhibition every ten years. The costs of putting on the most recent example in 1889 reached five million francs, and the profits were ten million.

In summary then, you get to see not only aspects of Western civilization but other things that it wouldn't be easy to locate unless you spent your entire life traveling and enduring all the hardships of travel. Things are brought together in Paris that are otherwise scattered across the globe among desert and urbanized societies—both primitive and advanced. The goods and products on display will never be collected in a single place such as this one or with broader scope for the inquiring mind that is interested in the states of the world's peoples, their customs, and their moral codes. One can investigate the causes of their progress and backwardness, and the factors influencing their happiness or misery. This collection of materials constitutes a market of the entire world, an 'Ukāẓ Fair for these periods of civilized society.[254] The significance of it all can be gauged from the decree issued by the French president, ordering the establishment of the exhibition this year. In it he says, "This exhibition will present to the entire world the products of the human mind; it will show how far mankind's initiatives have advanced in a hundred years of perfecting both knowledge and the arts. For scientists, intellectuals, philosophers, and sages it will undoubtedly offer a new gateway to sound strategies that will serve to guide mankind's ideas along a clear path through which truth will overtop fantasy. By so doing, the intellectual will be the inventor of a philosophical method to steer this century forward."

37.7 'Īsā ibn Hishām said: I noticed that the Pāshā's facial expression indicated a strong desire on his part to see the things at the exhibition that our Friend had been describing. The Pāshā looked at me, an obvious request evident in his expression:

PĀSHĀ By God, this is a huge opportunity for the inquiring scholar; no curious student should miss it! Maybe God will make it possible for us to see this "exposition" before it finishes, and we'll be able to examine what it has on offer.

'ĪSĀ IBN HISHĀM As long as you're that keen, I can't refuse or fail to respond to your request.

FRIEND If that's the case, we'll have to hurry. If you agree, I'll come with you. I've been thinking about it already. I can't imagine two more agreeable travel companions with whom to investigate the true nature of things, reveal those aspects that remain concealed behind a veil of fancy, and show the hidden consequences that emerge from mistaken ideas.

PĀSHĀ What a wonderful friend and fine companion!

FRIEND Let's make our preparations to travel. We'll need to start immediately by reserving places on a boat leaving this week.

Many passengers booked their places a month or two in advance, and I've heard that there are no vacant spots on any boat leaving this month.

ʿĪsā ibn Hishām said: No one can have been quicker than the Pāshā to get to his feet. We went with him to look for a place on any boat that was on the point of departing. After a good deal of checking and multiple visits we could only find a single boat with a few empty spaces. It was anchored at Port Suez from where it was heading for Marseille in France. So on Sunday we were to leave Cairo. It is from God that we request help, and upon Him that we rely. 37.8

Miṣbāḥ al-sharq 116, August 17, 1900[255]

38.1 This is the first episode of *Ḥadīth ʿĪsā ibn Hishām* concerning the visit to the Paris Exhibition. It has been sent to us by Muḥammad al-Muwayliḥī following his previous report on the visit of the Khedive of Egypt to Her Majesty the Queen of England.

Paris[256]

38.2 It was in Paris that we finally threw down our staff and reached our destination. We now started making our way along the network of streets and across broad squares. To tell the truth, no gathering on Judgment Day, no dead being raised, no living persons hastily summoned, no tribes gathering in assembly, no troops routed in the heat of battle, no people in the utmost panic—none of them could possibly rival the way people were crammed together, all shoving, pushing, clashing with, and jostling one another. They kept surging against one another so that even the broad expanse of earth was not spacious enough. They careened past us like a flood beneath lights that eliminated the dark. There was no night, and the lights were so bright that one would have to be worried about night blindness. Indeed the cock might have been deceived and started crowing to announce the arrival of morning.

If you surveyed the street from above, you would not consider it to be a hyperbole in stating that it was a veritable sea with crashing waves, with two shores of light on either side. Viewed from below, you would have said that they were desert flocks rising in the air amidst gleaming stars made up of electric lights. Over it all clustered trees, creating a green dome that replaced the heavenly dome itself. On either side there were lofty houses neatly arrayed; it was as though there was a kind of calligraphy in their harmony, with the flowers on their walls giving the letters shapes and dots. Their structures reached to the very clouds and tried to hang by ropes from the heavens. Compared with these, what can one say about Haman's construction for the Pharaoh, what Solomon's jinn erected for him, and what Sinmār built for Nuʿmān? And what, for that matter, concerning mountain slopes against anthills, the raging sea as compared to a gleaming mirage, the peaks of Mount Thabīr compared to mere camel humps, or celestial stars compared to a spider's web?

We watched as people hassled each other in such a close-packed situation, with everyone barging against everyone else—men both young and middle-aged, old folk and children, boys and girls—some of them riding, others on foot. Thousands of bicycles plunged through the crowd, clearing a path like arrows shot from a bow, seemingly flying as though powered by electricity, steam, or horses:

> And, when no animal challenged them,
> they chased their very shadows.[257]

They all seemed as frightened as sparrows, looking anxiously 38.3
around like scared sandgrouse in the desert. One false glance, and they would be dead; one slip of the foot, and blood would flow; a single disdainful stare, and perdition would soon ensue. They all stuck to the two sides of the street, like a drowning man clutching the shore. On either side the shops were loaded down with incredible wares, costly goods, things that would lead the most fervent ascetic astray and make him desire them, that would tempt the stingiest of misers into buying them. The bars alongside were all full of customers and crowds of people sitting down; everyone had a glass of wine in one hand and the evening newspaper in the other. In this kind of situation we were so shocked and befuddled that we almost

lost our minds; such was the anxiety we felt that we hardly knew where to turn:

In a square where even Luqmān the wise,
were he there, would not be so wise.[258]

Needing some place to rest, we headed for a bar in the square, but, such was the crowd that we could find nowhere to sit down. After spending some time on our feet, we were on the point of departing in despair, but some people got up to leave and go their way, so we took their places and sat in a spot from which we could observe the expressions on people's faces and watch passersby. We immediately noticed that there were more women than men and that they were handsome, attractive, and flirtatious, with curvaceous figures and rosy cheeks:

In a kaleidoscope of color they swaggered,
Bright yellow gleaming and deep red.[259]

Strutting their finery and hurrying along, these ladies kept outdoing each other in showing off skirts and hems:

As they smiled, they revealed pearly teeth,
as though their very necks were bedecked in smiles.[260]

They exuded too the sweet fragrance of perfume, the like of which no flower ever exuded on a dewy branch. They kept tapping the ground with their feet and clinking their jewels as much as possible, shooting forth arrowed glances that stirred latent sorrows;

Mouth gestures, the twitch of an eyebrow,
eyelids aflutter, and the wave of a hand.[261]

Peddlers kept coming and going, yelling and shouting like so many howling hyenas and barking dogs as they proffered their wares with their usual insistence.

38.4 Once we had come to our senses, the Pāshā started asking questions, as was his wont. He wanted to know precisely what was happening. "I've no doubt," he said, "that this must be a festival day for the people of this new world; either that or they're immigrants or soldiers returning from combat; now that they're no longer facing death, they're bringing back spoils and captives." "No," I replied, "the situation was just as people had described and those in the know were fully aware: this is 'the virtuous city,'[262] the mother of perfect civilization, the very haven of cultured urbanity, site of refinement and grace, homeland of honor and glory, and source of both calamity and felicity. For these people it was Iram with its many pillars, something the like of which no other country could possibly create. Were Chosroes Anushirwan, the builder of the famous portico, to set his eyes on this city, he would no longer be able to boast of portico or palace; he would judge his famous Madā'in to be a desert wasteland. If the Roman Caesar were to lay his eyes on it, he would rip the crown off his brow and the royal staff from his hand, then swear that the city of Rome itself, the world's capital, was a pathetic little village, the kind that he described in this way before he came to power: 'I would rather be the first person in a lowly village than the second in a Roman city.' Were Plato, the philosopher of his age, to have seen it, he would never have declared in olden times: 'I praise God for three blessings that the human tongue cannot laud sufficiently nor offer due thanks, namely that I was created a man and not an animal; then that I was made a man and not a woman; and thirdly that I am a citizen of Athens and not of any other country.' If Hārūt and Mārūt had been aware of it, they would never have argued with the notion that, compared with Paris, Babylon was a wasteland:

> Like paradise itself it pleases the viewer,
> scoffing at the palaces of Khuld and Surra Man Ra'ā.

"Today this city is the home of learning and excellence, the haven of peace and justice, the cradle of liberty and fairness, and sanctuary of unity and concord. It is that school where humanity encounters the rights of man and learns the different aspects of charity and 38.5

beneficence. All people have their own homeland, but this place is the homeland of homelands, the place from which the sun of guidance and knowledge radiates across the world. Minds are enlightened and insights are disclosed; anyone led astray and perplexed is guided out of the dark corners of ignorance. If it did not exist, mankind would not be aware of its own potential, nor would people feel safe from intrigue and assassination in their own homes. It wards off from people the ravages of injustice and compensates them against the calamities of debt. It educates them in the ways of generosity and the avoidance of burdens and taboos; how people living in hard times can still be content, devout, modest, and pure, all under the banner of 'liberté, égalité, fraternité.' Should any tyrant, no matter what gender or nation, proclaim that slogan, France will respond, We hear you! Death to injustice. There is to be no such thing today.

"As you can see, these are people who never sleep but are perpetually awake; they spend their entire lives on serious matters and work. One aspiration leads to another; where their ambition is concerned, nothing is impossible, no matter what the situation. Their resolution allows them to melt solid steel; a mere gesture on their part, and solid rocks disintegrate. They can melt air, write on water, plait ropes out of sand, level lofty peaks with feathered arrows, dry out entire seas with buckets, and defeat the darkness of night. For them it has no limit, and they can turn daytime into eternity.

Considered as a whole in comparison with others,
those people are a limitless riddle.
The difference between them and the rest of humanity
is like that between existence and nonexistence."[263]

38.6 As I was saying all this, the Pāshā sat there listening and thinking. Meanwhile the Friend was muttering and complaining. I turned to ask him what was on his mind, why was he so annoyed. Hardly had I posed my question before he burst into speech, regaling us like a flood from a lofty height:

Friend We're tired and fed up listening to this type of exaggerated talk and the way it's been repeated about these places for years and years. It's all more appropriate for someone who has never been here rather than people who are actually in this country now. You're an astute observer of things, used to unraveling obscurities and looking beneath the surface of things. The key thing for us to do now is to separate our ideas from descriptions like this and the kind of information that has burdened our imaginations for such a long time. We need to forget it all and not refer to it, so that our judgments can be founded on actual observation and not on preliminary information that has become fixed in our minds.

You're already aware that mankind tends to avoid precise inquiry and investigation; for the most part people only get involved as a last resort because it's much more comforting simply to accept things as they are and acknowledge them without any fuss. When something gets implanted in a person's mind, he'll accept it at once, then rely on it and subsequently approve anything in that category. If he disapproves of something, the same principle applies. Thus we see a lover admiring everything about his beloved and considering it all to be sublime and noble, even though in fact it is reprehensible and wrong; and all because of the primary instinct, his former approval and his ingrained predilection to be content and happy with his decisions. This is why it's been said that:

> The eye of pleasure is blind to all faults;
> the resentful eye likewise evinces evil deeds.[264]

You may see, for example, an erudite poet listening as you recite a line of poetry by Abū Tammām or Abū l-Ṭayyib al-Mutanabbī that he hasn't memorized. When you don't name the poet, he may scoff at it and refuse to acknowledge its qualities. But once you tell him the name, he changes his tune and praises it to the skies. If there actually are some reasons for criticizing the line, he'll start wheedling his way around things (and there exists an infinite number of such ruses). The reason is that he has to reconcile himself to the fact 38.7

that he habitually approves of any poetry by these two renowned poets.

That's why we can see that there exist numerous things to which humans either give their credulous approval or disapproval without close examinations that are bound to have a residual effect on them. Even when close investigation and evident proof make clear that their judgments are in error and based on false premises, they'll still find it hard to get rid of those preconceptions. People are frequently too proud and arrogant to change their opinions and disapprove of something that they previously regarded as good and vice versa, and all because they're afraid of earning a reputation for holding contradictory opinions and changing their minds.

From all this we can glean the extent of the good fortune and felicity that a person may acquire on this earth if his works manage to engender the approval of people, and, on the other hand, the degree of misery and revulsion that will result when the work meets with disapproval:

> When a person ventures forth in his destiny, his depictions
> of himself will be credited, though he be a liar.[265]

38.8 With regard to these Europeans in general and the French in particular, we've become inured to never leafing through a book, reading something they've written, or listening to a conversation of theirs without encountering encomiums concerning their civilization and boasts to the entire world about how well organized their life is. They're paragons of morality, lords of mankind. True guidance belongs to them, and anyone who opposes them is in error. Thanks to them people have emerged from darkness into light, from blindness to sight. Their statements about themselves have spread far and wide, duly assisted by those of us who have offered them help. We've believed what they've been telling us and granted them that everything they offer has to be good. For them we've opened a page stamped with approval on to which is imprinted everything they conceive for us and tell us about. So let's discard all the things they've said and described in such exaggerated terms. Instead let's now investigate things here as they really are. That way we'll be able to judge them according to their intrinsic merits rather than on the basis of whatever our fancies and imaginations have crafted for us. We have with us—thanks be to God!— the Pāshā, someone distinct from the rest of us in that he was far removed from such people and shielded from this world of ours by a considerable period of time. His mind is therefore uncluttered by the kind of information about this civilization that burdens our own minds. As a result his verdict now on the things he is observing will be more valid and his opinions more precise. If we can share such an untrammeled vision with him, ridding ourselves of other inclinations, we'll be able to point with complete accuracy to the elements of truth and falsehood, right and wrong, to be found within this system of Western civilization. That way we'll be better able to explain things to people in our country who ask about it.

'Īsā ibn Hishām You seem to want us to depart from consensus and go against the norm; to present and confront people with the unusual and unfamiliar. We'll be criticizing things which in their minds are entirely free of criticism and finding fault with what they believe to be flawless and innocent of any notion of disapproval or disgrace. They'll accuse us of misguided and biased opinions and narrowmindedness. And don't forget that many insightful people say that not every truth needs to be pronounced and not every sound judgment should be told. So isn't it a good idea for us to follow the lead of people who've visited this country before by blaming Eastern peoples for their lower cultural status and the superiority of the West? Shouldn't we be describing the powerful position and symptoms of greatness that we see in the pleasant circumstances in which the peoples of the West are living, while we remain stuck in our profound slumber, happy to remain recumbent in the caves of lassitude and apathy? They do the talking, and we listen. They give the orders, and we obey. They apportion our livelihood for us, and we're duly grateful. They purloin our lands, and we 38.9

give thanks. They occupy our territories, and we accept it all. Surely the least we can do is to research the reasons for their lofty position in the universe and go to great lengths to explore the bases upon which their civilization has been founded. In that way we'll be able to do likewise and follow their lead. Shouldn't we be encouraging our own people to throw off the dust of indolence and discard the garb of degradation so that they can start imitating these industrious Europeans who are assiduous in their pursuit of such perfection? Isn't it a good way of initiating such a process of encouragement to show this civilization in the best possible light and making them realize its great achievements? We can make our people aware of its enormous significance and use accounts of it to blame them for their own behavior. We'll be able to show how important this civilization is by making use of comparison in order to show how much lower our own is. The reproach will be all the stronger that way, the incentive to imitate will be more robust, and the stimulation will be more general. Mankind has only ever learned anything through competition, resistance, struggle, and the challenge to win. If a teacher only tells his student how well he's doing and never lets him know that he's not doing as well as others, do you imagine that he'll ever study hard or succeed in learning?

38.10 Friend To begin with, you're obviously well aware that all the people about whom you've been talking have visited this country and returned home again. They have talked about it all, written things, come to conclusions, and delivered their own verdict. They fall into specific categories:

The first group consists of students who have come here to study. They're all young and busy with their studies, and they encounter here a degree of license that they don't talk about in their own country. They content themselves with superficialities. They're hardly capable of any real research or of casting a discriminating eye on what is good and bad among the people in this Western civilization. Indeed it all emerges in a magnified light, and they paint the whole thing in glowing colors. When they get back to their families, they talk about it like a lover describing his beloved at the height of his passion. They try as hard as possible to show traces of this magnified culture so as to lessen the burdens it imposes and make light of its costs. They can then claim for themselves a bit of the aura of greatness that has been imprinted in their imaginations, an impression they use to impress other people as well. We don't belong to this particular group.

The second group consists of people who visit this country as tourists—for pleasure, and that's all. Such people rarely investigate the things they're observing. The only way they look at this Western civilization is based solely on visual impressions. If anyone does go to the trouble of checking further and uncovers some of its flaws or if he comes to realize the problem of having to change his mind and cancel his previous impressions, then he finds his frustrated hopes hard to bear. He comes back to his own country ready to round off the faulty opinions he had in the first place and indulges in hyperbole as a way of preparing his listeners to accept such talk with pleasure and satisfaction. To which you can add the difficulties attached to going against the grain of the familiar and the fact that listeners will much prefer to concentrate on favorable impressions. We don't belong to this second category either. 38.11

The third category consists of holders of government offices who spend a month or two escaping to France from the clutches of their jobs here—like prisoners loosed from their chains. Some of them have learned everything they know from representatives of my first category, so their attitude is obvious enough and their judgments are predictable. Unlike the first category, however, some of them have never studied in Europe, so they do their utmost to compete with them so they can join them, attach themselves to their coterie, and remove the distinction between the two categories. As a result, they copy their opinions and see everything through their eyes. At all events, people in this third category mostly have little spare time for research, contemplation, and evaluation regarding the things they are observing. So throughout the visit they all spend the entire 38.12

time preoccupied and perplexed about two important matters: one eye looking at the amount of time left on his visa; and the other checking on how much money he has left in his purse. We don't belong to this group either.

38.13 As we've noticed, all these groups have their eyes closed to research and naturally insist on exaggerating the things they describe. Since time immemorial people have only ascribed value to such accounts when things have been added. People obviously enjoy listening to stories about exotic and new phenomena. Rarely has mankind ever rejected a natural inclination to talk about strange and wonderful, fresh and exciting things from God's creation of Adam right up to the present day. Our forebears regularly talked about genies, demons, ghouls, and witches, all the way up to the tales of the *1001 Nights* and the Saga of ʿAntar and ʿAblah.

38.14 There may also be a fourth group, one that does do research, that investigates, pauses, and learns. However, it has its own particular motivation that prevents it from uncovering truths and leads it to overemphasize its goals and intentions. This group only shares the things that it narrates about this civilization in order to bolster and extol the things that it describes, be they true or false, and all in order to support a designated idea or a predetermined goal. Such people are accustomed to doing their utmost to extol foreigners and elevate the status of their civilization so that they too can gain in stature, lord it over us, and use the kind of prestige and power thus attained to achieve things that they could not otherwise do. People in this group believe that the process of imposing Western civilization on the East, the changes it brings to traditions and customs, and the triumph that it implies for a system of belief is what civilization comprises. Their support for and proselytization of civilization is exactly like that used by missionaries and advocates for a particular faith. We don't belong to this category either.

By now it should be clear to you that we don't belong to any of these groups. We've left our own homeland and have based our decision to travel on a desire to investigate things and subject them to analysis, criticism, and even opposition. We want to discuss every aspect of this civilization, its good and bad points, where things go astray and where they are appropriate, all by means of looking at things in the source culture—the land in which they've developed. I'm someone who's inclined to the view that everything true can be said, everything correct can be passed on. With that in mind, let's put aside all exaggeration and hyperbole and forget about fantasy when it comes to description. Let's now act on the terms we've imposed on ourselves. The Pāshā will be looking at things in a disinterested fashion. So let's ask him first what his impression is now that he's had his first glimpse of this world and what he's gleaned from it.

Pāshā I've not been able to make any distinctions on the basis of what I've seen so far. What I've observed is just throngs of people and perpetual bustle, with the buzz of the markets sounding like beehives and the bright lights hurting the eyes. I find myself baffled and confused, and that may explain why I can't make any judgments. I'd have preferred for us to choose a district of the city without all these crowds and this bustle. Then we could really get to know the area and the people who live here. 38.15

ʿĪsā ibn Hishām That wish of yours is not easy to fulfill. Every district of the city is crowded like this. The bustle doesn't end, night and day, which is only to be expected since the number of people living in the city is estimated between two and three million. You might say that the entire country is counted in the inhabitants of a single city.

Friend Yes, and the richness of property is obvious to everyone!

Pāshā If that's the case, then we really need someone to advise us, a guide who can show us things in whole and in part.

Friend You'll rarely find any of the city's inhabitants who won't be extolling his civilization's values. If we do find someone, his primary concern will be to tell us about his wonderful people and marvelous country in every conceivable detail, boasting in ways that we certainly don't need. All we'll get out of it will be yet more verbiage and minimal value.

38.16 ʿĪsā ibn Hishām said: Mealtime arrived, so we got up to go to a restaurant. We found it to be just as crowded as the streets. Once we had taken our seats at a table and chosen from the menu, we looked around and noticed three Parisians sitting at the next table. One of them was a thin young man, clearly very careful about the way he dressed, sporting a beard and mustache clipped in the latest fashion. The second was a portly man with a protruding stomach and ruddy complexion. The third was an older man of average height, simply dressed and unconcerned about his appearance. We listened to their conversation and discovered that they were arguing about politics and war. The young writer started banging on the table with his hand and tapping the ground with his feet. He was speaking angrily:

38.17 Young Man The time has come for civilization to put an end to savagery and eradicate barbarous behavior from the world. We need to promulgate the message that we've engaged ourselves to bring to other people. We can then improve the lot of human beings wherever they may be, lead them on the right path, and inculcate in them the principles of civilization that will propel the world to a life of perpetual ease and absolute contentment. Failing that, what can be the virtue of our struggle to achieve the heights of advancement and progress; what are the benefits of these inventions and innovations? If civilization's purpose is to perfect the development of war machines and to keep armed forces at the ready in order to kill each other and tear down our houses with our own hands, then so much the worse for civilization, sciences, and learning, things that have brought us to this degree of barbarity. A curse on the goals to which we have dedicated ourselves, wasting our entire lives in the process! Western people should be uniting, acting collectively, and using the power that scientists and the intelligentsia have provided for them to civilize the peoples of the rest of the world who are still living in ignorance to this very day. They'll be able to bring them out of the depths of their primitive existence and place them on a loftier human plane. Once that is achieved, every one of us will be able to boast that he's helped correct whatever's corrupt in nature, put a stop to its shortcomings, and set it on a new course. If European nations had been doing the right thing from the outset, they'd have followed the same policy with the peoples of Asia and Africa as they've done with China today. Europeans united against them and forgot about older hatreds and disputes. By uniting their forces, they were able to eradicate the vestiges of delusions and falsehoods stretching back through the ages to nature's earliest stages. If Europeans didn't act but instead chose to bother themselves about each other's business and forget about the need to spread civilization throughout the world, it would be a huge mistake and an enormous threat in the future. If our government would only show the same level of honor and astuteness as the German Emperor is doing today with regard to the Chinese problem, dispatching his soldiers on the risky journey to those regions, instructing them to take no prisoners, and telling them to do things that will make the Chinese shudder in fright every time they set eyes on a German in future centuries, then France would be doing its part for civilization, fulfilling the mission it has set for itself, and pledging to the entire world to carry it through. It would then have preserved for itself that high standing and prestige that it possesses in the minds of Eastern peoples.

SHORT MAN You're absolutely right. That has to be our policy. 38.18
If not, how are we supposed to make our goods available and find a market for our industry, the things for which our own country is too small and upon which our livelihood depends, if people like these weak, puny, yellow-faced Chinese dare to confront us? How can it be right for us to suffer and tire ourselves out devising and inventing things, crushing rocks to produce water and reaching the very heights of scientific achievement, when there exist in the world peoples who are content to sleep on top of piles of gold like guards over treasure without benefiting from them or letting

anyone else benefit? The boons and delights of nature should by right accrue to the people who have discovered their secrets and pointed the way to their uses for the benefit of everyone. But, in spite of their weakness and impotence, we leave them alone and let them scoff at people of our race, stand in the way of our aspirations, and confront those people who are trying to serve humanity by hoisting the standard of civilization. No one should be satisfied with the situation and no intelligent person should accept it.

38.19 OLD MAN If your conversation is about genuine civilization, one based on "liberté, égalité, fraternité," one that advocates both justice and charity as being traits on which depend the happiness of humanity in life, the quest for what is good in existence, and what provides people with the benefits of peace, serenity, security, welfare, and composure, then that same civilization is a complete failure in the conduct of our lives. We spend our time manufacturing lethal machinery, mustering troops, and preparing weapons, all of them activities that place us in need of things that are in the hands of other people and drain our country's resources. Greed and cupidity then propel us against other people; we embark upon destructive missions, kill human beings, lay waste to regions, and despoil them of their wealth. It's no part of civilization to consider ourselves as the world's angels and lords of the universe, to despise all those who oppose us—never satisfied unless such people alter their customs and morals, not to mention things that their natural habitat and climate dictate that they do at certain points in time. They're supposed to hand over their affairs to us and place all discretion in our hands. We can then serve as their regents and curators: we subdue them, and they're content; we enslave them, and they submit. It is no part of civilization for us to approach the Chinese people who are living with their families secure and content in their own homes, and to tell them, "We've brought you the true way. So come on! Destroy your statues, burn your books, change your clothing, eat different food, abolish your rituals, divorce your wives, remove the veil from your daughters' faces, and abandon your crafts. Instead be Europeans in old China, Westerners in the Far East."

A Chinese person might well reply, "You Westerners, I've no idea what it is you're inviting me to do. If this thing is civilization as you're claiming, then I've my own civilization too, one established among us by centuries of experience. Sons have inherited it from fathers, and fathers from their fathers. It's a well-known fact that the passage of time serves like a sieve, ridding culture of what is bad while preserving what is good. Nothing remains unless it's proven to have strong bases and firm structure. No ethics and customs can survive unless they are founded on fine principles and clear essentials. If you record your own existence on earth as dating back some seven thousand years, ours goes back hundreds of thousands. If your civilization is one hundred years old, then ours goes back dozens of centuries; thanks to it we have lived comfortably and enjoyed good lives. A primary characteristic of genuine civilization is that people should live in peace. No one should crave what does not belong to him, nor should anyone launch hostile attacks against others. You're well aware that we've lived for many centuries without engaging in warfare or invading territory. As evidence I can note that our people have not aspired to the ultimate in luxury and fripperies which only weaken the body and diminish the procreation of future generations. Our territories, as you know, have the largest number of citizens." To all that we would respond, "How wrong you are, and how feeble is your intelligence! Surely you realize that there's no real civilization apart from ours, the one that we've been inspired to develop through science and learning, to reach heights not achieved by any other humans. We're not content to see the rest of the world living in some other way. We've committed ourselves to draw humanity to our way and to use it as a guiding principle so that they can all live in unending happiness and bliss. This is the charge we have received from our great leaders, Gladstone, Gambetta, Lavigerie, and Hanotaux. Should you not accept, then 38.20

you should expect to encounter the charge that the guardians of our civilization, Krupp, Maxim, Nobel, and Mauser, have given us.

38.21 "If this is indeed the civilization that we're so proud of, then it's hardly surprising that Eastern peoples have come to view it as simply another means of conquest so that we can grab what we want and achieve our goals. It involves one race, one sect, one religion overcoming another. The Ottoman Muslim Sultan is right when he states that Europe is engaged in another Crusade, albeit in the guise of peace. No indeed, these are not the deeds of genuine civilization, but of raw aggression, savagery, and barbarism."

Young Man What's all this nonsense and confusion? You know full well that religion has no part in politics in our society and in the spread of civilization. Now everything's completely divorced from religion and matters of faith and belief. In our society now religious leaders are being persecuted, and the government stands with the people against them. England itself is currently fighting the Berbers who are Christians and the Chinese as well who are pagans.[266] It's all a matter of political expediency as part of the process of proclaiming the concept of civilization. We have to convince people with actions if they cannot be convinced with words alone. Force has to be used when people otherwise refuse to submit.

38.22 Old Man I'm well aware of the place that religion and belief have in our society. However, that's something that operates in our own country and should only apply in our midst. If on the other hand another foreign country is involved that we are in league with, even though we are not concerned about religious leaders here at home, our ambassadors and agents in every region are charged with the obligation of offering those leaders assistance and support in every situation. Don't forget what Gambetta had to say when the religious leaders in our country were being suppressed: "The suppression of religious authorities in our own country is not to be exported abroad." Now here's the German Emperor addressing his troops and energizing them to fight the Chinese, raising the standard of civilization and service to humanity throughout the world.

"You should know that the Christian religion is not the foundation and basis of every civilization. It is in fact a civilization in decline and on the path to extinction." Even Lord Salisbury from his rostrum today confirms that Christian missionaries in China have indulged in gross exaggerations in order to stir up the Chinese, and so they were duly expelled. Those missionaries were not content merely to call people to the faith, but went on to show contempt toward Chinese religion and show active hostility toward it. Everyone's aware, for instance, that the Chinese religion is founded on respect for the dead; that's the major principle of their faith system. They believe that if the dead person isn't shown respect in his grave he'll be angry with his family and community and will bring down all kinds of calamity on them—destruction and drought. The Christian missionaries deliberately targeted their religious principles; they grabbed cemetery land, scattered the bones of the dead, and constructed churches and monasteries on top of their shrines and temples, overtopping the royal palace itself. So please tell me, by God, would any of these missionaries dare to perpetrate this enormous insult against the religion of a people with over four hundred million souls if they didn't have an ambassador to support and assist them—he himself having guns and weaponry at his disposal?

What really matters is that all this may well lead to dire conse- 38.23
quences if Europe does not adopt a more balanced policy and put an end to this greed and violence. The frequency with which these events are happening may show the real extent of the power that Europe possesses and serve as a corrective to people's false ideas. What has happened in China shows us clearly that the severance of telegraph lines—itself a splendid invention of our own civilization—has thrust Europe into a very tense situation and caused everyone a good deal of grief and worry for a considerable period of time. Governments have started getting equipment ready in a rush so that, out of their total forces numbering in the millions, they can spare a mere thirty thousand soldiers, half of whom are Japanese, for the attack on China. And all that after the governments concerned have

previously been competing with each other to sell weapons from their armament factories to the Chinese.

38.24 ʿĪsā ibn Hishām said: At this point a beautiful young woman came strutting over and headed straight for the young man. She hit him with her umbrella. "Are you leaving me waiting," she chided him angrily, "while you sit here arguing about politics?" He leapt to his feet along with the short man. We listened as the Old Man, sad faced and dejected, ate up the remainder of his meal. "This is the civilization," he said, "whose government has announced to its people that it will pay two hundred francs to anyone who wishes to go and fight in China. Many of them are doing so, selling their livelihoods and leaving their wives as widows and their children as orphans for a tiny amount of money that women like this prostitute can use to buy a single blouse—wearing it one night and ripping it apart the next morning."

The Friend now turned to me. "I'm surprised at this old Frenchman," he said. "He seems to be prepared to tell the truth. We really need someone like him to accompany us." I looked toward the old man; he was staring in our direction, listening to our conversation in Arabic and apparently welcoming us. He talked to us and asked us which country we were from. We now opened a conversation and gathered that he was a professor of philosophy, something that he had studied and profited from, investigating the reality of things and not allowing desires and aspirations to divert his attention. He told us how interested he was in researching the ethics of peoples and finding out about their conditions. We then agreed to keep his company; we would tell him about the Orient and he would do the same for the West. We accepted his offer with gratitude and agreed to visit the Exhibition the next day.

Miṣbāḥ al-sharq 117, August 34, 1900[267]

Paris

39.1 ʿĪsā ibn Hishām said: So we set off for the renowned ʿUkāẓ Fair of countries and peoples, the market for values and ambitions, the site of everything marvelous and amazing, the display of powers and resolves, the fulcrum of creativity and invention, the domain of formation and ingenuity, the exhibition of foresight and enlightenment in the appropriate use of tradition and imitation. This particular exhibition has fifty gateways, some close, others more distant. We ourselves entered through the principal gate, the main entrance, which consisted of a gate resting on three pillars high enough to touch the clouds, like some hill vast in both its height and breadth. Beneath it flowed a veritable army all crammed together; the tops were separated, and there was a column on either side. The pillars bordered the very clouds scudding back and forth. On the top of each pillar a lamp turned, and what a lamp it was! Once illuminated, darkest night became like a firebrand, each column a flag with a fire at its peak. Night and day became the same. And how could al-Khansā's brother, Ṣakhr, possibly have elegized them, since he himself was thus mourned in the desert darkness:

> Ṣakhr is to be mourned by our chiefs,
> like a standard with fire at its pinnacle.[268]

But these were columns of dawn, not of stone.[269] They framed the statue of a beautiful woman, placed at the very top of this lofty dome. She had removed dress and girdle and appeared in morning garb, bare-breasted, svelte, with shapely legs and ample backside.

Her buttocks and breast prevented her blouse
from touching her belly or her back.[270]

39.2 It was as though the breeze were doing its best to lift her garment and remove its covering. She was using her hands to clutch it to her waist. When the light of her face was placed next to the moon, the latter's expression showed anguish; it hid its freckled visage behind the clouds and went into eclipse. Venus herself would have been jealous, like a rival wife, and would have angrily disappeared from view. Were al-Nābighah al-Dhubyānī to rise from his grave, he would testify that she was the statue whose naked form he describes in his poem:

Or a pearly shell, whose diver
is staggered and bows when he sees it gleam,
Or a marble statue,
constructed in blocks and mortar.
Were she to be presented to a hoary monk,
one who devotes himself unmarried to God,
He would delight in the sheer beauty of her image
and consider it proper though it were not.[271]

We learned that people regarded the statue as a marvel of the plastic arts and an outstanding example of representation. She was envisioned as the women of Paris welcoming visitors, greeting all those coming to see the exhibition. The entire gate was inlaid with pieces of crystal. When rays of light shone on them, you imagined that they were multicolored peacocks' tails or flowers blossoming on their branches. Or rather you could say they were necklaces of pearls and jewels, clusters of emeralds, all of them in reds, blues, and yellows, bezels of diamond, with the reflected glow of the sun in them. No wonder then that people regarded this gate as the very acme of craftsmanship and a perfect example of fine art.

Once past the gateway we found ourselves in a huge open space, a grassy valley, its grounds planted with lofty pavilions just as bowers sprout leafy branches. It was large enough for camel drivers to get lost and guides to be baffled. And no wonder, because this virtual city was so extensive that it could be divided up into separate regions. The exhibition all told was in fact an entire city in itself. We could see lofty golden domes that seemed to flash and gleam with their gilding. We made our way around grounds that were bedecked in garden plants and orchards, scented bushes and flowers, all interspersed with statues representing everything that body and imagination could conceive, so much so that they almost seemed to be addressing you or responding to an implicit question. 39.3

Once my eye had had its fill of such stunning wonders and my heart had been sufficiently overwhelmed by such superb vistas, I turned to my colleagues in order to ask them for their impressions and find out what they were thinking about such amazing sights. I noticed that the Pāshā was staring in amazement, examining everything but remaining silent. I could hear him talking to himself: "My God, how far-reaching is their construction, how amazing their creative and innovative talents! Their initiative shows such seriousness of intent to expand and increase in every area. They seem preoccupied with the basic level of things that mankind needs, the least they may want in terms of a life of ease. If humans were sure that the grave was their goal in life, then standards would never flutter over palaces; they would be more concerned about digging graves than building palaces. After all, man spends a long period residing elsewhere after death and only a short time on this earth. If only he realized that these gilded stones on lofty balconies would soon be turned into tablets for dilapidated tombs, he wouldn't behave like some immortal when in fact he's a hostage hanging between fate's claws: 39.4

> Eras long since demolished build
> houses out of breaths and hours."[272]

39.5 Our Friend's attitude to all this had not changed; his expression was still the same. The things that we were admiring so much he was observing like a peasant in his village and a bedouin over his campfire. Nothing he was seeing impressed him, nor was he at all fascinated by these stellar examples of mankind's skill:

There is no meaning to anything; nothing
wonderful was wonderful for him.[273]

Even so, I could see that he was disconsolate and restless, searching anxiously for an idea to detail his thoughts, something beyond his conception, so that he could gather his impressions and scattered reactions. I asked him what was bothering him, but he did not reply directly. Instead I heard him recite these lines:

39.6 How little we take note of time,
how much we are misled by desires!
Postures in banality, ventures down
misfortune's slippery slope.
Looking back on centuries past,
do we see today aught but a century wasted?
Where today is the Lord of Sadīr Castle and gleaming
Ḥīra, proud Chosroes with his famous portico;
Iron swords from the tribe of Badr,
mute lances from the Banū al-Rayyān?
Forebears from the family of Jafna,
their terrain firmly planted on the Golan.
They quaff dregs in cups of gold
like thirsty men at brooks.
Arrogant as they hurl curses as greetings
crowns intermesh.
You can see them in droves afar,
striking chests to chins
In decorous meads of tolerance
and mountains of dream serene.

For the thirsty they are water delicious
in its coolness; for those in despair they are fire.
No spiked hand, saber-edged, has
turned the fates away from them.
Destiny has lowered their branch, so that,
after much sifting, the fruits are at hand.
After their recalcitrance those fates have subdued
them with reins of submission and obedience.
For time there remains neither daredevil in pride
nor weakling in disgrace.[274]

The elderly Frenchman looked to either side and shrugged his shoulders. Looking in our direction, he said, "When it comes to boasts about things futile and ephemeral, how similar are the moderns to the ancients! No one bothers to pause and think that the amazing things he's seeing here, the huge buildings he's admiring, have cost enormous amounts of money and demanded incredible hardships and will last for years and years. However, the truth of the matter is that their existence can be counted in days and months; the only things that'll be left among all these constructions is those two palaces." He now pointed to two palaces opposite each other, each of them lofty enough to resemble mountain peaks. 39.7

The Pāshā now started asking him questions, while I served as his translator:

Pāshā Do you think this exhibition is the work of the government or the people?

Friend (*talking to himself*) The work of the Devil!

Frenchman All of the above.

Pāshā How much money has been spent to put on this exhibition?

Frenchman The French government has contributed twenty million francs and the municipality of Paris has put in another twenty million. An association was created that has contributed sixty million, added to which is sixty-five million from tickets which have been issued to people underwritten by the Agricultural Bank.

Pāshā And what is the exhibition's purpose?

Frenchman The primary purpose is a desire for profit and gain. But what they claim as the primary goal is to put things on display in order to showcase quite how far the French people have come from one point in time to another. People can clearly gauge how much physical exhaustion and sheer industry has been involved in achieving such continuous progress and how far they've come along the path of civilization and the process of taming nature completely to their demands.

Pāshā Will there be an enormous profit?

39.8 Frenchman People had hoped as much, but their hopes have been dashed. The company originally made an estimate of the number of visitors who would visit the exhibition during the period that it's open, namely two hundred and four days, at sixty-five million, but up till now only ten million have come; and the period's over half over. Not only that, but the number of people who'll come during the first half is bound to be greater than during the second. The entry ticket which costs a franc—or a hundred centimes—is now being sold at the Bourse for fifteen centimes. Up to today some fifty-eight companies have declared bankruptcy. The most recent one was just yesterday. I watched as they were auctioning off its exhibits and furniture in one corner of the exhibition as the result of a court order. It was called "the Cairo Street Company." It had occupied a wide space in one section of the exhibition and brought together everything that you would be likely to see on Cairo streets: monkeys playing, snakes coiled, Africans dancing, slaves singing, camels wandering, and a donkey market. I saw the three camels sold off for two hundred and fifty francs, and each of the twenty-nine donkeys went for forty francs. Anyone watching those poor animals being sold off for such cheap prices might have imagined seeing in their eyes regret over their fate and intense sorrow at their misfortune and the measly price they were worth abroad.

And please don't even ask me about the sorry state of the men and women who were accompanying the animals. The bankruptcy official has caught up with them and given each of them an amount of money to send them back to their homeland. All in all, the losses from this exhibition have been enormous. In my opinion they made a huge mistake in expanding the exhibition site and making exaggerated claims about it. To get round it even once demands a trek of no less than ten kilometers. But, even though only a few visitors were coming, they spread everything out and cut it all up into chunks. If only they had kept things modest, it would have been so much better for them.

FRIEND Is the company you've just mentioned the "Egyptian Exhibition Company" that we've heard about? 39.9

FRENCHMAN No, that's another French company. The company owners don't have to be from the country in question, even though they may claim to represent it.

PĀSHĀ Why couldn't they foresee what would happen with this exhibition since they are so sophisticated in such matters?

FRENCHMAN People assumed that the peoples of the world would flock to it from all over the place. They initially invited fifty-six countries to participate, but only thirty responded. They also assumed that the majority of the world's rulers would come and spend the wealth of their treasuries here. But among Western monarchs only the King of Sweden has come, while the Shah of Iran is the only one from Eastern countries.

ʿĪsā ibn Hishām said: By now we had reached the entrance to one of the two palaces noted above, built in order to display what they call "beaux arts," the building being known as the "Petit Palais." We decided to visit it first. When we entered, it was to find that its construction, ornamentation, decor, drawing, and painting were far superior to anything found in the palaces of monarchs or emperors. No wonder, when they had spent twelve million francs to build it. They were using it to display precious crafts preserved from as far 39.10

back as the Roman era all the way up to the eighteenth century: beaten metal pieces from the doors of churches, pottery vessels, clocks and rings, embroidered sandals, and embossed ivory. Here the pen fails in any attempt to describe and detail such beauty. With such incredible *objets d'art*, the written word can never substitute for the act of seeing with one's own eyes; the effect on the reader can in no way rival what the observer experiences. And all this was predicated on the very possibility of describing the enormous variety of objects on display in all their profusion. When we had done a tour of the rooms in the palace and looked at its displays, the Friend stopped the Pāshā and asked him about the things he had just seen:

PĀSHĀ I've just seen a lot of things, at least some of which were readily available in markets in the old days and also in the great mansions. I don't see any aspect of modern civilization in all this.

FRENCHMAN You should realize that what you're seeing here are the costliest and most precious examples of art in the entire world, something that people simply cannot fully appreciate. Take this clock for example, the one which we're standing beside but you haven't even noticed or looked at closely. Some people wanted to buy it and offered three million francs, but the owner refused.

39.11 ʿĪsā ibn Hishām said: With that we turned and took a closer look at the clock. It was shaped like a ball supported by three girls made of marble. It was displayed in a glass case only a meter tall and half a meter wide. We were duly amazed. Our Friend now continued:

FRIEND True enough, the way Western people preserve ancient objects is to their credit. They take a good deal of pleasure in it. Looking at such things leaves a powerful sense in the heart; it engenders a respect for people from ages past, serves as a useful reminder of the glory of previous generations, and offers a useful lesson that cannot be replicated in history books and narratives of the past. Not only that, but it preserves the link for industries in a way that benefits creative thinking and leads to improvements in working conditions. By contrast, people in the East, and especially the Muslim community, have completely neglected this particular sphere in an unforgivable fashion. You'll not be able to find anything that a person of the East finds more despicable than an ancient object; it has no value whatsoever for him, and he pays it no reverence or respect. Quite the contrary in fact, he regards it as useless stuff. As a result, with the passage of time monuments have crumbled and crafts have vanished. All we know about the lifestyle of our forebears is a set of names with no meanings attached. With us neglect has reached such a stage that such things are never mentioned in any books, the hope being that they can survive somehow, although they are forever lost. All that's left are names with no significance. God knows that if this particular clock had been left as a legacy in one of our illustrious households its fate would be that the family would probably have given it to the wet-nurse's son or the agent's daughter to play with until it was eventually destroyed.

Tell me, for heaven's sake, what would be more pleasing for the 39.12
eye and more poignant for the heart than the kind of thing that our sheer negligence has forever lost for us: ʿUmar's pearl, for example, ʿUthmān's shirt, ʿAmr ibn Maʿdī Karib's sword, ʿAlī's shield, Hārūn al-Rashīd's crown, al-Muʿizz's standard, and Muḥammad ʿAlī's clothing when he entered Egypt. But, in spite of all that, I still think that Western nations have gone much too far in their regard for these ancient objects, by assigning them so much value and fighting each other to possess them in a way that is utterly reprehensible. The price of this piece of marble is three million francs, and someone will purchase it in order to show it to his visitors in one of the rooms in his house. That money could be used to feed three million of the world's population, people who spend their nights starving and raising their cries of hardship from the depths of their hearts to the very heavens—almost bringing down punishment from on high. Can it be right for the owner of this object to deprive people of food for a piece of marble, at least if he's endowed with a modicum of mercy and sympathy?

Frenchman You're quite right. Westerners have gone to excessive lengths in silly boasting about their acquisitions. In their eyes ancient objects are so desirable because of their rarety and because they're bored with modern stuff that can be readily acquired by the majority of people. That's why these things have become so incredibly valuable. They've gone back to acquiring antique furniture and decorations for their homes, to such a degree that the price of wood has now become the equivalent of gold in this era of modern inventions, the so-called period of advancement in industrialization and progress in civilization.

39.13 ʿĪsā ibn Hishām said: Here the conversation came to an end, and we left before darkness fell.

Miṣbāḥ al-sharq 118, August 31, 1900[275]

Paris

40.1 ʿĪsā ibn Hishām said: We followed our visit to the Petit Palais with one to the Grand Palais, by which I mean the even greater wonder after the minor miracle, a building beautifully situated and perfectly constructed. These two buildings contained treasures such as had never been brought together by anyone before; no king or chieftain had ever possessed the like. Māriyah's bangles would be mere beads and date pits, the treasures of Qārūn would be but dust and pebbles, Alexander's multiple spoils the rags worn by holy men and lunatics, Dārā's finery would be no better than the fur skins worn by jurists, and ʿAmr's necklace a mere garland of dates.[276] The pens of the eloquent would be no more than women's spindles, should they even try to describe all this on paper and find elegant ways of depicting what they had seen. How can you possibly talk about the treasures of the inhabited world all residing in two buildings, the *objets d'art* from across the globe spread out between two walls? If a small portion of what we've selected were to be distributed to people on earth, almost no one would ever have to seek his livelihood; no one would ever complain about hardships of time and the toils of deprivation. Thanks to such things, the indigent would be wealthy, the very word "poverty" would be a thing of the past. Everyone would have the same status and position, and there would no longer be any need for trickery and deceit. Desiring and desired would no longer exist; the conqueror would not impose on the defeated, and the despoiler would no longer attack the despoiled. Crimes and felonies would no longer be committed. These two palaces then have been erected by their builders in the face of fate, witnesses to the vast extent of their prestige, the very acme of wealth and plenty.

40.2 We started walking through the various rooms of the palace, looking at the wonderful objects on display. Every time we looked at statues and paintings, their beauty fired and bolstered our enthusiasm. There were so many pictures of such perfection and intelligence that no written word could possibly replicate the effect on mind and understanding. They presented for you historical events and scenes, so you could imagine that you were actually there witnessing it all. It invoked the eloquence of Saḥbān to reveal for you the concealed passions and sorrows, all clearly presented with color and brush:

I show you desires, you craved them.
For you a phantom was crafted, then broke away.[277]

Whatever impact the objects had on you, they burnished rusty feelings and softened the sharp edges of your soul. On seeing them you felt a shudder of sheer joy; their appearances breathed in you a waft of magic. You found yourself sighing over the dead cavalier, empathizing with the man stricken with grief, begging God's mercy as much for the victim of passion as you did for one slain by the thrust of a sword. You looked at the beautiful girl and buxom virgin, and you dearly wished to woo her and fall in love, and yet you felt almost scared of her eagle-eyed guardians standing all around her.

40.3 Over there you could see the portrait of a lovely girl, her image steeped in beauty and antiquity, revealing love and passion in all their normality, her visage glowing with a chaste modesty. Her entire appearance suggested a staid dignity duly blended with a powerful disdain and determined resolution. Under her feet she had crushed an evil female ghoul who had a hundred mouths ready to mangle and kill; she had impaled the stomach with a spear and dispatched it to its death. Over the girl's head there hovered a cluster of victory angels awarding her the crown of glory and triumph. This picture was the portrait of "Virtue" in her conquest of "Depravity." To her right was another noble lady, also beautiful and august. To the viewer she showed the delight of someone proclaiming his party's success and relishing the achievement of his wishes and desires; this was "Wisdom," the only means of acquiring virtue and the only gate through which happiness could be obtained. To the left was another lady in whose appearance gleamed the power of knowledge and certainty, the sheer force of experience and potential. She was carrying a nursing child who was clasping a pen or reed in his hand as she clasped him. She was giving "Virtue" a gaze replete with awe and appreciation as a show of her reverence. This then was a portrait of "Knowledge" and its virtues, while the nursing child represented mankind in its ignorance.

Next you could see a woman of a certain age, clutching a nursing baby at each breast; as she held them, she kept kissing and smelling them. All around her were naked children whom she was inviting to sit on her lap and offering them shelter in her wrap. Her expression showed her joy, happiness and satisfaction, as though the very contents of time's own hand—outstanding beauty and craftsmanship—gleamed in her face. This was the portrait of "Charity and Beneficence."

Then you could see a lovely young girl, a beautiful pearl, her features as gorgeous as a wild cow or gazelle, her hair reaching below her waist and shielding her against both heat and cold: 40.4

> Tresses that bring the night in the full of day
>   and a face restoring day in darkest night.[278]

She appeared in the midst of a forest with branches of wood and musk amid fields of violets and roses. The floor was bedecked in scattered clusters of flowers while the ceiling consisted of tree bowers:

She sashayed her path amidst green emeralds
that gave forth scattered pearls.
Every hillock relished the dance,
clothed in a low covering of plants.[279]

40.5 Sunlight sprinkled golden dinar-beams on the ground as with brides, gold untouchable by human hands just as the poet al-Mutanabbī earlier described the same situation while riding through the Bawwān Pass, wishing that real coins might fall into his actual pocket, rather than empty favors on his clothing. And perhaps the poor poet died with such regrets as he repeated these words:

The eastern glow projected on my clothes
dinars that fled from my fingertips.[280]

It was as if all around her chirping birds and cooing doves were answering the maid who had asked about her beloved: Where had he gone, why had he left her and not returned?

They replied that like her, each dove among them had a love to rival the lover who was lost. All this made the girl yet more passionate, and she became alarmed, ignoring her flocks and herds. She was joining the doves in their cooing and expressing her desperate love in the open air. The observer would feel inclined to bow down in homage to nature's exquisite beauty and the superb skill shown in creation.

40.6 Next you would see Homer, the original Greek poet who was blind. Enveloped in a colorful wrap, his beard shone with the grey gleam of old age and filled your vision with an awesome spectacle. He was seated on a regal throne, but that of poetry rather than kingdoms, ruler of meters rather than countries. Other poet-djinn were crowning his head with victory garlands, while human poets stood before him in admiration and respect: Herodotus, Aeschylus, Horace, and Virgil, and to the poet's right, brave heroes and cavaliers of old, all humble and submissive, Achilles, Alexander, Aeneas, and Caesar. Above him were two buxom ladies, as beautiful as the purest pearl, similarly lovely in face and body but different in shape and size. They were his two muses, the ones whose path in poetry he had followed since the very beginnings of time. The other poets were standing there, being imbued with their twin culture and relishing their proximity. Circling them both were singing girls, playing on fifes and drums and performing their lays to the appropriate tune and rhythm. How can we talk adequately about this great poet and his colleagues, ancients and illustrious forebears, who manage to use their poetry to portray for us the images found in these paintings and parchments? For portraits are silent poetry, whereas poetry is a portrait that speaks.

When we had somewhat recovered from the sense of rapture and admiration, and our visit was almost at its end, we saw in front of us a shabbily dressed man, scrawny and disheveled, his djellaba in tatters: 40.7

> A traveler far and wide ejected by desert wastes
> so he looked disheveled and dust-covered.[281]

His head-hair and beard blended together, concealing his face and features, so it was difficult to make out his expression. He looked as thin as a sheep in pastureless terrain. His nails were long and curved like talons; they harbored so much dirt that they looked like kohl-sticks with a nib attached or mourning columns on newspaper pages. This man kept giving people, those arriving and leaving, contemptuous looks and adopting the posture of a creative artist. Even so, people kept greeting him with respect and honoring him. The Pāshā turned toward our colleague, the aged Frenchman, and asked him about this accumulation of dirt and pile of rubbish. How could they possibly be showing a devilish figure like him such respect amid such a collection of beautiful objects and sights. The two men started to engage in conversation on the topic, and I served as their translator as they asked and answered questions:

Pāshā Shouldn't people like him be kept away from costly locations like this so as to preserve their splendor, not squander their attraction for the viewing public, and debase the value of their embellishment. But maybe they're trying to avoid the proverbial "evil eye?"

40.8 Frenchman This man and others with the same appearance are part of a group of painters who are renowned for their skill as artists and painters. The government has spent a total of twenty-four million francs to erect this palace you're now seeing; its purpose is to display their glorious achievements and extol their reputation. These precious works of art that have so impressed you are the products of their skillful hands and issues of their genius. But don't be shocked by the difference in the two images that you see before you; after all, gold is extracted from soil, and diamonds from coal.

Pāshā But, if these are examples of their art, why don't you treat them properly? Why don't you give them enough to live decently, improve their appearance, and avoid looking so regrettably scruffy? If this artistic profession is so unprofitable in your country, then what's the point of constructing this building and all this decoration?

Frenchman These people you're seeing and sympathizing with are among our wealthiest and most prosperous citizens. Of all our people they're most likely to gain a great deal of money. Of the countless number of works hanging here a single canvas may be worth hundreds of thousands or even millions of francs. The price of even a small one would be quite enough to provide a reserve for life. Their general appearance is not because of poverty or need; it's merely that they don't bother about such things and act distracted. You need to realize that such delicate artistry demands a lot of thought, inspiration, and application. Some of them will concentrate so intensely and focus on a single notion that all their other faculties dwindle; they become so distracted that they forget about feeding and clothing themselves. Their circumstances get worse, their moral posture deteriorates, and they become so mean, stupid, reckless, and fickle that it's difficult to spend time with them. They've even persuaded some of their colleagues to adopt the same pose. They've now started putting on the same kind of airs that are used by certain religious types—self-denial, displays of piety, devoutness, and abstinence. Such people are called "artistes." It may in fact be the case that, for many of them, the only tools they have are their scruffy garb and filthy appearance.

FRIEND I'm constantly amazed at people who only use their heads as part of their work while neglecting their bodies to this extent. The traditional phrase, *mens sana in corpore sano* is well enough known, so how can anyone's body remain healthy if you don't keep it clean, properly nourished, well exercised, and generally well looked after? A thinker in the midst of his contemplations might smell something bad or witness something disgusting, in which case his entire being shrivels and his ideas dry up. How can it be for someone who can detect such things all the time in his own person and feel it on his own body? Any creative person who loves the fine arts and exerts his talents in that area has to possess an innate subtlety and gentleness so that their morals will be tolerant, their character will be pleasant, and their social traits will be friendly; and such a person should never behave or dress in a way different from other people. What can be the possible benefit of science, learning, intellectual talent, and expertise if they don't lead to the development of upright and good-natured behavior that can guarantee the kind of happy existence envisioned by the quest for knowledge and learning? It's totally wrong to imagine that the achievement of fame in a particular field (and fame is of all things the swiftest to be transformed) is enough to bring someone happiness in life, to please both God and mankind, and indeed to please his family and himself. We have among us a group of people who make all sorts of claims about being faithful, generous, and in the closest possible contact with God. Yet you'll find that they've the scruffiest appearance and present the ugliest of sights. People are 40.9

deceived by them and have no qualms about artists who portray living creatures in all their beauty and paint nature in all its loveliness. But, that said, how are flowers supposed to grow in a swamp or the gleam of light to shine forth from a grave?

Frenchman You're so right! Anyone who fails to monitor his own self cannot aspire to do so with other people.

40.10 Pāshā But what do these artists do with all the money they earn if they haven't been hording it?

Frenchman As a general rule they don't horde any of it. Their wealth gets squandered because of poor planning, stupid behavior, reckless desires, and general absentmindedness. Their art keeps them very close to women due to the delicacy of their craft and their passion for beauty. So you'll watch as the price for the canvas leaves the purse of the befuddled rich man to be placed first into the hands of its crazy creator, then into the pockets of a nasty harlot, and thereafter into the owner of a jewelry store. Some of them spend money on lots of models.

Pāshā What do you mean by "models"?

Frenchman A "model" is a woman chosen by the artist for her beauty. He can gaze at her and paint a likeness of her perfect proportions, the aim being that not for a single moment will the obvious and hidden aspects of the body be out of his vision. Whenever you enter an artist's studio, you will always find a woman in front of him, unclothed and naked, with every one of her limbs clearly exposed and totally uncovered.

Pāshā What is this disgusting debauchery?

40.11 Frenchman In our culture there's nothing shameful about it. It's completely acceptable, and for women it has become one of the respectable crafts and professions. In fact, there's a debate going on at the moment as to whether an artist needs to practice his profession away from public thoroughfares. Yesterday an artist decided that he wanted to portray resurrection from the grave, so he headed for one of the city's cemeteries and sat there with his paintbrushes and two models. He positioned them both, completely naked with their private parts exposed, with one bowed down and the other prostrate on the ground. He spent an hour or two gazing at the two women, contemplating, sketching, and then creating the painting. Right alongside the cemetery a house was under construction with builders standing on the wall. They were disgusted by what they were seeing and felt bashful about such a scandalous display. They went up to the painter and told him that what he was doing was wrong and they found the entire scene disgusting. But the painter not merely ignored their complaints and jeered at them but also carried on with his work for several days, still ignoring their complaints and disapproval. The construction workers raised the matter with the police and then took the matter to court in order to stop this scene from occurring before their very eyes and this lewd assembly from gathering every morning and afternoon. The entire matter is now before the courts, and newspapers have published different opinions on it: should such practices be prohibited or not. Some people say that the answer is "yes," basing their opinion on the law that punishes anyone for infringements of public morality on the streets and offending all guise of modesty and decency, but others claim that such prohibition is an infringement of personal liberty; everyone is free to practice his art and no one has the right to interfere in such a way as to impede his artistic creativity.

'Īsā ibn Hishām said: When I had translated all this for the Pāshā, 40.12
I noticed that his brow was covered in sweat, and he was using his hand to cover his face in sheer embarrassment. Seeking refuge in God, he indicated that we should leave. We now did so, walking from one room into the next till we almost got lost due to the sheer size of the palace. There were so many rooms, all filled with paintings and sculptures, and no nook or cranny was left unfilled. After we had found the exit and left the palace, we walked along the road between the two buildings, they being the centerpiece of the exhibition as a whole, wonderfully constructed. The Pāshā now turned to the Philosopher and asked him:

PĀSHĀ So what's going to happen to these two buildings when the exhibition comes to an end? Who'll be living there?

FRENCHMAN Nobody will be living in them. They're going to stay the way they are, ready to hold exhibitions of crafts and paintings created by artists every year.

FRIEND Every time I consider the amount of attention that you pay to art in this culture—raising it to the very heights, giving it enormous prestige, devoting almost exclusive and even exaggerated attention to it, and, by contrast, the minimal concern that we show in the East, I find myself astonished and unable to come up with a reason. If it's the consequence of a superior level of culture and civilization and of increasing affluence, I find that your culture has possessed such qualities since ancient times and that the earliest historical periods are very much current among you. Indeed, what is ancient may be more skillfully rendered than what is modern. What's the reason for the interest that you people show whereas we do not? And we do not in spite of the fact that, in your conception, the peoples of the East have shown far greater imagination and potential in portraiture.

40.13 FRENCHMAN You should be aware that all the objects that you see here that survive and persist among different peoples have either fulfilled some specific purpose or need or else responded to a fixed article of faith that has been inherited across generations for one reason or another. I've learned that, before the advent of the Christian faith, religious people in the West used to worship idols. Religious belief demanded the creation of paintings and statues. They were not capable of representing the majesty of the Creator, so they did their best to represent the concept according to their own limited thinking. However, they were unable to elevate their ideas to such an exalted plane, so instead they reduced the concept to their own level and made their images accordingly. Your own Egyptian ancestors left splendid portraits and statues. The trend spread widely during the Greek and Roman eras to such an extent that it went beyond the portrayal of gods to created beings. They put up statues to important men and great rulers. During the Greek era things reached such a pass that on the streets of Athens they put up three hundred statues for a single man who had acquired some fleeting fame and recognition among them. When he died, those statues did not even last three hundred days. One of the well-known stories in this connection tells how someone spoke to one of these worthy and noble citizens in these terms: "I'm amazed that the people of Athens have put up three hundred statues to this man, whereas they haven't put up a single one for you who are much more deserving and virtuous." The man replied that he would much rather have people wonder why he has no statue than have the same people equally surprised that he did have one. When the Christian faith developed, its adherents neither proscribed nor forbad this practice, so everyone continued the same way. In fact, the Christian community adopted the representational arts, portraying Jesus and his mother (peace be upon them both) at various stages in their lives and recording all kinds of stories from sacred history, as you can see here. Christians have remained interested in this field up to the present day, unlike the situation with regard to your own faith in particular, where, as far as I understand, such things are proscribed. Apart from that, it is widespread among other peoples—the Chinese, for example, the Japanese, and the Indians. Frankly, the widespread availability of such art does not bring great benefits to us now, that is, apart from the fact that it makes a small group of our people sufficiently crazy to satisfy the desires of a limited group who are prepared to spend enormous sums at the expense of the poor.

'Īsā ibn Hishām said: After leaving these twin palaces, we made our way to other institutions so we could get some impression of the famous sites. 40.14

Miṣbāḥ al-sharq 121, September 21, 1900[282]

PARIS

41.1 We entered the tree and flower pavilion. It was not constructed like other palaces and houses. The corners had no plaster over the stones, nor were bricks used to build its different rooms or wood for its doors and ceilings. Instead it consisted of domes and towers of polished crystal and glass. A construction like a polished bottle, it looked just like sea swell or the calm surface of a pond. If Bilqīs, the Sheban queen of old, had entered this building today, she would have uncovered her legs again.[283] In this building they had collected plants of every kind and from all corners of the globe, some of them poking out of ice, others growing on solid boulders; some plants that flourish in desert hills and some that grow in the lowlands of steppes, flowering amid snow and budding in extreme heat. Some emerge from places where streams and rivers flow, while others come from climes where goats and falcons are the denizens. Some come from regions where the mourning dove coos its melody in shady courts while others belong in places where the chameleon roams in the noonday heat—from nearest East to furthest East, and from one pole to the other. The flowers and plants were thus of every conceivable variety and from all the world's regions; some were coiled in a spiral while others climbed high and branched out. Yellow- and white-colored flowers opened up, as did others—silver and gold, bright and gleaming, all to enrapture you with their colors that flashed like jewels. What would the poet, Ibn al-Rūmī, have done as he contemplated their beauty? Relinquishing all pride and boast, he would have been forced to admit his failure to describe or compare them, and would even have been compelled to burn his poetry collection with its well-known simile:

How many a lapis lazuli in the meadows
  flaunts its blue color at the red ruby's expense,
As though both it and fragile stems were being
  supported by the initial flares on the tips of matches.[284]

Compared with flowers like these, what are rubies, emeralds, 41.2
tortoiseshells, carnelians, pearls, and corals? How can stones be compared to trees or dry gravel be measured against gently swaying boughs? How can what is fixed and immovable be preferred over what is ever growing and developing; movement over stasis, things spread over soil over those buried under ground; flora planted in a fertile meadow over what is interred in the dust? Were garlands like these to be strung for the necks of beauteous damsels and to deck the bosoms and throats of lovely ladies, then flowers like these should be found twixt breast and rib. How often have they refreshed body and soul with pleasant scents and lovely wafts.

We stood there, relishing the fragrant scent of different aromatic 41.3
plants till we felt intoxicated without wine and drunk without guilt. Had the blind poet of Maʿarrah, the ascetic Abū l-ʿAlāʾ, prison hostage, been in our company, he would have rejected his frigidity and blindness, emerging from his isolation and bewildered by his own poverty and lack. He would have realized that whatever is permitted can be just as intoxicating; he would have had no need to indulge in old vintages when he declared:

I wished for a wine that could engender an intoxication
  that could leave me ignorant as to why I feel so secure.
I am unaware of being on the edge in Iraq,
  all hopes lost and without companions or money.[285]

We stayed in this gorgeous garden, this splendid paradise, for a while, repeating the sighs of the devout worshipper: «Entering your own paradise, you must say: As God wills, there is no power unless it be through Him,»[286] and repeating the chant to the haven of Unity:

In every thing there is a sign of Him
revealing that He is One.[287]

When it was time to leave, we made our way out of this luxurious garden, just like our forebear, Adam, as he made his way out of the haven of eternity into the world of cares and misery. As we headed for other parts of the exhibition, things that had been delighting us thus far diminished in our eyes; whatever had previously been of concern to us now seemed insignificant. Every view now seemed less glamorous, and all that was rare and imposing now paled. The vistas we had seen were superior to all the various innovative and wonderful arts and crafts. For how can one compare human craft with that of the Creator? The products of factories can never rival the hand of the One Maker of all?

41.4 At this point the Pāshā was on the verge of going back the way we had come and confining his day's ration of visits to what he had already seen. But we heard the Frenchman talking to our Friend about the way this exhibition had been organized and arranged:

Frenchman That's right. The exhibition space is divided into two sectors. The one devoted to exhibits culled from both industry and nature, is open to the public without charge. There's also another section that's been set up for entertainment and public appeal by putting weird and amazing things on display. Entry to the second section involves paying a special fee.

Friend The things that I've heard about this latter section have shocked and amazed me. What I've read in the newspapers every day contains exaggerated accounts of the various inventions that it includes. The one thing that I'm anxious to see is the amazing telescope they've invented that allows you to see the moon just a meter away, so close that it looks as though you were sitting there watching it in a walled room. So, come on, let's go there.

FRENCHMAN It's not far. They call it the palace of lights and mirrors. As you say, newspapers have been writing about it in terms that make you want to go there. I haven't been there myself as yet, so we can go there now if you like.

PĀSHĀ Yes, let's hurry. If what they say about it is true, it must be a real wonder, if not a piece of magic! For my own part, I'm surprised that we wasted so much time visiting exhibits that we've already seen right in front of us in our own country in commercial locations and markets. We could have started by visiting this amazing palace which can bring the moon so amazingly close.

ʿĪsā ibn Hishām said: So we set out for this other building and eventually arrived at another palace, one so splendid and huge that princes and kings would have proudly showed off the like. Over the door decked with stars and planets was inscribed the following text in Latin: "From here mankind ascends to the stars and links with infinity." Once we had gone inside, we found it crowded with people. We joined them all and made our way into a huge room fifteen meters long and ten meters wide, divided up by triangular-shaped glass mirrors, each of which was two and a half meters high and a meter and a half wide. They were all separated by electric lamps. If you looked at the triangular shapes, you could see your image reflected hundreds of times. By walking just a few paces, you could lose your way completely. It was impossible to find a way out. Every time you thought you had discovered a way out and headed towards it, your face would bang against the glass; everyone would start laughing because they were just as lost. This process would go on for quite a while until by a stroke of luck you eventually reached the right path. If we had had in our company a poet, he would have had a great deal of scope for his imagination to describe the shapes of the female visitors and the impression left a thousand times by their images in the mirrors—much as a single woman can 41.5

leave an impression on the pages of men's hearts in the thousands as well.

41.6 Once we had made our way out of this room where the visitor can get as lost as any rider in desert wastes, we headed for other rooms. The Frenchman was talking to our Friend:

FRENCHMAN This idea of putting up places and buildings in maze-like patterns that will get people lost and not knowing the way out is an ancient one. We've learned that the ancient Egyptians were the first to construct buildings specifically so that people would get lost. Some traces of this type of temple that Herodotus saw and described in his history still exist. It contained three thousand interlocking rooms, constructed in such a way that anyone entering the temple without a guide would get so lost that he'd die of hunger; traces of it can still be seen by Lake Moeris next to the ancient city known as Crocodile City. The ancient Greeks copied the Egyptian model and erected a temple like it in Crete. One of their myths tells how a ghoul was causing all sorts of havoc on earth but then took refuge inside this labyrinth where no one could catch it. A Greek hero decided to go after it and kill it. To do so he had recourse to a piece of string that his beloved showed him. He tied one end to a door by the entrance before he went in, then entered the labyrinth, achieved his purpose, then made his way out. The major difference between what the ancients did long ago and modern people have been doing recently is that the ancients used stone whereas the moderns are using glass.

41.7 ʿĪsā ibn Hishām said: We now went into a number of smaller rooms; in each case, the pattern of reflected light in mirrors and the multiplicity of images was repeated. What you thought was a well turned out to be an entire sea, and so on. Finally we reached the room we were aiming for, the one where the moon could be viewed at a distance of a mere meter. No sooner had we made our way inside than the lights were all turned off, and we found ourselves in total darkness. They then projected rays of light on the wall, and a map of the moon's surface appeared in such a way as to show the moon's mountains and valleys; the former looked the size of a fingernail, while the latter were like the holes in a sieve. A man holding forth like a preacher was explaining to us the details of the image and asserting that it was a picture of the moon at a distance of seventy kilometers as seen through the telescope. This was the device that announcements had been claiming could show you the moon at a meter's distance, something that important articles in scientific and political journals had also been proclaiming to the world for years. As we left, the Friend was brushing his hands in surprise and amazement, as he asked the Frenchman to explain how such a piece of fraud and deceit was possible:

FRENCHMAN Don't act so shocked! There can be no justification for the kind of hyperbole in discussing matters that you tend to read in newspapers. They do it quite deliberately for a fixed price and for their own benefit, with no advantage accruing to the French people. They exaggerate in this way because they're eager for visitors to come to these exhibits because huge profits are involved for the people who set them up. All that makes such fraudulent claims permissible in their eyes, since it's supposed to be a service to both private and public interests. If only you realized that the person who embarked on the project to set up this exhibition was none other than your good friend, Monsieur Deloncle who's well known in your part of the world, you shouldn't be surprised. You know about his projects; this isn't his first one, even though he's lied and tricked his way on a formal basis in front of everyone. After he had got up and made a speech in the assembly in 1892 in which he asked for an agreement to mount this Universal Exhibition, he proceeded to announce that he had discovered the exhibit's Phoenix, one that would be mankind's greatest ever miracle, a telescope through which you could see the moon just one meter away. He's kept on talking about it and newspapers have kept on repeating it till in 1896 he'd founded a company consisting of astronomers who would make the telescope which they now say can show the moon at a 41.8

distance of seventy kilometers. They've built this structure—with all its vistas—in order to rake in the profits from the large number of visitors who would come to look at this amazing invention. This is the way things work with people in the world today, mouthing falsehoods and grossly exaggerating their accomplishments—to the extent of the difference between a single meter and seventy kilometers. The major profiteers in this process are the people who resort to deceit and trickery; the big winners habitually cheat and double-cross.

41.9 ʿĪsā ibn Hishām said: As we left, we were amazed to learn about this deputy who was not content just to use trickery in his political life and colonial policy, but had to raise it as far as the stars and planets.

Miṣbāḥ al-sharq 123, October 5, 1900[288]

Paris

42.1 ʿĪsā ibn Hishām said: We walked around the section of the exhibition called "sights and scenes" and went into one exhibit after another. Truth to tell, we did not find in any of them confirmation of the kind of things we had been hearing about; in fact, quite the opposite. But then we reached a lofty palace, beautifully constructed and laid out, which had been built for various types of dancing, revelry, gymnastics, and music—movements of every kind involving turns and pliés from way back in the distant past and up to the present day, from times of coarse and primitive living up to today's luxury and ornamentation. There were dances illustrating chivalry and heroism, and others that reflected aspects both charming and debauched. You could watch bedouin men dancing with swords in deathly postures, while young maidens behind them strummed on tambourines and clapped their hands, all to encourage the men to fight and stir them up and encourage them to confront their foes. With that the taste of fortitude would be as good as sipping wine, and they would be willing to quaff the cups of death just as eagerly as others did the sweet saliva of the beloved. Then you could watch the dances of people returning from a journey, as they relished their success and triumph amid the virgins and maids of the tribe and the prisoners and unassuaged enemy fighters. Their finger gestures spoke eloquently for themselves so as to reveal the love and yearnings that lay buried inside them, the zeal and defiance that filled hearts replete with honor and courage, spirits enough to make ravenous beasts cringe at the very sound of their voices and cause vicious lions and tigers to forget their own awesome repute. Even so they submitted to the svelte and buxom ladies and splintered off into separate groups, quavering in case a gesture of rejection or a suggestion of distaste should occur. Movements intended to fawn and flatter would be met with a chaste coquetry; a response to ardent love would be disdain and rejection. The most subtle of rebukes would be leveled through an exquisite plié. In their downcast eyes one could see the glow of purity. The women would spin, covering their exposed limbs as they did so, causing the infatuated observer to recoil and the admirer to admit defeat. How wonderful modesty looks on the cheek of the beautiful, like drops of water on a burnished sword; set in opposition to the bravery of an intrepid cavalier, it would lose its grip to the lady-wearer of bangles and anklets. It is as though, in the clutches of gorgeous maidens, the hero keeps reciting the words of the poet Abū ʿIbādah:

We are a folk undone by lovely eyes,
even though we can melt very steel.
To the demands of love are we led by pale beauties,
while we ourselves are governed by gruesome thrusts.[289]

42.2 We now observed various types of dancing and varieties of twisting and twirling, the kinds of thing commonly practiced in various faiths and encountered with idol-worshippers. It seemed almost as though the observer of these movements were like someone worriedly asking questions about cholera and nausea. The general purpose seemed to be to exhaust the human body so as to dampen lustful desires.

Following this spectacle we watched dancing of a more urban kind which seemed particularly indecent. There were bevies of women, like gazelle flocks, their bodies minimally covered in translucent, skin-colored garb which clung to their limbs like ostrich shell or snakeskin. To the observer they looked naked, just barely clothed. As they danced in the brilliant lighting they adopted poses that showed muscles and limbs, sometimes bending over, then straightening up again, performing pirouettes on point while staying in place. Some of them did high kicks so that their anklets clinked as they touched their very cheeks. Spectators kept showing their approval by applauding and demanding encores. They now introduced still another form of modern dance with its particular creativity, each dancer being dressed in a white gown with wide skirts; when each one did a turn, you imagined they were clouds in the sky with the full moon gleaming down or else an entire flock of doves hovering over a water pond. High above them from the ceiling, a stage light projected different shades and colors on their sleeves and dresses, all of which made the dancers look like bunches of flowers and clusters of jewels. So rapid was the change of color that the scene looked like sea foam stirred up by a passing ship, the shining sun reflected in its eddies with its seven different colors. Each dancer was carrying a staff that she waved in the air to reflect the electric light and let the brilliant beams shine forth like crystal flowers duly ripened. Everyone watching would imagine them to be cluster of mature grapes. Were the Pharaoh and Haman to have seen them, they would definitely have vouched for the virtues of the staff in every place and time.

Once these dances were at an end, the curtain came down. We 42.3
made our way out, duly amazed at what we had seen. The Pāshā turned to the Frenchman and said:

Pāshā I can see that you Western people hold dancing in high regard; it seems to be one of the treasures of your culture and fine arts. I suppose you all feel no sense of shame in such performances and movements, even though they're obviously the kind of thing that all decency forbids being celebrated and disseminated for your daughters and young women to watch.

Frenchman But dancing in your culture is more highly regarded and even more debauched than it is here. Our writers and critics keep on blaming your society for putting on the style of dance known as "belly dancing." Everyone who's gone into the Egyptian pavilion here and watched Egyptian women with bellies exposed, twisting and gyrating, has left with sweating brow in sheer embarrassment and feeling almost sick after seeing such a lewd and disgusting display. Your own culture stands accused of cultural backwardness, immodesty, and a total lack of good taste. Anyone from here who goes to nightclubs in your country won't find them full of people like himself. Whenever you decide to display your heritage in our homeland, such dancers are the very first thing you offer as your most precious commodity, and that's because they're considered a valuable asset and are afforded such a prestigious status in your society.

42.4 FRIEND Things are not as you imagine. Such dances are not widely known among women in our culture. It's only harlots who perform it. Such women practice all manner of fornication inside their own homes. The only reason why it can be seen in nightclubs is that foreigners who own such places can see no end of profit in encouraging such practices. The select public in my country are just as disgusted by it as you are here and totally disapprove of it. Every time people have tried to rouse the government into putting an end to it all, they've been unable to respond because the capitulations enjoyed by foreigners have stood in their way. In general the only people who go to watch belly dancing are idlers and debauchees and the only women involved are prostitutes. That's all there is to say about dance in our culture: it's certainly not part of our culture as is the case with you. In your cultural tradition, dance has deep roots, something that can be attended and practiced by men and women alike, boys and young girls, wives and spouses. There's hardly a single celebration or wedding here without this kind of dancing, with men clasping women around the waist, young men and virgin girls, while the women themselves are bare-armed and have their breasts exposed. This applies from the lowest levels of society all the way up to royalty and down again; it's a feature of every celebration and one of the hallmarks of a sparkling society.

I've heard about a really strange custom in a European country, namely that, when the dance is over and the male dancer takes his partner back to her place between husband, brother, mother, and children, she is supposed to give him a number of kisses. In your culture dance is a valued art form which men study in the same way as they do reading and writing and which women learn as they do sewing and embroidery. But things are not like that in our culture.

FRENCHMAN In its origins dance is not something to be dis- 42.5
approved of or castigated as you seem to imply. For mankind it is something perfectly natural. It aims at bodily harmony, something to calm the nervous system and keep it in good order whenever someone finds himself excited or deeply affected. Its influence goes far back in nature, and we can even detect its effects in birds. From earliest times until today you will rarely encounter a people that has no form of dance. It can be subdivided into four types: dances used in war, in hunting, in love stories through mime and gesture, and a fourth, in religious liturgies. A number of ancient civilizations have focused on dance, and Greeks in particular achieved a very high level of perfection. Their grandees and rulers were devoted to it and regarded it as a primary virtue. Some of them even specialized in dance and became well-known. The ambassador who plied between Athens and King Philip of Macedon, Alexander's father, was someone named Aristodemus who was a famous dancer and dance teacher. Indeed, the very same king married a well-known dancer named Larissa. Even Socrates, the famous philosopher, enjoyed dance and never expressed any disapproval of it or disdain for it. Epaminondas, one of the most famous philosophers, was an accomplished dancer.

The same was true for religious dance in the Roman Empire 42.6
from its earliest phases. Various categories of dance spread until the Christian religion was superimposed on Roman paganism. Even so, they didn't initially condemn the varieties of dance perfected by the Romans, despite all the debauched aspects that were characteristic of the latter days of their empire. Dance became part of the customs

of Western nations, and they kept it going, undaunted by the resistance of religious authorities on numerous occasions. People had grown used to it and could see nothing sinful or shameless about it. The fact that women in our culture are unveiled and mingle freely with men is the factor that makes dance seem so sinful in your eyes. Women in your cultural tradition are kept veiled from men's eyes, even though among your men and women there still exist two types of dance which in their sheer debauchery and lechery outperform the shoddiest dance halls in our culture. I'm truly amazed at the way your intellectuals and aristocrats who express their disapproval of European dance halls utterly fail to condemn the situation in their own culture.

42.7 ʿĪsā ibn Hishām said: Our conversation was interrupted when, as we were walking around, we noticed a place crammed with people. We found out that it was one of the most famous exhibits, one where they had built a huge boat that would take its passengers on a Mediterranean cruise, visiting large ports where they could see the buildings and inhabitants going about their daily work. We had already read a number of articles describing and extolling this exhibit in the major French newspapers like *Le Débat* and *Figaro*. After paying the price of admission we climbed a walkway and found ourselves inside a replica of a large boat. Once we were "on board," it started swaying like the two sides of a weighing scale, rocking just like a boat in a stormy sea. On both sides was a cloth wall with images of sea waves and ports like Naples and Venice—among others. The boat machine kept things moving at a fast pace, while the vessel stayed where it was, swaying from side to side. It all gave visitors the impression that they were actually at sea, being buffeted by the waves on the cloth and stopping at the various ports of call shown there. All in all, there seemed nothing particularly remarkable about the whole thing, that is, until the visitor looked at the machine pulling the cloth along and moving the vessel like a seesaw.

As we left this exhibit, we were amazed at the excessive nature of the allegedly amazing wonders to be witnessed at the Sights and Scenes section of the exhibition. It was clear to us that they were utterly phony, the kind of things that would only appeal to schoolboys; the only people impressed by it all would be people who were prepared to admire anything coming from Western societies, whether serious or frivolous. Once the Frenchman realized how little our Friend was bothering with the exhibits and learned what we really thought about them, he suggested that we visit the single exhibit in Sights and Scenes that had given him any satisfaction. It was a model village set up by some people from Switzerland, which showed their mountains, rivers, and village life, with its natural beauty and complete lack of artificial frippery. When we entered the exhibit and made the rounds, we were delighted by the wonderful spectacle with views of lofty mountain peaks; transferring the stonework had required some three hundred workers over a period of three years. Streams flowed downhill from mountain peaks to valleys below, with brooks and rivers branching off, enough to delight the eye and warm the heart. Interspersed between the water and greenery were simply built houses, surrounded by stores where various kinds of fruit, food dishes, and delicious meals were on sale. We could watch the famous cattle of the region at their feeding troughs, and young boys and girls whose features were bursting with the freshness of youth and the sheer beauty of country life would milk them by hand for any visitors who wanted some. We were delighted by the entire exhibit, with both men and women filling the eye with lovely scenes and soothing the soul with the sheer beauty of the surroundings. We spent a good deal of time talking about the virtues of a simple country life as opposed to urban industrialized existence. 42.8

Miṣbāḥ al-sharq 126, October 26, 1900[290]

Paris

43.1 ʿĪsā ibn Hishām said: As we were wandering around the various exhibits, we suddenly heard the sound of flute and drums, which aroused in us many memories and a sense of nostalgia. It made us feel a longing for our homeland, as a lover does with his beloved and a craver does with the object of his craving. We were like travel-weary camels amid lightning flashes that crash on the far horizon while conflicting urges are leading them to desert hollows and steppes. The exotic sounds made people turn around to glance in that direction. We too headed for its source, our hearts on fire with expectation, hoping perhaps to discover some traces of our country, something to show off to our peers and look on as samples of our prestige and glory; something to distract us from our nostalgia and console us from our pangs of emotion. We would be able to see how far Egypt and Egyptians had advanced and the ways in which the country and its inhabitants showed particular qualities of excellence.

43.2 When we reached the place where the flutes were being played, we discovered a crowd of people. Right in the middle was a coarse specimen of a man, grossly overweight. His face was a tissue of ugliness, so ugly that it seemed to roar like a herd of camels, and no wonder! It hit you like the clop of horses' hooves that stir up muck and blacken the air. He looked like a rock boulder or a chunk of ice. Had he been any more boorish, it would have been impossible to find the excess. He was wearing a tarboosh on his head that was caked in sweat and filth. Were the sun's rays to alight on it, it would have caught fire and burned. He kept on yelling in a foul voice and snorting like a desert camel. He was holding a fan with which he kept fanning himself whenever he ran out of breath. You could watch as he circled to right and left and swayed proudly from side to side. He kept shouting at people. We listened as he barked out his message:

"Come inside, folks! You'll have lots of fun and see enough to 43.3
satisfy all five senses, things to wipe corrosive cares from the soul and replace them with joy sufficient to banish all anxiety and guard against fate's calamities. Delicately crafted, beautifully shaped, there are things to banish sorrow and annul grief. Come on now, don't deprive yourselves of a sight unparalleled, a spectacle so amazing as to defy surmise or estimation, so dazzling as to surpass all imagination and conception. Come and witness how Egypt has bested all other nations in glory, so steeped in prestige as to overtop mountain peaks. And no wonder, for ever since time immemorial, Egypt has played a distinguished role among peoples and held a prominent position. So come now, here's a golden opportunity to be seized, a moment in time to be snatched. Anybody who fails to rush in is making a bad choice and condemning himself to be a loser and wasting two valuable commodities, time and money, by not seeing the beauties of this exhibit in its best light. Anyone who fails to see the skills of Zuhrah and Maʿtūqah will never in their life fully realize who wins and who loses; his only return will be disappointment both coming and going."

We made our way inside to see what things were like. At the door 43.4
we met an average-sized man wearing a clean djellaba and turban:

A wolf whom you see praying,
when you pass by, he makes a prostration.
He prays and prays,
but only as long as there's no prey.[291]

He greeted us and congratulated us on our safe arrival. We walked ahead, with him following us. When we got inside, we almost died of shock: we were obviously inside a gaming room, a place for music and entertainment. The curtain was drawn back to reveal a troupe of lewd women who started belly dancing, using all kinds of disgusting gestures and movements. For a moment we thought we had gone back in time and were still in the company of the Playboy and ʿUmdah.[292] We rushed for the door, our faces moist with tears of remorse and sheer embarrassment. As we hurried out, we were covering our faces with hands and sleeves, doing our utmost to conceal our association with our homeland and people and to rid ourselves of the stain of such an utterly vile display, one that only served to make other people look down on us with contempt. We rushed to put as much distance as possible between ourselves and this awful spectacle and to reject such a dreadful sight. We swore an oath not to pass by this sector of the exhibition again. However the Frenchman stopped to talk to us and upbraided us:

43.5 Frenchman Why are you in such a hurry? Don't you remember that this exhibition is divided into two separate parts: one for crafts and antiquities, and the other for sights and scenes? You shouldn't base your opinion of the Egyptian pavilion on a single visit to this part that has caused you so much distress and sorrow. This is the frivolous section of the exhibit. You need to visit the second section which is more serious. Maybe we'll be able to find there some nice examples of beautiful objects crafted by your hands to dispel the sorrow and aggravation you're feeling.

Pāshā I can only envisage this second section as being a prelude to the other. The person who's made such an appalling selection for the scenes section will undoubtedly do just as badly on the other section devoted to crafts. Anyone who stoops so low as to decide to display women's bellies and girls' breasts to all comers at this exhibition can hardly be expected to make a better selection for display and exhibition when it comes to relics and crafts.

FRIEND As I see it, it's the profit motive that has blinded these people to the sheer vileness of these presentations; they've been duped by the way stupid people flock to see them in Egypt, and that has aroused the jealousy of bar owners, not to mention the way that young heirs of families have squandered family resources in such nefarious haunts. They've not managed to control the profession in Egypt itself, so instead they've grabbed this opportunity to do it in a Western country. They imagine that people will flock to it as they do at home; that way they'll be able not only to make a huge profit but also avoid the opprobrium that they face in their own country. If you even mentioned the word "dance" to people in Egypt itself, they would cover their face and turn away, seeking God's help and expressing their outrage and condemnation, believing that dance halls are objectionable and forbidden by their faith. However, things have turned out exactly the opposite of what they had been expecting. Visitors to the exhibition, in all their variety, have enough taste to shun such disgusting displays and avoid watching such debauchery. So, as we can see, the entire place is empty; nobody's come to visit the exhibit. I'm astonished that the people who set up the Egyptian pavilion here, yet who would definitely refuse to establish such a dance hall as this for fear of their countrymen's condemnation, have felt no qualms about the blame that'll attach to their country and its citizens because of this exhibit. They simply don't care about the way other nations are condemning and poking fun at them. All they're bothered about is profit, and that has both blinded and deafened them. 43.6

ʿĪsā ibn Hishām said: Once outside, we followed the advice of our French friend and returned to the pavilion to visit the other part of the Egyptian exhibit. Once past the dance-hall structure, we found alongside it another building in the form of a mosque, with a wine-shop to its right overseen by an elderly Parisian woman surrounded by her children. By the mosque door was a man whose appearance 43.7

was such that a skullcap would have been more suitable attire than the turban he was wearing. In front of him was a table with an inkwell and paper on it. Around him were all kinds of people who came up to him one by one; after they had paid him a few dirhams, he would ask each one for his name and then write it out for him on the yellowing paper, along with a few pious prayers. We heard one of the visitors say to a woman who was with him, "Come on, let's get the shaykh to write us something from Muhammad's Qur'an." Once the crowd around the shaykh had gone away, we went over to talk to him, introduced ourselves, and asked him about himself. He was unable to hide from us the fact that he was not even a Muslim; it was the sheer need to earn a living that had forced him to change his usual dress in order to earn some money by setting this trap for visitors. I almost found it possible to forgive him, as I recalled a visit to a park in London called Kensington where I'd watched a man in a turban sitting with a circle of children; he was playing the part of a traditional teacher in a Qur'an school, reciting verses from the Opening Surah of the Qur'an, and teaching them how to sway in rhythm to the reading. English spectators, men and women, were standing around, utterly amazed at what they were seeing and poking fun at the whole thing. Some of them even sat down and learned how to recite, only to go back to the other spectators laughing at the whole thing. When I'd asked this turbaned shaykh what his name was, he replied "Shaykh Hasan." When I upbraided him for what he was doing, he replied that it was the need to earn a living that forced him do this, duly quoting the proverb, "Necessity legitimizes the forbidden."

43.8 We now left this Syrian to his writing and scripting and went inside the building. There we discovered a market just like the ones for festival days along with their various booths and stores. To the right there was a vendor of *libb* seeds and humus, while to the left licorice juice was on sale. In one corner someone was selling Syrian silks, in another halva, and still another shoes. When we asked whether all these things were authentic Egyptian products, we were assured that they were, and there were still more things on display along with industrial and agricultural products further inside. So we went further in and found ourselves in a wide space along the lines of ancient Egyptian temples, with produce from a typical perfumer's store brought over by its owner. In one corner was a bag full of cotton seeds, others with maize and hulba seeds, while further inside was a glass case with a gold-framed picture showing the uniform worn by "runners," the people who run in front of horses and vehicles in Egypt. All around we could see a number of pictures like this one showing types of cereals and various kinds of scents and perfumes.

As we turned to make our way out of this industrial and agricultural products section of the pavilion, we felt even more aggravated and distressed than when we had left the sights and scenes section. Our sense of shame at the sight of these relics and products was just as great as we had felt seeing the belly dancers. Anxious to get as far away as possible from this dreadful Egyptian exhibit, we were stopped by one of its regular clientele who told us that we should not miss seeing the wonder of wonders that it contained. Following his advice, we entered a curtained room where a screen revealed to us a Syrian girl with no arms using her feet to weave (and she could almost thread a needle with them) and perform a number of other functions. What we found so astonishing was that they could regard this as somehow miraculous in the context of the exhibition as a whole. 43.9

By now it was late afternoon, and so we left the Egyptian pavilion without glancing behind us. But we had hardly crossed the square in front before we were accosted by a group of women, some of them holding candles while others were shaking tambourines. In their midst was a girl wearing bridal costume; they were hitting her on the head with their tambourines and chanting the kind of wedding songs used at Egyptian nuptials. To us it seemed as if their goal was to bring a further, even more tangible, scandal down on the Egyptian people. We moved to one side in order to find out why they had left their section inside the exhibit and come outside to wander around the exhibition's streets. While we were watching our Friend noticed an Egyptian colleague of his who had come to see the exhibition. He stopped him and asked him if he had visited the Egyptian pavilion:

43.10 Egyptian Colleague Yes, I've visited it and seen the various disgraceful and shameful exhibits inside. Now here I am standing with you, watching this would-be wedding right in the midst of the exhibition.

Friend But tell me for heaven's sake, what's the purpose of the owners of this exhibit in putting on such a variety of scandalous spectacles? Isn't it enough for them to put such things on display inside the pavilion? Why have they decided now to bring such spectacles outside on to the public street for everyone to see? What on earth is making them do such a disgraceful thing?

Egyptian Colleague That's not the issue here. The primary motivating factor here is the poor returns they're getting and the fact that very few people are visiting the dancers and singers in the dance-hall exhibit inside. So every night they come outside several times and display themselves in public like this. The aim is to get people to notice the Egyptian pavilion; for them it's a kind of advertisement.

Friend I notice that you keep talking about "the Egyptian exhibit." What distresses us so much is what foreigners will say about Egyptian women. It completely ignores the damage that such a spectacle will cause. My experience with you suggests that you are a true Egyptian.

Egyptian Colleague In fact, I've investigated the truth about this Egyptian pavilion. What I've learned has lessened the sense of outrage that you've been feeling and may indeed calm the fears you have of the opprobrium that may be aimed at us. Even though the label "Egyptian" has been applied to the exhibit, Egypt itself is actually far removed from any involvement. Whereas every other exhibit here is the result of the official response of the government concerned, Egypt is an exception. The Egyptian government declined the invitation, which has been duly noted in newspapers and the official publications of the Exhibition. If you take a quick look at the women and men involved in the Egyptian exhibit, the only Egyptians are the Bey who is well known for speculating on exhibitions and two famous Egyptian female dancers. Apart from them everyone else is non-Egyptian. The women you see here acting like a flock of sheep are Syrians brought here by poverty and the need to earn a living. Incidentally this situation does not apply only to the Egyptian exhibit; it's the same with many of the exhibits from eastern countries, as you've probably noticed with the Turkish, Algerian, and other Middle East pavilions as well. These people have an excuse, in that they all need to earn a living while the reputation belongs elsewhere.

FRIEND Do you think the Egyptian pavilion will make a large profit for its sponsors to compensate for all the hardships and disgrace involved? 43.11

EGYPTIAN COLLEAGUE I don't think the company that set up the exhibit is going to lose anything or make any profit. The people who'll be losing are the shareholders. Current estimates put the losses to date at eighty thousand pounds. Maybe this time God will inflict sufficient losses on them that it'll serve as an object lesson. They won't be trying again to embark on projects like this which run the risk of not only their own loss but also the denigration of Egyptians.

ʿĪsā ibn Hishām said: With that we said our farewells to this Egyptian colleague, and he left. He had managed to lessen our pained feelings somewhat. 43.12

Miṣbāḥ al-sharq 130, November 23, 1900[293]

Paris

44.1 ʿĪsā ibn Hishām said: Our tour of the exhibition now took us to the pavilions of other nations. There we saw such wonderful things, both ancient and modern, that we stopped to admire their provenances and savor what they offered the eye. They vied with each other in fierce competition and tried to outrival the others in sheer excellence. Among them all, the German pavilion had the loftiest status and the greatest impact. It was as though the Germans were not content merely to show their superiority in warfare, but had also decided to outpace everyone else in learning, the goal being to beat everyone else in both spheres, war and peace. Evidence of this was the painting that the visitor saw at the entrance to the pavilion. It showed two girls like sisters dressed in the costumes of the two states, France and Germany. From the picture one could glean the idea of victory and potential, and assess the fate of those people in countries no longer under their suzerainty and now in the clutches of their enemies—forced to endure humiliation and shame. There were only two choices before them: greed and avarice, or contempt and instinct. What was most remarkable of all about the speed with which things change was that people who had spent twenty-five years enhancing their strength and power, every single day calling for raids of revenge—the kind of people who, whenever any one of them decided to stir up latent hatreds and jealousies, would stoke the flames of revenge. These people would dress their own daughter this way, namely in Alsatian costume. Then you would see hearts astir and minds on fire; it would be as if every single one of them was so enraged and belligerent that he turned into a fierce bull, flourishing his red uniform or, if you prefer, Caesar's own garb amid the Greeks.[294] If the comparison is valid, I would compare it to ʿUthmān's shirt seen by the Marwanids.[295] Today, however, these people are accustomed to seeing this all-powerful nation putting on such a display at this exhibit and scoffing at those so-called lions in their lairs. So all praise be to the Lord of Lords, the one who assigns monarchy to whomsoever He wills and similarly snatches it away when He so decides, raising up the one and humiliating the other.

Once the conversation reached this point, our French friend addressed us with a fiery passion: 44.2

Frenchman This modern civilization has its virtues, but it also has increased needs, multiplied desires, and instigated an excessive craving for luxury and comfort among both the elite and common people. It has left no vestige in the human heart for noble sentiments, laudable instincts, and sound principles. The fate of whole nations now resembles nothing so much as commerce where merchants are falling over each other in quest of gain and the means of profit making. Need and lack have now overwhelmed them, just like a starving wolf that has no idea which path to take or which corpse it has stumbled on. As I see it, this civilization of ours has now reached the same point as the Roman Empire did, when salacious acts reached such a stage that they were no longer considered sinful or blameworthy. All sorts of vile action and shortcomings came to have validity and legitimacy to the detriment of all virtues and laudable qualities. As their empire was drawing to a close, an erudite philosopher criticized the Roman emperor for imposing a tax on public toilets. The Emperor summoned him. After a brief conversation the philosopher was about to leave, but the Emperor, that mighty ruler, took a dinar out of his pocket and put it on the nose of his critic. "Let me ask you, by God," he asked the philosopher, "can you smell anything?" After sniffing several times, the philosopher replied that he could not smell anything. "In which case," the Emperor told him, "go away. Your criticism is baseless, so stop criticizing me. The intelligent person in quest of money should only be concerned about its true worth, not about the corrupt sources it may come from."

44.3 This then is the situation in which France finds itself today. The country's yearning and great need for profit from this exhibition has managed to divert all their attention away from their gut instinct, one that is blended with their very blood, to seek revenge, reveal dishonor, and retrieve what has been either lost or stolen. The French have entirely forgotten about the fire and destruction they intended to inflict on their victorious enemy and the raging anger they showed against the nation that has snatched away their land.[296] People have apparently thought nothing about raising Germany's prestige here in their own midst, helping it achieve its goals, and opening avenues for it. Tongues and pens are constantly heaping praise on Germans and extolling their virtues even though the Germans themselves basically ignore them and pay their opinions not the slightest respect. The Germans choose what they wish to emphasize, and that explains why they've put up this picture right at the front of their pavilion. Not only that, but they've made sure that every art and craft on display is precisely the kind of thing for which the French are renowned specialists, all with the explicit purpose of showing how superior their own products are and how much more advanced their culture is.

44.4 FRIEND Nor is that the only result of this exhibit. In the context of European politics we've noticed that your government has committed any number of blunders over the last decade, all out of concern that it might have a negative political impact on the exhibition and lead to its failure. And that's not even to mention the effect it's had on its political effectiveness on a world scale, particularly regarding the problem of Fashoda.[297] This exhibition may be a major and prestigious event, but it can never be a substitute for what the French people have lost in dealing with this problem and any number of other issues where France previously played a major role. France has now accepted to do something that it has previously refused to consider; it's reached such a point that French generals have agreed to send their soldiers to fight in the China War under the command of the German general. People who were telling themselves about the defeat of German armed forces and their commanders now find themselves controlled by their supreme commander who can send French troops wherever he wishes and throw them to the fates as he sees fit.

FRENCHMAN All of which shows you the kind of ignominy and shame that modern civilization has brought us, all based on a policy of caution and reliance on prevention. The consequences are dire. Control can be easily manipulated, leading policymakers inevitably to positions of weakness, humiliation, and contempt.

'Īsā ibn Hishām said: While we were conversing, we were suddenly aware of a loud noise that made the entire exhibition grounds shake. We watched as people fell on top of each other like roaring waves on a dark night. Everyone was in a complete panic; people were going crazy, yelling and screaming everywhere accompanied by wails and sobs of grief. Once we had calmed down amid so much chaos, we asked what had happened. They told us that the bridge at the entrance to the exhibition had collapsed, piling people on it on top of the people underneath. When we went over to the place in question, we were greeted by a horrendous, heart-rending sight, enough to evoke tears and rend the very heart. Over forty visitors to the exhibition were groaning under the pile of wreckage, some of them dead, others wounded, covered in blood, and with broken bones. There were all sorts of people—nursing mothers and weaned babies, young girls and boys, nubile girls and youths, and old men and women. Blood was flowing in torrents amid the jewelry, bangles, finery, and brocade. We watched as a father collected the broken limbs of his son, and a mother gathered her daughter's shattered limbs, blood pouring from them. People were throwing themselves 44.5

to the ground, anxious to find out if any of their relatives—fathers, daughters, in-laws, kinsfolk, family, relatives, friends, or colleagues—were among the dead or wounded. Each one of them was assuming the very worst, expecting to face a disaster and prepared to confront a dreadful truth. Everyone was crying and moaning while doctors kept doing their best to bandage wounds and health workers carried people away. As the crowd grew larger and the situation went from bad to worse, we found it increasingly difficult to watch such a disastrous occurrence and horrendous sight. The Pāshā grabbed hold of me and urged us to get away. We hurriedly accepted his suggestion that we leave this terrible situation. As we were walking, he said:

44.6 PĀSHĀ By God, all the wondrous and delightful spectacles we have seen at this exhibition and all the beautiful objects and relics designed to soothe the heart cannot in any way compensate for the anxiety and grief we've been feeling as we've watched this dreadful event. By God, I had the feeling that I was standing there unarmed on a battle day during a war when inevitably both dead and wounded and prisoners would be taken.

FRIEND You're right. Not only that, but the horrors of war have a lesser effect on people and cause less distress because war involves soldiers who have been trained and are used to it; they have been brought up in its midst and performed drills for it that have bloodied their bodies and given them a steely resolve. They are not surrounded by family and relatives, and no babies and children stand alongside them. No girls or women are to be seen in front of them, people whose bodies are used to the comforts of life and whose feelings are accustomed to a life of ease. The sight of a needle scares them, they hate being brushed by a feather, and scream when a frog croaks. It's not the same for the women we've just left behind us, groaning underneath the rubble and in the bridge's wreckage. This is a disaster involving civilized society at peace, and it's no less terrible than battles during wartime.

PĀSHĀ Let's head for the exit. There's no need to come back. Isn't it time now to have done with it all and to use our journey here for something else? We've gone back and forth, hither and yon, and now we're bored and tired. Up till now we've seen nothing among its marvels and wonders that we didn't know about already, nor are there any rareties that we haven't heard about.

FRENCHMAN As long as you've decided to end your visits to the exhibition as of today, you should certainly make your last inspection be to the miracle that is the masterpiece of all these remarkable exhibits, the source from which flow all the signs of civilization and shines the sun of refinement and culture.

ʿĪsā ibn Hishām said: We were attracted by what he was saying and followed behind him till we reached a splendid edifice. Once we had gone inside, we ended up by a deep hole in the ground. He invited us to go down. At the edge we found a machine that went up and down like a gigantic bucket. They put us in the bucket, and, before we knew what was happening, we were inside a very deep well. The experience made me forget everything human beings remember except for three verses that stayed with me while I descended into darkest night: 44.7

Once my feet had touched the ground, they demanded,
Hopefully alive or dead and a risk?
"Remove the ropes," I said, "they will not detect us."
I then took off into the night without delay.
My feet directed me from a massive height, like a
a rapacious, black-feathered falcon swooping down.[298]

But for our long acquaintance with the Frenchman and the confidence that we had in him, we would have said that he was trying to do away with us or else playing the same trick on us as the one used by Jacob's sons on their brother, Joseph.[299] Once we had recovered from our shock, we asked him where exactly we were. He informed us that we were in a place underground that was modeled on the concept of a coal mine; the aim was to show how miners extracted coal. When we stared into the darkness, we managed to make out 44.8

in front of us some men acting as workers who could only see what was right in front of them by the light of an electric lamp tied to their heads. They looked to us just like fireflies glowing in trees on a dark night. Heaven only knows how the electric lamps were supposed to pierce such utter darkness, so thick that it could almost grab hold of your hand. It was as though the lights were not there to illuminate the darkness but rather to demonstrate quite how dark it actually was. We made our way slowly forward and saw enough chambers, caves, and trenches to make even an adder get lost and coil up in despair. In every nook and cranny we spotted specters of human beings whose postures in their hundreds provided examples of the need to work in such mine shafts. In their hands they carried heavy and light pickaxes and spades, along with wooden planks that they put in place to stop the shaft walls from crumbling while they were being mined. Some of them were standing on tiptoe, others were lying on their side, others on their knees, and a few of them flat on their faces. Water poured over them from cracks and crevices in the rock face.

44.9 These are just some of the aches and pains to which the human body was being exposed, and God alone knows what expectations and worries the men had in their hearts and minds because of any number of threats they might face from lack of oxygen, and possibility of fire, inundation, drowning, and rockfalls. The tiniest crack in the lamps attached to their heads could ignite gas explosions. They were in three types of darkness: coal being hard and dark; darkness itself a liquid form of coal black; and the pitch-black livelihood of these men. So all praise be to the One who has set up mankind as He has. From the coal mine we now moved on to the gold mine, but the workers there were no better off or less burdened than the others had been. When the humidity began to clog the very blood inside our veins, we hurried toward the way up and emerged from the belly of the earth. Relieved to be above ground at last, we stayed where we were for a while adjusting our eyes to the light. We then left the place and started strolling in the fresh air, looking to left and right but not saying a word or even trying to speak.

All of a sudden our French Philosopher friend directed our attention to a spot where he showed us the barrel of the enormous gun overlooking the famous gun foundry renowned for its size and girth. Here's what he told us: 44.10

FRENCHMAN So this is the third of the major wonders of the exhibition and constituents of civilization. The first, as you have seen, is coal; the second is gold; and the third is this one, iron. They extract gold so they can buy coal and weld it into iron and steel. They use it to make weapons and all kinds of industrial instruments, not to mention the marvelous inventions and strange creations that you've seen here. All these dazzling and amazing objects with their incredible power and sophistication originate in that black coal which today constitutes civilization's bread and is the source of mankind's luxury and refinement, not to mention civilization's power and vigor. But a pox on mankind! How utterly evil is everything it makes and how disdainful everything it does! It sends people to the lowest levels of the earth to rip out its guts and destroy its inside, all in order to extract something that will wreak as much havoc on its surface as well. The claim is that they're striving for a decent way of life and contentment on earth, whereas mankind spends its life in such misery and suffering. Eventually death arrives to take them away, and all that after spending a short while on earth even more lost than animals—of which they are supposed to be the most superior.

PĀSHĀ Tell me, by God, what's the wage for coal miners who have to work in the conditions that we've just seen. What other rewards are there?

FRENCHMAN In France there are a hundred thousand miners working in coal mines. They extract twenty-seven million tons of coal which is sold for two hundred and sixty million francs per year. Miners work underground at a depth of hundreds of meters and feet and in dangerous conditions. Each year there are on average fifteen hundred mining accidents which cause a large number of deaths and injuries. Then there are the chest and lung diseases from 44.11

inhaling carbon and breathing foul air. Some work by day, others by night, and they're joined by sons and wives as well. For all this hardship the miner receives a wage of two to five francs.

PĀSHĀ So what happens to all the hundreds of millions earned from the coal that they extract at the cost of so much effort and exhaustion?

FRENCHMAN They go into the coffers of a select minority of company and concession owners. They spend the money on their own desires and the fripperies of civilized life, having deprived these poor, wretched laborers whose lives are no better than insects or pack animals. But don't even think that the few francs that a miner earns as a daily wage ever actually reach his own hand. The majority of companies construct housing and stores, so the miner lives in a company house, buys his food and clothing from a company store, in return for which the company deducts a certain amount from his salary. If a miner finishes the month with neither credit nor debt, he considers himself the happiest and luckiest of mortals.

FRIEND It's this situation that's given rise to socialist and anarchist movements. How is anyone supposed to live such a life, working like insects underground or crawling reptiles. How can anyone regard this enormous gap in lifestyle between the people in the country? And to such a degree that there are some who spend their lives buried underground, slaving away for some idiot living in the utmost luxury and lounging on plush cushions in the boudoirs of a mighty mansion lofty enough to reach the clouds and rival the very towers of heaven in their decoration?

44.12 ʿĪsā ibn Hishām said: We now reached the famous Eiffel Tower. We leaned our backs against one of its columns and started contemplating the strange achievements of mankind and varieties of insanity that have been perpetrated in every age, claiming all the while that man is the perfect creature and wise observer.

Miṣbāḥ al-sharq 133, December 14, 1900[300]

Paris

ʿĪsā ibn Hishām said: We stopped for a while to take a look at this imposing tower, a lofty structure whose sheer height amazed us and whose construction was astonishing. In the category of wondrous sights, amazing rarities, prized entities, lofty peaks, and highest summits, this was certainly a remarkable feat of design and engineering—obviously the precious maiden of the entire exhibit, albeit of a certain age. Castles and hills would bow down before it, mountains and flags would be prostrate. In comparison what could one say about the height of the pyramids or Haman's lofty tower? If the Pharaoh had seen it, he would have demolished everything he had built and erected. Nor would he have stated, "I am your lord most high." He would have turned on his builder, Haman, and flayed him a thousand times, then hung him from a tree. And how could you compare the fabled Tower of Babel with this Parisian tower that addresses the very constellations in the heavens and whose top looks down on twinkling Sirius itself? Were a vulture to alight on it, it would immediately become the third of the Two Vultures, building its nest in the twin stars of Ursa Minor. How could an imaginative person conceive of overtopping its lofty heights or a crafter of similes rise so far upwards as to find the appropriate epithets to depict it and detail the modes of its construction? Needless to say, words would fail him. For, in a context where comparison becomes 45.1

impossible, people liken the biggest to the smallest and the greatest to the lowliest, just as they have compared the daytime sun with a cup of wine, the full moon with a spring gushing into a swollen lake. The Pleiades have been compared to a cluster of grapes, the Gemini to a stick or piece of wood, stars in the heavens to strings of sea-shells, darkest night to black slaves, and dawn to spilt blood. On that basis we would say that we are depicting this tower as the letter *alif* in the alphabet of progress and development, while its vowel sign is the flag fluttering at the top against the distant horizon. Either that, or it comes first in the list of crafts and sciences; the needle that marks the spot of civilization on the map of the globe; the pen that draws on the new moon's surface to indicate the level of sophistication that this nation has achieved; or, as some people would claim, the bull's horn poking out of the earth's surface.

45.2 We all walked around it several times and duly admired it; it was awesome enough to silence all talk and baffle the mind. Our Friend turned to us and said:

FRIEND This is the way things have been since ancient times, the manner in which time behaves. Whenever one nation achieves superiority in civilization, it builds a monument that testifies to all mankind about the elevated status that has accrued to it in the realms of glory and prestige. It survives for a while to remind the present generation of people about previous centuries. Every single city was famous for a remarkable monument that was duly memorialized on the pages of prestige and glory and indicated its superiority in arts and sciences at the time. God alone knows that, by constructing this tower, Western civilization has presented the world with an incredible marvel, a monument to which others bow down in admiration, an amazing construction that can even surpass the seven wonders of the world, monuments that were also beautiful to observe and equally amazing to the mind according to what people have to say about the achievements of ancient peoples and the civilization of earlier centuries.

45.3 PĀSHĀ What are those seven wonders?

FRIEND The Pyramids in Egypt, the Hanging Gardens of Queen Semiramis, the Wall of Babylon, Pheidias's Statue of Zeus, the Colossus of Rhodes, the Temple of Diana at Ephesus, and the Tomb of Mausulos at Halicarnassus.

PĀSHĀ Do they still exist today?

FRIEND Only the Pyramids still exist today. You know them well and have seen them. The hands of decay have done their work on the rest of the wonders. All we know about them today comes from anecdotes and mentions in texts. That is what happens to mankind's works, however great they may have been. On the scale of time they don't last longer than seconds.

PĀSHĀ Do you know things about the wonders you can share with us? I find myself eager to talk about olden times and to learn about ancient monuments.

FRIEND The Pyramids are well known. 45.4

The Hanging Gardens were constructed on a hill that is now known by the name ʿUmrān ibn ʿAlī. The area is forty feddans wide, and the River Euphrates used to flow past at the bottom. Artificial shapes like mountains were used to trace miniature versions of the gardens on the top. The reason was that one of the king's wives felt nostalgic for the hilly features in her homeland, so he had a replica of nature built that would compensate for what she was missing and make her forget her nostalgia. Underneath was a park with interlocking domes over which were suspended trees and clusters of flowers on pillars and empty cylinders that would be filled with soil. Large flowering trees planted in the cylinders would spread their roots. The domes were equipped with staircases by which you could ascend to the rooftop where flowers and plants were growing, fruits were ripening, and waterwheels kept turning to raise the water from the Euphrates below to the top of the structure.

The Wall of Babylon was actually a number of interlinked walls 45.5 enclosing ninety-three square kilometers—in other words, large enough to contain seven cities the size of Paris. The wall was forty-eight meters high and twenty-seven meters wide, surrounded by an enormous trench, and with a number of towers one hundred and eight meters high. According to a number of historical accounts, the wall had a hundred gates made of iron.

The Statue of Zeus in Greece, he being the chief of the Greek gods, was the work of the famous sculptor Pheidias. It was fourteen meters high. The artist took great pains to make its proportions exact. The deity sat on a throne, crowned with olive garlands and holding a gold statue of the god of victory and an elephant's tooth in his right hand; in his left, was a scepter studded with all kinds of metals, and at its tip sat an eagle. The god's shawl and shoes were both made of pure gold, as were the throne itself and the elephant's tooth, which used ebony and marble as well. His two feet were placed on top of two lions, also made of gold. For the ancients this statue was the most valuable thing in the world, and every Greek considered himself unlucky if he died before being able to make a pilgrimage to see it.

45.6 The Colossus of Rhodes was an enormous statue of the god Apollo erected opposite the entrance to Rhodes Harbor. It was thirty-seven meters high, making it the tallest statue known to the Greeks and Romans. It fell in an earthquake, but bits of it remained until the seventh century when Arabs removed most of what remained of it.

The Temple of Diana at Ephesus was one whose structure, decoration, paintings, and detail knew no rival among all ancient temples of its type. An interesting historical anecdote tells how an evil Greek intellectual decided that he wanted to do something for which he would be remembered for all time; the thing he chose to do was to burn down this temple. He did indeed contrive to set it on fire, on the very same night that Alexander the Great was born. When the perpetrator of the crime informed the government that he was the one who had started the blaze, they realized that he was in quest of fame. The government ordered that he be tortured to death and that anyone who even mentioned the man's name would suffer the same fate. This requirement for rendering this episode eternal has remained in place. After that, Alexander wanted to rebuild the temple using his own money, a condition being that he put his own name on one of the walls; but the people refused since they did not want any foreigner to lord over them in their own temple. They themselves undertook the task of rebuilding and redecorating it, a project that lasted two hundred and twenty years. That is the way things stayed until Nero, the Roman Emperor, came and robbed the temple of all its treasures and transferred the mosaics to his own palaces in Rome. The whole thing came to an end when the Germans destroyed it during their wars.

The Tomb of King Mausolus is very famous. His wife had it built. 45.7
After his death, his sister gathered together all the skilled craftsmen in the known world and assigned each group a separate part of the project. It was forty-two meters high, with marble columns on which were portrayed major battles and other events. The statuary was the finest of its kind, and the tomb itself was covered with a piece of marble on which were carved images of important battles. The tomb survived intact until the fourth century, but gradually it fell into ruin, and parts of it were taken away to build the fortress of Bodrum in the sixteenth century. Pieces of its decorated marble remained on the site until earlier this century, when England purchased them and transferred them to the British Museum in London. The tomb was very famous; it is even mentioned as part of the dialogue between the King and the philosopher Diogenes. Once both of them were dead, the worth of the tomb became evident, as was the fact that the king regarded it as his greatest monument, even though there were many others.

PĀSHĀ That is all wonderful, my friend! You have given me 45.8
plentiful detail about wonders that existed far in the past. But I still have to ask you about the issue of dialogue among the dead.

FRIEND Certain philosophers made a habit of putting some of the theses they were advocating in the form of dialogues—some of them involved living people, others the dead—as object lessons and guides for people. As proof of the way that such dialogues remain fixed in the mind, I can tell you that pieces of wise counsel from those dialogues keep occurring to me personally in a number of different situations.

Pāshā I assume you won't stint in sharing such counsel.

Friend Diogenes had a meeting with King Mausolus in which they discussed the world of tombs:

45.9 "Diogenes How is it, Asian monarch, that I see you here strutting arrogantly around, as though you expected to occupy a loftier position than ours?

"King There's nothing surprising about that. I merit such a status by virtue of being a king with wide powers and also due to the fact that I have conquered so many countries; and not merely those things, but also because of my own beauty and elegance and the courage I've displayed. And, if all that isn't enough, then I can claim a distinction and rank above all others, thanks to my tomb which is superior to any other tomb in its perfect construction and craftsmanship. It alone is sufficient for a whole series of monarchs to be celebrated through the ages. With all that in mind, do you still think that I've no right to boast?

"Diogenes But, o thou handsome king, I notice that none of that former beauty and power is now left. If we were to adjudicate matters fairly, then your cranium and mine are the same size. Neither of them have eyes, our noses are cracked, and our teeth exposed. And, when it comes to that temple and all its fancy decoration, it brings you no benefit; that only accrues to the people still alive in your country who can boast about it to visitors and glean whatever kudos they wish from its existence. But I can't see anything accruing to you from the construction of that building. I can only see you as being in a worse situation here than all the rest of us because you have all those stones and rocks over your head.

"King What's this I'm hearing? Is then everything I've ever done completely wasted? Am I to merit no distinction because of it, and to be the equal of Diogenes?

"DIOGENES Don't claim to be my equal. Here you are, still suffering for the loss of what you had when you were alive and what you reckoned to be supreme happiness. What it all adds up to is that all you're left with is to have people walk past your tomb and say that it is indeed very beautiful. Diogenes on the other hand isn't bothered by the fact that they've buried him in a grave or tossed him out in the desert somewhere. But in the minds of virtuous and goodly people he's left behind a fine memory, compared with which your mighty kingdom and your beautiful tomb are worth nothing, you deluded servant!"

'Īsā ibn Hishām said: Once our Friend had finished talking, the Frenchman suggested that we should go up the tower. With that we entered an elevator at one side of the tower, and it took us from the ground level into the heavens in the blinking of an eye. It let us off at the second floor, where we found a large market with stalls and merchants selling a variety of goods. In the middle was a superb restaurant and a number of bars. We took seats close to the edge of the floor. When we looked down below us, people looked like ants, and all the lofty palaces and expansive mansions resembled mere anthills. The Pāshā now started asking for further details about the tower. The Frenchman responded by noting that the Eiffel Tower rises three hundred meters from the ground. It weighs nine million kilograms. It is made up of twelve thousand separate pieces, and there are two-and-a-half million rivets. The total amount spent on it comes to almost seven million francs, and the revenues from it during the exhibition are eight million francs. To complete his account the Frenchman told us that the person who designed this amazing structure, one that surpasses anything built by ancients or moderns, has landed up in bankruptcy court and has been sentenced to a prison term because of the infamous Panama crisis.[301] 45.10

PĀSHĀ How is it that science can rise to such heights of industrial production among you, and yet it fails to train people to behave 45.11

appropriately and keep their ethics in check? Isn't it amazing that this clever engineer can devise something to amaze the entire world for its science and knowledge and bring in abundant revenues, but then he gets involved in shady deals and bankruptcy. If this is the way that grandees and people of substance behave in your country, what are we supposed to say about those poor wretches whom we observed living like insects underground in dark mines?

FRIEND Don't be so surprised. This Western civilization may have achieved a level of education in technology unachieved by any culture before, but, when it comes to ethical training, it's certainly not achieved the kind of progress in science and knowledge that might have been anticipated. Above all, don't regard the people whom you see strutting around here in all their finery as being in any case morally superior to the coal-stained miners you saw.

> Humans search for wealth
>   in every conceivable place,
> Evil is rampant in both worlds,
>   lowland and mountain.[302]

45.12 ʿĪsā ibn Hishām said: As we were about to get up and leave the exhibition, the Frenchman finished by telling us:

FRENCHMAN Now you've seen our civilization—its various sights and the variety of exhibits of tools and machines that you've looked at both below ground and up the tower, all of them wonderful and amazing. But for the intelligent person there's something even more wonderful and curious, namely to learn about the way society lives and to study its transactions, morals, and customs. If after leaving the exhibition you don't want to go straight back to your country with some surface descriptions of what you've seen, then you should spend a few more days with me in Paris so that you can get a better idea of peoples' manner and customs, both good and bad. The intelligent person is never fooled by superficial frippery, but rather avoids it in order to see what really lies behind it all.

Just as everyone seems to be of equal status when you look down from the Eiffel Tower, so such a person needs to use his insight to consider people once they've been stripped of all pretense and deprived of different kinds of cover and affectation.

ʿĪsā ibn Hishām said: We gladly accepted his offer, on condition that he stay with us and accompany us. And that's how we came to leave the grounds of this exhibition of precious objects for the realms of customs and ethics. 45.13

Miṣbāḥ al-sharq 192, February 14, 1902[303]

Paris

46.1 ʿĪsā ibn Hishām said: Our coverage of the visit we paid to the mother of all European capitals and our stay in the hub of civilization finished with a description of the Great Exhibition: the different people we met there, the strange happenings day and night, the variety of exotic items, the precious and creative objects of every conceivable kind of craft that were on display, the nightclubs and music halls scattered across the grounds, the splendid views it afforded visitors, and the undesirable subtext out of sight. The Pāshā, our Friend, and I had emerged from it with a mixture of feelings: praise, criticism, and outright condemnation. We were still in the company of the sage Frenchman, his temples whitened by his willingness to share with us his culture and learning. We had used him as our guide through the unfamiliar terrain and had gladly accepted his enlightened views in explaining complicated issues for us. We followed him as camels do with their cameleer and a caravan does with its guide, praising the good fortune that had led him to accompany us and enabled him to meet our needs. We adopted his plan so as to be sure to make the transfer from the exhibition of precious objects to the realms of customs and ethics.

46.2 We spent months of the year as though in a dream, with our French colleague taking us round packed clubs and crowded meetings as we selected different moods and qualities from among the different classes of society in the city. Thus at one moment we would be ascending to the highest levels of exclusivity among the elite, then at another we would descend to the most plebeian of venues. One day we would be at a meeting with men of influence and prestige, and then it would be with artisans and laborers. Some meetings that we attended would involve power and politics; others would be concerned with prediction and observation. From visits to lofty palaces we would move to dilapidated ruins, from pulpits for homilies and speeches to gatherings of the debauched and facetious; from learned societies to music halls with songs, from literary salons to havens of the wretched and ignorant. Eventually there was not a single assembly where you could experience both virtues and vices and probe morality at its highest and lowest points that we had not experienced and learned from in some way. In everything that we did, our French colleague went to enormous lengths to provide reasons for what we saw and explain rationales. From every single issue he managed to provide us with a notable piece of wisdom and a much-needed axiom. His demeanor throughout was one of careful consideration, restraint, caution, and admonition, all of which provided sound guidance for any perspicacious person. We took it all in as sound common sense and useful counsel.

So here we are now going back to the previous conversations. 46.3
We will relate for readers what we saw and heard. We can begin with the Pāshā's questions and inquiries regarding rulers and laws:

Pāshā Now that we've finished observing all those sights and monuments and have filled our eyes with its vistas, let's now take a serious look at the bases and principles of this civilization: how nations establish their laws, and how their presidents and governments conduct themselves. What is the status of the king of this country and what does he do? What's his name, for example?

Frenchman For us in France, kingship has no name and no human form.

Pāshā So then you must be in a chaotic situation, like stray livestock or camels with no shepherd. How can you organize the work you do and keep society in order?

FRENCHMAN Heaven forfend! We have a ruler, but he is not a king who sits on the throne. He is called the President of the Republic.

PĀSHĀ What is this thing called "republic" that you seem to have devised? I've never heard the word before. It seems as though you Western people have decided to create some new-fangled entity to replace everything that's old. What's the name of this "president," and what's his ancestry and lineage? When did he inherit the position from his father?

FRENCHMAN The president's name is Monsieur Emile Loubet.

PĀSHĀ (*cackling*) My dear friend, I can see that you're poking fun at us today. How can your ruler possibly be called "Monsieur"? That's the term I've heard people using on the street to address each other.

46.4 FRENCHMAN I wasn't joking; what I've said is the absolute truth. Once you have learned about the form of government that we have, you'll see that there's no harm in referring to the president of the country in that way. He is no different from the cupper in his shop or the wine-seller in his bar. The purpose is to proclaim the principle of equality between the elite and lowly, old and young. For us, that's a primary principle of the way we're governed. The president's actually of peasant agricultural origins. The highest post he occupied in his local area was as mayor of the town where he was born. His mother still lives in the same house, just as she's always done. The presidency isn't inherited from either father or grandfather. It comes to someone following the death of his predecessor. Before becoming president he worked as a tanner.

PĀSHĀ If what you're telling us is in fact the case, then I can only assert in the strongest terms that you've reached a level of decadence that negates all the finery, creativity, and splendor with which you've previously been dazzling the world in the realms of industry and innovation. How could anyone conceive of consigning all the glory, pride, and splendor that we witness to a president who's just a peasant or tanner and who's supposed to rule this wonderful people and great nation? I can't imagine your system of government remaining stable for a long time. Instead, I can only envisage a continuous state of chaos and intrigue, the end result of which can only be division and discord followed by devastation and ruin.

FRENCHMAN Steady on now! If you knew what the word "republic" meant, you would not be going to such extremes in your opinions. I'm now going to give you a definition of the term and the way in which it functions in our country. In general terms "republic" implies the government of the people by the people by delegating a select group of them to serve as government and arbiters of the laws, which they compose and under which they operate as a law code just like the holy Shariah with you. They duly elect a group of people who will implement those laws and make sure that they're maintained. The head of such a group is the president of the French Republic, and he's elected by a voting majority of the two legislative houses, the Senate and the Chamber of Deputies, on a designated day whenever the presidency becomes vacant. The president's term is for seven years; for us he's just like a king in other countries. He's selected on the basis of an absolute majority. His duties include joining the members of the two houses in creating laws and regulations, then issuing orders for their implementation after they've been ratified by both houses; he also will oversee their implementation and the people's adherence to them. He has the right to issue pardons, to use discretion regarding military force, and to appoint governors and officials to both military and civilian positions. He presides at all official ceremonies and public festivals, and is the point of contact for ambassadors and delegates from foreign governments. Every document emerging from the president's office has to carry the signature of one of his ministers. 46.5

He's the one who nominates the consultative Council of State in conjunction with the ministers. By agreement with members of the Senate he can dissolve the Chamber of Deputies before the 46.6

conclusion of its term in office, its sole responsibility in that case being connected to some breach of the nation's best interests involving the president. The president is also the person who initiates negotiations on treaties and agreements pertaining to them, although he's required to present them to the two chambers provided that disclosing them does not involve disclosing what are known as "state interests." However, he's not allowed to agree to any treaties involving peace, commerce, and financial matters, along with other things involving French citizens and their property outside the country. He can only conclude such agreements after they have been presented to the Chamber and approved by it. In the same way, he's not allowed to relinquish or exchange any French territories unless he has prior agreement from the Chamber. He may not declare war without first consulting both chambers. If he should commit some act of treason against the people's best interests, then he may only be charged by the Chamber of Deputies, and his trial may only take place in the Senate. He also nominates the Prime Minister from among members of the Chamber of Deputies, and charges him with the selection of the cabinet of ministers and approves of his choices. They are all members of the Chamber of Deputies, except for the Minister of War and Marine, on some occasions. The prime minister is responsible to the Chamber of Deputies for all actions taken by the government. If it happens that the ministry loses the confidence of the Chamber of Deputies, then a petition demanding its resignation is submitted to the president of the republic in order that another ministry can be elected in its place. All in all, the rights of the president of the French Republic resemble those of other monarchs where such matters are tied to a parliamentary system. Where there's an absence of such responsibilities, the entire burden falls on the ministers regarding all matters pertaining to the country, and they are responsible to the Chamber of Deputies. The president's influence is basically limited to the appointment of the prime minister and other official functions.

Pāshā From all this detail, it's now clear to me that the president is in fact a monarch in all but name, and that executive authority lies entirely with the two chambers. You might not even feel the need for such a president were it not for the fact that, in matters of governance, you find it necessary to have a kind of monarchical figure over you. But you also want to govern yourselves, and you can only achieve that by creating an image of such a figure along the lines designed for this presidency. Otherwise what's the point of spending so much effort appointing a man whom you grant all the broad trappings and authority of monarchy, but then proceed to tie him down with procedures that impede the exercise of power? As long as executive authority reverts to the Chamber of Deputies and the Senate, why doesn't the whole thing rest in the hands of the heads of the two chambers? 46.7

Frenchman You should realize that in our country governmental authority is divided into two parts: the presidency and the ministry, which we term "executive authority," and the Chamber of Deputies and the Senate, termed "legislative authority." Governance may indeed be in the hands of the legislative branch, but they have to elect another group who will undertake to implement the laws as written and supervise their proper implementation.

Pāshā Now I see that the members of the two chambers are the ones with the real authority; each of them is a king in his own right, with no responsibility or ties restraining his actions. It's as though you've replaced a single monarch—someone who's supposed to control affairs, implement your rules, and question his suzerainty over you before God and people—with a number of monarchs who have no regal characteristics: they're not sultans, and they have neither the kind of experience in administration such as other presidents and rulers. How can they feel any notion of liability towards your state if discretion in such matters is shared with a group of people from the populace? In such circumstances how can there be any sort of organization that can be relied on? 46.8

Frenchman In that particular context we possess a number of linkages and restraints which guarantee that matters will be properly run and regulations will be observed. The members of both chambers are responsible to the populace at large. In order to understand that fully, you need to learn what the requirements are for nomination, how the two chambers are set up, and how affairs are conducted in them.

Miṣbāḥ al-sharq 193, February 21, 1902[304]

PARIS

47.1 ʿĪsā ibn Hishām said: While the French philosopher was sitting with the Pāshā and explaining to him the French Chamber of Deputies, the way it is organized, and the methods by which it conducts the affairs of state, the Friend interrupted him:

FRIEND (*to the Frenchman*) My dear learned colleague, I'd like to know what you yourself think of these parliamentary chambers and the way they administer your country's affairs at home and abroad. Before you go into even more detail with the Pāshā, I find myself having a good deal of information about incidentals, but too little about essentials. While you're explaining things in even greater detail, I'd like to have some principles for judgment at my disposal, something that will make it that much easier to form an opinion on things and to be more discriminating in reacting to your account.

47.2 FRENCHMAN I don't think it is necessary for me to express a personal opinion or pass indiviual judgment while I'm giving you information about various less obvious aspects of the system. That's not the way I've been dealing with you. My preferred method is to lay things out clearly for you and discuss current conditions so that I can assess the impact that my commentary has on you and hear the different judgments that you may make about them. In that way I myself can benefit from my own previous verdicts on things, whether it is to support or oppose them. However intelligent and clear-sighted someone may be, he should only have self-confidence to the extent that he views himself in the mirror of other people. That's the way you'll observe many people of discretion and sound judgment in public affairs settling problems and resolving knotty issues. They may well be eager to have the correct opinion about things that happen in their private lives, but the very fact that at heart they want their opinion to be the one that wins cannot spare them a good deal of confused thinking and indeed of fudging when it comes to making fair comparisons and coming to sound conclusions. You can see the principle in operation quite clearly in matters both large and small, both exalted and lowly, even among people who play time-wasting games like chess, backgammon, and other similar pastimes. An expert player will be making one mistake after another while right next to him someone who is much less proficient will be benefitting from his errors. On such matters there's a proverb which says, "He can see the squares, but he can't see the player." All of you are spared any desire to get involved in French affairs and far removed from the ups and downs involved. As a result there's an opportunity for us to benefit from your opinions and make use of your judgments. In the same way, I hope that you'll let me benefit from your explanations of your own situation and your elucidation of things that I don't know about your own culture. You should be aware that simply going along with my own opinions about my own society will deprive you of the ability to criticize things freely and present you with a biased viewpoint. That's precisely what I wish to avoid so that your views and opinions can be totally independent.

47.3 FRIEND While you may not want to share your own opinion with me, you can at least let us know what others have to say. What I'd like to know is whether this system of government that you have is the most complete and perfect way of governing people and directing the affairs of nations. Is this then the ultimate stage achieved by mankind regarding the way in which human society is to be organized and governed justly and fairly?

FRENCHMAN Your own critical abilities and lively interest are quite enough to make everything clear to you. You've already observed the kinds of thing that I'm explaining to you now; you've been able to compare what I say with what is actually happening, and have realized the differences that may exist between something good in theory but bad in application, all resulting from seeing the things I've told you about in their actual context. It seems inevitable to me that you'll come to realize a good deal concerning this topic on your own, but I'm completely untroubled by the effect it may have on you or the way in which I'm explaining everything to you.

Here is what the renowned English philosopher and sage, [Herbert] Spencer, a paragon of contemporary European thinking about ethics, national traits, and the modes of creating human societies, has to say about parliamentary chambers under whose regulations Western nations function in this era: 47.4

"Parliamentary chambers are like complex machinery, with many working parts that are neither unified, connected, or harmonious. Their course is only moderated through frequent adjustment and correction and a continuous process of change and alteration. But even that does not guarantee continuing order. For there exists a basic and ongoing flaw, namely that every single gear will only keep functioning as long as its motion does not impair the functioning of the machine as a whole. Even so, its flaws are far less than those of autocratic rule and much easier to tolerate than other absolute forms of government. Parliaments have one overriding advantage, namely that they ensure that every single individual has his fair share of justice and equality of rights in dealing with other people. The only thing that leads people to create such parliamentary chambers is a need to make sure that tyranny and autocratic rule are kept at bay. Experience has shown that this type of parliament is useful primarily for promulgating laws and regulations, and that the jurisdiction needs to be restricted to that and nothing beyond. If it so happens that they do go beyond those bounds, the negative effects on the country are considerable. The legislative function gets lost and distracted in a maze of administrative politics, which is currently the case with all Western governments."

47.5 Pāshā Let's put that aside for now and start on our inquiry. Tell me about the Chamber of Deputies, how it's made up and how it functions. I'd like to be able to respond to your description before I make too hasty a judgment.

Frenchman The Chamber of Deputies is made up of six hundred or more members who meet under the leadership of a chamber president whom they elect along with four vice presidents and four aides. They are then constituted into a number of departments and committees that focus on particular matters brought to their attention. Such matters are subdivided into two categories: one dealing with things forwarded from the government itself, known as the "statutes and laws" division; and the second that receives business from the Chamber deputies themselves, known as the "requests" division. Each of these committees handles the business relevant to their charge and then forwards a report to the Chamber session where it is debated and discussed, as a result of which there may be amendments, additions, and omissions, following which the measure will be either accepted or rejected by majority vote. There are a total of eleven such committees, and in each case membership is renewed every month. The most significant of the major committees consists of thirty-three members, namely those dealing with budget, administration, army, railways, education, navy, colonial affairs, commerce and industry, criminal law, property law, and government economics.

47.6 Each committee has its own president under whose authority it meets, and a person delegated to read its reports to the general meetings of the Chamber. Each of these committees meets two days a week. The means by which the government forwards projects to them is that the minister in whose jurisdiction the project lies forwards the proposal in the government's name to the administrative committee charged by the Chamber with the receipt of such documents. It is quickly printed and circulated to all the members of the Chamber. The chamber's president then forwards it to the committee that is charged to look into the matter. Requests received from chamber members themselves have to be submitted in the proper legal form, with clauses and materials, all preceded by an introduction that explains the reason for the request and the need for its submission. The chamber president sends all such requests to a committee that is prepared to receive them and considers their necessity and appropriateness. Should it become clear to the members of this committee that the request should be accepted, then they will duly forward it to the committee that deals with such matters. If not, the request is rejected.

Any report submitted by the relevant committees for consider- 47.7
ation by the Chamber of Deputies in general session is required to conform exactly with the stated purpose of the proposal in question and to reflect a comprehensive investigation of the issue in all its aspects. It should also conform to all clauses to be found in legal precedents, be in line with contemporary circumstances, and take into account future impacts of the measure in question. It needs to reflect debating points raised by members of the Chamber and to provide necessary clarification of arguments put forward by members of the Chamber, so that when the full chamber considers the issue, they do not need to go back and argue the points all over again. Every member receives a copy of the motion twenty-four hours before the session. The president opens the session by reading the minutes of the previous session and then detailing the items that are to be discussed in accordance with the agenda promulgated by the various committees. Every motion is thus identified, and the members are then at liberty to make speeches in which they either advocate for its approval or argue against it. Once no one else wishes to speak on the subject, the president then presents the measure to the Chamber to be discussed clause by clause. Assuming that the majority of members approve of the measure in general, they go through every clause. If there is general agreement, the measure is resubmitted five days later. If it is once again approved, then it becomes effective, actionable law; that is, once it has been published in the official gazette and approved by the Senate. If on

the other hand the majority does not approve of the measure, then the proposal and the report on it are both null and void.

47.8 Every member of the Chamber of Deputies has the right to ask questions regarding any event or matter on which he requires clarification, and without any restraints. He can question the government about its general policies and ask any minister about the workings of his particular ministry. Every minister is obliged to respond to such inquiries in a satisfactory fashion so as either to convince the majority of members of the Chamber so that they will vote in favor, or else the majority will not be convinced, in which case the government is forced to resign; either that, or else it has to dictate to the government the precise fashion in which it intends to proceed on that particular matter. In that case the person who raises the question in the first place submits his request to the president, and he in turn informs the relevant minister and requests discussion during the course of the session on a particular day. Any internal matter cannot be ignored for a period longer than one month.

47.9 There are several ways of casting votes. One involves standing and sitting in the Chamber itself in order to count the number of votes in favor and against. Others include raising hands or keeping them lowered, casting positive and negative ballots in an urn for that purpose, and using black and white pieces of paper. At any rate, there can be no majority without over half the members voting in favor, even if the majority is just one. Once a motion is passed in the Chamber of Deputies, it is forwarded to the Senate.

Pāshā And what exactly is the Senate?

Frenchman In its organization it is no different from the Chamber of Deputies, except in matters of election. Its function is to examine projects passed by the Chamber of Deputies. It consists of three hundred members. It can propose projects on its own and send them to the Chamber of Deputies for approval, just as is the case with the Chamber of Deputies sending proposals to the Senate. They are then forwarded to the president of the republic for his signature, all by means of the minister in whose sphere the project falls.

Pāshā In discussing both these chambers, you have kept talking about "elections." Please explain to me how that works. How do people elect each other, and what are the requirements that can guarantee that the people whom they elect will perform their duties in a proper fashion? 47.10

Frenchman I'll explain it all to you. I've started my explanation with the organization of the government from top to bottom so as not to confuse you. So I've talked about the president of the republic and the government itself. Now I'll explain the electoral process which marks the beginning and end of all governmental authority.

Miṣbāḥ al-sharq 196, March 14, 1902

Paris

48.1 ʿĪsā ibn Hishām said: The Frenchman continued with his explanation to the Pāshā about the electoral process for the Chamber of Deputies, the beginning and end of everything for the French people. Here is what he had to say:

Frenchman In every subdivision of every town and city in France there's a committee made up of the local chief, a delegate selected by the mayor, and another delegate selected by the town council. They're responsible for putting together the electoral roll containing the names of people who have the right to vote listed in alphabetical order. The requirements for such a right are that the man must be French, must be over twenty years old, and must have had a domicile in the town and lived there for at least six months. Civil servants and religious personnel do not have to meet the six months' residency requirement in the town. Military people are not permitted to vote while they are in service in accordance with the principle that requires the army to stay out of politics and not to involve itself in party differences.

48.2 Among factors that will prevent anyone having the right to vote are:

1) all bodily impairments, and other impairments that compromise walking and deprive citizens of their civil and political rights;

2) court verdicts that interdict the right of participation in elections;
3) prison terms imposed on compassionate grounds;
4) three-month prison terms on grounds of commercial fraud;
5) court verdicts for theft, perfidy, treason, embezzlement, and breach of public morality;
6) offences involving breaches of public decency, matters of religion, and assaults on ownership principles and social rights;
7) three-month prison terms for committing fraud on matters relating to elections and ballot rigging;
8) decisions made concerning the justifiable dismissal of public works officials, court clerks, and administrators;
9) regulations applying to beggars and vagrants;
10) a three-month sentence for anyone convicted of destroying public records, agricultural machinery, uprooting trees, or poisoning horses, cattle, or fish;
11) verdicts issued against anyone who kills a member of the Chamber as a means of avoiding military service;
12) decisions made regarding legal competence;
13) decisions made regarding bankruptcy.

The above-mentioned committee meets at the end of March every year. It then places on the electoral list anyone whose name has not come up in the previous year and omits the names of any people who are prevented because of one of the above-mentioned conditions. The list is then published and posted on the wall of the local town hall. When the time comes for the election itself, the president of the republic issues instructions for the people to participate in the election, and a committee is appointed to supervise the process. The people then vote for their favored candidates by secret ballot, and the person who wins the majority of votes becomes a member of the Chamber of Deputies. The first item of business those newly elected members have to undertake is to consider protests against anyone accused of fraud or corruption during the electoral process. 48.3

A vote is taken on every case, resulting either in the validation of his election or its annulment, in which case someone has to be selected to replace him.

PĀSHĀ Do the self-nominated candidates for election in this fashion come from any particular class of intellectuals and *penseurs*, people who have had experience in matters of administration and the like, things that will qualify them to pass laws and conduct policy for this great nation whose repute is so widespread?

48.4 FRENCHMAN When it comes to administering government affairs, we make no such class distinction, nor do we favor one sector over another. When it concerns the conduct of government business, we all have our own opinions and ways of doing things. We're all qualified to direct government affairs and exert authority over the millions of French citizens. It doesn't matter whether the person elected by the people is a nobleman or someone from the lower classes. In fact, a number of members of the Chamber of Deputies will often come from industry and the commercial classes rather than from the aristocracy. Many of them come from the more plebeian trades: hairdressers, shoe repairers, perfumiers, and the like.

PĀSHĀ Well then, tell me the kind of qualities for which members are elected. How do people choose one such person over another?

48.5 FRENCHMAN In France it's the custom for each group to form a political party that is directed by ambitious men who aspire to either fame or wealth by working in the political arena. Each party has a number of newspapers behind it, along with a cluster of public speakers who regale the populace with talk of their goals and ambitions, hold lavish receptions to get funds that they can spend in a variety of ways at election time and persuade voters to cast their ballots in favor of their candidates. For instance, they will distribute various kinds of pamphlets to people in an attempt to win them over. They also give bribes to influential people in order to bring them over to their point of view, and will spend money on the populace in general for the costs of wine that is served at their receptions and gatherings. Every candidate prepares a statement in which he outlines the agenda that he intends to follow in serving the people if they elect him to serve as their representative. If people need to have a new canal built, for example, to have their taxes lowered, or to have some particular service performed, the candidate will swear in his statement only to return to them from the Chamber of Deputies with their desires fulfilled and their needs answered.

Members spend the majority of their time and energy attacking 48.6
each other according to their different viewpoints and as part of this party affiliation. For example, you'll see someone who belongs to a party that advocates the return of the monarchy to France plastering walls all over the place with scurrilous attacks on any members nominated by another party that wants to bring back the Empire. A member who supports the Republican Party will attack both those other members—indeed the Republican Party is subdivided into a number of different groups, each of which attacks the other. These attacks are not concerned purely with public affairs, but involve private ones as well—people's personal lifestyles and households secrets. At election time, France turns into a battlefield for slanderous attacks and even fights. All sorts of scandal and misconduct are described, and everyone starts yelling and screaming. The whole thing now becomes totally chaotic and reckless, to such a degree that even the most sage of people lose their sense of perspective, and all notion of proportion is lost. Not only that, but during election season everyone in public positions, from ministers to local policemen, get together and help each other put pressure on voters—whether by incitement or threats—to vote for those candidates who represent the governing party and fly its flag. The other parties also get together and start blackening the government's reputation, denigrating the actions of the people who work there, and broadcasting their various faults and peccadilloes, not to mention the equally substantial number of taunts and slanders that they hurl at each other.

48.7 Pāshā I am astonished by this weird form of government that you describe, one that gives the general populace authority over the aristocracy. How can these members of the Chamber of Deputies manage to effectuate all the things that they promise people, when there are all these different parties, ideas, and goals, and there is so much dissension and strife among the elected members?

Frenchman Once the candidate has been elected, he goes to great lengths to break his promises and annul the virtual contract he made with the people, to the same extent in fact as he initially made exaggerated promises to do what the people wanted and on the basis of which they voted for him. Now that he is sitting on his member's chair in the Chamber of Deputies, he can treat their desires and interests with as much contempt as was demanded by the toadying behavior he adopted in order to win their votes in the first place. As long as he occupies his position, his only interest and concern is to intercede with his governmental bosses and plead for some influence with them in return for a few favors that may earn him some reward and profit. That is, of course, to assume that he doesn't instead say absolutely nothing and make do with collecting his yearly salary.

Pāshā How much does a member of the Chamber of Deputies earn each year?

48.8 Frenchman The French people pay each member of the Chamber of Deputies nine thousand francs a year. The president of the republic gets seventy-two thousand, and he lives with his family in the Council Palace. There are people in the lowly professions who work all year but don't make even a quarter of that amount.

Pāshā As far as I can see, this chamber and its members are a cross between an asylum and a factory. It can certainly not be a place for lawmaking or a seat of authority as long as the process of earning a living by it involves means that are so contradictory to probity and decent behavior, and clearly in breach of all notions of ethics and nobility of character. And that's not even to mention that the majority in it belong to the merchant class and the general populace.

FRENCHMAN The electoral process for the Senate only differs from that of the Chamber of Deputies in that people eligible for election come from a particular class. In each *département* of the country, the members of the Chamber of Deputies get together with the local council and select the person to serve in the Senate.

Now that I have finished explaining to you the way people are elected to the two houses and how our government functions, I think the time has now come to show you what you've heard about and let you see it for yourselves. Tomorrow I propose to take you all to the Chamber of Deputies to attend one of its sessions. Then you will be able to observe precisely how its two sides, investigation and debate, function.

ʿĪsā ibn Hishām said: We all agreed to his plan and thanked him for 48.9
all his efforts.[305]

Notes

1 This article and the three that follow it (0.2–0.4) are narrated by ʿĪsā ibn Hishām, a name that Muḥammad al-Muwayliḥī revived from the famous collection of picaresque narratives—*maqāmāt*—composed in the tenth century by Badīʿ al-Zamān al-Hamadhānī (d. 398/1007). They were all published in the al-Muwayliḥī newspaper *Miṣbāḥ al-sharq* in the weeks immediately before their author began to publish the lengthy series of articles entitled *Fatrah min al-Zaman* that, in edited form, was later to become the book *Ḥadīth ʿĪsā ibn Hishām* (1907). In such a context, two things are significant: firstly, that these four articles would appear to constitute some kind of "dry run" for the series that is to follow; and secondly, that these initial articles address the extremely topical subject of the war in the Sudan in 1898, something however that Muḥammad al-Muwayliḥī completely excluded from the eventual text of *Ḥadīth ʿĪsā ibn Hishām.*

2 In these articles and all those to follow, Muḥammad al-Muwayliḥī replicates the prosimetric tradition of the pre-modern *maqāmah* genre by regularly inserting lines of poetry into his narrative. While he will often provide the name of the poet whom he is citing, sometimes he will not do so. For this edition, every effort has been made to identify the original authors of the poetry, but given the paucity of referential resources on the topic, that has sometimes proved impossible. The poet in this case is Muḥammad ibn Wuhayb (a Shiʿi poet from Basra, dates unknown); see Abū l-Faraj al-Iṣfahānī, *Kitāb al-Aghānī*, 75.

3 The title "Sirdar" was given to the commanding officer of the British armed forces in Egypt. In 1898 it was Lord Kitchener, and he was succeeded in 1898 by Sir Reginald Wingate.

4 Latin for "I came, I saw, I conquered."

5 The Arabic text here invokes the Abjad numerical system, whereby the symbols of the Arabic alphabet are assigned numerical value. By adding up the values of the symbols in this line of poetry, the number 1316 is reached.

6 This refers to Parliamentary Papers. See e.g., Marlowe, *Cromer in Egypt*, 322.

7 These lines by an unknown poet are quoted anonymously in, among other sources, *al-Maḥāsin wa-l-aḍdād* by (ps.-[?]al-Jāḥiẓ, 118) and in *'Uyūn al-akhbār* (Ibn Qutaybah, 1:164).

8 The translation attempts to replicate the rhyming patterns of the original Arabic.

9 The minister's deficient knowledge of geography is illustrated here by his reference to the old Aswān Dam constructed in 1902. Fashoda, the site of a famous confrontation of British and French forces in 1898, is far to the South in Central Sudan.

10 In the Arabic text, al-Muwayliḥī inserts a parenthesis explaining that the surname of the French commander Jean-Baptiste Marchand means "merchant" in French.

11 Al-Muwayliḥī includes in the Arabic text a transliteration into Arabic of the French phrase, "marchand d'esclaves" (slave trader) before providing a translation.

12 Here again al-Muwayliḥī is playing on the minister's ignorance by punning on the surname of the French commander, Le Marquis Christian de Bonchamps—"bonchamps" meaning "good fields."

13 Yet again, al-Muwayliḥī is citing the basic meanings of these three proper names.

14 Since the Arabic word *fakhr* means "pride," there's a pun here.

15 This end structure mocks the Ottoman convention of bringing panegyrics to closure.

16 Abū Tammām, *Dīwān Abī Tammām*, 4:102.

17 Al-Muwayliḥī appears to have his particulars confused here. It is the Umayyad Caliph Yazīd who enters Damascus on a donkey. Furthermore, there is no caliph named "Abū Sufyān ibn Hishām." However, this might be a reference to the Umayyad Caliph Marwān II (r. 127–32/744–50) who was nicknamed *al-ḥimār* ("the donkey"), in which case his opponent in civil war was Sulaymān ibn Hishām.

18 From a line of poetry by Abū Nuwās. See *Dīwān*, ed. Ewald Wagner, 3:2–7.

19 Al-Maʿarrī, *Siqṭ al-zand* (1869), 1:209; (1948), 974.

20 Ibid. (1869), 2:8; (1948), 3:1021.

21 Al-Maʿarrī, *Al-Luzūmiyyāt*, 1:123.

22 The story is described in the Qur'an: Q Aʿrāf 7:138ff.

23 A well-known proverb. See Aḥmad Taymūr, *Al-Amthāl al-ʿāmmiyyah*, 320.

24 From Q Kahf 18:67–68, the passage in which Moses's encounter with al-Khiḍr is described.

25 This term originally meant "archer," but was also applied during the Ottoman period to military police and embassy guards.

26 Al-Maʿarrī; *Al-Luzūmiyyāt*, 1:416.

27 A line quoted anonymously in *al-Ḥujjāb*, which appears in al-Jāḥiẓ's *Rasāʾil*, 2:50; attributed to an *aʿrābī* in Ibn Ḥamdūn, *Tadhkirah*, 8:204.

28 According to a tradition attributed to the Prophet, "a Qurayshī is worth two men of any other tribe." See W. Montgomery Watt, *Muhammad at Mecca* (London: Oxford University Press, 1953), 153.

29 Moses's words to Al-Khidr: Q Kahf 18:73.

30 The Pāshā's reaction is the result of a pun on the two possible meanings of the Arabic verb *S-B-Q*: "to precede" and "to race," from which come both translations: "precedents" and "racing steeds."

31 There is yet another pun here, this time on the verbal root *Sh-H-D*. The Pāshā interprets "shahādah" (the word ʿĪsā uses for "certificate") to mean "martyrdom." In pre-modern times, "shahādah" meant "martyrdom," but in modern times, as ʿĪsā later explains, it has also come to be used to mean "certificate" or "degree."

32 *ʿUmdah*: the provincial village headman, a figure who is later to become a major character in this sequence of episodes.

33 While the original episode continues without a break here, this point marks the beginning of a new chapter in the text of *Ḥadīth ʿĪsā ibn Hishām*. The title "Al-Muḥāmī al-ahlī" ("The People's Court Lawyer") was added to the third edition of the book (1923).

34 Al-Maʿarrī, *Al-Luzūmiyyāt*, 1:224.

35 Lines of poetry by al-Nābighah al-Dhubyānī, from his poem *A-min āli Mayyata rāʾiḥun aw mughtadī*. See e.g., Ahlwardt, *The Diwans of the Six Ancient Arabic Poets*, 10.

36 *Humāyūn*: the Persian word meaning "empire," and with the adjectival ending here, "imperial" (Ottoman).

37 A reference to the al-Muwayliḥī newspaper in which these episodes were being published.

38 Joseph's words in Q Yūsuf 12:33.

39 A line of poetry by Umayya ibn Abī l-Ṣalt. See Al-Jāḥiẓ, *Kitāb al-Ḥayawān*, 49.

40 Al-Maʿarrī; *Al-Luzūmiyyāt*, 2:403.

41 A line of poetry allegedly by a poet named ʿAbd Allāh ibn al-Mubārak ibn Wāḍiḥ (d. 181/797), a merchant, traveler, *mujāhid*, and *muḥaddith*, from Khurāsān.

42 Q Raʿd 13:17.

43 Q Ḥijr 15:74 and Hūd 11:82.

44 From the Q Zukhruf 43:32.

45 Al-Maʿarrī, *Siqṭ al-Zand* (1869), 203; (1948), 3:955.

46 Abū Tammām, *Dīwān Abī Tammām*, 1:161.

47 A line of poetry by al-Mutanabbī (*Dīwān*, 636); the standard version is *fa-mā l-ḥadāthatu min ḥilmin . . . qad yūjadu l-ḥilmu . . . .*

48 A line of poetry by al-Ḥuṭayʾah; cited in *Kitāb Sībawayh*, 1:443.

49 Al-Mutanabbī, *Dīwān* (Beirut: 1882), 245.

50 Al-Buḥturī, *Dīwān*, 3:1980. The *Dīwān* reads *muẓlimu* instead of *aqtamu*.

51 There is some disagreement over the authorship of these lines. They are attributed to the caliph al-Muʿtamid in al-Shābushtī, *Diyārāt*, ed.

ʿAwwād (101); to "al-ʿAbbās" in al-Ḥuṣrī, *Zahr al-ādāb* (repr. Beirut: 1972), 827, meaning Ibn al-Muʿtazz; the lines are in his *Dīwān*, ed. Muḥammad Badīʿ Sharīf, 2:375. But quoting the lines in his *Jamʿ al-jawāhir*, ed. al-Bijāwī (Beirut: 1987), 157, al-Ḥuṣrī says: *qad qāla al-Muʿtamid . . . aw qīla ʿalā lisāni-hi.*

52 No source for this line of poetry has been identified.

53 This point marks the beginning of a new chapter in *Ḥadīth ʿĪsā ibn Hishām*: "Maḥkamat al-Istiʾnāf" ("The Court of Appeal").

54 This quarter is now downtown Cairo, with its broad streets and squares, as opposed to the older Fatimid city.

55 Al-Mutanabbī, *Dīwān* (1898), 281.

56 Ibid., 138.

57 A line of poetry by Abū Muḥammad al-Khāzin (poet of Isfahan and librarian to al-Ṣāḥib ibn ʿAbbād), in al-Thaʿālibī's *Yatīmah* (Cairo: 1947), 3:191.

58 In *Ḥadīth ʿĪsā ibn Hishām* this episode still forms part of the "Court of Appeal" chapter.

59 Al-Mutanabbī, *Dīwān* (1898), 381.

60 A reference to an injunction in the Q Tawbah 9:58ff.

61 These lines are attributed to "an Arab from the Asad tribe": see Al-Jāḥiẓ, *Kitāb al-Ḥayawān*, 3:86.

62 Line of poetry by Abū Firās al-Ḥamdānī, *Dīwān* (Leiden: 1895), 151.

63 This point marks the beginning of a new chapter in *Ḥadīth ʿĪsā ibn Hishām*: "Al-Waqf" ("The Endowment").

64 ʿAzzah's lover was the famous poet, Bashshār ibn Burd, while Nawār's lover (and husband) was the poet, al-Farazdaq. The line itself comes from *Dīwān Abī Tammām* (1905), 25; (1951–65), 164.

65 A line of poetry by Abū Tammām, *Dīwān Abī Tammām* (1905), 352; (1952–65), 4:42.

66 A famous line of poetry by al-Maʿarrī; see *Al-Luzūmiyyāt*, 63.

67 This point marks the beginning of a new chapter in *Ḥadīth ʿĪsā ibn Hishām*: "Abnāʾ al-kubarāʾ" ("Sons of Great Men").

68 These names all refer to consonants in the Arabic alphabet that are often mispronounced by non-native speakers.

69 *Bashibozuk* is a Turkish word used to describe an irregular soldier, a civilian serving in the military. In this context it obviously conveys pejorative significance.

70 This point marks the beginning of a new chapter in *Ḥadīth ʿĪsā ibn Hishām*: "Kubarāʾ min al-ʿAṣr al-māḍī" ("Great Men of the Past").

71 Al-Maʿarrī, *Al-Luzūmiyyāt*, 2:258.

72 On the night when the Prophet Muḥammad left Mecca in secret and traveled to Medina, his cousin ʿAlī stayed behind in Mecca and only traveled to Medina three days later.

73 This latter passage, describing Rāghib Pāshā's negative experiences with the Khedive Ismāʿīl, was omitted from the text of the fourth edition of *Ḥadīth ʿĪsā ibn Hishām*.

74 *Fulūs* means "cash," and *kurbāj* means "whip."

75 The entire section of this speech describing Muḥammad ʿAlī's conversations with the would-be governor of the Sudan and with the military reserve officers was omitted from the text of the fourth edition.

76 A line of poetry by Ibn Hāniʾ al-Andalusī, *Dīwān* (Dār Ṣādir), 131; in a *madīḥ* beginning *Taqūlu Banū l-ʿAbbāsi: hal futiḥat Miṣru? Fa-qul li-Banī l-ʿAbbāsi: qad quḍiya l-amrū.*

77 The function of the *muzawwir* was to show visitors round the tomb of the Prophet in Medina. Burckhardt, *Travels in Arabia*, 2:138; Burton, *Personal Narrative of a Pilgrimage*, 1:305.

78 The term *Ghawth*, meaning "aid," or "refuge," refers to the highest ranking saint (*walī*) in Islamic mysticism.

79 Q Zalzalah 99:7.

80 Al-Maʿarrī, *Al-Luzūmiyyāt*, 285.

81 "Abū Turāb" is ʿAlī ibn Abī Ṭālib's *kunyah*, or name theoretically referring to the bearer's firstborn. In this case, it is a name allegedly given to ʿAlī by the Prophet.

82 This point marks the beginning of a new chapter in *Ḥadīth ʿĪsā ibn Hishām*: "Al-Muḥāmī al-Sharʿī" ("The Shariah Court Lawyer").

83 In "Ḥadīth ʿĪsā ibn Hishām," 1018, Zakī Mubārak writes: "The division between wearers of the turban and tarboosh in al-Muwayliḥī's time was an object of seething dissension. The tarboosh wearers [those

civil servants who had often received a modern and/or European education] considered themselves as the vanguard of the modern generation, while the turban wearers [the more traditionally minded shaykhs] regarded themselves as the guardians of the true religion."

84 Al-Maʿarrī, *Al-Luzūmiyyāt*, 81.

85 Al-Maʿarrī, *Al-Luzūmiyyāt*, 1:71.

86 Q Anʿām 6:53.

87 Lines attributed to Suwayd ibn al-Ṣāmit; see al-Maʿarrī, *The Epistle of Forgiveness* (New York: NYUP, 2013), 71.

88 The second hemistich is found in a line by Abū l-Walīd al-Ḥimyarī, see his *al-Badīʿ fī waṣf al-rabīʿ*, ed. Pérès, 109, beginning *talawwunan wa-manẓaran*. Perhaps a misquotation by al-Muwayliḥī, or a coincidence.

89 This point marks the beginning of a new chapter in *Ḥadīth ʿĪsā ibn Hishām*: "Al-Daftarkhānah al-Sharʿiyyah" ("The Records Office of the Shariah Court"). The office was situated below the main entrance to the Citadel. The approach to the building is described in detail in J. Deny's *Sommaire des archives turques du Caire*, 19.

90 Both al-Muwayliḥīs were apparently members of the Freemasons lodge run by Jamāl al-dīn al-Afghānī; Landau, *Parliaments and Parties in Egypt*, 96.

91 Al-Maʿarrī, *Siqṭ al-Zand* (1869), 61; (1948), 1:263.

92 Abū Tammām, *Dīwān Abī Tammām*, 4:311.

93 Lines of poetry by Ibn Hāniʾ al-Andalusī; see al-Rikābī, *Fī l-Adab al-Andalusī*, 152.

94 *Dhimmīs*: non-Muslim inhabitants of Islamic countries, so called because the Islamic community offered them a *dhimmah* (contract of hospitality and protection) provided that they acknowledged the dominance of Islam and paid the poll tax (*jizyah*).

95 The Clerk now proceeds to list all the locations in Cairo where these particular courts were to be found. Many of them still exist, but others have disappeared over time.

96 This point marks the beginning of a new chapter in *Ḥadīth ʿĪsā ibn Hishām*: "Al-Maḥkamah al-Sharʿiyyah" ("The Shariah Court"). This

system of courts was the topic of a series of articles in *Miṣbāḥ al-sharq*, no. 27, October 20, 1898; and 81ff., November 16, 1899 et seq.

97 This line is often quoted anonymously, but is attributed to Majnūn Laylā by Abū l-Faraj al-Iṣfahānī in *Kitāb al-Aghānī*, 2:93.

98 The names of two palaces, often invoked in Arabic literature as symbols of former worldly glories and authority.

99 The first ʿUmar was the second caliph, succeeding Abū Bakr in 13/634; the second was one of the Umayyad caliphs (r. 98–101/717–20), renowned for his piety and frugality.

100 In Arabic the words representing these concepts have very similar consonantal patterns.

101 Al-Maʿarrī, *Siqṭ al-Zand*, (1869), 2: 223; (1948), 2066.

102 The author here is not only pointing out the inappropriateness of a Shariah Court official taking such inordinate interest in works of this category, but also parodying the flowery language which was used by Arab writers in order that their books should have titles, the two halves of which rhymed with each other.

103 No source for this line of poetry has been identified.

104 A line of poetry by Abū Tammām, *Dīwān Abī Tammām* (1905), 30; (1951), 186. I am grateful to Professor Geert Jan van Gelder for his assistance in interpreting this (one might say, typically) complex line by this poet.

105 A line of poetry by Ibn Abī ʿUyaynah; see Ibn ʿAbd Rabbihi, *Al-ʿIqd al-farīd*, 5:421.

106 Al-Buḥturī, *Dīwān*, 2:22.

107 Al-Buḥturī, *Dīwān*, 1:36.

108 Al-Maʿarrī, *Siqṭ al-Zand* (1869), 2:51; (1948), 3:1240.

109 A line of poetry attributed to Ḥamdah Bint Ziyād al-Mu'addib, a Spanish poetess; see al-Rikābī, *Fī l-Adab al-Andalusī*, 99.

110 Literally: "I am a well-known person and a climber of tortuous ways." It is part of a line of poetry by Suhaym ibn Wahb al-Riyāḥī, see "Min Shawārid al-Shawāhid," *Al-Risālah* no. 749 (1947): 1263.

111 This entire article was completely rewritten by the author for publication in the book, *Ḥadīth ʿĪsā ibn Hishām*. In the book's third

edition, the title "Al-Ṭibb wa-l-Aṭibbā'" ("Medicine and Doctors") is added.

112 While this original episode was published in 1898, Al-Muwayliḥī was to obtain direct information about this department when he became its director in 1910. There is presumably a direct reflection of his sentiments expressed here in the fact that he resigned his position in 1914.

113 Al-Mutanabbī, *Dīwān* (Beirut: 1882), 341. Most sources read *yakhtarimu* instead of *yakhtariqu.*

114 Apart from the first description in this article (until the end of 16.3), the remainder of the episode is totally omitted from the text of *Ḥadīth 'Īsā ibn Hishām*. Once again, the similarity of its format and topic to those of the initial four articles in this series will be noted. The different chapter in *Ḥadīth 'Īsā ibn Hishām* was entitled "Al-Ṭā'ūn" ("The Plague")—in the third edition and thereafter.

115 These lines of poetry seem to involve a range of possible sources. They are sometimes attributed to al-Sarī al-Raffā'; see Usāmah ibn Munqidh, *al-Badī' fī naqd al-shi'r*, 37, etc. (with *-rabī'i* instead of *-makāni*), but are apparently not found in the *Dīwān*. The second hemistich of the first line is taken from a line by al-Ḥusayn ibn Muṭayr and is often quoted (e.g., in Iṣfahānī, *al-Aghānī*). The second line is attributed to "al-Mu'arrij al-Nasafī" in al-Tha'ālibī, *Khāṣṣ al-khāṣṣ* (Beirut, n.d., 138) where the reading is *wa-wardun* instead of *wa-durrun*. In al-Tha'ālibī's *Man ghāba 'anhu l-muṭrib* (ed. Sha'lān, 30), this line is attributed to al-Mu'awwij al-Raqqī (Abū Bakr Muḥammad ibn al-Ḥasan—reading *wa-durrun*).

116 Lines of poetry by al-Ma'arrī, *al-Luzumiyyat* (a reprint of ed. Amin 'Abd al-'Aziz al-Khanji, Cairo: Maktabat al-Khanji, 1924, vol. I, p. 40).

117 This is a reference back to one of the four early articles above (0.2), published in *Miṣbāḥ al-sharq* (September 22, 1898), 23.

118 The term *qadhf* is used for a slanderous accusation of sexual misconduct against someone. Among the punishments for it is the withdrawal of eligibility to testify in court. I am grateful to Professor Joseph Lowry for this information and for that on Ḥanafī texts on jurisprudence below.

119 Meaning *Al-Durr al-mukhtār*. (See the Glossary for further details.)

120 The Ḥanafī sources cited here are: *Al-Fatāwā al-bazzāziyyah* of Ibn Bazzāz (d. 817/1414) and *Al-Nahr al-fā'iq: sharḥ kanz al-daqā'iq* of ʿUmar Ibn Nujaym (tenth/sixteenth century).

121 The *Kanz* is another source on Ḥanafī jurisprudence by al-Nasafī (d. 710/1310). *Al-Nahr al-fā'iq* a commentary on it (see n. 120).

122 This line of poetry is quoted anonymously in Ibn ʿArabshāh, *ʿAjā'ib al-maqdūr*, where it reads: *yakrahu an yashraba min fiḍḍatin* | *wa-yasriqu al-fiḍḍata in nāla-hā*.

123 The clash between modernists and conservatives at this time was often expressed as being between the tarboosh-wearing class of Western-educated civil servants, and the turban-wearing class of shaykhs and others educated along traditional Islamic lines.

124 Q Muḥammad 47:7.

125 Al-Saʿd here refers to Saʿd al-Dīn al-Taftazānī (d. 791/1389), the author of a commentary on al-Qazwīnī's (d. 739/1338) *Talkhīṣ Miftāḥ al-ʿulūm*, itself an abridgement of the famous and much cited work on rhetoric by al-Sakkākī (d. 626/1229) entitled *Miftāḥ al-ʿulūm*. The work by al-Anbābī (d. 1896), twice rector of al-Azhar in the nineteenth century, is a further commentary on al-Qazwīnī's abridgement.

126 Q Baqarah 2:195.

127 Q Nisā' 4:59.

128 Q Kahf 18:29; Baqarah 2:256; Qaṣaṣ 28:56; Yūnus 10:108; Isrā' 17:84.

129 Q Yūsuf 12:68.

130 Q Āl ʿImrān 3:27.

131 Al-Mutanabbī, *Dīwān* (1898), 109.

132 Q Yūnus 10:12.

133 Al-Mutanabbī, *Dīwān* (1898), 366.

134 Al-Maʿarrī, *Siqṭ al-Zand* (1869), 1:197; (1948), 2:922.

135 A line of poetry attributed to "an Omani"; see al-Jāḥiẓ, *Kitāb al-Ḥayawān*, 6:219.

136 This description of the plague epidemic in 1791 (with a few minor omissions) is an extract from ʿAbd al-Raḥmān al-Jabartī's account in his *ʿAjā'ib al-āthār fī al-tarājim wa-al-akhbār* (1906), 203; (1965), 4:185.

137 A reference to the *mawāqif*, the places in which all of mankind will have to stand on the Day of Judgment before they are summoned to appear before God in order to hear His judgment on the basis of their deeds on earth.

138 For Muʿallim Ghālī, secretary of Muhammad ʿAlī, see *Mashāhīr al-sharq* by Jurjī Zaydān [*Tarājim mashāhir al-sharq fī l-qarn al-tāsiʿ ʿashar* in the bibliography] (1910–11), 1:215ff.

139 Another quotation from ʿAbd al-Raḥmān al-Jabartī's account: *ʿAjāʾib al-āthār fī al-tarājim wa-al-akhbār* (1906), 4:187; (1965), 7:218ff.

140 A line of poetry by Abū Nuwās; see *Dīwān Abī Nuwās* (Cairo: 1898), 235.

141 Q Anfāl 8:60.

142 For a reference to this actual incident, see Muḥammad ʿUmar, *Ḥāḍir al-Miṣriyyīn aw sirr taʾakhkhurihim*, 174.

143 *Akalūnī al-barāghīth* ("fleas have eaten me") is cited in works of Arabic grammar as an example of mistaken usage.

144 The bulk of this episode of *Fatrah min al-Zaman* was not included in the text of *Ḥadīth ʿĪsā ibn Hishām*. The initial description was also used in a later chapter of the book, "Qaṣr al-Gīzah wa-al-mathaf" ("The Giza Palace and the Museum").

145 This is one of several versions of a line by Abū Muḥammad ibn Ruzayq al-Kūfī (Iraq, fourth/tenth century), which in al-Thaʿālibī's *Yatīmah* (2:377), is quoted differently. In Ibn Khallikān's *Wafayāt* (ed. ʿAbbās, 4:46), the line is attributed to Asad ibn Ruzayq (with *raʾaytu al-ʿizza wa-nqaraḍā*). In al-Tanūkhī's *Nishwār* (2:221), the second hemistich is *hādhī al-wisādati kāna al-ʿizzu fa-nqaraḍā*. There are yet other variants. Note that *wa-raʾaytu* (as used here by al-Muwayliḥī) is unmetrical.

146 Al-Maʿarrī, *al-Luzūmiyyāt*, 1:50.

147 This is a reference to an actual incident in which the British sent troops to al-Azhar in order to force them to comply with quarantine regulations. The affair and its aftermath were described in detail in *Miṣbāḥ al-sharq*. See also the reference in n. 143 above.

148 Q Naḥl 16:112.

149 Q Naḥl 16:43.

150 A line of poetry attributed to ʿUlayyah bint al-Mahdī in al-Ḥuṣrī in *Zahr al-ādāb* (44), with different rhyme: *wa-lā yuraḍḍī l-qātilā*.

151 Q Ṣāffāt 37:61.

152 This episode of *Fatrah min al-Zaman* and the one that follows it was subsantially reworked for publication in *Ḥadīth ʿĪsā ibn Hishām* as the chapter "Al-ʿUrs" ("The Wedding"). Not only that, but the reworked chapter was placed later in the ordering of events in the narrative.

153 Al-Maʿarrī, *Al-Luzūmiyyāt*, 2:292.

154 Ibn Hāniʾ al-Andalusī, *Dīwān*, 344 (reading *amīlu*).

155 Q Anbiyāʾ 21:63.

156 Q Aḥzāb 33:53.

157 Unlike the previous episode of *Fatrah min al-Zaman* which was not used in the text of *Ḥadīth ʿĪsā ibn Hishām*, this lengthy discussion of the status of singing in Islam is included (albeit in heavily edited form). What is interesting however is that in the book version of the text, the explicator of the history of the topic is not ʿĪsā ibn Hishām, but rather a "Shaykh" whose views on the interpretation of Islamic texts are clearly more in line with the more liberal views of one of al-Muwayliḥī's colleagues and mentors, Muḥammad ʿAbduh.

158 Anṣār: the people who "helped" the Prophet in his community in al-Madinah (as opposed to the Muhājirūn, those who emigrated with him from Mecca).

159 Recited by the young women (*jawārī*) of Mecca upon the arrival of the Prophet; al-Jāḥiẓ, *al-Bayān wa-al-tabyīn* (ed. Hārūn, 4:57). Other sources indicate they recited it on his arrival in Medina.

160 *Kāmil* and *wāfir* are the names of two of the meters noted down by al-Khalīl ibn Aḥmad (d. 175/791), the famous grammarian and prosodist of Basra, as part of his system of prosody. Saḥbān was a famous orator of the pre-Islamic period whose powers gave rise to the expression "more eloquent than Saḥbān." See al-Ziriklī, *Al-Aʿlām*, 3:123.

161 The speech that follows is intended as a parody of the verbiage employed on such occasions.

162 Without the insertion of the word "buffet," the lines of poetry are by Ibn Jad'ān; see Muḥammad ʿAbd al-Munʿim al-Khafājah, *Qiṣṣat al-adab fi l-Ḥijāz fī l-ʿaṣr al-jāhilī* (1958), 491.

163 A line of poetry by Laqīṭ ibn Zurārah (pre-Islamic), see al-Mubarrad, *Kāmil*, ed. Hindāwī, 1:180; also found in a poem by Muḥammad ibn al-Ashʿath, *Aghānī*, 15:60.

164 Al-Maʿarrī: *Siqṭ al-zand* (1869), 1:117; (1948), 2:559.

165 These lines are attributed to a member of the Banū Nashhāl. See Abū Tammām, *Al-Ḥamāsah* (Cairo: Būlāq, 1879), 1:50; airo, 1916, 24. In line 7 of this quotation, the reading *qawl* has been adopted.

166 Al-Maʿarrī, *Siqṭ al-zand* (1869), 40; (1948), 3:1174.

167 Lines by Qays ibn Khatīm; see Abū Tammām, *Al-Ḥamāsah* (Cairo: Būlāq, 1879), 95; (Cairo: 1916), 49.

168 A line of poetry by Ibn al-Rūmī, *Dīwān* 2:806 (where the reading *faqdā* is preferable to the unmetrical *fiqdān*).

169 A line of poetry by Sālim ibn Wābiṣah (d. 125/742); in Abū Tammām's *Ḥamāsah*, see al-Marzūqī, *Sharḥ Dīwān al-Ḥamāsah*, 1143.

170 Al-Mutanabbī, *Dīwān* (1882), 540; (1898), 375.

171 Al-Maʿarrī, *Al-Luzūmiyyāt*, 103.

172 Q Qamar 54:4–5.

173 Al-Maʿarrī, *Siqṭ al-zand* (1869), 1:144; (1948), 2:679ff.

174 This section (22.1–22.19) is one of the episodes/chapters that was omitted from the fourth edition of *Ḥadīth ʿĪsā ibn Hishām* (1927).

175 These initial two sections (22.1 and 22.2) are only to be found in the episodes of *Fatrah min al-Zaman*. The elaborate way in which each of the forthcoming sessions is described was obviously intended to form a vivid contrast with the actual situation that ʿĪsā and the Pāshā encounter in the episodes that now follow.

176 A quotation from a famous poem by Abū Nuwās; see *Dīwān*, ed. Ewald Wagner (1988), 3:2–7.

177 Q Kāfirūn 109:6.

178 A line of poetry quoted anonymously in several sources including al-Qalqashandī, *Ṣubḥ*; according to al-Damirī, *Ḥayāt al-ḥayawān al-kubrā* (Cairo: 1970, 2:90) in a chapter on *ʿanqāʾ mughrib*, often

quoted by al-Qāḍī al-Fāḍil. In *Majānī al-adab* by Luwīs Shaykhū (Beirut: 1885, 6:311), attributed to al-Qāḍī al-Fāḍil himself, possibly incorrectly.

179 For a discussion of this story, see Fedwa Malti-Douglas, *Woman's Body, Woman's Word* (Princeton: Princeton University Press, 1991), 84–110.

180 A reference to a work by Aḥmad ibn ʿAbdallāh al-Bakrī al-Baṣrī (fl. ca. 694/1295).

181 Q Raʿd 13:33.

182 A line of poetry by Abū l-Aswad al-Du'alī, according to ʿAbd al-Qādir al-Baghdādī, *Khizānat al-adab*, ed. Hārūn, 8:567. Anonymously in al-Jāḥiẓ, *Bayān* (4:63) and many other sources. All these sources read *fa-l-qawmu* instead of *fa-l-kullu.*

183 Line of poetry by al-Mutanabbī; see *The Poems of Al-Mutanabbī,* ed. A. J. Arberry (Cambridge: Cambridge University Press, 1967), 53.

184 My translation makes no effort to eradicate the complicated and verbose style of the original.

185 Al-Maʿarrī, *Al-Luzūmiyyāt*, 1:95.

186 Q Ḍuḥā 93:11.

187 Q Yūsuf 12:64.

188 This is a hadith of the Prophet Muḥammad. It is found in the two most famous collections, the *Ṣaḥīḥ* of al-Bukhari (d. 256/870) and Muslim ibn al-Ḥajjāj (d. 261/875).

189 Q Qaṣaṣ 28:56.

190 Q Āl ʿImrān 3:173.

191 The segment of this paragraph beginning with the words "nor would we be suffering"—with its reference to the British occupying forces (albeit without specifically mentioning them by name)—was omitted from the text of the fourth edition of *Ḥadīth ʿĪsā ibn Hishām.*

192 *Mustashār* refers to the British counselors who were attached to Egyptian ministries and whose function was to "advise" the minister on policy decisions.

193 Once again, the passage from "the boss gets annoyed" to the end of the paragraph was omitted from the text of the fourth edition.

194 Lines of poetry by Imru' al-Qays; see *Dīwān*, ed. Wilhelm Ahlwardt (London: Trubner, 1870), 154.

195 Al-Maʿarrī, *Al-Luzūmiyyāt*, 1:326. Qanbar is described in a footnote in this edition as ʿAlī's *mawlā*.

196 Lines 98 and 96 (in that order) of a long poem by Ibn al-Rūmī, *Dīwān*, i:70–71.

197 Lines of poetry by ʿUbayd Allāh ibn ʿAbd Allāh ibn Ṭāhir (d. 300/913); see Ibn Khallikān, *Wafayāt*, 3:121. Anonymously in al-Khālidiyyān, *al-Ashbāh wa-l-naẓā'ir* (Cairo, 1958–65), 1:101.

198 Zayd and ʿAmr are two names commonly used by Arab grammarians to illustrate syntactic usages in the language.

199 This entire chapter (25.1–25.14) was omitted from the fourth edition (1927).

200 Al-Maʿarrī, *Al-Luzūmiyyāt*, 1:65.

201 This point marks the beginning of a new chapter in *Ḥadīth ʿĪsā ibn Hishām*: the title "Al-ʿUmdah fī l-ḥadīqah" ("The ʿUmdah in the Gardens") was added to the text of the third edition of the book (1923).

202 A typically gnomic line of poetry by al-Mutanabbī, *Dīwān*, 197 (with *tatabayyanu*).

203 The book edition of *Ḥadīth ʿĪsā ibn Hishām* identifies the poet as Ḥabīb ibn ʿAws, i.e. Abū Tammām. See his *Dīwān Abī Tammām*, 198. The text there has *bikr* instead of *arḍ*. The Cairo 1951–65 edition has *ruʿā'* instead of *arḍ*.

204 The first hemistich is by al-Mutanabbī (*Dīwān*, 771), where it is the second hemistich of a line beginning *fa-bātat fawqahunna bilā ṣiḥābin*.

205 This is a near-verbatim quotation from Q Raḥmān 55:27.

206 No source for this line of poetry has been identified.

207 *ʿUmdah*: a provincial village headman.

208 Q Āl ʿImrān 3:173.

209 This point marks the beginning of a new chapter in *Ḥadīth ʿĪsā ibn Hishām*: the title "Al-ʿUmdah fī al-mujtamaʿ" ("The ʿUmdah in the Meeting Hall") was added to the text of the third edition of the book (1923).

210 The image of the sandgrouse (*qaṭā*) is frequently encountered in the depictions of the desert contexts of pre-Islamic poetry.

211 A line of poetry by Shihāb al-dīn Aḥmad al-Fayyūmī (d. 917/1511), in al-Shihāb al-Khafājī, *Rayḥānat al-alibbā'*. The first hemistich is also found anonymously in Ibn Dāwūd's *Zahrah*, ed. al-Sāmarrā'ī, 717.

212 The reference here is to the original Cairo Opera House, constructed during the reign of the Khedive Ismā'īl and dedicated in November 1869. Verdi had been commissioned to compose *Aida* for the occasion but it was not finished; *Rigoletto* was performed instead. The building was destroyed by fire in 1971.

213 Al-Buḥturī, *Dīwān*, 2:1160 (from his famous *qaṣīdah* on Īwān Kisrā).

214 The topic of the Stock Market (Bourse) was a sensitive one for the al-Muwayliḥī family, in that Muḥammad's father, Ibrāhīm, lost the entire family fortune in speculation and was only rescued through the generosity of the Khedive Ismā'īl. It is probably for that reason that Ibrāhīm al-Muwayliḥī makes the risks of the Stock Exchange a major theme of his companion piece to *Fatrah min al-Zaman*, *Mir'āt al-'Ālam* (later known as *Ḥadīth Mūsā ibn 'Iṣām* as an echo of the title of his son's work in book form).

215 Al-Arrajānī, *Dīwān*, ed. Muḥammad Qāsim Muṣṭafā, 1:32.

216 This point marks the beginning of a new chapter in *Ḥadīth 'Īsā ibn Hishām*: the title "Al-'Umdah fī l-maṭ'am" ("The 'Umdah in the Restaurant") was added to the text of the third edition of the book (1923).

217 Al-Ma'arrī, *al-Luzūmiyyāt*, 1:105.

218 Q Baqarah 2:30.

219 Al-Ma'arrī, *Saqṭ al-zand* (1869), 2:7; (1948), 3:1012.

220 Q Qalam 68:10–13.

221 Al-Ma'arrī, *al-Luzūmiyyāt*, 63.

222 The name of the street running from 'Atabah Square to al-Azhar Mosque.

223 This point marks the beginning of a new chapter in *Ḥadīth 'Īsā ibn Hishām*: the title "Al-'Umdah fī l-ḥān" ("The 'Umdah in the Tavern") was added to the text of the third edition of the book (1923).

224 Middle Eastern tradition includes a number of narratives related to King Solomon and the jinn. The relationship is cited in the text of the Qur'an, Q Naml 27:17 and Saba' 34:4. The tale "Madīnat al-nuḥās" ("The City of Brass") in *A Thousand and One Nights* is an elaborate morality tale centered around a quest for the bottles in which Solomon is alleged to have imprisoned the jinn.

225 In *Ḥadīth ʿĪsā ibn Hishām,* the name "Euclas" is replaced by "someone erecting hovels in a village."

226 Q Aʿrāf 7:116.

227 The joke involves using both of the sibilant "s" sounds in Arabic: with "ṣ" the meaning is "to accompany"; with "s," "to drag."

228 A feddan is a measure of area commonly used in Egypt, slightly larger than an acre.

229 This point marks the beginning of a new chapter in *Ḥadīth ʿĪsā ibn Hishām*: the title "Al-ʿUmdah fī l-marqaṣ" ("The ʿUmdah in the Dance Hall") was added to the text of the third edition of the book (1923). This chapter consists of three episodes from al-Muwayliḥī's *Fatrah min al-zaman, Miṣbāḥ al-sharq* 90, 91, and 92.

230 In pre-modern Arabic poetry, the epithet "Mashrafī" by itself was sufficient to refer to the very finest of swords.

231 Al-Maʿarrī, *al-Luzūmiyyāt*, 1:188.

232 Ibid., 1:165–166.

233 Lines of poetry cited anonymously (*qāla ākhar*) in Abū Tammām's *Ḥamāsah*; see al-Marzūqī, *Sharḥ Dīwān al-Ḥamāsah*, 1238 (beginning *wa-kunta matā arsalta*). Also attributed to a girl (*jāriyah*) in Ibn Qutaybah, *ʿUyūn al-akhbār*, 4:22.

234 Al-Maʿarrī, *al-Luzūmiyyāt*, 1:117.

235 A line of poetry by al-Khalīʿ al-Shāmī Abū ʿAbd Allāh Muḥammad ibn Abī l-Ghamr Aḥmad, in al-Thaʿālibī's *Yatīmah*, 1:271.

236 Al-Maʿarrī, *Saqṭ al-Zand* (1957), 286.

237 This point marks the beginning of a new chapter in *Ḥadīth ʿĪsā ibn Hishām*: the title "Al-ʿUmdah fī l-rahn" ("The ʿUmdah's Property in Pawn") was added to the text of the third edition of the book (1923). Since this episode follows the previous one after a gap of some three

months, it begins with a summary of the previous "Dance Hall" episodes.

238 This point marks the beginning of a new chapter in *Ḥadīth ʿĪsā ibn Hishām*: the title "Al-ʿUmdah fī l-ahrām" ("The ʿUmdah at the Pyramids") was added to the text of the third edition of the book (1923).

239 The reference is to Napoleon (whose name is included in the book versions of the text). The reference is to the Battle of the Pyramids fought in July, 1798.

240 An allusion to Q Qāriʿah 101:5, in which the Day of Judgment is depicted: «The mountains will be like carded wool»; also to Furqān 25:23, in which God will turn wrongdoers into «scattered dust.»

241 Parts of this account are to be found in al-Kisāʾī's *Qiṣaṣ al-Anbiyāʾ*, 233ff., and in al-Thaʿālibī's *Kitāb Qiṣaṣ al-anbiyāʾ*, 151ff.

242 This point marks the beginning of a new chapter in *Ḥadīth ʿĪsā ibn Hishām*: the title "Qaṣr al-gīzah wa-l-mat̤ḥaf" ("The Giza Palace and the Museum") was added to the text of the third edition of the book (1923). In the book edition, the Father/Son discussion appears first, followed by the dialogue between Pāshā and Friend.

243 Al-Maʿarrī, *Saqṭ al-zand* (1869), 2:198; (1948), 1987.

244 "Qaṣr al-Nīl" refers to the current Egyptian Museum on Taḥrīr Square in central Cairo.

245 Not coincidentally, the Amīriyyah Press was to be the publisher of the first edition of *Ḥadīth ʿĪsā ibn Hishām*.

246 A reference to *maysir*, the traditional game of chance in which arrows were used as lots.

247 The first book edition of *Ḥadīth ʿĪsā ibn Hishām* also includes the second half of this line: "Once we are gone, look to these relics."

248 Q Kahf 18:5.

249 Q Shuʿarāʾ 26:86.

250 This point marks the beginning of a new chapter in *Ḥadīth ʿĪsā ibn Hishām*: the title "Al-ʿUmdah fī l-malhā" ("The ʿUmdah at the Theater") was added to the text of the third edition of the book (1923).

251 The author is punning here on the dual meaning of the Arabic word *ghazālah*, both "a gazelle" and "the sun's disk."

252 Lines of poetry by Abū Bakr Muḥammad al-Khālidī (d. ca. 380/990) in al-Thaʿālibī's *Yatīmah*, 2:190.

253 This point marks the beginning of a new chapter in *Ḥadīth ʿĪsā ibn Hishām*: the title "Al-Madaniyyah al-gharbiyyah" ("Western Civilization") was added to the text of the third edition of the book (1923). This original version is considerably longer than the one now found in the book versions, no doubt because the author found it necessary to describe the Exposition Universelle in Paris for his Egyptian newspaper readers.

254 ʿUkāẓ, a town a short distance from Mecca, was the site of an annual fair in pre-Islamic times, famous, among other things, for its competitions in poetry.

255 This point marks the beginning of *al-Riḥlah al-thāniyah* (*The Second Journey*), referring to the trip that took the author to France following "The First Journey" around Cairo and Egypt. Chapter titles were added when these episodes were included in the text of *Ḥadīth ʿĪsā ibn Hishām* for the first time (in the fourth edition, 1927). This episode is entitled "Bārīs" ("Paris").

256 This title occurs in the original newspaper article.

257 Al-Maʿarrī, *Saqṭ al-zand*, 48.

258 Abū Tammām, *Dīwān Abī Tammām*, 3:266 (where the text reads *fī sāʿatin*).

259 A line of poetry attributed to Abū Tammām, see Muḥsīn al-ʿĀmilī, *Aʿyān al-shīʿah*, 4:531.

260 Al-Mutanabbī, *Dīwān*, 316.

261 This line is one of three sung by a girl to the Caliph al-Maʾmūn. See Ibn ʿAbd Rabbih, *al-ʿIqd al-Farīd*, 6:210; and al-Masʿūdī, *Murūj al-dhahab*, 4:307. Quoted by (and composed by?) Abū l-Faḍl Aḥmad ibn Abī Ṭāhir or al-Faḍl ibn Abī Ṭāhir in Ibn Dāwūd's *Zahrah*, 153.

262 In addition to the Western model of the ideal society offered by Plato, *al-Madīnah al-fāḍilah* is one of the principal works of the philosopher al-Fārābī (d. 339/950).

263 Ibn Hāniʾ al-Andalusī, *Dīwān*, 95 (where *fa-laghwun* is used in the first line).

264 A line of poetry by ʿAbd Allāh ibn Muʿāwiyah al-Jaʿfarī (d. 130/747). See al-Jāḥiẓ, *Ḥayawān*, 3:488 and many later sources, most of which have *wa-lākinna ʿayna*; some have *kamā ʿaynu* (e.g., al-Ibshīhī, *Mustaṭraf*, 1:213). *Kamā anna aʿyuna* is unmetrical.

265 Al-Maʿarrī, *al-Luzūmiyyāt*, 1:74.

266 Needless to say, neither of these statements is correct.

267 This point marks the beginning of a new episode of *al-Riḥlah al-thāniyah*: the chapter title "Al-Maʿraḍ" ("The Exhibition") was added to the text of the fourth edition of *Ḥadīth ʿĪsā ibn Hishām* (1927).

268 Al-Khansāʾ, *Dīwān*, [1986], 305; [1988], 386.

269 The name of the poet al-Khansāʾ's brother, Ṣakhr, killed in pre-Islamic tribal warfare, means "stone, rock."

270 A line of poetry cited anonymously in many sources, e.g. *Ḥamāsat Abī Tāmmām* (see al-Marzūqī, *Sharḥ*, 1284); Ibn ʿAbd Rabbih, *al-ʿIqd al-farīd*, 3:462 and 6:108; and al-Qālī, *Amālī*, 1:23.

271 Al-Nābighah al-Dhubyānī, *The Divans*, ed. Wilhelm Ahlwardt, 10–11 (vss. 15–16, 26–27). In the last line, other sources read *la-ranā* in place of *innā*.

272 Al-Maʿarrī, *al-Luzūmiyyāt*, 1:174.

273 A line of poetry by Abū Tammām, see ʿĀmilī, *Aʿyān al-shīʿah*, 4:480.

274 These lines are by al-Sharīf al-Raḍī, *Dīwān*, 2:877–80.

275 This point marks the beginning of a new episode of *al-Riḥlah al-thāniyah*: the chapter title "Al-Qaṣr al-kabīr" ("The Grand Palais") was added to the text of the fourth edition of *Ḥadīth ʿĪsā ibn Hishām* (1927).

276 While the names Alexander and Qārūn can be traced to particular figures (see the Glossary of Names and Places), the names Māriyah, Dārah, and ʿAmr may refer to multiple historical or mythical persons.

277 Al-Maʿarrī, *al-Luzūmiyyāt*, 1:66.

278 Al-Mutanabbī, *Dīwān*, 178.

279 Lines of poetry quoted anonymously (and in reversed order) in al-Muḥibbī, *Nafḥat al-rayḥānah*, and al-Shihāb al-Khafājī, *Rayḥānat al-alibbāʾ*. In the first line, the alternative reading is *takhtālu*.

280 Al-Mutanabbī, *Dīwān*, 767 (in his "Shiʿb Bawwān" *qaṣīdah* for ʿAḍud al-Dawlah).

281 A line of poetry by ʿUmar ibn Abī Rabīʿah, from his famous *rāʾiyyah*. See, among many other sources, al-Iṣfahānī, *Aghānī*, 1:80, 82.

282 This point marks the beginning of a new episode of *al-Riḥlah al-thāniyah*: the chapter title "Al-Ashjār wa-l-azhār" ("Trees and Flowers") was added to the text of the fourth edition of *Ḥadīth ʿĪsā ibn Hishām* (1927). It is interesting to note that Muḥammad al-Muwayliḥī seems to have taken longer than usual in sending this episode back to Cairo for publication. In the interim, number 119 of *Miṣbāḥ al-sharq* (September 7, 1900) includes an episode of Ibrāhīm al-Muwayliḥī's parallel narrative, entitled *Mirʾāt al-ʿĀlam*. For that text, see Ibrāhīm al-Muwayliḥī, *al-Muʾallafāt al-Kāmilah*, 161–202. My translation of this work into English is published in *Middle Eastern Literatures*, 15, no. 3 (December 2012): 318–36; and 16, no. 3 (December 2013): 1–17.

283 In the Qurʾan's account of the meeting of King Solomon and the Queen of Sheba, (Q Naml 27:44), the queen is shown an image of her throne. Since it shimmers like water, she bares her legs to avoid getting them wet.

284 These lines of poetry may be by Ibn al-Rūmī; see his *Dīwān*, 1:394, but they are also attributed to others. See the apparatus by Helmut Ritter in his edition of ʿAbd al-Qāhir al-Jurjānī, *Asrār al-balāghah*, 117. Also in Ibn al-Muʿtazz's *Dīwān*, 2:168; and the *Dīwān* by Abū l-Qāsim al-Zāhī, 72.

285 Al-Maʿarrī, *Saqṭ al-zand*, 232 (where *fa-adhhalu* is found instead of *fa-ajhalu*).

286 Q Kahf 18:39.

287 Abū l-ʿAtāhiyah, *Dīwān*, 104; al-Iṣfahānī, *Aghānī*, 4:35.

288 This point marks the beginning of a new episode of *al-Riḥlah al-thāniyah*: the chapter title "Al-Marāʾī wa-l-mashāhid" ("Sights and Scenes") was added to the text of the fourth edition of *Ḥadīth ʿĪsā ibn Hishām* (1927).

289 Lines of poetry attributed to ʿAbd Allāh ibn Ṭāhir ibn al-Ḥusayn Dhū l-Yamīnayn in Ibn Khallikān, *Wafayāt*, 3:85–86. The first line is attributed to Abū Dulaf in Ibn Wakīʿ, *al-Munṣif*, ed. al-Dāyah, 411.

290 This point marks the beginning of a new episode of *al-Riḥlah al-thāniyah*: the chapter title "Al-Iftirāʾ ʿalā al-waṭan" ("Slandering the Homeland") was added to the text of the fourth edition of *Ḥadīth ʿĪsā ibn Hishām* (1927).

291 Lines of poetry cited anonymously in al-Ṭurṭūshī, *Sirāj al-mulūk*, 167, 330–31; Yāqūt, *Muʿjam al-buldān* (Dār Ṣādir), 2:311. These sources read *mā li-l-farīsati* instead of *mā l-farīsatu*.

292 This is a reference to the previous episodes of *Fatrah min al-zaman* set in Cairo.

293 This point marks the beginning of a new episode of *al-Riḥlah al-thāniyah*: the chapter title "Khubz al-madaniyyah" ("Bread of Civilization") was added to the text of the fourth edition of *Ḥadīth ʿĪsā ibn Hishām* (1927).

294 Edward Lane's dictionary (s.v. *aṣfar*) explains that this use of "sons of yellow" refers to an early Greek king named al-Aṣfar ("son of Room, son of Eysoon" [Esau]).

295 A reference to the shirt worn by the third caliph ʿUthmān when he was assassinated. The bloody shirt was later publicly displayed in Damascus by its governor, Muʿawiyah, in order to provoke popular anger and public demands to avenge his kinsman's murder.

296 This, and the specific reference to the portrait of the girl wearing Alsatian costume, is a reference to the Franco-Prussian War (1870–1) which brought about a crushing defeat for the French army and the cession of much of Alsace to Germany.

297 The so-called "Fashoda incident" occurred in Sudan in 1898. French forces seeking to control the upper reaches of the River Nile and thus cause problems for the British in Egypt were confronted by a British force. As a result of vigorous diplomacy, the French were eventually forced to withdraw their claims. This incident was widely reported in the al-Muwayliḥī newspaper, *Miṣbāḥ al-sharq*, but references to the

incident in the original episodes of *Fatrah min al-Zaman* were omitted from the book version of *Ḥadīth ʿĪsā ibn Hishām*.

298 In the editions of *Ḥadīth ʿĪsā ibn Hishām* the author notes that these lines are by al-Farazdaq, *Dīwān*, 1:212.

299 The Joseph narrative is to be found in the Qurʾan, Surah 12 Yūsuf.

300 This point marks the beginning of a new episode of *al-Riḥlah al-thāniyah*: the chapter title, "al-Muʿjizah al-thāminah" ("The Eighth Wonder"), was added to the text of the fourth edition of *Ḥadīth ʿĪsā ibn Hishām* (1927).

301 The so-called Panama Scandals (1892) involved large-scale corruption in the construction of the Panama Canal. Gustave Eiffel was among those involved, but his jail sentence was later revoked.

302 Al-Maʿarrī, *al-Luzūmiyyāt*, 1:63–64.

303 This is the first of three episodes of *Fatrah min al-zaman* which were published after a gap of more than two years, and long after the author's return from Paris to Cairo (*Miṣbāḥ al-sharq* nos. 192, 193, 196). When the author prepared the episodes of *Fatrah min al-zaman* for publication in book form (1907), he added a new final chapter to the "Second Journey" entitled "Min al-Gharb ilā l-Sharq" ("From West to East") which was not part of the original episodes in *Miṣbāḥ al-sharq*. These three episodes were never included in any edition of *Ḥadīth ʿĪsā ibn Hishām* in its book form.

304 This is the second of the three episodes of *Fatrah min al-zaman* that were published after an interval of over two years. While the previous episode begins with a characteristic piece of virtuoso language in the traditional style of *sajʿ* (rhyming and cadenced prose), this episode and the one that follows it do not begin in that way but merely continue the Frenchman's description of the French governmental system.

305 Even though this episode of *Fatrah min al-zaman* ends, like all its predecessors, with the phrase "to be continued" (*wa-l-ḥadīth yutbaʿ*), no more episodes appeared.

Glossary of Names and Terms

ʿAbbās the First (1812–54) grandson of Muḥammad ʿAlī and, from 1849–54, his successor as *walī* of Egypt (nominally under Ottoman suzerainty).

ʿAbbāsiyyah suburb of Cairo which, in al-Muwayliḥī's time, was on the outer edge of the city.

ʿAbdallāh ibn Jaʿfar (d. between 81/700 and 85/704) nephew of ʿAlī ibn Abī Ṭālib, who tried to prevent ʿAlī's son, al-Ḥusayn, from going to al-Kūfah to be proclaimed Caliph.

Abū l-ʿAbbās Aḥmad Al-Rifāʿī (512–78/1118–82) founder of the Rifāʿiyyah order of Sufis, which originated in Iraq with rapid spreading to Syria and Egypt during the course of the seventh/thirteenth century.

Abū l-ʿAlāʾ al-Maʿarrī (363–449/973–1058) famous blind Syrian poet, whom al-Muwayliḥī admired greatly and who is quoted throughout this work. A picture of the poet used to hang in the hall of al-Muwayliḥī's house.

Abū Ḥanīfah (80–150/699–767) founder of the Sunnī Ḥanafī school of Islamic jurisprudence.

Abū Tammām (172–231/788–845) Ḥabīb ibn Aws al-Ṭāʾī, a renowned Arab poet, famous (and also much criticized) for the complexity of his imagery.

Abū l-Ṭayyib al-Mutanabbī (303–54/915–65) premodern Arab poet widely regarded as one of the greatest. He composed a large number of ringing odes—both praising (*madḥ*) and lampooning (*hijāʾ*) the most prominent rulers of his time as to have become proverbial in the centuries since his death.

Alexander (356–323 BC) “the Great,” King of Macedon, who launched a number of military campaigns and defeated the forces of the Persian Empire. He founded a number of cities named after himself, including Iskenderun and Alexandria.

ʿAlī ibn Abī Ṭālib (d. 40/661) cousin and son-in-law of the Prophet Muḥammad, and the fourth Caliph. In his name, the Shiʿah (originally *shīʿat ʿAlī*, “ʿAlī’s Party”) was established.

ʿAmr ibn Maʿdī Karib renowned Yemeni warrior-poet from the pre-Islamic era who lived on into the Islamic era and is alleged to have witnessed the Battle of Qādisiyyah in 15/636.

ʿAntar and ʿAblah renowned pre-Islamic poet ʿAntarah who is the subject of one of Arabic’s most famous popular sagas, *Sīrat ʿAntar*. ʿAblah is the name of his beloved, to win whose hand he undertakes a large number of difficult tasks.

al-ʿAqīq valley in central Arabia.

al-Asfarayīnī (Esfarayeni), Abū Bakr Khurasani physician and author of *Zubdat al-bayān fī ʿilm al-abdān* (*The Best Explanation in the Science of Bodies*), a work on the human body.

al-ʿAynī, Badr al-dīn (762–856/1360–1453) full name al-ʿAyntabī, Ḥanafī jurist who also served as *muḥtasib* (inspector of public morality) of Cairo during the Mamluk era.

Bāb al-Lūq district in central Cairo.

Baudry-Lacantinerie, G. (1837–1913) main compiler (with other collaborators) of *Traité de droit civile*, first published in 1895.

Bawwān Pass probably a reference to Shiʿb Bawwān, a well-forested area in Fars, Iran.

Baybars, Sulṭān al-Ẓāhir (620–76/1223–77) fourth Mamlūk Sultan of Egypt and a redoubtable warrior who defeated the forces of the Seventh Crusade under Louis IX of France and later those of the Mongol Hūlāgū Khān at the famous battle of ʿAyn Jālūt (Goliath’s Spring) in 658/1260. His exploits are celebrated in one of Arabic’s best-known popular sagas, *Sīrat al-Ẓāhir Baybars*.

Bilqīs, Queen of Sheba renowned queen, whose encounter with King Solomon is mentioned in both the Hebrew Bible and the Qur'an. The latter account occurs in Surahs 27 Naml ("The Ants") and 34 Sabā ("Sheba").

Bonchamps, Marquis Christian de (1860–1919) famous nineteenth-century French explorer of the African continent. In 1897 he was dispatched by the French government from Ethiopia to the Sudan to secure the region around Fashoda (see below).

Buṭrus Ghālī (1846–1910) prominent Egyptian politician and minister (later to be prime minister) who was assassinated in 1910. He interceded on al-Muwayliḥī's behalf when the latter was condemned to death for distributing nationalist literature in 1882 and obtained a commutation of sentence to one of exile.

Chosroes Anushirwan (r. AD 531–79) Sasanian emperor who built the city of Ctesiphon, the famous portico of which is celebrated in a poem by the poet al-Buḥturī (d. 284/897). The site is at al-Madā'in to the south of Baghdad.

Cromer, Lord (1841–1917) Evelyn Baring, major British diplomat and statesman. He was appointed Controller General of Egypt in 1879 (following the exile of the Khedive Ismāʿīl). After the quelling of the ʿUrābī Revolt of 1882, he became consul general (and virtual ruler) of Egypt until his resignation from the post in 1907 as the result of furious reactions to a notorious incident in the Egyptian village of Dinshaway, in which—whilst Cromer was on leave—several villagers were hung for challenging British officers engaged in a pigeon shoot. His two-volume study *Modern Egypt* (1908) presents his own view of the events of Egypt's recent history.

Dalloz, Victor (1795–1869) member of a prominent French legal family and author of *Jurisprudence générale.*

al-Dawlah, Sayf (303–56/915–67) the Ḥamdānid ruler, attracted to his court at Ḥalab (Aleppo) many famous writers, including the poet al-Mutanabbī and the philosopher al-Fārābī.

Day of Resurrection/Reckoning (*Yawm al-Qiyāmah*) in Islamic eschatology, the day when all believers will be called to account.

Deloncle, François (1856–1922) French politician and member of the French Chamber of Deputies who held a number of cabinet posts in the second half of the nineteenth century.

al-Dhubyānī, Al-Nābighah (ca. AD 535–604) prominent pre-Islamic poet, closely associated with the Lakhmid court at al-Ḥīrah.

Al-Durr al-Mukhtār work on Ḥanbalī jurisprudence by the Damascus scholar ʿAlāʾ al-dīn al-Ḥaṣkafī (d. 1088/1677) consisting of a commentary on an earlier work, *Tanwīr al-Abṣār*, composed by Muḥammad ibn ʿAbd Allāh al-Tamartāshī.

Euripides (ca. 490–406 BC) one of the three famous writers of Greek tragedy (along with Aeschylus and Sophocles). Among his most famous works are *Medea*, *Women of Troy*, and *The Bacchae*.

Ezbekiyyah Quarter district of Cairo named after Amir Ezbek al-Tutush, a general in the reign of the Mamluk Qāʾit Bāy. It contained a large park that separated the old city of Cairo from the modern (Ismāʿīliyyah) section constructed in the nineteenth century. In the late 1890s, the gardens were filled with trees and plants, and there was an ornamental lake in the middle of the area.

al-Faḍl ibn al-Rabīʿ (138–207/755–822) chamberlain and chief minister to two Abbasid Caliphs, Hārūn al-Rashīd and al-Amīn.

Fakhrī Pāshā, Ḥusayn (1843–1910) Egyptian cabinet minister and, for only three days in January 1893, Prime Minister of Egypt. On the orders of the Khedive Tawfīq, Fakhrī had replaced Muṣṭafā Fahmī who was considered too pro-British, but the order was rapidly rescinded.

al-Fārābī (ca. 295–338/908–50) renowned philosopher who wrote commentaries on the works of Aristotle, a study on the ideal society, *al-Madīnah al-fāḍilah* (*The Virtuous City*) modeled on the earlier work of Plato, and a series of treatises on music, of which the most famous and complex is *Kitāb al-mūsīqā al-kabīr* (*The Great Book on Music*).

Fashoda site in Sudan of a famous late nineteenth-century confrontation between British and French forces. The Marquis de Bonchamps was sent from Ethiopia and Major Jean-Baptiste Marchand from Brazzaville in the Congo to secure the region around Fashoda in the Sudan as French territory. When the British sent a flotilla down the River Nile, the confrontation led to an ignominious French withdrawal.

Gambetta, Léon (1838–82) French statesman and prime minister who came to prominence in the period during and after the Franco-Prussian War (1870–71).

Garraud, René (1849–1930) author of *Traité théorique et pratique du droit pénal français*.

Ghumdān a famous palace in Sanaa in the Yemen, which was legendary for its beauty.

Gladstone, William Ewart (1809–98) British Liberal politician who served as prime minister for four separate periods during the nineteenth century.

Gordon, Charles George (1833–85) British major-general, often known as "Gordon of Khartoum." He entered service for the Egyptian government in 1873 and was appointed commander-in-chief of the Sudanese army. He confronted a revolt by Muḥammad Aḥmad who declared himself the "Mahdī"; after evacuating a number of British troops from the Sudanese capital, Gordon decided to stay behind with a small force. When the British government did not intervene in time, the city fell and he was killed.

Griffith, George Richard (1857–1920) veterinary officer in the British army who was sent to the Sudan in 1884, took part in several campaigns there, and later served as general in charge of veterinary medicine for the Egyptian army between 1905 and 1907.

Haman mentioned in the Qur'an as being a minister of the Pharaoh at the time of Moses.

Hanotaux, Gabriel (1853–1944) French diplomat and statesman who, from 1894 to 1898, served as Minister of Foreign Affairs. Among his tasks as minister was to negotiate the colonization of Africa with the British, thus including the "Fashoda incident." (See above and below under *Fashoda*, *Bonchamps*, and *Marchand*.).

Hārūt and Mārūt two angels mentioned in the Qur'an, Q Baqarah 2:96. They taught men sorcery (*siḥr*) and, for their sins, they were punished by being imprisoned in Babel.

Hélie, Faustin (1799–1884) author of *Analyse et commentaire du code du procédure pénal.*

Homer name traditionally assigned to the "author" of two famous Greek epic poems *The Iliad* and the *The Odyssey.* Since both poems are the products of a lengthy process of oral transmission and performance, we have to assume that they constitute the result of multiple contributors.

Horace (65–8 BC) Quintus Horatius Flaccus, famous Roman lyric poet, best known for his set of *Odes.*

Ḥulwān town to the south of Cairo, the location of the al-Muwayliḥī family home.

Hunter, Archibald (1857–1939) British general in the Egyptian army who served in the Sudan from 1884 to 1899. He later moved on, first to India and then to South Africa.

Ibn ʿĀbidīn, Muḥammad Amīn (1198–1258/1784–1842) author of a legal textbook known as *Majmūʿat rasāʾil Ibn ʿĀbidīn* (*Collected Letters of Ibn ʿAbdīn*).

Ibn al-ʿArabī, Muḥyī al-dīn (560–638/1165–1240) Sufi author. one of the most famous figures in the history of Sufism, he has remained an inspirational and often controversial figure in the history of Islamic doctrine. Among his most famous works are *Fuṣūṣ al-Ḥikam* (*Bezels of Wisdom*) and *al-Futūḥāt al-Makkiyyah* (*The Meccan Illuminations*).

Ibn Malak (d. ca. 797/1395) also known as Ibn Firishteh, teacher of Islamic sciences under the Ottoman Sulṭān Bāyezīd (r. 792–805/1389–1402) in the town of Tīre in southwest Anatolia. A Ḥanafī jurist, he commented on the *Majmaʿ al-Baḥrayn* (see below) and other famous Ḥanafī law books.

Ibn al-Rūmī (221–83/836–96) Arabic poet of Byzantine descent who was born in Baghdad. While his poetic gifts were quickly recognized, his lampoons earned him enemies, in particular Al-Qāsim ibn ʿUbaydallāh, who is alleged to have had the poet poisoned.

Ibrāhīm (Abraham) patriarch in both the Hebrew Bible and the Qur'an. In the latter he earned the title "Khalīl Allāh" (friend of God) after enduring great hardship in his wars against King Namrūd. See Q Anbiyā' 21:51–72.

Ibrāhīm ibn al-Mahdī (162–224/779–839) son of the Abbasid Caliph al-Mahdī, and brother of Hārūn al-Rashīd. His prowess as a singer is discussed in detail in the famous work of Abū l-Faraj al-Isfahānī (283–356/897–967), *Kitāb al-Aghānī* (*Book of Songs*).

Ibrāhīm Pāshā (1789–1848) son of Muḥammad 'Alī who led the Egyptian army in victorious campaigns against the Wahhābīs in Arabia and the Ottoman army in Syria. When his father became mentally ill, he took over as regent, but died before his father in 1848. A statue of him riding a horse was a prominent feature of Opera Square in Cairo.

Imām ibn al-Wardī (691–749/1292–1349) author of a work entitled *Kharīdat al-'Ajā'ib wa-Farīdat al-Gharā'ib* (*Pearl of Wonders and Gem of Marvels*).

Imām Shāfi'ī Cemetery cemetery which surrounded the mausoleum of Imām Shāfi'ī (150–204/767–820) and lay outside the city walls of Cairo at that time. One of al-Muwayliḥī's ancestors was buried there.

Ismā'īl Bāy al-Kabīr (d. 1205/1791) Mamluk of Ibrāhīm Katkhudā (who was an influential figure in Egypt during the years 1156–67/1743–54). Ismā'īl Bāy joined himself to Muḥammad Bāy Abū Dhahab, who eventually overthrew 'Alī Bāy and, on his return to Egypt, became very powerful despite attempts by Murād Bāy to have him killed.

Ismā'īliyyah quarter the modern section of Cairo, constructed during the reign of the Egyptian Khedive Ismā'īl (r. 1863–79) along the lines of Haussmann's Paris.

al-'Izz ibn 'Abd al-Salām (Al-Sulamī) (578–660/1182–1261) famous Sufi and theologian of the Shāfi'ī School, known as "Sultan of the Religious Scholars."

Jabal Qāf proverbially distant mountain in early Arabic cosmology.

Ja'far al-Barmakī (150–87/767–803) vizier of Caliph Hārūn al-Rashīd, in both fact and fiction. He was a major patron of the arts and also a supporter of the translation movements during Hārūn's reign. His own downfall and that of his family is alleged to have resulted from his affair with the caliph's sister, ʿAbbāsah.

al-Jāḥiẓ (160–256/776–869) ʿAmr ibn Baḥr, the most illustrious composer of works in Arabic prose in the pre-modern era, given the nickname "goggle-eyed" by which he is known. A genuine polymath, he composed an enormous repertoire of works on a wide variety of topics.

Jayḥūn river known in Persian as the Amū Daryā and in European languages as the Oxus.

al-Jīlānī, ʿAbd al-Qādir (470–561/1078–1166) Ḥanbalī theologian who gave his name to the Qādiriyyah order of Sūfis.

Kaʿb al-Aḥbār (d. 32/652–53) Yemeni Jewish rabbi in the pre-Islamic era who converted to Islam. The epithet "Aḥbār" is an acknowledgment of his proverbial wisdom.

Kawthar traditionally a river in Paradise; some commentators discussing the Qur'an, Q 108 Kawthar, relate this word to the verbal root *K-Th-R* (with the meaning of "abundance").

Khān al-Khalīlī famous bazaar of Cairo in the Fatimid section of the city (also known to tourists as the "Muski").

al-Khansāʾ (first/seventh century) Tumāḍir bint ʿAmr ibn al-Ḥarth, one of Arabic literature's most famous elegaic poets. Many of her mosts famous elegies were in memory of her brother, Ṣakhr.

al-Khawarnak fortress near the town of Najaf in Iraq. It was originally constructed by al-Nuʿmān, the Lakhmid ruler of al-Ḥīrah.

al-Khiḍr mysterious figure who appears most prominently in the Qur'an in the Surah of the Cave (Q 18 Kahf), where he tests Moses in a series of complex situations. Al-Khiḍr is also a major reference-point in Sufi literature.

Khuld palace built by the Abbasid Caliph al-Manṣūr on the banks of the River Tigris.

kiswah black brocaded cloth used to cover the Kaaba in Mecca.

Kitchener, Horatio Herbert (1850–1916) British Field-Marshal and major figure in British colonial administration. Sent to the Sudan, he secured the country in 1898 and was appointed Chief-of-Staff (*Sirdār*) of the

Anglo-Egyptian armed forces there. He later participated in the Boer War in South Africa and was subsequently sent to India. In 1914 he was appointed as Secretary of State for War in England.

Kordofan province in the central regions of the Sudan. It was the site of vicious fighting between the forces of the Mahdī Muḥammad Aḥmad and the British army, but by 1898 it had become part of Sudan as a whole.

Krupp family from Essen who founded the renowned German steel producing company, which was thus heavily involved in the manufacture of ammunition and weapons.

Lavigerie, Cardinal Charles (1825–92) French priest and later cardinal, he was Primate of Africa (based in Tunisia and Algeria) and campaigned against slavery on the continent.

Lāẓoghly, Muḥammad Bey "katkhudā" to the ruler of Egypt, also known as Muḥammad Aghā. He played a major role in organizing the massacre of the Mamluks in the Cairo Citadel in 1811.

al-Maʿarrī See Abū l-ʿAlāʾ al-Maʿarrī.

al-Mahdī, al-ʿAbbāsī (1827–97) grand mufti of Egypt and author of *al-Fatāwā al-Mahdiyyah.*

Al-Majmaʿ *Majmaʿ al-baḥrayn wa-multaqā al-nayyirayn* (*Meeting-place of the Two Seas and Rendezvous of Sun and Moon*), a Ḥanafī law book by Muẓaffar al-dīn Aḥmad ibn ʿAbdallāḥ ibn Thaʿlab Ibn al-Sāʿātī (d. ca. 694/1295).

Mamlūk (lit. "owned," "a slave") dynasty of rulers in Egypt between 648/1250 and 922/1517. Drawn primarily from Turkic tribes in the Caucasus region, all those who assumed the position of "Sulṭān" were required to be manumitted slaves. Even after the Ottoman invasion of Egypt in 1516–17, the Mamlūks remained the primary authority in Egypt until Muḥammad ʿAlī organized their corporate massacre in the Cairo Citadel in 1811..

al-Mānastirlī, Ḥasan Pāshā prominent political figure during the reign of Muḥammad ʿAlī. He is best remembered for the elaborate palace (*sarāy*) that he had constructed at the southern tip of Roda Island in Cairo (completed in 1851).

al-Manīkalī, Aḥmad Pāshā Minister of War during the reign of Muḥammad ʿAlī. See ʿAbd al-Rahmān al-Rāfiʿī, *ʿAṣr Muḥammad ʿAlī* (Cairo, Maktabat al-Nahḍah al-Miṣriyyah, 1951), 191 and 308.

maqāmah, pl. maqāmāt picaresque narrative genre originated in the tenth century by Badīʿ al-Zamān al-Hamadhānī (358–98/969–1007), which became a widely used literary form in the ensuing centuries and which is invoked, along with al-Hamadhānī's narrator, ʿĪsā ibn Hishām, in this work of al-Muwayliḥī.

Marchand, Jean Baptiste (1863–1934) French explorer in Africa who was sent in 1897 to help secure the region around Fashoda in the Sudan. Once there, he and the French forces were confronted by British forces under Lord Kitchener and were eventually forced to withdraw.

Marwān, Marwānids name of several prominent members of the Umayyad dynasty, including two Caliphs.

Mauser German arms manufacturer, founded in the 1870s, that specialized in the production of bolt-action rifles and automatic pistols.

Maxim first recoil-operated machine gun, named after Hiram Stevens Maxim who invented it in 1884.

Maẓlūm Pāshā (1858–1928) Egyptian Minister of Justice in the 1890s who frequently clashed with the British occupation authorities on matters of law and its implementation.

Miles, Nelson A. (1839–1925) American Civil War general who was appointed Commanding General of the United States Army in 1895 and was thus involved in the invasions of both Cuba and Puerto Rico during the Spanish-American War.

Muʿallim Ghālī (1190–1237/1776–1822) Minister of Finance and Foreign Affairs in Egypt during the reign of Muḥammad ʿAlī.

Muḥammad ʿAlī (1183–1265/1769–1849) Ottoman soldier of Macedonian origins and later ruler of Egypt. He was originally sent to fight against the Napoleonic invasion of Egypt in 1798. Filling the vacuum left following the French army's withdrawal and following the massacre of the Mamluks at the Cairo Citadel in 1811, he became the ruler of Egypt and founder of what was to become its royal dynasty—lasting until the July Revolution of 1952. He was the initiator of a large number of reforms that turned Egypt into a major military power and also the fulcrum of a good deal of innovation and reform in the financial, social, educational, and cultural sectors of Egypt.

Muḥammad the Conqueror (Mehmet Fātiḥ) (835–86/1432–81) Ottoman sultan who conquered Constantinople in 1453, bringing the Byzantine Empire to a close.

al-Muʿizz (319–65/932–75) Faṭimid caliph who gave his name to a large section of the post-fourth/tenth-century city of Cairo.

Muskī area of Cairo lying between al-ʿAtabah al-Khadrāʾ Square and the mosque of al-Ḥusayn, still renowned for its artifacts of metal and leather. The term may perhaps be an arabization of the French word *mosquée* (mosque).

Muslim Ibn al-Walīd (ca. 130–208/748–823) celebrated early Abbasid love-poet in the tradition of pre-modern Arabic poetry, known as *ṣarīʿ al-ghawānī* ("victim of beautiful maidens").

al-Mutanabbī see Abū l-Ṭayyib al-Mutanabbī.

al-Muʿtaṣim (178–227/795–842) Abbasid Caliph, son of Hārūn al-Rashīd. Noted for his campaigns against the Byzantine forces in Anatolia, he also established a new caliphal city in Samarrāʾ.

Nobel, Alfred (1833–96) Swedish chemist and arms manufacturer who invented dynamite and was also the owner of the Bofors arms manufacturing company. His will established the set of prestigious prizes that are awarded annually in October.

Nuʿmān of al-Ḥīrah (r. ca. AD 580–602) last king of the Lakhmid house of al-Ḥīrah (in present-day Iraq), also known as Abū Qābūs.

Parquet (*Al-Niyābah*) agency within the system of French law (the Code Napoléon) that is responsible for the prosecution of crimes.

Qāʾim maqām Ottoman term used to describe the governor of a province.

Qanāṭir Khayriyyah barrage which spans the two branches of the River Nile some fifteen miles north of Cairo. The project was begun in 1843, but only finished in 1910.

qanṭar unit of weight.

Qārūn figure of legendary wealth described in the Qurʾan (Q Qaṣaṣ 28:76–82) as "of the people of Moses."

Qaṣbat Ruḍwān formerly a palace near the Ezbekiyyah gardens, although Stanley Lane-Poole reports in the late nineteenth century that it was "no more to be seen."

Questioning angels Munkar and Nakīr in Islamic eschatology, the two angels who question the dead concerning their deeds during their lifetime.

Raḍwā mountain in Saudi Arabia to the west of Medina.

Rāghib Pāshā (1819–84) official in various departments during the reigns of Muḥammad ʿAlī and Ismāʿīl. It is interesting to note that Ibrāhīm al-Muwayliḥī worked for him when he was Minister of Finance.

al-Rashīd, Hārūn (145–93/763?-809) most famous of the Abbasid Caliphs (a status further enhanced by his frequent presence in tales from *A Thousand and One Nights*), whose reign was marked by an efflorescence in scientific and cultural learning. He established the famous library Bayt al-Ḥikmah in Baghdad, which was to become the depository of a large number of works translated from Greek and Syriac.

al-Rāzī, Muḥammad ibn Zakariyā (250–313/864–925) renowned physician, chemist, and philosopher who wrote numerous works on medicine and other sciences.

Rhodes, Cecil (1853–1902) major figure in British imperial policy in Africa, and especially southern Africa where an entire country, Rhodesia (now Zimbabwe), was named after him.

Riḍwān the Angel of Paradise in Islam.

Mr. Rollo like the Suarez and Circurel families, the Rollos were prominent members of the Jewish business community in Egypt, with a lengthy history of involvement in the public affairs of the country.

al-Sadīr proverbially impressive fortress usually associated with the castle of Ukhayḍir in the Iraqi desert near Al-Karbalāʾ.

Saḥbān famous orator from the pre-Islamic era whose eloquence led to the coining of the phrase "more eloquent than Saḥbān."

Saʿīd Pāshā (1822–63) one of the sons of Muḥammad ʿAlī, the founder of the ruling dynasty in Egypt, Saʿīd, educated in France. He succeeded his murdered nephew, ʿAbbās, as viceroy (*walī*) of Egypt (nominally under Ottoman suzerainty) in 1854.

Sāmī Pāshā Muḥammad ʿAlī's private secretary.

San Stefano One of the most opulent districts of Alexandria, on the Mediterranean coast.

Sayf al-dīn prince of the Egyptian royal family. The case of his involvement in a shooting incident at a Cairo club was heavily covered in the al-Muwayliḥī newspaper. Attempts to have him declared legally incompetent failed, and he was sentenced to seven years in prison, later reduced to five. In December 1899 he was declared insane and sent to England for treatment.

Sayḥūn river known in Persian as Sir Daryā and in European languages as the Jaxartes.

Shamām presumably, like Raḍwā (see above), a proverbially high mountain peak.

al-Sīrah al-Ḥalabiyyah biography of the Prophet Muḥammad written by ʿAlī ibn Burhān al-dīn al-Ḥalabī (974–1044/1567–1635) and based on previous works by Ibn Sayyid al-Nās and Shams al-dīn al-Shāmī.

Solomon and the Jinn the Qurʾan contains a number of references to King Solomon and the jinn (e.g. Q Naml 27:17 and Q Sabaʾ 34:14). The tale in *A Thousand and One Nights* entitled "The City of Brass" (*Madīnat al-Nuḥās*) includes a quest for the bottles in which, according to legend, Solomon imprisoned the jinn.

Suarez famous Jewish family in Egypt, members of which were prominent participants in the foundation of the National Bank of Egypt in 1898.

Surra Man Raʾā literally "the viewer's delight," the city of Samarrāʾ, which was constructed by the Abbasid caliph, al-Muʿtaṣim, as a new capital to the north of Baghdad, beginning in 255/869.

al-Taʿāyishī (ca. 1846–99) "Khalīfa," or "successor" to the Mahdī Muḥammad Aḥmad, who took over leadership of the revolt in the Sudan in the 1890s.

Thabīr "a famous mountain," as al-Muwayliḥī puts it in a footnote, frequently mentioned in pre-Islamic poetry.

Tombs of the Caliphs name commonly given to the Eastern Cemetery in Cairo, although the people buried there are not actually "caliphs," but rather Mamluk Sultans from the eighth/fourteenth to tenth/sixteenth centuries.

ʿŪj ibn ʿUnuq mythical figure, concerning whom stories are to be found in the records of *Qiṣāṣ al-Anbiyāʾ* (*Stories of the Prophets*) by al-Kisāʾī and al-Thaʿālibī.

ʿUmar ibn al-Khaṭṭāb (d. 23/644) Companion of the Prophet Muḥammad and second caliph of Islam. He succeeded Abū Bakr in 13/634 and was assassinated in 23/644.

ʿUmar al-Khayyām (439–526/1048–1131) prominent Persian-born polymath, algebraist, philosopher, and poet. His collection of poetry, the *Rubāʿiyyāt* (*Quatrains*), was made famous through the rendering of at least part of their meaning into English by Edward Fitzgerald (1809–83).

ʿUthmān ibn ʿAffān (d. 35/656) Companion of the Prophet Muḥammad and third caliph of Islam (23–35/644–56).

Virgil (Publius Virgilius Maro) (70–19 BC) renowned Roman poet and composer of both the *Aeneid* and *Georgics*.

Wingate, Francis Reginald (1861–1953) British Army general. After service in India and Aden, he joined the Egyptian Army. He was involved in the operation to relieve Khartoum in 1885 and was later involved in campaigns in the Sudan, notably against the forces of the "Mahdī," Muḥammad Aḥmad.

Ziyād ibn Abīhi (d. 53/673) governor of Basra during the caliphate of Muʿawiyah.

al-Zubayr, Raḥmah Manṣūr (1830–1913) Sudanese slave-trader and nemesis of General Gordon who, following his imprisonment in Egypt, was eventually returned to his native country as its governor. In 1887 he returned to Cairo, but, after the successful conclusion of the Sudanese campaign in 1899, he was allowed to return to his homeland.

Bibliography

1. Works by the al-Muwayliḥīs

Ibrāhīm al-Muwayliḥī

"Al-Inshā' wa-l-'Aṣr." In *Mukhtārāt al-Manfalūṭī*, edited by Muṣṭafā Luṭfī al-Manfalūṭī, 181 ff. Cairo: Maṭba'a al-Sa'ādah, n.d.

Mā Hunālik. Cairo: Maṭba'at al-Muqaṭṭam, 1896.

"Mir'āt al-'Ālam." *Miṣbāḥ al-sharq* nos. 60, 61, 62, 109, 110, 111, 115, 119 (June-July 1899, June-September 1900); reprinted in *Kawkab al-sharq* (March-April 1930).

Al-Mu'allafāt al-Kāmilah. Cairo: Al-Majlis al-A'lā li-l-Thaqāfah, 2007.

"Der Spiegel der Welt." *Die Welt des Islams*, translated by Gottfried Widmer, N.s. 3 (1954): 58–126.

Hamzah, 'Abd al-Latīf. *Adab al-Maqālah al-Ṣaḥafiyyah fī Miṣr*. Cairo: Dār al-Fikr, 1965, 3: 83: 166 ff.

Ḥusayn, Ṭāhā, ed. *Al-Muntakhab min Adab al-'Arab*. Cairo: Wizārat al-Ma'ārif al-'Umūmiyyah, n.d. 1: 268 ff.; 2: 554 ff.

Zaydān, Jurjī. *Bunāt al-Nahḍah al-'Arabiyyah*, Kitāb al-Hilāl series no 72. Cairo: Dār al-Hilāl, 1957: 155 ff.

Muḥammad al-Muwayliḥī

"Ayyuhā al-Maḥzūn." In *Mukhtārāt al-Manfalūṭī*, edited by Muṣṭafā Luṭfī al-Manfalūṭī, 249 ff. Cairo: Maṭba'at al-Sa'ādah, n.d.

Ḥadīth 'Īsā ibn Hishām. 1st ed. Cairo: Maṭba'at al-Ma'ārif, 1907.

———. 2nd ed. Cairo: Al-Maktabah al-Azhariyyah, 1912.

———. 3rd ed. Cairo: Maṭba'at al-Sa'ādah, 1923.

———. 4th ed. Cairo: Maṭba'at Miṣr, 1927.

———. 5th ed. Cairo: Maṭbaʿat Miṣr, 1935.

———. 6th ed. Cairo: Maṭbaʿat al-Maʿārif, 1943.

———. 7th ed. Cairo: Maṭbaʿat al-Maʿārif, 1947.

———. 8th ed. 2 vols. Cairo: Dār al-Hilāl, 1959.

———. 9th ed. Cairo: Dār al-Qawmiyyah, 1964.

"Iktisāb Malakat al-Inshā' bi Ḥifẓ al-Ashʿār." *Al-Muqaṭṭam*, 18 August 1893.

ʿIlāj al-Nafs. Cairo: Al-Maṭbaʿah al-Amīriyyah, 1932; Dār al-Qawmiyyah, 1962.

"Jawhar al-Shiʿr." In *Mukhtārāt al-Manfalūṭī*, edited by Muṣṭafā Luṭfī al-Manfalūṭī, 196 ff. Cairo: Maṭbaʿat al-Saʿādah, n.d.

"Kalima Mafrūḍa." *Al-Mu'ayyad*, 9 February 1908.

"Naqd Dīwān Shawqī." In *Mukhtārāt al-Manfalūṭī*, edited by Muṣṭafā Luṭfī al-Manfalūṭī, 139 ff. Cairo: Maṭbaʿat al-Saʿādah, n.d.

"Ṣawt min al-ʿUzlah." *Al-Ahrām*, 30 December 1921.

2. References in Arabic

ʿAbbūd, Mārūn. *Badīʿ al-Zamān al-Hamadhānī*. Cairo: Dār al-Maʿārif, 1963.

ʿAbd al-Laṭīf, Muḥammad Fahmī. "Ibrāhīm al-Muwayliḥī." *Al-Thaqāfah*, no. 711 (1952): 7.

ʿAbduh, Ibrāhīm. *ʿAlām al-ṣiḥāfah al-ʿarabiyyah*. Cairo: Maktabat al-ʿArab, 1944.

———. *Taṭawwur al-ṣiḥāfah al-miṣriyyah*. Cairo, 1945.

Abū l-ʿAtāhiyah. *Dīwān*, ed. Shukrī Fayṣal. Damascus: Maṭbaʿat Jāmiʿat Dimashq, 1965.

Abū Rīḥ, Maḥmūd. *Jamāl al-dīn al-Afghānī*. Cairo: Dār al-Maʿārif, 1961.

Abū Tammām [Ḥabīb ibn Aws]. *Dīwān Abī Tammām*. Beirut: n.p., 1905.

Afghānī, Jamāl al-dīn, and Muḥammad ʿAbduh al-. *Al-ʿUrwah al-wuthqā*. Cairo: Dār al-ʿArab, 1957.

Aḥmad, ʿAbd al-Ilāh ʿAbd al-Muṭṭalib. *Al-Muwayliḥī al-ṣaghīr*. Cairo: Al-Hay'ah al-Miṣriyyah al-ʿĀmmah li-l-Kitāb, 1985.

ʿAlam, Muḥammad Mahdī. "Ṣafaḥāt min al-adab al-ʿarabī: Ḥadīth ʿĪsā ibn Hishām." *Al-Siyāsah al-Usbūʿiyyah*, 13 November 1943, 22 January 1944.

ʿĀmilī, Muḥsīn al-Ḥusaynī al-. *Aʿyān al-shīʿah*, 10 vols. Beirut: Dār al-Taʿāruf, 1983.
Amīn, Aḥmad. *Zuʿamāʾ al-iṣlāḥ fī l-ʿaṣr al-ḥadīth*. Cairo: Maktabat al-Nahḍah al-Miṣriyyah, 1948.
Amīn, Qāsim. *Taḥrīr al-marʾah*. Cairo: Maṭbaʿat ʿAyn Shams, 1899.
———. *Al-Marʾah al-jadīdah*. Cairo: Maktabat Muḥammad Zakī al-dīn, 1901.
ʿAqqād, ʿAbbās Maḥmūd al-. *Murājaʿāt fī l-adab wa-l-funūn*. Cairo: Al-Maṭbaʿah al-ʿAṣriyyah, 1926.
———. *Rijāl ʿaraftuhum*, Kitāb al-Hilāl no. 151. Cairo: Dār al-Hilāl, 1963.
Badawī, Aḥmad. *Rifāʿah al-Ṭahṭāwī Bey*. Cairo: Lajnat al-Bayān al-ʿArabī, 1950.
Badr, ʿAbd al-Muḥsin Ṭāhā. *Taṭawwur al-riwāyah al-ʿarabiyyah al-ḥadīthah fī miṣr*. Cairo: Dār al-Maʿārif, 1963.
Bishrī, ʿAbd al-ʿAzīz al-. "Muḥammad al-Muwayliḥī." *Al-Risālah*, nos. 72, 73, 74 (1934): 1886, 1927, 1966.
———. *Al-Mukhtār*. 2 vols. Cairo: Dār al-Maʿārif, 1959.
Buḥturī, Al-Walīd ibn ʿUbayd al-. *Dīwān*. Cairo: Maṭbaʿah Hindiyyah, 1911.
Ḍayf, Aḥmad. "Al-Adab al-miṣrī fī l-qarn al-tāsiʿ ʿashar." *Al-Muqtaṭaf*, May 1926: 543.
Ḍayf, Shawqī. *Al-Adab al-ʿarabī al-muʿaṣir fī miṣr*. Cairo: Dār al-Maʿārif, 1957.
———. *Al-Fakāhah fī miṣr*, Kitāb al-Hilāl series no. 83. Cairo: Dār al-Hilāl, 1958.
———. *Al-Maqāmah*. Cairo: Dār al-Maʿārif, 1954.
Dhihnī, Ṣalāḥ al-dīn al-. *Miṣr bayna l-iḥtilāl wa-l-thawrah*. Cairo: Maktabat al-Sharq al-Islāmiyyah, 1939.
Disūqī, ʿUmar al-. *Fī l-adab al-ḥadīth*. 2 vols. Cairo: Dār al-Fikr, 1966.
Farazdaq, al-. *Dīwān al-Farazdaq*, 2 vols. Beirut: Dār Ṣādir, 1966.
Fikrī, Amīn. *Al-Āthār al-fikriyyah*. Cairo: Al-Maṭbaʿah al-Amīriyyah, 1897.
———. *Irshād al-alibbāʾ ilā maḥāsin urūbbā*. Cairo: Maṭbaʿat al-Muqtaṭaf, 1892.
Ḥakīm, Tawfīq al-. *ʿAwdat al-rūḥ*. Cairo: Maktabat al-Ādāb, n.d.
———. *Yawmiyyāt nāʾib fī l-aryāf*. Cairo: Maktabat al-Ādāb, n.d.

Hamadhānī, Badī' al-Zamān al-. *Maqāmāt*. Edited by Muḥammad 'Abduh. Beirut: Al-Maṭba'ah al-Kathūlikiyyah, 1958.

Hamza, 'Abd al-Latīf. *Adab al-maqālah al-ṣaḥafiyyah fī miṣr*. Cairo: Dār al-Fikr, 1964.

———. *Mustaqbal al-ṣiḥāfah fī miṣr*. Cairo: Dār al-Fikr, 1961.

Ḥaqqī, Yaḥyā. *Fajr al-qiṣṣah al-miṣriyyah*. Cairo: Dār al-Qalam, 1960.

Ḥarīrī, Abū l-Qāsim al-. *Maqāmāt*. Beirut: Dār Ṣādir, 1958.

Hawārī, Aḥmad Ibrāhīm al-. *Naqd al-mujtama' fī Ḥadīth 'Īsā ibn Hishām li-l-Muwayliḥī*. Cairo: Dār al-Ma'ārif, 1981.

Ḥusayn, Ṭāhā. *Al-Ayyām*. 2 vols. Cairo: Maṭba'at al-Ma'ārif, 1939–44.

Ibn 'Abd Rabbihi. *Al-'Iqd al-farīd*. Cairo: Lajnat al-Ta'līf wa-l-Tarjamah wa-l-Nashr, 1946.

Ibn Dāwūd. *Zahrah*, 2 vols., ed. Ibrāhīm al-Sāmarrā'ī. Al-Zarqā', Jordan: Maktabat al-Manār, 1985.

Ibn al-Mu'tazz. *Dīwān Ibn al-Mu'tazz*, ed. Muḥammad Badī' Sharīf. Cairo: Dār al-Ma'ārif, 1977–78.

Ibn Qutaybah, 'Abd Allāh ibn Muslim. *Kitāb al-Shi'r wa-l-shu'arā'*. Edited by de Goeje. Leiden: E. J. Brill, 1902.

———. *'Uyūn al-akhbār*., 4 vols. Cairo: Dār al-Kutub al-Miṣriyyah, 1925–1930.

Ibn al-Rūmī. *Dīwān Ibn al-Rūmī*, 6 vols., ed. Ḥusayn Naṣṣār. Cairo: Maṭba'at Dār al-Kutub, 1973.

Ibrāhīm, Aḥmad Abū Bakr. "Ḥadīth 'Īsā ibn Hishām." *Al-Risālah*, 10 (1942): 1080.

Ibrāhīm, Ḥāfiẓ. *Dīwān*. Cairo: Maṭba'at Dār al-Kutub, 1937.

———. *Layālī saṭīḥ*. Cairo: Dār al-Qawmiyyah, 1964.

Ibshīhī, Muḥammad ibn Aḥmad al-. *al-Mustaṭraf fī kull fann mustaẓraf*. Cairo: Sharikat Matba'at wa-Maktabat Muṣṭafā al-Bābī al-Ḥalabī, 1952.

Iṣfahānī, Abū l-Faraj al-. *Kitāb al-Aghānī*. Cairo: Dār al-Kutub, 1927–61.

Jabartī, 'Abd al-Raḥmān al-. *'Ajā'ib al-āthār fī l-tarājim wa-l-akhbār*. Cairo: Dār al-Fikr, 1965–.

Jāhiẓ, 'Amr ibn Baḥr al-. *Kitāb al-Ḥayawān*. Cairo: Muṣṭafā al-Bābī al-Ḥalabī, 1938.

Jurjānī, ʿAbd al-Qāhir al-. *Asrār al-balāghah*, ed. Helmut Ritter. Istanbul: Govt. Press, 1954; Wiesbaden: F. Steiner, 1959.

Khafājī, Shihāb al-dīn Aḥmad ibn Muḥammad ibn ʿUmar al-. *Rayḥānat al-alibbāʾ wa-zahrat al-ḥayāt al-dunyā*, 2 vols., ed. ʿAbd al-Fattāḥ Muḥammad al-Ḥulw. Cairo: ʿIsā al-Bābī al-Ḥalabī, 1967.

Khansāʾ, al-. *Dīwān al-Khansāʾ*, ed. Ibrāhīm ʿAwḍayn. Cairo: Maṭbaʿat al-Saʿādah, 1986.

———. *Dīwān al-Khansāʾ*, ed. Anwar Abū Suwaylim. Amman: Dār ʿAmmār, 1988.

Khiḍr, ʿAbbās. *Al-Qiṣṣah al-qaṣīrah fī miṣr*. Cairo: Dār al-Qawmiyyah, 1966.

Kisāʾī, Muḥammad ibn ʿAbd Allāh al-. *Kitāb Qiṣaṣ al-anbiyāʾ*. Edited by Eisenberg. Leiden: E. J. Brill, 1922.

Labīd ibn Rabīʿah. *Der Dīwān des Labīd*. Vienna: C. Gerolds Sohn, 1880.

Maʿarrī, Abū l-ʿAlāʾ al-. *Al-Luzūmiyyāt*. Cairo: Maṭbaʿat al-Maḥrūsa, 1891.

———. *Siqṭ al-zand*. Cairo: Būlāq, 1869; Cairo: n.p., 1948–.

Marzūqī, Aḥmad ibn Muḥammad al-. *Sharḥ Dīwān al-Ḥamāsah*, ed. Aḥmad Amīn and ʿAbd al-Salām Hārūn. Cairo: Lajnat al-Taʾlīf wa-l-Tarjamah wa-l-Nashr, 1951–53.

Malṭī-Douglas, Fadwā. "Layālī Saṭīh." *Fuṣūl*, 3, no. 2 (Jan.-Mar. 1983): 109–117.

Manfalūṭī, Muṣṭafā Luṭfī al-. *Mukhtārāt al-Manfalūṭī*. Cairo: Maṭbaʿat al-Saʿādah, n.d.

———. *Al-Naẓārāt*. Al-Maktabah al-Tijāriyyah al-Kubrā, n.d.

Maqrīzī, Taqī al-dīn al-. *Al-Mawāʾidh wa-l-iʿtibār fī dhikr al-khiṭaṭ wa-l-āthār*. Cairo: Institut français d'archéologie orientale du Caire, 1911–13.

Masʿūdī, al-. *Murūj al-dhahab*, 7 vols., ed. Charles Pellat. Beirut: al-Jāmiʿah al-Lubnāniyyah, 1965–79.

Mubārak, ʿAlī. *ʿAlam al-dīn*. Alexandria: Maṭbaʿat Jarīdat al-Maḥrūsah, 1882.

———. *Al-Khiṭaṭ al-tawfīqiyyah al-jadīdah*. Cairo: Al-Maṭbaʿah al-Amīriyyah, 1887–88.

Mubārak, Zakī. "Ḥadīth ʿĪsā ibn Hishām." *Al-Risālah*, 10 (1942): 995, 1016, 1035.

Mutanabbī, Abū l-Ṭayyib al-. *Dīwān*, with commentary by al-Wāḥidī, ed. Friedrich Dieterici. 1861. Reprint, Baghdad: Maktabat al-Muthannā, 1964.

———. *al-ʿArf al-ṭayyib fī sharḥ dīwān Abī al-Ṭayyib*, 2 vols., ed. Nāṣīf al-Yāzijī. 1882–88. Reprint, Beirut: Dār Ṣādir, 1964.

Muwayliḥī, Ibrāhīm al-. "Hadīth ʿĪsā ibn Hishām." *Al-Risālah*, 10 (1942): 1042.

———. "Ibrāhīm al-Muwayliḥī." *Al-Risālah*, 6 (1939): 617, 658.

———. "Tarjamat al-Sayyid Muḥammad al-Muwayliḥī." Introduction to the 6th and 7th editions of *Ḥadīth ʿĪsā ibn Hishām*. Cairo: Dār al-Maʿārif, 1943, 1947.

Qālī, Abū ʿAlī Ismāʿīl ibn al-Qāsim al-. *Kitāb al-Amālī*. [need biblio info.]

Raḍī, al-Sharīf al-. *Dīwān al-Sharīf al-Raḍī*. Beirut: al-Maṭbaʿah al-Adabiyyah, 1890–92.

Rāfiʿī, ʿAbd al-Raḥmān al-. *ʿAṣr Ismāʿīl*. Cairo: Maktabat al-Nahḍah al-Miṣriyyah, 1948.

———. *ʿAṣr Muḥammad ʿAlī*. Cairo: Maktabat al-Nahḍah al-Miṣriyyah, 1951.

Rāʿī, ʿAlī al-. *Dirāsāt fī l-riwāyah al-miṣriyyah*. Cairo: Al-Muʾassasah al-Miṣriyyah al-ʿĀmmah li-l-Taʾlīf wa-l-Tarjamah wa-l-Ṭibāʿah wa-l-Nashr, n.d.

———. "Ḥadīth ʿĪsā ibn Hishām." *Kitābāt Miṣriyyah*, 2 (1956): 54.

Ramadī, Jamāl al-dīn al-. "Muḥammad al-Muwayliḥī." *Ṣawt al-Sharq*, November 1960.

Ramitch, Aḥmad Yūsuf. *Usrat al-Muwayliḥī*. Cairo: Dār al-Maʿārif, 1980.

Rikābī, Jawda al-. *Fī l-adab al-andalūsī*. Cairo: Dār al-Maʿārif, 1960.

Ṣābā, ʿĪsā Mīkhaʾil. *Nāṣīf al-Yāzijī*. Cairo: Dār al-Maʿārif, 1965.

Ṣabrī, Ismāʿīl. *Dīwān*. Cairo: Maṭbaʿat Lajnat al-Taʾlīf wa-l-Tarjamah wa-l-Ṭibāʿah wa-l-Nashr, 1938.

Ṣalāḥ, Bhoury. "Al-Maqāmah." *Bulletin des études arabes*, September-October 1948: 149–53.

Sarkīs, Yūsuf. *Muʿjam al-maṭbūʿāt al-ʿarabiyyah wa-l-muʿarrabah*. Cairo: Maṭbaʿat Sarkīs, 1928.

Sharqāwī, ʿAbd al-Raḥmān al-. *Al-Arḍ*. Cairo: Dār al-Kātib al-ʿArabī li-l-Ṭibāʿah wa-l-Nashr, 1968.

Shawkat, Maḥmūd. *Al-Fann al-qaṣaṣī fī l-adab al-miṣrī al-ḥadīth*. Cairo: Dār al-Fikr, 1963.

Shaykhū, Lūwīs. *Al-Ādāb al-ʿarabiyyah fī l-qarn al-tāsiʿ ʿashar*. Beirut: Al-Maṭbaʿah al-Kathūlikiyyah, 1908.

———. *Taʾrīkh al-ādāb al-ʿarabiyyah fī l-rubʿ al-awwal min al-qarn al-ʿishrīn*. Beirut: Maṭbaʿat al-Ābāʾ al-Yasūʿiyyīn, 1926.

Shayyāl, Jamāl al-dīn al-. *Rifāʿah al-Ṭahṭāwī*. Cairo: Dār al-Maʿārif, 1958.

Shidyāq, Aḥmad Fāris al-. *Al-Sāq ʿalā l-sāq fī mā huwa al-fāriyāq*. Paris: n.p., 1865.

Ṭāhir (anonymous). "Muḥammad al-Muwayliḥī." *Kull shayʾ wa-l-ʿālam*, 22 March 1930: 20, 40.

Ṭahṭāwī, Rifāʿah Rāfiʿ al-. *Takhlīṣ al-ibrīz fī talkhīṣ Bārīz*. Cairo: Dār al-Taqaddum, 1905.

Tarrāzī, Fīlīb dī. *Taʾrīkh al-Ṣiḥāfah al-ʿarabiyyah*. Cairo: Al-Maṭbaʿah al-Adabiyyah, Al-Maṭbaʿah al-Amrikiyyah, 1913–33.

Taymūr, Aḥmad. *Al-Amthāl al-ʿāmmiyyah*. Cairo: Dār al-Kutub, 1956; Maṭābiʿ al-Ahrām al-Tijāriyyah, 1970.

———. *Fann al-qiṣaṣ: dirāsāt fī l-qiṣṣah wa-l-masraḥ*. Cairo: Maktabat al-Ādāb, n.d.

———. *Nashr al-qiṣṣah wa-tatawwuruhā*. Cairo: Al-Maṭbaʿah al-Salafiyyah, 1936.

———. *Al-Qaṣaṣ fī adab al-ʿarab*. Cairo: Al-Maṭbaʿah al-Kamaliyyah, 1958.

———. *Shaykh Sayyid al-ʿabīt wa-aqāṣīṣ ukhrā*. Cairo: Al-Maṭbaʿah al-Salafiyyah, 1926.

Thaʿālibī, Aḥmad ibn Muḥammad al-. *Kitāb Qiṣaṣ al-anbiyāʾ*. Cairo: n.p., 1906.

———. *Yatīmah al-dahr fī maḥāsin ahl al-ʿaṣr*, 4 vols. Beirut: Dār al-Kutub al-ʿIlmiyyah, 1979.

Ṭurṭūshī, Muḥammad ibn al-Walīd al-. *Sirāj al-mulūk*, ed. Jaʿfar al-Bayātī. London: Riad el-Rayyes, 1990.

ʿUmar, Muḥammad. *Ḥāḍir al-miṣriyyīn aw sirr taʾakhkhurihim*. Cairo: Maṭbaʿat al-Muqtaṭaf, 1902.

Yāqūt ibn ʿAbd Allāh al-Ḥamawī. *Muʿjam al-buldān*. Beirut: Dār Ṣādir, 1955–57.

Yāzijī, Nāṣīf al-. *Majmaʿ al-baḥrayn*. Beirut: Dār Ṣādir, 1966.

Zaghlūl, Aḥmad Fathī. *Sirr taqaddum al-inklīz al-saksūniyyīn*. Cairo: Al-Maṭbaʿah al-Raḥmāniyyah, 1899.

Zāhī, Abū l-Qāsim al-. *A Poet of the Abbasid Period: Abū l-Qāsim al-Zāhī (ʿAlī b. Isḥāq b. Khalaf al-Zāhī) 313–352 AH/925–963 CE: his life and poetry, annotated, edited and with an introduction by Khalid Sindawi*. Wiesbaden: Harrassowitz Verlag, 2010.

Zakī, Aḥmad. *Al-Safar ilā l-muʾtamar*. Cairo: Al-Maṭbaʿah al-Amīriyyah, 1894.

Zaydān, Jurjī. *Bunāt al-nahḍah al-ʿarabiyyah*, Kitāb al-Hilāl no. 72. Cairo: Dār al-Hilāl, 1957.

———. *Tarājim mashāhir al-sharq fī l-qarn al-tāsiʿ ʿashar*. 2 vols. Cairo: Dār al-Hilāl, 1910–11.

———. *Taʾrīkh Ādāb al-lughah al-ʿarabiyyah*. 4 vols. Cairo: Dār al-Hilāl, 1937.

Ziriklī, Khayr al-dīn al-. *Al-Aʿlām*. Cairo: Maṭbaʿat Kustatsumas, 1954.

3. References in European Languages

Abdel-Meguid, Abdel Aziz. *The Modern Arabic Short Story*. Cairo: Dạr al-Maʿārif, 1955.

Abou-Saif, L. "Najīb al-Rīḥānī: From Buffoonery to Social Comedy." *Journal of Arabic Literature*, 4 (1973): 1–17.

About, Edmond. *Le fellah: Souvenirs d'Egypte*. Paris: Hachette, 1869.

———. *The Fellah*. Translated by Sir Randal Roberts. London: Chapman and Hall, 1870.

———. *L'homme à l'oreille cassée*. Paris: Hachette, 1935.

Abu Lughod, Ibrahim. *The Arab Rediscovery of Europe*. Princeton: Princeton University Press, 1963.

Adams, Charles. *Islam and Modernism in Egypt*. London: Oxford University Press, 1933.

Ahlwardt, Wilhelm, ed. *The Diwans of the Six Ancient Arabic Poets Ennabiga ʿAntara, Tharafa, Zuhair, ʿAlqama and Imruulqais*. London: Trübner, 1870.

Ahmed, Jamal. *The Intellectual Origins of Egyptian Nationalism*. London: Oxford University Press, 1960.

Allen, Roger. "The Early Arabic Novel." In *Cambridge History of Arabic Literature*, Vol. IV. Cambridge: Cambridge University Press, [forthcoming].

———. "Ḥadīth ʿĪsā ibn Hishām: The Excluded Passages." *Die Welt des Islams*, N.S. 12 (1969): 74–89, 163–81.

———. "Ḥadīth ʿĪsā ibn Hishām: A Reconsideration." *Journal of Arabic Literature*, 1 (1970): 88–108.

———. "Ibrāhīm al-Muwayliḥī." In *The Encyclopedia of Islam*, 2nd ed., 1954–[forthcoming].

———. "Ibrāhīm Al-Muwaylihī's *Mir'āt al-ʿĀlam*: Introduction and Translation." *Middle Eastern Literatures*, 15, no. 3 (December 2012): 318–36.

———. "Ibrāhīm Al-Muwaylihī's *Mir'āt al-ʿĀlam*: Introduction and Translation." *Middle Eastern Literatures*, 16, no. 3 (December 2013): 334–50.

———. "Muḥammad al-Muwayliḥī." In *The Encyclopedia of Islam*, 2nd ed., 1954–[forthcoming].

———. "Some New Al-Muwayliḥī Materials, or the Unpublished Ḥadīth of ʿĪsā ibn Hishām." *Humaniora Islamica*, 2 (1974): 139–80.

———. "Writings of Members of the Naẓlī Circle." *Journal of the American Research Center in Egypt*, 8 (1971): 79–84.

Ammar, Hamed. *Growing Up in an Egyptian Village*. London: Routledge and Kegan Paul, 1954.

Anderson, J. N. D. "Law Reform in Egypt, 1850–1950." In *Political and Social Change in Modern Egypt*, edited by P. M. Holt. Oxford: Oxford University Press, 1968.

Artin Bey, Yaʿqub. *L'instruction publique en Egypte*. Paris: E. Leroux, 1890.

Ayrout, Henri Habib. *The Egyptian Peasant*. Translated by J. Alden Williams. Boston: Beacon Press, 1963.

Baedecker, Karl. *Egypt, Handbook for Travellers*. Leipzig: Karl Baedecker, 1902, 1908.

Baer, Gabriel. *A History of Landownership in Modern Egypt 1800–1950*. London: Oxford University Press, 1952.
———. *Population and Society in the Arab East*. Translated by Hanna Szöke. London: Routledge & Kegan Paul, 1964.
———. "Social Change in Egypt, 1800–1914." In *Political and Social Change in Modern Egypt*, edited by P. M. Holt. London: Oxford University Press, 1968.
———. *Studies in the Social History of Modern Egypt*. Chicago: University of Chicago Press, 1969.
———. "Urbanization in Egypt, 1820–1907." In *Beginnings of Modernization in the Middle East*, edited by William Polk and Richard Chambers. Chicago: University of Chicago Press, 1968.
Baudry-Lacantinerie, G. et al. *Traité de droit civile*. Paris: L. Larose et L. Tenin, 1905–9.
Bencheneb, Saadeddine. "Edmond About et Al-Muwailiḥī." *Revue africaine*, 88 (1944): 270–73.
———. "Etudes de littérature arabe moderne: I. Muḥammad al-Muwailiḥī." *Revue africaine*, 83 (1939): 358–82; 84 (1940): 77–92.
Berger, Morroe. *Bureaucracy and Society in Modern Egypt*. Princeton: Princeton University Press, 1957.
Berque, Jacques. *Histoire sociale du village égyptien au XXième siècle*. Paris: Mouton, 1957.
———. *L' Egypte: Impérialisme et révolution*. Paris: Gallimard, 1967.
———. *Egypt: Imperialism and Revolution*. Translated by Jean Stewart. London: Faber and Faber, 1972.
———. "The Establishment of the Colonial Economy." In *Beginnings of Modernization in the Middle East*, edited by William Polk and Richard Chambers. Chicago: University of Chicago Press, 1968.
Blachère, Régis, and Pierre Masnou. *Al-Hamadhānī: Choix de maqāmāt*. Paris: Klincksieck, 1957.
Blunt, Wilfrid Scawen. *Gordon at Khartoum*. London: S. Swift and Co., 1911.
———. *My Diaries*. 2 vols. London: M. Seeker, 1919.
———. *Secret History of the Occupation of Egypt*. 2 vols. London: Unwin, 1907.

Bosworth, C. Edmund. *The Medieval Islamic Underworld*. Leiden: E. J. Brill, 1976.
Brinton, Jasper. *The Mixed Courts of Egypt*. New Haven: Yale University Press, 1930.
Brockelmann, Karl. *Geschichte der arabischen Literatur*. 3 Supplementbanden. Leiden: E. J. Brill, 1937–42.
Burckhardt, J. L. *Travels in Arabia, Comprehending an Account of Those Territories in Hedjaz Which the Mohammedans Regard as Sacred*. London: Henry Colburn, 1829.
Burton, Sir Richard. *Personal Narrative of a Pilgrimage to El-Medinah and Meccah*. London: Longman and Sons, 1855, 1857; W. Mullan and Son, 1879; G. Bell and Sons, 1898, 1906.
Chirol, Sir Valentine. *The Egyptian Problem*. London: MacMillan and Co., 1921.
Civil Code of Egypt-Native Tribunals. Cairo: Ministry of Justice, 1901.
Clerget, Marcel. *Le Caire: étude de géographic urbaine et d'histoire économique*. Cairo: Imprimerie E. et R. Schindler, 1934.
Code of Civil and Commercial Procedure. Cairo: Ministry of Justice, 1904–11.
Colvin, Sir Auckland. *The Making of Modern Egypt*. London: Seeley and Co., 1906.
Coulson, Noel. *Islamic Law*. Islamic Surveys, no. 2. Edinburgh: Edinburgh University Press, 1964.
Crecelius, Daniel. "The Organization of Waqf Documents in Cairo." *International Journal of Middle East Studies*, 2, no. 3 (July, 1971): 266–77.
Creswell, K. A. G. *The Muslim Architecture of Egypt*. 2 vols. Oxford: Oxford University Press, 1952.
Cromer, Lord. *Abbas II*. London: Macmillan and Co., 1915.
———. *Modern Egypt*. 2 vols. London: Macmillan and Co., 1908.
Dalloz, Victor. *Codes d'audience*. Paris: Dalloz, 1926.
———. *Jurisprudence générale*. Paris: Bureau de la jurisprudence générale, 1896.

David, René, and Henry de Vries. *The French Legal System*. New York: Columbia University Press, 1954.
Demolins, Edmond. *A quoi tient la superiorité des anglo-saxons?* Paris: Firmin-Didot et al, 1897.
Deny, Jean. *Sommaire des archives turques du Caire*. Cairo: Royal Geographical Society of Egypt, 1930.
Dodwell, H. *The Founder of Modern Egypt*. Cambridge: Cambridge University Press, 1931.
Elgood, P. *Bonaparte's Adventure in Egypt*. London: Oxford University Press, 1931.
———. *Egypt and the Army*. London: Oxford University Press, 1924.
Encyclopedia of Islam. 4 vols. Leiden: E. J. Brill, 1913–36; 2nd edition, 1954–[in process].
Ende, Werner. "Europabild und kulturelles Selbstbewusstsein bei den Muslimen am Ende des 19. Jahrhunderts, dargestellt an den Schriften der beiden ägyptischen Schriftsteller Ibrāhīm und Muḥammad al-Muwailiḥī." D. Phil. dissertation. Hamburg: Hamburg Universität, 1965.
Forster, E. M. *Aspects of the Novel*. London: Penguin Books, 1962.
Freytag, Gustav. *Arabum Proverbia*. Bonn: A. Marcus, 1838–43.
Garillot, J. Aristide. *La réforme judiciaire en Egypte*. Alexandria: n.p., 1893.
Garraud, René. *Traité théorique et pratique de droit pénale français*. Paris: L. Larose et L. Tenin, 1913–35.
Gendzier, Irene. *The Practical Vision of Yaʿqūb Sanūʿ*. Cambridge: Harvard University Press, 1966.
Gibb, Sir Hamilton A. R. *Modern Trends in Islam*. Chicago: University of Chicago Press, 1947.
———. *Studies on the Civilization of Islam*. Edited by Stanford Shaw. London: Routledge and Kegan Paul, 1962.
Gibb, Sir Hamilton A. R., and H. Bowen. *Islamic Society and the West*. 2 vols. London: Oxford University Press, 1950, 1957.
Goadby, Frederic. *Commentary on Egyptian Criminal Law and the Related Criminal Law of Palestine, Cyprus and Iraq*. Cairo: Government Press, 1924.

Gran, Peter. *The Islamic Roots of Capitalism: Egypt 1760–1840*. Austin: University of Texas Press, 1979.

von Grunebaum, Gustave. E. *Medieval Islam*. Chicago: University of Chicago Press, 1962.

———. *Modern Islam*. Berkeley: University of California Press, 1962.

———. "The Spirit of Islam as Shown in its Literature." *Studia Islamica*, 1 (1953): 101–19.

Hakim, Tawfiq al-. *The Maze of Justice*. Translated by Aubrey Eban. London: Harvill Press, 1947; Austin: University of Texas Press, 1989.

Halton, H. W. *An Elementary Treatise of the Egyptian Civil Codes*. Cairo: National Printing Department, 1904.

Ḥarīrī, Abū l-Qāsim al-. *The Assemblies of Al-Harīrī*. Translated by C. Chenery and F. Steingass. London: n.p., 1870; London: Gregg Reprint, 1970.

Hartmann, Martin. *The Arabic Press of Egypt*. London: Luzac and Co., 1899.

Hélie, Faustin Adolphe. *Analyse et commentaire du code de procédure pénal*. Paris: Librairies techniques, 1959.

Heyd, Uriel, ed. *Studies in Islamic Institutions and Civilization*. Jerusalem: Hebrew University Press, 1961.

Heyworth-Dunne, J. *Introduction to the History of Education in Modern Egypt*. London: Luzac and Co., 1938.

———. "Society and Politics in Modern Egyptian Literature." *Middle East Journal*, 2 (July 1948): 306–18.

Holt, P. M., ed. *Political and Social Change in Modern Egypt*. London: Oxford University Press, 1968.

Hourani, Albert. *Arabic Thought in the Liberal Age*. London: Oxford University Press, 1962.

Hussein, Taha. *A Stream of Days*. Translated by Hilary Wayment. Cairo: Dār al-Maʿārif, 1943.

de la Jonquière, Taffanel. *Journal de l'expedition de l'Egypte*. 5 vols. Paris: Henri Charles-Lavauzelle, 1904.

Keddie, Nikki. *Sayyid Jamāl ad-Dīn 'al-Afghani': a Political Biography*. Berkeley: University of California Press, 1972.

Khadduri, Majid, and H. J. Liebesny. *Law in the Middle East*. Washington: Middle East Institute, 1955.

Kirk, George. *Lord Cromer in Egypt: a Retrospect*. Cambridge: Harvard University Press, 1958.

Kurd ʿAlī, Muḥammad. *Memoirs*. Translated by Khalil Totah. American Council of Learned Societies Near Eastern Translation Program, No. 6. Washington: American Council of Learned Societies, 1954.

Lamplough, A., and R. Francis. *Cairo and Environs*. London: Sir Joseph Causton and Sons, 1909.

Landau, Jacob M. "Abu Naḍḍārah, an Egyptian Jewish Nationalist." *Journal of Jewish Studies*, 3 (1952): 30–44.

———. "An Insider's View of Istanbul: Ibrāhīm al-Muwayliḥī's *Mā Hunālika*." *Die Welt des Islams*, XXVII (1987): 70–81.

———. *Parliaments and Parties in Egypt*. Tel Aviv: Israel Publishing House, 1953.

———. "Prolegomena to a Study of Secret Societies in Modern Egypt." *Middle Eastern Studies*, 1, no. 2 (1965): 35–86.

Landes, David. "Bankers and Pashas." In *Men in Business: Essays in the History of Entrepreneurship*, edited by William Miller. Cambridge: Harvard University Press, 1952.

Lane, Edward. *The Manners and Customs of the Modern Egyptians*. London: Everyman ed., 1954.

Lane-Poole, Stanley. *Cairo Fifty Years Ago*. London: J. Murray, 1896.

———. *Cairo: Sketches of its History, Monuments, and Social Life*. London: J. S. Virtue and Co., 1898.

———. *The Story of Cairo*. London: J. M. Dent, 1902.

Lewis, Bernard. *The Middle East and the West*. Bloomington: Indiana University Press, 1964.

Liddell, R. *A Treatise on the Novel*. London: Jonathan Cape, 1947.

Little, Tom. *Egypt*. London: Ernest Benn, 1958.

Lubbock, Percy. *The Craft of Fiction*. London: Jonathan Cape, 1963.

Lutfi as-Sayyid, Afaf. *Egypt and Cromer: A Study in Anglo-Egyptian Relations*. London: John Murray, 1968.

———. *Egypt in the Reign of Muḥammad ʿAlī*. Cambridge: Cambridge University Press, 1984.
Malortie, Baron Carl von. *Egypt: Native Rulers and Foreign Interference*. London: W. Ridgeway, 1882.
Marcel, Jean-Jacques. *Les contes du Cheykh el-Mohdy*. Paris: Henri Dupuy, 1835.
Margoliouth, D. S. *Cairo, Jerusalem, and Damascus: Three Chief Cities of the Egyptian Sultans*. London: Chatto and Windus, 1907.
Marlowe, John. *Cromer in Egypt*. London: Elek, 1970.
———. *A History of Modern Egypt and Anglo-Egyptian Relations*. London: Cresset Press, 1954.
Marshall, J. E. *The Egyptian Enigma 1890–1928*. London: John Murray, 1928.
McCoan, J. *Egypt As It Is*. London: Cassell, Petter and Galpin, 1877, 1898.
———. *Egypt Under Ismail, A Romance of History*. London: Chapman and Hall, 1899.
Milner, Lord. *England in Egypt*. London: Edward Arnold, 1899.
Monroe, James. *The Art of Badīʿ al-Zamān al-Hamadhānī as Picaresque Narrative*. Beirut: American University in Beirut, 1983.
Moosa, Matti. *The Origins of Modern Arabic Fiction*. Washington: Three Continents Press, 1983.
Mūsā, Salāmah. *The Education of Salāmah Mūsā*. Translated by L. O. Schuman. Leiden: E. J. Brill, 1961.
Muwailihi, Ibrahim al-. "Ibrahim al-Muwailihi." *Cahiers d'histoire égyptienne*, 2 (1949): 313–28.
———. "Muḥammad al-Muwailihi." *Cahiers d'histoire égyptienne*, 6 (1954): 168 ff.
Nicholson, R. A. *A Literary History of the Arabs*. Cambridge: Cambridge University Press, 1907.
Penfield, F. *Present Day Egypt*. New York: The Century Co., 1899.
Pérès, Henri. "Editions successives de Hadīth ʿĪsā ibn Hishām." In *Mélanges Louis Massignon*, 3 (1957): 233–58.
———. "Les premières manifestations de la renaissance littéraire arabe en Orient au XIXième siècle: Nāṣīf al-Yāzijī et Fāris al-Shidyāk." *Annales de l'institut des études orientales*, 1 (1934–35): 232–56.

———. "Origines d'un roman célèbre de la littérature arabe moderne: Ḥadīth 'Īsā ibn Hishām." *Bulletin des études orientales*, 10 (1944): 101–18.

Polk, William, and Richard Chambers, eds. *Beginnings of Modernization in the Middle East*. Chicago: University of Chicago Press, 1968.

La réforme judiciaire en Egypte et les capitulations. Alexandria: n.p., 1874.

Report on Egypt. London: Intelligence Department War Office, 1882.

Safran, Nadav. *Egypt in Search of Political Identity*. Cambridge: Harvard University Press, 1962.

Sawa, George Dimitri. *Music Performance Practice in the Early 'Abbāsid Era 132–320 AH/750–932 AD*. Toronto: Pontifical Institute of Medieval Studies, 1989.

Scott, J. H. *The Law Affecting Foreigners in Egypt*. Edinburgh: William Green & Sons, 1907.

Senior, Nassau William. *Conversations and Journals in Egypt and Malta*. London: Sampson Low and Co., 1882.

Sharqāwī, 'Abd al-Raḥmān al-. *Egyptian Earth*. Translated by Desmond Stewart. London: Heinemann, 1962; Delhi: Hind Pocket Books, 1972.

Shaw, Stanford. *Ottoman Egypt in the Age of the French Revolution*. Cambridge: Cambridge University Press, 1964.

———. *The Financial and Administrative Organization and Development of Ottoman Egypt, 1517–1798*. Princeton: Princeton University Press, 1958.

Index

al-Yashkurī, Wāziʿ, §16.7
Yūsuf, ʿAlī, xviii, xxi–iii, xxvii, §16.12
Zaghlūl, Aḥmad Fatḥī, xviii
Zaghlūl, Saʿd, xxiv
Zaqāzīq, §24.15
Zaydān, Jūrjī, xl, 500n138
Ziyād ibn Abīhi, §16.7
Zubayr, Raḥmah Manṣūr, §6.5

About the NYU Abu Dhabi Institute

The Library of Arabic Literature is supported by a grant from the NYU Abu Dhabi Institute, a major hub of intellectual and creative activity and advanced research. The Institute hosts academic conferences, workshops, lectures, film series, performances, and other public programs directed both to audiences within the UAE and to the worldwide academic and research community. It is a center of the scholarly community for Abu Dhabi, bringing together faculty and researchers from institutions of higher learning throughout the region.

NYU Abu Dhabi, through the NYU Abu Dhabi Institute, is a world-class center of cutting-edge research, scholarship, and cultural activity. The Institute creates singular opportunities for leading researchers from across the arts, humanities, social sciences, sciences, engineering, and the professions to carry out creative scholarship and conduct research on issues of major disciplinary, multidisciplinary, and global significance.

About the Translator

Roger Allen retired in 2011 from his position as the Sascha Jane Patterson Harvie Professor at the University of Pennsylvania, where he served for forty-three years as Professor of Arabic and Comparative Literature. He is the author and translator of numerous publications on Arabic literature, modern fiction and drama, and language pedagogy. Among his studies devoted to the Arabic literary tradition are: *The Arabic Novel* (1995) and *The Arabic Literary Heritage* (1998; abridged version, *Introduction to Arabic Literature*, 2000).

The Library of Arabic Literature

For more details on individual titles, visit www.libraryofarabicliterature.org.

Classical Arabic Literature: A Library of Arabic Literature Anthology
Selected and translated by Geert Jan van Gelder

A Treasury of Virtues: Sayings, Sermons and Teachings of ʿAlī, by al-Qāḍī al-Quḍāʿī with the *One Hundred Proverbs* attributed to al-Jāḥiẓ
Edited and translated by Tahera Qutbuddin

The Epistle on Legal Theory, by al-Shāfiʿī
Edited and translated by Joseph E. Lowry

Leg over Leg, by Aḥmad Fāris al-Shidyāq
Edited and translated by Humphrey Davies

Virtues of the Imām Aḥmad ibn Ḥanbal, by Ibn al-Jawzī
Edited and translated by Michael Cooperson

The Epistle of Forgiveness, by Abū l-ʿAlāʾ al-Maʿarrī
Edited and translated by Geert Jan van Gelder and Gregor Schoeler

The Principles of Sufism, by ʿĀʾishah al-Bāʿūniyyah
Edited and translated by Th. Emil Homerin

The Expeditions: An Early Biography of Muḥammad, by Maʿmar ibn Rāshid
Edited and translated by Sean W. Anthony

Two Arabic Travel Books
Accounts of China and India, by Abū Zayd al-Sīrāfī
Edited and translated by Tim Mackintosh-Smith

Mission to the Volga, by Aḥmad ibn Faḍlān
Edited and translated by James Montgomery

Disagreements of the Jurists: A Manual of Islamic Legal Theory, by al-Qāḍī al-Nuʿmān
Edited and translated by Devin J. Stewart

Consorts of the Caliphs: Women and the Court of Baghdad, by Ibn al-Sāʿī
Edited by Shawkat M. Toorawa and translated by the Editors of the Library of Arabic Literature

What ʿĪsā ibn Hishām Told Us, by Muḥammad al-Muwayliḥī
Edited and translated by Roger Allen

The Life and Times of Abū Tammām, by Abū Bakr Muḥammad ibn Yaḥyā al-Ṣūlī
Edited and translated by Beatrice Gruendler

The Sword of Ambition: Bureaucratic Rivalry in Medieval Egypt, by ʿUthmān ibn Ibrāhīm al-Nābulusī
Edited and translated by Luke Yarbrough

Brains Confounded by the Ode of Abū Shādūf Expounded, by Yūsuf al-Shirbīnī
Edited and translated by Humphrey Davies

Light in the Heavens: Sayings of the Prophet Muḥammad, by al-Qāḍī al-Quḍāʿī
Edited and translated by Tahera Qutbuddin

Risible Rhymes, by Muḥammad ibn Maḥfūẓ al-Sanhūrī
Edited and translated by Humphrey Davies

A Hundred and One Nights
Edited and translated by Bruce Fudge

The Excellence of the Arabs, by Ibn Qutaybah
Edited by James E. Montgomery and Peter Webb
Translated by Sarah Bowen Savant and Peter Webb

Scents and Flavors: A Syrian Cookbook
Edited and translated by Charles Perry

Arabian Satire: Poetry from 18th-Century Najd, by Ḥmēdān al-Shwēʿir
Edited and translated by Marcel Kurpershoek

ENGLISH-ONLY PAPERBACKS

Leg over Leg: Volumes One and Two, by Aḥmad Fāris al-Shidyāq

Leg over Leg: Volumes Three and Four, by Aḥmad Fāris al-Shidyāq

The Expeditions: An Early Biography of Muḥammad, by Maʿmar ibn Rāshid

The Epistle on Legal Theory: A Translation of al-Shāfiʿī's Risālah, by al-Shāfiʿī

The Epistle of Forgiveness, by Abū l-ʿAlāʾ al-Maʿarrī

The Principles of Sufism, by ʿĀʾishah al-Bāʿūniyyah

A Treasury of Virtues: Sayings, Sermons and Teachings of ʿAlī, by al-Qāḍī al-Quḍāʿī with *The One Hundred Proverbs*, attributed to al-Jāḥiẓ

The Life of Ibn Ḥanbal, by Ibn al-Jawzī

Mission to the Volga, by Ibn Faḍlān

Accounts of China and India, by Abū Zayd al-Sīrāfī

Consorts of the Caliphs: Women and the Court of Baghdad, by Ibn al-Sāʿī

A Hundred and One Nights

Disagreements of the Jurists: A Manual of Islamic Legal Theory, by al-Qāḍī al-Nuʿmān

What ʿĪsā ibn Hishām Told Us, by Muḥammad al-Muwayliḥī

Printed and bound by CPI Group (UK) Ltd, Croydon, CR0 4YY

25/03/2025

14647335-0002